"...The Qur'an cannot be translated. ...The book is here rendered almost literally and every effort has been made to choose befitting language. But the result is not the Glorious Qur'an, that inimitable symphony, the very sounds of which move men to tears and ecstasy. It is only an attempt to present the meaning of the Qur'an and peradventure something of the charm in English. It can never take the place of the Qur'an in Arabic, nor is it meant to do so..."

Muhammad Marmaduke Pickthall, 1930

Table of Contents

Translator's Foreword 7

Editor's Introduction 8

1. *Al-Fatihah* 9

2. *Al-Baqarah* 9

3. *Al-'Imran* 36

4. *An-Nisa* 52

5. *Al-Ma'idah* 67

6. *Al-An'am* 78

7. *Al-A'raf* 90

8. *Al-Anfal* 104

9. *At-Taubah* 110

10. *Yunus* 121

11. *Hud* 128

12. *Yusuf* 136

13. *Ar-Ra'd* 143

14. *Ibrahim* 147

15. *Al-Hijr* 150

16. *An-Nahl* 154

17. *Bani Israel* 162

18. *Al-Kahf* 169

19. *Maryam* 176

20. *Ta-Ha* 182

21. *Al-Anbiya* 189

22. *Al-Hajj* 194

23. *Al-Mu'minun* 200

24. *An-Nur* 205

25. *Al-Furqan* 210

26. *Ash-Shu'ara* 214

27. *An-Naml* 221

28. *Al-Qasas* 226

29. *Al-'Ankabut* 232

30. *Ar-Rum* 236

31. *Luqman* 241

32. *As-Sajdah* 243

33. *Al-Ahzab* 245

34. *Saba* 252

35. *Al-Mala'ikah* 256

36. *Ya Sin* 259

37. *As-Saffat* 262

38. *Sad* 267

39. *Az-Zumar* 271

40. *Al-Mu'min* 276

41. *Fussilat* 281

42. *Ash-Shura* 284

43. *Az-Zukhruf* 288

44. *Ad-Dukhan* 292

45. *Al-Jathiya* 294

46. *Al-Ahqaf* 296

47. *Muhammad* 299

48. *Al-Fath* 302

49. *Al-Hujurat* 305

50. *Qaf* 307

51. *Adh-Dhariyat* 309

52. *At-Tur* 311

53. *An-Najm* 313

54. *Al-Qamar* 315

55. *Ar-Rahman* 317

56. *Al-Waqi'ah* 319

57. *Al-Hadid* 322

58. *Al-Mujadilah* 324

59. *Al-Hashr* 326

60. *Al-Mumtahanah* 329

61. *As-Saff* 330

62. *Al-Jummu'ah* 332

63. *Al-Munafiqun*	333		96. *Al-'Alaq*	368	
64. *At-Taghabun*	334		97. *Al-Qadr*	368	
65. *At-Talaq*	335		98. *Al-Bayyinah*	368	
66. *At-Tahrim*	336		99. *Al-Zalzalah*	369	
67. *Al-Mulk*	339		100. *Al-'Adiyat*	369	
68. *Al-Qalam*	340		101. *Al-Qari'ah*	370	
69. *Al-Haqqah*	342		102. *At-Takathur*	370	
70. *Al-Ma'arij*	344		103. *Al-'Asr*	370	
71. *Nuh*	345		104. *Al-Humazah*	371	
72. *Al-Jinn*	346		105. *Al-Fil*	371	
73. *Al-Muzzammil*	348		106. *Quraysh*	371	
74. *Al-Muddaththir*	349		107. *Al-Ma'un*	372	
75. *Al-Qiyamah*	351		108. *Al-Kauthar*	372	
76. *Al-Insan*	352		109. *Al-Kafirun*	372	
77. *Al-Mursalat*	353		110. *An-Nasr*	372	
78. *An-Naba*	354		111. *Al-Masad*	373	
79. *An-Nazi'at*	355		112. *Al-Ikhlas*	373	
80. *Abasa*	356		113. *Al-Falaq*	374	
81. *At-Takwir*	357		114. *An-Nas*	374	
82. *Al-Infitar*	358		*Brief Index of Subjects*	375	
83. *Al-Mutaffifin*	359				
84. *Al-Inshiqaq*	360				
85. *Al-Buruj*	360				
86. *At-Tariq*	361				
87. *Al-A'la*	362				
88. *Al-Ghashiyah*	363				
89. *Al-Fajr*	363				
90. *Al-Balad*	364				
91. *Ash-Shams*	365				
92. *Al-Lail*	365				
93. *Ad-Duha*	366				
94. *Ash-Sharh*	367				
95. *At-Tin*	367				

Translator's Foreword

by Muhammad Marmaduke Pickthall

The aim of this work is to present to English readers what Muslims the world over hold to be the meaning of the words of the Qur'an, and the nature of that Book, in not unworthy language and concisely, with a view to the requirements of English Muslims. It may be reasonably claimed that no Holy Scripture can be fairly presented by one who disbelieves its inspiration and its message; and this is the first English translation of the Qur'an by an Englishman who is a Muslim. Some of the translations include comments offensive to Muslims, and almost all employ a style of language which Muslims at once recognise as unworthy. The Qur'an cannot be translated. That is the belief of the old-fashioned Sheykhs and the view of the present writer. The Book is here rendered almost literally and every effort has been made to choose befitting language. But the result is not the Glorious Qur'an, that inimitable symphony, the very sounds of which move men to tears and ecstasy. It is only an attempt to present the meaning of the Qur'an - and perhaps something of the charm - in English. It can never take the place of the Qur'an in Arabic, nor is it meant to do so.

Before publication the work has been scrutinised word by word and thoroughly revised in Egypt with the help of one whose mother-tongue is Arabic, who has studied the Qur'an and who knows English; and when difficulties were encountered the translator had recourse to perhaps the greatest living authority on the subject. Every care has thus been taken to avoid unwarrantable renderings. On the one or two occasions where there is departure from the traditional interpretation, the traditional rendering will be found in a footnote.

The translator's thanks are due to Lord Lloyd for an introduction of great use in Egypt; to Dr. F. Krenkow for supplying him with old meanings of Arabic words not to be found in dictionaries; to Muhammad Ahmad Al-Ghamrawi Bey of the Cairo College of Medicine for his invaluable and patient help with the revision of the manuscript, a work which occupied three months; to the Sheykh Mustafa Al-Maraghi, former Rector of Al-Azhar University, for his advice and guidance in the revision; and to His Excellency Fuad Bey Salim al-Higazi, by whose efforts such revision was made possible

The Mushaf (copy of the Qur'an) which has been used throughout is a lithograph copy of that written by Al-Hajj Muhammad Shakarzadeh at the command of Sultan Muhmud of Turkey in 1246 A.H. In the introduction and the notes to individual Surahs, Ibn Hisham (Bulaq edn. 1295 A.H.) has been followed, with occasional reference to the much later, much abbreviated, but more critical Life of the Prophet by Ibn Khaldun (published as an appendix to his Tarikh, Bulaq edn.) Other Sirahs, like that of Abu 'l-Fida, late in date and uncritical, have been read but not followed. Of commentators Al-Beydawi and Zamakhshari must be mentioned, while for reference during the work of revision, the brief commentary of Al-Jalaleyn was kept at hand. Wahidi's Asbabu'n-Nuzul has been largely consulted, and for the authenticity of Traditions the translator has relied upon Bukhari.

Editor's Introduction

The Qur'an is no ordinary book. To Muslims it is the eternal word of God (Allah), dictated to the prophet Muhammad - peace be with him - via the angel Gabriel (*Jibreel*). Originally revealed in Arabic, its style is unrivalled, its language eloquent, its meaning deep. It is beyond any translation to render all this richness of expression in another language. Yet, the Qur'an is primarily a book of guidance and must, therefore, be accessible to those who seek the truth contained in it. Whilst a translation cannot be an authoritative replacement of the original, it can make the meaning of its verses available to a non-Arabic speaking readership.

The verses (*Ayahs*) of the Qur'an were revealed throughout the 23 years of prophet Muhammad's prophethood, often in connection with events of the time. They were then memorised, recorded in writing, collected and arranged into chapters (*Surahs*). Within those verses we find narratives describing the creation of the world from earliest times or recounting the missions of earlier prophets, we come across general exhortation to belief and righteous conduct, we are given the tools and principles for reflection and sound judgement in a multitude of life's situations, and we receive detailed rulings on important aspects of criminal and civil law. Thus the Qur'an is not only a text of inspiration but also the foundation of the legal and social structure of Islamic society.

The text of the Qur'an has not changed since the days the prophet Muhammad - peace be with him - received this revelation, yet its content retains its relevance, validity and dynamics and continues to inspire believers of every generation as well as challenge the status quo of human society. The convincing observations of the Qur'an which, after all, are a communication from our Maker, are a powerful call to action and a rebuttal of complacency. They appeal to both the mind and the heart of the reader or listener, they call for justice and compassion, they decry and defy falsehood, pretence and oppression. They represent an uncomfortable truth for those who would like to banish the courage of one's conviction and do not want us to use our intellect and power of reflection to guide us along our path in life.

Amongst the various translations of the Qur'an, this first translation by an indigenous English Muslim, Muhammad Marmaduke Pickthall, first published in 1930, remains a favourite amongst many English-speaking Muslims. Language, however, evolves, and to make the meaning of the divine revelation more accessible, IDCI has re-published Pickthall's translation in its present, modern English form, where it has been carefully adapted by Dr Sahib Mustaqim Bleher, replacing some of the more archaic terms with those in current usage, without generally altering the flow and register of the original work.

Surah 1: **Al-Fatihah**
(The Opening)

Al-Fatihah, "The Opening" Fatihatu'l Kitab, 'The Opening of the Scripture" or Ummu'l-Qur'an, "The Essence of the Qur'an" as it is variously named, has been called the Lord's Prayer of the Muslims. It is an essential part of the Muslims' worship, public and private, and no solemn contract or transaction is complete unless it is recited. The date of revelation is uncertain, but the fact that it has always, from the very earliest of times, formed a part of Muslim worship, there being no record or remembrance of its introduction, or of public prayer without it, makes it clear that it was revealed before the fourth year of the Prophet's Mission (the tenth year before the *Hijrah*); because we know for certain that by that time regular congregational prayers were offered by the little group of Muslims in Makkah. In that year, as the result of insult and attack[1] by the idolaters, the Prophet arranged for the services, which had till then been held out of doors, to take place in a private house.

This Surah is also often called *Saba'an min al-Muthani*, "Seven of the Oft-repeated" ("verses" being understood), Surah 15, *Al-Hijr*, v. 87, words which are taken as referring to this Surah.[2]

1. *In the name of Allah, the Beneficent, the Merciful.*

2. Praise be to Allah, Lord of the Worlds,

3. The Beneficent, the Merciful,

4. Master of the Day of Judgement,

5. You (alone) we worship; You (alone) we ask for help.

6. Show us the straight path,

7. The path of those whom You have favoured; not the (path) of those who earn Your anger, nor of those who go astray.

Surah 2: **Al-Baqarah**
(The Heifer)

Al-Baqarah, "The Cow" is so named from the story of the yellow heifer (vv. 67-71). As is the case with many other Surahs, the title is taken from some word or incident which surprised the listeners. All suggestions to the contrary notwithstanding, it seems probable that the whole of this Surah was revealed during the first four years after Hijrah, and that by far the greater portion of it was revealed in the first eighteen months of the Prophet's reign at Al-Madinah - that is to say, before the battle of Badr.[3]

The Jewish tribes, once paramount in Yathrib, had, not very long before the coming of *Al-Islam*, been reduced by the pagan Arab tribes of Aus and

---

1. Ibn Hisham *Sirah* (Cairo edn.), Part I, p. 88.

2. See Nöldeke, *Geschichte des Qorans*, Zweite Auflage, bearbeitet von Fr. Schwally, Part I, pp. 173 seq.

TRANSLATOR'S NOTE: I have retained the word Allah throughout, because there is no corresponding word in English. The word Allah (the stress is on the last syllable) has

neither feminine nor plural, and has never been applied to anything other than the unimaginable Supreme Being. I use the word "God" only where the corresponding word ilah is found in the Arabic. The words in brackets are interpolated to explain the meaning.

3. Th. Nöldeke, *Geschichte des Qorans*, Zweite Auflage, bearbeitet von Fr. Schwally, Part I, pp. 173 seq.

Khazraj, each Jewish tribe becoming an adherent of one or the other. But they had preserved a sort of intellectual ascendancy owing to their possession of the Scripture and their fame for occult science, the pagan Arabs consulting their rabbis on occasions and paying heed to what they said. Before the coming of *Al-Islam*,[4] these Jewish rabbis had often threatened them that when he came, (the Jews) would destroy the pagan Arabs as the tribes of A'ad and Thamud had been destroyed of old.[5] So plainly did they describe the coming Prophet that pilgrims from Yathrib recognised the Prophet, when he addressed them in Makkah, as the same who the Jewish doctors had described to them. But the Jewish idea of a Prophet was one who would give them dominion, not one who would make them brothers of every pagan Arab who chose to accept *Al-Islam*. When they found that they could not make use of the newcomer, they opposed him and tried to bewilder him with questions from their theology, speaking to him as men who possessed superior wisdom; failing to perceive that, from a Prophet's standpoint, theology is childish nonsense, the very opposite of religion, and its enemy; religion, for the Prophet, being not a matter of conjecture and speech, but of fact and conduct.

Ibn Ishaq[6] states definitely that vv. 1-141 were revealed concerning these Jewish rabbis and such of the new converts to *Al-Islam* as were half-hearted and inclined to them. There follows the order to change the *Qiblah* (the place towards which the Muslims turn their face in prayer) from Jerusalem to the Ka'bah at Makkah, which was built by Abraham, the choice of Jerusalem having led to a misunderstanding on the part of the Jews that the Prophet was groping his way towards their religion and stood in need of their guidance and instruction.

All through the Surah runs the note of warning, which sounds indeed throughout the whole Qur'an, that it is not the mere profession of a creed, but righteous conduct which is true religion. There is the repeated announcement that the religion of Abraham, to which Judaism and Christianity (which springs from Judaism) trace their origin, is the only true religion, and that religion consists in the surrender of a man's will and purpose to the Will and Purpose of the Lord of Creation as manifested in His creation and revealed by way of guidance through successive Prophets. Of sincerity in that religion the one test is conduct, and the standard of religion is for all alike.

At the time when this Surah was revealed at Al-Madinah, the Prophet's own tribe, the pagan Quraysh at Makkah, were preparing to attack the Muslims in their place of refuge. Cruel

---

4. *Al-Islam* means "The Surrender" - *i.e.* man's surrender to God's will and purpose.
5. Ibn Hisham (Cairo edn.), Part I, pp. 180 seq.

6. Apud Ibn Hisham, Sirah (Cairo edn.), pp. 189 seq.

persecution was the lot of Muslims who had stayed in Makkan territory or who journeyed there, and Muslims were being prevented from performing the pilgrimage. The possible necessity of fighting had been foreseen in the terms of the oath, taken at Al-'Aqabah by the Muslims of Yathrib before the emigration, to defend the Prophet as they would their own wives and children, and the first commandment to fight was revealed to the Prophet before his emigration from Makkah; but there was no actual fighting by the Muslims until the battle of Badr. Many of them were reluctant, having before been subject to a rule of strict nonviolence. It was with difficulty that they could accept the idea of fighting even in self-defence, as can be seen from several verses in this Surah, which contains also rules for fasting and the pilgrimage, bequests, almsgiving, divorce and contracts, and verses which discountenance usury, strong drink and gambling. It concludes with a statement of the universal character of *Al-Islam*, the religion of Allah's sovereignty, and a prayer for the forgiveness of shortcomings.

This Surah might be described as the Qur'an in small. It contains mention of all the essential points of the Revelation, which are elaborated elsewhere. This accounts for the precedence given to it in the arrangement of the Book.

The period of revelation is the years 1 and 2 A.H. for the most part, certain verses of legislation being considered as of later date.

In the name of Allah,
the Beneficent, the Merciful.

1. *Alif. Lam. Mim.*[7]

2. This is the Scripture of which there is no doubt, a guidance to those who ward off (evil);

3. Who believe in the Unseen, and establish worship, and spend of that We have bestowed upon them;

4. And who believe in that which is revealed to you (Muhammad) and that which was revealed before you, and are certain of the Hereafter.

5. These depend on guidance from their Lord. These are the successful.

6. As for the disbelievers, whether you warn them or you warn them not, it is all one for them; they believe not.

7. Allah has sealed their hearing and their hearts, and on their eyes there is a covering. Theirs will be an awful doom.

8. And of mankind are some who say: We believe in Allah and the Last Day, when they believe not.

9. They think they can deceive Allah and those who believe, but they deceive no one except themselves; but they perceive not.

10. In their hearts is a disease, and Allah increases their disease. A painful doom is theirs because they lie.

11. And when it is said to them: Make not mischief in the earth, they say: We are peacemakers only.

---

7. Three letters of the Arabic alphabet. Many Surahs begin thus with letters of the alphabet. Opinions differ as to their significance, but all Muslims are agreed that they indicate some mystic words or truths too far beyond the understanding of the people to bear statement.

12. Are not they indeed the mischief-makers? But they perceive not.

13. And when it is said to them: Believe as the people[8] believe, they say: shall we believe as the foolish believe? Surely they are indeed the foolish? But they know not.

14. And when they fall in with those who believe, they say: "We believe," but when they go apart to their devils they declare: "We are with you; surely we did only mock."

15. Allah (Himself) mocks them, leaving them to wander blindly on in their rebellion.

16. These are they who purchase error at the price of guidance, so their commerce did not prosper, neither are they guided.

17. Their likeness is as the likeness of one who kindles fire, and when it sheds its light around him Allah takes away their light and leaves them in darkness, where they cannot see,

18. Deaf, dumb and blind; and they return not.

19. Or like a rainstorm from the sky, in which is darkness, thunder and the flash of lightning. They thrust their fingers in their ears by reason of the thunder-claps, for fear of death. Allah encompasses the disbelievers (in His might).

20. The lightning almost snatches away their sight from them. As often as it flashes forth for them they walk in it, and when it darkens against them they stand still. If Allah willed, He could destroy their hearing and their sight. Allah is able to do all things.

21. O mankind! Worship your Lord, Who has created you and those before you, so that you may ward off (evil);

22. Who has appointed the earth a resting-place for you, and the sky a canopy; and causes water to pour down from the sky, by it producing fruits as food for you. And do not set up rivals to Allah when you know (better).

23. And if you are in doubt concerning that which We reveal to Our slave[9] (Muhammad), then produce a Surah of the like of it, and call your witnesses besides Allah if you are truthful.

24. And if you do it not - and you can never do it - then guard yourselves against the Fire prepared for disbelievers, whose fuel is of men and stones.

25. And give glad tidings (O Muhammad) to those who believe and do good works; that theirs are Gardens underneath which rivers flow; as often as they are entertained with food of the fruit of it, they say: "This is what was given us previously;"[10] and it is given to them in resemblance. There for them are pure companions; there forever they remain.

---

8. *i.e.* The people of Al-Madinah, most of whom were Muslims, vv. 8 to 19 refer to the "Hypocrites," or lukewarm Muslims of Al-Madinah, whose leader was Abdullah ibn Ubeyy. They pretended that their aim was to make peace between the Muslims and the Jewish rabbis, but they only embittered the controversy.

9. To be the slave of Allah is the proudest boast of the Muslim, bondage to Allah liberating from all other servitudes. In the Qur'an mankind are often called God's slaves or bondsmen, a stronger and more just expression than the word "servants" generally substituted in translations.

10. The joys of Paradise will recall, in a rapturous degree, the joys the righteous tasted in their life on earth.

26. Allah disdains not to coin the similitude even of a gnat. Those who believe know that it is the truth from their Lord; but those who disbelieve say: What does Allah wish (to teach) by such a similitude? He misleads many by it, and He guides many by it; and He misleads by it only miscreants;

27. Those who break the covenant of Allah after ratifying it, and sever that which Allah ordered to be joined, and (who) make mischief in the earth: those are they who are the losers.

28. How do you disbelieve in Allah when you were dead and He gave life to you? Then He will give you death, then life again, and then to Him you will return.

29. He it is Who created for you all that is in the earth. Then He turned to the heaven, and fashioned it as seven heavens. And He is Knower of all things.

30. And when your Lord said to the angels: I am about to place a viceroy in the earth, they said: Will you place in it one who will do harm in it and will shed blood, while we, we hymn Your praise and sanctify You? He said: Surely I know that which you know not.

31. And He taught Adam all the names, then showed them to the angels, saying: Inform Me of the names of these, if you are truthful.

32. They said: Be glorified! We have no knowledge except that which You have taught us. You, only You, are the Knower, the Wise.

33. He said: O Adam! Inform them of their names, and when he had informed them of their names, He said: Did I not tell you that I know the secret of the heavens and the earth? And I know that which you disclose and which you hide.

34. And when We said to the angels: Prostrate yourselves before Adam, they fell prostrate, all except Iblis. He demurred through pride, and so became a disbeliever.

35. We said: O Adam! Dwell you and your wife in the Garden, and eat you[11] freely (of the fruits) of it where you will; but come not near this tree lest you become wrongdoers.

36. But Satan caused them to deflect from it and expelled them from the (happy) state in which they were; and We said: Fall down,[12] one of you a foe to the other! There shall be for you on earth a habitation and provision for a time.

37. Then Adam received from his Lord words (of revelation), and He relented towards him. He is the Relenting, the Merciful.

38. We said: Go down, all of you, from here; so when there comes to you from Me a guidance, and who follows My guidance, no fear shall come upon them, neither shall they grieve.

39. But they who disbelieve, and deny Our revelations, such are rightful Peoples of the Fire. They will remain in it.

40. O Children of Israel! Remember My favour with which I favoured you, and fulfil your (part of the) covenant, I shall fulfil My (part of the) covenant, and fear Me.

---

11. Here the command is in the dual, as addressed to Adam and his wife.
12. Here the command is in the plural, as addressed to Adam's race.

41. And believe in that which I reveal, confirming that which you possess already (of the Scripture), and be not first to disbelieve in it, and part not with My revelations for a trifling price, and keep your duty to Me.

42. Mix not truth with falsehood, nor knowingly conceal the truth.

43. Establish worship, pay the poor-due,[13] and bow your heads with those who bow (in worship).

44. Do you enjoin righteousness upon mankind while you yourselves forget (to practise it)? And you are readers of the Scripture! Have you then no sense?

45. Seek help in patience and prayer; and truly it is hard, except for the humble-minded,

46. Who know that they will have to meet their Lord, and that to Him they are returning.

47. O Children of Israel! Remember My favour with which I favoured you and how I preferred you to (all) creatures.

48. And guard yourselves against a day when no soul will in anything benefit another, nor will intercession be accepted from it, nor will compensation be received from it, nor will they be helped.

49. And (remember) when We did deliver you from Pharaoh's people, who were afflicting you with dreadful torment, slaying your sons and sparing your women: that was a tremendous trial from your Lord.

50. And when We brought you through the sea and rescued you, and drowned the people of Pharaoh in your sight.

51. And when We did appoint for Moses forty nights (of solitude), and then you chose the calf when he had gone from you, and you were wrongdoers.

52. Then, even after that, We pardoned you in order that you might give thanks.

53. And when We gave to Moses the Scripture and the Criterion (of right and wrong), that you might be led aright.

54. And when Moses said to his people: O my people! You have wronged yourselves by your choosing of the calf (for worship), so turn in penitence to your Creator, and kill (the guilty) yourselves. That will be best for you with your Creator and He will relent towards you. He is the Relenting, the Merciful.

55. And when you said: O Moses! We will not believe in you till we see Allah plainly; and even while you gazed the lightning seized you.

56. Then We revived you after your extinction, that you might give thanks.

57. And We caused the white cloud to overshadow you and sent down on you the honey and the quails, (saying): Eat of the good things with which We have provided you - they wronged Us not, but they did wrong themselves.

58. And when We said: Go into this township and eat freely of that which is in it, and enter the gate prostrate, and say: "Repentance."[14] We will

---

13. *Az-Zakah:* A tax at a fixed rate in proportion to the worth of property, collected from the well-to-do and distributed among the poor Muslims.

14. According to a tradition of the Prophet, *Hittatun* is a word implying submission to Allah and repentance. The evil-doers changed it for a word of rebellion - *i.e.* they were disobedient.

forgive you your sins and will increase (reward) for the right-doers.

59. But those who did wrong changed the word which had been told them for another saying, and We sent down upon the evildoers wrath from heaven for their evil-doing.

60. And when Moses asked for water for his people, We said: Strike with your staff the rock. And there gushed out from it twelve springs (so that) each tribe knew their drinking-place. Eat and drink of that which Allah has provided, and do not act corruptly, making mischief in the earth.

61. And when you said: O Moses! We are weary of one kind of food; so call on your Lord for us that He bring out for us of that which the earth grows - of its herbs and its cucumbers and its corn and its lentils and its onions. He said: Would you exchange that which is higher for that which is lower? Go down to settled country, thus you shall get that which you demand. And humiliation and wretchedness were stamped upon them and they were visited with wrath from Allah. That was because they disbelieved in Allah's revelations and slew the prophets wrongfully. That was for their disobedience and transgression.

62. Those who believe (in that which is revealed to you, Muhammad), and those who are Jews, and Christians, and Sabaeans - whoever believes in Allah and the Last Day and does right - surely their reward is with their Lord, and there shall no fear come upon them, neither shall they grieve.

63. And (remember, O Children of Israel) when We made a covenant with you and caused the mount to tower above you, (saying): Hold fast that which We have given you, and remember that which is in it, that you may ward off (evil).

64. Then, even after that, you turned away, and if it had not been for the grace of Allah and His mercy you would have been among the losers.

65. And you know of those of you who broke the Sabbath, how We said to them: Be you apes, despised and hated!

66. And We made it an example to their own and to succeeding generations, and an admonition to the God-fearing.

67. And when Moses said to his people: Allah commands you that you sacrifice a cow, they said: Do you make fun of us? He answered: Allah forbid that I should be among the foolish!

68. They said: Pray for us to your Lord that He make clear to us what (cow) she is. (Moses) answered: He says, Surely she is a cow neither with calf nor immature; (she is) between the two conditions; so do that which you are commanded.

69. They said: Pray for us to your Lord that He make clear to us of what colour she is. (Moses) answered: He says: Surely she is a yellow cow. Bright is her colour, gladdening beholders.

70. They said: Pray for us to your Lord that He make clear to us what (cow) she is. Cows are much alike to us; and if Allah wills, we may be led aright.

71. (Moses) answered: He says: Surely she is a cow unyoked; she ploughs not the soil nor waters the tilth; whole and without mark. They said: Now you bring the truth. So they sacrificed her, though almost they did not.

72. And (remember) when you slew a man and disagreed concerning it and Allah brought out that which you were hiding.

73. And We said: Strike him with some of it. Thus Allah brings the dead to life and shows you His signs so that you may understand.

74. Then, even after that, your hearts were hardened and became as rocks, or worse than rocks, for hardness. For indeed there are rocks out of which rivers gush, and indeed there are rocks which split apart so that water flows from them. And indeed there are rocks which fall down for the fear of Allah. Allah is not unaware of what you do.

75. Have you any hope that they will be true to you when a party of them used to listen to the word of Allah, then used to change it, after they had understood it, knowingly?

76. And when they fall in with those who believe, they say: We believe. But when they go apart one with another they say: Do you talk to them of that which Allah has disclosed to you that they may contend with you before your Lord concerning it? Have you then no sense?

77. Are they then unaware that Allah knows that which they keep hidden and that which they proclaim?

78. Among them are unlettered people who know the Scripture not except from hearsay. They only guess.

79. Therefore woe be to those who write the Scripture with their hands and then say, "This is from Allah," that they may purchase a small gain with it. Woe to them for that which their hands have written, and woe to them for that which they earn by it.

80. And they say: The Fire (of punishment) will not touch us except for a certain number of days. Say: Have you received a covenant from Allah - truly Allah will not break His covenant - or do you tell concerning Allah that which you know not?

81. No, but whoever has done evil and his sin surrounds him: such are rightful owners of the Fire; they will remain in it.

82. And those who believe and do good works: such are rightful owners of the Garden. They will remain in it.

83. And (remember) when We made a covenant with the Children of Israel, (saying): Worship none except Allah (only), and be good to parents and to relatives and to orphans and the needy, and speak kindly to mankind; and establish worship and pay the poor-due. Then, after that, you slid back, except a few of you, being averse.

84. And when We made with you a covenant (saying): Shed not the blood of your people nor turn (a party of) your people out of your dwellings. Then you ratified (Our covenant) and you were witnesses (to it).[15]

85. Yet you it is who slay each other and drive out a party of your people from their homes, supporting one another against them by sin and transgression[16] - and if they came to you as captives you would ransom them, whereas their expulsion was itself unlawful for you - Do you believe in part of the Scripture and disbelieve in part of it? And what is the reward of those who do so except ignominy in the life of the world, and on the Day of Resurrection they will be consigned to the most grievous doom. For Allah is not unaware of what you do.

86. Such are those who buy the life of the world at the price of the Hereafter. Their punishment will not be lightened, neither will they have support.

87. And surely We gave to Moses the Scripture and We caused a succession of messengers to follow after him, and We gave to Jesus, son of Mary, clear proofs (of Allah's sovereignty), and We supported him with the Holy Spirit.[17] Is it ever so, that, when there comes to you a messenger (from Allah) with that which you yourselves desire not, you grow arrogant, and some you disbelieve and some you slay?

88. And they say: Our hearts are hardened. No, but Allah has cursed them for their unbelief. Little is that which they believe.

89. And when there comes to them a Scripture from Allah, confirming that which is in their possession - though before that they were asking for a signal triumph over those who disbelieved - and when there comes to them that which they know (to be the truth) they disbelieve in it. The curse of Allah is on disbelievers.

90. Evil is that for which they sell their souls: that they should disbelieve in that which Allah has revealed, envious that Allah should reveal of His bounty to whom He will of His bondsmen.[18] They have incurred anger upon anger. For disbelievers is a shameful doom.

91. And when it is said to them: Believe in that which Allah has revealed, they say: We believe in that which was revealed to us. And they disbelieve in that which comes after it, though it is the truth confirming that which they possess. Say (to them, O Muhammad): Why then did you slay the prophets of Allah previously, if you are (indeed) believers?

92. And Moses came to you with clear proofs (of Allah's Sovereignty), though, while he was away, you chose the calf (for worship) and you were wrongdoers.

93. And when We made with you a covenant and caused the Mount to tower above you, (saying): Hold fast by that which We have given you,

15. v. 83 is generally taken as referring to the Biblical covenant and v. 84 as referring to the solemn treaty which the Jews of Al-Madinah made with the Prophet in the year 1 A.H.

16. The reference is to wars between the Arab tribes of Al-Madinah in which the Jews used to take part as allies of one and the other, Jew waging war upon Jew.

17. "The Holy Spirit" is a term for the angel of Revelation, Gabriel (on whom be peace).

18. See v. 23, footnote.

and hear (Our Word), they said: We hear and we rebel. And (worship of) the calf was made to sink into their hearts because of their rejection (of the covenant). Say (to them): Evil is that which your belief enjoins on you, if you are believers.

94. Say (to them): If the abode of the Hereafter in the providence of Allah is indeed for you alone and not for others of mankind (as you pretend), then long for death (for you must long for death) if you are truthful.

95. But they will never long for it, because of that which their own hands have sent before them. Allah is aware of evildoers.

96. And you will find them greediest of mankind for life and (greedier) than the idolaters. (Each) one of them would like to be allowed to live a thousand years. And to live (a thousand years) would by no means remove him from the doom. Allah is Seer of what they do.

97. Say (O Muhammad, to mankind): Who is an enemy to Gabriel! For he it is who has revealed (this Scripture) to your heart by Allah's permission, confirming that which was (revealed) before it, and a guidance and glad tidings to believers;

98. Who is an enemy to Allah, and His angels and His messengers, and Gabriel and Michael! Then, Allah (Himself) is an enemy to the disbelievers.

99. Surely We have revealed to you clear signs, and only miscreants will disbelieve in them.

100. Is it ever so that when they make a covenant a party of them set it aside? The truth is, most of them believe not.

101. And when there comes to them a messenger from Allah, confirming that which they possess, a party of those who have received the Scripture fling the Scripture of Allah behind their backs as if they knew not,

102. And follow that which the devils falsely related against the kingdom of Solomon. Solomon disbelieved not; but the devils disbelieved, teaching mankind magic and that which was revealed to the two angels in Babel, Harut and Marut. Nor did they (the two angels) teach it to anyone till they had said: We are only a temptation, therefore disbelieve not (in the guidance of Allah). And from these two (angels) people learn that by which they cause division between man and wife; but they injure by it no-one except by Allah's permission. And they learn that which harms them and profits them not. And surely they do know that he who traffics in it will have no (happy) portion in the Hereafter; and surely evil is the price for which they sell their souls, if they only knew.[19]

103. And if they had believed and kept from evil, a recompense from Allah would be better, if they only knew.

104. O you who believe, say not (to the Prophet): "Listen to us"[20] but say "Look

19. The reference is to the occult science practised by the Jews, the origin of which was ascribed to Solomon.
20. The first word which the Muslims used to call the Prophet's attention respectfully, *Ra'ina*, the Jews could change into an insult by a slight mispronunciation.

upon us," and be you attentive listeners. For disbelievers is a painful doom.

105. Neither those who disbelieve among the people of the Scripture[21] nor the idolaters love that there should be sent down to you any good thing from your Lord. But Allah chooses for His mercy whom He will, and Allah is of Infinite Bounty.

106. Nothing of Our revelation (even a single verse) do We abrogate or cause to be forgotten, but We bring (in place) one better or the like of it. Do you not know that Allah is Able to do all things?

107. Do you not know that it is Allah to Whom belongs the Sovereignty of the heavens and the earth; and you have not, besides Allah, any guardian or helper?

108. Or would you question your messenger as Moses was questioned before? He who chooses disbelief instead of faith, surely he has gone astray from a plain road.

109. Many of the people of the Scripture long to make you disbelievers after your belief, through envy on their own account, after the truth has become manifest to them. Forgive and be indulgent (toward them) until Allah gives command. Allah is Able to do all things.

110. Establish worship, and pay the poor-due;[22] and whatever of good you send before (you) for your souls, you will find it with Allah. Allah is Seer of what you do.

21. *i.e.* Jews and Christians.
22. *Az-Zakah,* a tax at fixed rate in proportion to the worth of property, collected from the well-to-do and distributed among the poor Muslims.

111. And they say: No-one enters paradise unless he be a Jew or a Christian. These are their own desires. Say: Bring your proof (of what you state) if you are truthful.

112. No, but whoever surrenders his purpose to Allah while doing good, his reward is with his lord; and there shall no fear come upon them, neither shall they grieve.

113. And the Jews say the Christians follow nothing (true), and the Christians say the Jews follow nothing (true); though both are readers of the Scripture. Even thus speak those who know not. Allah will judge between them on the Day of Resurrection concerning that in which they differ.

114. And who does greater wrong than he who forbids the approach to the sanctuaries of Allah lest His name should be mentioned in it, and strives for their ruin? As for such, it was never meant that they should enter them except in fear. Theirs in the world is ignominy and theirs in the Hereafter is an awful doom.

115. To Allah belong the East and the West, and whichever way you turn, there is Allah's Countenance. Allah is All-Embracing, All-Knowing.

116. And they say: Allah has taken to Himself a son. Be He glorified! No, but whatever is in the heavens and the earth is His. All are subservient to Him.

117. The Originator of the heavens and the earth! When He decrees a thing, He says to it only: Be! and it is.

118. And those who have no knowledge say: Why does not Allah speak to us, or some sign come to us? Even thus, as they now speak, spoke those (who were) before them. Their hearts are all alike. We have made clear the revelations for people who are sure.

119. We have sent you (O Muhammad) with the truth, a bringer of glad tidings and a warner. And you will not be asked about the owners of Hell-fire.

120. And the Jews will not be pleased with you, nor will the Christians, till you follow their creed. Say: The guidance of Allah (Himself) is Guidance. And if you should follow their desires after the knowledge which has come to you, then you would have from Allah no protecting guardian nor helper.

121. Those to whom We have given the Scripture, who read it with the right reading, those believe in it. And who disbelieves in it, those are they who are the losers.

122. O Children of Israel! Remember My favour with which I favoured you and how I preferred you to (all) creatures.

123. And guard (yourselves) against a day when no soul will in anything benefit another, nor will compensation be accepted from it, nor will intercession be of use to it; nor will they be helped.

124. And (remember) when his Lord tried Abraham with (His) commands, and he fulfilled them, He said: I have appointed you a leader for mankind. (Abraham) said: And of my offspring (will there be leaders)? He said: My covenant includes not wrongdoers.

125. And when We made the House (at Makkah) a resort for mankind and sanctuary, (saying): Take as your place of worship the place where Abraham stood (to pray). And We imposed a duty upon Abraham and Ishmael, (saying): Purify My house for those who go around and those who meditate in it and those who bow down and prostrate themselves (in worship).

126. And when Abraham prayed: My Lord! Make this a region of security and bestow upon its people fruits, such of them as believe in Allah and the Last Day, He answered: As for him who disbelieves, I shall leave him in contentment for a while, then I shall compel him to the doom of Fire - an unhappy journey's end!

127. And when Abraham and Ishmael were raising the foundations of the House (Abraham prayed): Our Lord! Accept from us (this duty). You, only You, are the Hearer, the Knower.

128. Our Lord! And make us submissive to You, and of our seed a nation submissive to You, and show us our ways of worship, and relent towards us. You, only You, are the Relenting, the Merciful.

129. Our Lord! And raise up in their midst a messenger from among them who shall recite to them Your revelations, and shall instruct them in the Scripture and in wisdom and shall make them grow. You, only You, are the Mighty, Wise.

130. And who forsakes the religion of Abraham except him who fools himself? Surely We chose him in the world, and in the Hereafter he is among the righteous.

131. When his Lord said to him: Surrender! He said: I have surrendered to the Lord of the Worlds.

132. The same did Abraham enjoin upon his sons, and also Jacob, (saying): O my sons! Allah has chosen for you the (true) religion; therefore die not except as men who have surrendered (to Him).

133. Or were you present when death came to Jacob, when he said to his sons: What will you worship after me? They said: We shall worship your God, the God of your fathers, Abraham and Ishmael and Isaac, One God, and to Him we have surrendered.

134. Those are a people who have passed away. Theirs is that which they earned, and yours is that which you earn. And you will not be asked of what they used to do.

135. And they say: Be Jews or Christians, then you will be rightly guided. Say (to them, O Muhammad): No, but (we follow) the religion of Abraham, the upright, and he was not of the idolaters.

136. Say (O Muslims): We believe in Allah and that which is revealed to us and that which was revealed to Abraham, and Ishmael, and Isaac, and Jacob, and the tribes, and that which Moses and Jesus received, and that which the prophets received from their Lord. We make no distinction between any of them, and to Him we have surrendered.

137. And if they believe in the like of that which you believe, then they are rightly guided. But if they turn away,

then they are in schism, and Allah will suffice you (for defence) against them. He is the Hearer, the Knower.

138. (We take our) colour from Allah, and who is better than Allah at colouring? We are His worshippers.

139. Say (to the People of the Scripture): Do you dispute with us concerning Allah when He is our Lord and your Lord? Ours are our works and yours your works. We look to Him alone.

140. Or say you that Abraham, and Ishmael, and Isaac, and Jacob, and the tribes were Jews or Christians? Say: Do you know best, or does Allah? And who is more unjust than he who hides a testimony which he has received from Allah? Allah is not unaware of what you do.

141. Those are a people who have passed away; theirs is that which they earned and yours that which you earn. And you will not be asked of what they used to do.

142. The foolish of the people will say: What has turned them from the Qiblah[23] which they formerly observed? Say: To Allah belong the East and the West. He guides whom He will to a straight path.

143. Thus We have appointed you a middle nation, that you may be witnesses against mankind, and that the messenger may be a witness against

---

23. *i.e.* The place towards which the face is turned at prayer. The first *Qiblah* of the Muslims was Jerusalem, which gave rise to a misunderstanding on the part of the Jews of Al-Madinah, who wished to draw the Muslims into Judaism. This was the cause of the Prophet's anxiety mentioned in the next verse but one.

you. And We appointed the *Qiblah* which you formerly observed only that We might know him who follows the messenger, from him who turns on his heels. In truth it was a hard (test) except for those whom Allah guided. But it was not Allah's purpose that your faith should be in vain, for Allah is Full of Pity, Merciful towards mankind.

144. We have seen the turning of your face to heaven (for guidance, O Muhammad). And now surely We shall make you turn (in prayer) towards a *Qiblah* which is dear to you. So turn your face towards the Inviolable Place of Worship[24], and you (O Muslims), wherever you may be, turn your faces (when you pray) towards it. Those who have received the Scripture know that (this Revelation) is the Truth from their Lord. And Allah is not unaware of what they do.

145. And even if you bring to those who have received the Scripture all kinds of signs, they would not follow your *Qiblah*, nor can you be a follower of their *Qiblah*; nor are some of them followers of the *Qiblah* of others. And if you should follow their desires after the knowledge which has come to you, then surely you were of the evildoers.

146. Those to whom We gave the Scripture recognise (this revelation) as they recognise their sons. But a party of them knowingly conceal the truth.

147. It is the Truth from your Lord (O Muhammad), so be not you of those who waver.

148. And each one has a goal towards which he turns; so vie with one another

in good works. From wherever you may be, Allah will bring you all together. Allah is Able to do all things.

149. And from wherever you come out (for prayer, O Muhammad) turn your face towards the Inviolable Place of Worship. It is the Truth from your Lord. Allah is not unaware of what you do.

150. From wherever you come out turn your face toward the Inviolable Place of Worship; and wherever you may be (O Muslims) turn your faces towards it (when you pray) so that men may have no argument against you, except such of them as do injustice - Fear them not, but fear Me! - and so that I may complete My grace upon you, and that you may be guided.

151. Even as We have sent to you a Messenger from among you, who recites to you Our revelations and causes you to grow, and teaches you the Scripture and wisdom, and teaches you that which you knew not[25].

152. Therefore remember Me, I will remember you. Give thanks to Me, and reject Me not.

153. O you who believe! Seek help in steadfastness and prayer. Allah is with the steadfast.

154. And call not those who are slain in the way of Allah "dead." No, they are living, only you perceive not.

155. And surely We shall try you with something of fear and hunger, and loss of wealth and lives and crops; but give glad tidings to the steadfast,

---

24. The *Ka'bah* at Makkah.

25. See Abraham's prayer, v. 129.

156. Who say, when a misfortune strikes them: We are Allah's and to Him we are returning.

157. Such are they on whom are blessings from their Lord, and mercy. Such are the rightly guided.

158. (The mountains) As-Safa and Al-Marwah are among the indications of Allah. It is therefore no sin for him who is on pilgrimage to the House (of God) or visits it, to go around them (as the pagan custom is). And he who does good of his own accord, (for him) Allah is Responsive, Aware.

159. Those who hide the proofs and the guidance which We revealed, after We had made it clear to mankind in the Scripture: such are accursed of Allah and accursed of those who have the power to curse.

160. Except those who repent and amend and make manifest (the truth). These it is towards whom I relent. I am the Relenting, the Merciful.

161. Those who disbelieve, and die while they are disbelievers; on them is the curse of Allah and of angels and of men combined.

162. They ever dwell in it. The doom will not be lightened for them, neither will they be reprieved.

163. Your God is One God; there is no God except Him, the Beneficent, the Merciful.

164. In the creation of the heavens and the earth, and the difference of night and day, and the ships which run upon the sea with that which is of use to men, and the water which Allah sends

down from the sky, by it reviving the earth after its death, and dispersing all kinds of beasts in it, and (in) the ordinance of the winds, and the clouds obedient between heaven and earth: are signs (of Allah's sovereignty) for people who have sense.

165. Yet of mankind are some who take to themselves (objects of worship which they set as) rivals to Allah, loving them with a love like (that which is the due) of Allah (only) - Those who believe are stauncher in their love for Allah - Oh, that those who do evil had only known, (on the day) when they see the doom, that power belongs wholly to Allah, and that Allah is severe in punishment!

166. (On the day) when those who were followed disown those who followed (them), and they see the doom, and all their aims collapse with them.

167. And those who were only followers will say: If a return were possible for us, we would disown them even as they have disowned us. Thus will Allah show them their own deeds as anguish for them, and they will not emerge from the Fire.

168. O mankind! Eat of that which is lawful and wholesome in the earth, and follow not the footsteps of the devil. He is an open enemy for you.

169. He enjoins upon you only the evil and the foul, and that you should tell concerning Allah that which you know not.

170. And when it is said to them: Follow that which Allah has revealed, they say: We follow that in which we found our fathers. What! Even though their fathers were wholly unintelligent and had no guidance?

171. The likeness of those who disbelieve (in relation to the Messenger) is as the likeness of one who calls to that which hears nothing except a shout and cry. Deaf, dumb, blind, therefore they have no sense.

172. O you who believe! Eat of the good things with which We have provided you, and render thanks to Allah if it is (indeed) He Whom you worship.

173. He has forbidden you only carrion, and blood, and swine flesh, and that which has been sanctified to (the name of) any other than Allah. But he who is driven by necessity, neither craving nor transgressing, it is no sin for him. Allah is Forgiving, Merciful.

174. Those who hide anything of the Scripture which Allah has revealed and purchase a small gain with it, they eat into their bellies nothing else than fire. Allah will not speak to them on the Day of Resurrection, nor will He make them grow. Theirs will be a painful doom.

175. Those are they who purchase error at the price of guidance, and torment at the price of pardon. How constant are they in their strife to reach the Fire!

176. That is because Allah has revealed the Scripture with the truth. Those who find (a cause of) disagreement in the Scripture are in open schism.

177. It is not righteousness that you turn your faces to the East and the

West; but righteous is he who believes in Allah and the Last Day and the angels and the Scripture and the Prophets; and gives wealth, for love of Him, to kindred and to orphans and the needy and the wayfarer and to those who ask, and to set slaves free; and observes proper worship and pays the poor-due[26]. And those who keep their treaty when they make one, and the patient in tribulation and adversity and time of stress. Such are they who are sincere. Such are the God-fearing.

178. O you who believe! Retaliation is prescribed for you in the matter of the murdered; the freeman for the freeman, and the slave for the slave, and the female for the female. And for him who is forgiven somewhat by his (injured) brother, prosecution according to usage and payment to him in kindness. This is an alleviation and a mercy from your Lord. He who transgresses after this will have a painful doom.

179. And there is life for you in retaliation, O men of understanding, that you may ward off (evil).

180. It is prescribed for you, when death approaches one of you, if he leave wealth, that he leave an inheritance to parents and near relatives in kindness. (This is) a duty for all those who ward off (evil).

181. And who changes (the will) after he has heard it - the sin of it is only on those who change it. Allah is Hearer, Knower.

182. But he who fears from a testator some unjust or sinful clause, and makes peace between the parties,

26. See verse 43, footnote.

(it shall be) no sin for him. Allah is Forgiving, Merciful.

183. O you who believe! Fasting is prescribed for you, even as it was prescribed for those before you, that you may ward off (evil);

184. (Fast) a certain number of days; and (for) him who is sick among you, or on a journey, (the same) number of other days; and for those who can afford it there is a ransom: the feeding of a man in need - but who does good of his own accord, it is better for him: and that you fast is better for you if you only know -

185. The month of Ramadan in which was revealed the Qur'an, a guidance for mankind, and clear proofs of the guidance, and the Criterion (of right and wrong). And whoever of you is present, let him fast the month, and whoever of you is sick or on a journey, (let him fast the same) number of other days. Allah desires for you ease; He desires not hardship for you; and (He desires) that you should complete the period, and that you should magnify Allah for having guided you, and that perhaps you may be thankful.

186. And when My servants question you concerning Me, then surely I am near. I answer the prayer of the supplicant when he calls to Me. So let them hear My call and let them trust in Me, in order that they may be led aright.

187. It is made lawful for you to go to your wives on the night of the fast. They are garment for you and you are garment for them. Allah is aware that you were

deceiving yourselves[27] in this respect and He has turned in mercy towards you and relieved you. So hold intercourse with them and seek that which Allah has ordained for you, and eat and drink until the white thread becomes distinct to you from the black thread of the dawn. Then strictly observe the fast till nightfall and touch them not, but be at your devotions in the mosques. These are the limits imposed by Allah, so approach them not. Thus Allah explains His revelations to mankind that they may ward off (evil).

188. And eat not up your property among yourselves in vanity, nor seek by it to gain the hearing of the judges that you may knowingly devour a portion of the property of others wrongfully.

189. They ask you, (O Muhammad), of new moons. Say: They are fixed seasons for mankind and for the pilgrimage. It is not righteousness that you go to houses by the backs of them (as do the idolaters at certain seasons), but the righteous man is he who wards off (evil). So go to houses by the gates of them, and observe your duty to Allah, that you may be successful.

190. Fight in the way of Allah against those who fight against you, but begin not hostilities. Allah loves not aggressors.

---

27. Until this verse was revealed, the Muslims used to fast completely from the evening meal of one day till the evening meal of the next, and if they fell asleep before they had taken their meal they had considered it their duty to abstain from it, with the result that men fainted and came nearer to death. Intercourse with their wives had been similarly restricted.

191. And slay them wherever you find them, and drive them out of the places from where they drove you out, for persecution is worse than slaughter. And fight not with them at the Inviolable Place of Worship until they first attack you there, but if they attack you (there) then slay them. Such is the reward of disbelievers.

192. But if they desist, then Allah is Forgiving, Merciful.

193. And fight them until persecution is no more, and religion is for Allah. But if they desist, then let there be no hostility except against wrongdoers.

194. The forbidden month for the forbidden month, and forbidden things in retaliation. And one who attacks you, attack him in like manner as he attacked you. Observe your duty to Allah, and know that Allah is with those who ward off (evil).

195. Spend your wealth for the cause of Allah, and be not cast by your own hands to ruin; and do good. Allah loves the beneficent.

196. Perform the pilgrimage[28] and the visit (to Makkah) for Allah. And if you are prevented, then send such gifts as can be obtained with ease, and shave not your heads until the gifts have reached their destination. And whoever among you is sick or has an ailment of the head must pay a ransom of fasting or almsgiving or offering. And if you are in safety, then whoever contents himself with the visit for the pilgrimage (shall give) such gifts as can be had with ease. And whoever cannot find (such

gifts), then a fast of three days while on the pilgrimage, and of seven when you have returned; that is, ten in all. That is for him whose people are not present at the Inviolable Place of Worship. Observe your duty to Allah, and know that Allah is severe in punishment.

197. The pilgrimage is (in) the well-known months, and whoever is minded to perform the pilgrimage in it (let him remember that) there is (to be) no lewdness nor abuse nor angry conversation on the pilgrimage. And whatever good you do Allah knows it. So make provision for yourselves (hereafter); for the best provision is to ward off evil. Therefore keep your duty to Me, O men of understanding.

198. It is no sin for you that you seek the bounty of your Lord (by trading). But, when you press on in the multitude from 'Arafat, remember Allah by the sacred monument. Remember Him as He has guided you, although before you were of those astray.

199. Then hasten onward from the place from where the multitude hastens onward, and ask forgiveness of Allah. Allah is Forgiving, Merciful.

200. And when you have completed your devotions, then remember Allah as you remember your fathers[29] or with a more lively remembrance. But of mankind is he who says: "Our Lord! Give to us in the world," and he has no portion in the Hereafter.

201. And of them (also) is he who says: "Our Lord! Give to us in the world that

---

28. See also *Surah 22, Yusuf*, vv. 26 ff.

29. It was a custom of the Pagan Arabs to praise their forefathers at the conclusion of the pilgrimage.

which is good and in the Hereafter that which is good, and guard us from the doom of Fire."

202. For them there is in store a goodly portion out of that which they have earned. Allah is swift at reckoning.

203. Remember Allah through the appointed days. Then who hastens (his departure) by two days, it is no sin for him, and who delays, it is no sin for him; that is for him who wards off (evil). Be careful of your duty to Allah, and know that to Him you will be gathered.

204. And of mankind there is he whose conversation on the life of this world pleases you (Muhammad), and he calls Allah to witness as to that which is in his heart; though he is the most rigid of opponents.

205. And when he turns away (from you) his effort in the land is to make mischief in it and to destroy the crops and the cattle; and Allah loves not mischief.

206. And when it is said to him: Be careful of your duty to Allah, pride takes him to sin. Hell will settle his account, an evil resting-place.

207. And of mankind is he who would sell himself, seeking the pleasure of Allah; and Allah has compassion on (His) bondsmen.

208. O you who believe! Come, all of you, into submission (to Him); and follow not the footsteps of the devil. He is an open enemy for you.

209. And if you slide back after the clear proofs have come to you, then know that Allah is Mighty, Wise.

210. Do they wait for nothing else than that Allah should come to them in the shadows of the clouds with the angels? Then the case would be already judged. All cases go back to Allah (for judgement).

211. Ask of the Children of Israel how many a clear revelation We gave them! He who alters the grace of Allah after it has come to him, (for him) Allah is severe in punishment.

212. Beautified is the life of the world for those who disbelieve; they make fun of the believers. But those who keep their duty to Allah will be above them on the Day of Resurrection. Allah gives without limit to whom He will.

213. Mankind were one community, and Allah sent (to them) Prophets as bearers of good tidings and as warners, and revealed with that the Scripture with the truth that it might judge between mankind concerning that in which they differed. And only those to whom (the Scripture) was given differed concerning it, after clear proofs had come to them, through hatred one of another. And Allah by His Will guided those who believe to the truth of that concerning which they differed. Allah guides whom He will to a straight path.

214. Or do you think that you will enter paradise while yet there has not come to you the like of (that which came to) those who passed away before you? Affliction and adversity befell them, they were shaken as with earthquake, till the Messenger (of Allah) and those who believed along with him said: When comes Allah's help? Now surely Allah's help is near.

215. They ask you, (O Muhammad), what they shall spend. Say: That which you spend for good (must go) to parents and near relatives and orphans and the needy and the wayfarer. And whatever good you do, Allah is Aware of it.

216. Warfare is ordained for you, though it is hateful to you; but it may happen that you hate a thing which is good for you, and it may happen that you love a thing which is bad for you. Allah knows, you know not.

217. They question you (O Muhammad) with regard to warfare in the sacred month. Say: Warfare in it is a great (transgression), but to turn (men) from the way of Allah, and to disbelieve in Him and in the Inviolable Place of Worship, and to expel His people from there is a greater (transgression) with Allah; for persecution is worse than killing. And they will not cease from fighting against you till they have made you renegades from your religion, if they can. And who becomes a renegade and dies in his disbelief: such are they whose works have fallen both in the world and the Hereafter. Such are rightful owners of the Fire: they will remain in it.

218. Those who believe, and those who emigrate (to escape the persecution) and strive in the way of Allah, these have hope of Allah's mercy. Allah is Forgiving, Merciful.

219. They question you about strong drink and games of chance. Say: In both is great sin, and (some) utility for men; but the sin of them is greater than their usefulness. And they ask you what they ought to spend. Say: That which is superfluous. Thus Allah makes plain to you (His) revelations, that perhaps you may reflect.

220. Upon the world and the Hereafter. And they question you concerning orphans. Say: To improve their lot is best. And if you mingle your affairs with theirs, then (they are) your brothers. Allah knows the one who spoils from the one who improves. Had Allah willed He could have overburdened you. Allah is Mighty, Wise.

221. Do not marry idolatresses till they believe; for a believing bondwoman is better than an idolatress though she pleases you; and give not your daughters in marriage to idolaters till they believe, for a believing slave is better than an idolater though he please you. These invite to the Fire, and Allah invites to the Garden, and to forgiveness by His grace, and explains His revelations to mankind that perhaps they may remember.

222. They question you (O Muhammad) concerning menstruation. Say: It is an illness, so let women alone at such times and go not in to them till they are cleansed. And when they have purified themselves, then go in to them as Allah has enjoined upon you. Truly Allah loves those who turn to Him, and loves those who have a care for cleanliness.

223. Your women are a tilth for you (to cultivate), so go to your tilth as you will, and send (good deeds) before you for your souls, and fear Allah, and know that you will (one day) meet Him. Give glad tidings to believers, (O Muhammad).

224. And make not Allah, by your oaths, a hindrance to your being righteous and observing your duty to Him and making peace among mankind. Allah is Hearer, Knower.

225. Allah will not take you to task for that which is unintentional in your oaths. But He will take you to task for that which your hearts have amassed. Allah is Forgiving, Clement.

226. Those who renounce their wives must wait four months; then, if they change their mind, Allah is Forgiving, Merciful.

227. And if they decide upon divorce (let them remember that) Allah is Hearer, Knower.

228. Women who are divorced shall wait, keeping themselves apart, three (monthly) courses. And it is not lawful for them that they should conceal that which Allah has created in their wombs if they are believers in Allah and the Last Day. And their husbands would do better to take them back in that case if they desire a reconciliation. And they (women) have rights similar to those (of men) over them in kindness, and men are a degree above them. Allah is Mighty, Wise.

229. Divorce must be pronounced twice and then (a woman) must be retained in honour or released in kindness. And it is not lawful for you that you take from women anything of that which you have given them; except (in the case) when both fear that they may not be able to keep within the limits (imposed by) Allah. And if you fear that they may not be able to keep the limits of Allah, in that case it is no sin for either of them if the woman ransom herself. These are the limits (imposed by) Allah. Transgress them not. For who transgresses Allah's limits: such are wrongdoers.

230. And if he has divorced her (the third time), then she is not lawful to him after that until she has wedded another husband. Then if he (the other husband) divorce her it is no sin for both of them that they come together again if they consider that they are able to observe the limits of Allah. These are the limits of Allah. He manifests them for people who have knowledge.

231. When you have divorced women, and they have reached their term, then retain them in kindness or release them in kindness. Retain them not to their hurt so that you transgress (the limits). He who does that has wronged his soul. Make not the revelations of Allah a laughing-stock (by your behaviour), but remember Allah's grace upon you and that which He has revealed to you of the Scripture and of wisdom, by which He does exhort you. Observe your duty to Allah and know that Allah is Aware of all things.

232. And when you have divorced women and they reach their term, place not difficulties in the way of their marrying their husbands if it is agreed between them in kindness. This is an admonition for him among you who believes in Allah and the Last Day. That is more virtuous for you, and cleaner. Allah knows; you know not.

233. Mothers shall suckle their children for two whole years; (that is) for those who wish to complete the suckling. The duty of feeding and clothing nursing mothers in a seemly manner is upon the father of the child. No-one should be charged beyond his capacity. A mother should not be made to suffer because of her child, nor should he to whom the child is born (be made to suffer) because of his child. And on the (father's) heir is incumbent the like of that (which was incumbent on the father). If they desire to wean the child by mutual consent and (after) consultation, it is no sin for them; and if you wish to give your children out to nurse, it is no sin for you, provided that you pay what is due from you in kindness. Observe your duty to Allah, and know that Allah is Seer of what you do.

234. Such of you as die and leave behind them wives, they (the wives) shall wait, keeping themselves apart, four months and ten days. And when they reach the term (prescribed for them) then there is no sin for you in anything that they may do with themselves in decency. Allah is Informed of what you do.

235. There is no sin for you in that which you proclaim or hide in your minds concerning your engagement to women. Allah knows that you will remember them. But pledge not your engagement to women except by uttering a recognised form of words. And do not consummate the marriage until (the term) prescribed is run. Know that Allah knows what is in your minds, so beware of Him; and know that Allah is Forgiving, Clement.

236. It is no sin for you if you divorce women while you have not yet touched them, nor appointed to them a portion. Provide for them, the rich according to his means, and the straitened according to his means, a fair provision. (This is) a binding duty for those who do good.

237. If you divorce them before you have touched them and you have appointed to them a portion, then (pay the) half of that which you appointed, unless they (the women) agree to waive it, or he agrees to waive it in whose hand is the marriage tie.[30] To waive is nearer to piety. And forget not kindness among yourselves. Allah is Seer of what you do.

238. Be guardians of your prayers, and of the midmost prayer,[31] and stand up with devotion to Allah.

239. And if you go in fear, then (pray) standing or on horseback. And when you are again in safety, remember Allah, as He has taught you that which until then you knew not.

240. (In the case of) those of you who are about to die and leave behind them wives, they should leave to their wives a provision for the year without turning them out, but if they go out (of their own accord) there is no sin for you in that which they do of themselves within their rights. Allah is Mighty, Wise.

---

30. *i.e.* the bridegroom.
31. Meaning, probably, the best amid all forms of prayer; but some authorities think the reference is to the 'Asr (afternoon) prayer which Muslims are most apt to forget.

241. For divorced women a provision in kindness: a duty for those who ward off (evil).

242. Thus Allah explains to you His revelations so that you may understand.

243. Consider you not (O Muhammad) those of old, who went out from their habitations in their thousands, fearing death,[32] and Allah said to them: Die; and then He brought them back to life. Allah is a Lord of Kindness to mankind, but most of mankind give not thanks.

244. Fight in the way of Allah, and know that Allah is Hearer, Knower.

245. Who is it who will lend to Allah a goodly loan,[33] so that He may give it increase manifold? Allah tightens and enlarges. To Him you will return.

246. Consider the leaders of the Children of Israel after Moses, how they said to a prophet whom they had: Set up for us a king and we will fight in Allah's way. He said: Would you then refrain from fighting if fighting were prescribed for you? They said: Why should we not fight in Allah's way when we have been driven from our dwellings with our children? Yet, when fighting was prescribed for them, they turned away, all except a few of them. Allah is aware of evildoers.

247. Their Prophet said to them: Allah has raised up Saul to be a king for you. They said: How can he have kingdom over us when we are more deserving of the kingdom than he is, since he has not been given wealth enough? He said: Allah has chosen him above you, and has increased him abundantly in wisdom and stature. Allah bestows His Sovereignty on whom He will. Allah is All-Embracing, All Knowing.

248. And their Prophet said to them: The sign of his kingdom is that there shall come to you the ark in which is peace of reassurance from your Lord, and a remnant of that which the house of Moses and the house of Aaron left behind, the angels bearing it. In this shall be a sign for you if (in truth) you are believers.

249. And when Saul set out with the army, he said: Allah will try you by (the ordeal of) a river. Whoever therefore drinks of it he is not of me, and whoever tastes it not he is of me, except him who takes (of it) in the hollow of his hand. But they drank of it, all except a few of them. And after he had crossed (the river), he and those who believed with him, they said: We have no power this day against Goliath and his forces. But those who knew that they would meet Allah exclaimed: How many a little company has overcome a mighty force by Allah's permission! Allah is with the steadfast.

250. And when they went into the field against Goliath and his forces they said: Our Lord! Bestow on us endurance, make our foothold sure, and give us help against the disbelieving people.

251. So they routed them by Allah's permission and David slew Goliath; and Allah gave him the kingdom and

---

32. The reference is to the Exodus.

33. A loan without interest - *i.e.* without thought of gain.

wisdom, and taught him of that which He wills. And if Allah had not repelled some men by others, the earth would have been corrupted. But Allah is a Lord of Kindness to (His) creatures.

252. These are the signs of Allah which We recite to you (Muhammad) with truth, and you are of the number of (Our) messengers;

253. Of those messengers, some of whom We have caused to excel others, and of whom there are some to whom Allah spoke, while some of them He exalted (above others) in degree; and We gave Jesus, son of Mary, clear proofs (of Allah's Sovereignty) and We supported him with the Holy Spirit.[34] And if Allah had so willed it, those who followed after them would not have fought one with another after the clear proofs had come to them. But they differed, some of them believing and some disbelieving. And if Allah had so willed it, they would not have fought one with another; but Allah does what He will.

254. O you who believe! Spend of that with which We have provided you before a day when there will be no trafficking, nor friendship, nor intercession. The disbelievers, they are the wrongdoers.

255. Allah! There is no God except Him, the Alive, the Eternal. Neither slumber nor sleep overtakes Him. To Him belongs whatever is in the heavens and whatever is in the earth. Who is he that intercedes with Him except by His permission? He knows that which is in front of them and that which is behind them, while they encompass nothing of His knowledge except what He will. His throne includes the heavens and the earth, and He is never weary of preserving them. He is the Sublime, the Tremendous.

256. There is no compulsion in religion. The right direction is from now on distinct from error. And he who rejects false deities and believes in Allah has grasped a firm handhold which will never break. Allah is Hearer, Knower.

257. Allah is the Protecting Guardian of those who believe. He brings them out of darkness into light. As for those who disbelieve, their patrons are false deities. They bring them out of light into darkness. Such are rightful owners of the Fire. They will remain in it.

258. Consider him who had an argument with Abraham about his Lord, because Allah had given him the kingdom; how, when Abraham said: My Lord is He Who gives life and causes death, he answered: I give life and cause death. Abraham said: Allah causes the sun to rise in the East, so do you cause it to come up from the West? Thus was the disbeliever embarrassed. And Allah guides not wrongdoing people.

259. Or (consider) the like of him who, passing by a township which had fallen into utter ruin, exclaimed: How shall Allah give this township[35]

---

34. *i.e.* the angel Gabriel.

35. Most of the commentators agree that the reference here is to Jerusalem in ruins, while the following words tell of the vision of Ezekiel.

life after its death? And Allah made him die a hundred years, then brought him back to life. He said: How long have you stayed? (The man) said: I have stayed a day or part of a day. (He) said: No, but you have stayed for a hundred years. Just look at your food and drink which have not rotted! Look at your donkey! And, that We may make you a sign to mankind, look at the bones, how We adjust them and then cover them with flesh! And when (the matter) became clear to him, he said: I know now that Allah is Able to do all things.

260. And when Abraham said (to his Lord): My Lord! Show me how You give life to the dead, He said: Do you not believe? Abraham said: Yes, but (I ask) in order that my heart may be at ease. (His Lord) said: Take four of the birds and cause them to incline to you, then place some of them on each hill, then call them, they will come to you in haste, and know that Allah is Mighty, Wise.

261. The likeness of those who spend their wealth in Allah's way is as the likeness of a grain which grows seven ears, in every ear a hundred grains. Allah gives increase manifold to whom He will. Allah is All-Embracing, All-Knowing.

262. Those who spend their wealth for the cause of Allah and afterwards make not reproach and injury to follow that which they have spent; their reward is with their Lord, and there shall no fear come upon them, neither shall they grieve.

263. A kind word with forgiveness is better than almsgiving followed by injury. Allah is Absolute, Clement.

264. O you who believe! Render not vain your almsgiving by reproach and injury, like him who spends his wealth only to be seen of men and believes not in Allah and the Last Day. His likeness is as the likeness of a rock on which is dust of earth; a rainstorm strikes it, leaving it smooth and bare. They have no control of anything of that which they have gained. Allah guides not the disbelieving people.

265. And the likeness of those who spend their wealth in search of Allah's pleasure, and for the strengthening of their souls, is as the likeness of a garden on a height. The rainstorm strikes it and it brings forth its fruit twofold. And if the rainstorm strike it not, then the shower is sufficient. Allah is Seer of what you do.

266. Would any of you like to have a garden of palm-trees and vines, with rivers flowing underneath it, with all kinds of fruit for him in it; and old age has stricken him and he has feeble offspring; and a fiery whirlwind strikes it and it is (all) consumed by fire. Thus Allah makes plain His revelations to you, in order that you may give thought.

267. O you who believe! Spend of the good things which you have earned, and of that which We bring out from the earth for you, and seek not the bad (with intent) to spend of it (in charity) when you would not take it for yourselves except with contempt; and know that Allah is Absolute, Owner of Praise.

268. The devil promises you destitution and enjoins on you lewdness. But Allah promises you forgiveness from Himself with bounty. Allah is All-Embracing, All-knowing.

269. He gives wisdom to whom He will, and he to whom wisdom is given, he truly has received abundant good. But none remember except men of understanding.

270. Whatever alms you spend or vow you make, Allah knows it. Wrongdoers have no helpers.

271. If you publish your almsgiving, it is well, but if you hide it and give it to the poor, it will be better for you, and will atone for some of your ill-deeds. Allah is Informed of what you do.

272. The guiding of them is not your duty (O Muhammad), but Allah guides whom He will. And whatever good thing you spend, it is for yourselves, when you spend not except in search of Allah's Countenance; and whatever good thing you spend, it will be repaid to you in full, and you will not be wronged.

273. (Alms are) for the poor who are in difficulty for the cause of Allah, who cannot travel in the land (for trade). The unthinking man accounts them wealthy because of their restraint (modesty). You shall know them by their mark: They do not beg of men with annoyance. And whatever good thing you spend, Allah knows it.

274. Those who spend their wealth by night and day, secretly and openly, surely their reward is with their Lord, and no fear shall come upon them, neither shall they grieve.

275. Those who swallow usury cannot rise up except as he arises whom the devil has prostrated by (his) touch. That is because they say: Trade is just like usury; whereas Allah permits trading and forbids usury. He to whom an admonition from his Lord comes, and (he) refrains (in obedience to it), he shall keep (the profits of) that which is past, and his affair (from then on) is with Allah. As for him who returns (to usury) - such are rightful owners of the Fire. They will remain in it.

276. Allah has destroyed usury and made almsgiving fruitful. Allah loves not the impious and guilty.

277. Those who believe and do good works and establish worship and pay the poor-due, their reward is with their Lord and there shall no fear come upon them, neither shall they grieve.

278. O you who believe! Observe your duty to Allah, and give up what remains (due to you) from usury, if you are (in truth) believers.

279. And if you do not, then be warned of war (against you) from Allah and His messenger. And if you repent, then you have your principal (without interest). Wrong not, and you will not be wronged.

280. And if the debtor is in straitened circumstances, then (let there be) postponement to (the time of) ease; and that you remit the debt as almsgiving would be better for you if you did but know.

281. And guard yourselves against a day in which you will be brought back to Allah. Then every soul will be paid in full that which it has earned, and they will not be wronged.

282. O you who believe! When you contract a debt for a fixed term, record it in writing. Let a scribe record it in writing between you in (terms of) equity. No scribe should refuse to write as Allah has taught him, so let him write, and let him who incurs the debt dictate, and let him observe his duty to Allah his Lord, and diminish none of it. But if he who owes the debt is of low understanding, or weak, or unable himself to dictate, then let the guardian of his interests dictate in (terms of) equity. And call to witness, from among your men, two witnesses. And if two men be not (at hand) then a man and two women, of such as you approve as witnesses, so that if the one errs (through forgetfulness) the other will remember. And the witnesses must not refuse when they are summoned. Be not averse to writing down (the contract) whether it be small or great, with (record of) the term of it. That is more equitable in the sight of Allah and more sure for testimony, and the best way of avoiding doubt between you; except only in the case when it is actual merchandise which you transfer among yourselves from hand to hand. In that case it is no sin for you if you write it not. And have witnesses when you sell one to another, and let no harm be done to scribe or witness. If you do (harm to them) it is a sin in you. Observe your duty to Allah. Allah is teaching you. And Allah is Knower of all things.

283. If you are on a journey and cannot find a scribe, then a pledge

in hand (shall suffice). And if one of you entrusts to another let him who is trusted deliver up that which is entrusted to him (according to the pact between them) and let him observe his duty to Allah his Lord. Hide not testimony. He who hides it, surely his heart is sinful. Allah is Aware of what you do.

284. To Allah (belongs) whatever is in the heavens and whatever is in the earth; and whether you make known what is in your minds or hide it, Allah will bring you to account for it. He will forgive whom He will and He will punish whom He will. Allah is Able to do all things.

285. The messenger believes in that which has been revealed to him from his Lord and (so do) the believers. Each one believes in Allah and His angels and His scriptures and His messengers - we make no distinction between any of His messengers - and they say: We hear, and we obey. (Grant us) Your forgiveness, our Lord. To You is the journeying.

286. Allah tasks not a soul beyond its scope. For it (is only) that which it has earned, and against it (only) that which it has deserved. Our Lord! Condemn us not if we forget, or miss the mark! Our Lord! Lay not on us such a burden as You did lay on those before us! Our Lord! Impose not on us that which we have not the strength to bear! Pardon us, absolve us and have mercy on us, You, our Protector, and give us victory over the disbelieving people.

Surah 3: **Al-'Imran**
(The Family of 'Imran)

Al-'Imran takes its title from v. 33, where "the family of Imran" (the father of Moses) occurs as a generic name for all the Hebrew prophets from Moses to John the Baptist and Jesus Christ. This, with the mention of the mother of Mary as "the wife of Imran" (v. 35), and the words "sister of Aaron" addressed to Mary (19, 28), have given rise to a charge of anachronism - absurd because the whole of the rest of the Qur'an is against it - by Muir and other non-Muslim writers, who say that the Prophet confused Mary, the mother of Jesus, with Miriam, the sister of Moses. Most Muslims believe, on the authority of the Qur'an, that the grandfather of Jesus Christ was named Imran, which may also have been the name of the father of Moses. In Surah 19, 28, where Mary is addressed as "sister of Aaron", they hold the ancestral sense to be the more probable, while denying that there is any reason to suppose that the Virgin Mary had not a brother named Aaron.

If vv. 1 to 34 were, as tradition states, revealed on the occasion of the deputation from the Christians of Najran, which took place in the tenth year of the Hijrah ("the year of deputations", as it is called), then they are of much later date than the rest of the Surah, but it seems possible that they were only recited by the Prophet on that occasion, having been revealed before.

The Jews have become bolder and more bitter in opposition which, as Nöldeke points out, cannot have been the case, after the signal victory of Badr, until after the Muslims suffered a reverse at Uhud; a battle to which vv. 121 to 188 largely refer.

In the third year of the Hijrah the Makkans came against Al-Madinah, with an army of 3000 men to avenge their defeat at Badr in the previous year, and to wipe out the Muslims. The Prophet, against his own first plan, which was to defend Al-Madinah, at the insistence of his companions, went out to meet them at Mt. Uhud, posting his men carefully. He led an army of 1000 men, a third of whom under Abdullah ibn Ubeyy (the "Hypocrite" leader) deserted him before the battle, and said afterwards that they did not think there would be any fighting that day. The battle began well for the Muslims but was changed to something near defeat by the disobedience of a band of fifty archers placed to guard a certain point. Seeing the Muslims winning, they feared that they might lose their share of the spoils, and ran to join the others, leaving a way open for the Makkan cavalry. The idolaters then rallied and inflicted considerable losses upon the Muslims, the Prophet himself being wounded in the struggle. A cry arose that the Prophet had been slain, and the Muslims were in despair till someone recognised the Prophet and called out that he was living. The Muslims then rallied to his side, and retired in some sort of order. The army of Quraysh also retired after the battle.

In this battle the wives of the leaders of Quraysh, who had been brought with the army to give courage by their presence and their chanting, mutilated the Muslims slain, making necklaces and bracelets of ears and noses. Hind, the wife of Abu Sufyan, plucked out the liver of the Prophet's uncle, Hamzah, publicly, and tried to eat it. The Prophet, when he saw the condition of the slain, was moved to vow reprisals. But he was relieved of his vow by a revelation, and mutilation was forbidden to the Muslims.

On the day after the battle of Mt. Uhud, the Prophet again went out with such of the army as survived, in order that Quraysh might hear that he was in the field and perhaps be deterred from any project of attacking Al-Madinah in its weakened state. On that occasion many wounded men went out with him. Tradition tells how a friendly nomad met the Muslims and afterwards met the army of Quraysh. Questioned by Abu Sufyan, he said that the Prophet was seeking vengeance with an overwhelming force; and that report determined Abu Sufyan to march back to Makkah.

The period of revelation is the third and fourth years of the Hijrah.

In the name of Allah,
the Beneficent, the Merciful.

1. *Alif. Lam. Mim.*[36]

2. Allah! There is no God except Him, the Alive, the Eternal.

3. He has revealed to you (Muhammad) the Scripture with truth, confirming that

which was (revealed) before it, even as He revealed the Torah and the Gospel.

4. Before, a guidance to mankind; and has revealed the Criterion (of right and wrong). Those who disbelieve the revelations of Allah, theirs will be a heavy doom. Allah is Mighty, Able to Requite (the wrong).

5. Nothing in the earth or in the heavens is hidden from Allah.

6. He it is Who fashions you in the wombs as pleases Him. There is no God except Him, the Almighty, the Wise.

7. He it is Who has revealed to you (Muhammad) the Scripture in which are clear revelations - they are the substance of the Book - and others (which are) allegorical. But those in whose hearts is doubt pursue that which is allegorical seeking (to cause) dissension by seeking to explain it. None knows its explanation except Allah. And those who are of sound instruction say: We believe in it; the whole is from our Lord; but only men of understanding really heed.

8. Our Lord! Cause not our hearts to stray after You have guided us, and bestow upon us mercy from Your Presence. You, only You, are the Bestower.

9. Our Lord! It is You Who will gather mankind together to a Day of which there is no doubt. Allah fails not to keep the appointed time.

10. (On that Day) neither the riches nor the progeny of those who disbelieve will benefit them anything with Allah. They will be fuel for the Fire.

---

36. See *Surah 2, Al-Baqarah*, v. 1, footnote.

11. Like Pharaoh's people and those who were before them, they disbelieved Our revelations and so Allah seized them for their sins. And Allah is severe in punishment.

12. Say (O Muhammad) to those who disbelieve: You shall be overcome and gathered to Hell, an evil resting-place.

13. There was a sign for you in two armies which met,[37] one army fighting in the way of Allah, and another disbelieving, whom they saw as twice their number, clearly, with their very eyes. But Allah strengthens with His help whom He will. In this is a lesson for those who have eyes.

14. Beautified for mankind is love of the joys (that come) from women and offspring; and stored-up heaps of gold and silver, and horses branded (with their mark), and cattle and land. That is comfort of the life of the world. Allah! With Him is a more excellent abode.

15. Say: Shall I inform you of something better than that? For those who keep from evil, with their Lord, are Gardens underneath which rivers flow in which they will remain, and pure companions, and contentment from Allah. Allah is Seer of His bondsmen,

16. Those who say: Our Lord! We believe. So forgive us our sins and guard us from the punishment of Fire;

17. The steadfast, and the truthful, and the obedient, those who spend (and hoard not), those who pray for pardon in the watches of the night.

18. Allah (Himself) is Witness that there is no God except Him. And the angels and the men of learning (too are witness). Maintaining His creation in justice, there is no God except Him, the Almighty, the Wise.

19. Religion with Allah (is) the Surrender[38] (to His Will and Guidance). Those whoever (formerly) received the Scripture differed only after knowledge came to them, through transgression among themselves. Who disbelieves the revelations of Allah (will find that) Allah is swift at reckoning.

20. And if they argue with you, (O Muhammad), say: I have surrendered my purpose to Allah and (so have) those who follow me. And say to those who have received the Scripture and those who read not: Have you (too) surrendered? If they surrender, then truly they are rightly guided, and if they turn away, then it is your duty only to convey the message (to them). Allah is Seer of (His) bondsmen.

21. Those who disbelieve the revelations of Allah, and slay the prophets wrongfully, and slay those of mankind who enjoin equity: promise them a painful doom.

22. Those are they whose works have failed in the world and the Hereafter; and they have no helpers.

23. Have you not seen how those who have received a portion of the Scripture invoke the Scripture of Allah (in their disputes) that it may judge between them; then a faction of them turn away, being opposed (to it)?

---

37. The reference is to the battle of Badr.

38. Arabic - *Al-Islam*

24. That is because they say: The Fire will not touch us except for a certain number of days. That which they used to invent has deceived them regarding their religion.

25. How (will it be with them) when We have brought them all together to a Day of which there is no doubt, when every soul will be paid in full what it has earned, and they will not be wronged.

26. Say: O Allah! Owner of Sovereignty! You give sovereignty to whom You will, and You withdraw sovereignty from whom You will. You exalt whom You will, and You humiliate whom You will. In Your hand is the good. You are Able to do all things.

27. You cause the night to pass into the day, and You cause the day to pass into the night. And You bring out the living from the dead, and You bring out the dead from the living. And You give sustenance to whom You choose, without limit.

28. Let not the believers take disbelievers for their friends in preference to believers. Who does that has no connection with Allah unless (it be) that you only guard yourselves against them, taking (as it were) security. Allah orders you to beware (only) of Himself. To Allah is the journeying.

29. Say, (O Muhammad): Whether you hide that which is in your breasts or reveal it, Allah knows it. He knows that which is in the heavens and that which is in the earth, and Allah is Able to do all things.

30. On the Day when every soul will find itself confronted with all that it has

done of good and all that it has done of evil, (every soul) will long that there might be a mighty space of distance between it and that (evil). Allah orders you to beware of Him. And Allah is Full of Pity for (His) bondsmen.

31. Say, (O Muhammad, to mankind): If you love Allah, follow me; Allah will love you and forgive you your sins. Allah is Forgiving, Merciful.

32. Say: Obey Allah and the messenger. But if they turn away, Allah loves not the disbelievers (in His guidance).

33. Allah preferred Adam and Noah and the Family of Abraham and the Family of 'Imran above (all His) creatures.

34. They were descendants one of another. Allah is Hearer, Knower.

35. (Remember) when the wife of 'Imran said: My Lord! I have vowed to You that which is in my belly as a consecrated (offering). Accept it from me. You, only You, are the Hearer, the Knower!

36. And when she was delivered she said: My Lord! I am delivered of a female - Allah knew best of what she was delivered - the male is not as the female; and I have named her Mary, and I crave Your protection for her and for her offspring from Satan the outcast.

37. And her Lord accepted her with full acceptance and vouchsafed to her a goodly growth; and made Zechariah her guardian. Whenever Zechariah went into the sanctuary where she was, he found that she had food. He said: O Mary! From where comes to you this (food)? She answered: It is from Allah. Allah gives without limit to whom He will.

38. Then Zechariah prayed to his Lord and said: My Lord! Bestow upon me of Your bounty goodly offspring. You are the Hearer of Prayer.

39. And the angels called to him as he stood praying in the sanctuary: Allah gives you glad tidings of (a son whose name is) John[39], (who comes) to confirm a word from Allah, lordly, chaste, a prophet of the righteous.

40. He said: My Lord! How can I have a son when age has overtaken me already and my wife is barren? (The angel) answered: So (it will be). Allah does what He will.

41. He said: My Lord! Appoint a sign for me. (The angel) said: The sign to you (will be) that you shall not speak to mankind three days except by signs. Remember your Lord much, and praise (Him) in the early hours of night and morning.

42. And when the angels said: O Mary! Allah has chosen you and made you pure, and has preferred you above (all) the women of creation.

43. O Mary! Be obedient to your Lord, prostrate yourself and bow with those who bow (in worship).

44. This is of the tidings of things hidden. We reveal it to you (Muhammad). You were not present with them when they threw their pens (to know) which of them should be the guardian of Mary, nor were you present with them when they quarrelled (about it).

45. (And remember) when the angels said: O Mary! Allah gives you glad tidings of a word from him, whose name is the Messiah, Jesus, son of Mary, illustrious in the world and the Hereafter, and one of those brought near (to Allah).

46. He will speak to mankind in his cradle and in his manhood, and he is of the righteous.

47. She said: My Lord! How can I have a child when no mortal has touched me? He said: So (it will be). Allah creates what He will. If He decrees a thing, He says to it only: Be! and it is.

48. And He will teach him the Scripture and wisdom, and the Torah and the Gospel,

49. And will make him a messenger to the Children of Israel, (saying): I come to you with a sign from your Lord. I fashion for you out of clay the likeness of a bird, and I breathe into it and it is a bird, by Allah's permission. I heal him who was born blind, and the leper, and I raise the dead, by Allah's permission. And I announce to you what you eat and what you store up in your houses. In this verily is a sign for you, if you are to be believers.

50. And (I come) confirming that which was before me of the Torah, and to make lawful some of that which was forbidden to you. I come to you with a sign from your Lord, so keep your duty to Allah and obey me.

51. Allah is my Lord and your Lord, so worship Him. That is a straight path.

52. But when Jesus became conscious of their disbelief, he called: Who will be my helpers in the cause of Allah? The disciples said: We will be

39. Arabic: *Yahya*

Allah's helpers. We believe in Allah, and bear you witness that we have surrendered[40] (to Him).

53. Our Lord! We believe in that which You have revealed and we follow him whom You have sent. Enrol us among those who witness (to the truth).

54. And they (the disbelievers) schemed, and Allah schemed (against them): and Allah is the best of schemers.

55. (And remember) when Allah said: O Jesus! I am gathering you and causing you to ascend to Me, and am cleansing you of those who disbelieve and am setting those who follow you above those who disbelieve until the Day of Resurrection. Then to Me you will (all) return, and I shall judge between you as to that in which you used to differ.

56. As for those who disbelieve I shall chastise them with a heavy chastisement in the world and the Hereafter; and they will have no helpers.

57. And as for those who believe and do good works, He will pay them their wages in full. Allah loves not wrongdoers.

58. This (which) We recite to you is a revelation and a wise reminder.

59. The likeness of Jesus with Allah is as the likeness of Adam. He created him of dust, then He said to him: Be! and he is.

60. (This is) the truth from your Lord (O Muhammad), so be not you of those who waver.

61. And whoever disputes with you concerning him, after the knowledge which has come to you, say (to him): Come! We will summon our sons and your sons, and our women and your women, and ourselves and yourselves, then we will pray humbly (to our Lord) and (solemnly) invoke the curse of Allah upon those who lie.

62. This verily is the true narrative. There is no God except Allah, and Allah, is the Mighty, the Wise.

63. And if they turn away, then Allah is Aware of (who are) the corrupters.

64. Say: O People of the Scripture![41] Come to an agreement between us and you: that we shall worship none but Allah, and that we shall ascribe no partner to Him, and that none of us shall take others for lords beside Allah. And if they turn away, then say: Bear witness that we are they who have surrendered[42] (to Him).

65. O People of the Scripture! Why will you argue about Abraham, when the Torah and the Gospel were not revealed till after him? Have you then no sense?

66. You are those who argue about that of which you have some knowledge. Why then do you argue concerning that of which you have no knowledge? Allah knows. You know not.

67. Abraham was not a Jew, nor yet a Christian; but he was an upright man who had surrendered (to Allah), and he was not of the idolaters.

---

40. Or "are Muslims."

41. Jews and Christians.
42. Arabic: *Muslimun.*

68. Those of mankind who have the best claim to Abraham are those who followed him, and this Prophet and those who believe (with him); and Allah is the Protecting Guardian of the believers.

69. A party of the People of the Scripture long to make you go astray; and they make none to go astray except themselves, but they perceive not.

70. O People of the Scripture! Why disbelieve you in the revelations of Allah, when you (yourselves) bear witness (to their truth)?

71. O People of the Scripture! Why do you mix truth with falsehood and knowingly conceal the truth?

72. And a party of the People of the Scripture say: Believe in that which has been revealed to those who believe at the opening of the day, and disbelieve at the end of it, in order that they may return;[43]

73. And believe not except in one who follows your religion. Say (O Muhammad): The guidance is Allah's guidance - that anyone is given the like of that which was given to you or that they may argue with you in the presence of their Lord. Say (O Muhammad): The bounty is in Allah's hand. He bestows it on whom He will. Allah is All-Embracing, All-Knowing.

74. He selects for His mercy whom He will. Allah is of infinite bounty.

75. Among the People of the Scripture there is he who, if you trust him with a weight of treasure, will return it to you. And among them there is he who, if you trust him with a piece of gold, will not return it to you unless you keep standing over him. That is because they say: We have no duty to the Gentiles. They speak a lie concerning Allah, knowingly.

76. No, but (the chosen of Allah is) he who fulfils his pledge and wards off (evil); for Allah loves those who ward off (evil).

77. Those who purchase a small gain at the cost of Allah's covenant and their oaths,[44] they have no portion in the Hereafter. Allah will neither speak to them nor look upon them on the Day of Resurrection, nor will He make them grow. Theirs will be a painful doom.

78. And there is a party of them who distort the Scripture with their tongues, that you may think that what they say is from the Scripture, when it is not from the Scripture. And they say: It is from Allah, when it is not from Allah; and they speak a lie concerning Allah, knowingly.

79. It is not (possible) for any human being to whom Allah had given the Scripture and wisdom and the Prophethood that he should afterwards have said to mankind: Be slaves of me instead of Allah; but (what he said was): Be you faithful servants of the Lord by virtue of your constant teaching of the Scripture and of your constant study of it.

---

43. The reference is to some Jews of Al-Madinah, who feigned an interest in Al-Islam only in the hope of detaching some of the Muslims by their subtle arguments.

44. The Jews of Madinah had made a solemn treaty with the Prophet in the year 1 after Hijrah (A.H.)

80. And he commanded you not that you should take the angels and the Prophets for lords. Would he command you to disbelieve after you had surrendered (to Allah)?

81. When Allah made (His) covenant with the Prophets, (He said): Take that which I have given you of the Scripture and knowledge. And afterwards there will come to you a messenger, confirming that which you possess. You shall believe in him and you shall help him. He said: Do you agree, and will you take up My burden (which I lay upon you) in this (matter)? They answered: We agree. He said: Then bear you witness. I will be a witness with you.

82. Then whoever turns away after this: they will be wrongdoers.

83. Seek they other than the religion of Allah, when to Him submits whoever is in the heavens and the earth, willingly or unwillingly, and to Him they will be returned.

84. Say (O Muhammad): We believe in Allah and that which is revealed to us and that which was revealed to Abraham and Ishmael and Isaac and Jacob and the tribes, and that which was entrusted to Moses and Jesus and the prophets from their Lord. We make no distinction between any of them, and to Him we have surrendered.[45]

85. And whoever seeks as religion other than the Surrender[46] (to Allah) it will not be accepted from him, and he will be a loser in the Hereafter.

86. How shall Allah guide a people who disbelieved after their belief and (after) they bore witness that the messenger is true, and after clear proofs (of Allah's Sovereignty) had come to them. And Allah guides not wrongdoing people.

87. As for such, their reward is that on them rests the curse of Allah and of angels and of men combined.

88. They will remain in it (Hell). Their doom will not be lightened, neither will they be reprieved;

89. Except those who afterwards repent and do right. Allah is Forgiving, Merciful.

90. Those who disbelieve after their (profession of) belief, and afterwards grow violent in disbelief: their repentance will not be accepted. And such are those who are astray.

91. Those who disbelieve, and die in disbelief, the (whole) earth full of gold would not be accepted from such a one if it were offered as a ransom (for his soul). Theirs will be a painful doom and they will have no helpers.

92. You will not attain to piety until you spend of that which you love. And whatever you spend, Allah is aware of it.

93. All food was lawful to the Children of Israel, except that which Israel forbade himself, (in days) before the Torah was revealed. Say: Produce the Torah and read it (to us) if you are truthful.

94. And whoever invents a falsehood after that concerning Allah, they will be wrongdoers.

---

45. Almost identical to *Surah* 2 v. 136.
46. Arabic: *Al-Islam.*

95. Say: Allah speaks the truth. So follow the religion of Abraham, the upright. He was not of the idolaters.

96. The first Sanctuary appointed for mankind was that at Becca[47], a blessed place, a guidance to the peoples;

97. In which are plain memorials (of Allah's guidance); the place where Abraham stood up to pray; and whoever enters it is safe. And pilgrimage to the House is a duty to Allah for mankind, for him who can find a way there. As for him who disbelieves, (let him know that) Allah is Independent of (all) creatures.

98. Say: O People of the Scripture! Why do you disbelieve in the revelations of Allah, when Allah (Himself) is Witness of what you do?

99. Say: O People of the Scripture! Why do you drive back believers from the way of Allah, seeking to make it crooked, when you are witnesses (to Allah's guidance)? Allah is not unaware of what you do.

100. O you who believe! If you obey a party of those who have received the Scripture they will make you disbelievers after your belief.

101. How can you disbelieve, when it is you to whom Allah's revelations are recited, and His messenger is in your midst? He who holds fast to Allah, he indeed is guided to a right path.

102. O you who believe! Observe your duty to Allah with right observance, and die not except as those who have surrendered (to Him);

47. Makkah.

103. And hold fast, all of you together, to the rope of Allah, and do not separate. And remember Allah's favour to you: how you were enemies and He made friendship between your hearts so that you became as brothers by His grace; and (how) you were upon the brink of an abyss of fire, and He did save you from it. ʾ hus Allah makes clear His revelatioɪ s to you, that perhaps you may be guɪded,

104. And there may spring from you a nation who invite to goodness, and enjoin right conduct and forbid indecency. Such are they who are successful.

105. And be you not as those who separated and disputed after the clear proofs had come to them. For such there is an awful doom,

106. On the Day when (some) faces will be whitened and (some) faces will be blackened; and as for those whose faces have been blackened, it will be said to them: Did you disbelieve after your (profession of) belief? Then taste the punishment for that you disbelieved.

107. And as for those whose faces have been whitened, in the mercy of Allah they dwell forever.

108. These are revelations of Allah. We recite them to you in truth. Allah wills no injustice to (His) creatures.

109. To Allah belongs whatever is in the heavens and whatever is in the earth; and to Allah all things are returned.

110. You are the best community that has been raised up for mankind. You enjoin right conduct and forbid indecency; and you believe in Allah. And if the People of the Scripture had believed it had been better for them. Some of them are believers; but most of them are evil-livers.

111. They will not harm you except a slight hurt, and if they fight against you they will turn and flee. And afterwards they will not be helped.

112. Disgrace will be their portion wherever they are found except (where they grasp) a rope from Allah and a rope from men.[48] They have incurred anger from their Lord, and wretchedness is laid upon them. That is because they used to disbelieve the revelations of Allah, and slew the prophets wrongfully. That is because they were rebellious and used to transgress.

113. They are not all alike. Of the People of the Scripture there is a staunch community who recite the revelations of Allah in the night season, falling prostrate (before Him).

114. They believe in Allah and the Last Day, and enjoin right conduct and forbid indecency and vie one with another in good works. They are of the righteous.

115. And whatever good they do, they will not be denied the reward of it. Allah is Aware of those who ward off (evil).

116. The riches and the progeny of those who disbelieve will not benefit them anything against Allah; and such are rightful owners of the Fire. They will remain in it.

117. The likeness of that which they spend in this life of the world is as the likeness of a biting, icy wind which strikes the harvest of a people who have wronged themselves, and devastates it. Allah wronged them not, but they did wrong themselves.

118. O you who believe! Take not for intimates others than your own people, who would spare no pains to ruin you; they love to hamper you. Hatred is revealed by (the utterance of) their mouths, but that which their hearts hide is greater. We have made plain for you the revelations if you will understand.

119. You are those who love them though they love you not, and you believe in all the Scripture. When they fall in with you they say: We believe; but when they go apart they bite their finger-tips at you, for rage. Say: Perish in your rage! Allah is Aware of what is hidden in (your) hearts.

120. If a lucky chance befall you, it is evil to them, and if disaster strike you they rejoice at it. But if you persevere and keep from evil, their cunning will never harm you. Allah is Surrounding what they do.

121. And (remember) when you set out at daybreak from your household to assign to the believers their positions for the battle[49], Allah was Hearer, Knower.

122. When two parties of you almost fell away, and Allah was

---

48. *i.e.* When they keep the covenant which the Prophet had made with the Jews in Al-Madinah.

49. The battle of Mount Uhud, located near Al-Madinah, which took place in 3 A.H. (see introduction to this *Surah*).

their Protecting Friend. In Allah let believers put their trust.

123. Allah had already given you the victory at Badr, when you were weak. So observe your duty to Allah in order that you may be thankful.

124. When you said to the believers: Is it not sufficient for you that your Lord should support you with three thousand angels sent down (to your help)?

125. No, but if you persevere, and keep from evil, and (the enemy) attack you suddenly, your Lord will help you with five thousand angels sweeping on.

126. Allah ordained this only as a message of good cheer for you, and that by it your hearts might be at rest. Victory comes only from Allah, the Mighty, the Wise -

127. That He may cut off a part of those who disbelieve, or overwhelm them so that they retire, frustrated.

128. It is no concern at all of you (Muhammad) whether He relent toward them or punish them; for they are evildoers.

129. To Allah belongs whatever is in the heavens and whatever is in the earth. He forgives whom He will, and punishes whom He will, Allah is Forgiving, Merciful.

130. O you who believe! Devour not usury, doubling and quadrupling (the sum lent). Observe your duty to Allah, that you may be successful.

131. And ward off (from yourselves) the Fire prepared for disbelievers.

132. And obey Allah and the messenger, that you may find mercy.

133. And vie one with another for forgiveness from your Lord, and for a paradise as wide as are the heavens and the earth, prepared for those who ward off (evil);

134. Those who spend (of that which Allah has given them) in ease and in adversity, those who control their wrath and are forgiving towards mankind; Allah loves the good;

135. And those who, when they do an evil thing or wrong themselves, remember Allah and implore forgiveness for their sins - Who forgives sins except Allah only? - and will not knowingly repeat (the wrong) they did.

136. The reward of such will be forgiveness from their Lord, and Gardens underneath which rivers flow, in which they will remain forever - a bountiful reward for workers!

137. Systems have passed away before you. Do but travel in the land and see the nature of the consequence for those who did deny (the messengers).

138. This is a declaration for mankind, a guidance and an admonition to those who ward off (evil).

139. Do not lose courage nor grieve, for you will overcome them if you are (indeed) believers.

140. If you have received a blow, the (disbelieving) people have received a blow the like of it[50]. These are (only) the changes which We cause to follow one another for mankind, to the end that Allah may know those who

50. At the Battle of Badr.

believe and may choose witnesses[51] from among you; and Allah loves not wrongdoers.

141. And that Allah may prove those who believe, and may destroy the disbelievers.

142. Or did you think that you would enter paradise while yet Allah knows not those of you who really strive, nor knows those (of you) who are steadfast?

143. And verily you used to wish for death before you met it (in the field). Now you have seen it with your eyes!

144. Muhammad is only a messenger, messengers (the like of whom) have passed away before him. Will it be that, when he dies or is slain, you will turn back on your heels? He who turns back on his heels does no hurt to Allah, and Allah will reward the thankful.[52]

145. No soul can ever die except by Allah's permission and at a term appointed. Who desires the reward of the world, We bestow on him of it; and who desires the reward of the Hereafter, We bestow on him of it. We shall reward the thankful.

146. And with how many a prophet have there been a number of devoted men who fought (beside him). They feared not for anything that befell

them in the way of Allah, nor did they weaken, nor were they brought low. Allah loves the steadfast.

147. Their call was only that they said: Our Lord! Forgive us for our sins and wasted efforts, make our foothold sure, and give us victory over the disbelieving people.

148. So Allah gave them the reward of the world and the good reward of the Hereafter. Allah loves those whose deeds are good.

149. O you who believe! If you obey those who disbelieve, they will make you turn back on your heels, and you turn back as losers.

150. But Allah is your Protector, and He is the Best of Helpers.

151. We shall cast terror into the hearts of those who disbelieve because they ascribe to Allah partners, for which no authority has been revealed. Their habitation is the Fire, and unhappy is the abode of the wrongdoers.

152. Allah verily made good His promise to you when you routed them by His permission, until (the moment) when your courage failed you, and you disagreed about the order and you disobeyed, after He had shown you that for which you long.[53] Some of you desired the world, and some of you desired the Hereafter. Therefore He made you flee from them, that He might try you. Yet now He has forgiven you. Allah is a Lord of Kindness to believers.

---

51. Or Martyrs.

52. On the morning when the Prophet died, Abu Bakr came into the mosque at Al-Madinah and found all the people distracted, and Omar telling them that it was a sin to say the Prophet was dead. Abu Bakr went and ascertained the truth, and coming back into the mosque, called: **"As for him who worshipped Allah, Allah is alive and dies not."** Then he recited this verse "and it was as if the people had not known till then that such a verse had been revealed."

53. When the archers deserted their post to share in the spoils, thinking that the day was won.

153. When you climbed (the hill) and paid no heed to anyone, while the messenger, at your rear, was calling you (to fight). Therefore He rewarded you grief for (his) grief, that (He might teach) you not to sorrow either for that which you missed or for that which befell you. Allah is Informed of what you do.

154. Then, after grief, He sent down security for you. As slumber did it overcome a party of you, while (the other) party, who were anxious on their own account, thought wrongly of Allah, the thought of ignorance. They said: Have we any part in the cause? Say (O Muhammad): The cause belongs wholly to Allah. They hide within themselves (a thought) which they reveal not to you, saying: Had we had any part in the cause we should not have been slain here. Say: Even though you had been in your houses, those appointed to be slain would have gone out to the places where they were to lie. (All this has been) in order that Allah might try what is in your breasts and prove what is in your hearts. Allah is Aware of what is hidden in the breasts (of men).

155. Those of you who turned back on the day when the two hosts met, Satan alone it was who caused them to backslide, because of some of that which they have earned. Now Allah has forgiven them. Allah is Forgiving, Clement.

156. O you who believe! Be not as those who disbelieved and said of their brothers who went abroad in the land or were fighting in the field: If they had been (here) with us they would not have died or been killed: that Allah may make it anguish in their hearts. Allah gives life and causes death; and Allah is Seer of what you do.

157. And what if you were slain in Allah's way or die in it? Surely pardon from Allah and mercy are better than all that they amass.

158. What if you be slain or die, when to Allah you are gathered?

159. It was by the mercy of Allah that you were lenient with them (O Muhammad), for if you had been stern and fierce of heart they would have dispersed from round about you. So pardon them and ask forgiveness for them and consult with them on the conduct of affairs. And when you are resolved, then put your trust in Allah. Allah loves those who put their trust (in Him).

160. If Allah is your helper no one can overcome you, and if He withdraws His help from you, who is there who can help you after Him? In Allah let believers put their trust.

161. It is not for any Prophet to deceive. Whoever deceives will bring his deceit with him on the Day of Resurrection. Then every soul will be paid in full what it has earned; and they will not be wronged.

162. Is one who follows the pleasure of Allah as one who has earned condemnation from Allah, whose habitation is the Fire, an unhappy journey's end?

163. There are degrees (of grace and damnation) with Allah, and Allah is Seer of what they do.

164. Allah verily has shown grace to the believers by sending to them a messenger of their own who recites to them His revelations, and causes them to grow, and teaches them the Scripture and wisdom;[54] although before (he came to them) they were in flagrant error.

165. And was it so, when a disaster struck you, though you had smitten (them with a disaster) twice (as great),[55] that you said: How is this? Say (to them, O Muhammad): It is from yourselves. Allah is Able to do all things.

166. That which befell you, on the day when the two armies met, was by permission of Allah; that He might know the true believers;

167. And that He might know the hypocrites, to whom it was said: Come, fight in the way of Allah, or defend yourselves. They answered: If we knew anything of fighting we would follow you. On that day they were nearer disbelief than faith. They utter with their mouths a thing which is not in their hearts. Allah is Best Aware of what they hide.

168. Those who, while they sat at home, said of their brothers (who were fighting for the cause of Allah): If they had been guided by us they would not have been slain. Say (to them, O

54. In fulfilment of the prayer of Ibrahim (*Surah* 2, *Al-Baqarah*, v. 129)
55. At the Battle of Badr.

Muhammad): Then avert death from yourselves if you are truthful.

169. Think not of those, who are slain in the way of Allah, as dead. No, they are living. With their Lord they have provision.

170. Jubilant (are they) because of that which Allah has bestowed upon them of His bounty, rejoicing for the sake of those who have not joined them but are left behind: that no fear will come upon them, neither will they grieve.

171. They rejoice because of favour from Allah and kindness, and that Allah wastes not the wage of the believers.

172. As for those who heard the call of Allah and His messenger after the harm befell them (in the fight); for such of them as do right and ward off (evil), there is great reward.

173. Those to whom men said: The people have gathered against you, therefore fear them. (The threat of danger) only increased the faith of them and they called: Allah is Sufficient for us! Most Excellent is He in Whom we trust!

174. So they returned with grace and favour from Allah, and no harm touched them. They followed the good pleasure of Allah, and Allah is of Infinite Bounty.

175. It is only the devil who would make (men) fear his supporters. Fear them not; fear Me, if you are true believers.

176. Let not their conduct grieve you, who run easily to disbelief, for they injure Allah not at all. It is Allah's Will to assign them no portion in the Hereafter, and theirs will be an awful doom.

177. Those who purchase disbelief at the price of faith harm Allah not at all, but theirs will be a painful doom.

178. And let not those who disbelieve imagine that the rein We give them is good for their souls. We only give them rein that they may grow in sinfulness. And theirs will be a shameful doom.

179. It is not (the purpose) of Allah to leave you in your present state till He shall separate the wicked from the good. And it is not (the purpose of) Allah to let you know the Unseen. But Allah chooses of His messengers whom He will (to receive knowledge of it). So believe in Allah and His messengers. If you believe and ward off (evil), yours will be a vast reward.

180. And let not those who hoard up that which Allah has bestowed upon them of His bounty think that it is better for them. No, it is worse for them. That which they hoard will be their collar on the Day of Resurrection. Allah's is the heritage of the heavens and the earth, and Allah is Informed of what you do.

181. Verily Allah heard the saying of those who said, (when asked for contributions to the war): "Allah is poor, and we are rich!"[56] We shall record their saying with their slaying of the prophets wrongfully and We shall say: Taste you the punishment of burning!

56. Saying of some Jews in Al-Madinah.

182. This is on account of that which your own hands have sent before (you to the judgement). Allah is no oppressor of (His) bondsmen.

183. (The same are) those who say: Allah has charged us that we believe not in any messenger until he brings us an offering which fire (from heaven) will devour. Say (to them, O Muhammad): messengers came to you before me with miracles, and with that (very miracle) which you describe. Why then did you slay them? (Answer that) if you are truthful!

184. And if they deny you, even so did they deny messengers who were before you, who came with miracles and with the Psalms and with the Scripture giving light.

185. Every soul will taste death. And you will be paid on the Day of Resurrection only that which you have fairly earned. Whoever is removed from the Fire and is made to enter Paradise, he indeed is triumphant. The life of the world is only comfort of illusion.

186. Assuredly you will be tried in your property and in your persons, and you will hear much wrong from those who were given the Scripture before you, and from the idolaters. But if you persevere and ward off (evil), then that is of the steadfast heart of things.

187. And (remember) when Allah laid a charge on those who had received the Scripture (He said): You are to explain it to mankind and not to hide it. But they flung it behind their backs and bought by it a little gain. Verily evil is that which they have gained by it.

188. Do not think that those who exult in what they have given, and love to be praised for what they have not done - do not think that they are in safety from the doom. A painful doom is theirs.

189. To Allah belongs the Sovereignty of the heavens and the earth. Allah is Able to do all things.

190. In the creation of the heavens and the earth and (in) the difference of night and day are signs (of His Sovereignty) for men of understanding,

191. Such as remember Allah, standing, sitting, and reclining, and consider the creation of the heavens and the earth, (and say): Our Lord! You created not this in vain. Glory be to You! Preserve us from the doom of Fire.

192. Our Lord! Whom You cause to enter the Fire: him indeed You have disgraced. For evildoers there will be no helpers.

193. Our Lord! We have heard a caller calling to Faith: "Believe in your Lord!" So we believed. Our Lord! Therefore forgive us our sins, and remit from us our evil deeds, and make us die the death of the righteous.

194. Our Lord! And give us that which You have promised to us by Your messengers. Disgrace us not upon the Day of Resurrection. You break not the appointed time.

195. And their Lord has heard them (and He says): I suffer not the work of any worker, male or female, to be lost.

You proceed one from another.[57] So those who fled and were driven out from their homes and suffered damage for My cause, and fought and were slain, verily I shall remit their evil deeds from them and verily I shall bring them into Gardens underneath which rivers flow - a reward from Allah. And with Allah is the fairest of rewards.

196. Let not the fortune (of the success) of those who disbelieve in the land deceive you (O Muhammad).

197. It is only a brief comfort. And afterwards their habitation will be Hell, an ill abode.

198. But those who keep their duty to their Lord, for them are Gardens underneath which rivers flow, in which they will be safe forever. A gift of welcome from their Lord. That which Allah has in store is better for the righteous.

199. And of the People of the Scripture there are some who believe in Allah and that which is revealed to you and that which was revealed to them, humbling themselves before Allah. They purchase not a slight gain at the price of the revelations of Allah. Verily their reward is with their Lord. Allah is swift to take account.

200. O you who believe! Endure, outdo all others in endurance, be ready, and observe your duty to Allah, in order that you may succeed.

---

57. This expression, which recurs in the Qur'an, is a reminder to men that women are of the same human status as themselves.

Surah 4: *An-Nisa*
(The Women)

An-Nisa, "Women", is so called because it deals largely with women's rights. The period of revelation is the months following the battle of Uhud, or, as Nöldeke,[58] a careful critic, puts it, "between the end of the third year and the end of the fifth year" of the Prophet's reign at Al-Madinah. As the Surah contains no reference to the siege of Al-Madinah ("The War of the Trench") by the allied tribes, which took place in the fifth year, I should rather say, between the end of the third year and the beginning of the fifth year.

Many Muslims were killed at the battle of Uhud, hence the concern for orphans and widows in the opening verses which lead on to a declaration of some rights of women of which they were deprived among the pagan Arabs. The defection of the Hypocrites - as the lukewarm or purely time-serving adherents were called - had been the chief cause of the reverse at Uhud; and after that reverse some of the Jewish tribes, who had till then observed the letter of their treaty with the Prophet, became avowed supporters of the enemy, even going so far as to declare that the old Arab idolatry was preferable to *Al-Islam* as a religion, and giving help and information to the Quraysh, so that in the end the Muslims were obliged to make war on them. Both the Hypocrites and the rebellious Jews are dealt with incidentally in this

58. Nöldeke, Geschichte des Quorans (2nd edn.) Part 1, p. 195.

Surah, the former at some length. There is a reference to Christian beliefs in vv. 171-172 the period of revelation is the fourth year of the Hijrah.

═══════════════

In the name of Allah, the Beneficent, the Merciful.

1. O mankind! Be careful of your duty to your Lord Who created you from a single soul and from it created its mate and from them both has spread abroad a multitude of men and women. Be careful of your duty toward Allah in Whom you claim (your rights) of one another and toward the wombs (that carried you). Allah has been a watcher over you.

2. Give to orphans their wealth. Exchange not the good for the bad (in your management of it) nor absorb their wealth into your own wealth. That would be a great sin.

3. And if you fear that you will not deal fairly with the orphans, marry of the women, who seem good to you, two or three or four; and if you fear that you cannot do justice (to so many) then one (only) or (the captives) that your right hands possess. Thus it is more likely that you will not do injustice.

4. And give to the women (whom you marry) free gift of their marriage portions; but if they of their own accord remit to you a part of it, then you are welcome to absorb it (in your wealth).

5. Give not to the foolish (what is in) your (keeping of their) wealth, which Allah has given you to maintain; but feed and clothe them from it, and speak kindly to them.

6. Test orphans till they reach the marriageable age; then, if you find them of sound judgement, deliver over to them their fortune; and devour it not by squandering and in haste until they should grow up. Whoever (of the guardians) is rich, let him abstain generously (from taking of the property of orphans); and whoever is poor let him take of it in reason (for his guardianship). And when you deliver up their fortune to orphans, have (the transaction) witnessed in their presence. Allah suffices as a Reckoner.

7. To the men (of a family) belongs a share of that which parents and near relatives leave, and to the women a share of that which parents and near relatives leave, whether it be little or much - a legal share.

8. And when kindred and orphans and the needy are present at the division (of the heritage), bestow on them from it and speak kindly to them.

9. And let those fear (in their behaviour towards orphans) who if they left behind them weak offspring would be afraid for them. So let them mind their duty to Allah, and speak justly.

10. Those who devour the wealth of orphans wrongfully, they do but swallow fire into their bellies, and they will be exposed to the burning flame.

11. Allah charges you concerning (the provision for) your children: to the male the equivalent of the portion of two females, and if there are women more than two, then theirs is two-thirds of the inheritance, and if there be one (only) then the half. And to each of

his[59] parents a sixth of the inheritance, if he has a son; and if he has no son and his parents are his heirs, then to his mother belongs the third; and if he has brothers, then to his mother belongs the sixth, after any legacy he may have left behind, or debt (has been paid). Your parents and your children: you know not which of them is nearer to you in usefulness. It is an injunction from Allah. Allah is Knower, Wise.

12. And to you belongs a half of that which your wives leave, if they have no child; but if they have a child then to you the fourth of that which they leave, after any legacy they may have left behind, or debt (they may have contracted, has been paid). And to them belongs the fourth of that which you leave if you have no child, but if you have a child then the eighth of that which you leave, after any legacy you may have left behind, or debt (you may have contracted, has been paid). And if a man or a woman have a distant heir (having left neither parent nor child), and he (or she) has a brother or a sister (only on the mother's side) then to each of them both (the brother and the sister) the sixth, and if they be more than two, then they shall be sharers in the third, after any legacy that may have been left behind or debt (contracted) not injuring (the heirs by willing away more than a third of the heritage) has been paid. A commandment from Allah. Allah is Knower, Indulgent.

13. These are the limits (imposed by) Allah. Whoever obeys Allah and His

---

59. The deceased.

messenger, He will make him enter Gardens underneath which rivers flow, where such will dwell forever. That will be the great success.

14. And who disobeys Allah and His messenger and transgresses His limits, He will make him enter the Fire, where he will dwell forever; his will be a shameful doom.

15. As for those of your women who are guilty of lewdness, call to witness four of you against them. And if they testify (to the truth of the allegation) then confine them to the houses until death take them or (until) Allah appoint for them a way (through new legislation).[60]

16. And as for the two of you who are guilty of it, punish them both. And if they repent and improve, then let them be. Allah is ever relenting, Merciful.

17. Forgiveness is only incumbent on Allah towards those who do evil in ignorance (and) then turn quickly (in repentance) to Allah. These are they towards whom Allah relents. Allah is ever Knower, Wise.

18. The forgiveness is not for those who do ill-deeds until, when death comes to one of them, he says: I repent now; nor yet for those who die while they are disbelievers. For such We have prepared a painful doom.

19. O you who believe! It is not lawful for you forcibly to inherit the women (of your deceased relatives), nor (that) you should put constraint upon them that you may take away a part of that which you have given them, unless

60. See *Surah 24, An-Nur*, vv. 2-10.

they are guilty of flagrant lewdness. But consort with them in kindness, for if you hate them it may happen that you hate a thing in which Allah has placed much good.

20. And if you wish to exchange one wife for another and you have given to one of them a sum of money (however great), take nothing from it. Would you take it by way of deception and open wrong?

21. How can you take it (back) after one of you has gone in to the other, and they have taken a strong pledge from you?

22. And marry not those women whom your fathers married, except what has already happened (of that nature) in the past. It was ever lewdness and abomination, and an evil way.

23. Forbidden to you are your mothers, and your daughters, and your sisters, and your father's sisters, and your mother's sisters, and your brothers' daughters and your sisters' daughters, and your foster-mothers, and your foster-sisters, and your mothers-in-law, and your step-daughters who are under your protection (born) of your women to whom you have gone in - but if you have not gone in to them, then it is no sin for you (to marry their daughters) - and the wives of your sons who (spring) from your own loins. And (it is forbidden to you) that you should have two sisters together, except what has already happened (of that nature) in the past. Allah is ever Forgiving, Merciful.

24. And all married women (are forbidden to you) except those (captives) whom your right hands possess. It is a decree of Allah for you. Lawful to you are all beyond those mentioned, so that you seek them with your wealth in honest wedlock, not debauchery. And those of whom you seek (by marrying them), give to them their portions as a duty. And there is no sin for you in what you do by mutual agreement after the duty (has been done). Allah is ever Knower, Wise.

25. And whoever is not able to afford to marry free, believing women, let them marry from the believing maids whom your right hands possess. Allah knows best (concerning) your faith. You (proceed) one from another;[61] so marry them by permission of their people, and give to them their portions in kindness, they being honest, not debauched nor of loose conduct. And if when they are honourably married they commit lewdness, they shall incur half of the punishment (prescribed) for free women (in that case). This is for him among you who fears to commit sin. But to have patience would be better for you. Allah is Forgiving, Merciful.

26. Allah wishes to explain to you and guide you by the examples of those who were before you, and would turn to you in mercy. Allah is Knower, Wise.

27. And Allah wishes to turn to you in mercy; but those who follow vain desires would have you go tremendously astray.

---

61. This expression, which recurs in the Qur'an, is a reminder to men that women are of the same status as themselves.

28. Allah would make the burden light for you, for man was created weak.

29. O you who believe! Squander not your wealth among yourselves in vanity, except it be a trade by mutual consent, and kill not one another. Allah is ever Merciful to you.

30. Whoever does that through aggression and injustice, we shall cast him into the Fire, and that is ever easy for Allah.

31. If you avoid the great (things) which you are forbidden, We will remit from you your evil deeds and make you enter at a noble gate.

32. And desire not the thing in which Allah has made some of you excel others. To men a fortune from that which they have earned, and to women a fortune from that which they have earned. (Envy not one another) but ask Allah of His bounty. Allah is ever Knower of all things.

33. And to each We have appointed heirs of that which parents and near relations leave; and as for those with whom your right hands have made a covenant, give them their due. Allah is ever Witness over all things.

34. Men are in charge of women, because Allah has made the one of them to excel the other, and because they spend of their property (for the support of women). So good women are the obedient, guarding in secret that which Allah has guarded. As for those from whom you fear rebellion, admonish them and banish them to beds apart, and chastise them. Then if they obey you, seek not a way against them. Allah is ever High Exalted, Great.

35. And if you fear a breach between them both (the man and wife), appoint an arbiter from his people and an arbiter from her people. If they desire amendment Allah will make them of one mind. Allah is ever Knower, Aware.

36. And serve Allah. Ascribe no thing as partner to Him. (Show) kindness to parents, and to near relatives, and orphans, and the needy, and to the neighbour who is related (to you) and the neighbour who is not related, and the fellow-traveller and the wayfarer and (the slaves) whom your right hands possess. Allah loves not such as are proud and boastful,

37. Who hoard their wealth and enjoin avarice on others, and hide that which Allah has bestowed upon them of His bounty. For disbelievers We have prepared a shameful doom;

38. And (also) those who spend their wealth in order to be seen of men, and believe not in Allah nor the Last Day. Whoever takes Satan for a comrade, a bad comrade has he.

39. What have they (to fear) if they believe in Allah and the Last Day and spend (aright) of that which Allah has bestowed upon them, when Allah is ever Aware of them (and all they do)?

40. Allah wrongs not even of the weight of an ant; and if there is a good deed, He will double it and will give (the doer) from His presence an immense reward.

41. But how (will it be with them) when We bring of every people a witness, and We bring you (O Muhammad) a witness against these?

42. On that day those who disbelieved and disobeyed the messenger will wish that they were level with the ground, and they can hide no fact from Allah.

43. O you who believe! Draw not near to prayer when you are drunken, till you know that which you utter, nor when you are polluted, except when journeying upon the road, till you have bathed. And if you be ill, or on a journey, or one of you comes from the closet, or you have touched women, and you do not find water, then go to high clean soil and rub your faces and your hands (with it). Allah is Benign, Forgiving.

44. Do you not see those to whom a portion of the Scripture has been given, how they purchase error, and seek to make you (Muslims) err from the right way?

45. Allah knows best (who are) your enemies. Allah is sufficient as a Guardian, and Allah is sufficient as a Supporter.

46. Some of those who are Jews change words from their context and say: "We hear and disobey; hear you as one who hears not" and "Listen to us!"[62] distorting with their tongues and slandering religion. If they had said: "We hear and we obey: hear you, and look at us" it had been better for them, and more upright. But Allah has cursed them for their disbelief, so they believe not, except a few.

---

62. Devices of some of the Jews in Al-Madinah to annoy the Muslims by distorting words of Scripture. *Ra'ina* (meaning listen to us), by which the Muslims used to call the Prophet's notice, they turned by slight mispronunciation into a Hebrew word of insult. (cf. *Surah 2, Al-Baqarah,* v. 104, footnote).

47. O you to whom the Scripture has been given! Believe in what We have revealed confirming that which you possess, before We destroy faces so as to disgrace them, or curse them as We cursed the Sabbath-breakers (of old time). The commandment of Allah is always executed.

48. Allah forgives not that a partner should be ascribed to Him. He forgives (all) except that to whom He will. Whoever ascribes partners to Allah, he has indeed invented a tremendous sin.

49. Have you not seen those who praise themselves for purity? No, Allah purifies whom He will, and they will not be wronged even by the hair upon a date-stone.

50. See, how they invent lies about Allah! That of itself is flagrant sin.

51. Have you not seen those to whom a portion of the Scripture has been given, how they believe in idols and false deities, and how they say of those (idolaters) who disbelieve: "These are more rightly guided than those who believe."?

52. Those are they whom Allah has cursed, and he whom Allah has cursed, you (O Muhammad) will find for him no helper.

53. Or have they even a share in the Sovereignty? Then in that case, they would not give mankind even the speck on a date-stone.

54. Or are they jealous of mankind because of that which Allah of His bounty has bestowed upon them? For We bestowed upon the house of Abraham (of old) the Scripture and

wisdom, and We bestowed on them a mighty kingdom.

55. And of them were (some) who believed in it and of them were (some) who turned away from it. Hell is sufficient for (their) burning.

56. Those who disbelieve Our revelations, We shall expose them to the Fire. As often as their skins are consumed We shall exchange them for fresh skins that they may taste the torment. Allah is ever Mighty, Wise.

57. And as for those who believe and do good works, We shall make them enter Gardens underneath which rivers flow - to dwell in them forever; there for them are pure companions - and We shall make them enter plenteous shade.

58. Allah commands you that you restore deposits to their owners, and, if you judge between mankind, that you judge justly. Splendid is this which Allah admonishes you. Allah is ever Hearer, Seer.

59. O you who believe! Obey Allah, and obey the messenger and those of you who are in authority; and if you have a dispute concerning any matter, refer it to Allah and the messenger if you are (in truth) believers in Allah and the Last Day. That is better and more seemly in the end.

60. Have you not seen those who pretend that they believe in that which is revealed to you and that which was revealed before you, how they would go for judgement (in their disputes) to false deities when they have been ordered to renounce them? Satan would mislead them far astray.

61. And when it is said to them: Come to that which Allah has revealed and to the messenger, you see the hypocrites turn from you with aversion.

62. How would it be if a misfortune struck them because of that which their own hands have sent before (them)? Then they would come to you, swearing by Allah that they were seeking nothing but harmony and kindness.

63. Those are they, the secrets of whose hearts Allah knows. So oppose them and admonish them, and address them in plain terms about their souls.

64. We sent no messenger except that he should be obeyed by Allah's permission. And if, when they had wronged themselves, they had only come to you and asked forgiveness of Allah, and the messenger had asked forgiveness for them, they would have found Allah Forgiving, Merciful.

65. But no, by your Lord, they will not believe (in truth) until they make you judge of what is in dispute between them and find within themselves no dislike of that which you decide, and submit with full submission.

66. And if We had decreed for them: Lay down your lives or go out from your dwellings, only few of them would have done it; though if they did what they are exhorted to do it would be better for them, and more strengthening;

67. And then We should bestow upon them from Our presence an immense reward,

68. And should guide them to a straight path.

69. Whoever obeys Allah and the messenger, they are with those to whom Allah has shown favour, of the prophets and the saints and the martyrs and the righteous. The best of company are they

70. Such is bounty from Allah, and Allah suffices as Knower.

71. O you who believe! Take your precautions, then advance in groups, or advance all together.

72. Among you there is he who hesitates; and if disaster overtook you, he would say: Allah has been gracious to me since I was not present with them.

73. And if a bounty from Allah befell you, he would surely cry, as if there had been no love between you and him: Oh, would that I had been with them, then should I have achieved a great success!

74. Let those fight in the way of Allah who sell the life of the world for the other (i.e the Hereafter). Who fights in the way of Allah, be he slain or be he victorious, on him We shall bestow a vast reward.

75. How should you not fight for the cause of Allah and of the feeble among men and of the women and the children who are crying: Our Lord! Bring us out from out this town[63] of which the people are oppressors! Oh, give us from Your presence some protecting friend! Oh, give us from Your presence some defender!

76. Those who believe do battle for the cause of Allah; and those who

63. Makkah

58

disbelieve do battle for the cause of idols. So fight the helpers of the devil. The devil's strategy is ever weak.

77. Have you not seen those to whom it was said: Withhold your hands, establish worship and pay the poor-due, but when fighting was prescribed for them behold! a party of them fear mankind even as their fear of Allah or with greater fear, and say: Our Lord! Why have You ordained fighting for us? If only You would give us respite yet a while! Say (to them, O Muhammad): The comfort of this world is scant; the Hereafter will be better for him who wards off (evil); and you will not be wronged the hair upon a date-stone.

78. Wherever you may be, death will overtake you, even though you were in lofty towers. Yet if a happy thing befalls them they say: This is from Allah; and if an evil thing befalls them they say: This is of your doing (O Muhammad). Say (to them): All is from Allah. What is amiss with these people that they come not near to understand a happening?[64]

79. Whatever of good befalls you (O man) it is from Allah, and whatever of ill befalls you it is from yourself. We have sent you (Muhammad) as a messenger to mankind and Allah is sufficient as Witness.

80. Whoever obeys the messenger has obeyed Allah, and whoever turns away: We have not sent you as a guardian over them.

81. And they say: (It is) obedience; but when they have gone away from you a party of them spend the night in planning other than what you say. Allah records what they plan by night. So oppose them and put your trust in Allah. Allah is sufficient as Trustee.

82. Will they not then ponder on the Qur'an? If it had been from other than Allah they would have found in it much inconsistency.

83. And if any tidings, whether of safety or fear, come to them, they noise it abroad, whereas if they had referred it to the messenger and to such of them as are in authority, those among them who are able to think out the matter would have known it. If it had not been for the grace of Allah upon you and His mercy you would have followed Satan, except a few (of you).

84. So fight (O Muhammad) in the way of Allah - You are not taxed (with the responsibility for anyone) except for yourself - and urge on the believers. Maybe Allah will restrain the might of those who disbelieve. Allah is stronger in might and stronger in inflicting punishment.

85. Who intervenes in a good cause will have the reward of it, and who intervenes in an evil cause will bear the consequence of it. Allah oversees all things.

86. When you are greeted with a greeting, greet with a better than it or return it. Allah takes count of all things.

87. Allah! There is no God except Him. He gathers you all to a Day of Resurrection of which there is no doubt. Who is more true in statement than Allah?

---

64. The reference is to the reverse which the Muslims suffered at Mt. Uhud which was caused by their own disobedience to the Prophet's order.

88. What is the matter with you that you have become two parties regarding the hypocrites[65], when Allah cast them back (to disbelief) because of what they earned? Do you seek to guide him whom Allah has sent astray? He whom Allah sends astray, for him you (O Muhammad) cannot find a road.

89. They long that you should disbelieve even as they disbelieve, that you may be upon a level (with them). So choose not friends from them till they forsake their homes in the way of Allah; if they turn back (to enmity) then take them and kill them wherever you find them, and choose no friend nor helper from among them,

90. Except those who seek refuge with a people between whom and you there is a covenant, or (those who) come to you because their hearts forbid them to make war on you or make war on their own people. Had Allah willed He could have given them power over you so that assuredly they would have fought you. So, if they hold aloof from you and wage not war against you and offer you peace, Allah allows you no way against them.

91. You will find others who desire that they should have security from you, and security from their own people. As often as they are returned to hostility they are plunged in it. If they keep not aloof from you nor offer

you peace nor hold their hands, then take them and kill them wherever you find them. Against such We have given you clear authority.

92. It is not for a believer to kill a believer unless (it be) by mistake. He who has killed a believer by mistake must set free a believing slave, and pay the blood-money to the family of the slain, unless they remit it as a charity. If he (the victim) be of a people hostile to you, and he is a believer, then (the penance is) to set free a believing slave. And if he comes of a people between whom and you there is a covenant, then the blood-money must be paid to his people and (also) a believing slave must be set free. And who has not the means must fast two consecutive months. A penance from Allah. Allah is Knower, Wise.

93. Whoever slays a believer intentionally, his reward is Hell forever. Allah is angry with him and He has cursed him and prepared for him an awful doom.

94. O you who believe! When you go out (to fight) in the way of Allah, be careful to discriminate, and say not to one who offers you peace: "You are not a believer," seeking the chance profits of this life (so that you may plunder him). With Allah are plenteous spoils. Even thus (as he now is) were you before; but Allah has since then been gracious to you. Therefore take care to discriminate. Allah is ever Informed of what you do.

95. Those of the believers who sit still, other than those who have a (disabling) hurt, are not on an equality with those

---

65. According to Tradition, the reference here is not to the lukewarm section of the Muslims of Al-Madinah, but to a particular group of alleged converts from among the Arabs, who afterwards relapsed into idolatry, and concerning whom there where two opinions among the Muslims.

who strive in the way of Allah with their wealth and lives. Allah has conferred on those who strive with their wealth and lives a rank above the sedentary. To each Allah has promised good, but He has bestowed on those who strive a great reward above the sedentary;

96. Degrees of rank from Him, and forgiveness and mercy. Allah is ever Forgiving, Merciful.

97. As for those whom the angels take (in death) while they wrong themselves, (the angels) will ask: In what were you engaged? They will say: We were oppressed in the land. (The angels) will say: Was not Allah's earth spacious that you could have migrated in it? As for such, their habitation will be Hell, an evil journey's end;

98. Except the feeble among men, and the women, and the children, who are unable to devise a plan and are not shown a way.

99. As for such, it may be that Allah will pardon them. Allah is ever Clement, Forgiving.

100. Whoever migrates for the cause of Allah will find much refuge and abundance in the earth, and whoever forsakes his home, as an emigrant to Allah and His messenger, and death overtakes him, his reward is then incumbent on Allah. Allah is ever Forgiving, Merciful.

101. And when you go out in the land, it is no sin for you to curtail (your) worship if you fear that those who disbelieve may attack you. In truth the disbelievers are an open enemy to you.

102. And when you (O Muhammad) are among them and arrange (their) worship for them, let only a party of them stand with you (to worship) and let them take their arms. Then when they have performed their prostrations let them fall to the rear and let another party come that has not worshipped and let them worship with you, and let them take their precaution and their arms. Those who disbelieve long for you to neglect your arms and your baggage that they may attack you once for all. It is no sin for you to lay aside your arms, if rain impedes you or you are sick. But take your precaution. Allah prepares for the disbelievers shameful punishment.

103. When you have performed the act of worship, remember Allah, standing, sitting and reclining. And when you are in safety, observe proper worship. Worship at fixed times has been enjoined on the believers.

104. Relent not in pursuit of the enemy. If you are suffering, they suffer even as you suffer and you hope from Allah that for which they cannot hope. Allah is ever Knower, Wise.

105. We reveal to you the Scripture with the truth, that you may judge between mankind by that which Allah shows you. And do not be a pleader for the treacherous;

106. And seek forgiveness of Allah. Allah is ever Forgiving, Merciful.

107. And plead not on behalf of (people) who deceive themselves. Allah loves not one who is treacherous and sinful.

108. They seek to hide from men and seek not to hide from Allah. He is with them when by night they hold discourse displeasing to Him. Allah ever surrounds what they do.

109. You are they who pleaded for them in the life of the world. But who will plead with Allah for them on the Day of Resurrection, or who will then be their defender?

110. Yet who does evil or wrongs his own soul, then seeks pardon of Allah, will find Allah Forgiving, Merciful.

111. Who commits sin commits it only against himself. Allah is ever Knower, Wise.

112. And who commits a delinquency or crime, then throws (the blame) of it upon the innocent, has burdened himself with falsehood and a flagrant crime.

113. But for the grace of Allah upon you (Muhammad), and His mercy, a party of them had resolved to mislead you, but they will mislead only themselves and they will hurt you not at all. Allah reveals to you the Scripture and wisdom, and teaches you that which you knew not. The grace of Allah towards you has been infinite.

114. There is no good in much of their secret conferences except (in) him who enjoins almsgiving and kindness and peace-making among the people. Who does that, seeking the good pleasure of Allah, We shall bestow on him a vast reward.

115. And whoever opposes the messenger after the guidance (of Allah) has been manifested to him, and follows other than the believer's way, We appoint for him that to which he himself has turned, and expose him to Hell - an unhappy journey's end!

116. Allah pardons not that partners should be ascribed to Him. He pardons all except that to whom He will. Whoever ascribes partners to Allah has wandered far astray.

117. They invoke in His stead only females;[66] they pray to none else than Satan, a rebel

118. Whom Allah cursed, and he said: Surely I will take of Your bondsmen an appointed portion,

119. And surely I will lead them astray, and surely I will arouse desires in them, and surely I will command them and they will cut the cattle's ears, and surely I will command them and they will change Allah's creation. Whoever chooses Satan for a patron instead of Allah is verily a loser and his loss is manifest.

120. He promises them and stirs up desires in them, and Satan promises them only to deceive.

121. For such, their habitation will be Hell, and they will find no refuge from it.

122. But as for those who believe and do good works, We shall bring them into Gardens underneath which rivers flow, in which they will remain forever. It is a promise from Allah in truth; and who can be more truthful than Allah in utterance?

66. The idols which the pagan Arabs worshipped were all female.

123. It will not be in accordance with your desires, nor the desires of the People of the Scripture.[67] He who does wrong will have the recompense of it, and will not find against Allah any protecting friend or helper.

124. And whoever does good works, whether of male or female, and he (or she) is a believer, such will enter paradise and they will not be wronged the dent in a date-stone.

125. Who is better in religion than he who surrenders his purpose to Allah while doing good (to men) and follows the tradition of Abraham, the upright? Allah (Himself) chose Abraham for a friend.

126. To Allah belongs whatever is in the heavens and whatever is in the earth. Allah ever surrounds all things.

127. They consult you concerning women. Say: Allah gives you decree concerning them, and the Scripture which has been recited to you (gives decree), concerning female orphans and those to whom you give not that which is ordained for them though you desire to marry them, and (concerning) the weak among children, and that you should deal justly with orphans. Whatever good you do, Allah is ever Aware of it.

128. If a woman fears ill-treatment from her husband, or desertion, it is no sin for them both if they make terms of peace between themselves. Peace is better. But greed has been made present in the minds (of men). If

you do good and keep from evil, Allah is ever Informed of what you do.

129. You will not be able to deal equally between (your) wives, however much you wish (to do so). But turn not altogether away (from one), leaving her as in suspense. If you do good and keep from evil, Allah is ever Forgiving, Merciful.

130. But if they separate, Allah will compensate each out of His abundance. Allah is ever All-Embracing, All-Knowing.

131. To Allah belongs whatever is in the heavens and whatever is in the earth. And We charged those who received the Scripture before you, and (We charge) you, that you keep your duty towards Allah. And if you disbelieve, to Allah belongs whatever is in the heavens and whatever is in the earth, and Allah is ever Absolute, Owner of Praise.

132. To Allah belongs whatever is in the heavens and whatever is in the earth. And Allah is sufficient as Defender.

133. If He will, He can remove you, O people, and produce others (in your stead). Allah is Able to do that.

134. Who desires the reward of the world, (let him know that) with Allah is the reward of the world and the Hereafter. Allah is ever Hearer, Seer.

135. O you who believe! Be staunch in justice, witnesses for Allah, even though it is against yourselves or (your) parents or (your) relatives, whether (the case is of) a rich man or a poor man, for Allah is nearer to both

---

67. Jews and Christians.

(than you are). So follow not passion lest you lapse (from truth), and if you lapse or fall away, then Allah is ever Informed of what you do.

136. O you who believe! Believe in Allah and His messenger and the Scripture which He has revealed to His messenger, and the Scripture which He revealed before. Who disbelieves in Allah and His angels and His scriptures and His messengers and the Last Day, he verily has wandered far astray.

137. Those who believe, then disbelieve and then (again) believe, then disbelieve, and then increase in disbelief, Allah will never pardon them, nor will He guide them to a way.

138. Give to the hypocrites the tidings that for them there is a painful doom;

139. Those who chose disbelievers for their friends instead of believers! Do they look for power at their hands? All power belongs to Allah.

140. He has already revealed to you in the Scripture that, when you hear the revelations of Allah rejected and derided, (you) sit not with them (who disbelieve and mock) until they engage in some other conversation. In that case (if you stayed) you would be like them. Allah will gather hypocrites and disbelievers, all together, into Hell;

141. Those who wait upon occasion in regard to you and, if a victory comes to you from Allah, say: Are we not with you? And if the disbelievers meet with a success say: Had we not the mastery of you, and did we not protect you from the believers? - Allah will judge between you at the Day of Resurrection, and Allah will not give

the disbelievers any way (of success) against the believers.

142. The hypocrites seek to deceive Allah, but it is He Who deceives them. When they stand up to worship they perform it languidly and to be seen of men, and are mindful of Allah only little;

143. Swaying between this (and that), (belonging) neither to these nor to those. He whom Allah causes to go astray, you (O Muhammad) will not find a way for him.

144. O you who believe! Choose not disbelievers for (your) friends in place of believers. Would you give Allah a clear authority against you?

145. The hypocrites (will be) in the lowest depth of the Fire, and you will find no helper for them;

146. Except those who repent and amend and hold fast to Allah and make their religion pure for Allah (only). Those are with the believers. And Allah will bestow on the believers an immense reward.

147. What concern has Allah for your punishment if you are thankful (for His mercies) and believe (in Him)? Allah is ever Responsive, Aware.

148. Allah loves not the utterance of harsh speech except by one who has been wronged. Allah is ever Hearer, Knower.

149. If you do good openly or keep it secret, or forgive evil, Allah is ever Forgiving, Powerful.

150. Those who disbelieve in Allah and His messengers, and seek to make distinction between Allah and His messengers, and say: We believe in some and disbelieve in others, and seek to choose a way in between;

151. Such are disbelievers in truth; and for disbelievers We have prepared a shameful doom.

152. But those who believe in Allah and His messengers and make no distinction between any of them, to them Allah will give their wages; and Allah is ever Forgiving, Merciful.

153. The people of the Scripture ask of you that you should cause an (actual) Book to descend upon them from heaven. They asked a greater thing of Moses before, for they said: Show us Allah plainly. The storm of lightning seized them for their wickedness. Then (even after that) they chose the calf (for worship) after clear proofs (of Allah's Sovereignty) had come to them. And We forgave them that! And We bestowed on Moses evident authority.

154. And We caused the Mount to tower above them at (the taking of) their covenant: and We ordered them: Enter the gate, prostrate! and We ordered them: Transgress not the Sabbath! and We took from them a firm covenant.

155. Then because of their breaking of their covenant, and their disbelieving in the revelations of Allah, and their slaying of the Prophets wrongfully, and their saying: Our hearts are hardened - No, but Allah set a seal upon them for their disbelief, so that they believe not except a few -

156. And because of their disbelief and of their speaking against Mary a tremendous calumny;

157. And because of their saying: We slew the Messiah, Jesus son of Mary, Allah's messenger - they slew him not nor crucified him, but it appeared so to them; and those who disagree concerning it are in doubt of it; they have no knowledge of it except pursuit of a conjecture; they slew him not for certain.

158. But Allah took him up to Himself. Allah was ever Mighty, Wise.

159. There is not one of the People of the Scripture but will believe in him before his death, and on the Day of Resurrection he will be a witness against them -

160. Because of the wrongdoing of the Jews We forbade them good things which were (before) made lawful to them, and because of their much hindering from Allah's way,

161. And of their taking usury when they were forbidden it, and of their devouring people's wealth by false pretences, We have prepared for those of them who disbelieve a painful doom.

162. But those of them who are firm in knowledge and the believers believe in that which is revealed to you, and that which was revealed before you, especially the diligent in prayer and those who pay the poor-due, the believers in Allah and the Last Day. Upon these We shall bestow immense reward.

163. We inspire you as We inspired Noah and the Prophets after him, as We inspired Abraham and Ishmael and Isaac and Jacob and the tribes, and Jesus and Job and Jonah and Aaron and Solomon, and as We imparted to David the Psalms;

164. And messengers We have mentioned to you before and messengers We have not mentioned to you; and Allah spoke directly to Moses;

165. Messengers of good cheer and of warning, in order that mankind might have no argument against Allah after the messengers. Allah was ever Mighty, Wise.

166. But Allah (Himself) testifies concerning that which He has revealed to you; in His knowledge He has revealed it; and the angels also testify. And Allah is sufficient Witness.

167. Those who disbelieve and hinder (others) from the way of Allah, they verily have wandered far astray.

168. Those who disbelieve and deal in wrong, Allah will never forgive them, neither will He guide them to a road,

169. Except the road of Hell, in which they will remain forever. And that is ever easy for Allah.

170. O mankind! The messenger has come to you with the Truth from your Lord. Therefore believe; (it is) better for you. But if you disbelieve, still, to Allah belongs whatever is in the heavens and the earth. Allah is ever Knower, Wise.

171. O People of the Scripture! Do not exaggerate in your religion nor utter anything concerning Allah except the truth. The Messiah, Jesus son of Mary, was only a messenger of Allah, and His word which He conveyed to Mary, and a spirit from Him. So - believe in Allah and His messengers, and say not "Three" - Cease! (It is) better for you! - Allah is only One God. Far is it removed from His Transcendent Majesty that He should have a son. His is all that is in the heavens and all that is in the earth. And Allah is sufficient as Defender.

172. The Messiah will never scorn to be a slave to Allah, nor will the favoured angels. Whoever scorns His service and is proud, all such will He assemble to Him;

173. Then, as for those who believed and did good works, to them He will pay their wages in full, adding to them of His bounty; and as for those who were scornful and proud, them will He punish with a painful doom and they will not find for them, against Allah, any protecting friend or helper.

174. O mankind! Now a proof from your Lord has come to you, and We have sent down to you a clear light;

175. As for those who believe in Allah, and hold fast to Him, them He will cause to enter into His mercy and grace, and will guide them to Him by a straight road.

176. They ask you for a pronouncement. Say: Allah has pronounced for you concerning distant relatives. If a man dies childless and he has a sister, hers is half the heritage, and he would have inherited from her had she died childless. And if there are two sisters, then theirs are two-thirds of the heritage, and if they are brothers and sisters, to the male is the equivalent of the share of two females. Allah explains to you, so that you err not. Allah is Knower of all things.

Surah 5: **Al-Ma'idah**
(The Table Spread)

Al-Ma'idah, "The Table Spread", derives its name from vv. 112 ff., where it is told how the disciples of Jesus asked that a table spread with food might be sent down from Heaven, and their prayer was granted, a passage in which some have seen an allusion to the Eucharist. Many authorities regard it as the last Surah in order of revelation, and Rodwell has so placed it in his chronological arrangement; but the claim can only be established in the case of verse 3, which announces the completion of their religion for the Muslims, and the choice for them of *Al-Islam* (the Surrender to Allah) as their religion. That verse is undoubtedly the latest of the whole Qur'an. It was revealed during the Prophet's last pilgrimage ("The Farewell Pilgrimage", as it is called) to Makkah, and spoken by him in the course of his address to the assembled thousands at Arafat, when all Arabia had embraced *Al-Islam*, only a little while before his death. It is possible that, as Nöldeke supposes, two other verses near to it are of the same date, but the remainder of the revelations contained in this Surah belong rather to the period between the fourth and seventh years of the Hijrah. Its subject is observance of religious duties. The followers of former prophets had failed through breaking their covenant, and so Muslims are obliged to keep their covenant with God and all their obligations watchfully, because God's covenant is only with those who do right. There is more mention of the Christians here than in the former Surahs, from which some writers infer that this Surah must have been revealed at the time when the Prophet was at war with certain Christian tribes belonging to the Eastern Roman Empire. But there is no evidence for that either in Tradition or in the text itself.

The period of revelation is between the fifth and tenth years of the Hijrah.

In the name of Allah,
the Beneficent, the Merciful.

1. O you who believe! Fulfil your undertakings. The beast of cattle is made lawful to you (for food) except that which is announced to you (in here), game being unlawful when you are on the pilgrimage. Allah ordains that which pleases Him.

2. O you who believe! Profane not Allah's monuments nor the Sacred Month, nor the offerings, nor the garlands, nor those repairing to the Sacred House,[68] seeking the grace and pleasure of your Lord. But when you have left the sacred territory, then go hunting (if you will). And let not your hatred of a people who (once) stopped you going to the Inviolable Place of Worship seduce you to transgress; but help you one another to righteousness and pious duty. Help not one another to sin and transgression, but keep your duty to Allah. Allah is severe in punishment.

3. Forbidden to you (for food) are carrion and blood and swine flesh, and

---

68. *i.e.* The *Ka'bah* at Makkah.

that which has been dedicated to any other than Allah, and the strangled, and the dead through beating, and the dead through falling from a height, and that which has been killed by (the goring of) horns, and the devoured of wild beasts, except that which you make lawful (by the death-stroke), and that which has been immolated to idols. And (forbidden it is) that you swear by the divining arrows. This is an abomination. This day those who disbelieve are in despair of (ever harming) your religion; so fear them not, fear Me! This day I have perfected your religion for you and completed My favour to you, and have chosen for you as religion Al-Islam.[69] Whoever is forced by hunger, not by will, to sin: (for him) Allah is Forgiving, Merciful.

4. They ask you (O Muhammad) what is made lawful for them. Say: (all) good things are made lawful for you. And those beasts and birds of prey which you have trained as hounds are trained, you teach them that which Allah taught you; so eat of that which they catch for you and mention Allah's name upon it, and observe your duty to Allah. Allah is swift to take account.

5. This day (all) good things are made lawful for you. The food of those who have received the Scripture is lawful for you, and your food is lawful for them. And so are the virtuous women of the believers and the virtuous women of those who received the Scripture before you (lawful for you)

when you give them their marriage portions and live with them in honour, not in fornication, nor taking them as secret concubines. He who denies the faith, his work is vain and he will be among the losers in the Hereafter.

6. O you who believe! When you rise up for prayer, wash your faces, and your hands up to the elbows, and lightly rub your heads and (wash) your feet up to the ankles. And if you are unclean, purify yourselves. And if you are sick or on a journey, or one of you comes from the closet, or you have had (sexual) contact with women, and you do not find water, then go to clean, high ground and rub your faces and your hands with some of it. Allah would not place a burden on you, but He would purify you and would perfect His grace upon you, that you may give thanks.

7. Remember Allah's grace upon you and His covenant by which He bound you when you said: We hear and we obey; And keep your duty to Allah. He knows what is in the breasts (of men).

8. O you who believe! Be steadfast witnesses for Allah in equity, and let not hatred of any people seduce you that you deal not justly. Deal justly, that is nearer to your duty. Observe your duty to Allah. Allah is Informed of what you do.

9. Allah has promised those who believe and do good works: theirs will be forgiveness and immense reward.

10. And they who disbelieve and deny Our revelations, such are rightful owners of Hell.

---

69. *i.e.* "The Surrender" to Allah. Thus solemnly the religion which the Prophet had established received its name.

11. O you who believe! Remember Allah's favour to you, how a people were minded to stretch out their hands against you but He withheld their hands from you; and keep your duty to Allah. In Allah let believers put their trust.

12. Allah made a covenant of old with the Children of Israel and We raised among them twelve chieftains, and Allah said: I am with you. If you establish worship and pay the poor-due, and believe in My messengers and support them, and lend to Allah a kindly loan[70], surely I shall remit your sins, and surely I shall bring you into Gardens underneath which rivers flow. Whoever among you disbelieves after this will go astray from a plain road.

13. And because of their breaking their covenant, We have cursed them and made hard their hearts. They change words from their context and forget a part of that of which they were admonished. You will not cease to discover treachery from all except a few of them. But bear with them and pardon them. Allah loves the kindly.

14. And with those who say: "We are Christians", We made a covenant, but they forgot a part of that of which they were admonished. Therefore, We have stirred up enmity and hatred among them till the Day of Resurrection, when Allah will inform them of their handiwork.

15. O People of the Scripture! Now Our messenger has come to you, explaining to you much of that which you used to hide in the Scripture,

and forgiving much. Now there has come to you light from Allah and plain Scripture,

16. By which Allah guides him who seeks His good pleasure to paths of peace. He brings them out of darkness to light by His decree, and guides them to a straight path.

17. They indeed have disbelieved who say: Allah is the Messiah, son of Mary. Say: Who then can do anything against Allah, if He had willed to destroy the Messiah son of Mary, and his mother and everyone on earth? Allah's is the Sovereignty of the heavens and the earth and all that is between them. He creates what He will. And Allah is Able to do all things.

18. The Jews and Christians say: We are sons of Allah and His loved ones. Say: Why then does He chastise you for your sins? No, you are only mortals of His creating. He forgives whom He will, and chastises whom He will. Allah's is the Sovereignty of the heavens and the earth and all that is between them, and to Him is the journeying.

19. O People of the Scripture! Now Our messenger has come to you to make things plain to you after an interval (of cessation) of the messengers, lest you should say: There came not to us a messenger of cheer nor any warner. Now a messenger of cheer and a warner has come to you. Allah is Able to do all things.

20. And (remember) when Moses said to his people: O my people! Remember Allah's favour to you, how He placed among you Prophets, and

---

70. *i.e.* a loan without interest or thought of gain.

He made you kings, and gave you that (which) He gave not to any (other) of (His) creatures.

21. O my people! Go into the holy land which Allah has ordained for you. Turn not in flight, for surely you turn back as losers:

22. They said: O Moses! A giant people (dwell) in it and we go not in till they go out from there. When they go out from there, then we will enter (not till then).

23. Then spoke two of those who feared (their Lord, men) to whom Allah had been gracious: Enter in upon them by the gate, for if you enter by it, you will be victorious. So put your trust (in Allah) if you are indeed believers.

24. They said: O Moses! We will never enter (the land) while they are in it. So go you and your Lord and fight! We will sit here.

25. He said: My Lord! I have control of none but myself and my brother, so distinguish between us and the wrong-doing people.

26. (Their Lord) said: For this the land will surely be forbidden to them for forty years that they will wander in the earth, bewildered. So grieve not over the wrongdoing people.

27. But recite to them with truth the tale of the two sons of Adam, how they each offered a sacrifice, and it was accepted from one of them and it was not accepted from the other. (The one) said: I will surely kill you. (The other) answered: Allah accepts only from those who ward off (evil).

28. Even if you stretch out your hand against me to kill me, I shall not stretch out my hand against you to kill you, I fear Allah, the Lord of the Worlds.

29. I would rather you should bear the punishment of the sin against me and your own sin and become one of the owners of the Fire. That is the reward of evildoers.

30. But (the other's) mind imposed on him the killing of his brother, so he slew him and became one of the losers.

31. Then Allah sent a raven scratching up the ground, to show him how to hide his brother's naked corpse. He said: Woe to me! Am I not able to be as this raven and so hide my brother's naked corpse? And he became repentant.

32. For that cause We decreed for the Children of Israel that whoever kills a human being for other than killing or corruption in the earth, it would be as if he had killed all mankind, and whoever saves the life of one, it would be as if he had saved the life of all mankind. Our messengers came to them of old with clear proofs (of Allah's Sovereignty), but afterwards many of them became prodigals in the earth.

33. The only reward of those who make war on Allah and His messenger and strive after corruption in the land will be that they will be killed or crucified, or have their hands and feet on alternate sides cut off, or will be expelled from the land. Such will be their degradation in the world, and in the Hereafter theirs will be an awful doom;

34. Except those who repent before you overpower them. For know that Allah is Forgiving, Merciful.

35. O you who believe! Be mindful of your duty to Allah, and seek the way of approach to Him, and strive in His way in order that you may succeed.

36. As for those who disbelieve, if all that is in the earth were theirs, and as much again with it, to ransom them from the doom on the Day of Resurrection, it would not be accepted from them. Theirs will be a painful doom.

37. They will wish to come out from the Fire, but they will not come out from it. Theirs will be a lasting doom.

38. As for the thief, both male and female, cut off their hands. It is the reward of their own deeds, an exemplary punishment, from Allah. Allah is Mighty, Wise.

39. But whoever repents after his wrongdoing and amends, Allah will relent towards him. Allah is Forgiving, Merciful.

40. Do you not know that to Allah belongs the Sovereignty of the heavens and the earth? He punishes whom He will, and forgives whom He will. Allah is Able to do all things.

41. O Messenger! Let not them grieve you who vie one with another in the race in disbelief of such as say with their mouths: "We believe," but their hearts believe not, and of the Jews: listeners for the sake of falsehood, listeners on behalf of other people who come not to you, changing words from their context and saying: If this is given to you, receive it, but if this is not given to you,

then beware! He whom Allah dooms to sin, you (by your efforts) will benefit him nothing against Allah. Those are they for whom the Will of Allah is that He cleanse not their hearts. Theirs in the world will be ignominy, and in the Hereafter an awful doom;

42. Listeners for the sake of falsehood! Greedy for illicit gain! If then they have recourse to you (Muhammad) judge between them or disclaim jurisdiction. If you disclaim jurisdiction, then they cannot harm you at all. But if you judge, judge between them with equity. Allah loves the equitable.

43. How is it that they come to you for judgement when they have the Torah, in which Allah has delivered judgement (for them)? Yet even after that they turn away. Such (people) are not believers.

44. We did reveal the Torah, in which is guidance and a light, by which the Prophets who surrendered (to Allah) judged the Jews, and the rabbis and the priests (judged) by such of Allah's Scripture as they were commanded to observe, and to it they were witnesses. So fear not mankind, but fear Me. And barter not My revelations for a little gain. Who judges not by that which Allah has revealed: such are disbelievers.

45. And We prescribed for them in it: The life for the life, and the eye for the eye, and the nose for the nose, and the ear for the ear, and the tooth for the tooth, and for wounds retaliation. But who forgoes it (in the way of charity) it will be expiation for him. Who judges not by that which Allah has revealed: such are wrongdoers.

46. And We caused Jesus, son of Mary, to follow in their footsteps, confirming that which was (revealed) before him in the Torah, and We bestowed on him the Gospel in which is guidance and a light, confirming that which was (revealed) before it in the Torah - a guidance and an admonition to those who ward off (evil).

47. Let the People of the Gospel judge by that which Allah has revealed in it. Who judges not by that which Allah has revealed: such are evil-livers.

48. And to you We have revealed the Scripture with the truth, confirming whatever Scripture was before it, and a watcher over it. So judge between them by that which Allah has revealed, and follow not their desires away from the truth which has come to you. For each We have appointed a divine law and a traced-out way. Had Allah willed He could have made you one community. But that He may try you by that which He has given you (He has made you as you are). So vie one with another in good works. To Allah you will all return, and He will then inform you of that in which you differ.

49. So judge between them by that which Allah has revealed, and follow not their desires, but beware of them lest they seduce you from some part of that which Allah has revealed to you. And if they turn away, then know that Allah's Will is to strike them for some sin of theirs. Many of mankind are evil-livers.

50. Is it a judgement of the time of (pagan) ignorance that they are seeking? Who is better than Allah for judgement to a people who have certainty (in their belief)?

51. O you who believe! Take not the Jews and the Christians for friends. They are friends one to another. He among you who takes them for friends is (one) of them. Allah guides not wrongdoing people.

52. And you see those in whose heart is a disease race towards them, saying: We fear lest a change of fortune befall us. And it may happen that Allah will grant (to you) the victory, or a commandment from His presence. Then they will repent of their secret thoughts.

53. Then the believers will say (to the People of the Scripture): Are these they who swore by Allah their most binding oaths that they were surely with you? Their works have failed, and they have become the losers.

54. O you who believe! Whoever of you becomes a renegade from his religion, (know that in his stead) Allah will bring a people whom He loves and who love Him, humble towards believers, stern towards disbelievers, striving in the way of Allah, and fearing not the blame of any blamer. Such is the grace of Allah which He gives to whom He will. Allah is All-Embracing, All-Knowing.

55. Your guardian can be only Allah; and His messenger and those who believe, who establish worship and pay the poor-due, and bow down (in prayer).

56. And who takes Allah and His messenger and those who believe for guardian, (will know that) the party of Allah, they are the victorious.

57. O You who believe! Choose not for guardians such of those who received the Scripture before you, and of the disbelievers, as make a jest and sport of your religion. But keep your duty to Allah if you are true believers.

58. And when you call to prayer they take it for a jest and sport. That is because they are a people who understand not.

59. Say: O People of the Scripture! Do you blame us for anything else than that we believe in Allah and that which is revealed to us and that which was revealed before, and because most of you are evil-livers?

60. Shall I tell you of a worse (case) than theirs for retribution with Allah? (Worse is the case of him) whom Allah has cursed, him on whom His wrath has fallen and of whose sort Allah has turned some to apes and swine, and who serves idols. Such are in worse plight and further astray from the plain road.

61. When they come to you (Muslims), they say: We believe; but they came in unbelief and they went out in the same; and Allah knows best what they were hiding.

62. And you see many of them vying one with another in sin and transgression and their devouring of illicit gain. Evil is what they do.

63. Why do not the rabbis and the priests forbid their evil-speaking and their devouring of illicit gain? Evil is their handiwork.

64. The Jews say: Allah's Hand is fettered. Their hands are fettered and they are accursed for saying so. No,

but both His Hands are spread out wide in bounty. He bestows as He will. That which has been revealed to you from your Lord is certain to increase the rebellion and disbelief of many of them, and We have cast among them enmity and hatred till the Day of Resurrection. As often as they light a fire for war, Allah extinguishes it. Their effort is for corruption in the land, and Allah loves not corrupters.

65. If only the People of the Scripture would believe and ward off (evil), surely We should remit their sins from them and surely We should bring them into Gardens of Delight.

66. If they had observed the Torah and the Gospel and that which was revealed to them from their Lord, they would surely have been nourished from above them and from beneath their feet. Among them there are people who are moderate, but many of them are of evil conduct.

67. O Messenger! Make known that which has been revealed to you from your Lord, for if you do it not, you will not have conveyed His message. Allah will protect you from mankind. Allah guides not the disbelieving people.

68. Say O People of the Scripture! You have nothing (of guidance) till you observe the Torah and the Gospel and that which was revealed to you from your Lord. That which is revealed to you (Muhammad) from your Lord is certain to increase the rebellion and disbelief of many of them. But grieve not for the disbelieving people.

69. Those who believe, and those who are Jews, and Sabaeans, and Christians - Whoever believes in Allah and the Last Day and does right - no fear will come upon them neither will they grieve.[71]

70. We made a covenant of old with the Children of Israel and We sent to them messengers. As often as a messenger came to them with that which their souls desired not (they became rebellious). Some (of them) they denied and some they slew.

71. They thought no harm would come of it, so they were wilfully blind and deaf. And afterwards Allah turned (in mercy) towards them. Now (even after that) many of them are wilfully blind and deaf. Allah is Seer of what they do.

72. They surely disbelieve who say: Allah is the Messiah, son of Mary. The Messiah (himself) said: O Children of Israel, worship Allah, my Lord and your Lord. Who ascribes partners to Allah, for him Allah has forbidden paradise. His abode is the Fire. For evildoers there will be no helpers.

73. They surely disbelieve who say: Allah is the third of three; when there is no God except the One God. If they desist not from so saying, a painful doom will fall on those of them who disbelieve.

74. Will they not rather turn to Allah and seek forgiveness of Him? For Allah is Forgiving, Merciful.

75. The Messiah, son of Mary, was no other than a messenger, messengers (the like of whom) had passed away before him. And his mother was a saintly woman. And they both used to eat (earthly) food. See how We make

the revelations clear for them, and see how they are turned away!

76. Say: Do you serve in place of Allah that which possesses for you neither hurt nor use? Allah it is Who is the Hearer, the Knower.

77. Say: O People of the Scripture! Stress not in your religion other than the truth, and follow not the vain desires of people who erred of old and led many astray, and erred from a plain road.

78. Those of the Children of Israel who went astray were cursed by the tongue of David, and of Jesus, son of Mary. That was because they rebelled and used to transgress.

79. They restrained not one another from the wickedness they did. Verily evil was that which they used to do!

80. You see many of them making friends with those who disbelieve. Surely ill for them is that which they themselves send on before them: that Allah will be angry with them and in the doom they will remain.

81. If they believed in Allah and the Prophet and that which is revealed to him, they would not choose them for their friends. But many of them are of evil conduct.

82. You will find the most vehement of mankind in hostility to those who believe (to be) the Jews and the idolaters. And you will find the nearest of them in affection to those who believe (to be) those who say: We are Christians. That is because there are among them priests and monks,[72] and because they are not proud.

---

71. Almost identical with *Surah 2, Al-Baqarah*, v. 62.

72. *i.e.* persons entirely devoted to the service of God, as were the Muslims.

83. When they listen to that which has been revealed to the messengers, you see their eyes overflow with tears because of their recognition of the Truth. They say: Our Lord, we believe. Inscribe us as among the witnesses.

84. How should we not believe in Allah and that which has come to us of the Truth. And (how should we not) hope that our Lord will bring us in along with righteous people?

85. Allah has rewarded them on account of their saying - Gardens underneath which rivers flow, in which they will remain forever. That is the reward of the good.

86. But those who disbelieve and deny Our revelations, they are owners of Hell-fire.

87. O you who believe! Forbid not the good things which Allah has made lawful for you, and transgress not, Allah loves not transgressors.

88. Eat of that which Allah has bestowed on you as food lawful and good, and keep your duty to Allah in Whom you are believers.

89. Allah will not take you to task for that which is unintentional in your oaths, but He will take you to task for the oaths which you swear in earnest. The expiation of it is the feeding of ten of the needy with the average of that with which you feed your own people, or the clothing of them, or the liberation of a slave, and for him who finds not (the means to do so) then a three days' fast. This is the expiation of your oaths when you have sworn; and keep your oaths. Thus Allah explains to you His revelations in order that you may give thanks.

90. O you who believe! Strong drink and games of chance and idols and divining arrows are only an infamy of Satan's handiwork. Leave it aside in order that you may succeed.

91. Satan seeks only to cast among you enmity and hatred by means of strong drink and games of chance, and to turn you from remembrance of Allah and from (His) worship. Will you then desist?

92. Obey Allah and obey the messenger, and beware! But if you turn away, then know that the duty of Our messenger is only plain conveyance (of the message).

93. There shall be no sin (imputed) to those who believe and do good works for what they may have eaten (in the past). So be mindful of your duty (to Allah), and believe, and do good works; and again: be mindful of your duty, and believe; and once again: be mindful of your duty, and do right. Allah loves the good.

94. O you who believe! Allah will surely try you somewhat (in the matter) of the game which you take with your hands and your spears, that Allah may know him who fears Him in secret. Who transgresses after this, for him there is a painful doom.

95. O you who believe! Kill no wild game while you are on the pilgrimage. Whoever of you kills it intentionally, he shall pay its penalty in the equivalent of that which he has killed, of domestic animals, the judge to be two men among you known for justice, (the compensation) to be brought as an offering to the Ka'bah; or, for expiation, he shall feed poor persons, or the equivalent of it in fasting, that he may taste the evil consequences of his deed. Allah forgives whatever (of this kind) may have happened in the past, but he who relapses, Allah will take retribution from him. Allah is Mighty, Able to Requite (the wrong).

96. To hunt and to eat the fish of the sea is made lawful for you, a provision for you and for seafarers; but to hunt on land is forbidden for you so long as you are on the pilgrimage. Be mindful of your duty to Allah, to Whom you will be gathered.

97. Allah has appointed the Ka'bah, the Sacred House, a standard for mankind, and the Sacred Month and the offerings and the garlands. That is so that you may know that Allah knows whatever is in the heavens and whatever is in the earth, and that Allah is Knower of all things.

98. Know that Allah is severe in punishment, but that Allah (also) is Forgiving, Merciful.

99. The duty of the messenger is only to convey (the message). Allah knows what you proclaim and what you hide.

100. Say: The evil and the good are not alike even though the plenitude of evil attracts you. So be mindful of your duty to Allah, O men of understanding, that you may succeed.

101. O you who believe! Ask not of things which, if they were made known to you, would trouble you; but if you ask of them when the Qur'an is being revealed, they will be made known to you. Allah pardons this, for Allah is Forgiving, Clement.

102. A people before you asked (for such disclosures) and then disbelieved in it.

103. Allah has not appointed anything in the nature of a Bahirah or a Sa'ibah or a Wasilah or a Hami,[73] but those who disbelieve invent a lie against Allah. Most of them have no sense.

104. And when it is said to them: Come to that which Allah has revealed, and to the messenger, they say: Enough for us is that in which we found our fathers. What! Even though their fathers had no knowledge whatever, and no guidance?

105. O you who believe! You have charge of your own souls. He who errs cannot injure you if you are rightly guided. To Allah you will all return; and then He will inform you of what you used to do.

106. O you who believe! Let there be witnesses between you when death draws near to one of you, at the time of bequest - two witnesses, just men from among you, or two others from another tribe, in case you are campaigning in the land and the calamity of death befalls you. You shall enlist them both after the prayer, and, if you doubt, they shall be made to swear by Allah (saying): We will not take a bribe, even though it were (on behalf of) a near relative, nor will we hide the testimony of Allah, for then indeed we should be of the sinful.

---

73. Different classes of cattle liberated in honour of idols and revered by the pagan Arabs.

107. But then, if it is afterwards ascertained that both of them merit (the suspicion of) sin, let two others take their place of those nearly concerned, and let them swear by Allah, (saying): Verily our testimony is truer than their testimony and we have not transgressed (the bounds of duty), for then indeed we should be of the evildoers.

108. Thus it is more likely that they will bear true witness or fear that after their oaths the oaths (of others) will be taken. So be mindful of your duty (to Allah) and listen. Allah guides not the obstinate people.

109. On the day when Allah gathers together the messengers, and says: What was your response (from mankind)? they say: We have no knowledge. You, only You, are the Knower of Things Hidden,

110. When Allah says: O Jesus, son of Mary! Remember My favour to you and to your mother; how I strengthened you with the Holy Spirit, so that you spoke to mankind in the cradle as in maturity; and how I taught you the Scripture and Wisdom and the Torah and the Gospel; and how you did shape of clay as it were the likeness of a bird by My permission, and did blow upon it and it was a bird by My permission, and you did heal him who was born blind and the leper by My permission; and how you did raise the dead by My permission; and how I restrained the Children of Israel from (harming) you when you came to them with clear proofs, and those of

them who disbelieved exclaimed: This is nothing else than mere magic;

111. And when I inspired the disciples, (saying): Believe in Me and in My messenger, they said: We believe. Bear witness that we have surrendered (to You) "we are Muslims".

112. When the disciples said: O Jesus, son of Mary! Is your Lord able to send down for us a table spread with food from heaven? He said: Observe your duty to Allah, if you are true believers.

113. (They said:) We wish to eat of it, that we may satisfy our hearts and know that you have spoken truth to us, and that of it we may be witnesses.

114. Jesus, son of Mary, said: O Allah, Lord of us! Send down for us a table spread with food from heaven, that it may be a feast for us, for the first of us and for the last of us, and a sign from You. Give us sustenance, for You are the Best of Sustainers.

115. Allah said: I send it down for you. And who disbelieves of you afterwards, him surely I will punish with a punishment with which I have not punished any of (My) creatures.

116. And when Allah says: O Jesus, son of Mary! Did you say to mankind: Take me and my mother for two gods beside Allah? he says: Be glorified! It was not mine to utter that to which I had no right. If I used to say it, then You knew it. You know what is in my mind, and I know not what is in Your Mind. You, only You, are the Knower of Things Hidden.

117. I spoke to them only that which You commanded me, (saying): Worship Allah, my Lord and your Lord. I was a witness of them while I dwelt among them, and when You took me You were the Watcher over them. You are Witness over all things.

118. If You punish them, they are Your slaves, and if You forgive them (they are Your slaves). You, only You, are the Mighty, the Wise.

119. Allah says: This is a day in which their truthfulness profits the truthful, for theirs are Gardens underneath which rivers flow, in which they are secure forever, Allah taking pleasure in them and they in Him. That is the great triumph.

120. To Allah belongs the Sovereignty of the heavens and the earth and whatever is in it, and He is Able to do all things.

Surah 6: *Al-An'am*
(Cattle)

Al-An'am "Cattle" takes its name from a word in v. 136, repeated in vv. 138, 139, where cattle are mentioned in connection with superstitious practices condemned by *Al-Islam*.

With the possible exception of nine verses, which some authorities - e.g. Ibn Salamah - ascribe to the Madinah period, the whole of this Surah belongs to the year before the *Hijrah*. It is related, on the authority of Ibn 'Abbas, that it was revealed in a single visitation. It is placed here on account of the subject, vindication of the Divine Unity, which aptly follows

onto the subjects of the previous Surahs. The note of certain triumph is remarkable in the circumstances of its revelation, when the Prophet, after thirteen years of effort, saw himself obliged to leave from Makkah and seek help from strangers.

A late Makkan Surah.

═══════════════

In the name of Allah, the Beneficent, the Merciful.

1. Praise be to Allah, Who has created the heavens and the earth, and has appointed darkness and light. Yet those who disbelieve ascribe rivals to their Lord.

2. He it is Who has created you from clay, and has decreed a term for you. A term is fixed with Him. Yet still you doubt!

3. He is Allah in the heavens and in the earth. He knows both your secret and your utterance, and He knows what you earn.

4. Never came there to them a revelation of the revelations of Allah but they did turn away from it.

5. And they denied the truth when it came to them. But there will come to them the tidings of that which they used to deride.

6. See they not how many a generation We destroyed before them, whom We had established in the earth more firmly than We have established you, and We shed on them abundant showers from the sky, and made the rivers flow beneath them. Yet we destroyed them for their sins, and created after them another generation.

7. Had we sent down to you (Muhammad) (actual) writing upon parchment, so that they could feel it with their hands, those who disbelieve would have said: This is nothing else than mere magic.

8. They say: Why has not an angel been sent down to him? If We sent down an angel, then the matter would be judged; no further time would be allowed them (for reflection).

9. Had we appointed him (Our messenger) an angel, We assuredly had made him (as) a man (that he might speak to men); and (thus) obscured for them (the truth) they (now) obscure.

10. Messengers (of Allah) have been derided before you, but that at which they scoffed surrounded such of them as did deride.

11. Say (to the disbelievers): Travel in the land, and see the nature of the consequence for the rejecters!

12. Say: To whom belongs whatever is in the heavens and the earth? Say: To Allah. He has prescribed for Himself mercy, that He may bring you all together to the Day of Resurrection of which there is no doubt. Those who ruin their souls will not believe.

13. To Him belongs whatever rests in the night and the day. He is the Hearer, the Knower.

14. Say: Shall I choose for a protecting friend other than Allah, the Originator of the heavens and the earth, Who feeds and is never fed? Say: I am ordered to be the first to surrender (to Him). And be not you (O Muhammad) of the idolaters.

15. Say: I fear, if I rebel against my Lord, the retribution of an Awful Day.

16. He from whom (such retribution) is averted on that day, (Allah) has in truth had mercy on him. That will be the signal triumph.

17. If Allah touches you with affliction, there is none that can relieve you from it except Him, and if He touches you with good fortune (there is none that can impair it); for He is Able to do all things.

18. He is the Omnipotent over His slaves, and He is the Wise, the Knower.

19. Say (O Muhammad): What thing is of most weight in testimony? Say: Allah is Witness between me and you. And this Qur'an has been inspired in me, that I may warn with it, you and whomsoever it may reach. Do you really bear witness that there are gods beside Allah? Say: I bear no such witness. Say: He is only One God. I am innocent of that which you associate (with Him).

20. Those to whom We gave the Scripture recognise (this revelation) as they recognise their sons. Those who ruin their own souls will not believe.

21. Who does greater wrong than he who invents a lie against Allah or denies His revelations? The wrongdoers will not be successful.

22. And on the day We gather them together We shall say to those who ascribed partners (to Allah): Where are (now) those partners of your make-believe?

23. Then they will have no contention except that they will say: By Allah, our Lord, we never were idolaters.

24. See how they lie against themselves, and (how) the thing which they devised has failed them!

25. Of them are some who listen to you, but We have placed upon their hearts veils, lest they should understand, and in their ears a deafness. If they saw every sign they would not believe in it; to the point that, when they come to you to argue with you, the disbelievers say: This is nothing else than fables of the men of old.

26. And they forbid (men) from it and avoid it, and they ruin none except themselves, though they perceive not.

27. If you could see when they are set before the Fire and say: Oh, would that we might return! Then we would not deny the revelations of our Lord but we would be of the believers!

28. No, but that has become clear to them which before they used to hide. And if they were sent back they would return to that which they are forbidden. They are liars.

29. And they say: There is nothing except our life of the world, and we shall not be raised (again).

30. If you could see when they are set before their Lord! He will say: Is not this real? They will say: Yes verily, by our Lord! He will say: Taste now the retribution for that which you used to disbelieve.

31. They indeed are losers who deny their meeting with Allah until, when the Hour comes on them suddenly, they cry: Alas for us, that we neglected it! They bear upon their backs their burdens. Ah, evil is that which they bear!

32. Nothing is the life of the world except a pastime and a sport. Better far is the abode of the Hereafter for those who keep their duty (to Allah). Have you then no sense?

33. We know well how their talk grieves you, though in truth they deny not you (Muhammad), but evildoers flout the revelations of Allah.

34. Messengers indeed have been denied before you, and they were patient under the denial and the persecution till Our help reached them. There is none to alter the decisions of Allah. Already there has reached you (somewhat) of the tidings of the messengers (We sent before).

35. And if their aversion is grievous to you, then, if you can, seek a way down into the earth or a ladder to the sky that you may bring to them a sign (to convince them all)! - If Allah willed, He could have brought them all together to the guidance - So be not you among the foolish ones.

36. Only those can accept who hear. As for the dead, Allah will raise them up; then to Him they will be returned.

37. They say: Why has no sign been sent down upon him from his Lord? Say: Allah is Able to send down a sign. But most of them know not.

38. There is not an animal in the earth, nor a flying creature flying on two wings, but they are peoples like to you. We have neglected nothing in the Book (of Our decrees). Then to their Lord they will be gathered.

39. Those who deny Our revelations are deaf and dumb in darkness. Whom Allah will, He sends astray, and whom He will, He places on a straight path.

40. Say: Can you see yourselves, if the punishment of Allah comes upon you or the Hour comes upon you, (calling on other than Allah)? Do you then call (for help) to any other than Allah? (Answer that) if you are truthful.

41. No, but to Him you call, and He removes that because of which you call to Him, if He will, and you forget whatever partners you ascribed to Him.

42. We have sent already to peoples that were before you, and We visited them with tribulation and adversity, in order that they might grow humble.

43. If only, when Our disaster came on them, they had been humble! But their hearts were hardened and the devil made all that they used to do seem fair to them!

44. Then, when they forgot that of which they had been reminded, We opened to them the gates of all things till, even as they were rejoicing in that which they were given, We seized them unawares, and they were dumbfounded.

45. So of the people who did wrong the last remnant was cut off. Praise be to Allah, Lord of the Worlds!

46. Say: Have you considered, if Allah should take away your hearing and your sight and seal your hearts, Who is the God Who could restore it to you except Allah? See how We display the revelations to them! Yet still they turn away.

47. Say: Can you see yourselves, if the punishment of Allah comes upon you unawares or openly? Would any perish except wrongdoing people?

48. We send not the messengers except as bearers of good news and warners. Whoever believes and does right, there shall no fear come upon them, neither shall they grieve.

49. But as for those who deny Our revelations, torment will afflict them for that they used to disobey.

50. Say (O Muhammad, to the disbelievers): I say not to you (that) I possess the treasures of Allah, nor that I have knowledge of the Unseen; and I say not to you: I am an angel. I follow only that which is inspired in me. Say: Are the blind man and the seer equal? Will you not then take thought?

51. Warn with this those who fear (because they know) that they will be gathered to their Lord, for whom there is no protecting ally nor intercessor beside Him, that they may ward off (evil).

52. Repel not those who call upon their Lord in the morning and evening, seeking His Countenance. You are not accountable for them in any way, nor are they accountable for you in any way, that you should repel them and be of the wrongdoers.

53. And even so do We try some of them by others, that they say: Are these they whom Allah favours among us? Is not Allah best Aware of the thanksgivers?

54. And when those who believe in Our revelations come to you, say: Peace be to you! Your Lord has prescribed for Himself mercy, that whoever of you does evil through ignorance and repents afterwards of it and does right, (for him) He is Forgiving, Merciful.

55. Thus do We explain the revelations that the way of the unrighteous may be manifest.

56. Say: I am forbidden to worship those on whom you call instead of Allah. Say: I will not follow your desires, for then I should go astray and I should not be of the rightly guided.

57. Say: I am (relying) on clear proof from my Lord, while you deny Him. I have not that for which you are impatient. The decision is for Allah only. He tells the truth and He is the Best of Deciders.

58. Say: If I had that for which you are impatient, then the case (so far) would have been decided between me and you. Allah is Best Aware of the wrongdoers.

59. And with Him are the keys of the Invisible. None but He knows them. And He knows what is in the land and the sea. Not a leaf falls but He knows it, not a grain amid the darkness of the earth, nothing of wet or dry but (it is noted) in a clear record.

60. He it is Who gathers you at night and knows that which you commit by day. Then He raises you again to life in it, that the term appointed (for you) may be accomplished. And afterwards to Him is your return. Then He will proclaim to you what you used to do.

61. He is the Omnipotent over His slaves. He sends guardians over you

until, when death comes to one of you, Our messengers[74] receive him, and they neglect not.

62. Then they are restored to Allah, their Lord, the Just. Surely His is the judgement. And He is the most swift of reckoners.

63. Say: Who delivers you from the darkness of the land and the sea? You call on Him humbly and in secret, (saying): If we are delivered from this (fear) we truly will be of the thankful.

64. Say: Allah delivers you from this and from all affliction. Yet you attribute partners to Him.

65. Say: He is able to send punishment upon you from above you or from beneath your feet, or to bewilder you with dissension and make you taste the tyranny one of another. See how We display the revelations so that they may understand.

66. Your people (O Muhammad) have denied it, though it is the Truth. Say: I am not put in charge of you.

67. For every announcement there is a term, and you will come to know.

68. And when you see those who meddle with Our revelations, withdraw from them until they meddle with another topic. And if the devil causes you to forget, sit not, after the remembrance, with the congregation of wrongdoers.

69. Those who ward off (evil) are not accountable for them anyway, but the Reminder (must be given them) that perhaps they (too) may ward off (evil).

---

74. *i.e.* angels. The same word *Rusul* is used for angels and for Prophets.

70. And forsake those who take their religion for a pastime and a jest, and whom the life of the world distracts. Remind (mankind) with it lest a soul be destroyed by what it earns. It has besides Allah no protecting ally nor intercessor, and though it offer every compensation it will not be accepted from it. Those are they who perish because of their own deeds. For them is drink of boiling water and a painful doom, because they disbelieved.

71. Say: Shall we call, instead of to Allah, to that which neither profits us nor hurts us, and shall we turn back after Allah has guided us, like one bewildered whom the devils have possessed in the earth, who has companions who invite him to the guidance (saying): Come to us? Say: The guidance of Allah is Guidance, and we are ordered to surrender to the Lord of the Worlds,

72. And to establish worship and be dutiful to Him, and He it is to Whom you will be gathered.

73. He it is Who created the heavens and the earth in truth. In the day when He says: Be! it is. His Word is the Truth, and His will be the Sovereignty on the day when the trumpet is blown. Knower of the Invisible and the Visible, He is the Wise, the Aware.

74. (Remember) when Abraham said to his father Azar: Do you take idols for gods? I see you and your people in error manifest.

75. Thus did We show Abraham the kingdom of the heavens and the earth that he might be of those possessing certainty.

76. When the night grew dark upon him he saw a star. He said: This is my Lord. But when it set, he said: I love not things that set.

77. And when he saw the moon rising, he exclaimed: This is my Lord. But when it set, he said: Unless my Lord guides me, I surely shall become one of the people who are astray.

78. And when he saw the sun rising, he exclaimed: This is my Lord! This is greater! And when it set he exclaimed: O my people! I am free from all that you associate (with Him).

79. I have turned my face towards Him Who created the heavens and the earth, as one by nature upright, and I am not of the idolaters.

80. His people argued with him. He said: Dispute you with me concerning Allah when He has guided me? I fear not at all that which you set up besides Him unless my Lord wills in any way. My Lord includes all things in His knowledge. Will you not then remember?

81. How should I fear that which you set up besides Him, when you fear not to set up besides Allah that for which He has revealed to you no authority? Which of the two factions has more right to safety? (Answer me that) if you have knowledge.

82. Those who believe and obscure not their belief by wrongdoing, theirs is safety; and they are rightly guided.

83. That is Our argument. We gave it to Abraham against his people. We raise to degrees of wisdom whom We will. Your Lord is Wise, Aware.

84. And We bestowed upon him Isaac and Jacob; each of them We guided; and Noah We guided before; and of his seed (We guided) David and Solomon and Job and Joseph and Moses and Aaron. Thus do We reward the good.

85. And Zechariah and John and Jesus and Elias. Each one (of them) was of the righteous.

86. And Ishmael and Elisha and Jonah and Lot. Each one (of them) We preferred above (Our) creatures,

87. With some of their forefathers and their offspring and their brothers; and We chose them and guided them to a straight path.

88. Such is the guidance of Allah with which He guides whom He will of His bondsmen. But if they had set up (for worship) anything besides Him, (all) that they did would have been in vain.

89. Those are they to whom We gave the Scripture and Command and Prophethood. But if these disbelieve in it, then indeed We shall entrust it to a people who will not be disbelievers in it.

90. Those are they whom Allah guides, so follow their guidance. Say (O Muhammad, to mankind): I ask of you no fee for it. It is nothing but a Reminder to (His) creatures.

91. And they measure not the power of Allah its true measure when they say: Allah has revealed nothing to a human being. Say (to the Jews who speak thus): Who revealed the Book which Moses brought, a light and guidance for mankind, which you have put on parchments which you show, but you hide much (of it), and (by which) you were taught that which you knew not yourselves nor (did) your fathers (know it)? Say: Allah. Then leave them to their play of trivial objections.

92. And this is a blessed Scripture which We have revealed, confirming that which (was revealed) before it, that you may warn the Mother of Villages[75] and those around her. Those who believe in the Hereafter believe in it, and they are careful of their worship.

93. Who is guilty of more wrong than he who forges a lie against Allah, or says: I am inspired, when he is not inspired at all; and who says: I will reveal the like of that which Allah has revealed? If you could see, when the wrongdoers reach the pangs of death and the angels stretch their hands out (saying): Deliver up your souls. This day you are awarded doom of degradation for that which you spoke concerning Allah other than the truth, and used to scorn His signs.

94. Now you have come to Us solitary as We created you at the first, and you have left behind you all that We bestowed upon you, and We see not with you those of your intercessors of whom you claimed that they possessed a share in you. Now the bond between you is severed, and that which you presumed has failed you.

---

75. *i.e.* Makkah

95. Allah (it is) Who splits the grain of corn and the date-stone (for sprouting). He brings out the living from the dead, and is the One Who brings out the dead from the living. Such is Allah. How then are you perverted?

96. He is the Cleaver of the Daybreak, and He has appointed the night for stillness, and the sun and the moon for reckoning. That is the measuring of the Mighty, the Wise.

97. And He it is Who has set for you the stars that you may guide your course by them amid the darkness of the land and the sea. We have detailed Our revelations for a people who have knowledge.

98. And He it is Who has produced you from a single being, and (has given you) a habitation and a safe place. We have detailed Our revelations for a people who have understanding.

99. He it is Who sends down water from the sky, and with it We bring out buds of every kind; We bring out the green blade from which We bring out the thick-clustered grain; and from the date-palm, from the pollen of it, spring pendant bunches; and (We bring out) gardens of grapes, and the olive and the pomegranate, alike and unlike. Look upon the fruit of them, when they bear fruit, and upon its ripening. In this verily are signs for a people who believe.

100. Yet they ascribe as partners to Him the jinn, although He created them, and attribute falsely, without knowledge, sons and daughters to

Him. Glorified is He and High Exalted above (all) that they ascribe (to Him).

101. The Originator of the heavens and the earth! How can He have a child, when there is for Him no partner, when He created all things and is Aware of all things?

102. Such is Allah, your Lord. There is no God except Him, the Creator of all things, so worship Him. And He takes care of all things.

103. Vision comprehends Him not, but He comprehends (all) vision. He is the Subtle, the Aware.

104. Proofs have come to you from your Lord, so he who sees, it is for his own good, and he who is blind is blind to his own hurt. And I am not a keeper over you.

105. Thus do We display Our revelations that they may say (to you, Muhammad): "You have studied," and that We may make (it) clear for people who have knowledge.

106. Follow that which is inspired in you from your Lord; there is no God except Him; and turn away from the idolaters.

107. Had Allah willed, they would have not been idolatrous. We have not set you as a keeper over them, nor are you responsible for them.

108. Revile not those to whom they pray besides Allah, lest they wrongfully revile Allah through ignorance. Thus to every nation have We made their deed seem fair. Then to their Lord is their return, and He will tell them what they used to do.

109. And they swear a solemn oath by Allah that if there come to them a sign they will believe in it. Say: Signs are with Allah and (so is) that which tells you that if such came to them they would not believe.

110. We confuse their hearts and their eyes. As they believed not in it at the first, We let them wander blindly on in their rebellion.

111. And though We should send down the angels to them, and the dead should speak to them, and We should gather against them all things in array, they would not believe unless Allah so willed. Although, most of them are ignorant.

112. Thus We have appointed to every prophet an adversary - devils of humankind and jinn who inspire in one another plausible discourse through cunning. If your Lord willed, they would not do so; so leave them alone with their devising;

113. That the hearts of those who believe not in the Hereafter may incline to it, and that they may take pleasure in it, and that they may earn what they are earning.

114. Shall I seek other than Allah for judge, when He it is Who has revealed to you (this) Scripture, fully explained? Those to whom We gave the Scripture (before) know that it is revealed from your Lord in truth. So be not you (O Muhammad) of the waverers.

115. Perfected is the Word of your Lord in truth and justice. There is nothing that can change His words. He is the Hearer, the Knower.

116. If you obeyed most of those on earth they would mislead you far from Allah's way. They follow nothing but an opinion, and they do but guess.

117. Your Lord, He knows best who errs from His way; and He knows best (who are) the rightly guided.

118. Eat of that over which the name of Allah has been mentioned, if you are believers in His revelations.

119. How should you not eat of that over which the name of Allah has been mentioned, when He has explained to you that which is forbidden to you unless you are compelled to it. But many are led astray by their own lusts through ignorance. Your Lord, He is Best Aware of the transgressors.

120. Forsake the outwardness of sin and the inwardness of it. Those who amass sin will be awarded that which they have earned.

121. And eat not of that on which Allah's name has not been mentioned, for it is abomination. The devils inspire their helpers to dispute with you. But if you obey them, you will be in truth idolaters.

122. Is he who was dead and We have raised him to life, and set for him a light in which he walks among men, as him whose similitude is in utter darkness from where he cannot emerge? Thus is their conduct made fair-seeming for the disbelievers.

123. And thus We have made in every city great ones of its wicked ones, that they should plot in it. They do only plot against themselves, though they perceive not.

124. And when a sign comes to them, they say: We will not believe till we are given that which Allah's messengers are given. Allah knows best with whom to place His message. Humiliation from Allah and heavy punishment will strike the guilty for their scheming.

125. And whomsoever it is Allah's will to guide, He expands his bosom to the Surrender,[76] and whomsoever it is His Will to send astray, He makes his bosom close and narrow as if he were engaged in sheer ascent. Thus Allah lays disgrace upon those who believe not.

126. This is the path of your Lord, a straight path. We have detailed Our revelations for a people who take heed.

127. For them is the abode of peace with their Lord. He will be their Protecting Friend because of what they used to do.

128. On the day when He will gather them together (He will say): O you assembly of the jinn! Many of humankind did you seduce. And their adherents among humankind will say: Our Lord! We enjoyed one another, but now we have arrived at the appointed term which You appointed for us. He will say: Fire is your home. Remain in it forever, except him whom Allah wills (to deliver). Your Lord is Wise, Aware.

129. Thus We let some of the wrongdoers have power over others because of what they used to earn.

130. O you assembly of the jinn and humankind! Came there not to

you messengers of your own who recounted to you My signs and warned you of the meeting of this your Day? They will say: We testify against ourselves. And the life of the world tricked them. And they testify against themselves that they were disbelievers.

131. This is because your Lord destroys not the townships arbitrarily while their people are unconscious (of the wrong they do).

132. For all there will be ranks from what they did. Your Lord is not unaware of what they do.

133. Your Lord is the Absolute, the Lord of Mercy. If He wills, He can remove you and can cause what He wills to follow after you, even as He raised you from the seed of other people.

134. That which you are promised will surely come to pass, and you cannot escape.

135. Say (O Muhammad): O my people! Work according to your power. I too am working. Thus you will come to know for which of us will be the happy sequel. The wrongdoers will not be successful.

136. They assign to Allah, of the crops and cattle which He created, a portion, and they say: "This is Allah's" - in their make-believe - "and this is for (His) partners in regard to us." Thus that which (they assign) to His partners in them reaches not Allah and that which (they assign) to Allah goes to their (so-called) partners. Evil is their ordinance.

76. Arabic: *Al-Islam*

137. Thus have their (so-called) partners (of Allah) made the killing of their children to seem fair to many of the idolaters, that they may ruin them and make their faith obscure for them. Had Allah willed (it otherwise), they had not done so. So leave them alone with their devices.

138. And they say: Such cattle and crops are forbidden. No-one is to eat of them except whom we will - in their make-believe - cattle whose backs are forbidden, cattle over which they mention not the name of Allah. (All that is) a lie against Him. He will repay them for that which they invent.

139. And they say: That which is in the bellies of such cattle is reserved for our males and is forbidden to our wives; but if it is born dead, then they (all) may be partakers of it. He will reward them for their attribution (of such ordinances to Him).[77] He is Wise, Aware.

140. They are losers who, out of folly, have slain their children without knowledge[78] and have forbidden that which Allah bestowed upon them, inventing a lie against Allah. They indeed have gone astray and are not guided.

141. He it is Who produces gardens trellised and untrellised, and the date-palm, and crops of diverse flavours, and the olive and the pomegranate, like and unlike. Eat of the fruit of it when it ripens, and pay the due of it upon the harvest day, and do not be prodigal. Allah loves not the prodigals.

142. And of the cattle (He produces) some for burdens, some for food. Eat of that which Allah has bestowed upon you, and follow not the footsteps of the devil, for he is an open foe to you.

143. Eight pairs: Of the sheep two, and of the goats two. Say: Has He forbidden the two males or the two females, or that which the wombs of the two females contain? Explain to me (the case) with knowledge, if you are truthful.[79]

144. And of the camels two and of the oxen two. Say: Has He forbidden the two males or the two females, or that which the wombs of the two females contain; or were you there to witness when Allah commanded you (all) this? Then who does greater wrong than he who devises a lie concerning Allah, that he may lead mankind astray without knowledge. Allah guides not wrongdoing people.

145. Say: I find not in that which is revealed to me anything prohibited to an eater that he eat of it, except it be carrion, or blood poured forth, or swineflesh - for that verily is foul - or the abomination which was sanctified to the name of other than Allah. But who is compelled (to it), neither craving nor transgressing, (for him) your Lord is Forgiving, Merciful.

146. To those who are Jews We forbade every animal with claws. And of the oxen and the sheep We forbade to them the fat of it except that upon the backs or the entrails, or that which is mixed with the bone. That We awarded them for their rebellion. And We verily are truthful.

---

77. vv. 138 & 139 refer to customs of the Pagan Arabs.
78. The reference is to the burial alive of female children who were deemed superfluous, and the practice of human sacrifice to idols.

79. This and the following verses relate to superstitions of the pagan Arabs with regard to cattle used for food.

147. So if they lie to you (Muhammad), say: Your Lord is a Lord of All-Embracing Mercy, and His wrath will never be withdrawn from guilty people.

148. They who are idolaters will say: Had Allah willed, we had not ascribed (to Him) partners, neither had our fathers, nor had we forbidden anything. Thus did those who were before them give the lie (to Allah's messengers) till they tasted of the fear of Us. Say: Have you any knowledge that you can present for Us? You follow nothing but an opinion, You only guess.

149. Say - For Allah's is the final argument - Had He willed He could indeed have guided all of you.

150. Say: Come, bring your witnesses who can bear witness that Allah forbade (all) this. And if they bear witness, do not bear witness with them. Follow not the whims of those who deny Our revelations, those who believe not in the Hereafter and deem (others) equal with their Lord.

151. Say: Come, I will recite to you that which your Lord has made a sacred duty for you: That you ascribe no thing as partner to Him and that you do good to parents, and that you slay not your children because of destitution - We provide for you and for them - and that you draw not near to lewd things whether open or concealed. And that you slay not the life which Allah has made sacred, except in the course of justice. This He has commanded you, in order that you may discern.

152. And approach not the wealth of the orphan except with that which is better,

till he reaches maturity. Give full measure and full weight, in justice. We task not any soul beyond its scope. And if you give your word, do justice to it, even though it is (against) a relative; and fulfil the covenant of Allah. This He commands you that perhaps you may remember.

153. And (He commands you, saying): This is My straight path, so follow it. Follow not other ways, lest you be parted from His way. This He has ordained for you, that you may ward off (evil).

154. Again, We gave the Scripture to Moses, complete for him who would do good, an explanation of all things, a guidance and a mercy, that they might believe in the meeting with their Lord.

155. And this is a blessed Scripture which We have revealed. So follow it and ward off (evil), that you may find mercy.

156. Lest you should say: The Scripture was revealed only to two sects before us, and we in fact were unaware of what they read;

157. Or lest you should say: If the Scripture had been revealed to us, we surely had been better guided than they are. Now there has come to you a clear proof from your Lord, a guidance and mercy; and who does greater wrong than he who denies the revelations of Allah, and turns away from them? We award to those who turn away from Our revelations an evil doom because of their aversion.

158. Wait they, indeed, for nothing less than that the angels should come to them, or your Lord should come, or there should come one of the signs from your Lord? On the day when one of the signs from your Lord comes, its belief benefits nothing a soul which prior to it believed not, nor in its belief earned good (by works). Say: Wait you! We (too) are waiting.

159. As for those who divide their religion and become schismatics, no concern at all have you with them. Their case will go to Allah, Who then will tell them what they used to do.

160. Who brings a good deed will receive tenfold the like of it, while who brings an ill-deed will be awarded the like of it; and they will not be wronged.

161. Say: As for me, my Lord has guided me to a straight path, a right religion, the community of Abraham, the upright, who was no idolater.

162. Say: My worship and my sacrifice and my living and my dying are for Allah, Lord of the Worlds.

163. He has no partner. This am I commanded, and I am first of those who surrender (to Him).

164. Say: Shall I seek another than Allah for Lord, when He is Lord of all things? Each soul earns only on its own account, nor does anyone loaded bear another's load. Then to your Lord is your return and He will tell you that in which you differed.

165. He it is Who has placed you as viceroys of the earth and has exalted some of you in rank above others, that He may try you by (the test of) that which He has given you. Your Lord is swift in prosecution, and He verily is Forgiving, Merciful.

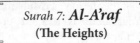

Surah 7: *Al-A'raf* (The Heights)

Al-A'raf, "The Heights", takes its name from a word in v. 46, "And on the Heights are men who know them all by their marks." The best authorities assign the whole of it to about the same period as Surah 6, *i.e.* the Prophet's last year in Makkah, though some consider vv. 163-167 to have been revealed at Al-Madinah. The subject may be said to be the opponents of God's will and purpose, from Satan onward, through the history of Divine Guidance.

A late Makkan Surah.

In the name of Allah, the Beneficent, the Merciful.

1. *Alif. Lam. Mim. Sad.*[80]

2. (It is) a Scripture that is revealed to you (Muhammad) - so let there be no heaviness in your heart from it - that you may warn by it, and (it is) a Reminder to believers.

3. (Saying): Follow that which is sent down to you from your Lord, and follow no protecting friends besides Him. Little do you recollect!

4. How many a township have We destroyed! As a raid by night, or while they slept at noon, Our terror came to them.

5. No plea had they, when Our terror came to them, except that they said: We were wrongdoers.

6. Then verily We shall question those to whom (Our message) has been

---

80. See *Surah 2, Al-Baqarah,* v. 1, footnote.

sent, and verily We shall question the messengers.

7. Then verily We shall narrate to them (the event) with knowledge, for We were not absent (when it came to pass).

8. The weighing on that day is the true (weighing). As for those whose scale is heavy, they are the successful.

9. And as for those whose scale is light: those are they who lose their souls because they used to wrong Our revelations.

10. And We have given you (mankind) power in the earth, and appointed for you in it your livelihoods. Little thanks you give!

11. And We created you, then fashioned you, then told the angels: Fall you prostrate before Adam! And they fell prostrate, all except Iblis, who was not of those who make prostration.

12. (Allah) said: What hindered you that you did not fall prostrate when I bade you? (Iblis) said: I am better than him. You created me of fire while him You created of mud.

13. (Allah) said: Then go down from here! It is not for you to show pride here, so go out! You are of those degraded.

14. (Iblis) said: Reprieve me till the day when they are raised (from the dead).

15. (Allah) said: You are of those reprieved.

16. (Iblis) said: Now, because You have sent me astray, verily I shall lurk in ambush for them on Your Right Path.

17. Then I shall come upon them from before them and from behind them and from their right hands and from

their left hands, and You will not find most of them grateful (to You).

18. He said: Go out from here, degraded, banished. As for such of them as follow you, surely I will fill Hell with all of you.

19. And (to man): O Adam! Dwell you and your wife in the Garden and eat from wherever you will, but come not near this tree lest you become wrongdoers.

20. Then Satan whispered to them that he might manifest to them that which was hidden from them of their shame, and he said: Your Lord forbade you from this tree only lest you should become angels or become of the immortals.

21. And he swore to them (saying): I am a sincere adviser to you.

22. Thus did he lead them on with cunning. And when they tasted of the tree their shame was manifest to them and they began to hide (by heaping) on themselves some of the leaves of the Garden. And their Lord called them, (saying): Did I not forbid you from that tree and tell you: Satan is an open enemy to you?

23. They said: Our Lord! We have wronged ourselves. If you forgive us not and have not mercy on us, surely we are of the lost!

24. He said: Go down (from here), one of you a foe to the other. There will be for you on earth a habitation and provision for a while.

25. He said: There you shall live, and there you shall die, and from there shall you be brought out.

26. O Children of Adam! We have revealed to you garment to conceal your shame, and splendid adornment, but the garment of restraint from evil, that is best. This is of the revelations of Allah, that they may remember.

27. O Children of Adam! Let not Satan seduce you as he caused your (first) parents to go out from the Garden and tore off from them their robe (of innocence) that he might manifest their shame to them. He sees you, he and his tribe, from where you see them not. We have made the devils protecting friends for those who believe not.

28. And when they do some lewdness they say: We found our fathers doing it and Allah has enjoined it on us. Say: Allah, verily, does not enjoin lewdness. Tell you concerning Allah that which you know not?

29. Say: My Lord enjoins justice. And set your faces upright (towards Him) at every place of worship and call upon Him, making religion pure for Him (only). As He brought you into being, so you return (to Him).

30. A party He has led aright, while error has just hold over (another) party, for they choose the devils for protecting supporters instead of Allah and deem that they are rightly guided.

31. O Children of Adam! Look to your adornment at every place of worship, and eat and drink, but be not prodigal. He loves not the prodigals.

32. Say: Who has forbidden the adornment of Allah which He has brought out for His bondsmen, and the good things of His providing? Say:

Such, on the Day of Resurrection, will be only for those who believed during the life of the world. Thus do We detail Our revelations for people who have knowledge.

33. Say: My Lord forbids only indecencies, such of them as are apparent and such as are within, and sin and wrongful oppression, and that you associate with Allah that for which no authority has been revealed, and that you tell concerning Allah that which you know not.

34. And every nation has its term, and when its term comes, they cannot put it off an hour nor yet advance (it).

35. O Children of Adam! When messengers of your own come to you who narrate to you My revelations, then whoever refrains from evil and amends - there shall no fear come upon them, neither shall they grieve.

36. But they who deny Our revelations and scorn them - each are rightful owners of the Fire; they will remain in it.

37. Who does greater wrong than he who invents a lie concerning Allah or denies Our signs. (For such) their appointed portion of the Book (of destiny) reaches them till, when Our messengers[81] come to gather them, they say: Where (now) is that to which you called besides Allah? They say: They have departed from us. And they testify against themselves that they were disbelievers.

38. He says: Enter into the Fire among nations of the jinn and humankind who passed away before you. Every

81. *i.e.* angels

time a nation enters, it curses its sister (nation) till, when they have all been made to follow one another there, the last of them says to the first of them: Our Lord! These led us astray, so give them double torment of the Fire. He says: For each one there is double (torment), but you know not.

39. And the first of them says to the last of them: You were no better than us, so taste the doom for what you used to earn.

40. They who deny Our revelations and scorn them, for them the gates of heaven will not be opened nor will they enter the Garden until the camel goes through the needle's eye. Thus do We repay the guilty.

41. Theirs will be a bed of Hell, and over them coverings (of Hell). Thus do We repay wrongdoers.

42. But (as for) those who believe and do good works - We tax not any soul beyond its scope - such are rightful owners of the Garden. They remain in it.

43. And We remove whatever rancour may be in their hearts. Rivers flow beneath them. And they say: The praise to Allah, Who has guided us to this. We could not truly have been led aright if Allah had not guided us. Verily the messengers of our Lord did bring the Truth. And it is called to them: This is the Garden. You inherit it for what you used to do.

44. And the dwellers of the Garden call to the dwellers of the Fire: We have found that which our Lord promised us (to be) the Truth. Have you (too) found that which your Lord promised

to be the Truth? They say: Yes, verily. And a caller in between them calls: The curse of Allah is on evildoers,

45. Who prevent (men) from the path of Allah and would have it crooked, and who are disbelievers in the Last Day.

46. Between them is a veil. And on the Heights are men who know them all by their marks. And they call to the dwellers of the Garden: Peace be to you! They enter it not although they hope (to enter).

47. And when their eyes are turned towards the dwellers of the Fire, they say: Our Lord! Place us not with the wrongdoing people.

48. And the dwellers on the Heights call to men whom they know by their marks (saying): What did your multitude and that in which you took your pride benefit you?

49. Are these they of whom you swore that Allah would not show them mercy? (To them it has been said): Enter the Garden. No fear shall come upon you, nor is it you who will grieve.

50. And the dwellers of the Fire call out to the dwellers of the Garden: Pour on us some water or some of that with which Allah has provided you. They say: Allah has forbidden both to disbelievers (in His guidance),

51. Who took their religion for a sport and pastime, and whom the life of the world distracted. So this day We have forgotten them even as they forgot the meeting of this their Day and as they used to deny Our signs.

52. Verily We have brought them a Scripture which We explained with knowledge, a guidance and a mercy for a people who believe.

53. Do they await anything except the fulfilment of it? On the day when the fulfilment of it comes, those who were before forgetful of it will say: The messengers of our Lord did bring the Truth! Have we any intercessors, that they may intercede for us? Or can we be returned (to life on earth), that we may act otherwise than we used to act? They have lost their souls, and that which they devised has failed them.

54. Your Lord is Allah Who created the heavens and the earth in six Days, then He mounted the Throne. He covers the night with the day, which is in haste to follow it, and has made the sun and the moon and the stars subservient by His command. His verily is all creation and commandment. Blessed be Allah, the Lord of the Worlds!

55. (O mankind!) Call upon your Lord humbly and in secret. He loves not aggressors.

56. Work not confusion in the earth after the fair ordering (of it), and call on Him in fear and hope. The mercy of Allah is near to the good.

57. And He it is Who sends the winds as tidings heralding His mercy, till, when they bear a cloud heavy (with rain), We lead it to a dead land, and then cause water to descend on it and by it bring forth fruits of every kind. Thus We bring out the dead. Perhaps you may remember.

58. As for the good land, its vegetation comes out by permission of its Lord; while as for that which is bad, only the useless comes out (from it). Thus do We recount the signs for people who give thanks.

59. We sent Noah (of old) to his people, and he said: O my people! Serve Allah. You have no other God except Him. I fear for you the retribution of an Awful Day.

60. The chieftains of his people said: We see you surely in plain error.

61. He said: O my people! There is no error in me, but I am a messenger from the Lord of the Worlds.

62. I convey to you the messages of my Lord and give good counsel to you, and know from Allah that which you know not.

63. Are you surprised that there should come to you a Reminder from your Lord by means of a man among you, that he may warn you, and that you may keep from evil, and that perhaps you may find mercy?

64. But they denied him, so We saved him and those with him in the ship, and We drowned those who denied Our signs. They were blind people.

65. And to (the tribe of) 'Aad (We sent) their brother, Hud.[82] He said: O my people! Serve Allah. You have no other God except Him. Will you not ward off (evil)?

66. The chieftains of his people, who were disbelieving, said: We surely see you in foolishness, and we deem you of the liars.

---

[82] An ancient Arab prophet

67. He said: O my people! There is no foolishness in me, but I am a messenger from the Lord of the Worlds.

68. I convey to you the messages of my Lord and I am for you a true adviser.

69. Are you surprised that there should come to you a Reminder from your Lord by means of a man among you, that he may warn you? Remember how He made you viceroys after Noah's people, and gave you growth of stature. Remember (all) the bounties of your Lord, that perhaps you may be successful.

70. They said: Have you come to us that we should serve Allah alone, and forsake what our fathers worshipped? Then bring upon us that with which you threaten us if you are of the truthful!

71. He said: Terror and wrath from your Lord have already fallen on you. Would you wrangle with me over names which you have named, you and your fathers, for which no authority from Allah has been revealed? Then await (the consequence), I (also) am of those awaiting (it).

72. And We saved him and those with him by a mercy from Us, and We cut the root of those who denied Our revelations and were not believers.

73. And to (the tribe of) Thamud (We sent) their brother Salih.[83] He said: O my people! Serve Allah. You have no other God except Him. A wonder from your Lord has come to you. This is the camel of Allah, a sign to you; so let her feed in Allah's earth, and touch her not with hurt lest painful torment seize you.

74. And remember how He made you viceroys after 'Aad and gave you station in the earth. You choose castles in the plains and hew the mountains into dwellings. So remember (all) the bounties of Allah and do not evil, making mischief in the earth.

75. The chieftains of his people, who were scornful, said to those whom they despised, to such of them as believed: Know you that Salih is one sent from his Lord? They said: In that with which he has been sent we are believers.

76. Those who were scornful said: In that which you believe we are disbelievers.

77. So they hamstrung the she-camel, and they flouted the commandment of their Lord, and they said: O Salih! Bring upon us that you threaten if you are indeed of those sent (from Allah).

78. So the earthquake seized them, and morning found them prostrate in their dwelling-place.

79. And (Salih) turned from them and said: O my people! I delivered my Lord's message to you and gave you good advice, but you love not good advisers.

80. And Lot! (Remember) when he said to his people: Will you commit abomination such as no creature ever did before you?

81. You come with lust to men instead of women. No, but you are immoral people.

82. And the answer of his people was only that they said (one to another): Turn them out of your township[84]. They are people who keep pure.

---

83. An ancient Arab prophet

84. The Arabic word *Qariah* means originally a settled community, polity or civilisation.

83. And We rescued him and his household, except his wife, who was of those who stayed behind.

84. And We rained a rain upon them. See now the nature of the consequence of evildoers!

85. And to Midian (We sent) their brother, Shu'eyb.[85] He said: O my people! Serve Allah. You have no other God except Him. A clear proof has come to you from your Lord; so give full measure and full weight and wrong not mankind in their goods, and work not confusion in the earth after the fair ordering of it. That will be better for you, if you are believers.

86. Lurk not on every road to threaten (wayfarers), and to turn away from Allah's path him who believes in Him, and to seek to make it crooked. And remember, when you were but few, how He did multiply you. And see the nature of the consequence for the corrupters!

87. And if there is a party of you which believes in that with which I have been sent, and there is a party which believes not, then have patience until Allah judges between us. He is the Best of all who deal in judgement.

88. The chieftains of his people, who were scornful, said: Surely we will drive you out, O Shu'eyb, and those who believe with you, from our township, unless you return to our religion. He said: Even though we hate it?

89. We should have invented a lie against Allah if we returned to your religion after Allah has rescued us

from it. It is not for us to return to it unless Allah our Lord should (so) will. Our Lord comprehends all things in knowledge. In Allah do we put our trust. Our Lord! Decide with truth between us and our people, for You are the best of those who make decision.

90. But the chieftains of his people, who were disbelieving, said: If you follow Shu'eyb, then truly you will be the losers.

91. So the earthquake seized them and morning found them prostrate in their dwelling-place.

92. Those who denied Shu'eyb became as though they had not dwelt there. Those who denied Shu'eyb, they were the losers.

93. So he turned from them and said: O my people! I delivered my Lord's messages to you and gave you good advice; then how can I sorrow for a people that rejected (truth)?

94. And We sent no prophet to any township but We did afflict its people with tribulation and adversity that perhaps they might grow humble.

95. Then We changed the evil plight for good till they grew affluent and said: Tribulation and distress did touch our fathers. Then We seized them unawares, when they perceived not.

96. And if the people of the townships had believed and kept from evil, surely We should have opened for them blessings from the sky and from the earth. But (to every messenger) they gave the lie, and so We seized them on account of what they used to earn.

85. Identified with Jethro.

97. Are the people of the townships then secure from the coming of Our wrath upon them as a night-raid while they sleep?

98. Or are the people of the townships then secure from the coming of Our wrath upon them in the daytime while they play?

99. Are they then secure from Allah's scheme? None considers himself secure from Allah's scheme except people that perish.

100. Is it not an indication to those who inherit the land after its people (who thus reaped the consequence of evil-doing) that, if We will, We can strike them for their sins and print upon their hearts so that they hear not?

101. Such were the townships. We relate some tidings of them to you (Muhammad). Their messengers verily came to them with clear proofs (of Allah's Sovereignty), but they could not believe because they had before denied. Thus does Allah print upon the hearts of disbelievers (that they hear not).

102. We found no (loyalty to any) covenant in most of them. No, most of them We found wrongdoers.

103. Then, after them, We sent Moses with our signs to Pharaoh and his chiefs, but they repelled them. Now, see the nature of the consequence for the corrupters!

104. Moses said: O Pharaoh! I am a messenger from the Lord of the Worlds,

105. Approved upon condition that I speak concerning Allah nothing but the truth. I come to you (lords of Egypt) with a clear proof from your Lord. So let the Children of Israel go with me.

106. (Pharaoh) said: If you come with a sign, then produce it, if you are of those who speak the truth.

107. Then he (Moses) flung down his staff and it was a serpent manifest;

108. And he pulled out his hand (from his garment), and it was white for the onlookers.

109. The chiefs of Pharaoh's people said: This is some knowing wizard,

110. Who would expel you from your land. Now what do you advise?

111. They said (to Pharaoh): Put him off (a while) - him and his brother - and send into the cities summoners,

112. To bring every knowing wizard to you.

113. And the wizards came to Pharaoh, saying: Surely there will be a reward for us if we are victors.

114. He answered: Yes, and surely you shall be of those brought near (to me).

115. They said: O Moses! Either throw (first) or let us be the first throwers.

116. He said: Throw! And when they threw, they cast a spell upon the people's eyes, and overawed them, and produced a mighty spell.

117. And We inspired Moses (saying): Throw your staff! And it swallowed up their lying show.

118. Thus the Truth was vindicated and that which they were doing was made vain.

119. Thus were they there defeated and brought low.

120. And the wizards fell down prostrate,

121. Exclaiming: We believe in the Lord of the Worlds,

122. The Lord of Moses and Aaron.

123. Pharaoh said: You believe in Him before I give you permission! This is the plot that you have plotted in the city that you may drive its people from it. But you shall come to know!

124. Surely I shall have your hands and feet cut off on alternate sides. Then I shall crucify you, every one.

125. They said: We are about to return to our Lord!

126. Do you take vengeance on us only inasmuch as we believed the signs of our Lord when they came to us. Our Lord! Grant to us steadfastness and make us die as men who have surrendered (to You).

127. The chiefs of Pharaoh's people said: (O King), will you suffer Moses and his people to make mischief in the land, and insult you and your gods? He said: We will slay their sons and spare their women, for we are in power over them.

128. And Moses said to his people: Seek help in Allah and endure. The earth is Allah's. He gives it for an inheritance to whom He will. And the sequel is for those who keep their duty (to Him).

129. They said: We suffered hurt before you came to us, and since you have come to us. He said: It may be that your Lord is going to destroy your adversary and make you viceroys in the earth, that He may see how you behave.

130. And We distressed Pharaoh's people with famine and shortage of fruits, that perhaps they might heed.

131. But whenever good befell them, they said: This is ours; and whenever evil struck them they ascribed it to the evil auspices of Moses and those with him. Surely their evil auspices were only with Allah. But most of them knew not.

132. And they said: Whatever sign you bring with which to bewitch us, we shall not put faith in you.

133. So We sent against them the flood and the locusts and the vermin and the frogs and the blood - a succession of clear signs. But they were arrogant and became a guilty people.

134. And when the terror fell on them they cried: O Moses! Pray for us to your Lord, because He has a covenant with you. If you remove the terror from us we verily will trust you and will let the Children of Israel go with you.

135. But when We did remove from them the terror for a term which they must reach, see! they broke their covenant.

136. Therefore We took retribution from them; therefore We drowned them in the sea: because they denied Our revelations and were heedless of them.

137. And We caused the people who were despised to inherit the eastern parts of the land and the western parts of it which We had blessed. And the fair word of your Lord was fulfilled for the Children of Israel because of their endurance; and We annihilated (all) that Pharaoh and his people had done and that they had contrived.

138. And We brought the Children of Israel across the sea, and they came to a people who were given up to idols which they had. They said: O Moses! Make for us a god just like they have gods. He said: You are a people who know not.

139. As for these, their way will be destroyed and all that they are doing is in vain.

140. He said: Shall I seek for you a god other than Allah when He has favoured you above (all) creatures?

141. And (remember) when We delivered you from Pharaoh's people who were afflicting you with dreadful torment, slaughtering your sons and sparing your women. That was a tremendous trial from your Lord.

142. And when We appointed for Moses thirty nights (of solitude), and added to them ten, and he completed the whole time appointed by his Lord of forty nights; and Moses said to his brother, Aaron: Take my place among the people. Do right, and follow not the way of mischief-makers.

143. And when Moses came to Our appointed time and his Lord had spoken to him, he said: My Lord! Show me (Your Self), that I may gaze upon You. He said: You will not see Me, but gaze upon the mountain! If it stands still in its place, then you will see Me. And when his Lord revealed (His) glory to the mountain He sent it crashing down. And Moses fell down senseless. And when he woke he said:

Glory to You! I turn to You repentant, and I am the first of (true) believers.

144. He said: O Moses! I have preferred you above mankind by My messages and by My speaking (to you). So hold that which I have given you, and be among the thankful.

145. And We wrote for him, upon the tablets, the lesson to be drawn from all things and the explanation of all things, then (told him): Hold it fast; and command your people (saying): Take the better (course made clear) in it. I shall show you the abode of the evil-livers.

146. I shall turn away from My revelations those who magnify themselves wrongfully in the earth, and if they see each sign believe it not, and if they see the way of righteousness choose it nor for (their) way, and if they see the way of error choose if for (their) way. That is because they deny Our revelations and are used to disregard them.

147. Those who deny Our revelations and the meeting of the Hereafter, their works are fruitless. Are they repaid anything except what they used to do?

148. And the people of Moses, after (he left them), chose a calf (for worship), (made) out of their ornaments, of saffron hue,[86] which gave a lowing sound. Did they not see that it spoke not to them nor guided them to any way? They chose it, and became wrongdoers.

---

86. Or a *body*. But, as the word in the Arabic (*jasad*) can only mean a body of flesh and blood, the meaning "saffron coloured" better fits the context.

149. And when they feared the consequences of it and saw that they had gone astray, they said: Unless our Lord has mercy on us and forgives us, we verily are of the lost.

150. And when Moses returned to his people, angry and grieved, he said: Evil is that (course) which you took after I had left you. Would you hasten on the judgement of your Lord? And he cast down the tablets, and he seized his brother by the head, dragging him towards him. He said: Son of my mother! The people judged me weak and almost killed me. Oh, make not my enemies to triumph over me and place me not among the evildoers.

151. He said: My Lord! Have mercy on me and on my brother; bring us into Your mercy, You are the Most Merciful of all who show mercy.

152. Those who chose the calf (for worship), terror from their Lord and humiliation will come upon them in the life of the world. Thus do We repay those who invent a lie.

153. But those who do ill-deeds and afterwards repent and believe - for them, afterwards, Allah is Forgiving, Merciful.

154. Then, when the anger of Moses subsided, he took up the tablets; in their inscription there was guidance and mercy for all those who fear their Lord.

155. And Moses chose of his people seventy men for Our appointed time and, when the trembling came on them, he said: My Lord! If You had willed, You could have destroyed them long before, and me with them. Will you destroy us for that which the ignorant among us did? It is but Your trial (of us). You send whom You will astray and guide whom You will: You are our Protecting Friend, therefore forgive us and have mercy on us, You, the Best of all who show forgiveness.

156. And ordain for us in this world that which is good, and in the Hereafter (that which is good), We have turned to You. He said: I strike with My punishment whom I will, and My mercy embraces all things, therefore I shall ordain it for those who ward off (evil) and pay the poor-due, and those who believe Our revelations;

157. Those who follow the messenger, the Prophet who can neither read nor write, whom they will find described in the Torah and the Gospel (which are) with them. He will enjoin on them that which is right and forbid them that which is wrong. He will make lawful for them all good things and prohibit for them only the foul; and he will relieve them of their burden and the fetters that they used to wear. Then those who believe in him, and honour him, and help him, and follow the light which is sent down with him: they are the successful.

158. Say (O Muhammad): O mankind! I am the messenger of Allah to you all - (the messenger of) Him to Whom belongs the Sovereignty of the heavens and the earth. There is no God except Him. He gives life and He gives death. So believe in Allah and His messenger, the Prophet who can neither read nor write,[87] who believes in Allah and

---

[87] I give the usual rendering. Some modern critics, while not denying the comparative illiteracy of the Prophet, would prefer the rendering "who is not of those who read the Scripture".

in His Words, and follow him that perhaps you may be led aright.

159. And of Moses' people there is a community who lead with truth and establish justice with it.

160. We divided them into twelve tribes, nations; and We inspired Moses, when his people asked him for water, saying: Strike with your staff the rock! And there gushed out from it twelve springs, so that each tribe knew their drinking-place. And we caused the white cloud to overshadow them and sent down for them the manna and the quails (saying): Eat of the good things with which we have provided you. They wronged Us not, but they used to wrong themselves.

161. And when it was said to them: Dwell in this township and eat from it from where you will, and say "Repentance,"[88] and enter the gate prostrate; We shall forgive you your sins; We shall increase (reward) for the right-doers.

162. But those of them who did wrong changed the word which had been told them for another saying, and We sent down upon them wrath from heaven for their wrongdoing.

163. Ask them (O Muhammad) of the township that was by the sea, how they did break the Sabbath, how their big fish came to them visibly upon their Sabbath day and on a day when they did not keep Sabbath they came not to them. Thus did We try them for that they were evil.

164. And when a community among them said: Why do you preach to a people whom Allah is about to destroy

or punish with an awful doom? They said: In order to be free from guilt before your Lord, and that perhaps they may ward off (evil).

165. And when they forgot that of which they had been reminded, We rescued those who forbade wrong, and visited those who did wrong with dreadful punishment because they were evil-livers.

166. So when they took pride in that which they had been forbidden, We said to them: Be you apes despised and loathed!

167. And (remember) when your Lord proclaimed that He would raise against them till the Day of Resurrection those who would lay on them a cruel torment. Verily your Lord is swift in prosecution and verily He is Forgiving, Merciful.

168. And We have divided them in the earth as (separate) nations. Some of them are righteous, and some far from that. And We have tried them with good things and evil things that perhaps they might return.

169. And a generation has succeeded them who inherited the scriptures. They grasp the goods of this low life (as the price of evil-doing) and say: It will be forgiven us. And if there came to them (again) the offer of the like, they would accept it (and would sin again). Has not the covenant of the Scripture been taken on their behalf that they should not speak anything concerning Allah except the truth? And they have studied that which is in it. And the abode of the Hereafter is better for those who ward off (evil). Have you then no sense?

88. See *Surah 2, Al-Baqarah*, v. 58, footnote.

170. And as for those who make (men) keep the Scripture, and establish worship - We squander not the wages of reformers.

171. And when We shook the Mount above them as if it were a covering, and they supposed that it was going to fall upon them (and We said): Hold fast to that which We have given you, and remember that which is in it, that you may ward off (evil).

172. And (remember) when your Lord brought out from the Children of Adam, from their loins, their seed, and made them testify of themselves, (saying): Am I not your Lord? They said: Yes, verily. We testify. (That was) lest you should say at the Day of Resurrection: Of this we were unaware;

173. Or lest you should say: (It is) only (that) our fathers ascribed partners to Allah of old and we were (their) seed after them. Will You destroy us on account of that which those who follow falsehood did?

174. Thus we detail the revelations, that perhaps they may return.

175. Recite to them the tale of him to whom We gave Our revelations, but he cast them off, so Satan overtook him and he became of those who lead astray.

176. And had We willed We could have raised him by their means, but he clung to the earth and followed his own lust. Therefore his likeness is as the likeness of a dog: if you attack him he pants with his tongue out, and if you leave him he pants with his tongue out. Such is the likeness of the people who deny Our revelations. Narrate to

them the history (of the men of old), that perhaps they may take thought.

177. Evil as an example are the people who denied Our revelations, and used to wrong themselves.

178. He whom Allah leads, he indeed is led aright, while he whom Allah sends astray - they indeed are losers.

179. Already We have urged to Hell many of the jinn and humankind, having hearts with which they understand not, and having eyes with which they see not, and having ears with which they hear not. These are as the cattle - no, but they are worse! These are the neglectful.

180. Allah's are the fairest names. Invoke Him by them. And leave the company of those who blaspheme His names. They will be repaid for what they do.

181. And of those whom We created there is a nation who guide with the Truth and establish justice with it.

182. And those who deny Our revelations - step by step We lead them on from where they know not.

183. I give them rein, (for) My scheme is strong.

184. Have they not considered (that) there is no madness in their comrade? He is but a plain warner.

185. Have they not considered the dominion of the heavens and the earth, and what things Allah has created, and that it may be that their own term draws near? In what fact after this will they believe?

186. Those whom Allah sends astray, there is no guide for them. He leaves them to wander blindly on in their rebellion.

187. They ask you of the (destined) Hour, when will it come to pass. Say: Knowledge of it is with my Lord only. He alone will manifest it at its proper time. It is heavy in the heavens and the earth. It comes not to you except unawares. They question you as if you could be well informed of it. Say: Knowledge of it is with Allah only, but most of mankind know not.

188. Say: For myself I have no power to benefit, nor power to hurt, except that which Allah wills. Had I knowledge of the Unseen, I should have abundance of wealth, and adversity would not touch me. I am but a warner, and a bearer of good tidings to people who believe.

189. He it is Who did create you from a single soul, and from it did make his mate that he might take rest in her. And when he covered her she carried a light burden, and she passed (unnoticed) with it, but when it became heavy they called to Allah, their Lord, saying: If you give us what is sound we shall be of the thankful.

190. But when He gave them what is sound, they ascribed to Him partners in respect of that which He had given them. High is He Exalted above all that they associate (with Him).

191. Attribute they as partners to Allah those who created nothing, but are themselves created,

192. And cannot give them help, nor can they help themselves?

193. And if you call them to the Guidance, they follow you not. Whether you call them or are silent is all one for you.

194. Those on whom you call besides Allah are slaves like you. Call on them

now, and let them answer you, if you are truthful!

195. Have they feet with which they walk, or have they hands with which they hold, or have they eyes with which they see, or have they ears with which they hear? Say: Call upon your (so-called) partners (of Allah), and then contrive against me, spare me not!

196. My Protecting Friend is Allah Who reveals the Scripture. He befriends the righteous.

197. They on whom you call besides Him have no power to help you, nor can they help you, nor can they help themselves.

198. And if you (Muslims) call them to the guidance they hear not; and you (Muhammad) see them looking towards you, but they see not.

199. Keep to forgiveness (O Muhammad), and enjoin kindness, and turn away from the ignorant.

200. And if a slander from the devil wound you, then seek refuge in Allah. He is Hearer, Knower.

201. Those who ward off (evil), when a spell from the devil troubles them, they do but remember (Allah's Guidance) and are seers!

202. Their brothers (the devils) plunge them further into error and cease not.

203. And when you bring not a verse for them they say: Why have you not chosen it? Say: I follow only that which is inspired in me from my Lord. This (Qur'an) is insight from your Lord, and a guidance and a mercy for a people who believe.

204. And when the Qur'an is recited, give ear to it and pay heed, that you may obtain mercy.

205. And (O Muhammad) remember your Lord within yourself humbly and with awe and silently, in the morning and evening. And be not of the neglectful.

206. Those who are with your Lord are not too proud to do Him service, but they praise Him and adore Him.

Surah 8: *Al-Anfal* (Spoils of War)

Al-Anfal, "The Spoils," takes its name from the first verse by which it is proclaimed that property in war belongs "to Allah and His messenger" - that is to say, to the theocratic State, to be used for the common good. The date of the revelation of this Surah is established, from the nature of the contents, as the time that elapsed between the battle of Badr and the division of the spoils - a space of only one month - in the second year of the Hijrah. The concluding verses are of later date and lead up to the subject of Surah 9.

A Makkan caravan was returning from Syria, and its leader, Abu Sufyan, fearing an attack from Al-Madinah, sent a camel-rider on to Makkah with a frantic appeal for help; which must have come too late, considering the distances, if, as some writers even among Muslims have alleged, the Prophet had always intended to attack the caravan. Ibn Ishaq (apud Ibn Hisham) when dealing with the Tabuk expedition, says that the Prophet announced the destination on that

occasion, whereas it was his custom to hide his real objective. Was not the real objective hidden in this first campaign? It is a fact that he only advanced when the army sent to protect the caravan, or rather (it is probable) to punish the Muslims for having plundered it, was approaching Al-Madinah. His little army of three hundred and thirteen men, ill-armed and roughly equipped, traversed the desert for three days till, when they halted near the water of Badr, they had news that the army of Quraysh was approaching on the other side of the valley. The rain fell heavily upon Quraysh so they could not advance further on account of the muddy state of the ground, lightly on the Muslims, who were able to advance to the water and secure it. At the same time Abu Sufyan, the leader of the caravan, which was also heading for the water of Badr, was warned by one of his scouts of the advance of the Muslims and turned back to the coast-plain. Before the battle against what must have appeared to all men overwhelming odds, the Prophet gave the Ansar, the men of Al-Madinah, whose oath of allegiance had not included fighting in the field, the chance of returning if they wished; but they were only hurt by the suggestion that they could possibly forsake him. On the other hand, several of the Quraysh, including the whole Zurhi clan, returned to Makkah when they heard the caravan was safe, having no grudge against the Prophet and his followers, whom they regarded as men who had been wronged.

Still the army of Quraysh outnumbered the Muslims by more than two to one, and was much better mounted and equipped, so that their leaders counted on an easy victory. When the Prophet saw them streaming down the sandhills, he called: "O Allah! Here are Quraysh with all their chivalry and pomp, who oppose you and deny Your messenger. O Allah! Make them bow this day!"

The Muslims were successful in the single combats with which Arab battles opened. But the melee at first went hard against them; and the Prophet stood and prayed under the shelter which they had put up to screen him from the sun, and called: "O Allah! If this little company is destroyed, there will be none left in the land to worship You." Then he fell into a trance and, when he spoke again, he told Abu Bakr, who was with him, that the promised help had come. Then he went out to encourage his people. Taking up a handful of gravel, he ran towards Quraysh and flung it at them, saying: "the faces are disgraced!" on which the tide of the battle turned in favour of the Muslims. The leader of the Quraysh and several of their greatest men were killed, many were taken prisoner, and their baggage and camels were captured by the Muslims. It was indeed a day to be remembered in the early history of Al-Islam, and there was great rejoicing in Al-Madinah. But the Muslims are warned in this Surah that it is only the beginning of their struggle against heavy odds. In fact in the following year at Mt Uhud (referred to in Surah 3), the enemy came against them with an army of three thousand, and in the fifth year of the Hijrah, an allied army of the pagan clans, amounting to 10,000, besieged Al-Madinah in the "War of the Trench" (see Surah 33, "The Clans").

The date of revelation is the second year of the Hijrah for the most part. Some good Arabic authorities hold that vv. 30-40, or some of them, were revealed at Makkah just before the Hijrah.

In the name of Allah, the Beneficent, the Merciful.

1. They ask you (O Muhammad) of the spoils of war. Say: The spoils of war belong to Allah and the messenger, so keep your duty to Allah, and adjust the matter of your difference, and obey Allah and His messenger, if you are (true) believers.

2. They only are the (true) believers whose hearts feel fear when Allah is mentioned, and when His revelations are recited to them they increase their faith, and who trust in their Lord;

3. Who establish worship and spend of that We have bestowed on them.

4. Those are they who are in truth believers. For them are grades (of honour) with their Lord, and pardon, and a bountiful provision.

5. Even as your Lord caused you (Muhammad) to go out from your home with the Truth, and a party of the believers were averse (to it).

6. Disputing with you of the Truth after it had been made manifest, as if they were being driven to visible death.

7. And when Allah promised you one of the two bands[89] (of the enemy) that it should be yours, and you longed that other than the armed one might be yours. And Allah willed that He should cause the Truth to triumph by His words, and cut the root of the disbelievers;

8. That He might cause the Truth to triumph and bring vanity to nothingness, however much the guilty might oppose;

9. When you sought help of your Lord and He answered you (saying): I will help you with a thousand of the angels, rank on rank.

10. Allah appointed it only as good tidings, and that your hearts by it might be at rest. Victory comes only by the help of Allah. Allah is Mighty, Wise.

11. When He made the slumber fall upon you as a reassurance from him and sent down water from the sky upon you, that by it He might purify you, and remove from you the fear of Satan, and make strong your hearts and firm (your) feet by it.

12. When your Lord inspired the angels, (saying): I am with you. So make those who believe stand firm. I will throw fear into the hearts of those who disbelieve. Then strike the necks and strike of them each finger.

13. That is because they opposed Allah and His messenger. Whoever opposes Allah and His messenger, (for him) Allah is severe in punishment.

14. That (is the award), so taste it, and (know) that for disbelievers is the torment of the Fire.

89. Either the army or the caravan.

15. O you who believe! When you meet those who disbelieve in battle, turn not your backs to them.

16. Whoever on that day turns his back to them, unless manoeuvring for battle or intent to join a company, he truly has incurred wrath from Allah, and his habitation will be Hell, an unhappy journey's end.

17. You (Muslims) slew them not, but Allah slew them. And you (Muhammad) threw not when you did throw, but Allah threw, that He might test the believers by a fair test from Him. Allah is Hearer, Knower.

18. That (is the case); and (know) that Allah (it is) Who makes weak the plan of disbelievers.

19. (O Quraysh!) If you sought a judgement, now the judgement has come to you. And if you cease (from persecuting the believers) it will be better for you, but if you return (to the attack) We also shall return. And your force will benefit you nothing, however numerous it be, and (know) that Allah is with the believers (in His Guidance).

20. O you who believe! Obey Allah and His messenger, and turn not away from him when you hear (him speak).

21. Be not as those who say, we hear, and they hear not.

22. The worst of beasts in Allah's sight are the deaf, the dumb, who have no sense.

23. Had Allah known of any good in them He would have made them hear, but had He made them hear they would have turned away, averse.

24. O you who believe! Obey Allah, and the messenger when He calls you to that which revives you, and know that Allah comes in between the man and his own heart, and that He it is to Whom you will be gathered.

25. And guard yourselves against a chastisement which cannot fall exclusively on those of you who are wrongdoers, and know that Allah is severe in punishment.

26. And remember, when you were few and reckoned feeble in the land, and were in fear lest men should uproot you, how He gave you refuge, and strengthened you with His help, and made provision of good things for you, that perhaps you might be thankful.

27. O you who believe! Betray not Allah and His messenger, nor knowingly betray your trusts.

28. And know that your possessions and your children are a test, and that with Allah is immense reward.

29. O you who believe! If you keep your duty to Allah, He will give you discrimination (between right and wrong) and will rid you of your evil thoughts and deeds, and will forgive you. Allah is of Infinite Bounty.

30. And when those who disbelieve plot against you (O Muhammad) to wound you fatally, or to kill you or to drive you out; they plot, but Allah (also) plots; and Allah is the best of plotters.

31. And when Our revelations are recited to them, they say: We have heard. If we wish we can speak the like of this. This is nothing but fables of the men of old.

32. And when they said: O Allah! If this indeed is the truth from You, then rain down stones on us or bring on us some painful doom!

33. But Allah would not punish them while you were with them, nor will He punish them while they seek forgiveness.

34. What (plea) have they that Allah should not punish them, when they prevent (His servants) from the Inviolable Place of Worship, though they are not its fitting guardians. Its fitting guardians are those only who keep their duty to Allah. But most of them know not.

35. And their worship at the (holy) House is nothing but whistling and hand-clapping. Therefore (it is said to them): Taste of the doom because you disbelieve.

36. Those who disbelieve spend their wealth in order that they may prevent (men) from the way of Allah. They will spend it, then it will become an anguish for them, then they will be conquered. And those who disbelieve will be gathered to Hell,

37. That Allah may separate the wicked from the good, The wicked will He place piece upon piece, and heap them all together, and consign them to Hell. Such verily are the losers.

38. Tell those who disbelieve that if they cease (from persecution of believers) that which is past will be forgiven them; but if they return (to it) then the example of the men of old has already gone (before them, for a warning).

39. And fight them until persecution is no more, and religion is all for Allah. But if they cease, then Allah is Seer of what they do.

40. And if they turn away, then know that Allah is your Befriender - a Transcendent Patron, a Transcendent Helper!

41. And know that whatever you take as spoils of war, a fifth of it is for Allah, and for the messenger[90] and for the relative (who has need) and orphans and the needy and the wayfarer, if you believe in Allah and that which We revealed to Our slave on the Day of Discrimination, the day when the two armies met. And Allah is Able to do all things.

42. When you were on the near bank (of the valley) and they were on the distant bank, and the caravan was below you (on the coast plain). And had you tried to meet one another you surely would have failed to keep the trial, but (it happened, as it did, without the forethought of either of you) that Allah might conclude a thing that must be done; that he who perished (on that day) might perish by a clear proof (of His Sovereignty) and he who survived might survive by a clear proof (of His Sovereignty). Allah in truth is Hearer, Knower.

43. When Allah showed them to you (O Muhammad) in your dream as few in number, and if He had shown them to you as many, you (Muslims) would have faltered and would have quarrelled over the affair. But Allah saved (you). He knows what is in the breasts (of men).

44. And when He made you (Muslims), when you met (them), see them with your eyes as few, and lessened you in their eyes, (it was) that Allah might conclude a thing that must be done. To Allah all things are brought back.

45. O you who believe! When you meet an army, hold firm and think of Allah much, that you may be successful.

46. And obey Allah and His messenger, and dispute not one with another lest you falter and your strength depart from you; but be steadfast! Allah is with the steadfast.

47. Be not as those who came out from their dwellings boastfully and to be seen of men, and prevent (men) from the way of Allah, while Allah is surrounding all they do.

48. And when Satan made their deeds seem fair to them and said: No-one of mankind can conquer you this day, for I am your protector. But when the armies came in sight of one another, he took flight, saying: I am guiltless of you. I see that which you see not. I fear Allah. And Allah is severe in punishment.

49. When the hypocrites and those in whose hearts is a disease said: Their religion has deluded them. Whoever puts his trust in Allah (will find that) Allah is Mighty, Wise.

50. If you could see how the angels receive those who disbelieve, striking their faces and their backs and (saying): Taste the punishment of burning!

51. This is for that which your own hands have sent before (to the

---

90. *i.e.* for the State, to be used for the common good.

Judgement), and (know) that Allah is not a tyrant to His slaves.

52. (Their way is) as the way of Pharaoh's people and those before them; they disbelieved the revelations of Allah, and Allah took them in their sins. Allah is Strong, severe in punishment.

53. That is because Allah never changes the grace He has bestowed on any people until they first change that which is in their hearts, and (that is) because Allah is Hearer, Knower.

54. (Their way is) as the way of Pharaoh's people and those before them; they denied the revelations of their Lord, so We destroyed them in their sins. And We drowned the people of Pharaoh. All were evildoers.

55. The worst of beasts in Allah's sight are the ungrateful who will not believe.

56. Those of them with whom you made a treaty, and then at every opportunity they break their treaty, and they keep not their duty (to Allah).

57. If you come on them in the war, deal with them so as to strike fear in those who are behind them, that perhaps they may remember.

58. And if you fear treachery from any people, then throw back to them (their treaty) fairly. Allah loves not the treacherous.

59. And let not those who disbelieve suppose that they can outstrip (Allah's Purpose). They cannot escape.

60. Make ready for them all you can of (armed) force and of horses tethered, that by it you may dismay the enemy of Allah and your enemy, and others

besides them whom you know not. Allah knows them. Whatever you spend in the way of Allah it will be repaid to you in full, and you will not be wronged.

61. And if they incline to peace, incline you also to it, and trust in Allah. He, even He, is the Hearer, the Knower.

62. And if they would deceive you, then Allah is Sufficient for you. He it is Who supports you with His help and with the believers,

63. And (as for the believers) has attuned their hearts. If you had spent all that is in the earth you could not have attuned their hearts, but Allah has attuned them. He is Mighty, Wise.

64. O Prophet! Allah is Sufficient for you and those who follow you of the believers.

65. O Prophet! Exhort the believers to fight. If there are of you twenty steadfast they shall overcome two hundred, and if there are of you a hundred (steadfast) they shall overcome a thousand of those who disbelieve, because they (the disbelievers) are a people without intelligence.

66. Now Allah has lightened your burden, for He knows that there is weakness in you. So if there are of you a steadfast hundred they shall overcome two hundred, and if there are of you a thousand (steadfast) they shall overcome two thousand by permission of Allah. Allah is with the steadfast.

67. It is not for any Prophet to have captives until he has made slaughter in the land. You desire the lure of the world and Allah desires (for you) the Hereafter, and Allah is Mighty, Wise.[91]

68. Had it not been for an ordinance of Allah which had gone before, an awful doom would have come upon you on account of what you took.

69. Now enjoy what you have won, as lawful and good, and keep your duty to Allah. Allah is Forgiving, Merciful.

70. O Prophet! Say to those captives who are in your hands: If Allah knows any good in your hearts He will give you better than that which has been taken from you, and will forgive you. Allah is Forgiving, Merciful.

71. And if they would betray you, they betrayed Allah before, and He gave (you) power over them. Allah is Knower, Wise.

72. Those who believed and left their homes and strove with their wealth and their lives for the cause of Allah, and those who took them in and helped them: these are protecting friends one of another. And those who believed but did not leave their homes, you have no duty to protect them till they leave their homes; but if they seek help from you in the matter of religion then it is your duty to help (them) except against a people between whom and you there is a treaty. Allah is Seer of what you do.

73. And those who disbelieve are protectors one of another - If you do not do so, there will be mischief in the land, and great corruption.

74. Those who believed and left their homes and strove for the cause of Allah, and those who took them in and helped them - these are the believers in truth. For them is pardon, and bountiful provision.

75. And those who afterwards believed and left their homes and strove along with you, they are of you; and those who are related are nearer one to another in the ordinance of Allah. Allah is Knower of all things.

Surah 9: *At-Taubah*
(Repentance)

At-Taubah, "Repentance," takes its name from v. 104. It is often called *Al-Bara'at* (The Immunity), from the first word. It is the only Surah which is without the *Bi'smillahi'r-Rahmani-Rahim* ("In the name of Allah the Beneficent, the Merciful") which is generally considered to be on account of the stern commandments against idolaters which it contains. Vv. 1-12, forming the proclamation of immunity from obligation towards the idolaters, were revealed after the pilgrims had started for Makkah in the ninth year of the Hijrah and sent by special messenger to Abu Bakr, leader of the pilgrimage, to be read out by Ali to the multitudes at Makkah. It signifies the end of idolatry in Arabia. The Christian Byzantine Empire had begun to move against the growing

91. Vv. 67-69 were revealed when the Prophet had decided to spare the lives of the prisoners taken at Badr and hold them to ransom, against the wish of Omar, who would have executed them for their past crimes. The Prophet took the verses as a reproach, and they are generally understood to mean that no clemency ought to have been given in that first battle.

Muslim power, and this Surah contains mention of a greater war to come and instructions with regard to it. Vv. 38-99 refer to the Tabuk campaign, and especially to those Arab tribes who failed to join the Muslims in that campaign. The "Hypocrites," as the half-hearted supporters of *Al-Islam* were called, had long been a thorn in the side of the Muslims. They had even at one time gone so far in dissent as forming a congregation and building a mosque of their own surreptitiously. On the Prophet's return from Tabuk they invited him to visit that mosque. This is referred to in vv. 107 ff.

The date of revelation is the ninth year of the *Hijrah*.

1. Freedom from obligation (is proclaimed) from Allah and His messenger towards those of the idolaters with whom you made a treaty:

2. Travel freely in the land four months, and know that you cannot escape Allah and that Allah will defeat the disbelievers (in His Guidance).

3. And a proclamation from Allah and His messenger to all men on the day of the Greater Pilgrimage that Allah is free from obligation to the idolaters, and (so is) His messenger. So, if you repent, it will be better for you; but if you are averse, then know that you cannot escape Allah. Give tidings (O Muhammad) of a painful doom to those who disbelieve,

4. Excepting those of the idolaters with whom you (Muslims) have a treaty, and who have since withdrawn nothing of your right nor have supported anyone against you. (As for these), fulfil their treaty to them till their term. Allah loves those who keep their duty (to Him).

5. Then, when the sacred months have passed, slay the idolaters wherever you find them, and take them (captive), and besiege them, and prepare for them each ambush. But if they repent and establish worship and pay the poor-due, then leave their way free. Allah is Forgiving, Merciful.

6. And if any one of the idolaters seeks your protection (O Muhammad), then protect him so that he may hear the Word of Allah, and afterwards convey him to his place of safety. That is because they are a people who know not.

7. How can there be a treaty with Allah and with His messenger for the idolaters except those with whom you made a treaty at the Inviolable Place of Worship? So long as they are true to you, be true to them. Allah loves those who keep their duty.

8. How (can there be any treaty for the others) when, if they have the upper hand of you, they regard not pact nor honour in respect of you? They satisfy you with their mouths whilst their hearts refuse. And most of them are wrongdoers.

9. They have purchased with the revelations of Allah a little gain, so they prevent (men) from His way. Evil is that which they are used to do.

10. And they observe towards a believer neither pact nor honour. These are they who are transgressors.

11. But if they repent and establish worship and pay the poor-due, then they are your brothers in religion. We detail Our revelations for a people who have knowledge.

12. And if they break their pledges after their treaty (has been made with you) and assail your religion, then fight the heads of disbelief - they have no binding oaths - in order that they may desist.

13. Will you not fight a people who broke their solemn pledges, and planned to drive out the messenger and did attack you first? What! Fear you them? Now Allah has more right that you should fear Him, if you are believers.

14. Fight them! Allah will chastise them at your hands, and He will lay them low and give you victory over them, and He will heal the breasts of people who are believers.

15. And He will remove the anger of their hearts. Allah relents towards whom He will. Allah is Knower, Wise.

16. Or did you think that you would be left (in peace) when Allah yet knows not those of you who strive, choosing for intimate friend none except Allah and His messenger and the believers? Allah is Informed of what you do.

17. It is not for the idolaters to tend Allah's sanctuaries, bearing witness against themselves of disbelief. As for such, their works are vain and in the Fire they will remain.

18. He only shall tend Allah's sanctuaries who believes in Allah and the Last Day and observes proper worship and pays the poor-due and fears none except Allah. For such

(only) is it possible that they can be of the rightly guided.

19. Do you count the quenching of a pilgrim's thirst and tending to the Inviolable Place of Worship as (equal to the worth of) him who believes in Allah and the Last Day, and strives in the way of Allah? They are not equal in the sight of Allah. Allah guides not wrongdoing people.

20. Those who believe, and have left their homes and striven with their wealth and their lives in Allah's way are of much greater worth in Allah's sight. These are they who are triumphant.

21. Their Lord gives them good tidings of mercy from Him, and acceptance, and Gardens where enduring pleasure will be theirs;

22. There they will remain forever. With Allah there is immense reward.

23. O you who believe! Choose not your fathers nor your brothers for friends if they take pleasure in disbelief rather than faith. Whoever of you takes them for friends, such are wrongdoers.

24. Say: If your fathers, and your sons, and your brothers, and your wives, and your tribe, and the wealth you have acquired, and merchandise for which you fear that there will be no sale,[92] and dwellings you desire are dearer to you than Allah and His messenger and striving in His way: then wait till Allah brings His command to pass. Allah guides not wrongdoing people.

---

92. It was objected that, if idolaters were forbidden to make the pilgrimage, the trade of Makkah would decline.

25. Allah has given you victory on many fields and on the day of Huneyn,[93] when you rejoiced in your multitude but it benefitted you nothing, and the earth, vast as it is, was narrowed for you; then you turned back in flight;

26. Then Allah sent His peace of reassurance down upon His messenger and upon the believers, and sent down hosts you could not see, and punished those who disbelieved. Such is the reward of disbelievers.

27. Then afterwards Allah will relent towards whom He will; for Allah is Forgiving, Merciful.

28. O you who believe! The idolaters are nothing but unclean. So let them not come near the Inviolable Place of Worship after this, their (final) year. If you fear poverty (from the loss of their merchandise) Allah shall preserve you of His bounty if He will. Allah is Knower, Wise.

29. Fight against such of those who have been given the Scripture as believe not in Allah nor the Last Day, and forbid not that which Allah has forbidden by His messenger, and follow not the Religion of Truth, until they pay the tribute readily, being brought low.

30. And the Jews say: Ezra is the son of Allah, and the Christians say: The Messiah is the son of Allah. That is their saying with their mouths. They imitate the saying of those who disbelieved of old. Allah's curse be on them: how they are deluded from the truth!

31. They have taken as lords beside Allah their rabbis and their monks and the Messiah son of Mary, when they were commanded to worship only One God. There is no god except Him. Be He Glorified from all that they ascribe as partner (to Him)!

32. Gladly would they put out the light of Allah with their mouths, but Allah despises (anything) except that He shall perfect His light, however much the disbelievers are averse.

33. He it is Who has sent His messenger with the guidance and the Religion of Truth, that He may cause it to prevail over all religions, however much the idolaters may be averse.

34. O you who believe! Many of the (Jewish) rabbis and the (Christian) monks devour the wealth of mankind unjustly and prevent (men) from the way of Allah. They who hoard up gold and silver and spend it not in the way of Allah, to them give tidings (O Muhammad) of a painful doom,

35. On the day when it will (all) be heated in the fire of Hell, and their foreheads and their flanks and their backs will be branded with it (and it will be said to them): Here is that which you hoarded for yourselves. Now taste of what you used to hoard.

36. The number of the months with Allah is twelve months by Allah's ordinance in the day that He created the heavens and the earth. Four of them are sacred: that is the right religion. So wrong not yourselves in them. And wage war on all of the idolaters as they are waging war on all

---

93. The Muslim army, ambushed at Huneyn, gained a great victory after being nearly routed.

of you. And know that Allah is with those who keep their duty (to Him).

37. Postponement (of a sacred month)[94] is only an excess of disbelief by which those who disbelieve are misled, they allow it one year and forbid it (another) year, that they may make up the number of the months which Allah has sanctified, so that they allow that which Allah has forbidden. The evil of their deeds is made fair-seeming to them. Allah guides not the disbelieving people.

38. O you who believe! What is the matter with you that when it is said to you: Go out in the way of Allah, you are bowed down to the ground with heaviness. Do you take pleasure in the life of the world rather than in the Hereafter? The comfort of the life of the world is but little in the Hereafter.

39. If you do not go out He will afflict you with a painful doom, and will choose instead of you a people other than you. You cannot harm Him at all. Allah is Able to do all things.

40. If you help him not, still Allah helped him when those who disbelieve drove him out, the second of two[95] when they both were in the cave, when he said to his comrade: Grieve not. Allah is with us. Then Allah caused His peace of reassurance to descend upon him and supported him with forces you cannot see, and made the word of those who disbelieved the lowermost, while

Allah's Word it was that became the uppermost. Allah is Mighty, Wise.

41. Go out, light-armed and heavy-armed, and strive with your wealth and your lives in the way of Allah! That is best for you if you but knew.

42. Had it been a near adventure and an easy journey they would have followed you, but the distance seemed too far for them.[96] Yet they swear by Allah (saying): If we had been able, we would surely have set out with you. They destroy their souls, and Allah knows that they verily are liars.

43. Allah forgive you (O Muhammad)! Why did you grant them permission before those who told the truth were clear to you and you did know the liars?

44. Those who believe in Allah and the Last Day ask no permission of you lest they should strive with their wealth and their lives. Allah is Aware of those who keep their duty (to Him).

45. They alone ask permission of you who believe not in Allah and the Last Day, and whose hearts feel doubt, so in their doubt they waver.

46. And if they had wished to go out they would assuredly have made ready some equipment, but Allah was averse to their being sent out and held them back and it was said (to them): Sit you with the sedentary!

47. Had they gone out among you they would have added to you nothing except trouble and would have hurried to and fro among you, seeking to

---

94. The idolaters would postpone a sacred month in which war was forbidden, when they wanted to make war, and make up for it by sanctifying another month
95. The Prophet and Abu Bakr during the emigration from Makkah to Al-Madinah.

96. The reference is to the Tabuk expedition. Tabuk is half-way between Al-Madinah and Damascus.

cause sedition among you; and among you there are some who would have listened to them. Allah is Aware of evildoers.

48. Before they sought to cause sedition and raised difficulties for you till the Truth came and the decree of Allah was made clear, though they were unwilling.

49. Of them is he who says: Grant me permission (to stay at home) and tempt me not.[97] Surely it is into temptation that they (thus) have fallen. Hell verily is all around the disbelievers.

50. If good befalls you (O Muhammad) it afflicts them, and if calamity befalls you, they say: We took precaution, and they turn away well pleased.

51. Say: Nothing befalls us except that which Allah has decreed for us. He is our Protecting Friend. In Allah let believers put their trust!

52. Say: Can you expect for us anything except one of two good things (death or victory in Allah's way)? while we expect for you that Allah will afflict you with a doom from Him or at our hands. Wait then! We are waiting with you.

53. Say: Pay (your contribution), willingly or unwillingly, it will not be accepted from you. You were ever obstinate people.

54. And nothing prevents that their contributions should be accepted from them except that they have disbelieved in Allah and in His messenger, and they come not to worship except as

---

97. The temptation here referred to is generally explained as being the beauty of the women of Syria, the country against which the campaign was directed.

idlers, and pay not (their contribution) except reluctantly.

55. So let not their riches nor their children please you (O Muhammad). Allah only intends to punish them by it in the life of the world and that their souls shall pass away while they are disbelievers.

56. And they swear by Allah that they are in truth of you, when they are not of you, but they are people who are afraid.

57. Had they but found a refuge, or caverns, or a place to enter, they surely would have resorted there swift as runaways.

58. And of them is he who defames you in the matter of the alms. If they are given of it they are content, and if they are not given of it, look! They are enraged.

59. (How much more seemly) if they had been content with that which Allah and His messenger had given them and had said: Allah suffices us. Allah will give us of His bounty, and (also) His messenger. To Allah we are suppliants.

60. The alms are only for the poor and the needy, and those who collect them, and those whose hearts are to be reconciled,[98] and to free the captives and the debtors, and for the cause of Allah, and (for) the wayfarer; a duty imposed by Allah. Allah is Knower, Wise.

61. And of them are those who annoy the Prophet and say: He is only a

---

98. A special portion of the alms was allotted to the people of Makkah, the former enemies of *Al-Islam*, who were converted *en masse* after the capture of the city, and whose "hearts were to be reconciled."

hearer. Say: A hearer of good for you, who believes in Allah and is true to the believers, and a mercy for such of you as believe. Those who annoy the messenger of Allah, for them there is a painful doom.

62. They swear by Allah to you (Muslims) to please you, but Allah, with His messenger, has more right that they should please Him if they are believers.

63. Know they not that who opposes Allah and His messenger, his portion verily is Hell, to remain in it? That is the extreme humiliation.

64. The hypocrites fear lest a Surah should be revealed concerning them, proclaiming what is in their hearts. Say: Mock (your fill)! Allah is disclosing what you fear.

65. And if you ask them (O Muhammad), they will say: We did but talk and jest. Say: Was it at Allah and His revelations and His messenger that you did mock?

66. Make no excuse. You have disbelieved after your (confession of) belief. If We forgive a party of you, a party of you We shall punish because they have been guilty.

67. The hypocrites, both men and women, proceed one from another. They enjoin the wrong, and they forbid the right, and they withhold their hands (from spending for the cause of Allah). They forget Allah, so He has forgotten them. The hypocrites, they are the transgressors.

68. Allah promises the hypocrites, both men and women, and the disbelievers fire of Hell for their abode. It will suffice them. Allah curses them, and theirs is lasting torment.

69. Even as those before you who were mightier than you in strength, and more affluent than you in wealth and children. They enjoyed their lot a while, so you enjoy your lot a while even as those before you did enjoy their lot a while. And you talk foolishly even as they talked foolishly. Such are they whose works have perished in the world and the Hereafter. Such are they who are the losers.

70. Has not the fame of those before them reached them - the people of Noah, 'Aad, Thamud, the people of Abraham, the dwellers of Midian and the disasters (which befell them)? Their messengers (from Allah) came to them with proofs (of Allah's Sovereignty). So Allah surely wronged them not, but they did wrong themselves.

71. And the believers, men and women, are protecting friends one of another; they enjoin the right and forbid the wrong, and they establish worship and they pay the poor-due, and they obey Allah and His messenger. As for these, Allah will have mercy on them. Allah is Mighty, Wise.

72. Allah promises to the believers, men and women, Gardens underneath which rivers flow, in which they will remain - blessed dwellings in Gardens of Eden. And - greater (far)! acceptance from Allah. That is the supreme triumph.

73. O Prophet! Strive against the disbelievers and the hypocrites! Be harsh with them. Their ultimate abode is Hell, an unhappy journey's end.

74. They swear by Allah that they said nothing (wrong), yet they did say the word of disbelief, and did disbelieve after their Surrender (to Allah). And they intended that which they could not attain, and they sought revenge only that Allah by His messenger should enrich them of His bounty. If they repent it will be better for them; and if they turn away, Allah will afflict them with a painful doom in the world and the Hereafter, and they have no protecting friend nor helper in the earth.

75. And of them is he who made a covenant with Allah (saying): If He gives us of His bounty we will give alms and become of the righteous.

76. Yet, when He gave them of His bounty, they hoarded it and turned away, averse;

77. So He has made the consequence (to be) hypocrisy in their hearts until the day when they will meet Him, because they broke their word to Allah that they promised Him, and because they lied.

78. Know they not that Allah knows both their secret and the thought that they confide, and that Allah is the Knower of Things Hidden?

79. Those who point at such of the believers as give the alms willingly and such as can find nothing to give but their endeavours, and deride them - Allah (Himself) derides them. Theirs will be a painful doom.

80. Ask forgiveness for them (O Muhammad), or ask not forgiveness for them; though you ask forgiveness for them seventy times Allah will not forgive them. That is because they disbelieved in Allah and His messenger, and Allah guides not wrongdoing people.

81. Those who were left behind rejoiced at sitting still behind the messenger of Allah, and were averse to striving with their wealth and their lives in Allah's way. And they said: Go not out in the heat! Say: The fire of Hell is more intense of heat, if they but understood.

82. Then let them laugh a little: they will weep much, as the reward of what they used to earn.

83. If Allah brings you back (from the campaign) to a party of them and they ask of you permission to go out (to fight), then say to them: You shall never more go out with me nor fight with me against a foe. You were content with sitting still the first time. So sit still, with the useless.

84. And never (O Muhammad) pray for one of them who dies, nor stand by his grave. They disbelieved in Allah and His messenger, and they died while they were evildoers.

85. Let not their wealth nor their children please you! Allah intends only to punish them by it in the world, and that their souls shall pass away while they are disbelievers.

86. And when a Surah is revealed (which says): Believe in Allah and strive along with His messenger, the men of wealth among them still ask permission of you and say: Suffer us to be with those who sit (at home).

87. They are content that they should be with the useless and their hearts are sealed, so that they apprehend not.

88. But the messenger and those who believe with him strive with their wealth and their lives. Such are they for whom are the good things. Such are they who are the successful.

89. Allah has made ready for them Gardens underneath which rivers flow, in which they will remain. That is the supreme triumph.

90. And those among the wandering Arabs who had an excuse came in order that permission might be granted them. And those who lied to Allah and His messenger sat at home. A painful doom will fall on those of them who disbelieve.

91. Not to the weak nor to the sick nor to those who can find nothing to spend is any fault (to be imputed though they stay at home) if they are true to Allah and His messenger. Not to the good is there any road (of blame). Allah is Forgiving, Merciful.

92. Nor to those whom, when they came to you (asking) that you should mount them, you did tell: I cannot find on which to mount you. They turned back with eyes flowing with tears, for sorrow that they could not find the means to spend.

93. The road (of blame) is only against those who ask for permission of you (to stay at home) when they are rich. They are content to be with the useless. Allah has sealed their hearts so that they know not.

94. They will make excuse to you (Muslims) when you return to them. Say: Make no excuse, for we shall not believe you. Allah has told us tidings of you. Allah and His messenger will see your conduct, and then you will be brought back to Him Who knows the invisible as well as the visible, and He will tell you what you used to do.

95. They will swear by Allah to you, when you return to them, that you may let them be. Let them be, for they are unclean, and their abode is Hell as the reward for what they used to earn.

96. They swear to you, that you may accept them. Though you accept them, Allah verily accepts not wrongdoing people.

97. The wandering Arabs are more hard in disbelief and hypocrisy, and more likely to be ignorant of the limits which Allah has revealed to His messenger. And Allah is Knower Wise.

98. And of the wandering Arabs there is he who takes that which he expends (for the cause of Allah) as a loss, and awaits (evil) turns of fortune for you (that he may be rid of it). The evil turn of fortune will be theirs. Allah is Hearer, Knower.

99. And of the wandering Arabs there is he who believes in Allah and the Last Day, and takes that which he expends and also the prayers of the messenger as acceptable offerings in the sight of Allah. Verily it is an acceptable offering for them. Allah will bring them into His mercy. Allah is Forgiving, Merciful.

100. And the first to lead the way, of the *Muhajirin*[99] and the *Ansar*,[100] and those who followed them in goodness - Allah is well pleased with them and they are well pleased with Him, and He has made ready for them Gardens underneath which rivers flow, in which they will remain forever. That is the supreme triumph.

101. And among those around you of the wandering Arabs there are hypocrites, and among the townspeople of Al-Madinah (there are some who) persist in hypocrisy whom you (O Muhammad) know not. We, We know them, and We shall chastise them twice; then they will be relegated to a painful doom.

102. And (there are) others who have acknowledged their faults. They mixed a righteous action with another that was bad. It may be that Allah will relent towards them. Allah is Forgiving, Merciful.

103. Take alms of their wealth, with which you may purify them and may make them grow, and pray for them. Your prayer is a relief for them. Allah is Hearer, Knower.

104. Do they not know that Allah is He Who accepts repentance from His bondsmen and takes the alms, and that Allah is He Who is the Relenting, the Merciful.

105. And say (to them): Act! Allah will see your actions, and (so will) His messenger and the believers, and you will be brought back to the Knower of the Invisible and the Visible, and He will tell you what you used to do.

106. And (there are) others who await Allah's decree, whether He will punish them or will forgive them. Allah is Knower, Wise.

107. And as for those who chose a place of worship out of opposition and disbelief, and in order to cause dissent among the believers, and as an outpost for those who warred against Allah and His messenger before, they will surely swear: We intended nothing except good. Allah bears witness that they verily are liars.

108. Never stand (to pray) there. A place of worship which was founded upon duty (to Allah) from the first day is more worthy that you should stand (to pray) in it. In it are men who love to purify themselves. Allah loves the purifiers.

109. Is he who founded his building upon duty to Allah and His good pleasure better; or he who founded his building on the brink of a crumbling, overhanging precipice so that it toppled with him into the fire of Hell? Allah guides not wrongdoing people.

110. The building which they built will never cease to be a misgiving in their hearts unless their hearts are torn to pieces. Allah is Knower, Wise.

111. Allah has bought from the believers their lives and their wealth because the Garden will be theirs: they will fight in the way of Allah and will slay and be slain. It is a promise which

---

99. The emigrants from Makkah to Al-Madinah.
100. The Muslims of Al-Madinah who welcomed the emigrants from Makkah and helped the Prophet with their wealth and defended him with their lives.

is binding on Him in the Torah and the Gospel and the Qur'an. Who fulfils His covenant better than Allah? Rejoice then in your bargain that you have made, for that is the supreme triumph.

112. (Triumphant) are those who turn repentant (to Allah), those who serve (Him), those who praise (Him), those who fast, those who bow down, those who fall prostrate (in worship), those who enjoin the right and who forbid the wrong and those who keep the limits (ordained) of Allah - And give glad tidings to believers!

113. It is not for the Prophet, and those who believe, to pray for the forgiveness of idolaters even though they may be relatives (to them) after it has become clear that they are people of Hell-fire.

114. The prayer of Abraham for the forgiveness of his father was only because of a promise he had promised him, but when it had become clear to him that he (his father) was an enemy to Allah, he (Abraham) disowned him. Abraham was soft of heart, long-suffering.

115. It was never Allah's (part) that He should send a people astray after He had guided them until He had made clear to them what they should avoid. Allah is Aware of all things.

116. Allah! To Him belongs the Sovereignty of the heavens and the earth. He gives life and He gives death. And you have, instead of Allah, no protecting friend nor helper.

117. Allah has turned in mercy to the Prophet, and to the *Muhajirin* and the *Ansar*[101] who followed him in the hour

of hardship. After the hearts of a party of them had almost swerved aside, then He turned to them in mercy. He is Full of Pity, Merciful for them.

118. And to the three also (did He turn in mercy) who were left behind, when the earth, vast as it is, was narrowed for them, and their own souls were narrowed for them till they thought that there is no refuge from Allah except towards Him. Then turned He to them in mercy that they (too) might turn (repentant to Him).[102] Allah! He is the Relenting, the Merciful.

119. O you who believe! Be careful of your duty to Allah, and be with the truthful.

120. It is not for the inhabitants of Al-Madinah and for those around them of the wandering Arabs to stay behind the messenger of Allah and prefer their lives to his life. That is because neither thirst nor toil nor hunger afflicts them in the way of Allah, nor do they take any step that angers the disbelievers, nor do they gain from the enemy a gain, but a good deed is recorded for them for it. Allah loses not the wages of the good.

121. Nor do they spend anything, small or great, nor do they cross a valley, but it is recorded for them, that Allah may repay them the best of what they used to do.

122. And the believers should not all go out to fight. Of every troop of them, a party only should go out, that they (who are left behind) may gain sound

---

101. See verse 100, footnotes

102. The reference is to three men of Al-Madinah who were ostracised on account of a misdeed, but afterwards repented and were forgiven.

knowledge in religion, and that they may warn their people when they return to them, so that they may beware.

123. O you who believe! Fight those of the disbelievers who are near to you, and let them find harshness in you, and know that Allah is with those who keep their duty (to Him).

124. And whenever a Surah is revealed there are some of them who say: Which one of you has thus increased in faith? As for those who believe, it has increased them in faith and they rejoice (for it).

125. But as for those in whose hearts is disease, it only adds wickedness to their wickedness, and they die while they are disbelievers.

126. Do they not see that they are tested once or twice in every year? Still they turn not in repentance, neither do they pay heed.

127. And whenever a Surah is revealed, they look one at another (as who should say): Does anybody see you? Then they turn away. Allah turns away their hearts because they are a people who understand not.

128. There has come to you a messenger, (one) of yourselves, and it grieves him when you are overburdened with anything; he is full of concern for you, and to believers full of compassion and mercy.

129. Now, if they turn away (O Muhammad) say: Allah suffices me. There is no God except Him. In Him I have put my trust, and He is Lord of the Tremendous Throne.

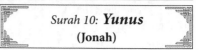

Surah 10: **Yunus** (Jonah)

Yunus derives its title from v. 98: "If only there had been a community (of those that were) destroyed of old that believed and profited by its belief as did the people of Jonah!" As is the case with nearly all the Makkan Surahs, the date of revelation is uncertain, on account of the scarcity of historical allusion. All that can with certainty be said is, that it belongs to the latest group of Makkan Surahs, and must therefore have been revealed at some time during the last four years before the Hijrah.

A late Makkan Surah, with the exception of three verses revealed at Al-Madinah.

In the name of Allah, the Beneficent, the Merciful.

1. *Alif. Lam. Ra.*[103] These are verses of the Wise Scripture.

2. Is it a wonder for mankind that We have inspired a man among them, saying: Warn mankind and bring to those who believe the good tidings that they have a sure footing with their Lord? The disbelievers say: This is a mere wizard.

3. Your Lord is Allah Who created the heavens and the earth in six Days,[104] then He established Himself upon the Throne, directing all things. There is no intercessor (with Him) except after His permission. That is Allah, your

103. See *Surah 2, Al-Baqarah*, v. 1, footnote.
104. See *Surah 22, Al-Hajj*, v. 47; *Surah 32, As-Sajdah*, v. 5 and *Surah 70, Al-Ma'arij*, v. 4.

Lord, so worship Him. Oh, will you not remember?

4. To Him is the return of all of you; it is a promise of Allah in truth. He produces creation, then reproduces it, that He may reward those who believe and do good works with equity; while, as for those who disbelieve, theirs will be a boiling drink and painful doom because they disbelieved.

5. He it is Who appointed the sun a splendour and the moon a light, and measured for her stages, that you might know the number of the years, and the reckoning. Allah created not (all) that except in truth. He details the revelations for people who have knowledge.

6. In the difference of day and night and all that Allah has created in the heavens and the earth are signs, verily, for people who ward off (evil).

7. Those who expect not the meeting with Us but desire the life of the world and feel secure in it, and those who are neglectful of Our revelations,

8. Their home will be the Fire because of what they used to earn.

9. Those who believe and do good works, their Lord guides them by their faith. Rivers will flow beneath them in the Gardens of Delight,

10. Their prayer in it will be: Glory be to You, O Allah! and their greeting in it will be: Peace. And the conclusion of their prayer will be: Praise be to Allah, Lord of the Worlds!

11. If Allah were to hasten on for men the ill (that they have earned) as they would hasten on the good, their

respite would already have expired. But We suffer those who look not for the meeting with Us to wander blindly on in their disobedience.

12. And if misfortune touches a man he calls to Us, (while reclining) on his side, or sitting or standing, but when We have relieved him of the misfortune he goes his way as though he had not called to Us because of a misfortune that afflicted him. Thus is what they do made (to seem) fair to the prodigal.

13. We destroyed the generations before you when they did wrong; and their messengers (from Allah) came to them with clear proofs (of His Sovereignty) but they would not believe. Thus do We reward the guilty people.

14. Then We appointed you viceroys in the earth after them, that We might see how you behave.

15. And when Our clear revelations are recited to them, they who look not for the meeting with Us say: "Bring a Lecture[105] other than this, or change it." Say (O Muhammad): It is not for me to change it of my accord. I only follow that which is inspired in me. If I disobey my Lord, I fear the retribution of an awful Day.

16. Say: If Allah had so willed I should not have recited it to you nor would He have made it known to you. I dwelt among you a whole lifetime before it (came to me). Have you then no sense?

17. Who does greater wrong than he who invents a lie concerning Allah and denies His revelations? The guilty never are successful.

105. Arabic: Qur'an

18. They worship besides Allah that which neither hurts them nor profits them, and they say: These are our intercessors with Allah. Say: Would you inform Allah of (something) that He knows not in the heavens or in the earth? Praised be He and High Exalted above all that you associate (with Him)!

19. Mankind were but one community; then they differed; and had it not been for a word that had already gone before from your Lord it would have been judged between them in respect of that in which they differ.

20. And they will say: If only a sign were sent down upon him from his Lord! Then say, (O Muhammad): The Unseen belongs to Allah. So wait! I am waiting with you.

21. And when We cause mankind to taste of mercy after some adversity which had afflicted them, see! They have some plot against Our revelations. Say: Allah is more swift in plotting. Our messengers write down that which you plot.

22. He it is Who makes you go on the land and the sea till, when you are in the ships and they sail with them with a fair breeze and they are glad in it, a wind-storm reaches them and the wave comes to them from every side and they think that they are overwhelmed in it; (then) they call to Allah, making their faith pure for Him only: If You deliver us from this, we truly will be of the thankful.

23. Yet when He has delivered them, look! They rebel in the earth wrongfully. O mankind! Your rebellion is only against yourselves. (You have)

enjoyment of the life of the world; then to Us is your return and We shall proclaim to you what you used to do.

24. The similitude of the life of the world is only as water which We send down from the sky, then the earth's growth of that which men and cattle eat mingles with it till, when the earth has taken on her ornaments and is embellished, and her people think that they are masters of her, Our commandment comes by night or by day and We make it as reaped corn as if it had not flourished yesterday. Thus do We explain the revelations for people who reflect.

25. And Allah summons to the abode of peace, and leads whom He will to a straight path.

26. For those who do good is the best (reward) and more (to it). Neither dust nor ignominy comes near their faces. Such are rightful owners of the Garden; they will remain in it.

27. And those who earn ill-deeds, (for them) repayment of each ill deed by the like of it; and ignominy overtakes them - They have no protector from Allah - as if their faces had been covered with a cloak of dark night. Such are rightful owners of the Fire; they will remain in it.

28. On the day when We gather them all together, then We say to those who ascribed partners (to Us): Stand back, you and your (pretended) partners (of Allah)! And We separate them, the one from the other, and their (pretended) partners say: It was not us you worshipped.

29. Allah suffices as a witness between us and you, that we were unaware of your worship.

30. There every soul experiences that which it did before, and they are returned to Allah, their rightful Lord, and that which they used to invent has failed them.

31. Say (to them, O Muhammad): Who provides for you from the sky and the earth, or Who owns hearing and sight; and Who brings out the living from the dead and brings out the dead from the living; and Who directs the course? They will say: Allah. Then say: Will you not then keep your duty (to Him)?

32. Such then is Allah, your rightful Lord. After the Truth, what is there except error? How then are you turned away!

33. Thus is the Word of your Lord justified concerning those who do wrong: that they do not believe.

34. Say: Is there of your partners (whom you ascribe to Allah) one that produces Creation and then reproduces it? Say: Allah produces Creation, then reproduces it. How then, are you misled!

35. Say: Is there of your partners (whom you ascribe to Allah) one that leads to the Truth? Say: Allah leads to the Truth. Is He Who leads to the Truth more deserving that He should be followed, or he who finds not the way unless he (himself) be guided. What is the matter with you? How do you judge?

36. Most of them follow nothing but conjecture. Assuredly, conjecture can by no means take the place of truth. Allah is Aware of what they do.

37. And this Qur'an is not such as could ever be invented in despite of Allah; but it is a confirmation of that which was before it and an exposition of that which is decreed for mankind - in it is no doubt - from the Lord of the Worlds.

38. Or do they say: He has invented it? Say: Then bring a Surah like it, and call (for help) on all you can besides Allah, if you are truthful.

39. No, but they denied that, the knowledge of which they could not comprehend, and of which the interpretation (in events) has not yet come to them. Even so did those before them deny. Then see what was the consequence for the wrongdoers!

40. And of them is he who believes in it, and of them is he who believes not in it, and your Lord is best aware of the corrupters.

41. And if they deny you, say: To me my work, and to you your work. You are innocent of what I do, and I am innocent of what you do.

42. And of them are some who listen to you. But can you make the deaf to hear even though they apprehend not?

43. And of them is he who looks towards you. But can you guide the blind even though they see not?

44. Allah does not wrong mankind in anything; but mankind wrong themselves.

45. And on the day when He will gather them together, (when it will seem) as though they had stayed but an hour of the day, recognising one another, those will verily have perished who denied the meeting with Allah and were not guided.

46. Whether We let you (O Muhammad) see something of that which We promise them or (whether We) cause you to die, still to Us is their return, and Allah, moreover, is Witness over what they do.

47. And for every nation there is a messenger. And when their messenger comes (on the Day of Judgement) it will be judged between them fairly, and they will not be wronged.

48. And they say: When will this promise be fulfilled, if you are truthful?

49. Say: I have no power to hurt or benefit myself, except that which Allah wills. For every nation there is an appointed time. When their time comes, then they cannot put it off an hour, nor hasten (it).

50. Say: Have you thought: When His doom comes to you as a raid by night, or in the (busy) day; what is there of it that the guilty ones desire to hasten?

51. Is it (only) then, when it has befallen you, that you will believe? What! (Believe) now, when (until now) you have been hastening it on (through disbelief)?

52. Then it will be said to those who dealt unjustly: Taste the torment of eternity. Are you repaid anything except what you used to earn?

53. And they ask you to inform them (saying): Is it true? Say: Yes, by my Lord, verily it is true, and you cannot escape.

54. And if each soul that does wrong had all that is in the earth it would seek to ransom itself with it; and they will feel remorse within them, when they see the doom. But it has been judged between them fairly and they are not wronged.

55. Verily all that is in the heavens and the earth is Allah's. Verily Allah's promise is true. But most of them know not.

56. He gives life and gives death, and to Him you will be returned.

57. O mankind! There has come to you an exhortation from your Lord, a healing for that which is in the hearts, a guidance and a mercy for believers.

58. Say: In the bounty of Allah and in His mercy: in it let them rejoice. It is better than what they hoard.

59. Say: Have you considered what provision Allah has sent down for you, how you have made of it lawful and unlawful? Has Allah permitted you, or do you invent a lie concerning Allah?

60. And what think those who invent a lie concerning Allah (will be their plight) on the Day of Resurrection? Allah truly is Bountiful towards mankind, but most of them do not give thanks.

61. And you (Muhammad) are not occupied with any business and you recite not a Lecture[106] from this (Scripture), and you (mankind) perform no act, but We are Witness of you when you are engaged in it. And not an atom's weight in the earth or in the sky escapes your Lord, nor what is less than that or greater than that, but it is (written) in a clear Book.

62. Verily the friends of Allah are (those) on whom fear (comes) not, nor do they grieve.

---

106. Arabic: *Qur'an*

63. Those who believe and keep their duty (to Allah).

64. Theirs are good tidings in the life of the world and in the Hereafter - there is no changing of the Words of Allah - that is the Supreme Triumph.

65. And let not their speech grieve you (O Muhammad). Power belongs wholly to Allah. He is the Hearer, the Knower.

66. Is it not to Allah that belongs whoever is in the heavens and whoever is in the earth? Those who follow anything instead of Allah follow not (His) partners. They follow only a conjecture, and they only guess.

67. He it is Who has appointed for you the night that you should rest in it and the day giving sight. In this verily are signs for a people that heed.

68. They say: Allah has taken (to Him) a son - Glorified is He! He has no needs! His is all that is in the heavens and all that is in the earth. You have no authority for this. Do you tell concerning Allah that which you know not?

69. Say: Verily those who invent a lie concerning Allah will not succeed.

70. This world's portion (will be theirs), then to Us is their return. Then We make them taste a dreadful doom because they used to disbelieve.

71. Recite to them the story of Noah, when he told his people: O my people! If my sojourn (here) and my reminding you by Allah's revelations are an offence to you, in Allah I have put my trust, so decide upon your course of action, you and your partners. Let not your course of action

be in doubt for you. Then decide about me, give me no respite.

72. But if you are averse, I have asked of you no wage. My wage is the concern of Allah only, and I am commanded to be of those who surrender (to Him).

73. But they denied him, so We saved him and those with him in the ship, and made them viceroys (in the earth), while We drowned those who denied Our revelations. See then the nature of the consequence for those who had been warned.

74. Then, after him, We sent messengers to their people, and they brought them clear proofs. But they were not ready to believe in that which they before denied. Thus We print on the hearts of the transgressors.

75. Then, after them, We sent Moses and Aaron to Pharaoh and his chiefs with Our revelations, but they were arrogant and were a guilty people.

76. And when the Truth from Our presence came to them, they said: This is mere magic.

77. Moses said: Do you speak (so) of the Truth when it has come to you? Is this magic? No, magicians thrive not.

78. They said: Have you come to us to pervert us from that (faith) in which we found our fathers, and that you two may be arrogant in the land? We will not believe you two.

79. And Pharaoh said: Bring every cunning wizard to me.

80. And when the wizards came, Moses said to them: Cast your spell!

81. And when they had cast, Moses said: That which you have brought is magic. Allah will make it vain. Allah upholds not the work of mischief-makers.

82. And Allah will vindicate the Truth by His words, however much the guilty are averse.

83. But no one trusted Moses, except some descendants of his people, (and they were) in fear of Pharaoh and their chiefs, that he would persecute them. Pharaoh was verily a tyrant in the land, and he verily was of the excessive.

84. And Moses said: O my people! If you have believed in Allah, then put trust in Him, if you have indeed surrendered (to Him)!

85. They said: In Allah we put trust. Our Lord! Oh, make us not a lure for the wrongdoing people;

86. And, of Your mercy, save us from the people who disbelieve.

87. And We inspired Moses and his brother, (saying): Appoint houses for your people in Egypt and make your houses oratories, and establish worship. And give good news to the believers.

88. And Moses said: Our Lord! You have given Pharaoh and his chiefs splendour and riches in the life of the world, Our Lord! That they may lead men astray from Your way. Our Lord! Destroy their riches and harden their hearts so that they believe not till they see the painful doom.

89. He said: Your prayer is heard. Both of you keep to the straight path, and follow not the road of those who have no knowledge.

90. And We brought the Children of Israel across the sea, and Pharaoh with his forces pursued them in rebellion and transgression, till, when the (fate of) drowning overtook him, he exclaimed: I believe that there is no God except Him in Whom the Children of Israel believe, and I am of those who surrender (to Him).

91. What! Now! When until then you have rebelled and been of the wrongdoers?

92. But this day We save you in your body that you may be a sign for those after you. Most of mankind are heedless of Our signs.

93. And We verily did allot to the Children of Israel a fixed abode, and did provide them with good things; and they differed not until the knowledge came to them. Your Lord will judge between them on the Day of Resurrection concerning that in which they used to differ.

94. And if you (Muhammad) are in doubt concerning that which We reveal to you, then question those who read the Scripture (that was) before you. Verily the Truth from your Lord has come to you. So do not be of the waverers.

95. And do not be of those who deny the revelations of Allah, for then you would be of the losers.

96. Those for whom the word of your Lord (concerning sinners) has effect will not believe,

97. Though every sign come to them, till they see the painful doom.

98. If only there had been a community (of all those that were destroyed of old) that believed and profited by its belief as did the people of Jonah! When they believed We drew off from them the torment of disgrace in the life of the world and gave them comfort for a while.

99. And if your Lord willed, all who are in the earth would have believed together. Would you (Muhammad) compel men until they are believers?

100. It is not for any soul to believe except by the permission of Allah. He has set uncleanness upon those who have no sense.

101. Say: Behold what is in the heavens and the earth! But revelations and warnings benefit not people who will not believe.

102. What expect they except the like of the days of those who passed away before them? Say: Expect then! I am with you among the expectant.

103. Then We shall save Our messengers and the believers, in like manner (as of old). It is incumbent upon Us to save believers.

104. Say (O Muhammad): O mankind! If you are in doubt of my religion, then (know that) I worship not those whom you worship instead of Allah, but I worship Allah Who causes you to die, and I have been commanded to be of the believers.

105. And, (O Muhammad) set your purpose resolutely for religion, as a man by nature upright, and be not of those who ascribe partners (to Allah).

106. And call not, besides Allah, to that which cannot profit you nor hurt you, for if you did so then you were of the wrongdoers.

107. If Allah afflicts you with some hurt, there is none who can remove it except Him; and if He desires good for you, there is none who can repel His bounty. He strikes with it whom He will of his bondsmen. He is the Forgiving, the Merciful.

108. Say: O mankind! Now the Truth from your Lord has come to you. So whoever is guided, is guided only for (the good of) his soul, and whoever errs, errs only against it. And I am not a guardian over you.

109. And (O Muhammad) follow that which is inspired in you, and forbear until Allah gives judgement. And He is the Best of Judges.

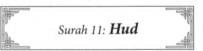

Surah 11: **Hud**

Hud takes its name from v. 50, which begins the story of Hud, of the tribe of 'Aad, one of the prophets of Arabia who is not mentioned in the Hebrew Scriptures. The Surah also contains the stories of two other Arab prophets, Salih, of the tribe of Thamud, and Shu'eyb of Midian (identified with Jethro), which, with those of Noah and Moses, are quoted as part of the history of Divine Revelation, the truth of which is here vindicated, in a manner supplementary to Surah 10, Yunus.

A late Makkan Surah, except v. 114 f., revealed at Al-Madinah.

In the name of Allah, the Beneficent, the Merciful.

1. *Alif. Lam. Ra.*[107] (This is) a Scripture the revelations of which are perfected and then explained. (It comes) from One Wise, Informed,

2. (Saying): Serve none but Allah. I am to you from Him a warner and a bringer of good tidings.

3. And (commanding you): Ask pardon of your Lord and turn to Him repentant. He will cause you to enjoy a fair estate until a time appointed. He gives His bounty to every bountiful one. But if you turn away, (then) I fear for you the retribution of an Awful Day.

4. To Allah is your return, and He is Able to do all things.

5. Now they fold up their hearts that they may hide (their thoughts) from Him. At the very moment when they cover themselves with their clothing, Allah knows that which they keep hidden and that which they proclaim. He is Aware of what is in the hearts (of men).

6. And there is not a beast in the earth but the sustenance of it depends on Allah. He knows its habitation and its repository. All is in a clear record.

7. And He it is Who created the heavens and the earth in six Days[108] - and His Throne was upon the water - that He might try you, which of you is best in conduct. Yet if you (O Muhammad) say: You will be raised again after death! Those who disbelieve will surely say: This is nothing but mere magic.

8. And if We delay for them the doom until a reckoned time, they will surely say: What withholds it? Verily, on the day when it comes to them, it cannot be averted from them, and that which they derided will surround them.

9. And if we cause man to taste some mercy from Us and afterwards withdraw it from him, he is despairing, thankless.

10. And if We cause him to taste grace after some misfortune that had befallen him, he says: The ills have gone from me. He is overjoyed, boastful;

11. Except those who persevere and do good works. Theirs will be forgiveness and a great reward.

12. A likely thing, that you would forsake anything of that which has been revealed to you, and that your chest should be tightened for it, because they say: Why has not a treasure been sent down for him, or an angel come with him? You are but a warner, and Allah is in charge of all things.

13. Or they say: He has invented it. Say: Then bring ten Surahs, the like of it, invented, and call on everyone you can besides Allah, if you are truthful!

14. And if they answer not your prayer, then know that it is revealed only in the knowledge of Allah; and that there is no God except Him. Will you then be (of) those who surrender?[109]

15. Whoever desires the life of the world and its pomp, We shall repay them their deeds in it, and in it they will not be wronged.

16. Those are they for whom there is nothing in the Hereafter except the Fire.

---

107. See *Surah 2, Al-Baqarah*, v. 1, footnote.
108. See *Surah 22, Al-Hajj*, v. 47; *Surah 32, As-Sajdah*, v. 5 and *Surah 70, Al-Ma'arij*, v. 4.

109. Arabic: *Muslimin*

(All) that they contrive here is vain and (all) that they used to do is fruitless.

17. Is he (to be counted equal with them) who relies on a clear proof from his Lord, and a witness from Him recites it, and before it was the Book of Moses, an example and a mercy? Such believe in it, and who disbelieves in it of the clans, the Fire is his appointed place. So be not you in doubt concerning it. It is the Truth from your Lord; but most of mankind believe not.

18. Who does greater wrong than he who invents a lie concerning Allah? Such will be brought before their Lord, and the witnesses will say: These are they who lied concerning their Lord. Now the curse of Allah is upon wrongdoers,

19. Who prevent (men) from the way of Allah and would have it crooked, and who are disbelievers in the Hereafter.

20. Such will not escape in the earth, nor have they any protecting friends besides Allah. For them the torment will be double. They could not bear to hear, and they used not to see.

21. Such are they who have lost their souls, and that which they used to invent has failed them.

22. Assuredly, in the Hereafter they will be the greatest losers.

23. Those who believe and do good works and humble themselves before their Lord: such are rightful owners of the Garden; they will remain in it.

24. The similitude of the two parties is as the blind and the deaf and the seer and the hearer. Are they equal in similitude? Will you not then be admonished?

25. And We sent Noah to his people (and he said): I am a plain warner to you.

26. That you serve none, except Allah. I fear for you the retribution of a painful Day.

27. The chieftains of his people, who disbelieved, said: We see you but a mortal like us, and we see not that any follow you except the most abject among us, without reflection. We see in you no merit above us - no, we consider you liars.

28. He said: O my people! Consider, if I rely on a clear proof from my Lord and there has come to me a mercy from His presence, and it has been made obscure to you, can we compel you to accept it when you are averse to it?

29. And O my people! I ask of you no wealth for it. My reward is the concern only of Allah, and I am not going to thrust away those who believe - they have to meet their Lord - but I see you a people who are ignorant.

30. And, O my people! Who would deliver me from Allah if I thrust them away? Will you not then reflect?

31. I say not to you: "I have the treasures of Allah" nor "I have knowledge of the Unseen", nor do I say: "I am an angel!" Nor do I say to those whom your eyes scorn that Allah will not give them good - Allah knows best what is in their hearts - then indeed I should be of the wrongdoers.

32. They said: O Noah! You have disputed with us and multiplied disputation with us; now bring upon us that with which you threaten us, if you are of the truthful.

33. He said: Only Allah will bring it upon you if He will, and you can by no means escape.

34. My counsel will not profit you if I were minded to advise you, if Allah's will is to keep you astray. He is your Lord and to Him you will be brought back.

35. Or do they say (again): He has invented it? Say: If I have invented it, upon me be my crimes, but I am innocent of (all) that you commit.

36. And it was inspired in Noah, (saying): No-one of your people will believe except him who has believed already. Be not distressed because of what they do.

37. Build the ship under Our eyes and by Our inspiration, and speak not to Me on behalf of those who do wrong. They will be drowned.

38. And he was building the ship, and every time that chieftains of his people passed him, they made fun of him. He said: Though you make fun of us, yet we mock at you even as you mock;

39. And you will know to whom a punishment that will humiliate him comes, and upon whom a lasting doom will fall.

40. (Thus it was) till, when Our commandment came to pass and the oven gushed out water,[110] We said: Load in it two of every kind, a pair (the male and female), and your household, except him against whom the word has gone out already, and

those who believe. And but a few were they who believed with him.

41. And he said: Embark in it! In the name of Allah be its course and its mooring. My Lord is Forgiving, Merciful.

42. And it sailed with them amid waves like mountains, and Noah called to his son - and he was standing aloof - O my son! Come ride with us, and be not with the disbelievers.

43. He said: I shall go to some mountain that will save me from the water. (Noah) said: This day there is none that is saved from the commandment of Allah except him on whom He has had mercy. And the wave came in between them, so he was among the drowned.

44. And it was said: O earth! Swallow your water and, O sky! be cleared of clouds! And the water was made to subside. And the commandment was fulfilled. And it (the ship) came to rest upon (the mount) Al-Judi and it was said: A far removal for wrongdoing people!

45. And Noah called to his Lord and said: My Lord! My son is of my household! Surely Your promise is the truth and You are the Most Just of Judges.

46. He said: O Noah! He is not of your household; he is of evil conduct, so do not ask of Me that of which you have no knowledge. I admonish you lest you will be among the ignorant.

47. He said: My Lord! In You I seek refuge (from the sin) that I should ask of You that of which I have no knowledge. Unless You forgive me and have mercy on me I shall be among the lost.

---

110. This was a sign of the deluge, water gushing up from underground as well as falling from the sky.

48. It was said (to him): O Noah! Go down (from the mountain) with peace from Us and blessings upon you and some nations (that will spring) from those with you. (There will be other) nations to whom We shall give enjoyment a long while and then painful doom from Us will overtake them.

49. This is of the tidings of the Unseen which We inspire in you (Muhammad). You yourself knew it not, nor did your people (know it) before this. Then have patience. The (good) outcome is for those who ward off (evil).

50. And to (the tribe of) 'Aad (We sent) their brother, Hud. He said: O my people! Serve Allah! You have no other God except Him. You do only invent!

51. O my people! I ask of you no reward for it. My reward is the concern only of Him Who made me. Have you then no sense?

52. And, O my people! Ask forgiveness of your Lord, then turn to Him repentant; He will cause the sky to rain abundance on you and will add to you strength to your strength. Turn not away, guilty!

53. They said: O Hud! You have brought us no clear proof and we are not going to forsake our gods on your (mere) saying, and we are not believers in you.

54. We say nothing except that one of our gods has possessed you in an evil way. He said: I call Allah to witness, and do you (too) bear witness, that I am innocent of (all) that you ascribe as partners (to Allah)

55. Besides Him. So (try to) circumvent me, all of you, give me no respite.

56. I have put my trust in Allah, my Lord and your Lord. Not an animal but He does grasp it by the forelock! My Lord is on a straight path.

57. And if you turn away, still I have conveyed to you that with which I was sent to you, and my Lord will set in place of you a people other than you. You cannot injure Him at all. My Lord is Guardian over all things.

58. And when Our commandment came to pass We saved Hud and those who believed with him by a mercy from Us; We saved them from a harsh doom.

59. And such were 'Aad. They denied the revelations of their Lord and flouted His messengers and followed the command of every disobedient ruler.

60. And a curse was made to follow them in the world and on the Day of Resurrection. 'Aad disbelieved in their Lord. A far removal for 'Aad, the people of Hud!

61. And to (the tribe of) Thamud (We sent) their brother Salih. He said: O my people! Serve Allah, you have no other God except Him. He brought you out from the earth and has made you cultivate it. So ask forgiveness of Him and turn to Him repentant. My Lord is Near, Responsive.

62. They said: O Salih! You have been among us till now the one in whom our hope was placed. Do you ask us not to worship what our fathers worshipped? We verily are in grave doubt concerning that to which you call us.

63. He said: O my people! Consider: if I am (acting) on clear proof from my Lord and there has come to me a mercy from Him, who will save me from Allah if I disobey Him? You would add to me nothing except ruin.

64. O my people! This is the camel of Allah, a sign to you, so allow her to feed in Allah's earth, and touch her not with harm lest a near torment seize you.

65. But they hamstrung her, and then he said: Enjoy life in your dwelling-place three days! This is a threat that will not be belied.

66. So, when Our commandment came to pass, We saved Salih, and those who believed with him, by a mercy from Us, from the ignominy of that day. Your Lord! He is the Strong, the Mighty.

67. And the (awful) Cry overtook those who did wrong, so that morning found them prostrate in their dwellings.

68. As though they had not dwelt there. Thamud disbelieved in their Lord. A far removal for Thamud!

69. And Our messengers came to Abraham with good news. They said: Peace! He answered: Peace! and delayed not to bring a roasted calf.

70. And when he saw their hands reached not to it, he mistrusted them and conceived a fear of them. They said: Fear not! We are sent to the people of Lot.

71. And his wife, standing by, laughed when We gave her good tidings (of the birth) of Isaac, and, after Isaac, of Jacob.

72. She said: Oh, woe is me! Shall I bear a child when I am an old woman, and this my husband is an old man? This is a strange thing!

73. They said: Do you wonder at the commandment of Allah? The mercy of Allah and His blessings be upon you, O people of the house! He is Owner of Praise, Owner of Glory!

74. And when the awe departed from Abraham, and the glad news reached him, he pleaded with Us on behalf of the people of Lot.

75. Abraham was mild, imploring, penitent.

76. (It was said) O Abraham! Forsake this! Your Lord's commandment has gone before, and there comes to them a doom which cannot be repelled.

77. And when Our messengers came to Lot, he was distressed and knew not how to protect them. He said: This is a distressful day.

78. And his people came to him, running towards him - and before then they used to commit abominations. He said: O my people! Here are my daughters! They are purer for you. Beware of Allah, and degrade me not in (the person of) my guests. Is there not among you any upright man?

79. They said: Well you know that we have no right to your daughters, and well you know what we want.

80. He said: Would that I had strength to resist you or had some strong support (among you)!

81. (The messengers) said: O Lot! We are messengers of your Lord; they will not reach you. So travel with your people in a part of the night, and let not one of you turn round - (all) except your wife. That which strikes them will strike her (also). Their appointed time is (for) the morning. Is not the morning near?

82. So when Our commandment came to pass We overthrew (that township) and rained upon it stones of clay, one after another,

83. Marked with fire in the providence of your Lord (for the destruction of the wicked). And they are never far from the wrongdoers.

84. And to Midian (We sent) their brother Shu'eyb. He said: O my people! Serve Allah. You have no other God except Him! And give not short measure and short weight. I see you well-to-do, and I fear for you the doom of a troubling Day.

85. O my people! Give full measure and full weight in justice, and wrong not people in respect of their goods. And do not do evil in the earth, causing corruption.

86. That which Allah leaves with you is better for you if you are believers; and I am not a keeper over you.

87. They said: O Shu'eyb! Does your way of prayer command you that we should forsake that which our fathers (used to) worship, or that we (should leave off) doing what we will with our own property? You are the mild, the guide to right behaviour.

88. He said: O my people! Consider: if I am (acting) on a clear proof from my Lord and He sustains me with fair sustenance from Him (how can I concede anything to you)? I desire not to do behind your backs that which I ask you not to do. I desire nothing except reform so far as I am able. My

welfare is only in Allah. In Him I trust and to Him I turn (repentant).

89. And, O my people! Let not the schism with me cause you to sin so that there befalls you that which befell the people of Noah and the people of Hud, and the people of Salih; and the people of Lot are not far off from you.

90. Ask pardon of your Lord and then turn to Him (repentant). My Lord is Merciful, Loving.

91. They said: O Shu'eyb! We understand not much of what you tell, and we behold you weak among us. But for your family, we should have stoned you, for you are not strong against us.

92. He said: O my people! Is my family more to be honoured by you than Allah? and you put Him behind you, neglected! My Lord surrounds what you do.

93. And, O my people! Act according to your power, I (too) am acting. You will soon know on whom there comes a doom that will humiliate him, and who it is who lies. And watch! I am a watcher with you.

94. And when Our commandment came to pass We saved Shu'eyb and those who believed with him by a mercy from Us; and the (Awful) Cry seized those who did injustice, and morning found them prostrate in their dwellings,

95. As though they had not dwelt there. A far removal for Midian, even as Thamud had been removed afar!

96. And verily We sent Moses with Our revelations and a clear authority,

97. To Pharaoh and his chiefs, but they followed the command of Pharaoh, and the command of Pharaoh was no right guide.

98. He will go before his people on the Day of Resurrection and will lead them to the Fire for a watering-place. Ah, unhappy is the watering-place (to which they are) led.

99. A curse is made to follow them in the world and on the Day of Resurrection. Unhappy is the gift (that will be) given (them).

100. That is (something) of the tidings of the townships[111] (which were destroyed of old). We relate it to you (Muhammad). Some of them are standing and some (already) cleared.

101. We did not wrong them, but they did wrong themselves; and their gods on whom they call besides Allah benefitted them nothing when your Lord's command came; they added to them nothing except ruin.

102. Even thus is the grasp of your Lord when He grasps the townships while they are doing wrong. His grasp is painful, very strong.

103. In this verily there is a sign for those who fear the doom of the Hereafter. That is a day to which mankind will be gathered, and that is a day that will be witnessed.

104. And We defer it only to a term already reckoned.

105. On the day when it comes no soul will speak except by His permission; some among them will be wretched, (others) glad.

111. Or "communities."

106. As for those who will be wretched (on that day) they will be in the Fire; sighing and wailing will be their portion in it,

107. Remaining there so long as the heavens and the earth endure, except for that which your Lord wills. Your Lord is Doer of what He will.

108. And as for those who will be glad (that day) they will be in the Garden, remaining there so long as the heavens and the earth endure, except for that which your Lord wills: a gift unfailing.

109. So be not in doubt concerning that which these (people) worship. They worship only as their fathers worshipped before. We shall pay them their whole due in full.

110. And we verily gave to Moses the Scripture, and there was dispute upon it; and had it not been for a Word that had already gone before from your Lord, the case would have been judged between them, and they are in grave doubt concerning it.

111. And to each your Lord will verily repay his works in full. He is Informed of what they do.

112. So tread the straight path as you are commanded, and those who turn (to Allah) with you, and transgress not. He is Seer of what you do.

113. And incline not towards those who do wrong lest the Fire touch you, and you have no protecting friends against Allah, and afterwards you would not be helped.

114. Establish worship at the two ends of the day and in some watches of the night. Good deeds annul evil deeds. This is a reminder for the mindful.

115. And have patience, (O Muhammad), for Allah loses not the wages of the good.

116. If only there had been among the generations before you men possessing a remnant (of good sense) to warn (their people) from corruption in the earth, as did a few of those whom We saved from them! The wrongdoers followed that by which they were made lifeless, and were guilty.

117. In truth, your Lord destroyed not the townships tyrannously while their people were doing right.

118. And if your Lord had willed, He verily would have made mankind one nation, yet they cease not differing,

119. Except him on whom your Lord has mercy; and for that He did create them. And the Word of your Lord has been fulfilled: Verily I shall fill Hell with the jinn and mankind together.

120. And all that We relate to you of the story of the messengers is in order that by it We may make firm your heart. And in this has come to you the Truth and an exhortation and a reminder for believers.

121. And say to those who believe not: Act according to your power. We (too) are acting.

122. And wait! We (too) are waiting.

123. And Allah's is the Invisible of the heavens and the earth, and to Him the whole matter will be returned. So worship Him and put your trust in Him. Your Lord is not unaware of what you (mortals) do.

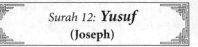

Surah 12: **Yusuf**
(Joseph)

Yusuf takes its name from its subject which is the life-story of Joseph. It differs from all other Surahs in having only one subject. The differences from the Bible narrative are striking. Jacob is here a Prophet, who is not deceived by the story of his son's death, but is distressed because, through a suspension of his clairvoyance, he cannot see what has become of Joseph. The real importance of the narrative, its psychic burden, is emphasised throughout, and the manner of narration, though astonishing to Western readers, is vivid.

Tradition says that it was recited by the Prophet at Makkah to the first converts from Yathrib (Al-Madinah), *i.e.* in the second year before the Hijrah; but that, as Nöldeke points out, does not mean that it was not revealed till then, but that it had been revealed by then.

A late Makkan Surah.

In the name of Allah,
the Beneficent, the Merciful.

1. *Alif. Lam. Ra.*[112] These are verses of the Scripture that makes plain.

2. We have revealed it, a Lecture[113] in Arabic, that you may understand.

3. We narrate to you (Muhammad) the best of narratives in that We have inspired in you this Qur'an, though before you were of the heedless.

112. See *Surah 2, Al-Baqarah,* v. 1, footnote.
113. Arabic: *Qur'an.*

4. When Joseph said to his father: O my father! I saw in a dream eleven planets and the sun and the moon, I saw them prostrating themselves to me.

5. He said: O my dear son! Tell not your brothers of your vision, lest they plot a plot against you. Satan is for man an open foe.

6. Thus your Lord will prefer you and will teach you the interpretation of events, and will perfect His grace upon you and upon the family of Jacob, as He perfected it upon your forefathers, Abraham and Isaac. Your Lord is Knower, Wise.

7. Verily, in Joseph and his brothers are signs (of Allah's Sovereignty) for the inquiring.

8. When they said: Verily, Joseph and his brother are dearer to our father than we are, though we are many. Our father is in plain error.

9. (One said): Kill Joseph or cast him to some (other) land, so that your father's favour may be all for you, and (that) you may afterwards be righteous people.

10. One among them said: Kill not Joseph but, if you must do it, fling him into the depth of the well; some caravan will find him.

11. They said: O our father! Why will you not trust us with Joseph, when we are good friends to him?

12. Send him with us tomorrow that he may enjoy himself and play. And we shall take good care of him.

13. He said: In truth, it saddens me that you should take him with you,

and I fear that the wolf devour him while you are heedless of him.

14. They said: If the wolf should devour him when we are (so strong) a band, then surely we should have already perished.

15. Then, when they led him off, and were of one mind that they should place him in the depth of the well, We inspired in him: You will tell them of this deed of theirs when they know (you) not.

16. And they came weeping to their father in the evening.

17. Saying: O our father! We went racing one with another, and left Joseph by our things, and the wolf devoured him, and you believe not our saying even when we speak the truth.

18. And they came with false blood on his shirt. He said: No, but your minds have deceived you into something. (My course is) beautiful patience. And Allah it is Whose help is to be sought in that (predicament) which you describe.

19. And there came a caravan, and they sent their water-drawer. He let down his bucket (into the well). He said: Good luck! Here is a youth. And they hid him as a treasure, and Allah was Aware of what they did.

20. And they sold him for a low price, a number of silver coins; and they attached no value to him.

21. And he of Egypt who purchased him said to his wife: Receive him honourably. Perhaps he may prove useful to us or we may adopt him as a son. Thus We established Joseph in the land that We might teach him the interpretation of events. And Allah was predominant in his career, but most of mankind know not.

22. And when he reached his prime We gave him wisdom and knowledge. Thus We reward the good.

23. And she, in whose house he was, asked of him an evil act. She bolted the doors and said: Come! He said: I seek refuge in Allah! He is my Lord, who has treated me honourably. Wrongdoers never prosper.

24. She verily desired him, and he would have desired her if it had not been that he saw the argument of his Lord. Thus it was, that We might ward off from him evil and lewdness. He was of Our chosen slaves.

25. And they raced with one another to the door, and she tore his shirt from behind, and they met her lord and master at the door. She said: What will be his reward, who wishes evil to your people, except prison or a painful doom?

26. (Joseph) said: She it was who asked of me an evil act. And a witness of her own people testified: If his shirt is torn from the front, then she speaks the truth and he is of the liars.

27. And if his shirt is torn from behind, then she has lied and he is of the truthful.

28. So when he saw his shirt torn from behind, he said: This is of the cunning of you women. The cunning of you is very great.

29. O Joseph! Turn away from this, and you, (O woman), ask forgiveness for your sin. You are of the sinful.

30. And women in the city said: The ruler's wife is asking of her slave-boy an ill-deed. Indeed he has smitten her to the heart with love. We see her in plain error.

31. And when she heard of their sly talk, she sent to them and prepared for them a cushioned couch (to lie on at the feast) and gave to every one of them a knife and said to (Joseph): Come out to them! And when they saw him they exalted him and cut their hands, exclaiming: Allah is Blameless! This is not a human being. This is no other than some gracious angel.

32. She said: This is he on whose account you blamed me. I asked of him an evil act, but he proved restrained, but if he does not obey my request he verily shall be imprisoned, and verily shall be of those brought low.

33. He said: O my Lord! Prison is more dear to me than that to which they urge me, and if You fend not off their seduction from me I shall incline to them and become of the foolish.

34. So his Lord heard his prayer and fended off their seduction from him. He is Hearer, Knower.

35. And it seemed good to them (the men) after they had seen the signs (of his innocence) to imprison him for a time.

36. And two young men went to prison with him. One of them said: I dreamed that I was pressing wine. The other said: I dreamed that I was carrying upon my head bread of which the birds were eating. Announce to us the interpretation, for we see you of those good (at interpretation).

37. He said: The food which you are given (daily) shall not come to you, but I shall tell you the interpretation before it comes to you. This is of that which my Lord has taught me. I have forsaken the religion of people who believe not in Allah and are disbelievers in the Hereafter.

38. And I have followed the religion of my fathers, Abraham and Isaac and Jacob. It never was for us to attribute anything as partner to Allah. This is of the bounty of Allah to us (the seed of Abraham) and to mankind; but most men give not thanks.

39. O my two fellow-prisoners! Are diverse lords better, or Allah the One, the Almighty?

40. Those whom you worship besides Him are only names which you have named, you and your fathers. Allah has revealed no sanction for them. The decision rests with Allah only, Who has commanded you that you worship none except Him. This is the right religion, but most men know not.

41. O my two fellow-prisoners! As for one of you, he will pour out wine for his lord to drink; and as for the other, he will be crucified so that the birds will eat from his head. Thus is the case judged concerning which you did inquire.

42. And he said to him of the two whom he knew would be released: Mention me in the presence of your lord. But Satan caused him to forget to mention it to his lord, so he (Joseph) stayed in prison for some years.

43. And the king said: I saw in a dream seven fat cows which seven lean were eating, and seven green ears of corn and another (seven) dry. O notables! Explain for me my vision, if you can interpret dreams.

44. They answered: Jumbled dreams! And we are not knowledgeable in the interpretation of dreams.

45. And he of the two who was released, and (now) finally remembered, said: I am going to announce to you the interpretation, therefore send me.

46. (And when he came to Joseph in the prison, he exclaimed): Joseph! O you truthful one! Explain for us the seven fat cows which seven lean were eating and the seven green ears of corn and the other (seven) dry, that I may return to the people, so that they may know.

47. He said: You will sow seven years as usual, but that which you reap, leave it in the ear, all except a little which you eat.

48. Then after that will come seven hard years which will devour all that you have prepared for them, except a little of that which you have stored.

49. Then, after that, will come a year when the people will have plenteous crops and when they will press (wine and oil).

50. And the king said: Bring him to me. And when the messenger came to him, he (Joseph) said: Return to your lord and ask him what was the case of the women who cut their hands. My Lord knows their cunning.

51. He (the king) (then sent for those women and) said: What happened when you asked an evil act of Joseph? They answered: Allah is Blameless! We know no evil of him. Said the wife of the ruler: Now the truth is out. I asked of him an evil act, and he is surely of the truthful.

52. (Then Joseph said: I asked for) this, that he (my lord) may know that I betrayed him not in secret, and that surely Allah guides not the stratagems of the betrayers.

53. I do not exonerate myself. The (human) soul enjoins to evil, except that on which my Lord has mercy. My Lord is Forgiving, Merciful.

54. And the king said: Bring him to me that I may attach him to my person. And when he had talked with him, he said: You are today in our presence established and trusted.

55. He said: Set me over the storehouses of the land. I am a skilled custodian.

56. Thus We gave power to Joseph in the land. He was the owner of it where he pleased. We reach with Our mercy whom We will. We lose not the reward of the good.

57. And the reward of the Hereafter is better, for those who believe and ward off (evil).

58. And Joseph's brothers came and presented themselves before him, and he knew them but they knew him not.

59. And when he provided them with their provision he said: Bring to me a brother of yours from your father. See you not that I fill up the measure and I am the best of hosts?

60. And if you bring him not to me, then there shall be no measure for you with me, nor shall you draw near.

61. They said: We will try to win him from his father: that we will surely do.

62. He said to his young men: Place their merchandise in their saddlebags, so that they may know it when they go back to their people, and so will come again.

63. So when they went back to their father they said: O our father! The measure is denied us, so send with us our brother that we may obtain the measure, surely we will guard him well.

64. He said: Can I entrust him to you other than I entrusted his brother to you before? Allah is better at guarding, and He is the Most Merciful of those who show mercy.

65. And when they opened their belongings, they discovered that their merchandise had been returned to them. They said: O our father! What (more) can we ask? Here is our merchandise returned to us. We shall get provision for our people and guard our brother, and we shall have the extra measure of a camel (load). This (that we bring now) is a light measure.

66. He said: I will not send him with you till you give me an undertaking in the name of Allah that you will bring him back to me, unless you are surrounded. And when they gave him their undertaking he said: Allah is the Guardian over what we say.

67. And he said: O my sons! Go not in by one gate; go in by different gates. I can benefit you nothing as against Allah. The decision rests with Allah only. In Him do I put my trust, and in Him let all the trusting put their trust.

68. And when they entered in the manner which their father had enjoined, it would have benefitted them nothing as against Allah, it was but a need of Jacob's soul which he thus satisfied;[114] and he was a lord of knowledge because We had taught him; but most of mankind know not.

69. And when they went in before Joseph, he took his brother to him, saying: I, even I, am your brother, therefore sorrow not for what they did.

70. And when he provided them with their provision, he put the drinking-cup in his brother's saddlebag, and then a caller called: O camel-riders! You are surely thieves!

71. They called, coming towards them: What is it you have lost?

72. They said: We have lost the king's cup, and he who brings it shall have a camel-load, and I (said Joseph) am answerable for it.

73. They said: By Allah, well you know we came not to do evil in the land, and are no thieves.

74. They said: And what shall be the penalty for it, if you prove liars?

75. They said: The penalty for it! He in whose bag (the cup) is found, he is the penalty for it. Thus we repay wrongdoers.

76. Then he (Joseph) began the search with their bags before his brother's bag, then he produced it from his brother's bag. Thus did We scheme

114. There was a prevalent superstition in the East that the members of a larger family ought not to appear all together, for fear of the ill luck that comes from envy in the hearts of others.

for Joseph. He could not have taken his brother according to the king's law unless Allah willed. We raise by grades (of mercy) whom We will, and over every lord of knowledge there is one more knowledgeable.

77. They said: If he steals, a brother of his stole before. But Joseph kept it secret in his soul and revealed it not to them. He said (within himself): You are in a worse case and Allah knows best (the truth of) that which you allege.

78. They said: O ruler of the land! He has a very aged father, so take one of us instead of him. We see you are of those who do kindness.

79. He said: Allah forbid that we should seize anyone except him with whom we found our property; then truly we should be wrongdoers.

80. So, When they despaired of (moving) him, they consulted together apart. The eldest of them said: Do you not know how your father took an undertaking from you in Allah's name and how you failed in the case of Joseph before? Therefore I shall not go out from the land until my father gives permission or Allah judges for me. He is the Best of Judges.

81. Return to your father and say: O our father! Your son has stolen. We testify only to that which we know; we are not guardians of the Unseen.

82. Ask the township where we were, and the caravan with which we travelled there. We speak the truth.

83. (And when they came to their father and had spoken thus to him) he said: No, but your minds have deceived you into something. (My course is) beautiful patience! It may be that Allah will bring them all to me. He, only He, is the Knower, the Wise.

84. And he turned away from them and said: Alas, my grief for Joseph! And his eyes were whitened with the sorrow that he was suppressing.

85. They said: By Allah, you will never cease remembering Joseph till your health is ruined or you are of those who perish!

86. He said: I expose my distress and anguish only to Allah, and I know from Allah that which you know not.

87. Go, O my sons, and ascertain concerning Joseph and his brother, and despair not of the Spirit of Allah. None despairs of the Spirit of Allah except disbelieving people.

88. And when they came (again) before him (Joseph) they said: O ruler! Misfortune has touched us and our people, and we bring only poor merchandise, so fill for us the measure and be charitable to us. Allah will repay the charitable,

89. He said: Do you know what you did to Joseph and his brother in your ignorance?

90. They said: Is it indeed you who are Joseph? He said: I am Joseph and this is my brother. Allah has shown us favour. He who wards off (evil) and endures (finds favour); for verily! Allah loses not the wages of the kindly.

91. They said: By Allah, verily Allah has preferred you above us, and we were indeed sinful.

92. He said: Have no fear this day! May Allah forgive you, and He is the Most Merciful of those who show mercy.

93. Go with this shirt of mine and lay it on my father's face, he will become (again) a seer; and come to me with all your people.

94. When the caravan departed, their father had said: Truly I am conscious of the breath of Joseph, though you call me senile.

95. (Those around him) said: By Allah, you are in your old error.

96. Then, when the bearer of glad tidings came, he laid it on his face and he became a seer once more. He said: Did I not say to you that I know from Allah that which you know not?

97. They said: O our father! Ask forgiveness of our sins for us, for we were sinful.

98. He said: I shall ask forgiveness for you of my Lord. He is the Forgiving, the Merciful.

99. And when they came in before Joseph, he took his parents to him, and said: Come into Egypt safe, if Allah wills?

100. And he placed his parents on the dais and they fell down before him prostrate, and he said: O my father! This is the interpretation of my dream of old. My Lord has made it true, and He has shown me kindness, since He took me out of the prison and has brought you from the desert after Satan had made discord between me and my brothers. My Lord is tender to whom He wills. He is the Knower, the Wise.

101. O my Lord! You have given me (something) of sovereignty and have taught me (something) of the interpretation of events - Creator of the heavens and the earth! You are my Protecting Friend in the world and the Hereafter. Make me to die submissive (to You), and join me to the righteous.

102. This is of the tidings of the Unseen which We inspire in you (Muhammad). You were not present with them when they fixed their plan and they were scheming.

103. And though you try much, most men will not believe.

104. You ask them no fee for it. It is nothing else than a reminder to the peoples.

105. How many a sign is there in the heavens and the earth which they pass by with their faces averted!

106. And most of them believe not in Allah except that they attribute partners (to Him).

107. Do they think themselves secure from the coming on them of a taste of Allah's punishment, or the coming of the Hour suddenly while they are unaware?

108. Say: This is my Way: I call on Allah with sure knowledge, I and who follows me - Glory be to Allah! - and I am not of the idolaters.

109. We sent not before you (any messengers) except men whom We inspired from among the people of the townships - have they not travelled in the land and seen the nature of the consequence for those who were before them? And verily the abode of the Hereafter, for those who ward off (evil), is best. Have you then no sense?

110. Till, when the messengers despaired and thought that they were denied, then came to them Our help, and whom We willed was saved. And Our wrath cannot be averted from the guilty.

111. In their history verily there is a lesson for men of understanding. It is no invented story but a confirmation of the existing (Scripture) and a detailed explanation of everything, and a guidance and a mercy for people who believe.

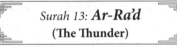

Surah 13: **Ar-Ra'd**
(The Thunder)

Ar-Ra'd, "The Thunder," takes its name from a word in v. 13 The subject is Divine guidance in relation to the law of consequences, it being explained here, as elsewhere in the Qur'an, that there is no partiality or aversion on the part of God, but that reward and punishment are the result of obeying or rejecting natural (or Divine) laws. According to some ancient authorities, it is a Makkan Surah with the exception of two verses revealed at Al-Madinah; according to others, a Madinan Surah with the exception of two verses revealed at Makkah. The very fact of such a wholesale difference of opinion favours the Makkan attribution because there could be no such doubt about a complete Madinan Surah, owing to the great number of witnesses. The Madinan ascription may have arisen from the recognition of some verses by those witnesses as having been revealed at Al-Madinah on a certain occasion.

A late Makkan Surah for the most part.

In the name of Allah,
the Beneficent, the Merciful.

1. *Alif. Lam. Mim. Ra.*[115] These are verses of the Scripture. That which is revealed to you from your Lord is the Truth, but most of mankind believe not.

2. Allah it is Who raised up the heavens without visible supports, then mounted the Throne, and compelled the sun and the moon to be of service, each runs to an appointed term; He orders the course; He details the revelations, that perhaps you may be certain of the meeting with your Lord.

3. And He it is Who spread out the earth and placed in it firm hills and flowing streams, and of all fruits He placed in it two spouses (male and female). He covers the night with the day. In this verily are signs for people who take thought.

4. And in the Earth are neighbouring tracts, vineyards and ploughed lands, and date-palms, like and unlike[116] which are watered with one water. And We have made some of them to excel others in fruit. In this verily are signs for people who have sense.

5. And if you wonder, then wondrous is their saying: When we are dust, are we then (to be raised) in a new creation? Such are they who disbelieve in their Lord; such have carcans on their necks; such are rightful owners of the Fire, they will remain in it.

6. And they ask you to hasten on the evil rather than the good, when exemplary punishments have indeed occurred before them. But your Lord is rich in pardon for mankind despite their wrong, and your Lord is strong in punishment.

7. Those who disbelieve say: If only some sign were sent down upon him from his Lord! You are a warner only, and for every people a guide.

8. Allah Knows that which every female bears and that which the wombs absorb and that which they grow. And everything with Him is measured.

9. He is the Knower of the Invisible and the Visible, the Great, the High Exalted.

10. Alike of you is he who hides the saying and he who noises it abroad, he who lurks in the night and he who goes freely in the daytime.

11. For him are angels ranged before him and behind him, who guard him by Allah's command.[117] Allah changes not the condition of a people until they (first) change that which is in their hearts; and if Allah wills misfortune for a people, there is none that can repel it, nor have they a defender besides Him.

12. He it is Who shows you the lightning, a fear and a hope,[118] and raises the heavy clouds.

13. The thunder hymns His praise and (so do) the angels in awe of Him. He launches the thunder-bolts and strikes

---

115. See *Surah* 2, *Al-Baqarah*, v. 1, footnote.
116. Or it may be, "growing thickly or alone".
117. This is taken by some commentators to refer to "he who goes freely in the daytime" in the previous verse. In that case it would read: "for whom are guards before him and behind him as if to guard him against Allah's commandment."
118. The fear is of the lightning, and the hope is of the rain.

with them whom He will while they dispute (in doubt) concerning Allah, and He is mighty in wrath.

14. To Him is the real prayer. Those to whom they pray besides Allah respond to them not at all, except as (is the response to) one who stretches out his hands towards water (asking) that it may come to his mouth, and it will never reach it. The prayer of disbelievers goes (far) astray.

15. And to Allah falls prostrate whoever is in the heavens and the earth, willingly or unwillingly, as do their shadows in the morning and the evening hours.

16. Say (O Muhammad): Who is Lord of the heavens and the earth? Say: Allah! Say: Do you then take (others) beside Him for protectors, which, even for themselves, have neither benefit nor hurt? Say: Is the blind man equal to the seer, or is darkness equal to light? Or do they assign to Allah partners who created the like of His creation so that the creation (which they made and His creation) seemed alike to them? Say: Allah is the Creator of all things, and He is the One, the Almighty.

17. He sends down water from the sky, so that valleys flow according to their measure, and the flood bears (on its surface) swelling foam - from that which they smelt in the fire in order to make ornaments and tools rises a foam like it - thus Allah coins (the similitude of) the true and the false. Then, as for the foam, it passes away as scum upon the banks, while, as for that which is of

use to mankind, it remains in the earth. Thus Allah coins the similitudes.

18. For those who answered Allah's call is bliss; and for those who answered not His call, if they had all that is in the earth, and with it the like of it, they would offer it as ransom. Such will have a woeful reckoning, and their habitation will be Hell, a dire abode.

19. Is he who knows that what is revealed to you from your Lord is the truth like him who is blind? But only men of understanding heed;

20. Such as keep the pact of Allah, and break not the covenant;

21. Such as unite that which Allah has commanded should be joined, and fear their Lord, and dread a woeful reckoning;

22. Such as persevere in seeking their Lord's Countenance and are regular in prayer and spend of that which We bestow upon them secretly and openly, and overcome evil with good. Theirs will be the sequel of the (heavenly) Home,

23. Gardens of Eden which they enter, along with all who do right of their fathers and their helpers and their seed. The angels enter to them from every gate,

24. (Saying): Peace be to you because you persevered. Ah, passing sweet will be the sequel of the (heavenly) Home.

25. And those who break the covenant of Allah after ratifying it, and sever that which Allah has commanded should be joined, and make mischief in the earth: theirs is the curse and theirs the ill abode.

26. Allah enlarges livelihood for whom He will, and tightens (it for whom He will); and they rejoice in the life of the world, whereas the life of the world is but brief comfort as compared with the Hereafter.

27. Those who disbelieve say: If only a sign were sent down upon him from his Lord! Say: Allah sends whom He will astray, and guides to Himself all who turn (to Him),

28. Who have believed and whose hearts have rest in the remembrance of Allah. Verily in the remembrance of Allah do hearts find rest!

29. Those who believe and do right: Joy is for them, and bliss (their) journey's end.

30. Thus We send you (O Muhammad) to a nation, before whom other nations have passed away, that you may recite to them that which We have inspired in you, while they are disbelievers in the Beneficent. Say: He is my Lord; there is no God except Him. In Him do I put my trust and to Him is my recourse.

31. Had it been possible for a Lecture[119] to cause the mountains to move, or the earth to be torn apart, or the dead to speak, (this Qur'an would have done so). No, but Allah's is the whole command. Do not those who believe know that, had Allah willed, He could have guided all mankind? As for those who disbelieve, disaster ceases not to strike them because of what they do, or it dwells near their home until the threat of Allah comes to pass. Allah fails not to keep the appointed time.

119. Arabic: *Qur'an.*

32. And verily messengers (of Allah) were mocked before you, but long I bore with those who disbelieved. At length I seized them, and how (awful) was My punishment!

33. Is He Who is aware of the outcome of every soul (as he who is aware of nothing)? Yet they ascribe to Allah partners. Say: Name them. Is it that you would inform Him of something which He knows not in the earth? Or is it only a way of speaking? No, but their scheming is made to seem fair for those who disbelieve and they are kept from the right road. He whom Allah sends astray, for him there is no guide.

34. For them there is torment in the life of the world, and verily the doom of the Hereafter is more painful, and they have no defender from Allah.

35. A similitude of the Garden which is promised to those who keep their duty (to Allah): Underneath it rivers flow; its food is everlasting, and its shade; this is the reward of those who keep their duty, while the reward of disbelievers is the Fire.

36. Those to whom We gave the Scripture rejoice in that which is revealed to you. And of the clans there are those who deny some of it. Say: I am commanded only that I serve Allah and ascribe to Him no partner. To Him I call, and to Him is my return.

37. Thus We have revealed it, a decisive utterance in Arabic; and if you should follow their desires after that which has come to you of knowledge, then truly you would have from Allah no protecting friend nor defender.

38. And verily We sent messengers (to mankind) before you, and We appointed for them wives and offspring, and it was not (given) to any messenger that he should bring a sign except by Allah's permission. For everything there is a time prescribed.

39. Allah erases what He will, and establishes (what He will), and with Him is the source of ordinance.

40. Whether We let you see something of that which We have promised them, or make you die (before its happening), yours is but conveyance (of the message). Ours the reckoning.

41. See they not how we aim to the land, reducing it of its outlying parts?[120] (When) Allah dooms there is none that can postpone His doom, and He is swift at reckoning.

42. Those who were before them plotted; but all plotting is Allah's. He knows that which each soul earns. The disbelievers will come to know for whom will be the sequel of the (heavenly) Home.

43. They who disbelieve say: You are no messenger (of Allah). Say: Allah, and whoever has knowledge of the Scripture, is sufficient witness between me and you.

Surah 14: **Ibrahim**
(Abraham)

Ibrahim, so-called from Abraham's prayer in vv. 35-41, at the time when he was establishing his son Ishmael,

---

the ancestor of the Arabs, in the "uncultivable valley" of Makkah. Otherwise the subject of the Surah is the same as that of other Makkan Surahs revealed during the last three years before the Hijrah. The reference in v. 46 to the plot of the idolaters makes it probable that it is among the last of the Makkan revelations.

A late Makkan Surah; except vv. 28-30, revealed at Al-Madinah.

═══════════════════

In the name of Allah,
the Beneficent, the Merciful

1. *Alif. Lam. Ra.*[121] (This is) a Scripture which We have revealed to you (Muhammad) that by it you may bring out mankind from darkness to light, by the permission of their Lord, to the path of the Mighty, the Owner of Praise,

2. Allah, to Whom belongs whatever is in the heavens and whatever is in the earth. And woe to the disbelievers from an awful doom;

3. Those who love the life of the world more than the Hereafter, and prevent (men) from the way of Allah and would have it crooked: such are far astray.

4. And We never sent a messenger except with the language of his people, that he might make (the message) clear for them. Then Allah sends whom He will astray, and guides whom He will. He is the Mighty, the Wise.

5. We verily sent Moses with Our revelations, saying: Bring your people out from darkness to light. And remind them of the days of Allah. In

---

120. If this is a Madinan verse, the reference would be to the spread of Al-Islam; if a Makkan verse it would be to the Persian and the Eastern Roman empires encroaching on Arabia.

121. See *Surah 2, Al- Baqarah,* v. 1, footnote.

it are revelations for each steadfast, thankful (heart).

6. And (remind them) how Moses said to his people: Remember Allah's favour to you when He delivered you from Pharaoh's people who were afflicting you with dreadful torment, and were slaying your sons and sparing your women; that was a tremendous trial from your Lord.

7. And when your Lord proclaimed: If you give thanks, I will give you more; but if you are thankless, My punishment is dire.

8. And Moses said: Though you and all who are in the earth prove thankless, Allah verily is Absolute, Owner of Praise.

9. Has not the history of those before you reached you: the people of Noah, and (the tribes of) 'Aad and Thamud, and those after them? None except Allah knows them. Their messengers came to them with clear proofs, but they thrust their hands into their mouths, and said: We disbelieve in that with which you have been sent, and we are in grave doubt concerning that to which you call us.

10. Their messengers said: Can there be doubt concerning Allah, the Creator of the heavens and the earth? He calls you that He may forgive you your sins and reprieve you to an appointed term. They said: You are but mortals like us, who would gladly turn us away from what our fathers used to worship. Then bring some clear authority.

11. Their messengers said to them: We are but mortals like you, but Allah gives

grace to whom He will of His slaves. It is not for us to bring you an authority unless by the permission of Allah. In Allah let believers put their trust!

12. How should we not put our trust in Allah when He has shown us our ways? We surely will endure the hurt you do us. In Allah let the trusting put their trust!

13. And those who disbelieved said to their messengers: Verily we will drive you out from our land, unless you return to our religion. Then their Lord inspired them, (saying): Verily we shall destroy the wrongdoers,

14. And verily We shall make you to dwell in the land after them. This is for him who fears My Majesty and fears My threats.

15. And they sought help (from their Lord) and every disobedient ruler was brought to nothing;

16. Hell is before him, and he is made to drink a festering water,

17. Which he sips but can hardly swallow, and death comes to him from every side while yet he cannot die, and before him is a harsh doom.

18. A similitude of those who disbelieve in their Lord: Their works are as ashes which the wind blows hard upon a stormy day. They have no control of anything that they have earned. That is the extreme failure.

19. Have you not seen that Allah has created the heavens and the earth with truth? If He will, He can remove you and bring (in) some new creation;

20. And that is no great matter for Allah.

21. They all come before their Lord. Then those who were despised say to those who were scornful: We were to you a following, can you then avert from us anything of Allah's doom? They say: Had Allah guided us, we would have guided you. Whether we rage or patiently endure is (now) all one for us; we have no place of refuge.

22. And Satan says, when the matter has been decided: Allah promised you a promise of truth; and I promised you, then failed you. And I had no power over you except that I called to you and you obeyed me. So blame me not, but blame yourselves. I cannot help you, nor can you help me, I disbelieved in that which you before ascribed to me. For wrongdoers is a painful doom.

23. And those who believed and did good works are made to enter Gardens underneath which rivers flow, in there remaining by permission of their Lord, their greeting in there: Peace!

24. Do you not see how Allah coins a similitude: A goodly saying, as a goodly tree, its root set firm, its branches reaching into heaven,

25. Giving its fruit at every season by permission of its Lord? Allah coins the similitudes for mankind in order that they may reflect.

26. And the similitude of a bad saying is as a bad tree, uprooted from upon the earth, possessing no stability.

27. Allah confirms those who believe by a firm saying in the life of the world and in the Hereafter, and Allah sends wrongdoers astray. And Allah does what He will.

28. Have you not seen those who gave the grace of Allah in exchange for thanklessness and led their people down to the Abode of Loss,

29. (Even to) Hell? They are exposed to it. An unhappy end!

30. And they set up rivals to Allah that they may mislead (men) from His Way. Say: Enjoy life (while you may) for your journey's end will be the Fire.

31. Tell My bondsmen who believe to establish worship and spend of that which We have given them, secretly and publicly, before a day comes when there will be neither bargaining nor befriending.

32. Allah is He Who created the heavens and the earth, and causes water to descend from the sky, by it producing fruits as food for you, and makes the ships to be of service to you, that they may run upon the sea at His command, and has made of service to you the rivers;

33. And makes the sun and the moon, constant in their courses, to be of service to you, and has made of service to you the night and the day.

34. And He gives you of all you ask of Him, and if you would count the bounty of Allah you cannot reckon it. Man is verily a wrong-doer, ungrateful.

35. And when Abraham said: My Lord! Make safe this territory, and preserve me and my sons from serving idols.

36. My Lord! They have led many of mankind astray. But he who follows me, he verily is of me. And he who disobeys me - still You are Forgiving, Merciful.

37. Our Lord! I have settled some of my posterity in an uncultivable valley near to Your holy House,[122] our Lord! That they may establish proper worship; so incline some hearts of men that they may be sympathetic towards them, and provide them with fruits in order that they may be thankful.

38. Our Lord! You know that which we hide and that which we proclaim. Nothing in the earth or in the heaven is hidden from Allah.

39. Praise be to Allah Who has given me, in my old age, Ishmael and Isaac! My Lord is indeed the Hearer of Prayer.

40. My Lord! Make me to establish proper worship, and some of my posterity (also); our Lord! and accept my prayer.

41. Our Lord! Forgive me and my parents and believers on the day when the account is cast.

42. Think not that Allah is unaware of what the wicked do. He only gives them a respite till a day when eyes will stare (in terror),

43. As they come hurrying on in fear, their heads raised, their gaze returning not to them, and their hearts as air.

44. And warn mankind of a day when the doom will come upon them, and those who did wrong will say: Our Lord! Reprieve us for a little while. We will obey Your call and will follow the messengers. (It will be answered): Did you not swear before that there would be no end for you?

45. And (have you not) dwelt in the dwellings of those who wronged

122. The valley of Makkah

themselves (of old) and (has it not) become plain to you how We dealt with them, and made examples for you?

46. Verily they have plotted their plot, and their plot is with Allah, though their plot was one by which the mountains should be moved.

47. So think not that Allah will fail to keep His promise to His messengers. Allah is Mighty, Able to Repay (the wrong).

48. On the day when the earth will be changed to other than the earth, and the heavens (also will be changed) and they will come before Allah, the One, the Almighty,

49. You will see the guilty on that day linked together in chains,

50. Their garment of pitch, and the Fire covering their faces,

51. That Allah may repay each soul what it has earned. Allah is swift at reckoning.

52. This is a clear message for mankind in order that they may be warned by it, and that they may know that He is only One God, and that men of understanding may take heed.

Surah 15: *Al-Hijr*

Al-Hijr (which I take to be a place-name) is so called from vv. 80-84, where the fate of the dwellers at that place is described. The date of revelation is earlier than that of any Makkan Surahs which precede it in the arrangement of the Book, though the subject and the tone are similar, which accounts for its position. Nöldeke places it in his middle group of Makkan Surahs, that is (as far as one can judge from the inclusions), those revealed after the eighth year and before the third year before the Hijrah, and in so doing confirms the judgement of the best Muslim authorities, though some Muslim authorities would place it among the earliest revelations.

It belongs to the middle group of Makkan Surahs.

═══════════

In the name of Allah, the Beneficent, the Merciful

1. *Alif. Lam. Ra.*[123] These are verses of the Scripture and a plain Reading.[124]

2. It may be that those who disbelieve wish ardently that they were Muslims.[125]

3. Let them eat and enjoy life, and let (false) hope deceive them. They will come to know!

4. And We destroyed no township but there was a known decree for it.

5. No nation can outstrip its term nor can they lag behind.

6. And they say: O you to whom the Reminder is revealed, you are indeed a madman!

7. Why do you not bring angels to us, if you are of the truthful?

8. We send not down the angels except with the Fact, and in that case (the disbelievers) would not be tolerated.

9. We, even We, reveal the Reminder, and We verily are its Guardian.

123. See *Surah 2, Al-Baqarah,* v. 1, footnote.
124. Arabic: *Qur'an.*
125. Or "those who have surrendered."

10. We verily sent (messengers) before you among the factions of the men of old.

11. And never came there to them a messenger but they did mock him.

12. Thus do We make it traverse the hearts of the guilty:

13. They believe not in it, though the example of the men of old has gone before.

14. And even if We opened to them a gate of heaven and they kept mounting through it,

15. They would say: Our sight is wrong - no, but we are people bewitched.

16. And verily in the heaven We have set mansions of the stars, and We have beautified it for onlookers.

17. And We have guarded it from every outcast devil,

18. Except him who steals the hearing, and them does a clear flame pursue.

19. And the earth We have spread out, and placed in it firm hills, and caused each beautiful thing to grow in it.

20. And we have given to you livelihoods in it, and to those for whom you provide not.

21. And there is not a thing but with Us are the stores of it. And we send it not down except in appointed measure.

22. And We send the winds fertilising, and cause water to descend from the sky, and give it you to drink. It is not you who are the holders of the store of it.

23. And it is We, even We, Who give life and give death, and We are the Inheritors.

24. And verily We know the eager among you and verily We know the laggards.

25. Your Lord will gather them together. He is Wise, Aware.

26. Verily We created man of potter's clay of black mud altered,

27. And the jinn We created before of essential fire.

28. And (remember) when your Lord said to the angels: I am creating a mortal out of potter's clay of black mud altered,

29. So, when I have made him and have breathed into him of My Spirit, do you fall down, prostrating yourselves to him.

30. So the angels fell prostrate, all of them together

31. Except Iblis. He refused to be among the prostrate.

32. He said: O Iblis! What is the matter with you that you are not among the prostrate?

33. He said: I am not one to prostrate myself to a mortal whom You have created out of potter's clay of black mud altered!

34. He said: Then go you out from here, for you are outcast.

35. And the curse shall be upon you till the Day of Judgement.

36. He said: My Lord! Reprieve me till the day when they are raised.

37. He said: Then you are of those reprieved

38. Till the Day of appointed time.

39. He said: My Lord! Because You have sent me astray, I verily shall adorn the path of error for them in the earth, and shall mislead them every one,

40. Except such of them as are Your perfectly devoted slaves.

41. He (Allah) said: This is a right course incumbent upon Me:

42. As for My slaves, you have no power over any of them except such of the obstinate as follow you,

43. And for all such, Hell will be the promised place.

44. It has seven gates, and each gate has an appointed portion.

45. Those who ward off (evil) are among gardens and water springs.

46. (And it is said to them): Enter them in peace, secure.

47. And We remove whatever resentment may be in their hearts. As brothers, face to face, (they rest) on couches raised.

48. Toil comes not to them there, nor will they be expelled from there.

49. Announce, (O Muhammad) to My slaves that verily I am the Forgiving, the Merciful,

50. And that My doom is the painful doom.

51. And tell them of Abraham's guests,

52. (How) when they came in to him, and said: Peace. He said: We are afraid of you.

53. They said: Be not afraid! We bring you good tidings of a boy possessing wisdom.

54. He said: Do you bring me good tidings (of a son) when old age has overtaken me? Of what then can you bring good tidings?

55. They said: We bring you good tidings in truth. So be not you of the despairing.

56. He said: And who despairs of the mercy of his Lord except those who are astray?

57. He said: And afterwards what is your business, O you messengers (of Allah)?

58. They said: We have been sent to a guilty people,

59. (All) except the family of Lot - from them we shall deliver everyone,

60. Except his wife, of whom We had decreed that she should be of those who stay behind.

61. And when the messengers came to the family of Lot,

62. He said: You are people unknown (to me).

63. They said: No, but we bring you that concerning which they keep disputing,

64. And bring you the Truth, and we are truth-tellers.

65. So travel with your household in a portion of the night, and follow their backs. Let none of you turn round, but go where you are commanded.

66. And We made plain the case to him, that the root of them (who did wrong) was to be cut off at early morn.

67. And the people of the city came, rejoicing at the news (of new arrivals).

68. He said: They are my guests. Offend me not!

69. And keep your duty to Allah, and shame me not!

70. They said; Have we not forbidden you from (entertaining) anyone?

71. He said: Here are my daughters, if you must be doing (so).

72. By your life (O Muhammad) they moved blindly in the frenzy of approaching death.

73. Then the (Awful) Cry overtook them at sunrise.

74. And We utterly defeated them, and We rained upon them stones of heated clay.

75. In it verily are signs for those who read the signs.

76. And it is upon a road still unerased.

77. In it is indeed a sign for believers.

78. And the dwellers in the wood[126] indeed were evildoers.

79. So we took vengeance on them; and they both are on a high-road plain to see.

80. And the dwellers in Al-Hijr denied (Our) messengers.

81. And we gave them Our revelations, but they were averse to them.

82. And they used to hew out dwellings from the hills, (in which they dwelt) secure.

83. But the (Awful) Cry overtook them at the morning hour,

84. And that which they used to count as gain benefitted them not.

85. We created not the heavens and the earth and all that is between them except with truth, and the Hour is surely coming. So forgive, (O Muhammad), with a gracious forgiveness.

86. Your Lord! He is the All-Wise Creator.

126. Another name for Midian.

87. We have given you seven of the oft-repeated (verses)[127] and the great Qur'an.

88. Strain not your eyes towards that which We cause some wedded pairs among them to enjoin, and be not grieved on their account, and lower your wing (in tenderness) for the believers.

89. And say: I, even I, am a plain warner,

90. Such as We send down for those who make division,

91. Those who break the Qur'an into parts.

92. Them, by your Lord, We shall question, every one,

93. Of what they used to do.

94. So proclaim that which you are commanded, and withdraw from the idolaters.

95. We defend you from the mockers,

96. Who set some other god along with Allah. But they will come to know.

97. Well do We know that your chest is oppressed by what they say,

98. But hymn the praise of your Lord, and be of those who make prostration (to Him).

99. And serve your Lord till the Inevitable[128] comes to you.

Surah 16: *An-Nahl*
(The Bee)

An-Nahl, "The Bee" takes its name from v. 68, where the activities of the Bee are mentioned as a type of duty and of usefulness. It calls attention to God's providence for creation, and to His guidance to mankind as a necessary part of it, and warns disbelievers in that guidance of a folly in rejecting which would be as great as the rejection of food and drink. The Surah is ascribed to the last Makkan group, though some ancient authorities regard the ascription as valid only for vv. 1-40, and consider the whole latter portion as revealed at Al-Madinah. The only verse in the Surah which is self-evidently of Madinan revelation is v. 110, where those who escaped persecution are said to have fought; for in the Makkan period fighting was unlawful for the Muslims, though many of them fled from persecution, taking refuge in Abyssinia.

A late Makkan Surah, with the exception of v. 110, which must have been revealed at Al-Madinah not earlier than the year 2 A.H., and possibly many other verses towards the end.

In the name of Allah, the Beneficent, the Merciful.

1. The commandment of Allah will come to pass, so seek not you to hasten it. Glorified and Exalted is He above all that they associate (with Him).

2. He sends down the angels with the Spirit of His command to whom He will of His bondsmen, (saying): Warn mankind that there is no God except Me, so keep your duty to Me.

3. He has created the heavens and the earth with truth. High is He Exalted above all that they associate (with Him).

---

127. According to a strong tradition, the reference is to *Surah 1, Al-Fatihah,* which consists of seven verses, and forms a part of every Muslim prayer.
128. *i.e.* death.

4. He has created man from a drop of fluid, yet behold! He is an open opponent.

5. And the cattle He has created, from which you have warm clothing and uses, and of which you eat;

6. And in which is beauty for you, when you bring them home, and when you take them out to pasture.

7. And they bear your loads for you to a land you could not reach except with great trouble to yourselves. Your Lord is Full of Pity, Merciful.

8. And horses and mules and donkeys (He has created) that you may ride them, and for ornament. And He creates that which you know not.

9. And Allah's is the direction of the way, and some (roads) go not straight. And had He willed He would have led you all aright.

10. He it is Who sends down water from the sky, from which you have drink, and from which are trees on which you send your beasts to pasture.[129]

11. With it He causes crops to grow for you, and the olive and the date-palm and grapes and all kinds of fruit. In this is indeed a sign for people who reflect.

12. And He has compelled the night and the day and the sun and the moon to be of service to you, and the stars are made subservient by His command. In this indeed are signs for people who have sense.

---

129. There being hardly any herbage in Arabia, the cattle eat the leaves of trees and shrubs.

13. And whatever He has created for you in the earth of diverse hues, in it is indeed a sign for people who take heed.

14. And He it is Who has compelled the sea to be of service so that you eat fresh meat from there, and bring out from there ornaments which you wear. And you see the ships ploughing it that you (mankind) may seek of His bounty and that perhaps you may give thanks.

15. And He has cast into the earth firm hills that it quake not with you, and streams and roads that you may find a way.

16. And landmarks (too), and by the star they find a way.

17. Is He then Who creates as him who creates not? Will you not then remember?

18. And if you would count the favour of Allah you cannot reckon it. Allah is indeed Forgiving, Merciful.

19. And Allah knows that which you keep hidden and that which you proclaim.

20. Those to whom they call besides Allah created nothing, but are themselves created.

21. (They are) dead, not living. And they know not when they will be raised.

22. Your God is One God. But as for those who believe not in the Hereafter, their hearts refuse to know, for they are proud.

23. Assuredly, Allah knows that which they keep hidden and that which they proclaim. He loves not the proud.

24. And when it is said to them: What has your Lord revealed? They say: (mere) fables of the men of old,

25. That they may bear their burdens undiminished on the Day of Resurrection, with somewhat of the burdens of those whom they mislead without knowledge. Ah! evil is that which they bear!

26. Those before them plotted, so Allah struck at the foundations of their building, and then the roof fell down upon them from above them, and the doom came on them from where they knew not;

27. Then on the Day of Resurrection He will disgrace them and will say: Where are My partners, for whose sake you opposed (My guidance)? Those who have been given knowledge will say: Disgrace this day and evil are upon the disbelievers,

28. Whom the angels cause to die while they are wronging themselves. Then they will make full submission (saying): We used not to do any wrong. No! Surely Allah is Knower of what you used to do.

29. So enter the gates of Hell, to dwell in it forever. Woeful indeed will be the lodging of the arrogant.

30. And it is said to those who ward off (evil): What has your Lord revealed? They say: Good. For those who do good in this world there is a good (reward), and the home of the Hereafter will be better. Pleasant indeed will be the home of those who ward off (evil) -

31. Gardens of Eden which they enter, underneath which rivers flow, in which they have what they will. Thus Allah repays those who ward off (evil),

32. Those whom the angels cause to die (when they are) good. They say: Peace be to you! Enter the Garden because of what you used to do.

33. Do they wait for anything except that the angels should come to them or your Lord's command should come to pass? Even so did those before them. Allah wronged them not, but they did wrong themselves,

34. So that the evil of what they did struck them, and that which they used to mock surrounded them.

35. And the idolaters say: Had Allah willed, we would not have worshipped anything beside Him, we and our fathers, nor would we have forbidden anything without (command from) Him. Even so did those before them. Are the messengers charged with anything except plain conveyance (of the message)?

36. And verily We have raised in every nation a messenger, (proclaiming): Serve Allah and shun false gods. Then some of them (there were) whom Allah guided, and some of them (there were) upon whom error had just hold. Do simply travel in the land and see the nature of the consequence for the deniers!

37. Even if you (O Muhammad) desire their right guidance, still Allah assuredly will not guide him who misleads. Such have no helpers.

38. And they swear by Allah their most binding oaths (that) Allah will not raise up him who dies. No, but it is a promise (binding) upon Him in truth, but most of mankind know not,

39. That He may explain to them that in which they differ, and that those who disbelieved may know that they were liars.

40. And Our word to a thing, when We intend it, is only that We say to it: Be! and it is.

41. And those who became emigrants for the cause of Allah after they had been oppressed, We verily shall give them goodly lodging in the world, and surely the reward of the Hereafter is greater, if they but knew;

42. Such as are steadfast and put their trust in Allah.

43. And We sent not (as Our messengers) before you other than men whom We inspired - ask the followers of the Remembrance if you know not! -

44. With clear proofs and writings; and We have revealed to you the Remembrance that you may explain to mankind that which has been revealed for them, and that perhaps they may reflect.

45. Are they who plan ill-deeds then secure that Allah will not cause the earth to swallow them, or that the doom will not come on them from where they know not?

46. Or that He will not seize them in their going to and fro so that there be no escape for them?

47. Or that He will not seize them with a gradual wasting? Your Lord is indeed Full of Pity, Merciful.

48. Have they not observed all things that Allah has created, how their shadows incline to the right and to the left, making prostration to Allah, and they are lowly?

49. And to Allah makes prostration whatever is in the heavens and whatever is in the earth of living creatures, and the angels (also), and they are not proud.

50. They fear their Lord above them, and do what they are commanded.

51. Allah has said: Choose not two gods. There is only One God. So of Me, Me only, be in awe.

52. To Him belongs whatever is in the heavens and the earth, and religion is His forever. Will you then fear any other than Allah?

53. And whatever of comfort you enjoy, it is from Allah. Then, when misfortune reaches you, to Him you call for help.

54. And afterwards, when He has rid you of the misfortune, look! a set of you attribute partners to their Lord,

55. So as to deny that which We have given them. Then enjoy life (while you may), for you will come to know.

56. And they assign a portion of that which We have given them to what they know not. By Allah! but you will indeed be asked concerning (all) that you used to invent.

57. And they assign to Allah daughters - May He be Glorified! - and to themselves what they desire;

58. If one of them receives tidings of the birth of a female, his face remains darkened, and he is angry inwardly.

59. He hides himself from the people because of the evil of that of which he has had tidings, (asking himself): Shall he keep it in contempt, or bury it beneath the dust. Verily evil is their judgement.

60. For those who believe not in the Hereafter is an evil similitude, and Allah's is the Sublime Similitude. He is the Mighty, the Wise.

61. If Allah were to take mankind to task for their wrong-doing, he would not leave on it a living creature, but He reprieves them to an appointed term, and when their term comes they cannot put (it) off an hour nor (yet) advance (it).

62. And they assign to Allah that which they (themselves) dislike, and their tongues explain the lie that the better portion will be theirs. Assuredly theirs will be the Fire, and they will be abandoned.

63. By Allah, We verily sent messengers to the nations before you, but the devil made their deeds fair-seeming to them. So he is their patron this day, and theirs will be a painful doom.

64. And We have revealed the Scripture to you only that you may explain to them that in which they differ, and (as) a guidance and a mercy for a people who believe.

65. Allah sends down water from the sky and with it revives the earth after her death. In this is indeed a sign for a people who hear.

66. And in the cattle there is a lesson for you. We give you to drink of that which is in their bellies, from between the refuse and the blood, pure milk palatable to the drinkers.

67. And of the fruits of the date-palm, and grapes, from which you derive strong drink and (also) good nourishment. In it is indeed a sign for people who have sense.

68. And your Lord inspired the bee, saying: Choose habitations in the hills and in the trees and in that which they thatch;

69. Then eat of all fruits, and follow the ways of your Lord, made smooth (for you). There comes out from their bellies a drink of diverse hues, in which is healing for mankind. In this is indeed a sign for people who reflect.

70. And Allah creates you, then causes you to die, and among you is he who is brought back to the most abject stage of life, so that he knows nothing after (having had) knowledge. Allah is Knower, Powerful.

71. And Allah has favoured some of you above others in provision. Now those who are more favoured will by no means hand over their provision to those (slaves) whom their right hands possess, so that they may be equal with them in respect of it. Is it then the grace of Allah that they deny?

72. And Allah has given you wives of your own kind, and has given you, from your wives, sons and grandsons, and has made provision of good things for you. Is it then in vanity that they believe and in the grace of Allah that they disbelieve?

73. And they worship besides Allah that which owns no provision whatever for them from the heavens or the earth, nor have they (whom they worship) any power.

74. So coin not similitudes for Allah. Allah knows; you know not.

75. Allah coins a similitude: (on the one hand) a (mere) slave, who has control of nothing, and (on the other hand) one on whom We have bestowed a fair provision from Us, and he spends of it secretly and openly. Are they equal? Praise be to Allah! But most of them know not.

76. And Allah coins a similitude: Two men, one of them dumb, having control of nothing, and he is a burden on his owner; whichever way he directs him to go, he brings no good. Is he equal with one who enjoins justice and follows a straight path (of conduct)?

77. And to Allah belongs the Unseen of the heavens and the earth, and the matter of the Hour (of Doom) is but as a twinkling of the eye, or it is nearer still. Allah is Able to do all things.

78. And Allah brought you out from the wombs of your mothers knowing nothing, and gave you hearing and sight and hearts, that perhaps you might give thanks.

79. Have they not seen the birds obedient[130] in mid-air? None holds them except Allah. In this, verily, are signs for a people who believe.

80. And Allah has given you in your houses an abode, and has given you (also), of the hides of cattle, houses[131] which you find light (to carry) on the day of migration and on the day of pitching camp; and of their wool and their fur and their hair, an ornament and comfort for a while.

81. And Allah has given you, of that which He has created, shelter from the sun; and has given you places of refuge in the mountains, and has given you coats to ward off the heat from you, and coats (of armour) to save you from your own foolhardiness. Thus does He perfect His favour to you, in order that you may surrender (to Him).

82. Then, if they turn away, your duty (O Muhammad) is but plain conveyance (of the message).

83. They know the favour of Allah and then deny it. Most of them are ungrateful.

84. And (consider) the day when We raise up of every nation a witness, then there is no leave for disbelievers, nor are they allowed to make amends.

85. And when those who did wrong see the doom, it will not be made light for them, nor will they be reprieved.

86. And when those who ascribed partners to Allah see those partners of theirs, they will say: Our Lord! these are our partners to whom we used to call instead of You. But they will fling at them the saying: You verily are liars!

87. And they offer to Allah submission on that day, and all that they used to invent has failed them.

---

130. *Lit.* made subservient - to the Law of Allah. 131. *i.e.* tents.

88. For those who disbelieve and prevent (men) from the way of Allah, We add doom to doom because they worked corruption,

89. And (consider) the day when We raise in every nation a witness against them of their own people, and We bring you (Muhammad) as a witness against these. And We reveal the Scripture to you as an exposition of all things, and a guidance and a mercy and good tidings for those who have surrendered (to Allah).

90. Allah enjoins justice and kindness, and giving to kindred, and forbids lewdness and abomination and wickedness. He exhorts you in order that you may take heed.[132]

91. Fulfil the covenant of Allah when you have covenanted, and break not your oaths after the affirmation of them, and after you have made Allah surety over you. Allah knows what you do.

92. And be not like her who unravels the thread, after she has made it strong, to thin filaments, making your oaths a deceit between you because of a nation being more numerous than (another) nation. Allah only tries you by it, and He verily will explain to you on the Day of Resurrection that in which you differed.

93. Had Allah willed He could have made you (all) one nation, but He sends whom He will astray and guides whom He will, and you will indeed be asked of what you used to do.

94. Make not your oaths a deceit between you, lest a foot should slip after being firmly planted and you should taste evil inasmuch as you prevented (men) from the way of Allah, and yours should be an awful doom.

95. And purchase not a small gain at the price of Allah's covenant. That which Allah has is better for you, if you did only know.

96. That which you have wastes away, and that which Allah has remains. And verily We shall pay those who are steadfast a recompense in proportion to the best of what they used to do.

97. Whoever does right, whether male or female, and is a believer, him verily we shall revive with good life, and We shall pay them a recompense in proportion to the best of what they used to do.

98. And when you recite the Qur'an, seek refuge in Allah from Satan the outcast.

99. He has no power over those who believe and put trust in their Lord.

100. His power is only over those who make a friend of him, and those who ascribe partners to Him (Allah).

101. And when We put a revelation in place of (another) revelation, - and Allah knows best what He reveals - they say: You are but inventing. Most of them know not.

102. Say: The Holy Spirit[133] has delivered it from your Lord with truth, that it may confirm (the faith of) those who believe, and as guidance

---

132. Since the time of Omar II the Omayyad, this verse has been recited at the end of every weekly sermon in all Sunni congregations.

133. *i.e.* Gabriel.

and good tidings for those who have surrendered[134] (to Allah).

103. And We know well that they say: Only a man teaches him. The speech of him at whom they falsely hint is foreign, and this is clear Arabic speech.[135]

104. Those who disbelieve the revelations of Allah, Allah guides them not and theirs will be a painful doom.

105. Only they invent falsehood who believe not Allah's revelations, and (only) they are the liars.

106. Whoever disbelieves in Allah after his belief - except him who is forced to it and whose heart is still content with the Faith - but who finds ease in disbelief: On them is wrath from Allah. Theirs will be an awful doom.

107. That is because they have chosen the life of the world rather than the Hereafter, and because Allah guides not the disbelieving people.

108. Such are they whose hearts and ears and eyes Allah has sealed. And such are the heedless.

109. Assuredly in the Hereafter they are the losers.

110. Then your Lord - for those who became emigrants after they had been persecuted, and then fought and were steadfast - your Lord afterwards is (for them) indeed Forgiving, Merciful.

111. On the Day when every soul will come pleading for itself, and every

soul will be repaid what it did, and they will not be wronged.

112. Allah coins a similitude: A township that dwelt secure and well content, its provision coming to it in abundance from every side, but it disbelieved in Allah's favours, so Allah made it experience the garment of shortage and fear because of what they used to do.

113. And verily there had come to them a messenger from among them, but they had denied him, and so the torment seized them while they were wrongdoers.

114. So eat of the lawful and good food which Allah has provided for you, and thank the bounty of your Lord if it is Him you serve.

115. He has forbidden for you only carrion and blood and swine flesh and that which has been sanctified in the name of any other than Allah; but he who is driven to it, neither craving nor transgressing, then Allah is Forgiving, Merciful.

116. And speak not, concerning that which your own tongues qualify (as clean or unclean), the falsehood: "This is lawful, and this is forbidden," so that you invent a lie against Allah. Those who invent a lie against Allah will not succeed.

117. A brief enjoyment (will be theirs); and theirs is a painful doom.

118. And to those who are Jews We have forbidden that which We have already related to you. And We wronged them not, but they used to wrong themselves.

134. Arabic: *Muslimin.*

135. Among the various attempts of the idolaters to deride the Qur'an was the charge that a Christian slave among the earliest converts taught it to the Prophet. The same slave suffered cruel persecution for his belief in the Divine Inspiration of the Qur'an.

119. Then your Lord - for those who do evil in ignorance and afterwards repent and amend - (for them) your Lord is afterwards indeed Forgiving, Merciful.

120. Abraham was a nation obedient to Allah, by nature upright, and he was not of the idolaters;

121. Thankful for His bounties; He chose him and He guided him to a straight path.

122. And We gave him good in the world, and in the Hereafter he is among the righteous.

123. And afterwards We inspired you (Muhammad, saying): Follow the religion of Abraham, as one by nature upright. He was not of the idolaters.

124. The Sabbath was appointed only for those who differed concerning it, and your Lord will judge between them on the Day of Resurrection concerning that in which they used to differ.

125. Call to the Way of your Lord with wisdom and fair exhortation, and reason with them in the best way. Your Lord is Best Aware of him who strays from His Way, and He is Best Aware of those who go aright.

126. If you punish, then punish with the like of that with which you were afflicted. But if you endure patiently, verily it is better for the patient.

127. Endure patiently (O Muhammad). Your endurance is only by (the help of) Allah. Grieve not for them, and be not in distress because of that which they devise.

128. Allah is with those who keep their duty to Him and those who are doers of good.

Surah 17: **Bani Israel** (The Children of Israel)

Bani Israel, "The Children of Israel," begins and ends with references to the Israelites. v. 1 relates to the Prophet's vision, in which he was carried by night upon a heavenly steed to the Temple of Jerusalem, from where he was carried up through the seven heavens to the very presence of God. The Surah may be taken as belonging to the middle group of Makkan Surahs, except v. 81, or, according to other commentators, vv. 76-82, revealed at Al-Madinah.

===

In the name of Allah, the Beneficent, the Merciful.

1. Glorified is He Who carried His servant by night from the Inviolable Place of Worship[136] to the Far distant place of worship[137] the neighbourhood of which We have blessed, that We might show him of Our signs! He, only He, is the Hearer, the Seer.

2. We gave to Moses the Scripture, and We appointed it a guidance for the children of Israel, saying: Choose no guardian besides Me.

3. (They were) the seed of those whom We carried (in the ship) along with Noah. He was a grateful slave.

4. And We decreed for the Children of Israel in the Scripture: You verily will work corruption in the earth twice, and you will become great tyrants.

136. Makkah.
137. Jerusalem.

5. So when the time for the first of the two came, We roused against you slaves of Ours of great might who ravaged (your) country, and it was a threat performed.

6. Then We gave you once again your turn against them, and We aided you with wealth and children and made you more in soldiery.

7. (Saying): If you do good, you do good for your own souls, and if you do evil, it is for them (in like manner). So, when the time for the second (of the judgements) came (We roused against you others of Our slaves) to ravage you, and to enter the Temple even as they entered it the first time, and to lay waste all that they conquered with an utter wasting.

8. It may be that your Lord will have mercy on you, but if you repeat (the crime) We shall repeat (the punishment), and We have appointed Hell a dungeon for the disbelievers.

9. This Qur'an guides to that which is straightest, and gives tidings to the believers who do good works that theirs will be a great reward.

10. And that those who believe not in the Hereafter, for them We have prepared a painful doom.

11. Man prays for evil as he prays for good; for man was ever hasty.

12. And We appoint the night and the day two signs. Then We make dark the sign of the night, and We make the sign of the day sight-giving, that you may seek bounty from your Lord, and that you may know the computation of the years, and the reckoning; and everything We have explained with a clear explanation.

13. And every man's fate We have fastened to his own neck, and We shall bring out for him on the Day of Resurrection a book which he will find wide open.

14. (And it will be said to him): Read your Book. Your soul suffices as reckoner against you this day.

15. Whoever goes right, it is only for (the good of) his own soul that he goes right, and whoever errs, errs only to his hurt. No laden soul can bear another's load, We never punish until We have sent a messenger.

16. And when We would destroy a township, We send commandment to its people who live at ease, and afterwards they commit abomination in it, and so the Word (of doom) has effect for it, and We annihilate it with complete annihilation.

17. How many generations have We destroyed since Noah! And Allah suffices as Knower and Beholder of the sins of His slaves.

18. Whoever desires that (life) which hastens away, We hasten for him in it what We will for whom We please. And afterwards We have appointed for him Hell; he will endure the heat of it, condemned, rejected.

19. And whoever desires the Hereafter and strives for it with the effort necessary, being a believer; for such, their effort finds favour (with their Lord).

20. Each We supply, both these and those, from the bounty of your Lord. And the bounty of your Lord can never be walled up.

21. See how We prefer one of them above another, and verily the Hereafter will be greater in degrees and greater in preferment.

22. Set not up with Allah any other god (O man) lest you sit down rebuked, forsaken.

23. Your Lord has decreed, that you worship none except Him, and (that you show) kindness to parents. If one of them or both of them attain old age with you, say not "Fie" to them nor repulse them, but speak to them a gracious word.

24. And lower to them the wing of submission through mercy, and say: My Lord! Have mercy on them both as they did care for me when I was little.

25. Your Lord is Best Aware of what is in your minds. If you are righteous, then He was ever Forgiving to those who turn (to Him).

26. Give the kinsman his due, and the needy, and the wayfarer, and squander not (your wealth) in wastefulness.

27. The squanderers were ever brothers of the devils, and the devil was ever ungrateful to his Lord.

28. But if you turn away from them, seeking mercy from your Lord, for which you hope, then speak to them a reasonable word.

29. And let not your hand be chained to your neck nor open it with a complete opening, lest you sit down rebuked, denuded.

30. Your Lord enlarges the provision for whom He wills, and tightens (it for whom He wills). He was ever Knower, Seer of His slaves.

31. Slay not your children, fearing a fall to poverty, We shall provide for them and for you. The slaying of them is a great sin.

32. And come not near to adultery. It is an abomination and an evil way.

33. And slay not the life which Allah has forbidden except with right. Who is slain wrongfully, We have given power to his heir, but let him not commit excess in slaying. He will be helped.

34. Come not near the wealth of the orphan except with that which is better, till he comes to strength; and keep the covenant. Of the covenant it will be asked.

35. Fill the measure when you measure, and weigh with a right balance; that is proper, and better in the end.

36. (O man), follow not that of which you have no knowledge. The hearing and the sight and the heart - of each of these it will be asked.

37. And walk not in the earth exultant. You cannot split the earth, nor can you stretch to the height of the hills.

38. The evil of all that is hateful in the sight of your Lord.

39. This is (part) of that wisdom with which your Lord has inspired you (O Muhammad). And set not up with Allah any other god, lest you be cast into Hell, rebuked, abandoned.

40. Has your Lord then distinguished you (O men of Makkah) by giving you sons, and has chosen for Himself females from among the angels? Verily you speak an awful word!

41. We verily have displayed (Our warnings) in this Qur'an that they may take heed, but it increases them in nothing except aversion.

42. Say (O Muhammad, to the disbelievers): If there were other gods along with Him, as they say, then they would have sought a way against the Lord of the Throne.

43. Glorified is He, and High Exalted above what they say!

44. The seven heavens and the earth and all that is in it praise Him, and there is not a thing but hymns His praise; but you understand not their praise. He is ever Clement, Forgiving.

45. And when you recite the Qur'an We place between you and those who believe not in the Hereafter a hidden barrier;

46. And We place upon their hearts veils lest they should understand it, and in their ears a deafness; and when you make mention of your Lord alone in the Qur'an, they turn their backs in aversion.

47. We are Best Aware of what they wish to hear when they give ear to you and when they take secret counsel, when the evildoers say: You only follow a man who is bewitched.

48. See what similitudes they coin for you, and thus are all astray, and cannot find a road!

49. And they say: When we are bones and fragments, shall we be raised up as a new creation?

50. Say: Be you stones or iron.

51. Or some created thing that is yet greater in your thoughts! Then they will say: Who shall bring us back (to life). Say: He Who created you at the first. Then they will shake their heads at you, and say: When will it be? Say: It will perhaps be soon;

52. A day when He will call you and you will answer with His praise, and you will think that you have stayed but a little while.

53. Tell My bondsmen to speak that which is better. The devil sows discord among them. The devil is for man an open foe.

54. Your Lord is Best Aware of you. If He will, He will have mercy on you, or if He will, He will punish you. We have not sent you (O Muhammad) as a guardian over them.

55. And your Lord is Best Aware of all who are in the heavens and the earth. And we preferred some of the prophets above others, and to David We gave the Psalms.

56. Say: Call to those (saints and angels) whom you assume (to be gods) beside Him, yet they have no power to rid you of misfortune nor to change.

57. Those to whom they call seek the way of approach to their Lord, which of them shall be the nearest; they hope for His mercy and they fear His doom. The doom of your Lord is to be shunned.

58. There is not a township[138] but We shall destroy it before the Day of Resurrection, or punish it with dire punishment. That is set out in the Book (of Our decrees).

138. Or "community".

59. Nothing hinders Us from sending signs, except that the people of old denied them. And We gave Thamud the she-camel - a clear sign - but they did wrong in respect of her. We send not signs except to warn.

60. And (it was a warning) when We told you: Your Lord encompasses mankind, and We appointed the vision[139] which We showed you as an ordeal for mankind, and (likewise) the Accursed Tree in the Qur'an.[140] We warn them, but it increases them in nothing except gross impiety.

61. And when We said to the angels: Fall down prostrate before Adam, and they fell prostrate all except Iblis, he said: Shall I fall prostrate before that which You have created of clay?

62. He said: Do You see this (creature) whom You have honoured above me, if You give me grace until the Day of Resurrection I verily will seize his seed, except a few.

63. He said: Go, and whoever of them follows you - Hell will be your payment, ample payment.

64. And excite any of them whom you can with your voice, and urge your horse and foot against them, and be a partner in their wealth and children, and promise them. Satan promises them only to deceive.

65. My (faithful) bondsmen - over them you have no power, and your Lord suffices as (their) guardian.

---

139. The Prophet's vision of his ascent through the seven heavens.
140. See *Surah* 44, *Ad-Dukhan*, vv. 43-49.

66. (O mankind), your Lord is He Who drives for you the ship upon the sea that you may seek of His bounty. He was ever Merciful towards you.

67. And when harm touches you upon the sea, all to whom you call (for help) fail except Him (alone), but when He brings you safe to land, you turn away, for man was ever thankless.

68. Do you then feel secure that He will not cause a slope of the land to engulf you, or send a sand-storm upon you, and then you will find that you have no protector?

69. Or do you feel secure that He will not return you to that (plight) a second time, and send against you a hurricane of wind and drown you for your thanklessness, and then you will not find in there that you have any avenger against Us?

70. Verily We have honoured the children of Adam. We carry them on the land and the sea, and have made provision of good things for them, and have preferred them above many of those whom We created with a marked preferment.

71. On the day when We shall summon all men with their record, whoever is given his book in his right hand - such will read their book and they will not be wronged a shred.

72. Whoever is blind here, will be blind in the Hereafter, and yet further from the road.

73. And they indeed strove hard to divert you (Muhammad) away from that with which We have inspired you, that you should invent other than it against Us; and then they would have accepted you as a friend.[141]

74. And if We had not made you wholly firm you might almost have inclined to them a little.

75. Then We would have made you taste a double (punishment) of living and a double (punishment) of dying, then you would have found no helper against Us.

76. And they indeed wished to scare you from the land that they might drive you out from there, and then they would have stayed (there) but a little after you.[142]

77. (Such was Our) method in the case of those whom We sent before you (to mankind), and you will not find for Our method anything of power to change

78. Establish worship at the going down of the sun until the dark of night, and (the recital of) the Qur'an at dawn. (The recital of) the Qur'an at dawn is ever witnessed.

79. And some part of the night awake for it, a largesse for you. It may be that your Lord will raise you to a praised rank.

80. And say: My Lord! Cause me to come in with a firm incoming and to go out with a firm outgoing. And give me from Your presence a sustaining Power.

81. And say: Truth has come and falsehood has vanished away. Falsehood is ever bound to vanish.[143]

82. And We reveal of the Qur'an that which is a healing and a mercy for believers though it increases the evildoers in nothing except ruin.

83. And when We make life pleasant to man, he turns away and is averse; and when ill touches him he is in despair.

84. Say: Each one does according to his rule of conduct, and your Lord is Best Aware of him whose way is right.

85. They are asking you concerning the Spirit. Say: The Spirit is by command of my Lord, and of knowledge you have been given but little.

86. And if We willed, We could withdraw that which We have revealed to you, then you would find no guardian for you against Us in respect of it.

87. (It is nothing) except mercy from your Lord. His kindness to you was ever great.[144]

88. Say: Verily, though mankind and the jinn should assemble to produce the like of this Qur'an, they could not produce the like of it though they were helpers one of another.

89. And verily We have displayed for mankind in this Qur'an all kinds of similitudes, but most of mankind refuse anything except disbelief.

---

141. The idolaters more than once offered to compromise with the Prophet.

142. If, as the *Jalaleyn* declare, vv. 76-82 were revealed at Al-Madinah the reference here is to the plotting of the Jews and Hypocrites.

143. These words were recited by the Prophet when he witnessed the destruction of the idols around the Ka'bah after the conquest of Makkah.

144. Vv. 85, 86 and 87 are said to have been revealed in answer to the third question which some Jewish rabbis prompted the idolaters to ask, the first two questions being answered in the following *Surah*.

90. And they say: We will not put faith in you till you cause a spring to gush out from the earth for us;

91. Or you have a garden of date-palms and grapes, and cause rivers to gush out in it abundantly;

92. Or you cause the heaven to fall upon us piecemeal, as you have pretended, or bring Allah and the angels as an authority;

93. Or you have a house of gold; or you ascend up into heaven, and even then we will put no faith in your ascension till you bring down for us a book that we can read. Say (O Muhammad): My Lord be Glorified! Am I anything except a mortal messenger?

94. And nothing prevented mankind from believing when the guidance came to them, except that they said: Has Allah sent a mortal as (His) messenger?

95. Say: If there were in the earth angels walking secure, We would have sent down for them from heaven an angel as messenger.

96. Say: Allah suffices for a witness between me and you. He is Knower, Seer of His slaves.

97. And he whom Allah guides, he is led aright; while, as for him whom He sends astray, for them you will find no protecting friends besides Him, and We shall assemble them on the Day of Resurrection on their faces, blind, dumb and deaf; their habitation will be Hell; whenever it subsides, We increase the flame for them.

98. That is their reward because they disbelieved Our revelations and said:

When we are bones and fragments will we be raised up as a new creation?

99. Have they not seen that Allah Who created the heavens and the earth is Able to create the like of them, and has appointed for them an end of which there is no doubt? But the wrongdoers refuse anything except disbelief.

100. Say (to them): If you possessed the treasures of the Mercy of my Lord, you would surely hold them back for fear of spending; for man is ever miserly.

101. And verily We gave to Moses nine signs, clear proofs (of Allah's Sovereignty). Do simply ask the Children of Israel how he came to them, then Pharaoh said to him: I consider you one bewitched, O Moses.

102. He said: In truth you know that none sent down these (signs) except the Lord of the heavens and the earth as proofs, and (for my part) I consider you lost, O Pharaoh.

103. And he wished to scare them from the land, but We drowned him and those with him, all together.

104. And We said to the Children of Israel after him: Dwell in the land; but when the promise of the Hereafter comes to pass, We shall bring you as a crowd gathered out of various nations.[145]

105. With truth We have sent it down, and with truth it has descended. And We have sent you as nothing else except a bearer of good tidings and a warner.

---

145. A reference to the dispersal of the Jews as the consequence of their own deeds after God had established them in the land.

106. And (it is) a Qur'an that We have divided, that you may recite it to mankind at intervals, and We have revealed it by (successive) revelation.

107. Say: Believe in it or believe not, those who were given knowledge before it, when it is read to them, fall down prostrate on their faces, adoring,

108. Saying: Glory to our Lord! Verily the promise of our Lord must be fulfilled.

109. They fall down on their faces, weeping, and it increases humility in them.

110. Say (to mankind): Call to Allah, or call to the Beneficent,[146] to whichsoever you call (it is the same). His are the most beautiful names. And you (Muhammad), be not loud-voiced in your worship nor yet silent in it, but follow a way in between.

111. And say: Praise be to Allah, Who has not taken to Himself a son, and Who has no partner in the Sovereignty, nor has He any protecting friend through dependence. And magnify Him with all magnificence.

Surah 18: *Al-Kahf* (The Cave)

Al-Kahf, "The Cave," takes its name from the story of the youths who took refuge from persecution in a cave (vv. 10-27) and were preserved there as if asleep for a long period - a story which

is generally identified by Western writers (e.g. Gibbon) with the legend of the Seven Sleepers of Ephesus. But a strong tradition in the Muslim world asserts that this story and that of Dhu'l Qarneyn ("The Two-Horned One"), vv. 83-98, possibly also that of Moses and the angel, vv. 60-82, were revealed to the Prophet to enable him to answer the questions which the Jewish doctors of Yathrib had instructed the idolaters to ask him, as a test of Prophethood.

The questions were three: "Ask him," said the Rabbis, "of some youths who were of old, what was their fate, for they have a strange story; and ask him of a much travelled man who reached the sunrise regions of the earth and the sun-set regions of it, what was his history; and ask him of the spirit, what it is."

The tormentors of the Prophet, who had been to Yathrib to get hints from the Jews, on their return to Makkah put these questions to the Prophet, after having told the people that it was to be a crucial test. The Prophet said that he would surely answer them in the morning, without adding "If God wills," as though he could command God's revelation. As a reproach for that omission, the wished-for revelation was withheld from him for some days, and when it came included the rebuke contained in verse 24.[147] There is no reason whatever to doubt the truth of the tradition which connects this chapter with three questions set by the Jewish rabbis, and the answers must have been considered satisfying, or

---

146. The idolaters had a peculiar objection to the name of *Ar-Rahman,* "The Beneficent," in the Qur'an. They said: "We do not know this *Rahman.*" Some of them thought that *Ar-Rahman* was a man living in Yamamah.

147. Ibn Hisham (Cairo edn.), Part 1, pp. 102, 103.

at least silencing, or the Jews would certainly have made fun of them when they were taunting the Prophet daily after his emigration to Yathrib (Al-Madinah). That being so, it would seem rash to identify the story with that of the Christian Seven Sleepers; it must belong, as the story of the "Two-Horned One" actually does belong, to rabbinical tradition. The third of the question is answered in Surah 17, vv. 85 ff. It belongs to the middle group of Makkan Surahs.

═══════════════

In the name of Allah,
the Beneficent, the Merciful.

1. Praise be to Allah Who has revealed the Scripture to His slave, and has not placed in it any crookedness,

2. (But has made it) straight, to give warning of stern punishment from Him, and to bring to the believers who do good works the news that theirs will be a fair reward,

3. In which they will remain forever;

4. And to warn those who say: Allah has chosen a son,

5. (A thing) of which they have no knowledge, nor (had) their fathers. Dreadful is the word that comes out of their mouths. They speak nothing but a lie.

6. Yet it may be, if they believe not in this statement, that you (Muhammad) will torment your soul with grief over their footsteps.

7. We have placed all that is on the earth as an ornament of it that We may try them: which of them is best in conduct.

8. And We shall make all that is on it a barren mound.

9. Or do you think that the People of the Cave and the Inscription are a wonder among Our signs?

10. When the young men fled for refuge to the Cave and said: Our Lord! Give us mercy from Your presence, and shape for us right conduct in our plight.

11. Then We sealed up their hearing in the Cave for a number of years.

12. And afterwards We raised them up that We might know which of the two parties would best calculate the time that they had stayed.

13. We narrate to you their story with truth. They were young men who believed in their Lord, and We increased them in guidance.

14. And We made firm their hearts when they stood up and said: Our Lord is the Lord of the heavens and the earth. We call to no God besides Him, for then should we utter an enormity.

15. These, our people, have chosen (other) gods besides Him though they bring no clear authority (given) to them. And who does greater wrong than he who invents a lie concerning Allah?

16. And when you withdraw from them and that which they worship except Allah, then seek refuge in the Cave; your Lord will spread for you of His mercy and will prepare for you a pillow in your plight.

17. And you might have seen the sun when it rose move away from their cave to the right, and when it set go past them on the left, and they were in the gap between it. That was (one) of the signs of Allah. He whom Allah guides, he indeed is led aright, and he whom He sends astray, for him you will not find a guiding friend.

18. And you would have thought them awake though they were asleep, and We caused them to turn over to the right and the left, and their dog stretching out his paws on the threshold. If you had observed them closely you would have assuredly turned away from them in flight, and had been filled with awe of them.

19. And in like manner We awakened them that they might question one another. A speaker from among them said: How long have you stayed? They said: We have stayed a day or some part of a day, (Others) said: Your Lord best knows how long you have stayed. Now send one of you with this your silver coin to the city, and let him see what food is purest there and bring you a supply of it. Let him be courteous and let no man know of you.

20. For they, if they should come to know of you, will stone you or turn you back to their religion; then you will never prosper.

21. And in like manner We disclosed them (to the people of the city) that they might know that the promise of Allah is true, and that, as for the Hour, there is no doubt concerning it. When (the people of the city) disputed of their case among themselves, they said: Build over them a building; their Lord knows best concerning them. Those who won

their point said: We verily shall build a place of worship over them.

22. (Some) will say: They were three, their dog the fourth, and (some) say: Five, their dog the sixth, guessing at random; and (some) say: Seven, and their dog the eighth. Say (O Muhammad): My Lord is Best Aware of their number. None knows them except a few. So contend not concerning them except with an outward contending, and ask not any of them to pronounce concerning them.

23. And say not of anything: I shall do that tomorrow,

24. Except if Allah wills. And remember your Lord when you forget, and say: It may be that my Lord guides me to a nearer way of truth than this.

25. And (it is said) they stayed in their cave three hundred years and add nine.

26. Say: Allah is Best Aware how long they stayed. His is the (knowledge of the) Invisible of the heavens and the earth. How clear of sight is He and keen of hearing! They have no protecting friend besides Him, and He makes none to share in His government.

27. And recite that which has been revealed to you of the Scripture of your Lord. There is none who can change His words, and you will find no refuge besides Him.

28. Restrain yourself along with those who call to their Lord in the morning and evening, seeking His Countenance; and let not your eyes overlook them, desiring the pomp of the life of the world; and obey not him whose heart We have made heedless of Our remembrance, who follows his own lust and whose case has been abandoned.

29. Say: (It is) the truth from the Lord of you (all). Then whoever will, let him believe, and whoever will, let him disbelieve. We have prepared for disbelievers Fire. Its tent encloses them. If they ask for showers, they will be showered with water like molten lead which burns the faces. Calamitous the drink and ill the resting-place!

30. As for those who believe and do good works - We suffer not the reward of one whose work is goodly to be lost.

31. As for such, theirs will be Gardens of Eden, in which rivers flow beneath them; in it they will be given armlets of gold and will wear green robes of finest silk and gold embroidery, reclining upon thrones in it. Blessed the reward, and fair the resting-place!

32. Coin for them a similitude: Two men, to one of whom We had assigned two gardens of grapes, and We had surrounded both with date-palms and had put between them tillage.

33. Each of the gardens gave its fruit and withheld nothing of it. And We caused a river to gush out in it.

34. And he had fruit. And he said to his comrade, when he spoke with him: I am more than you in wealth, and am stronger in respect of men.

35. And he went into his garden, whilst having wronged himself. He said: I do not think that all this will ever perish.

36. I think not that the Hour will ever come, and if indeed I am brought back to my Lord I surely shall find better than this as a resort.

37. His comrade, when he (thus) spoke with him, exclaimed: Do you disbelieve in Him Who created you of dust, then of a drop (of seed), and then fashioned you into a man?

38. But He is Allah, my Lord, and I ascribe to my Lord no partner.

39. If only, when you entered your garden, you had said: That which Allah wills (will come to pass)! There is no strength except in Allah! Though you see me as less than you in wealth and children,

40. Yet it may be that my Lord will give me better than your garden, and will send on it a bolt from heaven, and some morning it will be a smooth hillside,

41. Or some morning the water of it will be lost in the earth so that you cannot make search for it.

42. And his fruit was beset (with destruction). Then he began to wring his hands for all that he had spent upon it, when (now) it was all ruined on its trellises, and to say: Would that I had ascribed no partner to my Lord!

43. And he had no troop of men to help him against Allah, nor could he save himself.

44. In this case protection is only from Allah, the True, He is Best for reward, and Best for consequence.

45. And coin for them the similitude of the life of the world as water which We send down from the sky, and the vegetation of the earth mingles with it and then becomes dry twigs that the winds scatter. Allah is Able to do all things.

46. Wealth and children are an ornament of the life of the world. But the good deeds which endure are better in your Lord's sight for reward, and better in respect of hope.

47. And (consider) the Day when We remove the hills and you see the earth emerging, and We gather them together so as to leave not one of them behind.

48. And they are set before your Lord in ranks (and it is said to them): Now verily you have come to Us as We created you first. But you thought that We had set no appointed time for you.

49. And the Book is placed, and you see the guilty fearful of that which is in it, and they say: What kind of a Book is this that leaves not a small thing nor a great thing but has counted it! And they find all that they did confronting them, and your Lord wrongs no-one.

50. And (remember) when We said to the angels: Fall prostrate before Adam, and they fell prostrate, all except Iblis. He was of the jinn,[148] so he rebelled against his Lord's command. Will you choose him and his seed for your protecting friends instead of Me, when they are an enemy to you? Calamitous is the exchange for evildoers.

---

148. The fact that *Iblis* or Satan is *jinn* and not of the angels, though he was among the latter, explains his disobedience; jinn, like men, can choose their path of conduct.

51. I made them not to witness the creation of the heavens and the earth, nor their own creation; nor do I choose misleaders for (My) helpers.

52. And (be mindful of) the Day when He will say: Call those partners of Mine whom you pretended. Then they will call to them, but they will not hear their prayer, and We shall set a gulf of doom between them.

53. And the guilty shall behold the Fire and know that they are about to fall in it, and they find no way of escape from there.

54. And verily We have displayed for mankind in this Qur'an all manner of similitudes, but man is more than anything contentious.

55. And nothing hinders mankind from believing when the guidance comes to them, and from asking forgiveness of their Lord unless (it is that they wish) that the judgement of the men of old should come upon them or (that) they should be confronted with the Doom.

56. We send not the messengers except as bearers of good news and warners. Those who disbelieve contend with falsehood in order to refute the Truth by it. And they take Our revelations and that with which they are threatened as a jest.

57. And who does greater wrong than he who has been reminded of the revelations of his Lord, yet turns away from them and forgets what his hands send forward (to the Judgement)? On their hearts We have placed coverings so that they understand not, and in their ears a deafness. And though you call them to the guidance, in that case they can never be led aright.

58. Your Lord is the Forgiver, Full of Mercy. If He took them to task (now) for what they earn, He would hasten on the doom for them; but theirs is an appointed term from which they will find no escape.

59. And (all) those townships! We destroyed them when they did wrong, and We appointed a fixed time for their destruction.

60. And when Moses said to his servant: I will not give up until I reach the point where the two rivers meet, though I march on for ages.

61. And when they reached the point where the two met, they forgot their fish, and it took its way into the waters, being free.

62. And when they had gone further, he said to his servant: Bring us our breakfast. Verily we have found fatigue in this our journey.

63. He said: Did you see, when we took refuge on the rock, and I forgot the fish - and none but Satan caused me to forget to mention it - it took its way into the waters by a marvel.

64. He said: This is that which we have been seeking. So they retraced their steps again.

65. Then they found one of Our slaves, to whom We had given mercy from Us, and had taught him knowledge from Our presence.

66. Moses said to him: May I follow you, to the end that you may teach me

right conduct of that which you have been taught?

67. He said: You cannot bear with me.

68. How can you bear with that of which you cannot comprehend any knowledge?

69. He said: Allah willing, you shall find me patient and I shall not in anything contradict you.

70. He said: Well, if you go with me, ask me not concerning anything till I myself make mention of it to you.

71. So the two set out till, when they were in the ship, he made a hole in it. (Moses) said: Have you made a hole in it to drown the people of it? You verily have done a dreadful thing.

72. He said: Did I not tell you that you could not bear with me?

73. (Moses) said: Be not angry with me that I forgot, and be not hard upon me for my fault.

74. So the two journeyed on till, when they met a lad, he slew him. (Moses) said: What! Have you slain an innocent soul who has slain no man? Verily you have done a horrid thing.

75. He said: Did I not tell you that you could not bear with me?

76. (Moses) said: If I ask you after this concerning anything, keep not company with me. You have received an excuse from me.

77. So the two journeyed on till, when they came to the people of a certain township, they asked its people for food, but they refused to make them guests. And they found in it a wall upon the point of falling into ruin, and he repaired it. (Moses) said: If you had wished, you could have taken payment for it.

78. He said: This is the parting between you and me! I will announce to you the interpretation of that which you could not bear with patience.

79. As for the ship, it belonged to poor people working on the river,[149] and I wished to damage it, for there was a king behind them who is taking every ship by force.

80. And as for the lad, his parents were believers and we feared lest he should oppress them by rebellion and disbelief.

81. And we intended that their Lord should change him for them for one better in purity and nearer to mercy.

82. And as for the wall, it belonged to two orphan boys in the city, and there was beneath it a treasure belonging to them, and their father had been righteous, and your Lord intended that they should come to their full strength and should bring out their treasure as a mercy from their Lord; and I did it not upon my own command. Such is the interpretation of that with which you could not bear.

83. They will ask you of Dhu'l-Qarneyn. Say: I shall recite to you a remembrance of him.

84. We made him strong in the land and gave him to everything a road.

85. And he followed a road,

86. Till, when he reached the setting-place of the sun, he found it setting in

149. Or, it might be, "sea."

a muddy spring, and found a people there. We said: O Dhu'l-Qarneyn! Either punish or show them kindness.

87. He said: As for him who does wrong, we shall punish him, and then he will be brought back to his Lord, Who will punish him with awful punishment!

88. But as for him who believes and does right, good will be his reward, and We shall speak to him a mild command.

89. Then he followed a road,

90. Till, when he reached the rising-place of the sun, he found it rising on a people for whom We had appointed no shelter from it.

91. So (it was). And We knew all concerning him.

92. Then he followed a road,

93. Till, when he came between the two mountains, he found on their nearer side a people who scarcely could understand a word.

94. They said: O Dhu'l-Qarneyn! Gog and Magog are spoiling the land. So may we pay you tribute on condition that you set a barrier between us and them?

95. He said: That in which my Lord has established me is better (than your tribute). Do but help me with strength (of men), I will set between you and them a bank.

96. Give me pieces of iron - till, when he had levelled up (the gap) between the cliffs, he said: Blow! - till, when he had made it a fire, he said: Bring me molten copper to pour on it.

97. And (Gog and Magog) were not able to surmount, nor could they pierce (it).

98. He said: This is a mercy from my Lord; but when the promise of my Lord comes to pass, He will lay it low, for the promise of my Lord is true.

99. And on that day We shall let some of them surge against others, and the Trumpet will be blown. Then We shall gather them together in one gathering.

100. On that day We shall present Hell to the disbelievers, plain to view,

101. Those whose eyes were hoodwinked from My Reminder, and who could not bear to hear.

102. Do the disbelievers reckon that they can choose My bondsmen as protecting friends besides Me? We have prepared Hell as a welcome for the disbelievers.

103. Say: Shall We inform you who will be the greatest losers by their works?

104. Those whose effort goes astray in the life of the world, and yet they reckon that they do good work.

105. Those are they who disbelieve in the revelations of their Lord and in the meeting with Him. Therefore their works are in vain, and on the Day of Resurrection We assign no weight to them.

106. That is their reward: Hell, because they disbelieved, and made a jest of Our revelations and Our messengers.

107. Those who believe and do good works, theirs are the Gardens of Paradise for welcome,

108. In which they will abide, with no desire to be removed from there.

109. Say: Though the sea became ink for the Words of my Lord, verily the sea would be used up before the words of my Lord were exhausted, even though We brought the like of it to help.

110. Say: I am only a mortal like you. My Lord inspires in me that your God is only One God. And whoever hopes for the meeting with his Lord, let him do righteous work, and make none sharer of the worship due to his Lord.

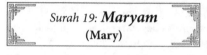

Surah 19: *Maryam*
(Mary)

Maryam takes its name from v. 16 ff. That it is of quite early Makkan revelation is established by the following tradition:

In the fifth year of the Prophet's mission (the ninth before the Hijrah, or emigration to Al-Madinah) a number of poorer converts were allowed by the Prophet to emigrate to Abyssinia, a Christian country, where they would not be subject to persecution for their worship of the one God. This is known as the first Hijrah. The rulers of Makkah sent ambassadors to ask the Negus for their extradition, accusing them of having left the religion of their own people without entering the Christian religion, and of having done wrong in their own country. The Negus (against the wish of the envoys) sent for the spokesperson of the refugees and, in the presence of the bishops of his realm, questioned them about their religion. Ja'far ibn Abi Talib, cousin of the Prophet, answered: (I translate from the account given by Ibn Ishaq).[150]

"We were people immersed in ignorance, worshipping idols, eating carrion, given to lewdness, severing the ties of kinship, bad neighbours, the strong among us preying on the weak; thus we were till Allah sent to us a messenger of our own, whose lineage, honesty, trustworthiness and chastity we knew, and he called us to Allah that we should acknowledge His unity and worship Him and eschew all the stones and idols that we and our fathers used to worship besides Him; and ordered us to be truthful and to restore the pledge and observe the ties of kinship, and be good neighbours, and to abstain from things forbidden, and from blood, and forbade us lewdness and false speech, to prey upon the wealth of orphans, or to accuse good women; and commanded us to worship Allah only, ascribing nothing to Him as a partner, and enjoined upon us prayer and legal alms and fasting. (And he enumerated for him the teachings of Islam.)

"So we trusted and we believed in Him and followed that which he had brought from Allah, and we worshipped Allah only, and ascribed no thing as a partner to Him. And we refrained from that which was forbidden to us, and indulged in that which was made lawful for us. And our people became hostile to us and tormented us, and sought to turn us from our religion that they might bring us back to the worship of idols from the worship of Allah Most High, and that we might

150. Ibn Hisham, Part 1, pp. 119 and 120.

indulge in those iniquities which before we had deemed lawful.

"And when they persecuted and oppressed us, and hemmed us in, and kept us from the practice of our religion, we came out to your land, and chose you above all others, and your protection, and hoped that we should not be troubled in your land, O King!"

"Then the Negus asked him: Have you anything with you of that which he brought from Allah? Ja'far answered: Yes. Then the Negus said: Relate it to me, and Ja'far recited to him the beginning of *Kaf, Ha, Ya, A'in, Sad*" - the Arabic letters with which this Surah begins, such letters being generally used instead of titles by the early Muslims. Therefore this Surah must have been revealed and well known before the departure of the emigrants for Abyssinia.

An early Makkan Surah, with the possible exception of vv. 59 and 60, which, according to some authorities, were revealed at Al-Madinah.

═══════════

In the name of Allah,
the Beneficent, the Merciful.

1. *Kaf. Ha. Ya. 'Ain. Sad.*[151]

2. A mention of the mercy of your Lord to His servant Zechariah.

3. When he called to his Lord a call in secret

4. Saying: My Lord! My bones grow feeble and my head is shining with grey hair, and I have never been unblessed in prayer to You, my Lord.

151. See *Surah 2, Al-Baqarah,* v. 1, footnote.

5. I fear for my relatives after me, since my wife is barren. Oh, give me from Your presence a successor,

6. Who shall inherit of me and inherit (also) of the house of Jacob. And make him, my Lord, acceptable (to You).

7. (It was said to him): O Zechariah! We bring you tidings of a son whose name is John;[152] We have given the same name to no one before (him).

8. He said: My Lord! How can I have a son when my wife is barren and I have reached infirm old age?

9. He said: So (it will be). Your Lord says: It is easy for Me, even as I created you before, when you were nothing.

10. He said: My Lord! Appoint for me some sign. He said: Your sign is that you, with no bodily defect, shall not speak to mankind three nights.

11. Then he came out to his people from the sanctuary, and signified to them: Glorify your Lord at break of day and fall of night.

12. (And it was said to his son): O John! Hold fast the Scripture. And We gave him wisdom when a child,

13. And compassion from Our Presence, and purity; and he was devout,

14. And dutiful towards his parents. And he was not arrogant, rebellious.

15. Peace on him the day he was born, and the day he dies and the day he will be raised alive!

16. And make mention of Mary in the Scripture, when she had withdrawn from her people to a chamber looking East,

17. And had chosen seclusion from them. Then We sent to her Our Spirit and it assumed for her the likeness of a perfect man.

18. She said: I seek refuge in the Beneficent One from you, if you are God-fearing.

19. He said: I am only a messenger of your Lord, that I may bestow on you a faultless son.

20. She said: How can I have a son when no mortal has touched me, neither have I been unchaste?

21. He said: So (it will be). Your Lord says: It is easy for Me. And (it will be) that We may make of him a revelation for mankind and a mercy from Us, and it is a thing ordained.

22. And she conceived him, and she withdrew with him to a far place.

23. And the pangs of childbirth drove her to the trunk of the palm-tree. She said: Oh, would that I had died before this and had become a thing of nothing, forgotten!

24. Then (one) called to her from below her, saying: Grieve not! Your Lord has placed a stream beneath you,

25. And shake the trunk of the palm-tree towards you, you will cause ripe dates to fall upon you.

26. So eat and drink and be consoled. And if you meet any mortal, say: I have vowed a fast to the Beneficent, and may not speak this day to any mortal.

27. Then she brought him to her own people, carrying him. They said: O Mary! You have come with an amazing thing.

152. Arabic: *Yahya*

28. O sister of Aaron![153] Your father was not a wicked man nor was your mother a harlot.

29. Then she pointed to him. They said: How can we talk to one who is in the cradle, a young boy?

30. He spoke: I am the slave of Allah. He has given me the Scripture and has appointed me a Prophet,

31. And has made me blessed wherever I may be, and has enjoined upon me prayer and almsgiving so long as I remain alive,

32. And (has made me) dutiful towards her who bore me, and has not made me arrogant, unblessed.

33. Peace on me the day I was born, and the day I die, and the day I shall be raised alive!

34. Such was Jesus, son of Mary: (this is) a statement of the truth concerning which they doubt.

35. It befits not (the Majesty of) Allah that He should take to Himself a son. Glory be to Him! When He decrees a thing, He says to it only: Be! and it is.

36. And Allah is my Lord and your Lord. So serve Him. That is the right path.

37. The sects among them differ: but woe to the disbelievers from the meeting of an Awful Day.

38. See and hear them on the Day they come to Us! Yet the evildoers are to-day in error manifest.

39. And warn them of the Day of anguish when the case has been decided. Now they are in a state of carelessness, and they believe not.

40. We, only We, inherit the earth and all who are on it, and to Us they are returned.

41. And make mention (O Muhammad) in the Scripture of Abraham. He was a saint, a prophet

42. When he said to his father: O my father! Why worship you that which hears not nor sees, nor can in anyway benefit you?

43. O my father! There has come to me knowledge that which came not to you. So follow me, and I will lead you on a right path.

44. O my father! Serve not the devil. The devil is a rebel to the Beneficent.

45. O my father! I fear lest a punishment from the Beneficent overtake you so that you become a comrade of the devil.

46. He said: Will you reject my gods, O Abraham? If you cease not, I shall surely stone you. Depart far from me!

47. He said: Peace be to you! I shall ask forgiveness of my Lord for you. He was ever gracious to me.

48. I shall withdraw from you and that to which you pray besides Allah, and I shall pray to my Lord. It may be that, in prayer to my Lord, I shall not be unblessed.

49. So, when he had withdrawn from them and that which they were worshipping besides Allah, We gave him Isaac and Jacob. Each of them We made a prophet.

50. And we gave them of Our mercy, and assigned to them a high and true honour.

153. See *Surah* 3, *Al-'Imran*, introduction.

51. And make mention in the Scripture of Moses. He was chosen, and he was a messenger (of Allah), a prophet.

52. We called him from the right slope of the Mount, and brought him near in communion.

53. And We bestowed upon him of Our mercy his brother Aaron, a prophet (likewise).

54. And make mention in the Scripture of Ishmael. He was a keeper of his promise, and he was a messenger (of Allah), a prophet.

55. He enjoined upon his people worship and almsgiving, and was acceptable in the sight of his Lord.

56. And make mention in the Scripture of Idris.[154] He was a saint, a prophet;

57. And We raised him to a high station.

58. These are they to whom Allah showed favour from among the Prophets, of the seed of Adam and of those whom We carried (in the ship) with Noah, and of the seed of Abraham and Israel, and from among those whom We guided and chose. When the revelations of the Beneficent were recited to them, they fell down, adoring and weeping.

59. Now there has succeeded them a later generation who have ruined worship and have followed lusts. But they will meet deception.

60. Except him who shall repent and believe and do right. Such will enter the Garden, and they will not be wronged in anything -

61. Gardens of Eden, which the Beneficent has promised to His slaves

154. Identified with Enoch.

in the unseen. His promise is ever sure of fulfilment -

62. They hear in it no idle talk, but only Peace; and in it they have food for morning and evening.

63. Such is the Garden which We cause the devout among Our bondsmen to inherit.

64. We (angels) come not down except by commandment of your Lord. To Him belongs all that is before us and all that is behind us and all that is between those two, and your Lord was never forgetful -

65. Lord of the heavens and the earth and all that is between them! Therefore, worship Him and be steadfast in His service. Do you know one that can be named along with Him?

66. And man says: When I am dead, shall I really be brought out alive?

67. Does not man remember that We created him before, when he was nothing?

68. And, by your Lord, verily We shall assemble them and the devils, then We shall bring them, crouching, around Hell.

69. Then We shall pluck out from every sect whichever of them was most stubborn in rebellion to the Beneficent.

70. And surely We are Best Aware of those most worthy to be burned in it.

71. There is not one of you but shall approach it. That is a fixed ordinance of your Lord.

72. Then We shall rescue those who kept from evil, and leave the evildoers crouching there.

73. And when Our clear revelations are recited to them, those who disbelieve say to those who believe: Which of the two parties (yours or ours) is in a better position, and more imposing as an army?

74. How many a generation have We destroyed before them, who were more imposing in respect of equipment and outward appearance!

75. Say: As for him who is in error, the Beneficent will verily prolong his span of life until, when they behold that which they were promised, whether it is punishment (in the world), or the Hour (of doom), they will know who is worse in position and who is weaker as an army.

76. Allah increases in right guidance those who walk aright, and the good deeds which endure are better in your Lord's sight for reward, and better for resort.

77. Have you seen him who disbelieves in Our revelations and says: Assuredly I shall be given wealth and children?

78. Has he examined the Unseen, or has he made a pact with the Beneficent?

79. No, but We shall record that which he says and prolong for him a span of torment.

80. And We shall inherit from him that of which he spoke, and he will come to Us, alone (without his wealth and children).

81. And they have chosen (other) gods besides Allah that they may be a (source of) power for them.

82. No, but they will deny their worship of them, and become opponents to them.

83. Do you not see that We have set the devils on the disbelievers to confuse them with confusion?

84. So make no haste against them (O Muhammad). We do only give to them a sum (of days).

85. On the day when We shall gather the righteous to the Beneficent, a goodly company,

86. And drive the guilty to Hell, a weary herd,

87. They will have no power of intercession, except him who has made a covenant with his Lord.

88. And they say: The Beneficent has taken to Himself a son.

89. Assuredly you utter a disastrous thing

90. By which almost the heavens are torn, and the earth is split apart and the mountains fall in ruins,

91. That you ascribe to the Beneficent a son,

92. When it is not proper for (the Majesty of) the Beneficent that He should choose a son.

93. There is none in the heavens and the earth but comes to the Beneficent as a slave.

94. Verily He knows them and numbers them with (right) numbering.

95. And each one of them will come to Him on the Day of Resurrection, alone.

96. Those who believe and do good works, the Beneficent will appoint for them love.

97. And We make (this Scripture) easy on your tongue, (O Muhammad) only that you may bear good tidings with it to those who ward off (evil), and warn with it the obstinate people.

98. And how many a generation before them have We destroyed! Can you (Muhammad) see a single man of them, or hear from them the slightest sound?

Surah 20: *Ta-Ha*

Ta-Ha takes its name from the Arabic letters which form the first verse. As in the case of Surah 19, the early date of revelation is established by a strong tradition.

Omar ibn Al-Khattab, who afterwards became Caliph, was among the bitterest opponents of Islam in the early days. He set out one day, sword in hand, with the intention of killing the Prophet - "this Sabaean who has split the unity of Quraysh, calls their ideals foolish and their religion shameful, and blasphemes their gods"- when a friend who met him dissuaded him, reminding him that if he slew the Prophet he would have to reckon with the vengeance of a powerful clan: "Do you think that the Banu 'Abd Munaf would let you walk on the earth if you had slain Muhammad?"- for tribal pride survived religious difference. "Is it not better for you to return to the people of your own house and keep them straight?" Omar asked: "Which of the people of my house?" "Your brother-in-law and cousin, Sa'id ibn Zeyd, and your sister,

Fatimah daughter of Al-Khattab, for, by Allah, they have become Muslims and followers of Muhammad in his religion, so look you to them."

Then Omar returned, enraged against his sister and brother-in-law, and there was with them in the house Khabab ibn 'Arit, having with him a leaf on which was written *Ta Ha* (this Surah) which he was reading aloud to them. When they heard the noise of Omar's coming, Khabab hid in a closet that they had in the house and Fatimah took the leaf and hid it under her thigh. But Omar had heard the sound of Khabab's reading as he drew near the house, and when he entered he said: "What was that mumbling which I heard?" They said: "You heard nothing." Omar said: "Yes, by Allah! And I have already been informed that you have become followers of Muhammad in his religion." Then he attacked his brother-in-law Sa'id ibn Zeyd, but Fatimah sprang to keep him off her husband and he struck and wounded her. And when he had done that, his sister and his brother-in-law said to him: "Yes, we are Muslims and we believe in Allah and His messenger, so do what you will!" But when Omar saw the blood upon his sister he was sorry for what he had done, and he said to his sister: "Give me that leaf from which I heard you reading just now, that I may see what this is that Muhammad has brought." And Omar was a scribe. When he said that, his sister said: "We fear to trust you with it." He said: "Fear not!" and swore by his gods that he would return it to her when he had read it. And when he said that, she hoped for his conversion to *Al-Islam*, but said: "O my brother, you are unclean on account of your idolatry and none may touch it except the purified." Then Omar went out and washed himself, and she gave him the leaf on which *Ta Ha* was written and he read it. And when he had read it he said: "How excellent are these words!" and praised it highly. And when he heard that, Khabab came out to him and said: "O Omar, I hope that Allah has brought you in answer to the prayer of the Prophet, for only yesterday I heard him saying: O Allah! Strengthen *Al-Islam* with Abu'l-Hakam ibn Hisham or Omar ibn Al-Khattab; and Allah is Allah, O Omar!" At that he said: "O Khabab, direct me to Muhammad that I may go to him and make surrender."[155]

The conversion of Omar took place in the fifth year of the Prophet's mission (ninth before the Hijrah) soon after the departure of the emigrants to Abyssinia. At that time this Surah was already written down and in circulation.

An early Makkan Surah.

In the name of Allah, the Beneficent, the Merciful.

1. *Ta-Ha.*[156]

2. We have not revealed to you (Muhammad) this Qur'an that you should be distressed,

3. But as a reminder to him who fears,

4. A revelation from Him Who created the earth and the high heavens,

5. The Beneficent One, Who is established on the Throne.

6. To Him belongs whatever is in the heavens and whatever is in the earth, and whatever is between them, and whatever is beneath the soil.

7. And if you speak aloud, then He knows the secret (thought) and (that which is yet) more hidden.

8. Allah! There is no God except Him. His are the most Beautiful Names.

9. Has there come to you the story of Moses?

10. When he saw a fire and said to his people: Wait! I see a fire in the distance. Perhaps I may bring you a flame from it or may find guidance at the fire.

11. And when he reached it, he was called by name: O Moses!

12. I, even I, am your Lord, So take off your shoes, for you are in the holy valley of Tuwa.

13. And I have chosen you, so listen to that which is inspired.

14. I, even I, am Allah, There is no God except Me. So serve Me and establish worship for My remembrance.

15. The Hour is surely coming. But I will to keep it hidden, that every soul may be rewarded for that which it strives (to achieve).

16. Therefore, let not him turn you aside from (the thought of) it who believes not in it but follows his own desire, lest you perish.

---

155. Ibn Hisham, Part 1, pp.119 and 120.
156. See *Surah 2, Al-Baqarah*, v. 1, footnote.

17. And what is that in your right hand, O Moses?

18. He said: This is my staff on which I lean, and with which I bear down branches for my sheep, and in which I find other uses.

19. He said: Cast it down, O Moses!

20. So he cast it down, and it was a serpent, gliding.

21. He said: Grasp it and fear not. We shall return it to its former state.

22. And thrust your hand within your armpit, it will come out white without hurt. (That will be) another sign.

23. That We may show you (some) of Our greater signs,

24. Go you to Pharaoh! He has transgressed (the bounds).

25. (Moses) said: My Lord! Relieve my mind

26. And ease my task for me;

27. And loosen a knot from my tongue,

28. That they may understand my speech.

29. Appoint for me a supporter from my people,

30. Aaron, my brother.

31. Confirm my strength with him

32. And let him share my task,

33. That we may glorify You much

34. And much remember You.

35. You are ever Seeing us.

36. He said: You are granted your request, O Moses.

37. And indeed, another time, already We have shown you favour,

38. When we inspired in your mother that which is inspired,

39. Saying: Drop him into the chest, and drop it into the river, then the river shall drop it on to the bank, and there an enemy to Me and an enemy to him shall take him. And I endued you with love from Me that you might be trained according to My will,

40. When your sister went and said: Shall I show you one who will nurse him?, and We restored you to your mother that her eyes might be refreshed and might not sorrow. And you killed a man and We delivered you from great distress, and tried you with a heavy trial. And you did stay years among the people of Midian. Then you came (here) by (My) providence, O Moses,

41. And I have attached you to Myself.

42. Go, you and your brother, with My signs, and be not weak in remembrance of Me.

43. Go, both of you, to Pharaoh. He has transgressed (the bounds).

44. And speak to him a gentle word, that perhaps he may heed or fear.

45. They said: Our Lord! We fear that he may be rash with us or that he may play the tyrant.

46. He said: Fear not. I am with you both, Hearing and Seeing.

47. So go you to him and say: We are two messengers of your Lord. So let the children of Israel go with us, and torment them not. We bring you a sign from your Lord. And peace will be for him who follows right guidance.

48. It has been revealed to us that the doom will be for him who denies and turns away.

49. (Pharaoh) said: Who then is the Lord of you both, O Moses?

50. He said: Our Lord is He Who gave to everything its nature, then guided it aright.

51. He said: What then is the state of the generations of old?

52. He said: The knowledge of it is with my Lord in a Record. My Lord neither errs nor forgets,

53. Who has appointed the earth as a bed and has threaded roads for you in it and has sent down water from the sky and by it We have brought out diverse kinds of vegetation,

54. (Saying): Eat you and feed your cattle. In this verily are signs for men of thought.

55. Of it We created you, and to it We return you, and from it We bring you out a second time.

56. And verily We did show him all Our signs, but he denied them and refused.

57. He said: Have you come to drive us out from our land by your magic, O Moses?

58. But we surely can produce for you magic the like of it; so appoint an appointed time between us and you, which neither we nor you shall fail to keep, at a place convenient (to us both).

59. (Moses) said: Your appointed time shall be the day of the feast, and let the people assemble when the sun has risen high.

60. Then Pharaoh went and gathered his strength, then came (to the appointed time).

61. Moses said to them: Woe to you! Invent not a lie against Allah, lest He destroy you by some punishment. He who lies fails miserably.

62. Then they debated one with another what they must do, and they kept their counsel secret.

63. They said: These are two wizards who would drive you out from your country by their magic, and destroy your best traditions;

64. So arrange your plan, and come in battle line. Who is uppermost this day will be indeed successful.

65. They said: O Moses! Either throw first, or let us be the first to throw?

66. He said: No, do you throw! Then their cords and their staffs, by their magic, appeared to him as though they ran.

67. And Moses conceived a fear in his mind.

68. We said: Fear not! You are the higher.

69. Throw that which is in your right hand! It will eat up that which they have made. That which they have made is but a wizard's artifice, and a wizard shall not be successful to whatever point (of skill) he may attain.

70. Then the wizards were (all) flung down prostrate, exclaiming: We believe in the Lord of Aaron and Moses.

71. (Pharaoh) said: You put faith in him before I give you permission. He is your chief who taught you magic. Now surely I shall cut off your hands and your feet alternately, and I shall crucify you on the trunks of palm trees, and you shall know for certain which of us has sterner and more lasting punishment.

72. They said: We choose you not above the clear proofs that have come to us, and above Him Who created us. So decree what you will decree. You will end for us only this life of the world.

73. We believe in our Lord, that He may forgive us our sins and the magic to which you did force us. Allah is better and more lasting.

74. Whoever comes guilty to his Lord, verily for him is Hell. There he will neither die nor live.

75. But whoever comes to Him a believer, having done good works, for such are the high stations;

76. Gardens of Eden underneath which rivers flow, in which they will remain forever. That is the reward of him who grows.

77. And verily We inspired Moses, saying: Take away My slaves by night and strike for them a dry path in the sea, fearing not to be overtaken, neither being afraid (of the sea).

78. Then Pharaoh followed them with his forces and there covered them that which did cover them of the sea.

79. And Pharaoh led his people astray, he did not guide them.

80. O Children of Israel! We delivered you from your enemy, and we made a covenant with you on the holy mountain's side, and sent down on you the manna and the quails,

81. (Saying): Eat of the good things with which We have provided you, and

transgress not in respect of it lest My wrath come upon you: and he on whom My wrath comes, he is lost indeed.

82. And verily I am Forgiving towards him who repents and believes and does good, and afterward walks aright.

83. And (it was said): What has made you hasten from your people, O Moses?

84. He said: They are close upon my track. I hastened to You, my Lord, that You might be well pleased.

85. He said: We have tried your people in your absence, and As-Samiri has misled them.

86. Then Moses went back to his people, angry and sad. He said: O my people! Has not your Lord promised you a fair promise? Did the time appointed then appear too long for you, or did you wish that wrath from your Lord should come upon you, that you broke the appointed time with me?

87. They said: We broke not the appointed time with you of our own will, but we were laden with burdens of ornaments of the people, then cast them (in the fire), for thus As-Samiri proposed.

88. Then he produced for them a calf, of saffron hue,[157] which gave a lowing sound. And they called: This is your god and the god of Moses, but he has forgotten.

89. Do they not see, then, that it returns no saying to them and possesses for them neither hurt nor use?

157. Or "a body." See *Surah 7, Al-A'raf,* v. 148, footnote.

90. And Aaron indeed had told them beforehand: O my people! You are but being seduced with it, for your Lord is the Beneficent, so follow me and obey my order.

91. They said: We shall by no means cease to be its devotees till Moses returns to us.

92. He (Moses) said: O Aaron! What held you back when you did see them gone astray,

93. That you followed me not? Have you then disobeyed my order?

94. He said: O son of my mother! Clutch not my beard nor my head! I feared lest you should say: You have caused division among the Children of Israel, and have not waited for my word.

95. (Moses) said: And what have you to say, O Samiri?

96. He said: I perceived what they perceive not, so I seized a handful from the footsteps of the messenger, and then threw it in. Thus my soul commended to me.[158]

97. (Moses) said: Then go! and in this life it is for you to say: Touch me not! and there is for you an appointed time you cannot break. Now look upon your god of which you have remained a devotee. Verily we will burn it and will scatter its dust over the sea.

---

158. The explanation usually given is that As-Samiri had seen the angel Gabriel pass by, and had taken some of the dust which he had sanctified, and thrown it into the image of the calf, thus giving it a semblance of life. Others say that As-Samiri was an adept of Egyptian idolatry who had believed for a little while and halfheartedly in the God of Moses.

98. Your God is only Allah, than Whom there is no other God. He embraces all things in His knowledge.

99. Thus We relate to you (Muhammad) some tidings of that which happened of old, and We have given you from Our presence a reminder.

100. Whoever turns away from it, he verily will bear a burden on the Day of Resurrection,

101. Remaining under it - an evil burden for them on the Day of Resurrection,

102. The day when the Trumpet is blown. On that day We assemble the guilty white-eyed (with terror),

103. Murmuring among themselves: You have stayed but ten (days).

104. We are Best Aware of what they utter when their best in conduct say: You have stayed but a day.

105. They will ask you of the mountains (on that day). Say: My Lord will break them into scattered dust.

106. And leave it as an empty plain,

107. In which you see neither curve nor ruggedness.

108. On that day they will follow the summoner who deceives not, and voices are hushed for the Beneficent, and you hear but a faint murmur.

109. On that day no intercession benefits except (that of) him to whom the Beneficent has given permission and whose word He accepts.

110. He knows (all) that is before them and (all) that is behind them, while they cannot comprehend it in knowledge.

111. And faces humble themselves before the Living, the Eternal. And he who bears (a burden of) wrongdoing is indeed a failure (on that day).

112. And he who has done some good works, being a believer, he fears not injustice nor withholding (of his wage).

113. Thus we have revealed it as a Lecture[159] in Arabic, and have displayed in it certain threats, that perhaps they may keep from evil or that it may cause them to take heed.

114. Then exalted be Allah, the True King! And hasten not (O Muhammad) with the Qur'an before its revelation has been perfected to you, and say: My Lord! Increase me in knowledge.

115. And verily We made a covenant of old with Adam, but he forgot, and We found no constancy in him.

116. And when We said to the angels: Fall prostrate before Adam, they fell prostrate (all) except Iblis; he refused.

117. Therefore We said: O Adam! This is an enemy to you and to your wife, so let him not drive you both out of the Garden so that you come to toil.

118. It is (promised) to you that you hunger not in it nor are naked,

119. And that you thirst not in it nor are exposed to the sun's heat.

120. But the devil whispered to him, saying: O Adam! Shall I show you the tree of immortality and power that wastes not away?

121. Then they both ate of it, so that their shame became apparent to them,

and they began to hide by heaping on themselves some of the leaves of the Garden. And Adam disobeyed his Lord, so he went astray.[160]

122. Then his Lord chose him, and relented towards him, and guided him.

123. He said: Go down from here, both of you, one of you a foe to the other. But when there comes to you from Me a guidance, then whoever follows My guidance, he will not go astray nor will he grieve.[161]

124. But he who turns away from remembrance of Me, his will be a narrow life, and I shall bring him blind to the assembly on the Day of Resurrection.

125. He will say: My Lord! Why have You gathered me (here) blind, when I used to see?

126. He will say: So (it must be). Our revelations came to you but you did forget them. In like manner you are forgotten this Day.

127. Thus do We reward him who is prodigal and believes not the revelations of his Lord; and verily the doom of the Hereafter will be sterner and more lasting.

128. Is it not a guidance for them (to know) how many generations We destroyed before them, amid whose dwellings they walk? In it verily are signs for men of thought.

159. Arabic: *Qur'an.*

160. Cf. *Surah 7, Al-A'raf,* v. 20 ff
161. Cf. *Surah 2, Al-Baqarah,* v. 38, and the passage leading up to it.

129. And but for a decree that had already gone before from your Lord, and a term already fixed, the judgement would have been inevitable (in this world).

130. Therefore (O Muhammad), bear with what they say, and celebrate the praise of your Lord before the rising of the sun and before the going down of it. And glorify Him some hours of the night and at the two ends of the day, that you may find acceptance.

131. And strain not your eyes towards that which We cause some wedded pairs among them to enjoy, the flower of the life of the world, that We may try them by it. The provision of your Lord is better and more lasting.

132. And enjoin upon your people worship, and be constant in it. We ask not of you a provision: We provided for you. And the sequel is for righteousness.

133. And they say: If only he would bring us a miracle from his Lord! Has there not come to them the proof of what is in the former scriptures?

134. And if We had destroyed them with some punishment before it, they would assuredly have said: Our Lord! If only You had sent to us a messenger, so that we might have followed Your revelations before we were (thus) humbled and disgraced!

135. Say: Each is awaiting; so await you! You will come to know who are the owners of the path of equity, and who is right.

Surah 21: *Al-Anbiya*
(The Prophets)

Al-Anbiya, "The Prophets," is named from its subject, the history of the former Prophets. The speaker in v. 4 and v. 112 is every Prophet. There is no historical reference or tradition to enable us to fix the date. It is undoubtedly of Makkan revelation, and lacks the characteristics of the latest and earliest Makkan Surahs. It may, therefore, be taken as belonging to the middle group of Makkan Surahs.

In the name of Allah, the Beneficent, the Merciful.

1. Their reckoning draws near for mankind, while they turn away in heedlessness.

2. Never comes there to them a new reminder from their Lord but they listen to it while they play,

3. With hearts preoccupied. And they consult in secret. The wrongdoers say: Is this other than a mortal like you? Will you then succumb to magic when you see (it)?

4. He says: My Lord knows what is spoken in the heaven and the earth. He is the Hearer, the Knower

5. No, say they, (these are but) muddled dreams; No, he has only invented it; No, he is only a poet. Let him bring us a sign even as those of old (who were God's messengers) were sent (with signs).

6. Not a township believed of those which We destroyed before them (though We sent them signs): would they then believe?

7. And We sent not (as Our messengers) before you other than men, whom We inspired. Ask the followers of the Reminder[162] if you know not?

8. We did not give them bodies that would not eat food, nor were they immortals.

9. Then We fulfilled the promise to them. So We delivered them and whom We would, and We destroyed the prodigals.

10. Now We have revealed to you a Scripture in which is your Reminder. Have you then no sense?

11. How many a community that dealt unjustly have We shattered, and raised up after them another people!

12. And, when they felt Our might, you see them fleeing from it!

13. (But it was said to them): Flee not, but return to that (existence) which pampered you and to your dwellings, that you may be questioned.

14. They cried: Alas for us! We were wrongdoers.

15. And this their crying ceased not till We made them as reaped corn, extinct.

16. We created not the heaven and the earth and all that is between them in play.

17. If We had wished to find a pastime, We could have found it in Our presence - if We ever did.

18. No, but We hurl the true against the false, and it does break its head and it vanishes. And yours will be woe for that which you ascribe (to Him).

19. To Him belongs whoever is in the heavens and the earth. And those who dwell in His presence are not too proud to worship Him, nor do they weary;

20. They glorify (Him) night and day; they tire not.

21. Or have they chosen gods from the earth who raise the dead?

22. If there were in it gods besides Allah, then verily both (the heavens and the earth) would have been disordered. Glorified be Allah, the Lord of the Throne, from all that they ascribe (to Him).

23. He will not be questioned as to that which He does, but they will be questioned.

24. Or have they chosen other gods besides Him? Say: Bring your proof (of their godhead). This is the Reminder of those with me and those before me, but most of them know not the Truth and so they are averse.

25. And We sent no messenger before you but We inspired him, (saying): There is no God except Me (Allah), so worship Me.

26. And they say: The Beneficent has taken to Himself a son. Be He Glorified! No, but (those whom they call sons) are honoured slaves;

27. They speak not until He has spoken, and they act by His command.

28. He knows what is before them and what is behind them, and they cannot intercede except for him whom He accepts, and they tremble for awe of Him.

29. And if one of them should say: I am a god beside Him, that one We should repay with Hell. Thus We repay wrongdoers.

---

162. *i.e.* the Jewish Scripture.

30. Have not those who disbelieve known that the heavens and the earth were of one piece, then We parted them, and we made every living thing of water? Will they not then believe?

31. And We have placed in the earth firm hills lest it quake with them, and We have placed in it ravines as roads that perhaps they may find their way.

32. And We have made the sky a roof withheld (from them). Yet they turn away from its signs.

33. And He it is Who created the night and the day, and the sun and the moon. They float, each in an orbit.

34. We appointed immortality for no mortal before you. What! if you die, can they be immortal!

35. Every soul must taste death, and We try you with evil and with good, for ordeal. And to Us you will be returned.

36. And when those who disbelieve see you, they only choose you out for mockery, (saying): Is this he who makes mention of your gods? And they would deny all mention of the Beneficent.

37. Man is made of haste. I shall show you My signs, but ask Me not to hasten.

38. And they say: When will this promise (be fulfilled), if you are truthful?

39. If those who disbelieved only knew the time when they will not be able to drive off the fire from their faces and from their backs, and they will not be helped!

40. No, but it will come upon them unawares so that it will stupefy them,

and they will be unable to repel it, neither will they be reprieved.

41. Messengers before you, indeed, were mocked, but that at which they mocked surrounded those who jeered at them.

42. Say: Who guards you in the night or in the day from the Beneficent? No, but they turn away from mention of their Lord!

43. Or have they gods who can shield them from Us? They cannot help themselves nor can they be defended from Us.

44. No, but We gave these and their fathers ease until life grew long for them. Do they not see how We aim to the land, reducing it of its outlying parts?[163] Can they then be the victors?

45. Say (O Muhammad, to mankind): I warn you only by the Inspiration. But the deaf hear not the call when they are warned.

46. And if a breath of your Lord's punishment were to touch them, they assuredly would say: Alas for us! We were wrongdoers.

47. And We set a just balance for the Day of Resurrection so that no soul is wronged in anything. Though it be of the weight of a grain of mustard seed, We bring it. And We suffice for reckoners.

48. And We verily gave Moses and Aaron the Criterion (of right and wrong) and a light and a Reminder for those who keep from evil,

49. Those who fear their Lord in secret and who dread the Hour (of doom).

---

163. See *Surah 8, Al-Anfal*, v. 41, note.

50. This is a blessed Reminder that we have revealed: Will you then reject it?

51. And We verily gave Abraham of old his proper course, and We were Aware of him,

52. When he said to his father and his people: What are these images to which you pay devotion?

53. They said: We found our fathers worshippers of them.

54. He said: Verily you and your fathers were in plain error.

55. They said: Do you bring to us the truth, or are you some jester?

56. He said: No, but your Lord is the Lord of the heavens and the earth, Who created them; and I am of those who testify to that.

57. And, by Allah, I shall circumvent your idols after you have gone away and turned your backs.

58. Then he reduced them to fragments, all except the chief of them, that perhaps they might have recourse to it.

59. They said: Who has done this to our gods? Surely it must be some evil-doer.

60. They said: We heard a youth make mention of them, who is called Abraham.

61. They said: Then bring him (here) before the people's eyes that they may testify.

62. They said: Is it you who has done this to our gods, O Abraham?

63. He said: But this, their chief has done it. So question them, if they can speak.

64. Then they gathered separately and said: You yourselves are the wrongdoers.

65. And they were utterly confused, and they said: Well you know that these speak not.

66. He said: Do you then worship instead of Allah that which cannot profit you at all, nor harm you?

67. Fie on you and all that you worship instead of Allah! Have you then no sense?

68. They called: Burn him and stand by your gods, if you will.

69. We said: O fire, be coolness and peace for Abraham,

70. And they wished to set a trap for him, but We made them the greater losers.

71. And We rescued him and Lot (and brought them) to the land which We have blessed for (all) peoples.

72. And We bestowed upon him Isaac, and Jacob as a grandson. Each of them We made righteous.

73. And We made them chiefs who guide by Our command, and We inspired in them the doing of good deeds and the right establishment of worship and the giving of alms, and they were worshippers of Us (alone).

74. And to Lot we gave judgement and knowledge, and We delivered him from the community that did abominations. They were people of evil, lewd.

75. And We brought him in to Our mercy. He was of the righteous.

76. And Noah, when he called of old, We heard his prayer and saved him and his household from the great affliction.

77. And delivered him from the people who denied Our revelations. They were people of evil, therefore We drowned them all.

78. And David and Solomon, when they gave judgement concerning the field, when people's sheep had strayed and browsed in it by night; and We were witnesses to their judgement.

79. And We made Solomon understand (the case); and to each of them We gave judgement and knowledge. And we subdued the hills and the birds to hymn (His) praise along with David. We were the doers (of it).

80. And We taught him the art of making garments (of mail) to protect you in your daring. Are you then thankful?

81. And to Solomon (We subdued) the wind in its raging. It set by his command toward the land which We had blessed. And of everything We are Aware.

82. And of the evil ones[164] (We subdued to him) some who dived (for pearls) for him and did other work, and We were guardians to them.

83. And Job, when he called to his Lord, (saying): Adversity afflicts me, and You are Most Merciful of all who show mercy.

84. Then We heard his prayer and removed that adversity from which he suffered, and We gave him his household (that he had lost) and the like of it along with them, a mercy from Our store, and a remembrance for the worshippers;

85. And (mention) Ishmael, and Idris, and Dhu'l-Kifl.[165] All were of the steadfast.

86. And We brought them in to Our mercy. They are among the righteous.

87. And (mention) Dhu'n-Nun,[166] when he went off in anger and deemed that We had no power over him, but he called out in the darkness, saying: There is no God except You. Be You Glorified! I have been a wrong-doer.

88. Then We heard his prayer and saved him from the anguish. Thus We save believers.

89. And Zechariah, when he called to his Lord: My Lord! Leave me not childless, though You are the Best of inheritors.

90. Then We heard his prayer, and bestowed upon him John, and adjusted his wife (to bear a child) for him. They used to vie one with the other in good deeds, and they called to Us in longing and in fear, and were submissive to Us.

91. And she who was chaste,[167] therefore We breathed into her (something) of Our Spirit and made her and her son a sign for (all) peoples.

92. This, your religion, is one religion, and I am your Lord, so worship Me.

93. And they have broken their religion (into fragments) among them, (yet) all are returning to Us.

94. Then who does some good works and is a believer, there will be no rejection of his effort. We record (it) for him.

---

164. Arabic: *Shayatin, lit.* "devils"

165. A prophet famous among the Arabs, whose story resembles that of Ezekiel.
166. *Lit.* "Lord of the Fish" - Jonah.
167. The reference here is to the Virgin Mary.

95. And there is a ban upon any community which We have destroyed: that they shall not return.

96. Until, when Gog and Magog are let loose, and they hasten out of every mound,

97. And the True Promise draws near; then see them, staring wide (in terror), the eyes of those who disbelieve! (They say): Alas for us! We (lived) in forgetfulness of this. Ah, but we were wrongdoers!

98. You (idolaters) and that which you worship besides Allah are fuel of Hell. To it you will come.

99. If these had been gods they would not have come there, but all will remain therein.

100. In it wailing is their portion, and in it they hear not.

101. Those to whom kindness has gone out before from Us, they will be far removed from there.

102. They will not hear the slightest sound of it, while they remain in that which their souls desire.

103. The Supreme Horror will not grieve them, and the angels will welcome them, (saying): This is your Day which you were promised;

104. The Day when We shall roll up the heavens as a recorder rolls up a written scroll. As We began the first creation, We shall repeat it. (It is) a promise (binding) upon Us. We are to perform it.

105. And verily, We have written in the Scripture, after the Reminder: My righteous slaves will inherit the earth:

106. There is a plain statement for people who are devout.

107. We sent you not except as a mercy for the peoples.

108. Say: It is only inspired in me that your God is One God. Will you then surrender (to Him)?

109. But if they are averse, then say: I have warned you all alike, although I know not whether near or far is that which you are promised.

110. He knows that which is said openly, and that which you conceal.

111. And I know not but that this may be a trial for you, and enjoyment for a while.

112. He says: My Lord! Judge You with truth. Our Lord is the Beneficent, Whose help is to be implored against that which you ascribe (to Him).

Surah 22: **Al-Hajj**
(The Pilgrimage)

Al-Hajj, "The Pilgrimage," takes its name from vv. 26-38 relating to the pilgrimage to Makkah. This Surah is ascribed by some authorities to the Makkan period, by others to the Madinah period. The copy of the Qur'an which I have followed throughout has the Madinah ascription, and, as it was copied long before the days of "higher" criticism, and was authorised for use throughout the Ottoman Empire, I retain that ascription. Vv. 11-13, 25-30, 39-41 and 58-60 were, according to all authorities, revealed at Al-Madinah. Nöldeke, greatest of the "higher" critics, says that the ascription is justified on account of the importance of the verses in this Surah which must, from the nature of their contents, have been revealed at Al-Madinah, while holding that much of the Surah belongs to the last Makkan period.

═══════════════════

In the name of Allah, the Beneficent, the Merciful.

1. O mankind! Fear your Lord. The earthquake of the Hour (of Doom) is a tremendous thing.

2. On the day when you see it, every nursing mother will forget her nursling and every pregnant one will be delivered of her burden, and you (Muhammad) will see mankind as drunken, yet they will not be drunken, but the Doom of Allah will be strong (upon them).

3. Among mankind is he who disputes concerning Allah without knowledge, and follows each obstinate devil;

4. For him it is decreed that whoever takes him for a friend, he verily will mislead him and will guide him to the punishment of the Flame.

5. O mankind! if you are in doubt concerning the Resurrection, then We have created you from dust, then from a drop of seed, then from a clot, then from a little lump of flesh shapely and shapeless, that We may make (it) clear for you. And We cause what We will to remain in the wombs for an appointed time, and afterwards We bring you out as infants, then (give you growth) that you attain your full strength. And among you there is he

who dies (young), and among you there is he who is brought back to the most abject time of life, so that, after knowledge, he knows nothing. And you (Muhammad) see the earth barren, but when We send down water on it, it does thrill and swell and put forth every lovely kind[168] (of growth).

6. That is because Allah, He is the Truth, and He gives life to the dead, and He is Able to do all things;

7. And because the Hour will come, there is no doubt of it; and because Allah will raise those who are in the graves.

8. And among mankind is he who disputes concerning Allah without knowledge or guidance or a scripture giving light,

9. Turning away in pride to deceive (men) from the way of Allah. For him in this world is ignominy, and on the Day of Resurrection We make him taste the doom of burning.

10. (And to him it will be said): This is for that which your two hands have sent before, and because Allah is no oppressor of His slaves.

11. And among mankind is he who worships Allah upon a narrow verge so that if good befalls him he is content with it, but if a trial befalls him, he falls away utterly. He loses

---

168. Or "every lovely pair." Prof. Ghamrawi, who helped me in the revision of the text, kept exclaiming on the subtlety and wealth of meaning of every expression used in the Qur'an concerning natural phenomena. Thus the word "pair" occurs often in the sense of "species", commemorating the fact that every growth of the earth exists as male and female. See particularly *Surah 36, Ya Sin,* v. 36 - Tr.

both the world and the Hereafter. That is the sheer loss.[169]

12. He calls, besides Allah, to that which hurts him not nor benefits him. That is the far error.

13. He calls to him whose harm is nearer than his benefit; verily an evil patron and verily an evil friend!

14. Allah causes those who believe and do good works to enter Gardens underneath which rivers flow. Allah does what He intends.

15. Whoever thinks (through envy) that Allah will not give him (Muhammad) victory in the world and the Hereafter (and is enraged at the thought of his victory), let him stretch a rope up to the roof (of his dwelling), and let him hang himself. Then let him see whether his strategy dispels that at which he rages![170]

16. Thus We reveal it as plain revelations, and verily Allah guides whom He will.

17. Those who believe (this revelation), and those who are Jews, and the Sabaeans and the Christians and the Magians and the idolaters - Allah will decide between them on the Day of Resurrection. Allah is Witness over all things.

169. Tradition says that the reference is to certain Arabs who came to the Prophet at Al-Madinah and professed Al-Islam; then, if they prospered in a worldly sense, they were content, but if they had to suffer at all they relapsed to idolatry.
170. The meaning is that Allah will undoubtedly cause the Prophet to triumph in both worlds, and therefore his opponents have no strategy except that of despair.

18. Have you not seen that to Allah pays adoration whoever is in the heavens and whoever is in the earth, and the sun, and the moon, and the stars, and the hills, and the trees and the beasts, and many of mankind, while there are many to whom the doom is justly due. He whom Allah disgraces, there is none to give him honour. Allah does what He will.

19. These two (the believers and the disbelievers) are two opponents who argue concerning their Lord. But as for those who disbelieve, garments of fire will be cut out for them; boiling fluid will be poured down on their heads,

20. By which that which is in their bellies, and their skins too, will be melted;

21. And for them are hooked rods of iron.

22. Whenever, in their anguish, they would go out from there they are driven back into it and (it is said to them): Taste the doom of burning.

23. Allah will cause those who believe and do good works to enter Gardens underneath which rivers flow, in which they will be allowed armlets of gold, and pearls, and their garments in it will be silk.

24. They are guided to gentle speech; they are guided to the path of the Owner of Praise.

25. Those who disbelieve and prevent (men) from the way of Allah and from the Inviolable Place of Worship, which We have appointed for mankind together, the dweller in it and the nomad: whoever seeks wrongful partiality in it, him We shall cause to taste a painful doom.

26. And (remember) when We prepared for Abraham the place of the (holy) House, saying: Ascribe nothing as partner to Me, and purify My House for those who make the round (of it) and those who stand and those who bow and make prostration.

27. And proclaim to mankind the pilgrimage.[171] They will come to you on foot and on very lean camel; they will come from every deep ravine,

28. That they may witness things that are of benefit to them, and mention the name of Allah on appointed days over the (sacrificial) beast of cattle that He has bestowed upon them. Then eat of it and feed with it the poor unfortunate.

29. Then let them make an end of their unkemptness and pay their vows and go around the ancient House.

30. That (is the command). And whoever magnifies the sacred things of Allah, it will be well for him in the sight of his Lord. The cattle are lawful to you except that which has been told you. So shun the filth of idols, and shun lying speech,

31. Turning to Allah (only), not ascribing partners to Him; for whoever ascribes partners to Allah, it is as if he had fallen from the sky and the birds had snatched him or the wind had blown him to a far-off place.

32. That (is the command). And whoever magnifies the offerings consecrated to Allah, it surely is from devotion of the hearts.

---

171. See *Surah 2, Al-Baqarah*, v. 196, footnote.

33. In it are benefits for you for an appointed term; and afterwards they are brought for sacrifice[172] to the ancient House.

34. And for every nation We have appointed a ritual, that they may mention the name of Allah over the beast of cattle that He has given them for food;[173] and your God is One God, therefore surrender to Him. And give good tidings (O Muhammad) to the humble,

35. Whose hearts fear when Allah is mentioned, and the patient of whatever may befall them, and those who establish worship and who spend of that which We have bestowed on them.

36. And the camels! We have appointed them among the ceremonies of Allah. In them you have much good. So mention the name of Allah over them when they are drawn up in lines. Then when their flanks fall (dead), eat of it and feed the beggar and the suppliant. Thus We have made them subject to you, that perhaps you may give thanks.

37. Their flesh and their food do not reach Allah, but the devotion from you reaches Him. Thus We have made them subject to you that

---

172. The slaughter of animals for food for the poor which is one of the ceremonies of the Muslim pilgrimage is not a conciliatory sacrifice, but is in commemoration of the sacrifice of Abraham which marked the end of human sacrifices for the Semitic race, and which made it clear that the only sacrifice which God requires of man is the Surrender of his will and purpose - *i.e.* Al-Islam.
173. In order that they may realise the awfulness of taking life, and the solemn nature of the trust which Allah has imposed on them in the permission to eat animal food.

you may magnify Allah that He has guided you. And give good tidings (O Muhammad) to the good.

38. Allah defends those who are true. Allah loves not each treacherous ingrate.

39. Sanction is given to those who fight because they have been wronged; and Allah is indeed Able to give them victory;

40. Those who have been driven from their homes unjustly only because they said: Our Lord is Allah - For had it not been for Allah's repelling some men by means of others, cloisters and churches and oratories and mosques, in which the name of Allah is oft mentioned, would assuredly have been pulled down. Verily Allah helps the one who helps Him. Allah is Strong, Almighty -

41. Those who, if We give them power in the land, establish worship and pay the poor-due and enjoin kindness and forbid iniquity. And Allah's is the sequel of events.

42. If they deny you (Muhammad), even so the people of Noah, and (the tribes of) A'ad and Thamud, before you, denied (Our messengers);

43. And the people of Abraham and the people of Lot;

44. (And) the dwellers in Midian. And Moses was denied; but I indulged the disbelievers a long while, then I seized them, and how (terrible) was My abhorrence!

45. How many a township have We destroyed while it was sinful, so that it lies (to this day) in ruins, and (how many) a deserted well and lofty tower!

46. Have they not travelled in the land, and have they hearts with which to feel and ears with which to hear? For indeed it is not the eyes that grow blind, but it is the hearts, which are within the bosoms, that grow blind.

47. And they will ask you to hasten on the Doom, and Allah fails not His promise, but a Day with Allah is as a thousand years of what you reckon.

48. And how many a township did I suffer long though it was sinful! Then I grasped it. To Me is the return.

49. Say: O mankind! I am only a plain warner to you.

50. Those who believe and do good works, for them is pardon and a rich provision;

51. While those who strive to thwart Our revelations, such are rightful owners of the Fire.

52. Never sent We a messenger or a prophet before you but when He recited (the message) Satan proposed (opposition) in respect of that which he recited of it. But Allah abolishes that which Satan proposes. Then Allah establishes His revelations. Allah is Knower, Wise;

53. That He may make that which the devil proposes a temptation for those in whose hearts is a disease, and those whose hearts are hardened - the evildoers are in open schism -

54. And that those who have been given knowledge may know that it is the truth from your Lord, so that they may believe in it and their hearts may submit humbly to Him. Allah verily is guiding those who believe to a right path.

55. And those who disbelieve will not cease to be in doubt of it until the Hour comes upon them unawares, or there comes to them the doom of a disastrous day.

56. The Sovereignty on that day will be Allah's, He will judge between them. Then those who believed and did good works will be in Gardens of Delight,

57. While those who disbelieved and denied Our revelations, for them will be a shameful doom.

58. Those who fled their homes for the cause of Allah and then were slain or died, Allah verily will provide for them a good provision. Allah, He verily is Best of all who make provision.

59. Assuredly He will cause them to enter by an entry that they will love. Allah verily is Knower, Indulgent.

60. That (is so). And whoever has retaliated with the like of that which he was made to suffer and then has (again) been wronged, Allah will help him. Allah verily is Mild, Forgiving.

61. That is because Allah makes the night to pass into the day and makes the day to pass into the night, and because Allah is Hearer, Seer.

62. That is because Allah, He is the True, and that on which they call instead of Him, it is the false, and because Allah, is the most High, the Great.

63. Do you not see how Allah sends down water from the sky and then the earth becomes green in the morning? Allah is Subtle, Aware.

64. To Him belongs all that is in the heavens and all that is in the earth. Allah, He verily is the Absolute, the Owner of Praise.

65. Have you not seen how Allah has made all that is in the earth subservient to you? And the ship runs upon the sea by His command, and He holds back the heaven from falling on the earth unless by His leave. Allah is, for mankind, Full of Pity, Merciful.

66. And He it is Who gave you life, then He will cause you to die, and then will give you life (again). Man is verily ungrateful.

67. To each nation We have given sacred rites which they are to perform; so let them not dispute with you of the matter, but summon you to your Lord. You indeed follow right guidance.

68. And if they wrangle with you, say: Allah is Best Aware of what you do.

69. Allah will judge between you on the Day of Resurrection concerning that in which you used to differ.

70. Have you not known that Allah knows all that is in the heaven and the earth? It is in a record. That is easy for Allah.

71. And they worship instead of Allah that for which He has sent down no authority, and that of which they have no knowledge. For evildoers there is no helper.

72. And when Our revelations are recited to them, you know the denial in the faces of those who disbelieve; they all but attack those who recite Our revelations to them. Say: Shall

I proclaim to you worse than that? The Fire! Allah has promised it for those who disbelieve. An unhappy journey's end!

73. O mankind! A similitude is coined, so pay heed to it: Those on whom you call besides Allah will never create a fly though they combine together for the purpose. And if the fly took something from them, they could not rescue it from it. So weak are (both) the seeker and the sought!

74. They measure not Allah His rightful measure. Allah is Strong, Almighty.

75. Allah chooses from the angels messengers, and (also) from mankind. Allah is Hearer, Seer.

76. He knows all that is before them and all that is behind them, and to Allah all things are returned.

77. O you who believe! Bow down and prostrate yourselves, and worship your Lord, and do good, that perhaps you may prosper.

78. And strive for Allah with the endeavour which is His right. He has chosen you and has not laid upon you in religion any hardship; the faith of your father Abraham (is yours). He has named you Muslims[174] before and in this (Scripture), that the messenger may be a witness against you, and that you may be witnesses against mankind. So establish worship, pay the poor-due, and hold fast to Allah. He is your Protecting friend. A blessed Patron and a blessed Helper!

---

174. "Those who have surrendered."

Surah 23: *Al-Mu'minun*
(The Believers)

Al-Mu'minun, "The Believers," is so named from a word occurring in the first verse or, it may be said, from its subject, which is the triumph of believers. It is considered to be the last of the Surahs revealed at Makkah, immediately before the Prophet's flight to Yathrib (Al-Madinah).

A late Makkan Surah.

In the name of Allah, the Beneficent, the Merciful.

1. Successful indeed are the believers.

2. Who are humble in their prayers,

3. And who shun vain conversation,

4. And who are payers of the poor-due;

5. And who guard their modesty -

6. Except from their wives or the (slaves) whom their right hands possess, for then they are not blameworthy,

7. But whoever craves beyond that, such are transgressors -

8. And who are shepherds of their pledge and their covenant,

9. And who pay heed to their prayers.

10. These are the heirs

11. Who will inherit paradise. There they will remain.

12. Verily We created man from a product of wet earth;

13. Then placed him as a drop (of seed) in a safe lodging;

14. Then We fashioned the drop into a clot, then We fashioned the clot into a little lump, then We fashioned the little lump bones, then clothed the bones with flesh, and then produced it as another creation. So blessed be Allah, the Best of Creators!

15. Then, after that, you shall surely die.

16. Then, on the Day of Resurrection, you are raised (again).

17. And We have created above you seven paths, and We are never unmindful of creation.

18. And we send down from the sky water in measure, and We give it lodging in the earth, and We are Able to withdraw it.

19. Then We produce for you with it gardens of date-palms and grapes, in which is much fruit for you, and of which you eat;

20. And a tree that springs out from Mount Sinai that grows oil and relish for the eaters.

21. And in the cattle there is verily a lesson for you. We give you to drink of that which is in their bellies, and many uses have you in them, and of them do you eat;

22. And on them and on ships you are carried.

23. And We verily sent Noah to his people, and he said: O my people! Serve Allah. You have no other God except Him. Will you not ward off (evil)?

24. But the chieftains of his people, who disbelieved, said: This is only a mortal like you who would make himself superior to you. Had Allah

willed, He surely could have sent down angels. We heard not of this in the case of our fathers of old.

25. He is only a man in whom is a madness, so watch him for a while.

26. He said: My Lord! Help me because they deny me.

27. Then We inspired in him, saying: Make the ship under Our eyes and Our inspiration. Then, when Our command comes, and the oven gushes out water, introduce in it of every (kind) two spouses, and your household, except him of it against whom the Word has already gone before. And plead not with Me on behalf of those who have done wrong. They will be drowned.

28. And when you are on board the ship, you and whoever is with you, then say: Praise be to Allah Who has saved us from the wrongdoing people!

29. And say: My Lord! Cause me to land at a blessed landing-place, for You are Best of all who bring to land.

30. In this verily are signs, for We are ever putting (mankind) to the test.

31. Then, after them, We brought out another generation;

32. And We sent among them a messenger of their own, saying: Serve Allah, You have no other God except Him. Will you not ward off (evil)?

33. And the chieftains of his people, who disbelieved and denied the meeting of the Hereafter, and whom We had made soft in the life of the world, said: This is only a mortal like you, who eats of that of which you eat and drinks of that of which you drink.

34. If you were to obey a mortal like yourselves, then, you surely would be losers.

35. Does he promise you that when you are dead and have become dust and bones, you will (again) be brought out?

36. Away, away, with that which you are promised!

37. There is nothing but our life of the world; we die and we live, and we shall not be raised (again).

38. He is only a man who has invented a lie about Allah. We are not going to put faith in him.

39. He said: My Lord! Help me because they deny me.

40. He said: In a little while they surely will become repentant.

41. So the (Awful) Call overtook them rightfully, and We made them like wreckage (that a torrent hurls). A far removal for wrongdoing people!

42. Then after them We brought out other generations.

43. No nation can outstrip its term, nor yet postpone it.

44. Then We sent our messengers one after another. Whenever its messenger came to a nation, they denied him; so We caused them to follow one another (to disaster), and We made them myths. A far removal for people who believe not!

45. Then We sent Moses and his brother Aaron with Our signs and a clear authority

46. To Pharaoh and his chiefs, but they despised (them) and they were despotic people.

47. And they said: Shall we put faith in two mortals like ourselves, and whose people are servile to us?

48. So they denied them, and became of those who were destroyed.

49. And We verily gave Moses the Scripture, that perhaps they might go aright.

50. And We made the son of Mary and his mother a sign, and We gave them refuge on a height, a place of flocks and water springs.

51. O you messengers! Eat of the good things, and do right. I am Aware of what you do.

52. And this your religion is one religion and I am your Lord, so keep your duty to Me.

53. But they (mankind) have broken their religion among them into sects, each group rejoicing in its tenets.

54. So leave them in their error till a time.

55. Do they think that in the wealth and sons with which We provide them

56. We hasten to them with good things? No, but they perceive not.

57. Those who go in awe for fear of their Lord,

58. And those who believe in the revelations of their Lord,

59. And those who ascribe not partners to their Lord,

60. And those who give that which they give with hearts afraid because they are about to return to their Lord,

61. These race for the good things, and they shall win them in the race.

62. And we task not any soul beyond its scope, and with Us is a Record which speaks the truth, and they will not be wronged.

63. No, but their hearts are in ignorance of this (Qur'an), and they have other works, besides, which they are doing;

64. Till when We grasp their luxurious ones with the punishment, look! They supplicate.

65. Supplicate not this day! Assuredly you will not be helped by Us.

66. My revelations were recited to you, but you used to turn back on your heels,

67. In contempt of it. Nightly did you rave together.

68. Have they not pondered the Word, or has that come to them which came not to their fathers of old?

69. Or know they not their messenger, and so reject him?

70. Or do they say: There is a madness in him? No, but he brings them the Truth; and most of them are haters of the Truth.

71. And if the Truth had followed their desires, verily the heavens and the earth and who is in it would have been corrupted. No, We have brought them their Reminder, but from their Reminder they now turn away.

72. Or do you ask of them (O Muhammad) any tribute? But the bounty of your Lord is better, for He is Best of all who make provision.

73. And you summon them indeed to a straight path.

74. And those who believe not in the Hereafter are indeed astray from the path.

75. Though We had mercy on them and relieved them of the harm afflicting them, they still would wander blindly on in their rebellion.

76. Already We have grasped them with punishment, but they humble not themselves to their Lord, nor do they pray,

77. Until, when We open for them the gate of extreme punishment, look! they are aghast at it.

78. He it is Who has created for you ears and eyes and hearts. Small thanks do you give!

79. And He it is Who has spread you out in the earth, and to Him you will be gathered.

80. And He it is Who gives life and causes death, and His is the difference of night and day. Have you then no sense?

81. No, but they say the like of that which the men of old said;

82. They say: When we are dead and have become (mere) dust and bones, shall we then be raised again?

83. We were already promised this, we and our forefathers. This is nothing but fables of the men of old.

84. Say: To Whom (belongs) the earth and whoever is in it, if you have knowledge?

85. They will say: To Allah. Say: Will you not then remember?

86. Say: Who is Lord of the seven heavens, and Lord of the Tremendous Throne?

87. They will say: To Allah (all that belongs). Say: Will you not then keep duty (to Him)?

88. Say: In Whose hand is the dominion over all things and He protects, while against Him there is no protection, if you have knowledge?

89. They will say: To Allah (all that belongs). Say: How then are you bewitched?

90. No, but We have brought them the Truth, and they are liars.

91. Allah has not chosen any son, nor is there any god along with Him; else each god would have assuredly championed that which he created, and some of them would assuredly have overcome others. Glorified is Allah above all that they allege.

92. Knower of the Invisible and the Visible! and Exalted is He over all that they ascribe as partners (to Him)!

93. Say: My Lord! If You would show me that which they are promised.

94. My Lord! then set me not among the wrongdoing people.

95. And verily We are Able to show you that which We have promised them.

96. Repel evil with that which is better. We are Best Aware of that which they allege.

97. And say: My Lord! I seek refuge in You from suggestions of the evil ones,

98. And I seek refuge in You, my Lord, lest they be present with me,

99. Until, when death comes to one of them, he says: My Lord! Send me back,

100. That I may do right in that which I have left behind! But no! It is but a word that he speaks; and behind them is a barrier until the day when they are raised.

101. And when the trumpet is blown there will be no kinship among them that day, nor will they ask of one another.

102. Then those whose scales are heavy, they are the successful.

103. And those whose scales are light are those who lose their souls, remaining in Hell.

104. The fire burns their faces, and they are glum in it.

105. (It will be said): Were not My revelations recited to you, and then you used to deny them?

106. They will say: Our Lord! Our evil fortune conquered us, and we were erring people.

107. Our Lord! Oh, bring us out from here! If we return (to evil) then indeed we shall be wrongdoers.

108. He says: Away with you in it, and speak not to Me.

109. There was a party of My slaves who said: Our Lord! We believe, therefore forgive us and have mercy on us for You are Best of all who show mercy;

110. But you chose them for a laughing-stock until they caused you to forget remembrance of Me, while you laughed at them.

111. I have rewarded them this day inasmuch as they were steadfast in that they, even they, are the triumphant.

112. He will say: How long did you stay in the earth, counting by years?

113. They will say: We stayed a day or part of a day. Ask of those who keep count!

114. He will say: You stayed but a little if you only knew.

115. Did you then think that We had created you for nothing, and that you would not be returned to Us?

116. Now Allah be Exalted, the True King! There is no God except Him, the Lord of the Throne of Grace.

117. He who calls to any other god along with Allah has no proof of it. His reckoning is only with his Lord. Disbelievers will not be successful.

118. And (O Muhammad) say: My Lord! Forgive and have mercy, for You are Best of all who show mercy.

Surah 24: *An-Nur*
(Light)

An-Nur, "Light," takes its name from vv. 35-40 descriptive of the Light of God as it should shine in the homes of believers, the greater part of the Surah being legislation for the purifying of home life. All its verses were revealed at Al-Madinah. Tradition says that vv. 11-20 relate to the slanderers of Ayeshah in connection with an incident which occurred in the fifth year of the Hijrah when the Prophet was returning from the campaign against the Bani'l-Mustaliq; Ayeshah, having been left behind on a march, was found and brought back by a young soldier who let her mount his camel and himself led the camel. A weaker tradition places the revelation of vv. 1-10 as late as the ninth year of the Hijrah.

The period of revelation is the fifth and sixth years of the Hijrah.

In the name of Allah,
the Beneficent, the Merciful.

1. (Here is) a surah which We have revealed and enjoined, and in which We have revealed plain signs, that perhaps you may take heed.

2. The adulterer and the adulteress, beat you each one of them (with) a hundred strokes. And let not pity for the two withhold you from obedience to Allah, if you believe in Allah and the Last Day. And let a party of believers witness their punishment.

3. The adulterer shall not marry except an adulteress or an idolatress, and the adulteress none shall marry except an adulterer or an idolater. All that is forbidden to believers.

4. And those who accuse honourable women but bring not four witnesses, beat them (with) eighty strokes and never (afterwards) accept their testimony - they indeed are evildoers -

5. Except those who afterwards repent and make amends. (For such) Allah is Forgiving, Merciful.

6. As for those who accuse their wives but have no witnesses except themselves; let the testimony of one of them be four testimonies, (swearing) by Allah that he is of those who speak the truth;

7. And yet a fifth, invoking the curse of Allah on him if he is of those who lie.

8. And it shall avert the punishment from her if she bears witness before Allah four times that the thing he says is indeed false,

9. And a fifth (time) that the wrath of Allah be upon her if he speaks the truth.

10. And had it not been for the grace of Allah and His mercy to you, and that Allah is Clement, Wise, (you would have been undone).

11. They who spread the slander are a gang among you. Consider it not a bad thing for you; no, it is good for you. To every man of them (will be paid) that which he has earned of the sin; and as for him among them who had the greater share in it, his will be an awful doom.

12. Why did not the believers, men and women, when you heard it, think good of their own people, and say: It is a manifest untruth?

13. Why did they not produce four witnesses? Since they produce not witnesses, they verily are liars in the sight of Allah.

14. Had it not been for the grace of Allah and His mercy to you in the world and the Hereafter an awful doom would have overtaken you for that of which you murmured.

15. When you welcomed it with your tongues, and uttered with your mouths that of which you had no knowledge, you counted it a trivial matter. In the sight of Allah it is very great.

16. Why, when you heard it, did you not say: It is not for us to speak of this. Glory be to You (O Allah)! This is awful slander.

17. Allah admonishes you that you repeat not the like of it ever, if you are (in truth) believers.

18. And He explains to you the revelations. Allah is Knower, Wise.

19. Those who love that slander should be spread concerning those who believe, theirs will be a painful punishment in the world and the Hereafter. Allah knows. You know not.

20. Had it not been for the grace of Allah and His mercy to you, and that Allah is Clement, Merciful, (you would have been undone).

21. O you who believe! Follow not the footsteps of the devil. To whomsoever follows the footsteps of the devil, he commands filthiness and wrong. Had it not been for the grace of Allah and His mercy to you, not one of you would ever have grown pure. But Allah causes whom He will to grow. And Allah is Hearer, Knower.

22. And let not those who possess dignity and ease among you swear not to give to the relatives and to the needy, and to emigrants for the cause of Allah.[175] Let them forgive and show indulgence. Do you not desire that Allah may forgive you? Allah is Forgiving, Merciful.

---

175. Tradition says that Abu Bakr, when he heard that a relative of his own whom he had supported had been among the slanderers of his daughter Ayeshah, swore no longer to support him, and that this verse was revealed on that occasion.

23. As for those who defame virtuous, believing women (who are) unaware, cursed are they in the world and the Hereafter. Theirs will be an awful doom

24. On the day when their tongues and their hands and their feet testify against them as to what they used to do,

25. On that day Allah will pay them their just due, and they will know that Allah, He is the Manifest Truth.

26. Vile women are for vile men, and vile men for vile women. Good women are for good men, and good men for good women; such are innocent of that which people say: For them is pardon and a bountiful provision.

27. O you who believe! Enter not houses other than your own without first announcing your presence and invoking peace upon the people of it. That is better for you, that you may be heedful.

28. And if you find no-one in it, still enter not until permission has been given. And if it be said to you: Go away again, then go away, for it is purer for you. Allah knows what you do.

29. (It is) no sin for you to enter uninhabited houses in which is comfort for you. Allah knows what you proclaim and what you hide.

30. Tell the believing men to lower their gaze and be modest. That is purer for them. Allah is aware of what they do.

31. And tell the believing women to lower their gaze and be modest, and to display of their adornment only that which is apparent, and to draw their veils over their chests, and not to reveal their adornment except to their own husbands or fathers or husbands' fathers, or their sons or their husbands' sons, or their brothers or their brothers' sons or sisters' sons, or their women, or their slaves, or male attendants who lack vigour, or children who know nothing of women's nakedness. And let them not stamp their feet so as to reveal what they hide of their adornment. And turn to Allah together, O believers, in order that you may succeed.

32. And marry such of you as are single and the pious of your slaves and maid-servants. If they be poor, Allah will enrich them of His bounty. Allah is of ample means, Aware.

33. And let those who cannot find a match keep chaste till Allah gives them independence by His grace. And such of your slaves as seek a writing (of emancipation), write it for them if you are aware of anything of good in them, and bestow upon them of the wealth of Allah which He has bestowed upon you. Force not your slave-girls to whoredom that you may seek enjoyment of the life of the world, if they would preserve their chastity. And if one forces them, then (to them), after their compulsion, Allah will be Forgiving, Merciful.

34. And verily We have sent down for you revelations that make plain, and the example of those who passed away before you. An admonition to those who ward off (evil).

35. Allah is the Light of the heavens and the earth. The similitude of His light is as a niche in which is a lamp. The lamp is in a glass. The glass is as it were a shining star. (This lamp is) kindled from a blessed tree, an olive neither of the East nor of the West, whose oil would almost glow (of itself) though no fire touched it. Light upon light. Allah guides to His light whom He will. And Allah speaks to mankind in allegories, for Allah is Knower of all things.

36. (This lamp is found) in houses which Allah has allowed to be exalted and that His name shall be remembered there. There, do offer praise to Him at morning and evening,

37. Men whom neither merchandise nor sale distracts from remembrance of Allah and constancy in prayer and paying to the poor their due; who fear a day when hearts and eyeballs will be overturned;

38. That Allah may reward them with the best of what they did, and increase reward for them of His bounty. Allah gives blessings without limit to whom He will.

39. As for those who disbelieve, their deeds are as a mirage in a desert. The thirsty one supposes it to be water till he comes to it and finds it nothing, and finds, in the place of it, Allah Who pays him his due; and Allah is swift at reckoning.

40. Or as darkness on a vast, abysmal sea. There covers him a wave, above which is a wave, above which is a cloud. Layer upon layer of darkness. When he holds out his hand he can scarcely see it. And he for whom Allah has not appointed light, for him there is no light.

41. Have you not seen that it is Allah, Whom all who are in the heavens and the earth praise, and the birds in their flight? Of each He knows verily the worship and the praise; and Allah is Aware of what they do.

42. And to Allah belongs the Sovereignty of the heavens and the earth, and to Allah is the journeying.

43. Have you not seen how Allah wafts the clouds, then gathers them, then makes them layers, and you see the rain come out from between them; He sends down from the heaven mountains in which is hail, and strikes with it whom He will, and averts it from whom He will. The flashing of His lightning all but snatches away the sight.

44. Allah causes the revolution of the day and the night. In this is indeed a lesson for those who see.

45. Allah has created every animal from water. Of them is (a kind) that goes upon its belly and (a kind) that goes upon two legs and (a kind) that goes upon four. Allah creates what He will. Allah is Able to do all things.

46. Verily We have sent down revelations and explained them. Allah guides whom He will to a straight path.

47. And they say: We believe in Allah and the messenger, and we obey; then after that a faction of them turn away. Such are not believers.

48. And when they appeal to Allah and His messenger to judge between them, a faction of them are averse,

49. But if right had been with them they would have come to him willingly.

50. Is there in their hearts a disease, or have they doubts, or fear they lest Allah and His messenger should wrong them in judgement? No, but such are evildoers.

51. The saying of (all true) believers when they appeal to Allah and His messenger to judge between them is only that they say: We hear and we obey. And such are the successful.

52. He who obeys Allah and His messenger, and fears Allah, and keeps his duty (to Him): such indeed are the victorious.

53. They swear by Allah solemnly that, if you order them, they will go out. Say: Swear not; known obedience (is better). Allah is Informed of what you do.

54. Say: Obey Allah and obey the messenger. But if you turn away, then (it is) for him (to do) only that with which he has been charged, and for you (to do) only that with which you have been charged. If you obey him, you will go aright. But the messenger has no other duty than to convey (the message) plainly.

55. Allah has promised such of you as believe and do good work that He will surely make them to succeed (the present rulers) in the earth even as He caused those who were before them to succeed (others); and that He will surely establish for them their religion which He has approved for them, and will give them in exchange safety after their fear. They serve Me. They ascribe no thing as partner to Me. Those who disbelieve afterwards, they are the miscreants.

56. Establish worship and pay the poor-due and obey the messenger, that perhaps you may find mercy.

57. Think not that the disbelievers can escape in the land. Fire will be their home - an unhappy journey's end!

58. O you who believe! Let your slaves, and those of you who have not come to puberty, ask prior permission of you at three times (before they come into your presence): Before the prayer of dawn, and when you lay aside your garment for the heat of noon, and after the prayer of night.[176] Three times of privacy for you. It is no sin for them or for you at other times, when some of you go round attendant upon others (if they come into your presence without prior permission). Thus Allah makes clear the revelations for you. Allah is Knower, Wise.

59. And when the children among you come to puberty then let them ask permission even as those before them used to ask it. Thus Allah makes clear His revelations for you. Allah is Knower, Wise.

60. As for women past child-bearing, who have no hope of marriage, it is no sin for them if they discard their (outer) clothing in such a way as not to show adornment. But to refrain is better for them. Allah is Hearer, Knower.

61. No blame is there upon the blind nor any blame upon the lame nor any blame upon the sick nor on yourselves if you eat from your houses, or the houses of your fathers, or the houses of your mothers, or the houses of your

---

176. The prayer to be offered when the night has fully come.

brothers, or the houses of your sisters, or the houses of your fathers' brothers, or the houses of your fathers' sisters, or the houses of your mothers' brothers, or the houses of your mothers' sisters, or (from that) of which you hold the keys, or (from the house) of a friend. No sin shall it be for you whether you eat together or apart. But when you enter houses, salute one another with a greeting from Allah, blessed and sweet. Thus Allah makes clear His revelations for you, that perhaps you may understand.

62. They only are the true believers who believe in Allah and His messenger and, when they are with him on some common errand, go not away until they have asked permission of him. Those who ask permission of you, those are they who believe in Allah and His messenger. So, if they ask your permission for some affair of theirs, give permission to whom you will of them, and ask for them forgiveness of Allah. Allah is Forgiving, Merciful.

63. Make not the calling of the messenger among you as your calling one of another. Allah knows those of you who steal away, hiding themselves. And let those who conspire to evade orders beware lest grief or painful punishment befall them.

64. Verily to Allah belongs whatsoever is in the heavens and the earth. He knows your condition. And (He knows) the Day when they are returned to Him so that He may inform them of what they did. Allah is Knower of all things.

Surah 25: *Al-Furqan*
(The Criterion)

Al-Furqan, "The Criterion," takes its name from a word occurring in v. 1 The subject is the folly of superstition and the craving for miraculous events despite the wonders of God's creation.

It belongs to the middle group of Makkan Surahs, except vv. 68-70 which were revealed at Al-Madinah.

In the name of Allah,
the Beneficent, the Merciful.

1. Blessed is He Who has revealed to His slave the Criterion (of right and wrong), that he may be a warner to the peoples.

2. He to Whom belongs the Sovereignty of the heavens and the earth, He has chosen no son nor has He any partner in the Sovereignty. He has created everything and has meted out for it a measure.

3. Yet they choose besides Him other gods who create nothing but are themselves created, and possess not hurt nor profit for themselves, and possess not death nor life, nor power to raise the dead.

4. Those who disbelieve say: This is nothing but a lie that he has invented, and other people have helped him with it, so that they have produced a slander and a lie.

5. And they say: Fables of the men of old which he has had written down so that they are dictated to him in the morning and evening.

6. Say (to them, O Muhammad): He who knows the secret of the heavens and the earth has revealed it. He is ever Forgiving, Merciful.

7. And they say: What is the matter with this messenger (of Allah) that he eats food and walks in the markets? Why is an angel not sent down to him, to be a warner with him.

8. Or (why is not) treasure thrown down to him, or why has he not a paradise from where to eat? And the evildoers say: You are only following a man bewitched.

9. See how they coin similitudes for you, so that they are all astray and cannot find a road!

10. Blessed is He Who, if He wills, will assign you better than (all) that - Gardens underneath which rivers flow - and will assign you mansions.

11. No, but they deny (the coming of) the Hour, and for those who deny (the coming of) the Hour We have prepared a flame.

12. When it sees them from afar, they hear the crackling and the roar of it.

13. And when they are flung into a narrow place of it, chained together, they pray for destruction there.

14. Pray not that day for one destruction, but pray for many destructions!

15. Say: Is that (doom) better or the Garden of Immortality which is promised to those who ward off (evil)? It will be their reward and journey's end.

16. In it remaining, they have all that they desire. It is for your Lord a promise that must be fulfilled.

17. And on the day when He will assemble them and that which they worship instead of Allah and will say: Was it you who misled these my slaves or did they (themselves) wander from the way?

18. They will say: Be You Glorified! it was not for us to choose any protecting friends besides You; but You did give them and their fathers ease till they forgot the warning and became lost people.

19. Thus they will give you the lie regarding what you say, then you can neither avert (the doom) nor obtain help. And whoever among you does wrong, We shall make him taste great torment.

20. We never sent before you any messengers but they verily ate food and walked in the markets. And We have appointed some of you a test for others: Will you be steadfast? And your Lord is ever Seer.

21. And those who look not for a meeting with Us say: Why are angels not sent down to us and (why) do we not see our Lord! Assuredly, they think too highly of themselves and are contemptuous with great pride.

22. On the day when they see the angels, on that day there will be no good tidings for the guilty; and they will call: A forbidding ban!

23. And We shall turn to the work they did and make it scattered dust.

24. Those who have earned the Garden on that day will be better in their home and happier in their place of noonday rest;

25. A day when the heaven with the clouds will be rent asunder and the angels will be sent down, a grand descent.

26. The Sovereignty on that day will be the True (Sovereignty) belonging to the Beneficent One, and it will be a hard day for disbelievers.

27. On the day when the wrongdoer bites his hands, he will say: Ah, If only I had chosen a way together with the messenger (of Allah)!

28. Alas for me! Ah, if only I had never taken such a one for friend!

29. He verily led me astray from the Reminder after it had reached me. Satan was ever man's deserter in the hour of need.

30. And the messenger says: O my Lord! My own people make this Qur'an of no account.

31. Even so We have appointed to every prophet an opponent from among the guilty; but Allah suffices for a Guide and Helper.

32. And those who disbelieve say: Why is the Qur'an not revealed to him all at once? (It is revealed) thus that We may strengthen your heart with it; and We have arranged it in right order.

33. And they bring you no similitude but We bring you the Truth (as against it), and better (than their similitude) as argument.

34. Those who will be gathered on their faces to Hell: such are worse in plight and further from the right road.

35. We verily gave Moses the Scripture and placed with him his brother Aaron as supporter.

36. Then We said: Go together to the people who have denied Our revelations. Then We destroyed them, a complete destruction.

37. And Noah's people, when they denied the messengers, We drowned them and made of them a sign for mankind. We have prepared a painful doom for evildoers.

38. And (the tribes of) 'Aad and Thamud, and the dwellers in Ar-Rass,[177] and many generations in between.

39. Each (of them) We warned by examples, and each (of them) We brought to utter ruin.

40. And indeed they have passed by the township on which was rained the fatal rain.[178] Can it be that they have not seen it? No, but they hope for no resurrection.

41. And when they see you (O Muhammad) they treat you only as a jest (saying): Is this he whom Allah sends as a messenger?

42. He would have led us far away from our gods if we had not been staunch to them. They will know, when they see the doom, who is more astray as to the road.

43. Have you seen him who chooses for his god his own lust? Would you then be guardian over him?

44. Or do you think that most of them hear or understand? They are as the cattle - no, they are farther astray.

45. Have you not seen how your Lord has spread the shades - and if He willed

---

177. Said to have been a town in Yamamah.
178. The great trade caravans from Makkah into Syria passed by the Dead Sea.

He could have made it still - then We have made the sun its guide;

46. Then We withdraw it to Us, a gradual withdrawal?

47. And He it is Who makes night a covering for you, and sleep repose, and makes day a resurrection.

48. And He it is Who sends the winds, glad tidings heralding His mercy, and We send down purifying water from the sky,

49. That We may give life by it to a dead land, and We give many beasts and men that We have created to drink of it.

50. And verily We have repeated it among them that they may remember, but most of mankind deny anything except ingratitude.

51. If We willed, We could raise up a warner in every village.

52. So obey not the disbelievers, but strive against them with this with a great endeavour.

53. And He it is Who has given independence to the two seas[179] (though they meet); one palatable, sweet, and the other saltish, bitter; and has set a bar and a forbidding ban between them.

54. And He it is Who has created man from water, and has appointed for him relatives by blood and relatives by marriage; for your Lord is ever Powerful.

55. Yet they worship instead of Allah that which can neither benefit them nor hurt them. The disbeliever was ever a partisan against his Lord.

56. And We have sent you (O Muhammad) only as a bearer of good tidings and a warner.

57. Say: I ask of you no reward for this, except that whoever will may choose a way to his Lord.

58. And trust in the Living One Who dies not, and hymn His praise. He suffices as the Knower of His bondsmen's sins,

59. Who created the heavens and the earth and all that is between them in six Days,[180] then He mounted the Throne. The Beneficent! Ask anyone informed concerning Him!

60. And when it is said to them: Adore the Beneficent! they say: And what is the Beneficent? Are we to adore whatever you (Muhammad) ask us? And it increases aversion in them.

61. Blessed is He Who has placed in the heavens mansions of the stars, and has placed in it a great lamp and a moon giving light!

62. And He it is Who has appointed night and day in succession, for him who desires to remember, or desires thankfulness.

63. The (faithful) slaves of the Beneficent are they who walk upon the earth modestly, and when the foolish ones address them, they answer: Peace;

64. And who spend the night before their Lord, prostrate and standing,

65. And who say: Our Lord! Avert from us the doom of Hell; the doom of it is anguish;

---

179. *i.e.* the two kinds of water in the earth

180. See *Surah* 22, *Al-Hajj*, v. 47; *Surah* 32, *As-Sajdah*, v. 5 and *Surah* 70, *Al-Ma'arij*, v. 4.

66. It is wretched as an abode and as a stopping place;

67. And those who, when they spend, are neither prodigal nor reluctant; and there is ever a firm position between the two;

68. And those who call not to any other god along with Allah, nor take the life which Allah has forbidden except in (the course of) justice, nor commit adultery - and whoever does this shall pay the penalty;

69. The doom will be doubled for him on the Day of Resurrection, and he will remain in it despised forever;

70. Except him who repents and believes and does righteous work; as for such, Allah will change their evil deeds to good deeds. Allah is ever Forgiving, Merciful.

71. And whoever repents and does good, he verily repents towards Allah with true repentance -

72. And those who will not witness vanity, but when they pass near senseless play, pass by with dignity.

73. And those who, when they are reminded of the revelations of their Lord, fall not deaf and blind at it.

74. And who say: Our Lord! Grant us comfort of our wives and our offspring, and make us examples for (all) those who ward off (evil).

75. They will be awarded the high place inasmuch as they were steadfast, and they will meet in it with welcome and the protection of peace,

76. Remaining there forever. Happy is it as an abode and stopping place!

77. Say (O Muhammad, to the disbelievers): My Lord would not concern Himself with you but for your prayer. But now you have denied (the Truth), therefore there will be judgement.

Surah 26: *Ash-Shu'ara*
(The Poets)

Ash-Shu'ara, "The Poets," takes its title from v. 224 ff., where the difference between poets and a Prophet is concisely pointed out; poets being those who say what they do not mean, while a Prophet always practises what he preaches. The pagan Arabs and their poets believed the poetic inspiration to be the work of Jinn.

The story of a number of former Prophets is here given to console the believers at a time of persecution, with the assurance that it is no new thing for a messenger of God to be persecuted, but that the persecutors always suffer in the end. It shows also that all the messengers of God came with the same message.

It belongs to the middle group of Makkan Surahs, with the exception of vv. 224-227, which were revealed at Al-Madinah.

In the name of Allah,
the Beneficent, the Merciful.

1. *Ta. Sin. Mim.*[181]

2. These are revelations of the Scripture that makes plain.

3. It may be that you torment yourself (O Muhammad) because they believe not.

181. See *Surah 2, Al-Baqarah*, v. 1, footnote.

214

4. If We will, We can send down on them from the sky a sign so that their necks would remain bowed before it.

5. Never comes there to them a fresh reminder from the Beneficent One, except that they turn away from it.

6. Now they have denied (the Truth); but there will come to them tidings of that at which they used to jeer.

7. Have they not seen the earth, how much of every fruitful kind We make to grow in it?

8. In this is indeed a sign; yet most of them are not believers.

9. And your Lord! He is indeed the Mighty, the Merciful.

10. And when your Lord called Moses, saying: Go to the wrongdoing people,

11. The people of Pharaoh. Will they not ward off (evil)?

12. He said: My Lord! I fear that they will deny me,

13. And I shall be embarrassed, and my tongue will not speak plainly, therefore send for Aaron (to help me).

14. And they have a crime against me, so I fear that they will kill me.

15. He said: No, verily. So go both of you with Our signs. We shall be with you, Hearing.

16. And come together to Pharaoh and say: We bear a message of the Lord of the Worlds,

17. (Saying): Let the Children of Israel go with us.

18. (Pharaoh) said (to Moses): Did we not rear you among us as a child?

And you did dwell many years of your life among us,

19. And you did that deed of yours which you did, and you were one of the ungrateful.

20. He said: I did it then, when I was of those who are astray.

21. Then I fled from you when I feared you, and my Lord gave me a command and appointed me (of the number) of those sent (by Him).

22. And this is the past favour with which you reproach me: that you have enslaved the Children of Israel.

23. Pharaoh said: And what is the Lord of the Worlds?

24. (Moses) said: Lord of the heavens and the earth and all that is between them, if you only had sure belief.

25. (Pharaoh) said to those around him: Do you not hear?

26. He said: Your Lord and the Lord of your fathers.

27. (Pharaoh) said: Your messenger who has been sent to you is indeed a madman!

28. He said: Lord of the East and the West and all that is between them, if you only understand.

29. (Pharaoh) said: If you choose a god other than me, I assuredly shall place you among the prisoners.

30. He said: Even though I show you something plain?

31. (Pharaoh) said: Produce it then, if you are of the truthful!

32. Then he flung down his staff and it became a serpent manifest,

33. And he pulled out his hand and it was white to the onlookers.

34. (Pharaoh) said to the chiefs about him: This is verily a knowing wizard,

35. Who would drive you out of your land by his magic. Now what do you advise?

36. They said: Put him off, (him) and his brother, and send into the cities summoners

37. Who will bring to you every knowing wizard.

38. So the wizards were gathered together at a set time on a day appointed.

39. And it was said to the people: Are you (also) gathering?

40. (They said): Yes, so that we may follow the wizards if they are the winners.

41. And when the wizards came they said to Pharaoh: Will there surely be a reward for us if we are the winners?

42. He said: Yes, and you will then surely be of those brought near (to me).

43. Moses said to them: Throw what you are going to throw!

44. Then they threw down their cords and their staffs and said: By Pharaoh's might, we verily are the winners.

45. Then Moses threw his staff and it swallowed that which they did falsely show.

46. And the wizards were flung prostrate,

47. Calling: We believe in the Lord of the Worlds,

48. The Lord of Moses and Aaron.

49. (Pharaoh) said: You put your faith in him before I give you permission. He doubtless is your chief who taught you magic! But verily you shall come to know. Verily I will cut off your hands and your feet alternately, and verily I will crucify you, every one.

50. They said: It is no hurt, for to our Lord we shall return.

51. We ardently hope that our Lord will forgive us our sins because we are the first of the believers.

52. And We inspired Moses, saying: Take away My slaves by night, for you will be pursued.

53. Then Pharaoh sent into the cities summoners,

54. (Who said): These indeed are only a little troop,

55. And they are offenders against us.

56. And we are a ready host.

57. Thus did We take them away from gardens and watersprings,

58. And treasures and a fair estate.

59. Thus (were those things taken from them) and We caused the Children of Israel to inherit them.

60. And they overtook them at sunrise.

61. And when the two forces saw each other, those with Moses said: We are indeed caught.

62. He said: No, verily! for my Lord is with me. He will guide me.

63. Then We inspired Moses, saying: Strike the sea with your staff. And it parted, and each part was as a vast mountain.

64. Then We brought the others near to that place.

65. And We saved Moses and those with him, every one;

66. And We drowned the others.

67. In this is indeed a sign, yet most of them are not believers.

68. And your Lord! He is indeed the Mighty, the Merciful.

69. Recite to them the story of Abraham:

70. When he said to his father and his people: What do you worship?

71. They said: We worship idols, and are ever devoted to them.

72. He said: Do they hear you when you call?

73. Or do they benefit or harm you?

74. They said: No, but we found our fathers acting in this way.

75. He said: See now that which you worship,

76. You and your forefathers!

77. They are (all) an enemy to me, except the Lord of the Worlds,

78. Who created me, and He guides me,

79. And Who feeds me and waters me.

80. And when I fall ill, then He heals me,

81. And Who causes me to die, then gives me life (again),

82. And Who, I ardently hope, will forgive me my sin on the Day of Judgement.

83. My Lord! Grant me wisdom and unite me to the righteous.

84. And give to me a good report in later generations.

85. And place me among the inheritors of the Garden of Delight,

86. And forgive my father. He is of those who err.

87. And disgrace me not on the day when they are raised,

88. The day when wealth and sons benefit not (any man)

89. Except him who brings to Allah a whole heart.

90. And the Garden will be brought near for those who ward off (evil).

91. And Hell will appear plainly to the erring.

92. And it will be said to them: Where is (all) that you used to worship

93. Instead of Allah? Can they help you or help themselves?

94. Then they will be hurled in it, they and the seducers

95. And the forces of Iblis, together.

96. And they will say, when they are quarrelling in it:

97. By Allah, truly we were in error manifest

98. When we made you equal with the Lord of the Worlds.

99. It was but the guilty who misled us.

100. Now we have no intercessors

101. Nor any loving friend.

102. Oh, that we had another turn (on earth), that we might be of the believers!

103. In this is indeed a sign, yet most of them are not believers!

104. And your Lord! He is indeed the Mighty, the Merciful.

105. Noah's people denied the messengers (of Allah),

106. When their brother Noah said to them: Will you not ward off (evil)?

107. I am a faithful messenger to you,

108. So keep your duty to Allah, and obey me.

109. And I ask of you no wage for it; my wage is the concern only of the Lord of the Worlds.

110. So keep your duty to Allah, and obey me.

111. They said: Shall we put faith in you, when the lowest (of the people) follow you?

112. He said: And what knowledge have I of what they may have been doing (in the past)?

113. Their reckoning is my Lord's concern, if you only knew;

114. And I am not (here) to repulse believers.

115. I am only a plain warner.

116. They said: If you cease not, O Noah, you will surely be among those stoned (to death).

117. He said: My Lord! My own people deny me.

118. Therefore judge between us, a (conclusive) judgement, and save me and those believers who are with me.

119. And We saved him and those with him in the laden ship.

120. Then afterwards We drowned the others.

121. In this is indeed a sign, yet most of them are not believers.

122. And your Lord, He is indeed the Mighty, the Merciful.

123. (The tribe of) 'Aad denied the messengers (of Allah).

124. When their brother Hud said to them: Will you not ward off (evil)?

125. I am a faithful messenger to you,

126. So keep your duty to Allah and obey me.

127. And I ask of you no wage for it; my wage is the concern only of the Lord of the Worlds.

128. Do you build on every high place a monument for vain delight?

129. And do you seek out strongholds, that perhaps you may last forever?

130. And if you seize by force, do you seize as tyrants?

131. Rather keep your duty to Allah, and obey me.

132. Keep your duty towards Him Who has aided you with (the good things) that you know,

133. Has aided you with cattle and sons.

134. And gardens and watersprings.

135. I fear for you the retribution of an awful day.

136. They said: It is all one to us whether you preach or are not of those who preach;

137. This is only a fable of the men of old,

138. And we shall not be doomed.

139. And they denied him; therefore We destroyed them. In this is indeed a sign, yet most of them are not believers.

140. And your Lord, He is indeed the Mighty, the Merciful.

141. (The tribe of) Thamud denied the messengers (of Allah)

142. When their brother Salih said to them: Will you not ward off (evil)?

143. I am a faithful messenger to you,

144. So keep your duty to Allah and obey me.

145. And I ask of you no wage for it; my wage is the concern only of the Lord of the Worlds.

146. Will you be left secure in that which is here before us,

147. In gardens and watersprings.

148. And tilled fields and heavy-sheathed palm-trees,

149. Though you hew out dwellings in the mountain, being skilful?

150. Therefore keep your duty to Allah and obey me,

151. And obey not the command of the prodigals,

152. Who spread corruption in the earth, and do not reform.

153. They said: You are only one of the bewitched;

154. You are only a mortal like us. So bring some sign if you are of the truthful.

155. He said: (See) this she-camel. She has the right to drink (at the well), and you have the right to drink, (each) on an appointed day.

156. And touch her not with ill lest there come on you the retribution of an awful day.

157. But they hamstrung her, and then were penitent.

158. So the retribution came on them. In this is indeed a sign, yet most of them are not believers.

159. And your Lord! He is indeed the Mighty, the Merciful.

160. The people of Lot denied the messengers (of Allah),

161. When their brother Lot said to them: Will you not ward off (evil)?

162. I am a faithful messenger to you,

163. So keep your duty to Allah and obey me.

164. And I ask of you no wage for it; my wage is the concern only of the Lord of the Worlds.

165. What! Of all creatures do you come to the males,

166. And leave the wives your Lord created for you? No, but you are obstinate people.

167. They said: If you cease not, O Lot, you will soon be of the outcast.

168. He said: I am in truth of those who hate your conduct.

169. My Lord! Save me and my household from what they do.

170. So We saved him and his household, every one,

171. Except an old woman among those who stayed behind.

172. Then afterwards We destroyed the others.

173. And We rained on them a rain. And dreadful is the rain of those who have been warned.

174. In this is indeed a sign, yet most of them are not believers.

175. And your Lord, He is indeed the Mighty, the Merciful.

176. The dwellers in the wood (of Midian) denied the messengers (of Allah),

177. When Shu'eyb said to them: Will you not ward off (evil)?

178. I am a faithful messenger to you,

179. So keep your duty to Allah and obey me.

180. And I ask of you no wage for it; my wage is the concern only of the Lord of the Worlds.

181. Give full measure, and be not of those who give less (than the due).

182. And weigh with the true balance.

183. Wrong not mankind in their goods, and commit not evil, making mischief, in the earth.

184. And keep your duty to Him Who created you and the generations of the men of old.

185. They said: You are but one of the bewitched;

186. You are only a mortal like us, and we think of you amongst the liars.

187. Then make fragments of the heaven fall upon us, if you are of the truthful.

188. He said: My Lord is Best Aware of what you do.

189. But they denied him, so there came on them the retribution of the day of gloom. It was the retribution of an awful day.

190. In this is indeed a sign; yet most of them are not believers.

191. And your Lord! He is indeed the Mighty, the Merciful.

192. And it is a revelation of the Lord of the Worlds,

193. Which the True Spirit has brought down

194. Upon your heart, that you may be (one) of the warners,

195. In plain Arabic speech.

196. And it is in the Scriptures of the men of old.

197. Is it not a sign for them that the scholars of the Children of Israel[182] know it?

198. And if We had revealed it to one of any other nation than the Arabs,

199. And he had read it to them, they would not have believed in it.

200. Thus do We make it traverse the hearts of the guilty.

201. They will not believe in it till they behold the painful doom,

202. So that it will come upon them suddenly, when they perceive not.

203. Then they will say: Are we to be reprieved?

204. Would they (now) hasten on Our doom?

---

182. The Jews knew, from their Scripture, that a Prophet had been promised to the Arabs.

205. Have you then seen, if We give them enjoyment for (long) years,

206. And then comes that which they were promised,

207. (How) that with which they enjoyed themselves benefits them nothing?

208. And We destroyed no township but it had its warners

209. For reminder, for We never were oppressors.

210. The devils did not bring it down.

211. It is not proper for them, nor is it in their power,

212. Verily they are banished from the hearing.

213. Therefore invoke not with Allah another god, lest you be one of the doomed.

214. And warn your tribe of near relatives,

215. And lower your wing (in kindness) to those believers who follow you.

216. And if they (your relations) disobey you, say: I am innocent of what they do.

217. And put your trust in the Mighty, the Merciful.

218. Who sees you when you stand up (to pray)

219. And (sees) your humility among those who fall prostrate (in worship).

220. He, only He, is the Hearer, the Knower.

221. Shall I inform you upon whom the devils descend?

222. They descend on every sinful, false one.

223. They listen eagerly, but most of them are liars.

224. As for poets, the erring follow them.

225. Have you not seen how they stray in every valley,

226. And how they say that which they do not do?

227. Except those who believe and do good works, and remember Allah much, and vindicate themselves after they have been wronged. Those who do wrong will come to know by what a (great) reverse they will be overturned!

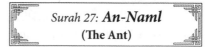

Surah 27: *An-Naml*
(The Ant)

An-Naml, "The Ant," takes its name from the ant mentioned in v. 18. Some commentators, objecting to the miraculous, seek to explain the ants, in the story of Solomon, as an old Arab tribe, the birds as cavalry, Hudhud (the hoopoe) as a man's name, and the Jinn as foreign troops.

It belongs to the middle group of Makkan Surahs.

In the name of Allah,
the Beneficent, the Merciful.

1. *Ta. Sin.*[183] These are revelations of the Qur'an and a Scripture that makes plain;

2. A guidance and good tidings for believers,

---

183. See *Surah 2, Al-Baqarah,* v. 1, footnote.

3. Who establish worship and pay the poor-due and are sure of the Hereafter.

4. As for those who believe not in the Hereafter, We have made their works fair-seeming to them so that they are all astray.

5. Those are they for whom is the worst of punishment, and in the Hereafter they will be the greatest losers.

6. As for you (Muhammad), you verily receive the Qur'an from the presence of One Wise, Aware.

7. (Remember) when Moses said to his household: I spy in the distance a fire; I will bring you tidings from there, or bring to you a borrowed flame that you may warm yourselves.

8. But when he reached it, he was called, saying: Blessed is Whoever is in the fire and Whoever is around it! And Glorified is Allah, the Lord of the Worlds!

9. O Moses! It is I, Allah, the Mighty, the Wise.

10. And throw down your staff! But when he saw it writhing as if it were a demon, he turned to flee headlong; (but it was said to him): O Moses! Fear not! the emissaries fear not in My presence,

11. Except who has done wrong and afterwards he has changed evil for good.[184] And I am Forgiving, Merciful.

12. And put your hand into the inside of your robe. It will come out white but unhurt. (This will be one) among nine signs to Pharaoh and his people. They were ever evil-living people.

13. But when Our signs came to them, plain to see, they said: This is mere magic,

14. And they denied them, though their souls acknowledged them, for spite and arrogance. Then see the nature of the consequence for the wrongdoers!

15. And We verily gave knowledge to David and Solomon, and they said: Praise be to Allah, Who has preferred us above many of His believing slaves!

16. And Solomon was David's heir. And he said: O mankind! We have been taught the language of birds, and have been given (abundance) of all things. This surely is evident favour.

17. And there were gathered together to Solomon his armies of the jinn and humankind, and of the birds, and they were set in battle order;

18. Till, when they reached the Valley of the Ants, an ant exclaimed: O ants! Enter your dwellings lest Solomon and his armies crush you, unperceiving.

19. And (Solomon) smiled, laughing at her speech, and said: My Lord, cause me to be thankful for Your favour with which You have favoured me and my parents, and to do good that shall be pleasing to You, and include me in (the number of) Your righteous slaves.

20. And he searched among the birds and said: How is it that I do not see the hoopoe, or is he among the absent?

21. I verily will punish him with hard punishment or I verily will slay him, or he verily shall bring me a plain excuse.

22. But he was not long in coming, and he said: I have found out (a thing)

---

184. Moses had been guilty of a crime in Egypt.

that you apprehend not, and I come to you from Sheba with sure tidings.

23. I found a woman ruling over them, and she has been given (abundance) of all things, and hers is a mighty throne.

24. I found her and her people worshipping the sun instead of Allah; and Satan makes their works fair-seeming to them, and prevented them from the way (of Truth), so that they do not go aright;

25. So that they worship not Allah, Who brings out the hidden in the heavens and the earth, and knows what you hide and what you proclaim,

26. Allah; there is no God except Him, the Lord of the Tremendous Throne.

27. (Solomon) said: We shall see whether you speak truth or whether you are of the liars.

28. Go with this my letter and throw it down to them; then turn away and see what (answer) they return,

29. (The Queen of Sheba) said (when she received the letter): O chieftains! There has been thrown to me a noble letter.

30. It is from Solomon, and it is: In the name of Allah, the Beneficent, the Merciful;

31. Exalt not yourselves against me, but come to me as those who surrender.

32. She said: O chieftains! Pronounce for me in my case. I decide no case till you are present with me.

33. They said: We are lords of might and lords of great prowess, but it is for you to command; so consider what you will command.

34. She said: Kings, when they enter a township, ruin it and make the honour of its people shame. Thus will they do.

35. But I am going to send a present to them, and to see with what (answer) the messengers return.

36. So when (the envoy) came to Solomon, (the King) said: What! Would you help me with wealth? But that which Allah has given me is better than that which He has given you. No it is you (and not I) who rejoice in your gift.

37. Return to them. We verily shall come to them with forces that they cannot resist, and we shall drive them out from there with shame, and they will be humiliated.

38. He said: O chiefs! Which of you will bring me her throne before they come to me, surrendering?

39. A stalwart of the jinn said: I will bring it to you before you can rise from your place. I verily am strong and trusty for such work.

40. One with whom was knowledge of the Scripture said: I will bring it you before your gaze returns to you. And when he saw it set in his presence, (Solomon) said: This is of the bounty of my Lord, that He may try me whether I give thanks or am ungrateful. Whoever gives thanks he only gives thanks for (the good of) his own soul; and whoever is ungrateful (is ungrateful only to his own soul's hurt). For my Lord is Absolute in independence, Bountiful.

41. He said: Disguise her throne for her that we may see whether she will go aright or be of those not rightly guided.

42. So, when she came, it was said (to her): Is your throne like this? She said: (It is) as though it were the very one. And (Solomon said): We were given the knowledge before her and we had surrendered (to Allah).

43. And (all) that she used to worship instead of Allah hindered her, for she came of disbelieving people.

44. It was said to her: Enter the hall. And when she saw it she thought it was a pool and bared her legs. (Solomon) said: It is a hall, made smooth, of glass. She said: My Lord! I have wronged myself, and I surrender with Solomon to Allah, the Lord of the Worlds.

45. And We verily sent to Thamud their brother Salih, saying: Worship Allah. And they (then) became two parties quarrelling.

46. He said: O my people! Why will you hasten on the evil rather than the good? Why will you not ask pardon of Allah, that you may receive mercy?

47. They said: We predict evil of you and those with you. He said: Your evil prediction is with Allah. No, but you are people who are being tested.

48. And there were in the city nine people who made mischief in the land and reformed not.

49. They said: Swear one to another by Allah that we verily will attack him and his household by night, and afterwards we will surely say to his friend: We witnessed not the destruction of his household. And we are truth tellers.

50. So they plotted a plot: and We plotted a plot, while they perceived not.

51. Then see the nature of the consequence of their plotting, for We destroyed them and their people, everyone.

52. See, over there are their dwellings empty and in ruins because they did wrong. In this is indeed a sign for a people who have knowledge.

53. And We saved those who believed and used to ward off (evil).

54. And Lot! when he said to his people: Will you commit abomination knowingly?

55. Must you lust after men instead of women? No, but you are people who act senselessly.

56. But the answer of his people was nothing except that they said: Expel the household of Lot from your township, for they are people who would keep clean!

57. Then We saved him and his household except his wife; We destined her to be of those who stayed behind.

58. And We rained a rain upon them. Dreadful is the rain of those who have been warned.

59. Say (O Muhammad): Praise be to Allah, and peace be on His slaves whom He has chosen! Is Allah best, or (all) that you ascribe as partners (to Him)?

60. Is not He (best) Who created the heavens and the earth, and sends down for you water from the sky with which We cause to emerge joyous orchards, whose trees it never has been yours to cause to grow. Is there any God besides Allah? No, but they are people who ascribe equals (to Him)!

61. Is not He (best) Who made the earth a fixed abode, and placed rivers in the folds of it, and placed firm hills in it, and has set a barrier between the two seas? Is there any God besides Allah? No, but most of them know not!

62. Is not He (best) Who answers the wronged one when he cries to Him and removes the evil, and has made you viceroys of the earth? Is there any God besides Allah? Little do they reflect!

63. Is not He (best) Who guides you in the darkness of the land and the sea, He Who sends the winds as heralds of His mercy? Is there any God beside Allah? High Exalted be Allah from all that they ascribe as partner (to Him)!

64. Is not He (best) Who produces creation, then reproduces it, and Who provides for you from the heaven and the earth? Is there any God besides Allah? Say: Bring your proof, if you are truthful!

65. Say (O Muhammad): None in the heavens and the earth knows the Unseen except Allah; and they know not when they will be raised (again).

66. No, but does their knowledge reach to the Hereafter? No, for they are in doubt concerning it. No, for they cannot see it.

67. Yet those who disbelieve say: When we have become dust like our fathers, shall we verily be brought out (again)?

68. We were promised this, we and our fathers. (All) this is nothing but fables of the men of old.

69. Say (to them, O Muhammad): Travel in the land and see the nature of the outcome for the guilty!

70. And do not grieve for them, nor be in distress because of what they plot (against you).

71. And they say: When (will) this promise (be fulfilled), if you are truthful?

72. Say: It may be that a part of that which you would hasten on is close behind you.

73. Your Lord is full of bounty for mankind, but most of them do not give thanks.

74. Your Lord knows surely all that their chests hide, and all that they proclaim.

75. And there is nothing hidden in the heaven or the earth but it is in a clear Record.

76. This Qur'an narrates to the Children of Israel most of that concerning which they differ.

77. And it is a guidance and a mercy for believers.

78. Your Lord will judge between them of His wisdom, and He is the Mighty, the Wise.

79. Therefore (O Muhammad) put your trust in Allah, for you (stand) on the plain Truth.

80. You cannot make the dead hear, nor can you make the deaf hear the call when they have turned to flee;

81. Nor can you lead the blind out of their error. You can make no one hear, except those who believe Our revelations and who have surrendered.

82. And when the Word is fulfilled concerning them, We shall bring out a beast of the earth to speak to them because mankind had not faith in Our revelations.

83. And (remind them of) the Day when We shall gather out of every nation a group of those who denied Our revelations, and they will be set in array;

84. Till, when they come (before their Lord), He will say: Did you deny My revelations when you could not comprehend them in knowledge, or what was it that you did?

85. And the Word will be fulfilled concerning them because they have done wrong, and they will not speak.

86. Have they not seen how We have appointed the night that they may rest in it, and the day sight-giving? In it verily are signs for a people who believe.

87. And (remind them of) the Day when the Trumpet will be blown, and all who are in the heavens and the earth will start in fear, except him whom Allah wills. And all come to Him, humbled.

88. And you see the hills you deem solid flying with the flight of clouds: the doing of Allah Who perfects all things. He is Informed of what you do.

89. Whoever brings a good deed will have better than its worth; and such are safe from fear that Day.

90. And whoever brings an ill-deed, such will be flung down on their faces in the Fire. Are you rewarded anything except what you did?

91. (Say): I (Muhammad) am commanded only to serve the Lord

of this land which He has sanctified, and to Whom all things belong. And I am commanded to be of those who surrender (to Him),

92. And to recite the Qur'an. And whoever goes right, goes right only for (the good of) his own soul; and as for him who goes astray - (To him) say: I am only a warner.

93. And say: Praise be to Allah Who will show you His signs so that you shall know them. And your Lord is not unaware of what you (mortals) do.

Surah 28: **Al-Qasas**
(The Story)

Al-Qasas, "The Story," takes its name from a word in v. 25 The name is moreover justified by the nature of the Surah, which consists mostly of the story of Moses, his early struggles and ultimate triumph, revealed at a time when the Prophet's case seemed desperate. It is one of the last Makkan Surahs. Some Arabic writers even say that it was revealed during the Hijrah, while others are of the opinion that v. 85 only was revealed during the migration.

A late Makkan Surah, except v. 85 revealed during the Prophet's emigration from Makkah to Al-Madinah, and vv. 52-55 revealed at Al-Madinah.[185]

In the name of Allah,
the Beneficent, the Merciful.

1. *Ta. Sin. Mim.*[186]

---

185. *Tafsir al-Jalaleyn.*
186. See *Surah 2, Al-Baqarah,* v. 1, footnote.

2. These are revelations of the Scripture that makes plain.

3. We narrate to you (somewhat) of the story of Moses and Pharaoh with truth, for people who believe.

4. Pharaoh exalted himself in the earth and made its people castes. A tribe among them he oppressed, killing their sons and sparing their women. He was of those who work corruption.

5. And We desired to show favour to those who were oppressed in the earth, and to make them examples and to make them the inheritors,

6. And to establish them in the earth, and to show Pharaoh and Haman and their forces that which they feared from them.

7. And We inspired the mother of Moses, saying: Suckle him and, when you fear for him, then throw him into the river and fear not nor grieve. We shall bring him back to you and shall make him (one) of Our messengers.

8. And the family of Pharaoh took him up, that he might become for them an enemy and a sorrow, Pharaoh and Haman and their forces were ever sinning.

9. And the wife of Pharaoh said: (He will be) a consolation for me and for you. Kill him not. Perhaps he may be of use to us, or we may choose him for a son. And they perceived not.

10. And the heart of the mother of Moses became empty, and she would have betrayed him if We had not fortified her heart, that she might be of the believers.

11. And she said to his sister: Trace him. So she observed him from afar, and they perceived not.

12. And We had before forbidden foster-mothers for him, so she (the sister) said: Shall I show you a household who will rear him for you and take care of him?

13. So We restored him to his mother that she might be comforted and not grieve, and that she might know that the promise of Allah is true. But most of them know not.

14. And when he reached his full strength and was mature, We gave him wisdom and knowledge. Thus do We reward the good.

15. And he entered the city at a time of carelessness of its people, and he found in it two men fighting, one of his own caste, and the other of his enemies; and he who was of his caste asked him for help against him who was of his enemies. So Moses struck him with his fist and killed him. He said: This is of the devil's doing. He is an enemy, a mere misleader.

16. He said: My Lord! I have wronged my soul, so forgive me. Then He forgave him. He is the Forgiving, the Merciful.

17. He said: My Lord! Inasmuch as You have favoured me, I will never again be a supporter of the guilty.

18. And morning found him in the city, fearing, vigilant, when he who had appealed to him the day before called out to him for help. Moses said to him: You are indeed a mere hothead.

19. And when he would have fallen upon the man who was an enemy to them both, he said: O Moses! Would you kill me as you did kill a person yesterday? You would be nothing but a tyrant in the land, you would not be of the reformers.

20. And a man came from the uttermost part of the city, running. He said: O Moses! The chiefs take counsel against you to slay you; therefore escape. I am of those who give you good advice.

21. So he escaped from there, fearing, vigilant. He said: My Lord! Deliver me from the wrongdoing people.

22. And when he turned his face towards Midian, he said: Perhaps my Lord will guide me on the right road.

23. And when he came to the water of Midian, he found there a whole tribe of men, watering. And he found apart from them two women keeping back (their flocks). He said: What troubles you? The two said: We cannot give (our flocks) to drink till the shepherds return from the water; and our father is a very old man.

24. So he watered (their flock) for them. Then he turned aside into the shade, and said: My Lord! I am needy of whatever good You send down for me.

25. Then there came to him one of the two women, walking shyly. She said: My father asks you, that he may reward you with a payment for watering (the flock) for us. Then, when he came to him and told him the (whole) story, he said: Fear not! You have escaped from the wrongdoing people.

26. One of the two women said: O my father! Hire him! For the best (man) that you can hire is the strong, the trustworthy.

27. He said: I intend to marry you to one of these two daughters of mine on condition that you hire yourself to me for (the term of) eight years. Then if you complete ten it will be of your own accord, for I would not make it hard for you. Allah willing, you will find me of the righteous.

28. He said: That (is settled) between you and me. Whichever of the two terms I fulfil, there will be no injustice to me, and Allah is Surety over what we say.

29. Then, when Moses had fulfilled the term, and was travelling with his family, he saw in the distance a fire and said to his family: Wait (here). I see in the distance a fire; perhaps I shall bring you tidings from there, or a flame from the fire that you may warm yourselves.

30. And when he reached it, he was called from the right side of the valley in the blessed field, from the tree: O Moses! I, even I, am Allah, the Lord of the Worlds;

31. Throw down your staff. And when he saw it writhing as it had been a demon, he turned to flee headlong, (and it was said to him): O Moses! Draw near and fear not. You are of those who are secure.

32. Put your hand into the inside of your robe. It will come out white without hurt. And guard your heart from fear. Then these shall be two proofs from your Lord to Pharaoh and his chiefs. They are evil-living people.

33. He said: My Lord! I killed a man among them and I fear that they will kill me.

34. My brother Aaron is more eloquent than me in speech. Therefore send him with me as a helper to confirm me. I fear that they will give the lie to me.

35. He said: We will strengthen your arm with your brother, and We will give to you both power so that they cannot reach you for Our signs. You both, and those who follow you, will be the winners.

36. But when Moses came to them with Our clear signs, they said: This is nothing but invented magic. We never heard of this among our fathers of old.

37. And Moses said: My Lord is Best Aware of him who brings guidance from His presence, and whose will be the sequel of the Home (of bliss). The wrongdoers will not be successful.

38. And Pharaoh said: O chiefs! I know not that you have a god other than me, so kindle for me (a fire), O Haman, to bake the mud; and set up for me a lofty tower in order that I may survey the God of Moses; and I consider him of the liars.

39. And he and his forces were haughty in the land without right, and thought that they would never be brought back to Us.

40. Therefore We seized him and his forces, and abandoned them to the sea. See the nature of the consequence for evildoers!

41. And We made them examples that invite to the Fire, and on the Day of Resurrection they will not be helped.

42. And We made a curse to follow them in this world, and on the Day of Resurrection they will be among the hated.

43. And We verily gave the Scripture to Moses after We had destroyed the generations of old: clear testimonies for mankind, and a guidance and a mercy, that perhaps they might reflect.

44. And you (Muhammad) were not on the western side (of the Mount) when We explained to Moses the commandment, and you were not among those present;

45. But We brought out generations, and their lives dragged on for them. And you were not a dweller in Midian, reciting to them Our revelations, but We kept sending (messengers to men).

46. And you were not beside the Mount when We did call; but (the knowledge of it is) a mercy from your Lord that you may warn a people to whom no warner came before you, that perhaps they may give heed.

47. Otherwise, if disaster should afflict them because of that which their own hands have sent before (them), they might say: Our Lord! Why did You not send a messenger to us, that we might have followed Your revelations and been of the believers?

48. But when there came to them the Truth from Our presence, they said: Why is he not given the like of what was given to Moses? Did they not

disbelieve in that which was given to Moses of old? They say: Two magics[187] that support each other; and they say: In both we are disbelievers.

49. Say (to them, O Muhammad): Then bring a scripture from the presence of Allah that gives clearer guidance than these two (that) I may follow it, if you are truthful.

50. And if they answer you not, then know that what they follow is their lusts. And who goes farther astray than he who follows his lust without guidance from Allah. Allah guides not wrongdoing people.

51. And now verily We have caused the Word to reach them, that perhaps they may give heed.

52. Those to whom We gave the Scripture before it, they believe in it,

53. And when it is recited to them, they say: We believe in it. It is the Truth from our Lord. Even before it we were of those who surrender (to Him).

54. These will be given their reward twice over, because they are steadfast and repel evil with good, and spend of that with which We have provided them,

55. And when they hear vanity they withdraw from it and say: To us our works and to you your works. Peace be to you! We desire not the ignorant.

56. You (O Muhammad) do not guide whom you love, but Allah guides whom He will. And He is Best Aware of those who walk aright.

57. And they say: If we were to follow the Guidance with you we

should be torn out of our land. Have We not established for them a sure sanctuary,[188] to which the produce of all things is brought (in trade), a provision from Our presence? But most of them do not understand.

58. And how many a community have We destroyed that was thankless for its means of livelihood! And over there are their dwellings, which have not been inhabited after them except a little. And We, even We, were the inheritors.

59. And never did your Lord destroy the townships till He had raised up in their mother(-town) a messenger reciting to them Our revelations. And never did We destroy the townships unless the people of it were evildoers.

60. And whatever you have been given is a comfort of the life of the world and an ornament of it; and that which Allah has is better and more lasting. Have you then no sense?

61. Is he whom We have promised a fair promise which he will find (true) like him whom We suffer to enjoy a while the comfort of the life of the world, then on the Day of Resurrection he will be of those summoned?

62. On the day when He will call to them and say: Where are My partners whom you imagined?

63. Those concerning whom the Word will have come true will say: Our Lord! These are they whom we led astray. We led them astray even as we ourselves were astray. We declare our innocence before You: us they never worshipped.

---

187. *i.e.* the Scripture of Moses and the Qur'an.

188. The sacred territory of Makkah.

64. And it will be said: Call to your (so-called) partners (of Allah). And they will call to them, and they will give no answer to them, and they will see the Doom. Ah, if they had only been guided!

65. And on the Day when He will call to them and say: What answer did you give to the messengers?

66. On that day (all) tidings will be dimmed for them, nor will they ask one of another,

67. But as for him who repents and believes and does right, he perhaps may be one of the successful.

68. Your Lord brings to pass what He wills and chooses. They have never any choice. Glorified be Allah and Exalted above all that they associate (with Him)!

69. And your Lord knows what their hearts conceal, and what they publish.

70. And He is Allah; there is no God except Him. His is all praise in the former and the latter (state), and His is the command, and to Him you will be brought back.

71. Say: Have you thought, if Allah made night everlasting for you till the Day of Resurrection, who is a god besides Allah who could bring you light? Will you not then hear?

72. Say: Have you thought, if Allah made day everlasting for you till the Day of Resurrection, who is a god besides Allah who could bring you night in which you rest? Will you not then see?

73. Of His mercy has He appointed for you night and day, that in it you may rest, and that you may seek His bounty, and that perhaps you may be thankful.

74. And on the Day when He will call to them and say: Where are My partners whom you pretended (to exist)?

75. And We shall take out from every nation a witness and We shall say: Bring your proof. Then they will know that Allah has the Truth, and all that they invented will have failed them.

76. Now Korah was of Moses' people, but he oppressed them; and We gave him so much treasure that the stores of it would verily have been a burden for a troop of mighty men. When his own people said to him: Do not rejoice (over your wealth); Rejoice not; Allah loves not the jubilant;

77. But seek the abode of the Hereafter in that which Allah has given you, and neglect not your portion of the world, and be kind even as Allah has been kind to you, and seek not corruption in the earth; Allah loves not corrupters,

78. He said: I have been given it only on account of knowledge I possess. Did he not know that Allah had destroyed already of the generations before him men who were mightier than him in strength and greater in respect of following? The guilty are not questioned about their sins.

79. Then he went out before his people in his pomp. Those who were desirous of the life of the world said: Ah, would that we had the like of what has been given to Korah! He is a lord of rare good fortune.

80. But those who had been given knowledge said: Woe to you! The reward of Allah for him who believes and does right is better, and only the steadfast will obtain it.

81. So We caused the earth to swallow him and his dwelling-place. Then he had no force to help him against Allah, nor was he of those who can save themselves.

82. And morning found those who had coveted his place but yesterday calling: Ah! Allah enlarges the provision for whom He will of His slaves and tightens it (for whom He will). If Allah had not been gracious to us He would have caused it to swallow us (also). Ah, the disbelievers never prosper.

83. As for that Abode of the Hereafter, We assign it to those who seek not oppression in the earth, nor yet corruption. The sequel is for those who ward off (evil).

84. Whoever brings a good deed, he will have better than the same; while as for him who brings an ill-deed, those who do ill-deeds will be repaid only what they did.

85. He Who has given you the Qur'an for a law will surely bring you home again.[189] Say: My Lord is Best Aware of him who brings guidance and him who is in manifest error.

86. You had no hope that the Scripture would be inspired in you; but it is a mercy from your Lord, so never be a helper to the disbelievers.

87. And let them not divert you from the revelations of Allah after they have been sent down to you; but call (mankind) to your Lord, and be not of those who ascribe partners (to Him).

88. And call not to any other god along with Allah. There is no God except Him. Everything will perish except His countenance. His is the command, and to Him you will be brought back.

Surah 29: *Al-'Ankabut* (The Spider)

Al-'Ankabut, "The Spider," takes its name from v. 41 where false beliefs are likened to the spider's web for frailty. Most of this Surah belongs to the middle or last Makkan period. Some authorities consider vv. 7 and 8, others the whole latter portion of the Surah,[190] to have been revealed at Al-Madinah. It gives comfort to the Muslims in a time of persecution. A late Makkan Surah.

In the name of Allah, the Beneficent, the Merciful.

1. *Alif. Lam. Mim.*[191]

2. Do men imagine that they will be left (at ease) because they say, We believe, and will not be tested with affliction?

3. We tested those who were before you. Thus Allah knows those who are sincere, and knows those who pretend.

4. Or do those who do ill-deeds imagine that they can outstrip Us? Evil (for them) is that which they decide.

---

189. A tradition says that this verse was revealed during the Prophet's emigration from Makkah to Al-Madinah.

190. *An-Nasikh wal-Mansukh* by Ibn Salamah
191. See *Surah 2, Al-Baqarah,* v. 1, footnote.

5. Whoever looks forward to the meeting with Allah (let him know that) Allah's reckoning is surely near, and He is the Hearer, the Knower.

6. And whoever strives, strives only for himself, for Allah is altogether Independent of (His) creatures.

7. And as for those who believe and do good works, We shall remit from them their evil deeds and shall repay them the best that they did.

8. We have enjoined on man kindness to parents; but if they strive to make you join with Me that of which you have no knowledge, then obey them not. To Me is your return and I shall tell you what you used to do.

9. And as for those who believe and do good works, We verily shall make them enter among the righteous.

10. Of mankind is he who says: We believe in Allah, but, if he is made to suffer for the sake of Allah, he mistakes the persecution of mankind for Allah's punishment; and then, if victory comes from your Lord, he will say: We were with you (all the while). Is not Allah Best Aware of what is in the hearts of (His) creatures?

11. Verily, Allah knows those who believe, and verily, He knows the hypocrites.

12. Those who disbelieve say to those who believe: Follow our way (of religion) and we verily will bear your sins (for you). They cannot bear anything of their sins. They verily are liars.

13. But they verily will bear their own loads and other loads besides their own, and they verily will be questioned on the Day of Resurrection concerning that which they invented.

14. And verily We sent Noah (as Our messenger) to his people, and he continued with them for a thousand years except fifty years; and the flood engulfed them, for they were wrongdoers.

15. And We rescued him and those with him in the ship, and made of it a sign for the peoples.

16. And Abraham! (Remember) when he said to his people: Serve Allah, and keep your duty to Him; that is better for you if you only knew.

17. You serve instead of Allah only idols, and you only invent a lie. Those whom you serve instead of Allah own no provision for you. So seek your provision from Allah, and serve Him, and give thanks to Him, (for) to Him you will be brought back.

18. But if you deny, then nations have denied before you. The messenger is only to convey (the message) plainly.

19. See they not how Allah produces creation, then reproduces it? For Allah that is easy.

20. Say (O Muhammad): Travel in the land and see how He originated creation, then Allah brings out the later growth. Allah is Able to do all things.

21. He punishes whom He will and shows mercy to whom He will, and to Him you will be turned.

22. You cannot escape (from Him) in the earth or in the sky, and besides Allah there is for you no friend or helper.

23. Those who disbelieve in the revelations of Allah and in (their) Meeting with Him, such have no hope of My mercy. For such there is a painful doom.

24. But the answer of his people was only that they said: "Kill him" or "Burn him." Then Allah saved him from the Fire. In this verily are signs for people who believe.

25. He said: You have chosen only idols instead of Allah. The love between you is only in the life of the world. Then on the Day of Resurrection you will deny each other and curse each other, and your abode will be the Fire, and you will have no helpers.

26. And Lot believed him, and said: I am emigrating to my Lord. He, only He, is the Mighty, the Wise.

27. And We bestowed on him Isaac and Jacob, and We established the prophethood and the Scripture among his seed, and We gave him his reward in the world, and in the Hereafter he verily is among the righteous.

28. And Lot! (Remember) when he said to his people: You commit lewdness such as no creature did before you.

29. For do you not come in to males, do you not cut the road (for travellers), and do you not commit abomination in your meetings? But the answer of his people was only that they said: Bring Allah's doom upon us if you are a truth-teller!

30. He said: My Lord! Give me victory over people who work corruption.

31. And when Our messengers brought Abraham the good news,[192] they said: We are about to destroy the people of that township, for its people are wrongdoers.

32. He said: Lot is there. They said: We are best aware of who is there. We are to deliver him and his household, all except his wife, who is of those who stay behind.

33. And when Our messengers came to Lot, he was troubled upon their account, for he could not protect them; but they said: Fear not, nor grieve! We are to deliver you and your family, (all) except your wife, who is of those who stay behind.

34. We are about to bring down upon the people of this township a fury from the sky because they are evil-livers.

35. And verily of that We have left a clear sign for people who have sense.

36. And to Midian We sent Shu'eyb, their brother. He said: O my people! Serve Allah, and look forward to the Last Day, and commit not evil, making mischief in the earth.

37. But they denied him, and the dreadful earthquake took them, and morning found them prostrate in their dwelling place.

38. And (the tribes of) 'Aad and Thamud! (Their fate) is manifest to you from their (ruined and deserted) dwellings. Satan made their deeds seem fair to them and so prevented them from the Way, though they were keen observers.

192. That he was to have a son.

39. And Korah, Pharaoh and Haman! Moses came to them with clear proofs (of Allah's Sovereignty), but they were boastful in the land. And they were not winners (in the race).

40. So We took each one in his sin; of them was he on whom We sent a hurricane, and of them was he who was overtaken by the (Awful) Call, and of them was he whom We caused the earth to swallow, and of them was he whom We drowned. It was not for Allah to wrong them, but they wronged themselves.

41. The likeness of those who choose patrons other than Allah is as the likeness of the spider when she takes to herself a house, and the frailest of all houses is the spider's house, if they only knew.

42. Allah knows what thing they invoke instead of Him. He is the Mighty, the Wise.

43. As for these similitudes, We coin them for mankind, but none will grasp their meaning except the wise.

44. Allah created the heavens and the earth with truth. In it is indeed a sign for believers.

45. Recite that which has been inspired in you of the Scripture, and establish worship. Worship preserves from lewdness and iniquity, but verily remembrance of Allah is more important. And Allah knows what you do.

46. And argue not with the People of the Scripture unless it is in (a way) that is better, except with such of them as do wrong; and say: We believe in that which has been revealed to us and revealed to you; our God and your God is One, and to Him we surrender.

47. In like manner We have revealed to you the Scripture, and those to whom We gave the Scripture before will believe in it; and of these (also)[193] there are some who believe in it. And none deny Our revelations except the disbelievers.

48. And you (O Muhammad) were not a reader of any scripture before it, nor did you write it with your right hand, for then might those have doubted who follow falsehood.

49. But it is clear revelations in the hearts of those who have been given knowledge, and none deny Our revelations except wrongdoers.

50. And they say: Why are not signs sent down upon him from his Lord? Say: Signs are with Allah only, and I am only a plain warner.

51. Is it not enough for them that We have sent down to you the Scripture which is read to them? In this verily is mercy, and a reminder for people who believe.

52. Say (to them, O Muhammad): Allah suffices for witness between me and you. He knows whatever is in the heavens and the earth. And those who believe in vanity and disbelieve in Allah, they are those who are the losers.

53. They ask you to hasten on the doom (of Allah). And if a term had not been appointed, the doom would assuredly have come to them (before

193. *i.e.* the people of Makkah.

235

now). And verily it will come upon them suddenly when they perceive not.

54. They ask you to hasten on the doom, when Hell verily will encompass the disbelievers

55. On the day when the doom will overwhelm them from above them and from underneath their feet, and He will say: Taste what you used to do!

56. O my bondsmen who believe! My earth is spacious. Therefore serve Me only.

57. Every soul will taste of death. Then to Us you will be returned.

58. Those who believe and do good works, them verily We shall house in lofty dwellings of the Garden underneath which rivers flow. There they will dwell secure. How sweet the reward of the workers,

59. Who persevere, and put their trust in their Lord!

60. And how many an animal there is that bears not its own provision! Allah provides for it and for you. He is the Hearer, the Knower.

61. And if you were to ask them: Who created the heavens and the earth, and compelled the sun and the moon (to their appointed work)? they would say: Allah. How then are they turned away?

62. Allah makes the provision wide for whom He will of His bondsmen, and tightens it for whom (He will). Allah is Aware of all things.

63. And if you were to ask them: Who causes water to come down from the sky, and with it revives the earth after its death? They verily would say: Allah.

Say: Praise be to Allah! But most of them have no sense.

64. The life of the world is but a pastime and a game. The home of the Hereafter - that is Life, if they only knew.

65. And when they mount upon the ships they pray to Allah, making their faith pure for Him only, but when He brings them safe to land, look! they ascribe partners (to Him),

66. That they may disbelieve in that which We have given them, and that they may take their ease. But they will come to know.

67. Have they not seen that We have appointed a sanctuary immune (from violence),[194] while mankind are being destroyed all around them? Do they then believe in falsehood and disbelieve in the bounty of Allah?

68. Who does greater wrong than he who invents a lie concerning Allah, or denies the truth when it comes to him? Is there not a home in Hell for disbelievers?

69. As for those who strive in Us (Our cause), We surely guide them to Our paths, and Allah is with the good.

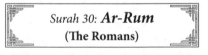

Surah 30: *Ar-Rum*
(The Romans)

Ar-Rum, "The Romans," takes its name from a word in the second verse.

The armies of the Eastern Roman Empire had been defeated by the Persians in all the territories near Arabia.

In the year A.D. 613 Jerusalem and Damascus fell, and in the following year

194. *i.e.* the people of Makkah.

Egypt. A Persian army invaded Anatolia and was threatening Constantinople itself in the year A.D. 615 or 616 (the sixth or seventh year before the Hijrah) when, according to the best authorities, this Surah was revealed at Makkah. The pagan Arabs triumphed in the news of Persian victories over the Prophet and his little band of followers, because the Christian Romans were believers in the One God, whereas the Persians were not. They argued that the power of Allah could not be supreme and absolute, as the Prophet kept proclaiming it to be, since the forces of a pagan empire had been able to defeat His worshippers.

The Prophet's answer was provided for him in this grand assertion of Theocracy, which shows the folly of all those who think of Allah as a partisan. It opens with two prophecies: that the Romans would be victorious over the Persians, and that the little persecuted company of Muslims in Arabia would have reason to rejoice, "within ten years."[195] In fact, in A.D. 624 the Roman armies entered purely Persian territory, and in the same year a little army of Muslims, led by the Prophet, overthrew the flower of Arab chivalry upon the field of Badr.

But the prophecies are only the prelude to a proclamation of God's universal kingdom, which is shown to be an actual Sovereignty. The laws of nature are explained as the laws of Allah in the physical sphere, and in the moral and political spheres mankind is informed that there are similar laws of life and death, of good and evil, action and inaction, and their consequences - laws which no one can escape by wisdom or by cunning. His mercy, like His law, surrounds all things, and the standard of His judgement is the same for all. He is not remote or indifferent, partial or unpredictable. Those who do good earn His favour, and those who do ill earn His wrath, no matter what may be their creed or race; and no one, by the mere profession of a creed, is able to escape His law of consequences.

It belongs to the middle group of Makkan Surahs.

In the name of Allah, the Beneficent, the Merciful.

1. *Alif. Lam. Mim.*[196]

2. The Romans have been defeated

3. In the nearer land, and they, after their defeat will be victorious

4. Within a few years (from now) - Allah's is the command in the former case and in the latter - and in that day believers will rejoice

5. In Allah's help to victory. He helps to victory whom He will. He is the Mighty, the Merciful.

6. It is a promise of Allah. Allah fails not His promise, but most of mankind know not.

7. They know only some appearance of the life of the world, and are heedless of the Hereafter.

---

195. The word in the Arabic *(bida)* implies a space of not less than three, and not more than nine, years.

196. See *Surah 2, Al-Baqarah*, v. 1, footnote.

8. Have they not pondered upon themselves? Allah created not the heavens and the earth, and that which is between them, except with truth and for a destined end. But truly many of mankind are disbelievers in the meeting with their Lord.

9. Have they not travelled in the land and seen the nature of the consequence for those who were before them?[197] They were stronger than these in power, and they dug the earth and built upon it more than these have built. Messengers of their own came to them with clear proofs (of Allah's Sovereignty). Surely Allah wronged them not, but they did wrong themselves.

10. Then evil was the consequence for those who dealt in evil, because they denied the revelations of Allah and made a mockery of them.

11. Allah produces creation, then He reproduces it, then to Him you will be returned.

12. And on the day when the Hour rises the unrighteous will despair.

13. There will be none to intercede for them of those whom they made equal with Allah. And they will reject their partners (whom they ascribed to Him).

14. On the day when the Hour comes, on that day they will be divided.

---

197. To those who journeyed out from Makkah, northward into Mesopotamia and Syria, or southward to the Yaman and Hadramaut, appeared the ruins of old civilisations which, tradition said, had been destroyed on account of their corruption and disobedience to the will of God.

15. As for those who believed and did good works, they will be made happy in a Garden.

16. But as for those who disbelieved and denied Our revelations, and denied the meeting of the Hereafter, such will be brought to doom.

17. So glory be to Allah when you enter the night and when you enter the morning -

18. To Him be praise in the heavens and the earth! - and at the sun's decline and at noon.

19. He brings out the living from the dead, and He brings out the dead from the living, and He revives the earth after her death. And even so you will be brought out.

20. And of His signs is this: He created you of dust, and there you are human beings, ranging widely!

21. And of His signs is this: He created for you companions from yourselves that you might find rest in them, and He ordained between you love and mercy. In this indeed are signs for people who reflect.

22. And of His signs is the creation of the heavens and the earth, and the difference of your languages and colours. In this indeed are signs for men of knowledge.

23. And of His signs is your slumber by night and by day, and your seeking of His bounty. In this indeed are signs for people who heed.

24. And of His signs is this: He shows you the lightning for a fear and for a hope, and sends down water from the sky, and by it revives the earth after her death. In this indeed are signs for people who understand.

25. And of His signs is this: The heavens and the earth stand fast by His command, and afterwards, when He calls you, from the earth you will emerge.

26. To Him belongs whoever is in the heavens and the earth. All are obedient to Him.

27. He it is Who produces creation, then reproduces it, and it is easy for Him. His is the Sublime Similitude in the heavens and the earth. He is the Mighty, the Wise.

28. He coins for you a similitude of yourselves. Have you, from among those whom your right hands possess,[198] partners in the wealth We have bestowed upon you, equal with you in respect of it, so that you fear them as you fear each other (that you ascribe to Us partners out of that which We created)? Thus We display the revelations for people who have sense.

29. No, but those who do wrong follow their own lusts without knowledge. Who is able to guide him whom Allah has sent astray? For such there are no helpers.

30. So set your purpose (O Muhammad) for religion as a man by nature upright - the nature (framed) of Allah, in which He has created man. There is no altering (the laws of) Allah's creation. That is the right religion, but most men know not -

198. *i.e.* the slaves.

31. Turning to Him (only); and be careful of your duty to Him and establish worship, and be not of those who ascribe partners (to Him);

32. Of those who split up their religion and became schismatics, each sect rejoicing in its tenets.

33. And when harm touches men they call to their Lord, turning to Him in repentance; then, when they have tasted of His mercy, some of them attribute partners to their Lord.

34. So as to disbelieve in that which We have given them. (To such it is said): Enjoy yourselves for a while, but you will come to know.

35. Or have We revealed to them any authority which speaks of that which they associate with Him?

36. And when We cause mankind to taste of mercy they rejoice in it; but if an evil thing befalls them as the consequence of their own deeds, they are in despair!

37. Do they not see that Allah enlarges the provision for whom He wills, and tightens (it for whom He wills). In this indeed are signs for people who believe.

38. So give to the relative his due, and to the needy, and to the wayfarer. That is best for those who seek Allah's Countenance. And such are they who are successful.

39. That which you give in usury in order that it may increase on (other) people's property has no increase with Allah; but that which you give in charity, seeking Allah's Countenance, has increase manifold.

40. Allah is He Who created you and then sustained you, then causes you to die, then gives life to you again. Is there any of your (so-called) partners (of Allah) that does anything of that? Praised and Exalted is He above what they associate (with Him)!

41. Corruption appears on land and sea because of (the evil) which men's hands have done, that He may make them taste a part of that which they have done, in order that they may return.

42. Say (O Muhammad, to the disbelievers): Travel in the land, and see the nature of the consequence for those who were before you! Most of them were idolaters.

43. So set your purpose resolutely for the right religion, before the inevitable day comes from Allah. On that day mankind will be separated;

44. Whoever disbelieves must (then) bear the consequences of his disbelief, while those who do right make provision for themselves -

45. That He may reward out of His bounty those who believe and do good works. He loves not the disbelievers (in His guidance).

46. And of His signs is this: He sends announcing winds to make you taste His mercy, and that the ships may sail at His command, and that you may seek his favour, and that perhaps you may be thankful.

47. Verily We sent before you (Muhammad) messengers to their own people. Then we took vengeance upon those who were guilty (in regard to them). To help believers is ever incumbent upon Us.

48. Allah is He Who sends the winds so that they raise clouds, and spreads them along the sky as pleases Him, and causes them to break and you see the rain pouring down from within them. And when He makes it to fall on whom He will of His bondsmen, they rejoice;

49. Though before that, even before it was sent down upon them, they were in despair.

50. Look, therefore, at the prints of Allah's mercy (in creation): how He revives the earth after her death. He verily is the Reviver of the Dead, and He is Able to do all things.

51. And if We sent a wind and they saw it yellow, they verily would still continue in their disbelief.

52. For verily you (Muhammad) cannot make the dead hear, nor can you make the deaf hear the call when they have turned to flee.

53. Nor can you guide the blind out of their error. You can make none hear except those who believe in Our revelations so that they surrender (to Him).

54. Allah is He Who shaped you out of weakness, then appointed after weakness strength, then, after strength, appointed weakness and grey hair. He creates what He will. He is the Knower, the Mighty.

55. And on the day when the Hour rises the guilty will vow that they did stay but an hour - thus were they ever deceived.

56. But those to whom knowledge and faith are given will say: The truth is, you have stayed, by Allah's decree, until the Day of Resurrection. This is the Day of Resurrection, but you did not know.

57. On that day their excuses will not profit those who did injustice, nor will they be allowed to make amends.

58. Verily We have coined for mankind in this Qur'an all kinds of similitudes; and indeed if you came to them with a miracle, those who disbelieve would verily exclaim: You are only tricksters!

59. Thus does Allah seal the hearts of those who know not.

60. So have patience (O Muhammad)! Allah's promise is the very truth, and let not those who have no certainty make you impatient.

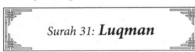

Surah 31: *Luqman*

Luqman takes its name from v. 12 ff., which contains mention of the wisdom of Luqman, a sage whose memory Arabs revered, but who is unknown to Jewish Scripture. He is said to have been a Negro slave, and the fables associated with his name are so like those of Aesop that the usual identification seems justified. The Surah conveys assurance of success to the Muslims at a time of persecution.

It belongs to the middle or last group of Makkan Surahs; except vv. 27 and 28 which were revealed at Al-Madinah.

In the name of Allah,
the Beneficent, the Merciful.

1. *Alif. Lam. Mim.*[199]

199. See *Surah 2, Al-Baqarah,* v. 1, footnote.

2. These are revelations of the wise Scripture,

3. A guidance and a mercy for the good,

4. Those who establish worship and pay the poor-due and have sure faith in the Hereafter.

5. Such have guidance from their Lord. Such are the successful.

6. And of mankind is he who pays for mere pastime of discourse, that he may mislead from Allah's way without knowledge, and makes it the butt of mockery. For such there is a shameful doom.

7. And when Our revelations are recited to him he turns away in pride as if he heard them not, as if there were a deafness in his ears. So give him tidings of a painful doom.

8. Those who believe and do good works, for them are the Gardens of delight,

9. In which they will remain. It is a promise of Allah in truth. He is the Mighty, the Wise.

10. He has created the heavens without supports that you can see, and has cast into the earth firm hills, so that it does not quake with you; and He has dispersed in it all kinds of beasts. And We send down water from the sky and We cause (plants) of every goodly kind to grow in it.

11. This is the Creation of Allah. Now show me that which those (you worship) besides Him have created. No, but the wrongdoers are in manifest error!

12. And verily, We gave Luqman wisdom, saying: Give thanks to Allah; and whoever gives thanks, he gives thanks for (the good of) his soul. And whoever refuses, Allah is Absolute, Owner of Praise.

13. And (remember) when Luqman said to his son, when he was exhorting him: O my dear son! Ascribe no partners to Allah. To ascribe partners (to Him) is a tremendous wrong-

14. And We have enjoined upon man concerning his parents - His mother bears him in weakness upon weakness, and his weaning is in two years - Give thanks to Me and to your parents. To Me is the journeying.

15. But if they strive with you to make you ascribe to Me as partner that of which you have no knowledge, then obey them not. Give them company in the world kindly, and follow the path of him who repents to Me. Then to Me will be your return, and I shall tell you what you used to do -

16. O my dear son! Though it is only the weight of a grain of mustard-seed, and though it is in a rock, or in the heavens, or in the earth, Allah will bring it out. Allah is Subtle, Aware.

17. O my dear son! Establish worship and enjoin kindness and forbid iniquity, and persevere with whatever may befall you. That is of the steadfast heart of things.

18. Turn not your cheek in mockery towards people, nor walk with impudence in the land. Allah loves not the braggart boaster.

19. Be modest in your conduct and subdue your voice. The harshest of all voices is the voice of the donkey.

20. Do you not see how Allah has made serviceable to you whatever is in the skies and whatever is in the earth and has loaded you with His favours both without and within? Yet of mankind is he who disputes concerning Allah, without knowledge or guidance or a Scripture giving light.

21. And if it be said to them: Follow that which Allah has revealed, they say: No, but we follow that in which we found our fathers. What! Even though the devil were inviting them to the doom of flame?

22. Whoever surrenders his purpose to Allah while doing good, he verily has grasped the firm hand-hold. To Allah belongs the sequel of all things.

23. And whoever disbelieves, let not his disbelief afflict you (O Muhammad). To Us is their return, and We shall tell them what they did. Allah is Aware of what is in the hearts (of men).

24. We give them comfort for a little, and then We drive them to a heavy doom.

25. If you should ask them: Who created the heavens and the earth? They would answer: Allah. Say: Praise be to Allah! But most of them know not.

26. To Allah belongs whatever is in the heavens and the earth. Allah, He is the Absolute, the Owner of Praise.

27. And if all the trees in the earth were pens, and the sea, with seven more seas to help it, (were ink), the words of Allah could not be exhausted. Allah is Mighty, Wise.

28. Your creation and your raising (from the dead) are only as (the creation and the raising of) a single soul. Allah is Hearer, Seer.

29. Have you not seen how Allah causes the night to pass into the day and causes the day to pass into the night, and has subdued the sun and the moon (to do their work), each running to an appointed term; and that Allah is Informed of what you do?

30. That (is so) because Allah, He is the True, and that which they invoke beside Him is the False, and because Allah, He is the Sublime, the Great.

31. Have you not seen how the ships glide on the sea by Allah's grace, that He may show you of His wonders? In it indeed are signs for every steadfast, grateful (heart).

32. And if a wave enshrouds them like awnings, they call to Allah, making their faith pure for Him only. But when He brings them safe to land, some of them compromise. No one denies Our signs except every ungrateful traitor.

33. O mankind! Keep your duty to your Lord and fear a Day when the parent will not be able to avail the child in anything, nor the child to avail the parent. Allah's promise is the very truth. Let not the life of the world deceive you, nor let the deceiver deceive you, in regard to Allah.

34. Allah! With Him is knowledge of the Hour. He sends down the rain, and knows that which is in the wombs. No soul knows what it will earn tomorrow, and no soul knows in what land it will die. Allah is Knower, Aware.

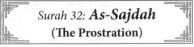

Surah 32: *As-Sajdah*
(The Prostration)

As-Sajdah, "The Prostration," takes its name from a word in v. 15.

It belongs in the middle group of Makkan Surahs.

In the name of Allah,
the Beneficent, the Merciful.

1. *Alif. Lam. Mim*[200]

2. The revelation of the Scripture of which there is no doubt is from the Lord of the Worlds.

3. Or do they say: He has invented it? No, but it is the Truth from your Lord, that you may warn a people to whom no warner came before you, that perhaps they may walk aright.

4. Allah it is Who created the heavens and the earth, and that which is between them, in six Days. Then He mounted the Throne. You have not, besides Him, a protecting friend or mediator. Will you not then remember?

5. He directs the ordinance from the heaven to the earth; then it ascends to Him in a Day, of which the measure is a thousand years of that you reckon.

6. Such is the Knower of the Invisible and the Visible, the Mighty, the Merciful,

7. Who made all things good which He created, and He began the creation of man from clay;

8. Then He made his seed from an extract of despised fluid;

200. See *Surah* 2, *Al-Baqarah,* v. 1, footnote.

9. Then He fashioned him and breathed into him of His Spirit; and appointed for you hearing and sight and hearts. Small thanks do you give!

10. And they say: When we are lost in the earth, how can we then be re-created? No but they are disbelievers in the meeting with their Lord.

11. Say: The angel of death, who has charge concerning you, will gather you, and afterwards to your Lord you will be returned.

12. Could you but see when the guilty hang their heads before their Lord, (and say): Our Lord! We have now seen and heard, so send us back; we will do right, now we are sure.

13. And if We had so willed, We could have given every soul its guidance, but the word from Me concerning evildoers took effect: that I will fill Hell with the jinn and mankind together.

14. So taste (the evil of your deeds). Inasmuch as you forgot the meeting of this your day, We forget you. Taste the doom of immortality because of what you used to do.

15. Only those believe in Our revelations who, when they are reminded of them, fall down prostrate and hymn the praise of their Lord, and they are not contemptuous,

16. Who forsake their beds to call to their Lord in fear and hope, and spend of that which We have bestowed on them.

17. No soul knows what is kept hidden for them of joy, as a reward for what they used to do.

18. Is he who is a believer like him who is an evil-liver? They are not alike.

19. But as for those who believe and do good works, for them are the Gardens of Retreat - a welcome (in reward) for what they used to do.

20. And as for those who do evil, their retreat is the Fire. Whenever they desire to come out from there, they are brought back into it. To them it is said: Taste the torment of the Fire which you used to deny.

21. And verily We make them taste the lower punishment[201] before the greater, that perhaps they may return.

22. And who does greater wrong than he who is reminded of the revelations of his Lord, then turns from them. We shall repay the guilty.

23. We verily gave Moses the Scripture; so be not you in doubt of his receiving it; and We appointed it a guidance for the Children of Israel.

24. And when they became steadfast and believed firmly in Our revelations, We appointed from among them leaders who guided by Our command.

25. Your Lord will judge between them on the Day of Resurrection concerning that in which they used to differ.

26. Is it not a guidance for them (to observe) how many generations We destroyed before them, amid whose dwelling places they do walk? In it verily are signs! Will they not then heed?

27. Have they not seen how We lead the water to the barren land and with it bring out crops of which their cattle

---

201. *i.e.* Punishment in this world.

244

eat, and they themselves? Will they not then see?

28. And they say: When comes this victory (of yours) if you are truthful?

29. Say (to them): On the day of the victory the faith of those who disbelieve (and who then will believe) will not benefit them, neither will they be reprieved.

30. So withdraw from them (O Muhammad), and await (the event). They (also) are awaiting (it).

Surah 33: *Al-Ahzab*
(The Clans)

Al-Ahzab, "The Clans," takes its name from the army of the allied clans which came against Yathrib (Al-Madinah) in the fifth year of the Hijrah (vv. 9-25). Certain of the Bani Nadir, a Jewish tribe whom the Prophet had expelled from Yathrib on the ground of treason (see Surah 59), went first to the leaders of Quraysh in Makkah and then to the chiefs of the great desert tribe of Ghatafan, urging them to destroy the Muslims and promising them help from the Jewish population of Yathrib. As a result of their efforts, Quraysh with all their clans, and Ghatafan with all their clans marched to destroy Yathrib.

When the Prophet had news of their plan, he ordered a trench to be dug before the city, and he himself led the work of digging it. The trench was finished when the clans arrived, 10,000 strong. The Prophet went out against them with his army of 3000, the trench being between the

two armies. For nearly a month the Muslims were exposed to showers of arrows, in constant expectation of attack by much superior forces; and, to make matters worse, news came that the Jewish tribe of Bani Qureyzah in their rear had broken their alliance with the Muslims and made common cause with Quraysh.

The women and children had been put in strongholds - towers like the peel towers of Northern England, of which every family of note had one for refuge in time of raids. These were practically unguarded, and some of the Muslims asked permission of the Prophet to leave the battle front and go to guard them, though they were not then in danger because the Bani Qureyzah were not likely to show their treachery until the victory of the clans was certain.

The case of the Muslims seemed, humanly speaking, hopeless. But a secret sympathiser in the enemy camp managed to sow distrust between the Bani Qureyzah and the chiefs of the clans, making both feel uneasy. The obstacle of the trench was unexpected and seemed formidable; and when a fierce, bitter wind from the sea blew for three days and nights so furiously that they could not keep a shelter up, or light a fire, or boil a pot, Abu Sufian, the leader of Quraysh, raised the siege in disgust. And when Ghatafan one morning found Quraysh had gone, they too departed for their homes.

On the very day when the Muslims returned from the trench, began the siege of the traitorous Bani

Qureyzah in their towers of refuge. It lasted for twenty-five days. When they at length surrendered, some of the tribe of Aus, whose adherents they were, asked the Prophet to show them the same grace that he had shown to the tribe of Khazraj, in the case of Bani Naḍir, in allowing them to intercede for their dependants.

The Prophet said: "Would you like that one of you should decide concerning them?" They said: "Yes," and he appointed Sa'd ibn Mu'adh, a great chief of Aus, who had been wounded and was being cared for in the Mosque. Sa'd was sent for and he ordered their men to be put to death, their women and children to be made captive, and their property to be divided among the Muslims at the Prophet's will.

I have taken this account from the narrative of Ibn Khaldun, which is concise, rather than from that in Ibn Hisham, which is exceedingly diffuse, the two accounts being in absolute agreement.

Vv. 26 and 27 refer to the punishment of Bani Qureyzah.

In v. 37 the reference is to the unhappy marriage of Zeyd, the Prophet's freedman and adopted son, with Zeynab, the Prophet's cousin, a proud lady of Quraysh. The Prophet had arranged the marriage with the idea of breaking down the old barrier of pride of caste, and had shown little consideration for Zeynab's feelings. Tradition says that both she and her brother were averse to the match, and that she had always wished to

marry the Prophet. For Zeyd, the marriage was nothing but a cause of embarrassment and humiliation. When the Prophet's attention was first called to their unhappiness, he urged Zeyd to keep his wife and not divorce her, being apprehensive of the talk that would arise if it became known that a marriage arranged by him had proved unhappy. At last, Zeyd did actually divorce Zeynab, and the Prophet was commanded to marry her in order, by his example, to disown the superstitious custom of the pagan Arabs, in such matters, of treating their adopted sons as their real sons, which was against the laws of God (*i.e.* the laws of nature); whereas in arranging a marriage, the woman's inclinations ought to be considered. Unhappy marriage was no part of Allah's ordinance, and was not to be held sacred in Islam.

The Surah contains further references to the wives of the Prophet in connection with which it may be mentioned that from the age of twenty-five till the age of fifty he had only one wife, Khadijah, fifteen years his senior, to whom he was devotedly attached and whose memory he cherished till his dying day. With the exception of 'Ayeshah, the daughter of his closest friend, Abu Bakr, whom he married at her father's request when she was still a child, all his later marriages were with widows whose state was pitiable for one reason or another. Some of them were widows of men killed in war. One was a captive, when he made the marriage the excuse for emancipating all the conquered tribe and restoring their property. Two were daughters of his enemies, and his alliance with them was a cause of peace. It is noteworthy that the period of these marriages was also the period of his greatest activity, when he had little rest from campaigning, and was always busy with the problems of a growing empire.

The period of revelation is between the end of the fifth and the end of the seventh years of the Hijrah.

=====

In the name of Allah, the Beneficent, the Merciful.

1. O Prophet! Keep your duty to Allah and obey not the disbelievers and the hypocrites. Allah is Knower, Wise.

2. And follow that which is inspired in you from your Lord. Allah is Aware of what you do.

3. And put your trust in Allah, for Allah is sufficient as Trustee.

4. Allah has not assigned to any man two hearts within his body, nor has He made your wives whom you declare (to be your mothers) your mothers,[202] nor has He made those whom you claim (to be your sons) your sons. This is but a saying of your mouths. But Allah says the truth and He shows the way.

5. Proclaim their real parentage. That will be more equitable in the sight of Allah. And if you know not their fathers, then (they are) your brothers in the faith, and your dependants. And there is

no sin for you in the mistakes that you make unintentionally, but what your hearts intend (that will be a sin for you). Allah is ever Forgiving, Merciful.

6. The Prophet is closer to the believers than their own selves, and his wives are (as) their mothers. And the owners of kinship are closer one to another in the ordinance of Allah than (other) believers and the emigrants (who emigrated from Makkah), except that you should do kindness to your friends.[203] This is written in the Book (of nature).

7. And when We exacted a covenant from the Prophets, and from you (O Muhammad) and from Noah and Abraham and Moses and Jesus son of Mary. We took from them a solemn covenant;

8. That He may ask the loyal of their loyalty. And He has prepared a painful doom for the unfaithful.

9. O you who believe! Remember Allah's favour to you when there came against you forces, and We sent against them a great wind and forces you could not see. And Allah is ever Seer of what you do.

10. When they came upon you from above you and from below you, and when eyes grew wild and hearts reached to the throats, and you were imagining vain thoughts concerning Allah.

---

202. The reference is to a custom of the pagan Arabs by which a man could put away his wife by merely saying: "your back is as my mother's back for me."

203. The Prophet had ordained brotherhood between individuals of the Ansar (Muslims of Al-Madinah) and the Muhajirin (emigrants from Makkah), a brotherhood which was closer than relationship by blood. This verse abolished such brotherhood, insofar as inheritance was concerned.

11. There were the believers sorely tried, and shaken with a mighty shock.

12. And when the hypocrites, and those in whose hearts is a disease, were saying: Allah and His messenger promised us nothing but delusion.

13. And when a party of them said: O people of Yathrib! There is no stand (possible) for you, therefore turn back. And certain of them (even) sought permission of the Prophet, saying: Our homes lie open (to the enemy). And they did not lie open. They only wished to flee.

14. If the enemy had entered from all sides and they had been exhorted to treachery, they would have committed it, and would have hesitated upon it but a little.

15. And verily they had already sworn to Allah that they would not turn their backs (to the foe). An oath to Allah must be answered for.

16. Say: Flight will not benefit you if you flee from death or killing, and then you dwell in comfort just a little while.

17. Say: Who is he who can preserve you from Allah if He intends harm for you, or intends mercy for you. They will not find that they have any friend or helper other than Allah.

18. Allah already knows those of you who hinder, and those who say to their brothers: "Come here to us!" and they only come to the stress of battle for a little while,

19. Being sparing of their help to you (believers). But when the fear comes, then you (Muhammad) see them regarding you with rolling eyes like one who faints to death. Then, when the fear departs, they scald you with sharp tongues in their greed for wealth (from the spoil). Such have not believed. Therefore Allah makes their deeds fruitless. And that is easy for Allah.

20. They hold that the clans have not retired (for good); and if the clans should advance (again), they would rather be in the desert with the wandering Arabs, asking for news of you; and if they were among you, they would not give battle, except a little.

21. Verily in the messenger of Allah you have a good example for him who looks to Allah and the Last Day, and remembers Allah much.

22. And when the true believers saw the clans, they said: This is that which Allah and His messenger promised us. Allah and His messenger are true. It only confirmed them in their faith and resignation.

23. Of the believers there are men who are true to that which they covenanted with Allah. Some of them have paid their vow by death (in battle), and some of them still are waiting; and they have not altered in the least;

24. That Allah may reward the true men for their truth, and punish the hypocrites if He will or relent toward them (if He will). For Allah is Forgiving, Merciful.

25. And Allah repulsed the disbelievers in their wrath; they gained no good. Allah averted their attack from the believers. Allah is ever Strong, Mighty.

26. And He brought those of the People of the Scripture who supported them down from their strongholds, and cast panic into their hearts. Some you slew, and some you made captive.

27. And He caused you to inherit their land and their houses and their wealth, and land you have not trodden. Allah is ever Able to do all things.

28. O Prophet! Say to your wives: If you desire the world's life and its adornment, come! I will content you and will release you with a fair release.

29. But if you desire Allah and His messenger and the abode of the Hereafter, then Allah has prepared for the good among you an immense reward.

30. O you wives of the Prophet! Whoever of you commits manifest lewdness, the punishment for her will be doubled, and that is easy for Allah.

31. And whoever of you is submissive to Allah and His messenger and does right, We shall give her reward twice over, and We have prepared for her a rich provision.

32. O you wives of the Prophet! You are not like any other women. If you keep your duty (to Allah), then be not soft of speech, lest he in whose heart is a disease aspire (to you), but utter customary speech.

33. And stay in your houses. Ornament not yourselves with the ornaments of the Time of Ignorance. Be regular in prayer, and pay the poor-due, and obey Allah and His messenger. Allah's wish is only to remove uncleanness far from you, O people of the Household, and cleanse you with a thorough cleansing.

34. And bear in mind that which is recited in your houses of the revelations of Allah and wisdom. Allah is Subtle, Aware.

35. Men who surrender to Allah, and women who surrender, and men who believe and women who believe, and men who obey and women who obey, and men who speak the truth and women who speak the truth, and men who persevere (in righteousness) and women who persevere, and men who are humble and women who are humble, and men who give alms and women who give alms, and men who fast and women who fast, and men who guard their modesty and women who guard (their modesty), and men who remember Allah much and women who remember - Allah has prepared for them forgiveness and a vast reward.

36. And it is not proper for a believing man or a believing woman, when Allah and His messenger have decided an affair (for them), that they should (after that) claim any say in their affair; and whoever is rebellious to Allah and His messenger, he verily goes astray in manifest error.

37. And when you said to him on whom Allah has conferred favour and you have conferred favour: Keep your wife to yourself, and fear Allah. And you hid in your mind that which Allah was to bring to light, and you feared mankind whereas Allah has a better right that you should fear Him. So when Zeyd had performed that necessary formality (of divorce) from her, We gave her to you in marriage, so that (from there on) there may be no sin for believers in respect of wives of their adopted sons, when the latter have performed the necessary formality (of release) from them. The commandment of Allah must be fulfilled.

38. There is no reproach for the Prophet in that which Allah makes his due. That was Allah's way with those who passed away of old - and the commandment of Allah is certain destiny -

39. Who delivered the messages of Allah and feared Him, and feared none except Allah. Allah keeps good account.

40. Muhammad is not the father of any man among you, but he is the messenger of Allah and the Seal of the Prophets; and Allah is ever Aware of all things.

41. O you who believe! Remember Allah with much remembrance.

42. And glorify Him morning and night.

43. He it is Who blesses you, and His angels (bless you), that He may bring you out from darkness to light; and He is ever Merciful to the believers.

44. Their salutation on the day when they will meet Him will be: Peace. And He has prepared for them a goodly recompense.

45. O Prophet! We have sent you as a witness and a bringer of good tidings and a warner.

46. And as a summoner to Allah by His permission, and as a lamp that gives light.

47. And announce to the believers the good tidings that they will have great bounty from Allah.

48. And incline not towards the disbelievers and the hypocrites. Disregard their noxious talk, and put your trust in Allah. Allah is sufficient as Trustee.

49. O you who believe! If you marry believing women and divorce them before you have touched them, then there is no period that you should reckon. But content them and release them handsomely.

50. O Prophet! We have made lawful to you your wives to whom you have paid their dowries, and those whom your right hand possesses of those whom Allah has given you as spoils of war, and the daughters of your uncle on the father's side and the daughters of your aunts on the father's side, and the daughters of your uncle on the mother's side and the daughters of your aunts on the mother's side who emigrated with you, and a believing woman if she gives herself to the Prophet and the Prophet desires to ask her in marriage - a privilege for you only, not for the (rest of) believers - We are Aware of that which We enjoined upon them concerning their wives and those whom their right hands possess - that you may be free from blame, for Allah is ever Forgiving, Merciful.

51. You can defer whom you will of them and receive to you whom you will, and whomsoever you desire of those whom you have set aside (temporarily), it is no sin for you (to receive her again); that is better; that they may be comforted and not grieve, and may all be pleased with what you give them. Allah knows what is in your hearts (O men), and Allah is ever Forgiving, Clement.

52. It is not allowed for you to take (other) women after that, nor that you should change them for other wives even though their beauty might please you, except those whom your right hand possesses. And Allah is ever Watcher over all things.

53. O You who believe! Enter not the dwellings of the Prophet for a meal without waiting for the proper time, unless permission be granted you. But if you are invited, enter, and, when your meal is ended, then disperse. Linger not for conversation. That would cause annoyance to the Prophet, and he would be shy of (asking) you (to go); but Allah is not shy of the truth. And when you ask of them (the wives of the Prophet) anything, ask it of them from behind a curtain. That is purer for your hearts and for their hearts. And it is not for you to cause annoyance to the messenger of Allah, nor that you should ever marry his wives after him. That in Allah's sight would be an enormity.

54. Whether you reveal a thing or keep it hidden, Allah is ever Knower of all things.

55. It is no sin for them (your wives) (to converse freely) with their fathers, or their sons, or their brothers, or their brothers' sons, or the sons of their sisters or of their own women, or their slaves. O women! Keep your duty to Allah. Allah is ever Witness over all things.

56. Allah and His angels shower blessings on the Prophet. O you who believe! Ask blessings on him and salute him with a worthy salutation.

57. Those who malign Allah and His messenger, Allah has cursed them in the world and the Hereafter, and has prepared for them the doom of the disdained.

58. And those who malign believing men and believing women undeservedly, they bear the guilt of slander and manifest sin.

59. O Prophet! Tell your wives and your daughters and the women of the believers to draw their cloaks close around them (when they go out). That will be better, so that they may be recognised and not annoyed. Allah is ever Forgiving, Merciful.

60. If the hypocrites, and those in whose hearts is a disease, and the alarmists in the city do not cease, We verily shall urge you on against them, then they will be your neighbours in it but a little while.

61. Accursed, they will be seized wherever they are found and will be slain with a (fierce) slaughter.

62. That was the way of Allah in the case of those who passed away of old; you will not find for the way of Allah any power to change.

63. Men ask you of the Hour. Say: The knowledge of it is with Allah only. What can convey (the knowledge) to you? It may be that the Hour is near.

64. Allah has cursed the disbelievers, and has prepared for them a flaming Fire,

65. In which they will remain forever. They will find (then) no protecting friend nor helper.

66. On the day when their faces are turned over in the Fire, they say: Oh, if only we had obeyed Allah and had obeyed His messenger!

67. And they say: Our Lord! We obeyed our princes and great men, and they misled us from the Way.

68. Our Lord! Oh, give them double torment and curse them with a mighty curse.

69. O you who believe! Be not as those who slandered Moses, but Allah proved his innocence of that which they alleged, and he was well esteemed in Allah's sight.

70. O you who believe! Guard your duty to Allah, and speak words straight to the point;

71. He will adjust your works for you and will forgive you your sins. Whoever obeys Allah and His messenger, he verily has gained a signal victory.

72. We offered the trust to the heavens and the earth and the hills, but they shrank from bearing it and were afraid of it. And man assumed it. He has proved a tyrant and a fool.

73. So Allah punishes hypocritical men and hypocritical women, and idolatrous men and idolatrous women. But Allah pardons believing men and believing women, and Allah is ever Forgiving, Merciful.

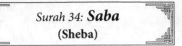

Surah 34: **Saba**
(Sheba)

Saba, "Sheba," takes its name from v. 15 ff., where Sheba (Saba), a region in the Yaman, is mentioned as having been devastated by a flood. It warns of the effects of luxury.

An early Makkan Surah.

In the name of Allah, the Beneficent, the Merciful.

1. Praise be to Allah, to Whom belongs whatever is in the heavens and whatever is in the earth. His is the praise in the Hereafter, and He is the Wise, the Aware.

2. He knows that which goes into the earth and that which comes out from it, and that which descends from the heaven and that which ascends into it. He is the Merciful, the Forgiving.

3. Those who disbelieve say: The Hour will never come to us. Say: No, by my Lord, but it is coming to you surely. (He is) the Knower of the Unseen. Not an atom's weight, or less than that or greater, escapes Him in the heavens or in the earth, but it is in a clear Record,

4. That He may reward those who believe and do good works. For them is pardon and a rich provision.

5. But those who strive against Our revelations, challenging (Us), theirs will be a painful doom of wrath.

6. Those who have been given knowledge see that what is revealed to you from your Lord is the truth and leads to the path of the Mighty, the Owner of Praise.

7. Those who disbelieve say: Shall we show you a man who will tell you (that) when you have become dispersed in dust, completely, still, even then, you will be created anew?

8. Has he invented a lie concerning Allah, or is there in him a madness? No, but those who disbelieve in the Hereafter are in torment and far error.

9. Have they not observed what is before them and what is behind them of the sky and the earth? If We will, We can make the earth swallow them, or cause obliteration from the sky to fall on them. In this surely is a sign for every slave who turns (to Allah) repentant.

10. And assuredly We gave David grace from Us, (saying): O you hills and birds, echo his psalms of praise! And We made the iron supple to him,

11. Saying: Make long coats of mail and measure the links (of it). And do right. I am Seer of what you do.

12. And to Solomon (We gave) the wind, of which the morning course was a month's journey and the evening course a month's journey, and We caused the fount of copper to gush out for him, and (We gave him) certain of the jinn who worked for him by permission of his Lord. And such of them as deviated from Our command, them We caused to taste the punishment of flaming Fire.

13. They made for him what he willed: synagogues and statues, basins like wells and boilers built into the ground.

Give thanks, O House of David! Few of My bondsmen are thankful.

14. And when We decreed death for him, nothing showed his death to them except a creeping creature of the earth which gnawed away his staff. And when he fell the jinn saw clearly how, if they had known the Unseen, they would not have continued in despised toil.

15. There was indeed a sign for Sheba in their dwelling-place: Two gardens on the right hand and the left (as who should say): Eat of the provision of your Lord and render thanks to Him. A fair land and an indulgent Lord!

16. But they were obstinate, so We sent on them the flood of 'Arim, and in exchange for their two gardens gave them two gardens bearing bitter fruit, the tamarisk and here and there a lote-tree.

17. This We awarded them because of their ingratitude. Do We ever punish any except the ungrateful?

18. And We set, between them and the towns which We had blessed, towns easy to be seen, and We made the distance between them easy, (saying): Travel in them safely both by night and day.

19. But they said: Our Lord! Make the distance between our journeys longer. And they wronged themselves, therefore We made them myths (in the land) and scattered them abroad, a total scattering. In this verily are signs for each steadfast, grateful (heart).

20. And Satan indeed found his calculation true concerning them, for they follow him, all except a group of true believers.

21. And he had no authority whatever against them, except that We would know him who believes in the Hereafter from him who is in doubt of it; and your Lord (O Muhammad) takes note of all things.

22. Say (O Muhammad): Call upon those whom you set up besides Allah! They possess not an atom's weight either in the heavens or in the earth, nor have they any share in either, nor has He a helper among them.

23. No intercession benefits with Him except for him whom He permits. Yet, when fear is banished from their hearts, they say: What was it that your Lord said? They say: The Truth. And He is the Sublime, the Great.

24. Say: Who gives you provision from the sky and the earth? Say: Allah, We or you assuredly are rightly guided or in manifest error.

25. Say: You will not be asked of what we committed, nor shall we be asked of what you do.

26. Say: Our Lord will bring us all together, then He will judge between us with truth. He is the All-Knowing Judge.

27. Say: Show me those whom you have joined to Him as partners. No (you dare not)! For He is Allah, the Mighty, the Wise.

28. And We have not sent you (O Muhammad) except as a bringer of good tidings and a warner to all mankind; but most of mankind know not.

29. And they say: When is this promise (to be fulfilled) if you are truthful?

30. Say (O Muhammad): Yours is the promise of a Day which you cannot postpone nor hasten by an hour.

31. And those who disbelieve say: We believe not in this Qur'an nor in that which was before it; but oh, if you could see, when the wrongdoers are brought up before their Lord, how they cast the blame one to another; how those who were despised (in the earth) say to those who were proud: But for you, we would have been believers.

32. Those who were proud say to those who were despised: Did we drive you away from the guidance after it had come to you? No, but you were guilty.

33. Those who were despised say to those who were proud: No but (it was your) scheming night and day, when you commanded us to disbelieve in Allah and set up rivals to Him. And they are filled with remorse when they see the doom; and We place shackles on the necks of those who disbelieved. Are they repaid anything except what they used to do?

34. And We sent not to any township a warner, but its pampered ones declared: We are disbelievers in that with which you have been sent.

35. And they say: We are more (than you) in wealth and children. We are not the punished!

36. Say (O Muhammad): My Lord enlarges the provision for whom He will and narrows it (for whom He will). But most of mankind know not.

37. And it is not your wealth nor your children that will bring you near to Us, but he who believes and does good (he draws near). As for such, theirs will be a twofold reward for what they did and they will dwell secure in lofty halls.

38. And as for those who strive against Our revelations, challenging, they will be brought to the doom.

39. Say: My Lord enlarges the provision for whom He will of His bondsmen, and narrows (it) for him. And whatever you spend (for good) He replaces it. And He is the Best of Providers.

40. And on the day when He will gather them all together, He will say to the angels: Did these worship you?

41. They will say: Be You Glorified. You (alone) are our Guardian, not them! No, but they worshipped the jinn; most of them were believers in them.

42. That day you will possess no use nor hurt one for another. And We shall say to those who did wrong: Taste the doom of the Fire which you used to deny.

43. And if Our revelations are recited to them in plain terms, they say: This is nothing else than a man who would turn you away from what your fathers used to worship; and they say: This is nothing else than an invented lie. Those who disbelieve say of the truth when it reaches them: This is nothing else than mere magic.

44. And We have given them no scriptures which they study, nor did We send to them, before you, any warner.

45. Those before them denied, and these have not attained a fraction of that which

We bestowed on them (of old); yet they denied My messengers. How intense then was My abhorrence (of them)!

46. Say (to them, O Muhammad): I exhort you to one thing only: that you awake, for Allah's sake, by twos and singly, and then reflect: There is no madness in your comrade. He is nothing else than a warner to you in the face of a terrific doom.

47. Say: Whatever reward I might have asked of you is yours. My reward is the affair of Allah only. He is Witness over all things.

48. Say: My Lord pronounces the truth. (He is) the Knower of Things Hidden.

49. Say: The Truth has come, and falsehood shows not its face and will not return.

50. Say: If I err, I err only to my own loss, and if I am rightly guided it is because of that which my Lord has revealed to me. He is Hearer, Near.

51. If you could only see when they are terrified with no escape, and are seized from near at hand,

52. And say: We (now) believe in it (*i.e.* the truth). But how can they reach (faith) from a distance,

53. When they disbelieved in it long ago and aim at the unseen from a distance.

54. And a gulf is set between them and that which they desire, as was done for people of their kind of old. They were in hopeless doubt.

Surah 35: **Al-Mala'ikah**
(The Angels)

Al-Mala'ikah, "The Angels," also called Al-Fatir, "The Creator," takes its name in either case from a word in v. 1. An early Makkan Surah.

In the name of Allah,
the Beneficent, the Merciful.

1. Praise be to Allah, the Creator of the heavens and the earth, Who appoints the angels as messengers having wings two, three and four. He multiplies in creation what He wills. Allah is Able to do all things.

2. That which Allah opens to mankind out of mercy no one can withhold it; and that which He withholds no one can release after it. He is the Mighty, the Wise.

3. O mankind! Remember Allah's grace towards you! Is there any creator other than Allah who provides for you from the sky and the earth? There is no God except Him. Where then are you turned?

4. And if they deny you, (O Muhammad), messengers (of Allah) were denied before you. To Allah all things are brought back.

5. O mankind! The promise of Allah is true. So let not the life of the world deceive you, and let not the (avowed) deceiver deceive you with regard to Allah.

6. The devil is an enemy for you, so treat him as an enemy. He only summons his faction to be owners of the flaming Fire.

7. Those who disbelieve, theirs will be an awful doom; and those who believe and do good works, theirs will be forgiveness and a great reward.

8. Is he, the evil of whose deeds is made fair-seeming to him so that he considers it good, (other than Satan's fool)? Allah verily sends whom He will astray, and guides whom He will; so let not your soul expire in sighing for them. Allah is Aware of what they do!

9. And Allah it is Who sends the winds and they raise a cloud; then We lead it to a dead land and revive with it the earth after its death. Such is the Resurrection.

10. Whoever desires power (should know that) all power belongs to Allah. To Him good words ascend, and the pious deed He exalts; but those who plot iniquities, theirs will be an awful doom; and the plotting of such (people) will come to nothing.

11. Allah created you from dust, then from a little fluid, then He made you pairs (the male and female). No female bears or gives birth except with His knowledge. And no-one grows old who grows old, nor is anything lessened of his life, but it is recorded in a Book. That is easy for Allah.

12. And the two seas[204] are not alike: this, fresh, sweet, good to drink, this (other) bitter salt. And from them both you eat fresh meat and derive the ornaments that you wear. And you see the ship cleaving them with its prow that you may seek of His bounty, and that perhaps you may give thanks.

---

204. *i.e.,* the two kinds of water on the earth.

13. He makes the night pass into the day and He makes the day pass into the night. He has subdued the sun and moon to service. Each runs to an appointed term. Such is Allah, your Lord; His is the Sovereignty; and those to whom you pray instead of Him own not so much as the white spot on a date-stone.

14. If you pray to them they hear not your prayer, and if they heard they could not grant it to you. On the Day of Resurrection they will disown association with you. No one can inform you like Him Who is Aware.

15. O mankind! You are poor in your relation to Allah. And Allah! He is the Absolute, the Owner of Praise.

16. If He will, He can be rid of you and bring (instead of you) some new creation.

17. That is not a hard thing for Allah.

18. And no burdened soul can bear another's burden, and if one who is heavy laden calls for (help with) his load, nothing of it will be lifted even though he (to whom he calls) be a relative. You warn only those who fear their Lord in secret, and have established worship. He who grows (in goodness), grows only for himself, (he cannot by his merit redeem others). To Allah is the journeying.

19. The blind man is not equal to the seer;

20. Nor is darkness (tantamount to) light;

21. Nor is the shadow equal to the sun's full heat;

22. Nor are the living equal to the dead. Allah makes whom He will hear. You cannot reach those who are in the graves.

23. You are but a warner.

24. We have sent you with the Truth, a bearer of glad tidings and a warner; and there is not a nation but a warner has passed among them.

25. And if they deny you, those before them also denied. Their messengers came to them with clear proofs (of Allah's Sovereignty), and with the Psalms and the Scripture giving light.

26. Then I seized those who disbelieved, and how intense was My abhorrence!

27. Have you not seen that Allah causes water to fall from the sky, and We produce with it fruit of diverse hues; and among the hills are streaks white and red, of diverse hues, and (others) raven-black;

28. And of men and beasts and cattle, in like manner, diverse hues? The learned among His bondsmen fear Allah alone. Allah is Mighty, Forgiving.

29. Those who read the Scripture of Allah, and establish worship, and spend of that which We have bestowed on them secretly and openly, they look forward to imperishable gain,

30. That He will pay them their wages and increase them with His grace. He is Forgiving, Responsive.

31. As for that which We inspire in you of the Scripture, it is the Truth confirming that which was (revealed) before it. Allah is indeed Observer, Seer of His slaves.

32. Then We gave the Scripture as inheritance to those whom We elected of Our bondsmen. But of them are some who wrong themselves and of them are some who are lukewarm, and of them are some who outstrip (others) through good deeds, by Allah's permission. That is the great favour!

33. Gardens of Eden! They enter them wearing armlets of gold and pearl and their garment in there is silk.

34. And they say: Praise be to Allah Who has put grief away from us. Our Lord is Forgiving, Bountiful,

35. Who, of His grace, has installed us in the mansion of eternity, where toil touches us not nor can weariness affect us.

36. But as for those who disbelieve, for them is fire of Hell; it takes not complete effect upon them so that they can die, nor is its torment lightened for them. Thus We punish every ungrateful one.

37. And they call for help there, (saying): Our Lord! Release us; we will do right, not (the wrong) that we used to do. Did not We grant you a life long enough for him who reflected to reflect in it? And the warner came to you. Now taste (the flavour of your deeds), for evildoers have no helper.

38. Allah is the Knower of the Unseen of the heavens and the earth. He is Aware of the secret of (men's) hearts.

39. He it is Who has made you regents in the earth; so he who disbelieves, his disbelief be on his own head. Their disbelief increases for the disbelievers, in their Lord's sight, nothing except abhorrence. Their disbelief increases for the disbelievers nothing except loss.

40. Say: Have you seen your partner-gods to whom you pray besides Allah?

Show me what they created of the earth! Or have they any portion in the heavens? Or have We given them a scripture so they act on clear proof from it? No, the evildoers promise one another only to deceive.

41. Allah grasps the heavens and the earth that they deviate not, and if they were to deviate there is not one that could grasp them after Him. He is ever Clement, Forgiving.

42. And they swore by Allah, their most binding oath, that if a warner came to them they would be more compliant than any of the nations; yet, when a warner came to them it then aroused in them nothing except repugnance,

43. (Shown in their) behaving arrogantly in the land and plotting evil; and the evil plot only encloses the men who make it. Then, can they expect anything except the treatment of the people of old? You will not find for Allah's way of treatment any substitute, nor will you find for Allah's way of treatment anything of power to change.

44. Have they not travelled in the land and seen the nature of the consequence for those who were before them, and they were mightier than these in power? Allah is not such that anything in the heavens or in the earth escapes Him. He is the Wise, the Mighty.

45. If Allah took mankind to task by that which they deserve, He would not leave a living creature on the surface of the earth; but He reprieves them to an appointed term, and when their term comes - then verily (they will know that) Allah is ever Seer of His slaves.

Surah 36: **Ya Sin**

Ya Sin takes its name from the two letters of the Arabic alphabet which stand as the first verse and are generally held to signify Ya Insan ("O Man"). This Surah is regarded with special reverence, and is recited in times of adversity, illness, fasting and on the approach of death.

It belongs to the middle group of Makkan Surahs.

In the name of Allah, the Beneficent, the Merciful.

1. *Ya Sin.*[205]

2. By the wise Qur'an,

3. You are of those sent

4. On a straight path,

5. A revelation of the Mighty, the Merciful,

6. That you may warn a people whose fathers were not warned, so they are heedless.

7. Already the judgement has, (for their infidelity) proved true of most of them, for they believe not.

8. We have put on their necks collars reaching to the chins, so that they are made stiff-necked.

9. And We have set a bar before them and a bar behind them, and (thus) have covered them so that they see not.

10. Whether you warn them or you warn them not, it is alike for them, for they believe not.

205. See *Surah 2, Al-Baqarah,* v. 1, footnote.

11. You warn only him who follows the Reminder and fears the Beneficent in secret. To him bring tidings of forgiveness and a rich reward.

12. It is We Who bring the dead to life. We record that which they send before (them), and their footprints. And all things We have kept in a clear Register.

13. Coin for them a similitude: The people of the city when those sent (from Allah) came to them;

14. When We sent them two messengers, and they denied them both, so We reinforced them with a third, and they said: We have been sent to you.

15. They said: You are only mortals like us. The Beneficent has nothing revealed. You only lie!

16. They answered: Our Lord knows that we are indeed sent to you,

17. And our duty is only plain conveyance (of the message).

18. (The people of the city) said: We predict ill of you. If you desist not, we shall surely stone you, and grievous torture will befall you at our hands.

19. They said: Your evil prediction is with you! Is it because you are reminded (of the truth)? No, but you are obstinate people!

20. And there came from the uttermost part of the city a man running. He called: O my people! Follow those who have been sent!

21. Follow those who ask of you no fee, and who are rightly guided.

22. For what reason should I not serve Him Who has created me, and to Whom you will be brought back?

23. Shall I take (other) gods in place of Him when, if the Beneficent should wish me any harm, their intercession will benefit me nothing, nor can they save?

24. Then truly I would be in manifest error.

25. I have believed in your Lord, so hear me!

26. It was said (to him): Enter paradise. He said: Would that my people knew

27. With what (generosity) my Lord has pardoned me and made me of the honoured ones!

28. We sent not down against his people after him a force from heaven, nor do We ever send.

29. It was but one Shout, and they were extinct.

30. Ah, the anguish for the bondsmen! Never came there to them a messenger but they did mock him!

31. Have they not seen how many generations We destroyed before them, which indeed returned not to them;

32. But all, without exception, will be brought before Us.

33. A sign to them is the dead earth. We revive it, and We bring out from it grain so that they eat of it;

34. And We have placed in it gardens of the date-palm and grapes, and We have caused springs of water to gush out in it,

35. That they may eat of the fruit of it, and their hands made it not. Will they not, then, give thanks?

36. Glory be to Him Who created all the sexual pairs, of that which the earth grows, and of themselves, and of that which they know not!

37. A sign to them is the night. We strip it of the day, and they are in darkness.

38. And the sun runs on to a resting-place for him. That is the measuring of the Mighty, the Wise.

39. And for the moon We have appointed mansions till she returns like an old shrivelled palm-leaf.

40. It is not for the sun to overtake the moon, nor does the night outstrip the day. They float each in an orbit.

41. And a sign to them is that We bear their offspring in the laden ship,

42. And have created for them of the like of it on which they ride.

43. And if We will, We drown them, and there is no help for them, neither can they be saved;

44. Unless by mercy from Us and as comfort for a while.

45. When it is said to them: Beware of that which is before you and that which is behind you, that perhaps you may find mercy (they are heedless).

46. Never came a sign of the signs of their Lord to them, but they did turn away from it!

47. And when it is said to them: Spend of that with which Allah has provided you, those who disbelieve say to those who believe: Shall we feed those whom

Allah, if He willed, would feed? You are in nothing else than manifest error.

48. And they say: When will this promise be fulfilled, if you are truthful?

49. They await but one Shout, which will surprise them while they are disputing.

50. Then they cannot make bequest, nor can they return to their own people.

51. And the trumpet is blown and from the graves they hurry to their Lord,

52. Calling: Woe upon us! Who has raised us from our place of sleep? This is that which the Beneficent did promise, and the messengers spoke truth.

53. It is but one Shout, and you see them brought together before Us!

54. This day no soul is wronged in anything; nor are you repaid anything except what you used to do.

55. Those who merit paradise this day are happily employed,

56. They and their wives, in pleasant shade, on thrones reclining;

57. Theirs the fruit (of their good deeds) and theirs (all) that they ask;

58. The word from a Merciful Lord (for them) is: Peace!

59. But away with you, O you guilty, this day!

60. Did I not charge you, O you sons of Adam, that you worship not the devil - He is your open enemy! -

61. But that you worship Me? That was the right path.

62. Yet he has led astray of you a great multitude. Had you then no sense?

63. This is Hell which you were promised (if you followed him).

64. Burn in it this day because you disbelieved.

65. This day We seal up their mouths, and their hands speak out to Us and their feet bear witness as to what they used to earn.

66. And had We willed, We verily could have extinguished their eyesight so that they should struggle for the way. Then how could they have seen?

67. And had We willed, We verily could have fixed them in their place, making them powerless to go forward or turn back.[206]

68. He whom we bring to old age, We reverse him in creation (making him go back to weakness after strength). Have you then no sense?

69. And We have not taught him (Muhammad) poetry, nor is it proper for him. This is nothing else than a Reminder and a Lecture making plain,

70. To warn whoever lives, and that the word may be fulfilled against the disbelievers.

71. Have they not seen how We have created for them of Our handiwork the cattle, so that they are their owners,

72. And have subdued them to them, so that some of them they have for riding, some for food?

---

206. But they have sight and power of motion so they can choose their way.

73. Benefits and (diverse) drinks have they from them. Will they not then give thanks?

74. And they have taken (other) gods besides Allah, in order that they may be helped.

75. It is not in their power to help them; but they (the worshippers) are to them a force in arms.

76. So let not their speech grieve you (O Muhammad). We know what they conceal and what they proclaim.

77. Has not man seen that We have created him from a drop of seed? Yet he is an open opponent.

78. And he has coined for Us a similitude, and has forgotten the fact of his creation, saying: Who will revive these bones when they have rotted away?

79. Say: He will revive them Who produced them at the first, for He is Knower of every creation,

80. Who has appointed for you fire from the green tree, and see! you kindle from it.

81. Is not He Who created the heavens and the earth Able to create the like of them? Indeed, that He is! for He is the All-Wise Creator,

82. But His command, when He intends a thing, is only that He says to it: Be! and it is.

83. Therefore Glory be to Him in Whose Hand is the dominion over all things! To Him you will be brought back.

Surah 37: *As-Saffat* (Those Who Set The Ranks)

As-Saffat takes its name from a word in the first verse. The reference in the first three verses is to the angels, as is made clear by vv. 164-166, where the revealing angel speaks in person. Tradition says that soothsayers and astrologers throughout the East were bewildered at the time of the Prophet's coming by the appearance in the heavens of a comet and many meteors which baffled all their science and made them afraid to sit at nights on high peaks to watch the stars, as was their general custom. They told enquirers that their families could no longer guide them, being themselves completely at a loss and terrified. This is the explanation usually given of vv. 7-9, and of a passage of similar meaning in Surah 72, vv. 8-10.

It stands early in the middle group of Makkan Surahs.

In the name of Allah, the Beneficent, the Merciful.

1. By those who set the ranks in battle order

2. And those who drive away (the wicked) with reproach

3. And those who read (the Word) for a reminder,

4. Your Lord is surely One;

5. Lord of the heavens and of the earth and all that is between them, and Lord of the sun's risings.

6. We have adorned the lowest heaven with an ornament, the stars;

7. With security from every rebellious devil.

8. They cannot listen to the Highest Chiefs for they are pelted from every side,

9. Outcast, and theirs is a perpetual torment;

10. Except him who snatches a fragment, and there pursues him a piercing flame.[207]

11. Then ask them (O Muhammad): Are they stronger as a creation, or those (others) whom We have created? We created them of shaped clay.

12. No, but you are surprised when they mock,

13. And heed not when they are reminded,

14. And seek to scoff when they see a sign.

15. And they say: This is mere magic;

16. When we are dead and have become dust and bones, shall we then be raised (again)?

17. And our forefathers?

18. Say (O Muhammad): Yes, in truth; and you will be brought low.

19. There is but one Shout, and they see,

20. And say: Ah, woe for us! This is the Day of Judgement.

21. This is the Day of Separation, which you used to deny.

22. (And it is said to the angels): Assemble those who did wrong, together with their wives and what they used to worship

23. Instead of Allah, and lead them to the path to Hell;

24. And stop them, for they must be questioned.

25. What is the matter with you that you help not one another?

26. No, but this day they make full submission.

27. And some of them draw near to others, mutually questioning.

28. They say: You used to come to us, imposing, (swearing that you spoke the truth).

29. They answer: No, but you (yourselves) were not believers.

30. We had no power over you, but you were headstrong people.

31. Now the Word of our Lord has been fulfilled concerning us. We are about to taste (the doom).

32. Thus we misled you. We were (ourselves) astray.

33. Then this day they (both) are sharers in the doom.

34. Thus We deal with the guilty.

35. For when it was said to them, There is no God except Allah, they were contemptuous

36. And said: Shall we forsake our gods for a mad poet?

37. No, but he brought the Truth, and he confirmed those sent (before him).

---

207. *Surah 72, Al-Jinn,* vv 8-10; *Surah 67, Al-Mulk,* v. 5.

38. (Now) verily you taste the painful doom -

39. You are repaid nothing except what you did -

40. Except single-minded slaves of Allah;

41. For them there is a known provision,

42. Fruits. And they will be honoured

43. In the Gardens of delight,

44. On couches facing one another;

45. A cup from a gushing spring is brought round for them,

46. White, delicious to the drinkers,

47. In which there is no headache nor are they made mad by it.

48. And with them are those of modest gaze, with lovely eyes,

49. (Pure) as if they were hidden eggs (of the ostrich).

50. And some of them draw near to others, mutually questioning.

51. A speaker of them says: I had a comrade

52. Who used to say: Are you in truth of those who put faith (in his words)?

53. Can we, when we are dead and have become mere dust and bones - can we (then) verily be brought to book?

54. He says: Will you look?

55. Then he looks and sees him in the depth of Hell.

56. He says: By Allah, you verily did all but cause my ruin,

57. And had it not been for the favour of my Lord, I too would have been of those dragged out (to doom).

58. Are we then not to die

59. Except our former death, and are we not to be punished?

60. This is the supreme triumph.

61. For the like of this, then, let the workers work.

62. Is this better as a welcome, or the tree of Zaqqum?[208]

63. We have appointed it as a torment for wrongdoers.

64. It is a tree that springs in the heart of Hell.

65. Its crop is as it were the heads of devils

66. And they verily must eat of it, and fill (their) bellies with it.

67. And afterwards, they have a drink of boiling water

68. And afterwards, their return is surely to Hell.

69. They indeed found their fathers astray,

70. But they make haste (to follow) in their footsteps.

71. And verily most of the men of old went astray before them,

72. And verily We sent among them warners.

73. Then see the nature of the consequence for those warned,

74. Except single-minded slaves of Allah;

75. And Noah verily prayed to Us, and gracious was the Hearer of his prayer

76. And We saved him and his household from the great distress,

77. And made his seed the survivors,

---

208. *Surah 44, Ad-Dukhan,* v. 43; *Surah 56, Al-Waqi'ah,* v. 52.

78. And left for him among the later people (the salutation):

79. Peace be to Noah among the peoples!

80. Thus do We reward the good.

81. He is one of Our believing slaves.

82. Then We drowned the others.

83. And of his persuasion verily was Abraham

84. When he came to his Lord with a whole heart;

85. When he said to his father and his people: What is it that you worship?

86. Is it a falsehood - gods beside Allah - that you desire?

87. What then is your opinion of the Lord of the Worlds?

88. And he glanced a glance at the stars.

89. Then said: I feel sick!

90. And they turned their backs and went away from him.

91. Then he turned to their gods and said: Will you not eat?

92. What is the matter with you that you do not speak?

93. Then he attacked them, striking with his right hand.

94. And (his people) came towards him, hastening.

95. He said: Do you worship that which you yourselves do carve

96. When Allah has created you and what you make?

97. They said: Build for him a building and fling him in the red-hot fire.

98. And they designed a trap for him, but We made them the lowest.

99. And he said: I am going to my Lord Who will guide me.

100. My Lord! Grant me of the righteous.

101. So We gave him tidings of a gentle son.

102. And when (his son) was old enough to walk with him, (Abraham) said: O my dear son, I have seen in a dream that I must sacrifice you. So look, what do you think? He said: O my father! Do that which you are commanded. Allah willing, you will find me of the steadfast.

103. Then, when they had both surrendered (to Allah), and he had flung him down upon his face,

104. We called to him: O Abraham!

105. You have already fulfilled the vision. Thus do We reward the good.

106. That verily was a clear test.

107. Then We ransomed him with a tremendous sacrifice.

108. And We left for him among the later people (the salutation):

109. Peace be to Abraham!

110. Thus do We reward the good.

111. He is one of Our believing slaves.

112. And we gave him tidings of the birth of Isaac, a Prophet of the righteous.

113. And We blessed him and Isaac. And of their seed are some who do good, and some who plainly wrong themselves.

114. And We verily gave grace to Moses and Aaron,

115. And saved them and their people from the great distress,

116. And helped them so that they became the victors.

117. And We gave them the clear Scripture

118. And showed them the right path.

119. And We left for them among the later people (the salutation):

120. Peace be to Moses and Aaron!

121. Thus do We reward the good.

122. They are two of Our believing slaves.

123. And Elias was of those sent (to warn),

124. When he said to his people: Will you not ward off (evil)?

125. Will you call to *Ba'l* and forsake the Best of creators,

126. Allah, your Lord and Lord of your forefathers?

127. But they denied him, so they surely will be dragged out (to the doom)

128. Except single-minded slaves of Allah.

129. And we left for him among the later people (the salutation):

130. Peace be to Elias!

131. Thus do We reward the good.

132. He is one of our believing slaves.

133. And Lot verily was of those sent (to warn).

134. When We saved him and his household, every one,

135. Except an old woman among those who stayed behind;

136. Then We destroyed the others.

137. And you verily pass by (the ruin of) them in the morning

138. And at night-time; have you then no sense?

139. And Jonah verily was of those sent (to warn)

140. When he fled to the laden ship,

141. And then drew lots and was of those rejected;

142. And the fish swallowed him while he was blameworthy;

143. And if he had not been one of those who glorify (Allah)

144. He would have stayed in its belly till the day when they are raised;

145. Then We cast him on a desert shore while he was sick;

146. And We caused a tree of gourd to grow above him;

147. And We sent him to a hundred thousand (people) or more.

148. And they believed, therefore We gave them comfort for a while.

149. Now ask them (O Muhammad): Does your Lord have daughters whereas they have sons?

150. Or did We create the angels females while they were present?

151. It is of their falsehood that they say:

152. Allah has begotten. Allah! verily they tell a lie.

153. (And again of their falsehood): He has preferred daughters to sons.

154. What is the matter with you? How do you judge?

155. Will you not then reflect?

156. Or have you a clear authority?

157. Then produce your proof, if you are truthful.

158. And they imagine kinship between him and the jinn, whereas the jinn know well that they will be brought before (Him).

159. Glorified is Allah from that which they attribute (to Him),

160. Except single-minded slaves of Allah.

161. Verily, you and that which you worship,

162. You cannot excite (anyone) against Him.

163. Except he who is to burn in Hell.

164. There is not one of us[209] but has his known position.

165. We, even We are they who set the ranks,

166. We, even we are they who hymn His praise.

167. And indeed they used to say:

168. If we only had a reminder from the men of old

169. We would be single-minded slaves of Allah.

170. Yet (now that it is come) they disbelieve in it; but they will come to know.

---

209. Here the revealing angel speaks in person.

171. And verily Our word went before of old to Our bondsmen sent (to warn)

172. That they verily would be helped,

173. And that Our host, they verily would be the victors.

174. So withdraw from them (O Muhammad) a while,

175. And watch, for they will (soon) see.

176. Would they hasten on Our doom?

177. But when it comes home to them, then it will be an unhappy morning for those who have been warned.

178. Withdraw from them a while

179. And watch, for they will (soon) see.

180. Glorified be your Lord, the Lord of Majesty, from that which they attribute (to Him),

181. And peace be to those sent (to warn).

182. And praise be to Allah, Lord of the Worlds!

Surah 38: *Sad*

Sad. This Surah takes its name from the letter of the Arabic Alphabet which stands alone at the beginning of the first verse. Tradition says that the first ten verses were revealed when the leaders of Quraysh tried to persuade Abu Talib to withdraw his protection from the Prophet, or when Abu Talib died. The former is the more probable. Its place is in the middle group of Makkan Surahs.

In the name of Allah,
the Beneficent, the Merciful.

1. Sad.[210] By the renowned Qur'an,

2. No, but those who disbelieve are in false pride and schism.

3. How many a generation We destroyed before them, and they cried out when it was no longer the time for escape!

4. And they are surprised that a warner from among themselves has come to them, and the disbelievers say: This is a wizard, a charlatan.

5. Does he make the gods One God? That is an astounding thing.

6. The chiefs among them go about, exhorting: Go and be staunch to your gods! This is a thing designed (against you).

7. We have not heard of this in later religion. This is nothing but an invention.

8. Has the reminder been to him (alone) among us? No, but they are in doubt concerning My reminder; no, but they have not yet tasted My doom.

9. Or are theirs the treasures of the mercy of your Lord, the Mighty, the Bestower?

10. Or is the kingdom of the heavens and the earth and all that is between them theirs? Then let them ascend by ropes!

11. A defeated force are (all) the factions that are there.

12. The people of Noah before them denied (their messenger) and (so did the tribe of) 'Aad, and Pharaoh firmly planted,

13. And (the tribe of) Thamud, and the people of Lot, and the dwellers in the wood:[211] these were the factions.

14. Not one of them but did deny the messengers, therefore My doom was justified,

15. These wait for just one Shout, there will be no second to it.

16. They say: Our Lord! Hasten on for us our fate before the Day of Reckoning.

17. Bear with what they say, and remember Our bondsman David, lord of might, He was always turning in repentance (towards Allah).

18. We subdued the hills to hymn the praises (of their Lord) with him at nightfall and sunrise,

19. And the birds assembled; all were turning to Him.

20. We made his kingdom strong and gave him wisdom and decisive speech.

21. And has the story of the litigants come to you? How they climbed the wall into the royal chamber;

22. How they burst in upon David, and he was afraid of them. They said: Be not afraid! (We are) two litigants, one of whom has wronged the other, therefore judge aright between us; be not unjust; and show us the fair way.

23. This my brother has ninety and nine ewes while I had one ewe; and he said: Entrust it to me, and he conquered me in speech.

24. (David) said: He has wronged you in demanding your ewe in addition to

210. See *Surah 2, Al-Baqarah*, v. 1, footnote.   211. Midian.

his ewes, and many partners oppress one another, except such as believe and do good works, and they are few. And David guessed that We had tried him, and he sought forgiveness of his Lord, and he bowed himself and fell down prostrate and repented.

25. So We forgave him that; and he had access to Our presence and a happy journey's end.

26. (And it was said to him): O David! We have set you as a viceroy in the earth; therefore judge aright between mankind, and follow not desire so that it might deceive you from the way of Allah. Those who wander from the way of Allah have an awful doom, inasmuch as they forgot the Day of Reckoning.

27. And We did not create the heaven and the earth and all that is between them in vain. That is the opinion of those who disbelieve. And woe to those who disbelieve, from the Fire!

28. Shall We treat those who believe and do good works as those who spread corruption in the earth; or shall We treat the pious as the wicked?

29. (This is) a Scripture that We have revealed to you, full of blessing, that they may ponder its revelations, and that men of understanding may reflect.

30. And We bestowed on David, Solomon. How excellent a slave! He was always turning in repentance (towards Allah).

31. When there were shown to him at evening light footed coursers

32. And he said: I have preferred the good things (of the world) to the remembrance of my Lord; till they were taken out of sight behind the curtain.

33. (Then he said): Bring them back to me, and he fell to slashing (with his sword their) legs and necks.

34. And verily We tried Solomon, and set upon his throne a (mere) body. Then did he repent.

35. He said: My Lord! Forgive me and bestow on me sovereignty such as shall not belong to any after me. You are the Bestower.

36. So We made the wind subservient to him, setting fair by his command wherever he intended.

37. And the unruly,[212] every builder and diver (We made subservient),

38. And others linked together in chains,

39. (Saying): This is Our gift, so bestow, or withhold, without reckoning.

40. And he has favour with Us, and a happy journey's end.

41. And make mention (O Muhammad) of Our bondsman Job, when he called to his Lord (saying): The devil afflicts me with distress and torment.

42. (And it was said to him): Strike the ground with your foot. This (spring) is a cool bath and a refreshing drink.

43. And We bestowed on him (again) his household and with it the like of it, a mercy from Us, and a memorial for men of understanding.

212. Lit, "devils".

44. And (it was said to him): Take in your hand a branch and strike with it, and break not your oath. We found him steadfast, how excellent a slave! He was always turning in repentance (to his Lord).

45. And make mention of Our bondsmen, Abraham, Isaac and Jacob, men of ability and vision.

46. We purified them with a pure thought, remembrance of the Home (of the Hereafter).

47. In Our sight they are verily of the elect, the excellent.

48. And make mention of Ishmael and Elisha and Dhu'l-Kifl.[213] All are of the chosen.

49. This is a reminder. And for those who ward off (evil), there is a happy journey's end,

50. Gardens of Eden, of which the gates are opened for them,

51. In which, reclining, they call for plenteous fruit and cool drink (that is) in it.

52. And with them are those of modest gaze, companions.

53. This it is that you are promised for the Day of Reckoning.

54. This in truth is Our provision, which will never waste away.

55. This (is for the righteous). And for the transgressors there will be an evil journey's end,

56. Hell, where they will burn, an evil resting-place.

---

213. A prophet of the Arabs whose story is like that of Ezekiel.

57. Here is a boiling and an ice-cold draught, so let them taste it,

58. And other (torment) of the kind in pairs (the two extremes)!

59. Here is an army rushing blindly with you. (Those who are already in the Fire say): No word of welcome for them. They will roast in the Fire.

60. They say: No, but you (misleaders), for you there is no word of welcome. You prepared this for us (by your misleading). Now unhappy is the plight.

61. They say: Our Lord! Whoever did prepare this for us, oh, give him double portion of the Fire!

62. And they say: What is the matter with us that we see not men whom we used to count among the wicked?

63. Did we take them (wrongly) for a laughing-stock, or have our eyes missed them?

64. That is the very truth: the arguing of the dwellers in the Fire.

65. Say (to them, O Muhammad): I am only a warner, and there is no God except Allah, the One, the Absolute,

66. Lord of the heavens and the earth and all that is between them, the Mighty, the Pardoning.

67. Say: It is tremendous tidings

68. Why do you turn away!

69. I had no knowledge of the Highest Chiefs when they disputed;

70. It is revealed to me only that I may be a plain warner.

71. When your Lord said to the angels: I am about to create a mortal out of mud,

72. And when I have fashioned him and breathed into him of My Spirit, then fall down before him prostrate,

73. The angels fell down prostrate, every one,

74. Except Iblis; he was contemptuous and became one of the disbelievers.

75. He said: O Iblis! What hinders you from falling prostrate before that which I have created with both My hands? Are you too proud or are you of the high exalted?

76. He said: I am better than him. You created me of fire, whilst him You created of clay.

77. He said: Go out from here, for you are outcast,

78. And My curse is on you till the Day of Judgement.

79. He said: My Lord! Reprieve me till the day when they are raised.

80. He said: You are of those reprieved

81. Until the day of the time appointed.

82. He said: Then, by Your might, I surely will deceive them every one,

83. Except Your single-minded slaves among them.

84. He said: The Truth is, and the Truth I speak,

85. That I shall fill Hell with you and with such of them as follow you, together.

86. Say (O Muhammad, to mankind): I ask of you no fee for this, and I am no imposter.

87. It is nothing else than a reminder for all peoples

88. And you will come in time to know the truth of it.

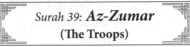

Surah 39: *Az-Zumar*
(The Troops)

Az-Zumar, "The Troops," takes its name from a peculiar word, meaning troops or companies, which occurs in v. 71, and again in v. 73. Some authorities think that vv. 53 and 54 were revealed at Al-Madinah.

It seems manifestly to belong to the middle group of Makkan Surahs, though Nöldeke places it in his last group.

In the name of Allah,
the Beneficent, the Merciful.

1. The revelation of the Scripture is from Allah, the Mighty, the Wise.

2. We have revealed the Scripture to you (Muhammad) with truth; so worship Allah, making religion pure for Him (only).

3. Surely pure religion is for Allah only. And those who choose protecting friends besides Him (say): We worship them only that they may bring us near to Allah. Allah will judge between them concerning that in which they differ. Allah guides not him who is a liar, ungrateful.

4. If Allah had willed to choose a son, He could have chosen what He would of that which He has created. Be He Glorified! He is Allah, the One, the Absolute.

5. He has created the heavens and the earth with truth. He makes night succeed day, and He makes day succeed night, and He constrains the sun and the moon to give service, each running on for an appointed term. Is not He the Mighty, the Forgiver?

6. He created you from one being, then from that (being) He made its mate; and He has provided for you of cattle eight kinds. He created you in the wombs of your mothers, creation after creation, in a threefold darkness. Such is Allah, your Lord. His is the Sovereignty. There is no God except Him. How then are you turned away?

7. If you are thankless, Allah is Independent of you, though He is not pleased with thanklessness from His bondsmen; and if you are thankful He is pleased with it. No laden soul will bear another's load. Then to your Lord is your return; and He will tell you what you used to do. He knows what is in the hearts (of men).

8. And when some hurt touches man, he calls to his Lord, turning to Him (repentant). Then, when He grants him a blessing from Him he forgets that for which he called to Him before, and sets up rivals to Allah that he may deceive (men) from His Way. Say (O Muhammad, to such a one): Take pleasure in your disbelief for a while. You are of the owners of the Fire.

9. Is he who pays adoration in the watches of the night, prostrate and standing, bewaring of the Hereafter and hoping for the mercy of his Lord, (to be accounted equal with a disbeliever)? Say (to them, O Muhammad): Are those who know equal to those who know not? But only men of understanding will pay heed.

10. Say: O My bondsmen who believe! Observe your duty to your Lord. For those who do good in this world there is good, and Allah's earth is spacious. Verily the steadfast will be paid their wages without limit.

11. Say (O Muhammad): I am commanded to worship Allah, making religion pure for Him (only).

12. And I am commanded to be the first of those who are Muslims (surrender to Him).

13. Say: If I should disobey my Lord, I fear the doom of a tremendous Day.

14. Say: Allah I worship, making my religion pure for Him (only).

15. Then worship what you will besides Him. Say: The losers will be those who lose themselves and their housefolk on the Day of Resurrection. Ah, that will be the manifest loss!

16. They have an awning of fire above them and beneath them a dais (of fire). With this Allah frightens His bondsmen. O My bondsmen, therefore fear Me!

17. And those who put away false gods lest they should worship them and turn to Allah in repentance, for them there are glad tidings. Therefore give good tidings (O Muhammad) to My bondsmen

18. Who hear advice and follow the best of it. Such are those whom Allah guides, and such are men of understanding.

19. Is he on whom the word of doom is fulfilled (to be helped), and can you (O Muhammad) rescue him who is in the Fire?

20. But those who keep their duty to their Lord, for them there are lofty halls with lofty halls above them, built (for them), beneath which rivers flow. (It is) a promise of Allah. Allah fails not His promise.

21. Have you not seen how Allah has sent down water from the sky and has caused it to penetrate the earth as water springs, and afterwards by it produces crops of diverse hues; and afterwards they wither and you see them turn yellow; then He makes them chaff. In this verily is a reminder for men of understanding.

22. Is he whose heart Allah has expanded for the Surrender[214] (to Him), so that he follows a light from his Lord, (as he who disbelieves)? Then woe to those whose hearts are hardened against remembrance of Allah. Such are in plain error.

23. Allah has (now) revealed the fairest of statements, a Scripture consistent, (in which promises of reward are) paired (with threats of punishment), at which creeps the flesh of those who fear their Lord, so that their flesh and their hearts soften to Allah's reminder. Such is Allah's guidance, with which He guides whom He wills. And he whom Allah sends astray, for him there is no guide.

24. Is he then, who will strike his face against the awful doom upon the Day of Resurrection (as he who does right)? And it will be said to the wrongdoers: Taste what you used to earn.

25. Those before them denied, and so the doom came on them from where they knew not.

26. Thus Allah made them taste humiliation in the life of the world, and verily the doom of the Hereafter will be greater if they did but know.

27. And verily We have coined for mankind in this Qur'an all kinds of similitudes, that perhaps they may reflect;

28. A Lecture[215] in Arabic, containing no crookedness, that perhaps they may ward off (evil).

29. Allah coins a similitude: A man in relation to whom are several part-owners, quarrelling, and a man belonging wholly to one man. Are the two equal in similitude? Praise be to Allah! But most of them know not.

30. You will die, and they will die;

31. Then on the Day of Resurrection, you will dispute before your Lord.

32. And who does greater wrong than he who tells a lie against Allah, and denies the truth when it reaches him? Will the home of disbelievers not be in Hell?

33. And who brings the truth and believes in it - such are the dutiful.

34. They shall have what they will of their Lord's bounty. That is the reward for the good:

35. That Allah will remit from them the worst of what they did, and will pay them as reward the best they used to do.

36. Will not Allah defend His slave? Yet they would frighten you with those besides Him. He whom Allah sends astray, for him there is no guide.

37. And he whom Allah guides, for him there can be no misleader. Is Allah not Mighty, Able to Repay (the wrong)?

214. Arabic: Al-Islam.

215. Arabic: Qur'an.

38. And verily, if you should ask them: Who created the heavens and the earth? they will say: Allah. Say: Consider then those you worship besides Allah, if Allah willed some hurt for me, could they remove from me His hurt; or if He willed some mercy for me, could they restrain His mercy? Say: Allah is my all. In Him do (all) the trusting put their trust.

39. Say: O my people! Act in your manner. I (too) am acting. Thus you will come to know

40. Who it is to whom comes a doom that will humiliate him, and on whom there falls everlasting doom.

41. We have revealed to you (Muhammad) the Scripture for mankind with truth. Then whoever goes right, it is for his soul, and whoever strays, strays only to its hurt. And you are not a guardian over them.

42. Allah receives (men's) souls at the time of their death, and that (soul) which dies not (yet) in its sleep. He keeps that (soul) for which He has ordained death and dismisses the rest till an appointed term. In this verily are signs for people who take thought.

43. Or do they choose intercessors other than Allah? Say: What! Even though they have power over nothing and have no intelligence?

44. Say: To Allah belongs all intercession. His is the Sovereignty of the heavens and the earth. And afterwards to Him you will be brought back.

45. And when Allah alone is mentioned, the hearts of those who believe not in the Hereafter are repelled, and when those (whom they worship) beside Him are mentioned, see! They are glad.

46. Say: O Allah! Creator of the heavens and the earth! Knower of the Invisible and the Visible! You will judge between Your slaves concerning that in which they used to differ.

47. And though those who do wrong possess all that is in the earth, and with it as much again, they verily will seek to ransom themselves with it on the Day of Resurrection from the awful doom; and there will appear to them, from their Lord, that with which they never reckoned.

48. And the evils that they earned will appear to them, and that at which they used to poke fun will surround them.

49. Now when hurt touches a man he calls to Us, and afterward when We have granted him a blessing from Us, he says: Only by force of knowledge I obtained it. No, but it is a test. But most of them know not.

50. Those before them said it, yet (all) that they had earned benefitted them not;

51. But the evils that they earned struck them; and such of these as do wrong, the evils that they earn will strike them; they cannot escape.

52. Do they not know that Allah enlarges provision for whom He wills, and tightens it (for whom He wills).

In this verily are signs for people who believe.

53. Say: O My slaves who have been prodigal to their own hurt! Despair not of the mercy of Allah, Who forgives all sins. He is the Forgiving, the Merciful.

54. Turn to your Lord repentant, and surrender to Him, before there come to you the doom, when you cannot be helped.

55. And follow the better (guidance) of that which is revealed to you from your Lord, before the doom comes on you suddenly when you know not,

56. Lest any soul should say: Alas, my grief that I was unmindful of Allah, and I was indeed among the mockers!

57. Or should say: If Allah had only guided me I would have been among the dutiful!

58. Or should say, when it sees the doom: Oh, that I had but a second chance so that I might be among the righteous!

59. (But now the answer will be): No, for My revelations came to you, but you did deny them and were contemptuous and were among the disbelievers.

60. And on the Day of Resurrection you (Muhammad) see those who lied concerning Allah with their faces blackened. Is not the home of the contemptuous in Hell?

61. And Allah delivers those who ward off (evil) because of what they earned. Evil touches them not, nor do they grieve.

62. Allah is Creator of all things, and He is Guardian over all things.

63. His are the keys of the heavens and the earth, and they who disbelieve the revelations of Allah - such are they who are the losers.

64. Say (O Muhammad, to the disbelievers): Do you ask me to serve other than Allah? O you fools!

65. And verily it has been revealed to you as to those before you (saying): If you ascribe a partner to Allah your work will fail and you indeed will be among the losers.

66. No, but, you must serve Allah, and be among the thankful!

67. And they esteem not Allah as He has the right to be esteemed, when the whole earth is His handful on the Day of Resurrection, and the heavens are rolled in His right hand. Glorified is He and High Exalted from all that they ascribe as partner (to Him).

68. And the trumpet is blown, and all who are in the heavens and all who are in the earth disappear, except he whom Allah wills. Then it is blown a second time, and you see them standing waiting!

69. And the earth shines with the light of her Lord, and the Book is set up. And the prophets and the witnesses are brought, and it is judged between them with truth, and they are not wronged.

70. And each soul is paid in full for what it did. And He is Best Aware of what they do.

71. And those who disbelieve are driven to Hell in troops till, when they reach it and the gates of it are opened, and the guardians of it say to them: Did there not come to you messengers of your own, reciting to you the revelations of your Lord and warning you of the meeting of this your Day? They say: Yea, verily. But the word of doom of disbelievers is fulfilled.

72. It is said (to them): Enter the gates of Hell to dwell in it. Thus unhappy is the journey's end of the contemptuous.

73. And those who keep their duty to their Lord are driven to the Garden in troops till, when they reach it, and the gates of it are opened, and the guardians of it say to them: Peace be to you! You are good, so enter (the Garden of delight), to dwell in it;

74. They say: Praise be to Allah, Who has fulfilled His promise to us and has made us inherit the land, sojourning in the Garden where we will! So bounteous is the wage of workers.

75. And you (O Muhammad) see the angels gathered around the Throne, hymning the praises of their Lord. And they are judged aright. And it is said: Praise be to Allah, the Lord of the Worlds!

Surah 40: *Al-Mu'min*
(The Believer)

Al-Mu'min, "The Believer," takes its name from vv. 28-45, which describe the attempt of a believer, in the house of Pharaoh, to dissuade his people from opposing Moses and Aaron. It is the first of seven Surahs beginning with the Arabic letters *Ha, Mim,* all of which are sometimes referred to as *Ha, Mim.*

It belongs to the middle group of Makkan Surahs. Some authorities hold vv. 56 and 57 to have been revealed at Al-Madinah.

In the name of Allah, the Beneficent, the Merciful.

1. *Ha. Mim.*[216]

2. The revelation of the Scripture is from Allah, the Mighty, the Knower,

3. The Forgiver of sin, the Accepter of repentance, the Stern in punishment, the Bountiful. There is no God except Him. To Him is the journeying.

4. None argue concerning the revelations of Allah except those who disbelieve, so let not their turn of fortune in the land deceive you (O Muhammad).

5. The people of Noah and the factions after them denied (their messengers) before these, and every nation purposed to seize their messenger and argued falsely, (thinking) by it to refute the Truth. Then I seized them, and how (awful) was My punishment.

6. Thus was the word of your Lord concerning those who disbelieve fulfilled: that they are owners of the Fire.

7. Those who bear the Throne, and all who are round about it, hymn the praises of their Lord and believe in Him and ask forgiveness for those who believe (saying): Our Lord! You comprehend all things in mercy and knowledge, therefore forgive those who repent and follow Your way. Ward off from them the punishment of Hell.

---

216. See *Surah 2, Al-Baqarah,* v. 1, footnote.

8. Our Lord! And make them enter the Gardens of Eden which you have promised them, with such of their fathers and their wives and their descendants as do right. You, only You, are the Mighty, the Wise.

9. And ward off from them ill-deeds; and he from whom You ward off ill-deeds that day, him verily You have taken into mercy. That is the supreme triumph.

10. (On that day) those who disbelieve are informed by proclamation: Verily Allah's abhorrence is more terrible than your abhorrence one of another, when you were called to the faith but did refuse.

11. They say: Our Lord! Twice You have made us die, and twice You have made us live. Now we confess our sins. Is there any way to go out?

12. (It is said to them): This is (your plight) because, when Allah only was invoked, you disbelieved, but when some partner was ascribed to Him you were believing. But the command belongs only to Allah, the Sublime, the Great.

13. He it is Who shows you His signs, and sends down for you provision from the sky. No one pays heed except he who turns (to Him) repentant.

14. Therefore (O believers) pray to Allah, making religion pure for Him (only), however much the disbelievers may be averse -

15. The Exalter of Ranks, the Lord of the Throne. He casts the Spirit of His command upon whom He will of His slaves, that He may warn of the Day of Meeting,

16. The day when they come out, nothing of them being hidden from Allah. Whose is the Sovereignty this day? It is Allah's, the One, the Almighty.

17. This day is each soul repaid that which it has earned; no wrong (is done) this day. Allah is swift at reckoning.

18. Warn them (O Muhammad) of the Day of the approaching (doom), when the hearts will be choking the throats, (when) there will be no friend for the wrongdoers, nor any intercessor who will be heard.

19. He knows the traitor of the eyes, and that which the chests hide.

20. Allah judges with truth, while those to whom they call instead of Him judge not at all. Allah, He is the Hearer, the Seer.

21. Have they not travelled in the land to see the nature of the consequence for those who disbelieved before them? They were mightier than these in power and (in the) traces (which they left behind them) in the earth. Yet Allah seized them for their sins, and they had no protector from Allah.

22. That was because their messengers kept bringing them clear proofs (of Allah's Sovereignty) but they disbelieved; so Allah seized them. He is Strong, severe in punishment.

23. And verily We sent Moses with Our revelations and a clear authority

24. To Pharaoh and Haman and Korah, but they said: A lying sorcerer!

25. And when he brought them the Truth from Our presence, they said: Slay the sons of those who believe with him, and spare their women. But the plot of disbelievers is in nothing but error.

26. And Pharaoh said: Leave me to kill Moses, and let him call to his Lord. I fear that he will alter your religion or that he will cause confusion in the land.

27. Moses said: I seek refuge in my Lord and your Lord from every derider who believes not in a Day of Reckoning.

28. And a believing man of Pharaoh's family, who hid his faith, said: Would you kill a man because he says: My Lord is Allah, and has brought you clear proofs from your Lord? If he is lying, then his lie is upon him; and if he is truthful, then some of that with which he threatens you will strike you. Allah guides not one who is a prodigal, a liar.

29. O my people! Yours is the kingdom today, you being uppermost in the land. But who would save us from the wrath of Allah should it reach us? Pharaoh said: I only show you what I think, and I only guide you to wise policy.

30. And he who believed said: O my people! I fear for you a fate like that of the factions (of old);

31. A plight like that of Noah's people, and 'Aad and Thamud, and those after them, and Allah wills no injustice for (His) slaves.

32. And, O my people! I fear for you a Day of Summoning,

33. A day when you will turn to flee, having no preserver from Allah: and he whom Allah sends astray, for him there is no guide.

34. And verily Joseph brought you of old clear proofs, yet you ceased not

to be in doubt concerning what he brought you till, when he died, you said: Allah will not send any messenger after him. Thus Allah deceives him who is a prodigal, a doubter.

35. Those who argue concerning the revelations of Allah without any authority that has come to them, it is greatly hateful in the sight of Allah and in the sight of those who believe. Thus does Allah print on every arrogant, disdainful heart.

36. And Pharaoh said: O Haman! Build for me a tower that perhaps I may reach the roads,

37. The roads of the heavens, and may look upon the God of Moses, though verily I think him a liar. Thus was the evil that he did made fair-seeming to Pharaoh, and he was prevented from the (right) way. The plot of Pharaoh ended only in ruin.

38. And he who believed said: O my people! Follow me. I will show you the way of right conduct.

39. O my people! The life of the world is but a passing comfort, and the Hereafter, that is the enduring home.

40. Whoever does an ill-deed, he will be repaid the like of it, while he who does right, whether male or female, and is a believer, (all) such will enter the Garden, where they will be nourished without limit.

41. And, O my people! Why should I call you to deliverance when you call me to the Fire?

42. You call me to disbelieve in Allah and ascribe to Him as partners that

of which I have no knowledge, while I call you to the Mighty, the Forgiver.

43. Assuredly that to which you call me has no claim in the world or in the Hereafter, and our return will be to Allah, and the prodigals will be owners of the Fire.

44. And you will remember what I say to you. I confide my cause to Allah. Allah is Seer of (His) slaves.

45. So Allah warded off from him the evils which they plotted, while a dreadful doom encompassed Pharaoh's people,

46. The Fire; they are exposed to it morning and evening; and on the day when the Hour rises (it is said): Cause Pharaoh's people to enter the most awful doom.

47. And when they argue in the Fire, the weak say to those who were proud: We were a following to you; will you therefore rid us of a portion of the Fire?

48. Those who were proud say: We are all (together) in this. Allah has judged between (His) slaves.

49. And those in the Fire say to the guards of Hell: Beg your Lord to relieve us of a day of the torment.

50. They say: Did not your messengers come to you with clear proofs? They say: Yea, verily. They say: Then pray, although the prayer of disbelievers is in vain.

51. We verily help Our messengers, and those who believe, in the life of the world and on the day when the witnesses arise,

52. The day when their excuses benefit not the evildoers, and theirs is the curse, and theirs the ill abode.

53. And We verily gave Moses the guidance, and We caused the Children of Israel to inherit the Scripture,

54. A guide and a reminder for men of understanding.

55. Then have patience (O Muhammad). The promise of Allah is true. And ask forgiveness for your sin, and hymn the praise of your Lord at fall of night and in the early hours.

56. Those who argue concerning the revelations of Allah without an authority having come to them, there is nothing else in their hearts except pride which they will never attain. So take refuge in Allah. He, only He, is the Hearer, the Seer.

57. Assuredly, the creation of the heavens and the earth is greater than the creation of mankind; but most of mankind know not.

58. And the blind man and the seer are not equal, neither are those who believe and do good works (equal with) the evil-doer. Little do you reflect!

59. The Hour is surely coming, there is no doubt of it; yet most of mankind believe not.

60. And your Lord has said: Pray to Me and I will hear your prayer. Those who despise My service, they will enter Hell, disgraced.

61. Allah it is Who has appointed for you night that you may rest in it, and day for seeing. Allah is a Lord of bounty for mankind, yet most of mankind give not thanks.

62. Such is Allah, your Lord, the Creator of all things, There is no God except Him. How then are you perverted?

63. Thus are they perverted who deny the revelations of Allah.

64. Allah it is Who appointed for you the earth for a dwelling-place and the sky for a canopy, and fashioned you and perfected your shapes, and has provided you with good things. Such is Allah, your Lord. Then blessed be Allah, the Lord of the Worlds!

65. He is the Living One. There is no God except Him. So pray to Him, making religion pure for Him (only). Praise be to Allah, the Lord of the Worlds!

66. Say (O Muhammad): I am forbidden to worship those to whom you call besides Allah since there have come to me clear proofs from my Lord, and I am commanded to surrender to the Lord of the Worlds.

67. He it is Who created you from dust, then from a drop (of seed) then from a clot, then brings you out as a child, then (ordains) that you attain full strength and afterwards that you become old men - though some among you die before - and that you reach an appointed term, that perhaps you may understand.

68. He it is Who gives life and gives death. When He ordains a thing, He says to it only: Be! and it is.

69. Have you not seen those who argue concerning the revelations of Allah, how they are turned away? -

70. Those who deny the Scripture and that with which We send Our messengers. But they will come to know,

71. When collars are about their necks and chains. They are dragged

72. Through boiling waters; then they are thrust into the Fire.

73. Then it is said to them: Where are (all) that you used to make partners (in the Sovereignty)

74. Besides Allah? They say: They have failed us; but we used not to pray to anything before. Thus does Allah send astray the disbelievers (in His guidance).

75. (And it is said to them): This is because you rejoiced in the earth without right, and because you were petulant.

76. Enter the gates of Hell, to dwell in it. Evil is the habitation of the contemptuous.

77. Then have patience (O Muhammad). The promise of Allah is true. And whether we let you see a part of that which We promise them, or (whether) We cause you to die, still to Us they will be brought back.

78. Verily We sent messengers before you, among them those of whom We have told you, and some of whom We have not told you; and it was not given to any messenger that he should bring a sign except by Allah's permission, but when Allah's commandment comes (the cause) is judged aright, and the followers of vanity will then be lost.

79. Allah it is Who has appointed for you cattle, that you may ride on some of them, and eat of some -

80. (Many) benefits you have from them - and that you may satisfy by their means a need that is in your hearts, and may be borne upon them as upon the ship.

81. And He shows you His signs. Which, then, of the signs of Allah do you deny?

82. Have they not travelled in the land to see the nature of the consequence for those before them? They were more numerous than these, and mightier in power and (in the) traces (which they left behind them) in the earth. But all that they earned did not benefit them.

83. And when their messengers brought them clear proofs (of Allah's Sovereignty) they rejoiced in the knowledge they (themselves) possessed. And that which they used to mock befell them.

84. Then, when they saw Our doom, they said: We believe in Allah only and reject (all) that we used to associate (with Him).

85. But their faith could not benefit them when they saw Our doom. This is Allah's law which has ever taken course for His bondsmen. And then the disbelievers will be ruined.

Surah 41: *Fussilat*
(They Are Explained)

Fussilat, "They Are Explained," derives its title from a word in v. 3. It is also often called *Ha, Mim, As-Sajdah,* from a word in v. 37, *Ha Mim* being added to distinguish it from Surah 32, which is called *As-Sajdah.*

It belongs to the middle group of Makkan Surahs.

In the name of Allah,
the Beneficent, the Merciful.

1. *Ha. Mim.*[217]

2. A revelation from the Beneficent, the Merciful,

3. A Scripture of which the verses are explained, a Lecture[218] in Arabic for people who have knowledge,

4. Good tidings and a warning. But most of them turn away so that they hear not.

5. And they say: Our hearts are protected from that to which you (O Muhammad) call us, and in our ears there is a deafness, and between us and you there is a veil. Act, then. We also shall be acting.

6. Say (to them O Muhammad): I am only a mortal like you. It is inspired in me that your God is One God, therefore take the straight path to Him and seek forgiveness of Him. And woe to the idolaters,

7. Who do not give the poor-due, and who are disbelievers in the Hereafter.

8. As for those who believe and do good works, for them is a lasting reward.

9. Say (O Muhammad, to the idolaters): Do you disbelieve in Him Who created the earth in two Days, and you ascribe rivals to Him? He (and none else) is the Lord of the Worlds.

10. He placed in it firm hills rising above it, and blessed it and measured in it its sustenance in four Days, alike for (all) who ask;

217. See *Surah 2, Al-Baqarah,* v. 1, footnote.
218. Arabic: *Qur'an.*

11. Then He turned to the heaven when it was smoke, and said to it and to the earth: Come both of you, willingly or reluctantly. They said: We come, obedient.

12. Then He ordained them seven heavens in two Days[219] and inspired in each heaven its mandate; and We adorned the nearer heaven with lamps, and rendered it inviolable[220]. That is the measuring of the Mighty, the Knower.

13. But if they turn away, then say: I warn you of a thunderbolt like the thunderbolt (which fell of old upon the tribes) of A'ad and Thamud;

14. When their messengers came to them from before them and behind them, saying: Worship none but Allah! they said: If our Lord had willed, He surely would have sent down angels (to us), so we are disbelievers in that with which you have been sent.

15. As for 'Aad, they were arrogant in the land without right, and they said: Who is mightier than us in power? Could they not see that Allah Who created them, He was mightier than them in power? And they denied Our revelations.

16. Therefore We let loose on them a raging wind in evil days, that We might make them taste the torment of disgrace in the life of the world. And verily the doom of the Hereafter will be more shameful, and they will not be helped.

17. And as for Thamud, We gave them guidance, but they preferred blindness to the guidance, so the bolt of the doom of humiliation overtook them because of what they used to earn.

18. And We delivered those who believed and used to keep their duty to Allah.

19. And (make mention of) the day when the enemies of Allah are gathered to the Fire; they are driven on

20. Till, when they reach it, their ears and their eyes and their skins testify against them as to what they used to do.

21. And they say to their skins: Why do you testify you against us? They will say: Allah has given us speech, He Who gives speech to all things, and Who created you at the first, and to Whom you are returned.

22. You did not hide yourselves lest your ears and your eyes and your skins should testify against you, but you deemed that Allah knew not much of what you did.

23. That, your thought which you had about your Lord, has ruined you; and you find yourselves (this day) among the lost.

24. And though they are resigned, yet the Fire is still their home; and if they ask for favour, yet they are not of those to whom favour can be shown.

25. And We assigned them comrades (in the world), who made their present and their past fair-seeming to them. And the Word concerning nations of the jinn and humankind who passed away before them has effect for them. They were always losers.

---

219. *Surah 37, As-Saffat,* vv. 6-10; *Surah 72, Al-Jinn,* vv. 8-10.
220. See *Surah 22, Al-Hajj,* v. 47; *Surah 32, As-Sajdah,* v. 5 and *Surah 70, Al-Ma'arij,* v. 4.

26. Those who disbelieve say: Heed not this Qur'an, and drown the hearing of it; perhaps you may conquer.

27. But verily We shall cause those who disbelieve to taste an awful doom, and verily We shall repay them the worst of what they used to do.

28. That is the reward of Allah's enemies: the Fire. In it is their immortal home, payment inasmuch as they denied Our revelations.

29. And those who disbelieve will say: Our Lord! Show us those who deceived us of the jinn and humankind. We will place them underneath our feet that they may be among the lowest.

30. Those who say: Our Lord is Allah, and afterwards are upright, the angels descend upon them, saying: Fear not nor grieve, but hear good tidings of the paradise which you are promised.

31. We are your protecting friends in the life of the world and in the Hereafter. There you will have (all) that your souls desire, and there you will have (all) for which you pray.

32. A gift of welcome from One Forgiving, Merciful.

33. And who is better in speech than he who prays to his Lord and does right, and says: I am of those who surrender[221] (to Him).

34. The good deed and the evil deed are not alike. Repel the evil deed with one which is better, then he, between whom and you there was enmity (will become) as though he was a dear friend.

35. But no one is granted it except those who are steadfast, and no one is granted it except the owner of great happiness.[222]

36. And if a whisper from the devil should reach you (O Muhammad) then seek refuge in Allah. He is the Hearer, the Knower.

37. And of His signs are the night and the day and the sun and the moon. Adore not the sun nor the moon; but adore Allah Who created them, if it is in truth Him Whom you worship.

38. But if they are too proud - still those who are with your Lord glorify Him night and day, and do not tire (to do so).

39. And of His signs (is this): that you see the earth plain, but when We send down water on it, it thrills and grows. He Who revives it is verily the Receiver of the Dead. He is Able to do all things.

40. Those who distort Our revelations are not hidden from Us. Is he who is hurled into the Fire better, or he who comes secure on the Day of Resurrection? Do what you will. He is Seer of what you do.

41. Those who disbelieve in the Reminder when it comes to them (are guilty), for it is an unassailable Scripture.

42. Falsehood cannot come at it from before it or from behind it. (It is) a revelation from the Wise, the Owner of Praise.

43. Nothing is said to you (Muhammad) except what was said to

---

221. Arabic: *Muslimin*

222. *i.e.* not everyone is able to practise such forgiveness.

the messengers before you. Your Lord is Owner of forgiveness, and Owner (also) of dire punishment.

44. And if We had appointed it a Lecture[223] in a foreign tongue, they would assuredly have said: If only its verses were explained (so that we might understand). What! A foreign tongue and an Arab? - Say to them (O Muhammad): For those who believe, it is a guidance and a healing; and as for those who disbelieve, there is deafness in their ears, and it is blindness for them. Such are called to from afar.

45. And We verily gave Moses the Scripture, but there has been dispute concerning it; and but for a Word that had already gone before from your Lord, it would before now have been judged between them; but they are in hopeless doubt concerning it.

46. Whoever does right, it is for his soul, and whoever does wrong, it is against it. And your Lord is not at all a tyrant to His slaves.

47. To Him is referred (all) knowledge of the Hour. And no fruits burst out from their sheaths, and no female carries or gives birth, but with His knowledge. And on the day when He calls to them: Where are My partners now? they will say: We confess to You, not one of us is a witness (for them).

48. And those to whom they used to call of old have failed them, and they perceive they have no place of refuge.

49. Man tires not of praying for good, and if ill touches him, then he is disheartened, desperate.

223. Arabic: *Qur'an.*

50. And verily, if We cause him to taste mercy after some hurt that has touched him, he will say: This is my own; and I think not that the Hour will ever rise, and if I am brought back to my Lord, I surely shall be better off with Him - But We verily shall tell those who disbelieve (all) that they did, and We verily shall make them taste hard punishment.

51. When We show favour to man, he withdraws and turns aside, but when ill touches him then he abounds in prayer.

52. Consider: If it is from Allah and you reject it - Who is further astray than one who is in open feud (with Allah)?

53. We shall show them Our signs on the horizons and within themselves until it will be manifest to them that it is the Truth. Does your Lord not suffice, since He is Witness over all things?

54. How! Are they still in doubt about the meeting with their Lord? Is not He surrounding all things?

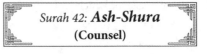

Surah 42: *Ash-Shura* (Counsel)

Ash-Shura, "Counsel," takes its name from a word in v. 38 It belongs to the middle group of Makkan Surahs.

In the name of Allah, the Beneficent, the Merciful.

1. *Ha. Mim.*

2. *'Ain. Sin. Qaf.*[224]

224. See *Surah 2, Al-Baqarah,* v. 1, footnote.

3. Thus Allah the Mighty, the Wise inspires you (Muhammad) as (He inspired) those before you.

4. To Him belongs all that is in the heavens and all that is in the earth, and He is the Sublime, the Tremendous.

5. Almost might the heavens above be split apart while the angels hymn the praise of their Lord and ask forgiveness for those on the earth. Allah, He is the Forgiver, the Merciful.

6. And as for those who choose protecting friends besides Him, Allah is Guardian over them, and you are in no way a guardian over them.

7. And thus We have inspired in you a Lecture[225] in Arabic, that you may warn the mother-town[226] and those around it, and may warn of a day of assembly of which there is no doubt. A party will be in the Garden, and a host of them in the Flame.

8. Had Allah willed, He could have made them one community, but Allah brings whom He will into His mercy. And the wrongdoers have no friend nor helper.

9. Or have they chosen protecting friends besides Him? But Allah, He (alone) is the protecting Friend. He revives the dead, and He is Able to do all things.

10. And in whatever you differ, the verdict in it belongs to Allah. Such is my Lord, in Whom I put my trust, and to Whom I turn.

225. Arabic: *Qur'an.*
226. *i.e.* Makkah

11. The Creator of the heavens and the earth. He has made for you pairs of yourselves, and of the cattle also pairs, by which He multiplies you. Nothing is as His likeness; and He is the Hearer, the Seer.

12. His are the keys of the heavens and the earth. He enlarges provision for whom He will and tightens (it for whom He will). He is Knower of all things.

13. He has ordained for you that religion which He commended to Noah, and that which We inspire in you (Muhammad), and that which We commended to Abraham and Moses and Jesus, saying: Establish the religion, and be not divided in it. Dreadful for the idolaters is that to which you call them. Allah chooses for Himself whom He will, and guides to Himself him who turns (towards Him).

14. And they were not divided until after the knowledge came to them, through rivalry among themselves; and had it not been for a Word that had already gone before from your Lord for an appointed term, it surely would have been judged between them. And those who were made to inherit the Scripture after them are verily in hopeless doubt concerning it.

15. To this, then, summon (O Muhammad). And be upright as you are commanded, and follow not their lusts, but say: I believe in whatever scripture Allah has sent down, and I am commanded to be just among you. Allah is our Lord and your Lord. To us our works and to you your works; no argument between us and you. Allah will bring us together, and to Him is the journeying.

16. And those who argue concerning Allah after He has been acknowledged, their argument has no weight with their Lord, and wrath is upon them and theirs will be an awful doom.

17. Allah it is Who has revealed the Scripture with truth, and the Balance. How can you know? It may be that the Hour is near.

18. Those who believe not in it seek to hasten it, while those who believe are fearful of it and know that it is the Truth. Are not they who dispute, in doubt concerning the Hour, far astray?

19. Allah is gracious to His slaves. He provides for whom He will. And He is the Strong, the Mighty.

20. Whoever desires the harvest of the Hereafter, We give him increase in its harvest. And whoever desires the harvest of the world, We give him of it, and he has no portion in the Hereafter.

21. Or have they partners (of Allah) who have made lawful for them in religion that which Allah allowed not? And but for a decisive Word (gone before already), it would have been judged between them. For wrongdoers is a painful doom.

22. You see the wrongdoers fearful of that which they have earned, and it will surely befall them, while those who believe and do good works (will be) in flowering meadows of the Gardens,

having what they wish from their Lord. This is the great preferment.

23. It is this which Allah announces to His bondsmen who believe and do good works. Say (O Muhammad, to mankind): I ask of you no fee for it, except loving kindness among relatives. And whoever does a good deed We add to its good for him. Allah is Forgiving, Responsive.

24. Or do they say: He has invented a lie concerning Allah? If Allah willed, He could have sealed your heart (against them). And Allah will wipe out the lie and will vindicate the truth by His words. He is Aware of what is hidden in the hearts (of men).

25. And He it is Who accepts repentance from His bondsmen, and pardons evil deeds, and knows what you do.

26. And accepts those who do good works, and gives increase to them of His bounty. And as for disbelievers, theirs will be an awful doom.

27. And if Allah were to enlarge the provision for His slaves they would surely rebel in the earth, but He sends down by measure as He wills. He is Informed, a Seer of His bondsmen.

28. And He it is Who sends down the saving rain after they have despaired, and spreads out His mercy. He is the Protecting Friend, the Praiseworthy.

29. And of His signs is the creation of the heaven and the earth, and of whatever beasts He has dispersed in it. And He is Able to gather them when He wills.

30. Whatever of misfortune strikes you, it is what your right hands have earned. And He forgives much.

31. You cannot escape in the earth, for besides Allah you have no protecting friend nor any helper.

32. And of His signs are the ships, like banners on the sea;

33. If He will, He calms the wind so that they keep still upon its surface - In this verily are signs for every steadfast grateful (heart).

34. Or He causes them to perish on account of that which they have earned - And He forgives much -

35. And so that those who argue concerning Our revelations may know they have no refuge.

36. Now whatever you have been given is but a passing comfort for the life of the world, and that which Allah has is better and more lasting for those who believe and put their trust in their Lord,

37. And those who shun the worst of sins and indecencies and, when they are angry, forgive,

38. And those who answer the call of their Lord and establish worship, and whose affairs are a matter of counsel, and who spend of what We have bestowed on them,

39. And those who, when great wrong is done to them, defend themselves,

40. The reward of an ill-deed is an ill the like of it. But whoever pardons and amends, his wage is the affair of Allah. He loves not wrongdoers.

41. And whoever defends himself after he has suffered wrong - for such, there is no way (of blame) against them.

42. The way (of blame) is only against those who oppress mankind, and wrongfully rebel in the earth. For such there is a painful doom.

43. And verily whoever is patient and forgives - that, verily, is (of) the steadfast heart of things.

44. He whom Allah sends astray, for him there is no protecting friend after Him. And you (Muhammad) will see the evildoers when they see the doom, (how) they say: Is there any way of return?

45. And you will see them exposed to (the Fire), made humble by disgrace, and looking with veiled eyes. And those who believe will say: The (eternal) losers are they who lose themselves and their families on the Day of Resurrection. Are not the wrongdoers in perpetual torment?

46. And they will have no protecting friends to help them instead of Allah. He whom Allah sends astray, for him there is no road.

47. Answer the call of your Lord before there comes to you from Allah a Day which there is no averting. You have no refuge on that Day, nor have you any (power of) refusal.

48. But if they are averse, We have not sent you as a guardian over them. Your duty is only to convey (the message). And when We cause man to taste of mercy from Us, he rejoices for it. And if some evil strikes them because of that which their own hands have sent before, then man is ungrateful.

49. To Allah belongs the Sovereignty of the heavens and the earth. He creates what He will. He bestows female (offspring) upon whom He will, and bestows male (offspring) upon whom He will;

50. Or He mingles them, males and females, and He makes barren whom He will. He is Knower, Powerful.

51. And it was not (given) to any mortal that Allah should speak to him unless (it be) by revelation or from behind a veil, or (that) He sends a messenger to reveal what He will by His permission. He is Exalted, Wise.

52. And thus have We inspired in you (Muhammad) a Spirit of Our command. You knew not what the Scripture was, nor what the Faith was. But We have made it a light by which We guide whom We will of Our bondsmen. And you verily guide to a right path,

53. The path of Allah, to Whom belongs whatsoever is in the heavens and whatsoever is in the earth. Do not all things reach Allah at last?

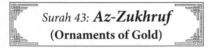

Surah 43: *Az-Zukhruf*
(Ornaments of Gold)

Az-Zukhruf, "Ornaments of Gold," is the fourth of the *Ha Mim* Surahs. It takes its name from a word meaning golden ornaments which occurs in v. 35.

It belongs to the middle group of Makkan Surahs.

In the name of Allah,
the Beneficent, the Merciful.

1. *Ha. Mim.*[227]

2. By the Scripture which makes plain,

3. We have appointed it as a Lecture,[228] in Arabic that perhaps you may understand.

4. And in the Source of Decrees, which We possess, it is indeed sublime, decisive.

5. Shall We utterly ignore you because you are an excessive people?

6. How many a Prophet did We send among the men of old!

7. And never came there to them a prophet but they used to mock him.

8. Then We destroyed men mightier than these in prowess; and the example of the men of old has gone (before them).

9. And if you (Muhammad) ask them: Who created the heavens and the earth, they will surely answer: The Mighty, the Knower created them;

10. Who made the earth a resting-place for you, and placed roads for you in it, that perhaps you may find your way;

11. And Who sends down water from the sky in (due) measure, and We revive a dead land with it. Even so you will be brought out;

12. He Who created all the pairs, and appointed for you ships and cattle upon which you ride,

13. That you may mount upon their backs, and may remember your Lord's favour when you mount on them, and

---

227. See *Surah 2, Al-Baqarah,* v. 1, footnote.
228. Arabic: *Qur'an.*

may say: Glorified be He Who has subdued these to us, and we were not capable (of subduing them);

14. And to our Lord we surely are returning.

15. And they allot to Him a portion of His bondsmen! Man is verily ungrateful.

16. Or does He choose daughters of all that He has created, and honours you with sons?

17. And if one of them has tidings of that which he likens to the Beneficent One,[229] his countenance becomes black and he is full of inward rage.

18. (Liken they then to Allah) that which is brought up in outward show, and in dispute cannot make itself plain?

19. And they make the angels, who are the slaves of the Beneficent, females. Did they witness their creation? Their testimony will be recorded and they will be questioned.

20. And they say: If the Beneficent One had (so) willed, we should not have worshipped them. They have no knowledge whatever of that. They only guess.

21. Or have We given them any scripture before (this Qur'an) so that they are holding fast to it?

22. No, for they only say: We found our fathers following a religion, and we are guided by their footprints.

23. And even so, We sent not a warner before you (Muhammad) into any township but its wealthy ones said: We

found our fathers following a religion, and we are following their footprints.

24. (And the warner) said: What! Even though I bring you better guidance than that you found your fathers following? They answered: In what you bring we are disbelievers.

25. So We repaid them. Then see the nature of the consequence for the rejecters!

26. And when Abraham said to his father and his people: I am innocent of what you worship

27. Except Him Who created me, for He will surely guide me.

28. And he made it a word enduring among his seed, that perhaps they might return.

29. No, but I let these and their fathers enjoy life (only) till there should come to them the Truth and a messenger making plain.

30. And now that the Truth has come to them, they say: This is mere magic, and we are disbelievers in it.

31. And they say: If only this Qur'an had been revealed to some great man of the two towns![230]

32. Is it they who apportion your Lord's mercy? We have apportioned among them their livelihood in the life of the world, and raised some of them above others in rank that some of them may take labour from others; and the mercy of your Lord is better than (the wealth) that they amass.

229. i.e. tidings of the birth of a girl-child.

230. The two towns were Makkah and Ta'if.

33. And were it not that mankind would have become one community,[231] We might well have appointed, for those who disbelieve in the Beneficent, roofs of silver for their houses and stairs (of silver) by which to mount,

34. And for their houses doors (of silver) and couches of silver on which to recline,

35. And ornaments of gold. Yet all that would have been only a provision of the life of the world. And the Hereafter with your Lord would have been for those who keep from evil.

36. And he whose sight is dim to the remembrance of the Beneficent, We assign to him a devil who becomes his comrade;

37. And they surely turn them from the way of Allah, and yet they think that they are rightly guided;

38. Till, when he comes to Us, he says (to his comrade): Ah, would that between me and you there were the distance of the two horizons[232] - an evil comrade!

39. And it profits you not this day, because you did wrong, that you will be sharers in the doom.

40. Can you (Muhammad) make the deaf hear, or can you guide the blind or him who is in manifest error?

41. And if We take you away, We surely shall take vengeance on them,

42. Or (if) We show you that with which We threaten them; for We have complete command of them.

43. So hold fast to that which is inspired in you. You are on a right path.

44. And it is in truth a Reminder for you and for your people; and you will be questioned.

45. And ask those of Our messengers whom We sent before you: Did We ever appoint gods to be worshipped besides the Beneficent?

46. And verily We sent Moses with Our revelations to Pharaoh and his chiefs, and he said: I am a messenger of the Lord of the Worlds.

47. But when he brought them Our signs, see! They laughed at them.

48. And every sign that We showed them was greater than its sister (sign), and We grasped them with the torment, that perhaps they might turn again.

49. And they said: O wizard! Entreat your Lord for us by the pact that He has made with you. We verily will walk aright.

50. But when We eased them of the torment, see! They broke their word.

51. And Pharaoh caused a proclamation to be made among his people saying: O my people! Is not mine the sovereignty of Egypt and these rivers flowing under me? Can you not then discern?

52. I am surely better than this fellow, who is despicable and can hardly make (his meaning) plain!

53. Why, then, have armlets of gold not been set upon him, or angels sent along with him?

---

231. Through love of riches.
232. *Lit.* the two Easts.

54. Thus he persuaded his people to make light (of Moses), and they obeyed him. They were an excessive people.

55. So, when they angered Us, We punished them and drowned them, every one.

56. And We made them a thing past, and an example for those after (them).

57. And when the son of Mary is quoted as an example, see! The people laugh aloud,

58. And say: Are our gods better, or is he? They raise not the objection except for argument. No! But they are a contentious people.

59. He is nothing but a slave[233] on whom We bestowed favour, and We made him an example for the Children of Israel.

60. And had We willed We could have set among you angels to be viceroys in the earth.

61. And verily there is knowledge of the Hour. So doubt not concerning it, but follow Me. This is the right path.

62. And let not Satan turn you aside. He is an open enemy for you.

63. When Jesus came with clear proofs (of Allah's Sovereignty), he said: I have come to you with wisdom, and to make plain some of that concerning which you differ. So keep your duty to Allah, and obey me.

64. Allah, He is my Lord and your Lord. So worship Him. This is a right path.

65. But the factions among them differed. Then woe to those who do wrong from the doom of a painful day.

66. Do they wait for anything except the Hour, that it shall come upon them suddenly, when they know not?

67. Friends on that day will be foes one to another, except those who kept their duty (to Allah).

68. O My slaves! For you there is no fear this day, nor is it you who grieve;

69. (You) who believed Our revelations and were self-surrendered,

70. Enter the Garden, you and your wives, to be made glad.

71. In it are brought round for them trays of gold and goblets, and in it is all that souls desire and eyes find sweet. And you are immortal in it.

72. This is the Garden which you are made to inherit because of what you used to do.

73. In it for you is fruit in plenty from which to eat.

74. The guilty are immortal in Hell's torment.

75. It is not relaxed for them, and they despair in it.

76. We wronged them not, but it was they who did the wrong.

77. And they call: O master! Let your Lord make an end of us. He says: Here you must remain.

78. We verily brought the Truth to you, but you were, most of you, averse to the Truth.

---

233. *Abd Allah,* "slave of God," is a proud designation with the Muslims, bondage to Allah implying liberation from all earthly servitudes.

79. Or do they determine anything (against the Prophet)? We (also) are determining.

80. Or do they think that We cannot hear their secret thoughts and private confidences? No, but Our envoys, present with them, do record.

81. Say (O Muhammad): If the Beneficent One has a son, then I shall be first among the worshippers. (But there is no son).

82. Glorified be the Lord of the heavens and the earth, the Lord of the Throne, from that which they ascribe (to Him)!

83. So let them flounder (in their talk) and play until they meet the Day which they are promised.

84. And He it is Who in the heaven is God, and in the earth God. He is the Wise, the Knower.

85. And blessed is He to Whom belongs the Sovereignty of the heavens and the earth and all that is between them, and with Whom is knowledge of the Hour, and to Whom you will be returned.

86. And those to whom they call instead of Him possess no power of intercession, except him who bears witness to the Truth knowingly.

87. And if you ask them who created them, they will surely say: Allah. How then are they turned away?

88. And he says: O my Lord! These are a people who believe not.

89. Then bear with them (O Muhammad) and say: Peace. But they will come to know.

Surah 44: **Ad-Dukhan** (The Smoke)

Ad-Dukhan, "The Smoke," takes its name from a word in v. 10. Tradition says that smoke here refers prophetically to the haze of dust which surrounded Makkah at the time of the great drought and famine which preceded the Muslim conquest of Makkah and facilitated it. It belongs to the middle group of Makkan Surahs.

In the name of Allah, the Beneficent, the Merciful.

1. *Ha. Mim.*[234]

2. By the Scripture that makes plain

3. We revealed it on a blessed night - We are always warning -

4. On which every wise command is made clear

5. As a command from Our presence - We are always sending -

6. A mercy from your Lord. He, even He is the Hearer, the Knower,

7. Lord of the heavens and the earth and all that is between them, if you would be sure.

8. There is no God except Him. He gives life and gives death; your Lord and Lord of your forefathers.

9. No, but they play in doubt.

10. But watch (O Muhammad) for the day when the sky will produce visible smoke

234. See *Surah 2, Al-Baqarah,* v. 1, footnote.

11. That will envelop the people.[235] This will be a painful torment.

12. (Then they will say): Our Lord relieve us of the torment. We are believers.

13. How can there be remembrance for them, when a messenger making plain (the Truth) had already come to them,

14. And they had turned away from him and said: One taught (by others), a madman?

15. We withdraw the torment a little. You return (to disbelief).

16. On the day when We shall seize them with the greater seizure, (then) in truth We shall punish.

17. And verily We tried before them Pharaoh's people, when there came to them a noble messenger,

18. Saying: Give up to me the slaves of Allah. I am a faithful messenger to you.

19. And saying: Be not proud against Allah. I bring you a clear authority.

20. And I have sought refuge in my Lord and your Lord, lest you stone me to death.

21. And if you put no faith in me, then let me go.

22. And he called to his Lord (saying): These are guilty people.

23. Then (his Lord commanded): Take away My slaves by night. You will be followed,

24. And leave the sea behind at rest, for they are a drowned force.

25. How many were the gardens and the water-springs that they left behind,

26. And the cornfields and the goodly sites,

27. And pleasant things in which they took delight!

28. Even so (it was), and We made it an inheritance for other people;

29. And the heaven and the earth wept not for them, nor were they reprieved.

30. And We delivered the Children of Israel from the shameful doom;

31. (We delivered them) from Pharaoh. He was a tyrant of the excessive ones.

32. And We chose them, purposely, above (all) creatures.

33. And We gave them signs in which was a clear trial.

34. These, indeed, are saying:

35. There is nothing but our first death, and we shall not be raised again.

36. Bring back our fathers, if you speak the truth!

37. Are they better, or the people of Tubb'a[236] and those before them? We destroyed them, for surely they were guilty.

38. And We did not create the heavens and the earth, and all that is between them, in play.

39. We did not create them except in truth; but most of them know not.

40. Assuredly the Day of Decision is the term for all of them,

41. A day when a friend cannot benefit a friend in anything, nor can they be helped,

42. Except him on whom Allah has mercy. He is the Mighty, the Merciful.

---

235. Of Makkah

236. A name for many kings of Himyar (the South Arabians), each of whom was called Tubb'a just as every king of Egypt was called Pharaoh.

43. The tree of Zaqqum[237]

44. The food of the sinner!

45. Like molten brass, it seethes in their bellies

46. As the seething of boiling water.

47. (And it will be said): Take him and drag him to the midst of Hell,

48. Then pour upon his head the torment of boiling water.

49. (Saying): Taste! You were indeed the mighty, the noble!

50. This is that of which you used to doubt.

51. Those who kept their duty will be in a place secure,

52. Amid gardens and water springs,

53. Attired in silk and silk embroidery, facing one another.

54. Even so (it will be). And We shall wed them to fair ones with wide, lovely eyes.

55. They call in it for every fruit in safety.

56. They taste not death in it, except the first death. And He has saved them from the doom of Hell,

57. A bounty from your Lord. That is the supreme triumph.

58. And We have made (this Scripture) easy in your language only that they may heed.

59. Wait then (O Muhammad). They (too) are waiting.

237. *Surah 27, An-Naml*, v. 62; *Surah 56, Al-Waqi'ah*, v. 52.

Surah 45: *Al-Jathiya* (Crouching)

Al-Jathiyah, "Crouching," takes its name from a word in v. 28 It belongs to the middle group of Makkan Surahs.

In the name of Allah, the Beneficent, the Merciful.

1. *Ha. Mim.*[238]

2. The revelation of the Scripture is from Allah, the Mighty, the Wise.

3. In the heavens and the earth are signs for believers.

4. And in your creation, and all the beasts that He scatters in the earth, are signs for a people whose faith is sure.

5. And the difference of night and day and the provision that Allah sends down from the sky and by it revives the earth after her death, and the ordering of the winds, are signs for a people who have sense.

6. These are the signs of Allah which We recite to you (Muhammad) with truth. Then in what fact, after Allah and His signs, will they believe?

7. Woe to each sinful liar,

8. Who hears the revelations of Allah recited to him, and then continues in pride as though he heard them not. Give him tidings of a painful doom.

9. And when he knows anything of Our revelations, he makes it a jest. For such there is a shameful doom.

10. Beyond them there is Hell, and that which they have earned will not benefit

238. See *Surah 2, Al-Baqarah*, v. 1, footnote.

them at all, nor those whom they have chosen for protecting friends besides Allah. Theirs will be an awful doom.

11. This is guidance. And those who disbelieve the revelations of their Lord, for them there is a painful doom of wrath.

12. It is Allah Who has made the sea of service to you that the ships may run on it by His command, and that you may seek of His bounty, and that perhaps you may be thankful;

13. And He has made of service to you whatever is in the heavens and whatever is in the earth; it is all from Him. In this verily are signs for a people who reflect.

14. Tell those who believe to forgive those who hope not for the days of Allah; in order that He may repay people what they used to earn.

15. Whoever does right, it is for his soul, and whoever does wrong, it is against it. And afterwards to your Lord you will be brought back.

16. And verily we gave the Children of Israel the Scripture and the Command and the Prophethood, and provided them with good things and favoured them above (all) peoples;

17. And gave them plain commandments. And they differed not until after the knowledge came to them, through rivalry among themselves. Your Lord will judge between them on the Day of Resurrection concerning that in which they used to differ.

18. And now We have set you (O Muhammad) on a clear road of (Our) commandment; so follow it, and follow not the whims of those who know not.

19. They cannot benefit you against Allah. And as for the wrongdoers, some of them are friends of others; and Allah is the Friend of those who ward off (evil).

20. This is clear indication for mankind, and a guidance and a mercy for a people whose faith is sure.

21. Or do those who commit ill-deeds suppose that We shall make them like those who believe and do good works, the same in life and death? Bad is their judgement!

22. And Allah has created the heavens and the earth with truth, and that every soul may be repaid what it has earned. And they will not be wronged.

23. Have you seen him who makes his desire his god, and Allah sends him astray purposely, and seals up his hearing and his heart, and sets on his sight a covering? Then who will lead him after Allah (has condemned him)? Will you not then heed?

24. And they say: There is nothing except our life of the world; we die and we live, and nothing destroys us except time; when they have no knowledge whatever of (all) that; they do only guess.

25. And when Our clear revelations are recited to them, their only argument is that they say: Bring (back) our fathers then, if you are truthful.

26. Say (to them, O Muhammad): Allah gives life to you, then causes you to die, then gathers you to the Day of Resurrection of which there is no doubt. But most of mankind know not.

27. And to Allah belongs the Sovereignty of the heavens and the earth; and on the day when the Hour rises, on that day those who follow falsehood will be lost.

28. And you will see each nation crouching, each nation summoned to its record. (And it will be said to them): This day you are repaid what you used to do.

29. This Our Book pronounces against you with truth. We have caused (all) that you did to be recorded.

30. Then, as for those who believed and did good works, their Lord will bring them in to His mercy. That is the evident triumph.

31. And as for those who disbelieved (it will be said to them): Were Our revelations not recited to you? But you were contemptuous and became a guilty people.

32. And when it was said: Allah's promise is the truth, and there is no doubt of the Hour's coming, you said: We know not what the Hour is. We deem it nothing but a conjecture, and we are by no means convinced.

33. And the evils of what they did will appear to them, and that which they used to deride will befall them.

34. And it will be said: This day We forget you, even as you forgot the meeting of this your day; and your habitation is the Fire, and there is no one to help you.

35. This, inasmuch as you made the revelations of Allah a jest, and the life of the world deceived you. Therefore this Day they come not out from there, nor can they make amends.

36. Then praise be to Allah, Lord of the heavens and Lord of the earth, the Lord of the worlds.

37. And to Him (alone) belongs Majesty in the heavens and the earth, and He is the Mighty, the Wise.

Surah 46: *Al-Ahqaf*
(The Wind-Curved Sandhills)

Al-Ahqaf, "The Wind-Curved Sandhills" (a formation which will be familiar to all desert travellers, and which especially characterised the region in which the tribe of 'Aad were said originally to have lived), takes its name from a word in v. 21 and is the last of the *Ha Mim* group.

It belongs to the middle group of Makkan Surahs, with the exception of v. 10, vv. 15-18, and v. 35, which were revealed at Al-Madinah.

In the name of Allah,
the Beneficent, the Merciful.

1. *Ha. Mim.*[239]

2. The revelation of the Scripture is from Allah the Mighty, the Wise.

3. We created not the heavens and the earth and all that is between them except with truth, and for a term appointed. But those who disbelieve turn away from that of which they are warned.

---

239. See *Surah 2, Al-Baqarah,* v. 1, footnote.

4. Say (to them, O Muhammad): Have you thought about all that you invoke besides Allah? Show me what they have created of the earth. Or have they any portion in the heavens? Bring me a scripture before this (Scripture), or some trace of knowledge (in support of what you say), if you are truthful.

5. And who is further astray than those who, instead of Allah, pray to such as hear not their prayer until the Day of Resurrection, and are unconscious of their prayer,

6. And when mankind are gathered (to the Judgement) they will become enemies for them, and will become deniers of having been worshipped.

7. And when Our clear revelations are recited to them, those who disbelieve say of the Truth when it reaches them: This is mere magic.

8. Or do they say: He has invented it? Say (O Muhammad): If I have invented it, still you have no power to support me against Allah. He is Best Aware of what you say among yourselves concerning it. He suffices for a witness between me and you. And He is the Forgiving, the Merciful.

9. Say: I am nothing new among the messengers (of Allah), nor do I know what will be done with me or with you. I only follow that which is inspired in me, and I am only a plain warner.

10. Consider: If it is from Allah and you disbelieve in it, and a witness of the Children of Israel[240] has already

testified to the like of it and has believed, and you are too proud (what plight is yours)? Allah guides not wrongdoing people.

11. And those who disbelieve say of those who believe: If it had been (any) good, they would not have been before us in attaining it. And since they will not be guided by it, they say: This is an ancient lie;

12. When before it there was the Scripture of Moses, an example and a mercy; and this is a confirming Scripture in the Arabic language, that it may warn those who do wrong and bring good tidings for the righteous.

13. Those who say: Our Lord is Allah, and after it walk aright, no fear shall come upon them neither shall they grieve.

14. Such are rightful owners of the Garden, immortal in it, as a reward for what they used to do.

15. And We have commended to man kindness toward parents. His mother bears him with reluctance, and brings him out with reluctance, and the bearing of him and the weaning of him is thirty months, till, when he attains full strength and reaches forty years, he says: My Lord! Cause me to give thanks for the favour with which You have favoured me and my parents, and that I may do what is right and acceptable to You. And be gracious to me in the matter of my seed. I have

---

240. Abdullah ibn Salam, a learned Jew of Al-Madinah, who became a devout Muslim. This is the usual explanation, though the verse is still considered as of Makkan revelation.

turned to You repentant, and I am of those who surrender[241] (to You).

16. Those are they from whom We accept the best of what they do, and overlook their evil deeds. (They are) among the owners of the Garden. This is the true promise which they were promised (in the world).

17. And whoever says to his parents: Fie upon you both! Do you threaten me that I shall be brought out (again) when generations before me have passed away? And they both call to Allah for help (and say): Woe to you! Believe! The promise of Allah is true. But he says: This is nothing except fables of the men of old.

18. Such are those on whom the Word concerning nations of the jinn and mankind which have passed away before them has effect. They are the losers.

19. And for all there will be ranks from what they do, that He may pay them for their deeds, and they will not be wronged.

20. And on the day when those who disbelieve are exposed to the Fire (it will be said): You squandered your good things in the life of the world and sought comfort in it. Now this day you are rewarded with the doom of ignominy because you were disdainful in the land without a right, and because you used to transgress.

21. And make mention (O Muhammad) of the brother of 'Aad[242] when he warned his people among the wind-curved sandhills - and verily

warners came and went before and after him - saying: Serve none but Allah. I fear for you the doom of a tremendous Day.

22. They said: Have you come to turn us away from our gods? Then bring upon us that with which you threaten us, if you are truthful.

23. He said: The knowledge is with Allah only. I convey to you that with which I have been sent, but I see you are a people who know not.

24. Then, when they saw it as a dense cloud coming towards their valleys, they said: Here is a cloud bringing us rain. No, but it is that which you did seek to hasten, a wind in which is painful torment,

25. Destroying all things by commandment of its Lord. And morning found them so that nothing could be seen except their dwellings. Thus We reward the guilty people.

26. And verily We had empowered them with that with which We have not empowered you, and had assigned them ears and eyes and hearts; but their ears and eyes and hearts benefitted them nothing since they denied the revelations of Allah; and what they used to mock befell them.

27. And verily We have destroyed townships around you, and displayed (for them) Our revelation, that perhaps they might return.

28. Then why did those whom they had chosen for gods as a way of approach (to Allah) not help them? No, but they failed them utterly. And

---

241. Arabic: *Muslimin*
242. The Prophet Hud.

(all) that was their lie, and what they used to invent.

29. And when We inclined towards you (Muhammad) certain of the jinn, who wished to hear the Qur'an and, when they were in its presence, said: Give ear! and, when it was finished, turned back to their people, warning.

30. They said: O our people! We have heard a Scripture which has been revealed after Moses,[243] confirming that which was before it, guiding to the truth and a right road.

31. O our people! respond to Allah's summoner and believe in Him. He will forgive you some of your sins and guard you from a painful doom.

32. And whoever responds not to Allah's summoner he can in no way escape in the earth, and he has no protecting friends instead of Him. Such are in manifest error.

33. Have they not seen that Allah, Who created the heavens and the earth and was not wearied by their creation, is Able to give life to the dead? Yes, He verily is Able to do all things.

34. And on the day when those who disbelieve are exposed to the Fire (they will be asked): Is not this real? They will say: Yes, by our Lord. He will say: Then taste the doom for that you disbelieved.

35. Then have patience (O Muhammad) even as the stout of

---

243. From the mention of Moses it has been conjectured by some commentators that these jinn were foreign (*i.e.* non-Arabian) Jews, the word jinn in old Arabic being often applied to clever foreigners.

heart among the messengers (of old) had patience, and seek not to hasten on (the doom) for them. On the day when they see that which they are promised (it will seem to them) as though they had stayed only an hour of daylight. A clear message. Shall any be destroyed except evil-living people?

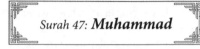

Surah 47: *Muhammad*

Muhammad, This Surah takes its name from the mention of the Prophet by name in v. 2. Most commentators agree that v. 18 was revealed when the Prophet, forced to emigrate from Makkah, looked back, weeping, for a last sight of his native city. Some have considered the whole Surah to be a Makkan revelation, but with no good reason.

It belongs to the first and second years after the Hijrah, with the exception of v. 18, which was revealed during the Hijrah.

In the name of Allah,
the Beneficent, the Merciful

1. Those who disbelieve and turn (men) from the way of Allah, He renders their actions vain.

2. And those who believe and do good works and believe in that which is revealed to Muhammad - and it is the truth from their Lord - He rids them of their ill-deeds and improves their state.

3. That is because those who disbelieve follow falsehood and because those who believe follow the truth from their Lord. Thus Allah coins their similitudes for mankind.

4. Now when you meet in battle those who disbelieve, then it is striking of the necks until, when you have routed them, then making fast of bonds; and afterwards either grace or ransom till the war lay down its burdens. That (is the ordinance). And if Allah willed He could have punished them (without you) but (thus it is ordained) that He may try some of you by means of others. And those who are slain in the way of Allah, He renders not their actions vain.

5. He will guide them and improve their state,

6. And bring them in to the Garden which He has made known to them.

7. O you who believe! If you help Allah, He will help you and will make your foothold firm.

8. And those who disbelieve, damnation is for them, and He will make their actions vain.

9. That is because they are averse to that which Allah has revealed, therefore He makes their actions fruitless.

10. Have they not travelled in the land to see the nature of the consequence for those who were before them? Allah wiped them out. And for the disbelievers there will be the like of it.

11. That is because Allah is patron of those who believe, and because the disbelievers have no patron.

12. Allah will cause those who believe and do good works to enter Gardens underneath which rivers flow; while those who disbelieve

take their comfort in this life and eat even as the cattle eat, and the Fire is their habitation.

13. And how many a township stronger than your township (O Muhammad) which has cast you out, have We destroyed, and they had no helper!

14. Is he who relies on a clear proof from his Lord like those for whom the evil that they do is beautified while they follow their own lusts?

15. A similitude of the Garden which those who keep their duty (to Allah) are promised: In it there are rivers of unpolluted water, and rivers of milk of which the flavour does not change, and rivers of wine delicious to the drinkers, and rivers of clear-run honey; in it for them is every kind of fruit, with pardon from their Lord. (Are those who enjoy all this) like those who are immortal in the Fire and are given boiling water to drink so that it tears their bowels?

16. Among them are some who give ear to you (Muhammad) till, when they go out from your presence they say to those who have been given knowledge: What was that he said just now? Those are they whose hearts Allah has sealed, and they follow their own lusts.

17. As for those who walk aright, He adds to their guidance, and gives them their protection (against evil).

18. Do they wait for anything except the Hour, that it should come upon them unawares? And the beginnings of it have already come. But how, when it has come upon them, can they take their warning?

19. So know (O Muhammad) that there is no God except Allah, and ask forgiveness for your sin, and for believing men and believing women. Allah knows (both) your place of turmoil and your place of rest.

20. And those who believe say: If only a Surah were revealed! But when a decisive Surah is revealed and war is mentioned in it, you see those in whose hearts is a disease looking at you with the look of men fainting to death. Therefore woe to them!

21. Obedience and a civil word. Then, when the matter is determined, if they are loyal to Allah it will be well for them.

22. Would you then, if you were given the command, work corruption in the land and sever your ties of kinship?

23. Such are they whom Allah curses so that He deafens them and makes blind their eyes.

24. Will they then not meditate on the Qur'an, or are there locks on the hearts?

25. Those who turn back after the guidance has been manifested to them, Satan has seduced them, and He gives them the rein.

26. That is because they say to those who hate what Allah has revealed: We will obey you in some matters; and Allah knows their secret talk.

27. Then how (will it be with them) when the angels gather them, striking their faces and their backs!

28. That will be because they followed that which angers Allah, and hated that which pleases Him. Therefore He has made their actions vain.

29. Or do those in whose hearts is a disease think that Allah will not bring to light their (secret) hates?

30. And if We would, We could show them to you (Muhammad) so that you should know them surely by their marks. And you shall know them by the burden of their talk. And Allah knows your deeds.

31. And verily We shall try you till We know those of you who strive hard (for the cause of Allah) and the steadfast, and till We test your record.

32. Those who disbelieve and turn from the way of Allah and oppose the messenger after the guidance has been manifested to them, they hurt Allah not a jot, and He will make their actions fruitless.

33. O you who believe! Obey Allah and obey the messenger, and do not render your actions vain.

34. Those who disbelieve and turn from the way of Allah and then die as disbelievers, Allah surely will not pardon them.

35. So do not falter and call out for peace when you (will be) the uppermost, and Allah is with you, and He will not withhold (the reward for) your actions.

36. The life of the world is only a sport and a pastime. And if you believe and ward off (evil), He will give you your wages, and will not ask of you your worldly wealth.

37. If He should ask it of you and insist, you would hoard it, and He would bring to light your (secret) hates.

38. You are those who are called to spend in the way of Allah, yet among you there are some who hoard. And as for him who hoards, he hoards only from his soul. And Allah is the Rich, and you are the poor. And if you turn away He will exchange you for some other people, and they will not be the likes of you.

Surah 48: *Al-Fath* (Victory)

Al-Fath, takes its name from the word Fath meaning "Victory" which occurs several times, and refers, not to the conquest of Makkah, but to the truce of Al-Hudeybiyeh, which, though at the time it seemed a set-back to the Muslims, proved in fact the greatest victory for *Al-Islam.*

In the sixth year of the Hijrah, the Prophet set out with some 1400 Muslims from Al-Madinah and the surrounding country, in the clothing of pilgrims, not for war but to visit the Ka'bah. When they drew near to Makkah, they were warned that Quraysh had gathered their allies against them, and that their cavalry under Khalid ibn Al-Walid was on the road before them. Making a detour through gullies of the hills, they escaped the cavalry and, coming into the valley of Makkah, encamped at Al-Hudeybiyeh below the city. The Prophet resolutely refused to give battle and persisted in attempts to negotiate with Quraysh who had sworn not to let him reach the Ka'bah. The Muslims were all the while in a position of some danger. Finally Othman ibn 'Affan was sent into the city, as the man most likely to be well received on account of his relationships. Othman was detained by the Makkans, and news that he had been murdered reached the Muslims in their camp.[244]

It was then that the Prophet, sitting under a tree, took from his comrades the oath (referred to in v. 18) that they would hold together and fight to the death.[245] Then it became known that the rumour of Othman's death was false, and Quraysh at length agreed to a truce of which the terms were favourable to them. The Prophet and his multitude were to give up the project of visiting the sanctuary for that year, but were to make the pilgrimage the following year when the idolaters undertook to evacuate Makkah for three days to allow them to do so. Emigrants from Quraysh to the Muslims were to be returned, but not renegades from the Muslims to Quraysh; and there was to be no hostility between the parties for ten years.

"And there was never a victory," says Ibn Khaldun, "greater than this victory; for, as Az-Zuhri says, when it was war the peoples did not meet, but when the truce came and war laid down its burdens and people felt safe one with another, then they met and indulged in conversation and discussion. And no man spoke of *Al-Islam* to another

244. Ibn Hisham, Part 2, pp. 176-178
245. Ibn Hisham Part 2, p. 179.

but the latter explained it, so that there entered *Al-Islam* in those two years (*i.e.*, between Al-Hudeybiyeh and the breaking of the truce by Quraysh) as many as all those who had entered it before, or more."[246]

The date of revelation is the sixth year of the Hijrah.

In the name of Allah, the Beneficent, the Merciful

1. We have given you (O Muhammad) a signal victory,

2. That Allah may forgive you of your sin that which is past and that which is to come, and may perfect His favour to you, and may guide you on a right path,

3. And that Allah may help you with strong help -

4. He it is Who sent down peace of reassurance into the hearts of the believers that they might add faith to their faith. Allah's are the forces of the heavens and the earth, and Allah is the Knower, Wise -

5. That He may bring the believing men and the believing women into Gardens underneath which rivers flow, in which they will remain, and may remit from them their evil deeds - That, in the sight of Allah, is the supreme triumph -

6. And may punish the hypocritical men and the hypocritical women, and the idolatrous men and the idolatrous women, who think an evil thought concerning Allah. For them is the evil

turn of fortune, and Allah is angry with them and has cursed them, and has made ready for them Hell, an unhappy journey's end.

7. Allah's are the forces of the heavens and the earth, and Allah is the Mighty, Wise.

8. We have sent you (O Muhammad) as a witness and a bearer of good tidings and a warner,

9. That you (mankind) may believe in Allah and His messenger, and may honour Him, and may revere Him, and may glorify Him at early dawn and at the close of day.

10. Those who swear allegiance to you (Muhammad), swear allegiance only to Allah. The Hand of Allah is above their hands. So whoever breaks his oath, breaks it only to his soul's hurt; while whoever keeps his covenant with Allah, on him will He bestow immense reward.

11. Those of the wandering Arabs who were left behind will tell you: Our possessions and our households occupied us, so ask forgiveness for us! They speak with their tongues that which is not in their hearts. Say: Who can benefit you anything against Allah, if He intend you hurt or intend you profit? No, but Allah is ever Aware of what you do.

12. No, but you thought that the messenger and the believers would never return to their own people, and that was made fair-seeming in your hearts, and you did think an evil thought, and you were worthless people.

---

246. Ibn Khaldun, *Tarikh,* Supplement to Part II, Bulaq 1284 A.H. He follows Ibn Hisham.

13. And so for him who believes not in Allah and His messenger - We have prepared a flame for disbelievers.

14. And Allah's is the Sovereignty of the heavens and the earth. He forgives whom He wills, and punishes whom He wills. And Allah is ever Forgiving, Merciful.

15. Those who were left behind will say, when you set out to capture booty: Let us go with you. They would like to change the verdict of Allah. Say (to them, O Muhammad): You shall not go with us. Thus has Allah said beforehand. Then they will say: You are envious of us. No, but they understand not, except a little.

16. Say to those of the wandering Arabs who were left behind: You will be called against a people of mighty prowess,[247] to fight them until they surrender; and if you obey, Allah will give you a fair reward; but if you turn away as you did turn away before, He will punish you with a painful doom.

17. There is no blame for the blind, nor is there blame for the lame, nor is there blame for the sick (that they do not go out to war). And whoever obeys Allah and His messenger, He will make him enter Gardens underneath which rivers flow; and whoever turns back, him will He punish with a painful doom.

18. Allah was well pleased with the believers when they swore allegiance to you beneath the tree, and He knew what was in their hearts, and He sent down peace of reassurance on them, and has rewarded them with a near victory;

247. This prophecy is taken to refer to the war with the Persian or the Byzantine empire.

19. And much booty that they will capture. Allah is ever Mighty, Wise.

20. Allah promises you much booty that you will capture, and has given you this in advance, and has withheld men's hands from you, that it may be a sign for the believers, and that He may guide you on a right path.

21. And other (gain), which you have not been able to achieve, Allah will accomplish it, Allah is Able to do all things.

22. And if those who disbelieve join battle with you they will take to flight, and afterward they will find no protecting friend nor helper.

23. It is the law of Allah which has taken course before. You will not find for the law of Allah any power to change.

24. And He it is Who has withheld men's hands from you, and has withheld your hands from them, in the valley of Makkah, after He had made you victors over them. Allah is Seer of what you do.

25. These it was who disbelieved and debarred you from the Sacred Mosque, and debarred the offering from reaching its goal. And if it had not been for believing men and believing women, whom you know not - lest you should tread them under foot and thus incur guilt for them unknowingly; that Allah might bring into His mercy whom He will - If (believers and the disbelievers) had been clearly separated We surely had punished those of them who disbelieved with painful punishment.

26. When those who disbelieve had set up in their hearts zealotry, the zealotry of the Age of Ignorance, then Allah sent down His peace of reassurance upon His messenger and upon the believers and imposed on them the word of self-restraint, for they were worthy of it and suited for it. And Allah is Aware of all things.

27. Allah has fulfilled the vision[248] for His messenger in very truth. You shall indeed enter the Inviolable Place of Worship, if Allah wills, secure, (having your hair) shaven and cut, not fearing. But He knows that which you know not, and has given you a near victory beforehand.

28. He it is Who has sent His messenger with the guidance and the religion of truth, that He may cause it to prevail over all religion. And Allah suffices as a Witness.

29. Muhammad is the messenger of Allah. And those with him are hard against the disbelievers and merciful among themselves. You (O Muhammad) see them bowing and falling prostrate (in worship), seeking bounty from Allah and (His) acceptance. The mark of them is on their foreheads from the traces of prostration. Such is their likeness in the Torah and their likeness in the Gospel - like as sown corn that sends out its shoot and strengthens it and rises firm upon its stalk, delighting the sowers - that He may enrage the disbelievers with (the sight of) them. Allah has promised, to such of them as believe and do good works, forgiveness and immense reward.

---

248. The Prophet had a vision that he was entering the Sanctuary at Makkah in peace and safety.

Surah 49: *Al-Hujurat* (The Private Apartments)

Al-Hujurat takes its name from v. 4, which, with the following verse, is said to refer to the behaviour of a deputation at a time when deputations from all parts of Arabia were coming to Al-Madinah to profess allegiance to the Prophet. The whole Surah, dealing as it does with manners, and particularly with behaviour towards the Prophet, evidently belongs to a period when there were many seeking audience, among them many who were quite uncivilised.

The date of revelation is the ninth year of the Hijrah, "the year of deputations," as it is called.

In the name of Allah, the Beneficent, the Merciful

1. O you who believe! Be not forward in the presence of Allah and His messenger, and keep your duty to Allah. Allah is Hearer, Knower.

2. O you who believe! Lift not up your voices above the voice of the Prophet, nor shout when speaking to him as you shout one another, lest your works be rendered vain while you perceive not.

3. They who subdue their voices in the presence of the messenger of Allah, those are they whose hearts Allah has proven to righteousness. Theirs will be forgiveness and immense reward.

4. Those who call you from behind the private apartments, most of them have no sense.

5. And if they had had patience till you came out to them, it would have been better for them. And Allah is Forgiving, Merciful.

6. O you who believe! If an evil-liver brings you tidings,[249] verify it, lest you strike some people in ignorance and afterwards repent of what you did.

7. And know that the messenger of Allah is among you. If he were to obey you in much of the government, you would surely be in trouble; but Allah has endeared the faith to you and has beautified it in your hearts, and has made disbelief and lewdness and rebellion hateful to you. Such are they who are the rightly guided.

8. (It is) a bounty and a grace from Allah; and Allah is Knower, Wise.

9. And if two parties of believers fall to fighting, then make peace between them. And if one party of them does wrong to the other, fight you the one which does wrong till it returns to the ordinance of Allah; then, if it returns, make peace between them justly, and act equitably. Allah loves the equitable.

10. The believers are nothing else than brothers. Therefore make peace between your brothers and observe your duty to Allah that perhaps you may obtain mercy.

249. The reference is to a man who brought false news of a revolt of the subject Jews at Kheybar.

11. O you who believe! Let not a people deride a people who may be better than they (are), let not women (deride) women who may be better than they are; neither defame one another, nor insult one another by nicknames. Bad is the name of lewdness after faith. And who turns not in repentance, such are evildoers.

12. O you who believe! Shun much suspicion; for some suspicion is a crime. And spy not, neither backbite one another. Would one of you love to eat the flesh of his dead brother? You abhor that (so abhor the other)! And keep your duty (to Allah). Allah is Relenting, Merciful.

13. O mankind! We have created you from a male and a female, and have made you nations and tribes that you may know one another. The noblest of you, in the sight of Allah, is the best in conduct. Allah is Knower, Aware.

14. The wandering Arabs say: We believe. Say (to them, O Muhammad): You believe not, but rather say "We submit," for the faith has not yet entered into your hearts. Yet, if you obey Allah and His messenger, He will not withhold from you anything of (the reward of) your deeds. Allah is Forgiving, Merciful.

15. The (true) believers are those only who believe in Allah and His messenger and afterwards doubt not, but strive with their wealth and their lives for the cause of Allah. Such are the sincere.

16. Say (to them, O Muhammad): Would you teach Allah your religion, when Allah knows all that is in the heavens and all that is in the earth, and Allah is Aware of all things?

17. They make it a favour to you (Muhammad) that they have surrendered (to Him). Say: Think not your Surrender a favour to me; no, but Allah confers a favour on you, inasmuch as He has led you to the Faith, if you are earnest.

18. Allah knows the Unseen of the heavens and the earth. And Allah is Seer of what you do.

Surah 50: *Qaf*

Qaf takes its name from the letter of the Arabic alphabet which stands alone at the beginning of the first verse. It belongs to the middle group of Makkan Surahs.

In the name of Allah,
the Beneficent, the Merciful.

1. *Qaf.* By the Glorious Qur'an,

2. No, but they are surprised that a warner of their own has come to them; and the disbelievers say: This is a strange thing:

3. When we are dead and have become dust (shall we be brought back again)? That would be a far return!

4. We know that which the earth takes of them,[250] and with Us is a recording Book.

---

250. *i.e.* those of them who die and are buried in the earth.

---

5. No, but they have denied the truth when it came to them, therefore they are now in a troubled state.

6. Have they not then observed the sky above them, how We have constructed it and beautified it, and how there are no rifts in it?

7. And the earth We have spread out, and have flung firm hills in it, and have caused of every lovely kind to grow on it,

8. A vision and a reminder for every penitent slave.

9. And We send down from the sky blessed water by which We give growth to gardens and the grain of crops,

10. And lofty date-palms with ranged clusters,

11. Provision (made) for men; and with it We revive a dead land. Even so will be the resurrection of the dead.

12. The people of Noah denied (the truth) before them, and (so did) the dwellers at Ar-Rass and (the tribe of) Thamud,

13. And (the tribe of) 'Aad, and Pharaoh, and the brothers of Lot,

14. And the dwellers in the wood,[251] and the people of Tubb'a:[252] every one denied their messengers, therefore My threat took effect.

15. Were We then worn out by the first creation? Yet they are in doubt about a new creation.

16. We verily created man and We know what his soul whispers to him, and We are nearer to him than his jugular vein.

---

251. Midian.
252. The name of a famous dynasty in Al-Yaman.

---

17. When the two Receivers receive (him), seated on the right hand and on the left,

18. He utters no word but there is with him an observer ready.

19. And the agony of death comes in truth. (And it is said to him): This is that which you used to shun.

20. And the trumpet is blown. This is the threatened Day.

21. And every soul comes, along with it a driver and a witness.

22. (And to the evil-doer it is said): You were in heedlessness of this. Now We have removed from you your covering, and piercing is your sight this day.

23. And (to the evil-doer) his comrade says: This is that which I have ready (as testimony).

24. (And it is said): Do you both[253] hurl to Hell each ungrateful rebel,

25. Hinderer of good, transgressor, doubter,

26. Who sets up another god along with Allah. Do you both hurl him to the dreadful doom.

27. His comrade says: Our Lord! I did not cause him to rebel, but he was (himself) far gone in error.

28. He says: Dispute not in My presence, when I had already given to you the warning.

29. The sentence that comes from Me cannot be changed, and I am in no way a tyrant to the slaves.

30. On the day when We say to Hell: Are you filled? and it says: Can there be more to come?

31. And the Garden is brought near for those who kept from evil, no longer distant.

32. (And it is said): This is that which you were promised. (It is) for every penitent and heedful one,

33. Who fears the Beneficent in secret and comes with a humble heart.

34. Enter it in peace. This is the day of immortality.

35. There they have all that they desire, and there is more with Us.

36. And how many a generation We destroyed before them, who were mightier than these in prowess so that they overran the lands! Had they any place of refuge (when the Judgement came)?

37. In it verily is a reminder for him who has a heart, or gives ear with full intelligence.

38. And verily We created the heavens and the earth, and all that is between them, in six Days,[254] and nothing of weariness touched Us.

39. Therefore (O Muhammad) bear with what they say, and hymn the praise of your Lord before the rising and before the setting of the sun;

40. And in the night-time hymn His praise, and after the (prescribed) prostrations.

---

253. The driver and the witness (v. 21) or the two Receivers (v. 17).

254. See *Surah 22, Al-Hajj*, v. 47; *Surah 32, As-Sajdah*, v. 5 and *Surah 70, Al-Ma'arij*, v. 4.

41. And listen on the day when the caller calls from a near place,

42. The day when they will hear the (Awful) Cry in truth. That is the day of coming out (from the graves).

43. It is We Who give life and give death, and to Us is the journeying.

44. On the day when the earth splits apart from them, hastening out (they come). That is a gathering easy for Us (to make).

45. We are Best Aware of what they say, and you (O Muhammad) are in no way a compeller over them. But warn by the Qur'an him who fears My threat.

Surah 51: **Adh-Dhariyat** (The Winnowing Winds)

Adh-Dhariyat, "The Winnowing Winds," takes its name from a word in v. 1. I have followed the usual interpretation of the first four verses, but they may also be taken as all referring to winds or to angels.

An early Makkan Surah.

In the name of Allah,
the Beneficent, the Merciful.

1. By those that winnow with a winnowing,

2. And those that bear the burden (of the rain),

3. And those that glide with ease (upon the sea),

4. And those who distribute (blessings) by command,

5. That with which you are threatened is indeed true,

6. And the judgement will indeed befall.

7. By the heaven full of paths,

8. You, indeed, are of various opinions (concerning the truth).

9. He is made to turn away from it who is (himself) averse.

10. Accursed be the conjecturers,

11. Who are careless in an abyss!

12. They ask: When is the Day of Judgement?

13. (It is) the Day when they will be tormented at the Fire,

14. (And it will be said to them): Taste your torment (which you inflicted). This is what you sought to hasten.

15. Those who keep from evil will dwell amid gardens and watersprings,

16. Taking that which their Lord gives them; for previously they were doers of good;

17. They used to sleep but little of the night,

18. And before the dawning of each day would seek forgiveness,

19. And in their wealth the beggar and the outcast had due share.

20. And in the earth are signs for those whose faith is sure.

21. And (also) in yourselves. Can you then not see?

22. And in the heaven is your provision and that which you are promised;

23. And by the Lord of the heavens and the earth, it is the truth, even as (it is true) that you speak.

24. Has the story of Abraham's honoured guests reached you (O Muhammad)?

25. When they came in to him and said: Peace! he answered, Peace! (and thought): People unknown (to me).

26. Then he went away to his family so that they brought a fatted calf;

27. And he set it before them, saying: Will you not eat?

28. Then he conceived a fear of them. They said: Fear not! and gave him tidings of (the birth of) a wise son.

29. Then his wife came forward, moaning, and struck her face, and exclaimed: A barren old woman!

30. They said: Even so, says your Lord. He is the Wise, the Knower.

31. (Abraham) said: And (afterwards) what is your errand, O you sent (from Allah)?

32. They said: We are sent to a guilty people,

33. That we may send upon them stones of clay,

34. Marked by your Lord for (the destruction of) the excessive.

35. Then We brought out such believers as were there.

36. But We found there but one house of those surrendered[255] (to Allah).

37. And We left behind in it a sign for those who fear a painful doom.

38. And in Moses (too, there is a sign) when We sent him to Pharaoh with clear authority,

39. But he withdrew (confiding) in his might, and said: A wizard or a madman.

40. So We seized him and his forces, rejected.

41. And in (the tribe of) 'Aad (there is a sign) when We sent the fatal wind against them.

42. It spared nothing that it reached, but made it (all) as dust.

43. And in (the tribe of) Thamud (there is a sign) when it was said to them: Take your ease a while.

44. But they rebelled against their Lord's decree, and so the thunderbolt overtook them even while they gazed;

45. And they were unable to rise up, nor could they help themselves.

46. And the people of Noah before. They were licentious people.

47. We have built the heaven with might, and We it is Who make the vast extent (of it).

48. And the earth We have laid out, how gracious is the Spreader (of it)!

49. And all things We have created by pairs, that perhaps you may reflect.

50. Therefore flee to Allah; I[256] am a plain warner to you from Him.

51. And set not any other god along with Allah; I am a plain warner to you from Him.

52. Even so there came no messenger to those before them but they said: A wizard or a madman!

255. Arabic: *Muslimin.*

256. The revealing angel, it would appear.

53. Have they handed down (the saying) as an heirloom one to another? No, but they are obstinate people.

54. So withdraw from them (O Muhammad), for you are in no way blameworthy,

55. And warn, for warning profits believers.

56. I created the jinn and humankind only that they might worship Me.

57. I seek no livelihood from them, nor do I ask that they should feed Me.

58. Allah! He it is that gives livelihood, the Lord of unbreakable might.

59. And for those who (now) do wrong, there is an evil day like the evil day (which came for) their likes (of old); so let them not ask Me to hasten on (that day).

60. And woe to those who disbelieve, from (that) their day which they are promised.

Surah 52: **At-Tur**
(The Mount)

At-Tur, "The Mount," takes name from the opening verse.

An early Makkan Surah.

===

In the name of Allah,
the Beneficent, the Merciful.

1. By the Mount,

2. And a Scripture inscribed

3. On fine parchment unrolled,

4. And the House frequented,

5. And the roof exalted,

6. And the sea kept filled,

7. The doom of your Lord will surely come to pass;

8. There is none who can ward it off.

9. On the day when the heaven will heave with (awful) heaving,

10. And the mountains move away with (awful) movement,

11. Then woe that day to the deniers

12. Who play in talk of grave matters;

13. The day when they are thrust with a (disdainful) thrust, into the fire of Hell,

14. (And it is said to them): This is the Fire which you used to deny.

15. Is this magic, or do you not see?

16. Endure the heat of it, and whether you are patient of it or impatient of it is all one for you. You are only being paid for what you used to do.

17. Those who kept their duty dwell in gardens and delight,

18. Happy because of what their Lord has given them, and (because) their Lord has warded off from them the torment of Hell-fire.

19. (And it is said to them): Eat and drink in health (as a reward) for what you used to do,

20. Reclining on ranged couches. And we wed them to fair ones with wide, lovely eyes.

21. And they who believe and whose seed follow them in faith, We cause their seed to join them (there), and We deprive them of nothing of their (life's) work. Every man is a pledge for that which he has earned.

22. And We provide them with fruit and meat such as they desire.

23. There they pass from hand to hand a cup in which is neither vanity nor cause of sin.

24. And there go round, waiting on them, menservants of their own, like hidden pearls.

25. And some of them draw near to others, questioning,

26. Saying: Before, when we were with our families, we were always anxious;

27. But Allah has been gracious to us and has preserved us from the torment of the breath of Fire.

28. We used to pray to Him before. He is the Benign, the Merciful.

29. Therefore warn (men, O Muhammad). By the grace of Allah you are neither soothsayer nor madman.

30. Or do say they: (he is) a poet, (one) for whom we may expect the accident of time?

31. Say (to them): Expect (your fill)! I am with you among the expectant.

32. Do their minds command them to do this, or are they an outrageous people?

33. Or say they: He has invented it? No, but they will not believe!

34. Then let them produce speech the like of it, if they are truthful.

35. Or were they created out of nothing? Or are they the creators?

36. Or did they create the heavens and the earth? No, but they are sure of nothing!

37. Or do they own the treasures of your Lord? Or have they been given charge (of it)?

38. Or have they any stairway (to heaven) by means of which they overhear (decrees)? Then let their listener produce some manifest authority!

39. Or has He daughters whereas you have sons?

40. Or you (Muhammad) ask a fee from them so that they are plunged into debt?

41. Or do they possess the Unseen so that they can write (it) down?

42. Or do they seek to trap (the messenger)? But those who disbelieve, they are the trapped!

43. Or have they any god beside Allah? Glorified is Allah from all that they ascribe as partner (to Him)!

44. And if they were to see a fragment of the heaven falling, they would say: A heap of clouds.

45. Then let them be (O Muhammad), till they meet their day, in which they will be thunderstruck,

46. A day in which their deception will not benefit them anything, nor will they be helped.

47. And verily, for those who do wrong, there is a punishment beyond that. But most of them know not.

48. So wait patiently (O Muhammad) for your Lord's decree, for surely you are in Our sight; and hymn the praise of your Lord when you stand up.

49. And in the night-time also hymn His praise, and at the setting of the stars.

Surah 53: **An-Najm**
(The Star)

An-Najm, "The Star," takes its name from a word in the first verse.

An early Makkan Surah.

In the name of Allah,
the Beneficent, the Merciful.

1. By the Star when it sets,

2. Your comrade errs not, nor is deceived;

3. Nor does he speak of (his own) desire.

4. It is nothing except an inspiration that is inspired,

5. Which one of mighty powers has taught him,

6. One vigorous; and he grew clear to view,[257]

7. When he was on the uppermost horizon.

8. Then he drew near and came down

9. Till he was (distant) two bows' length or even nearer,

10. And He revealed to His slave that which He revealed.

11. The heart lied not (in seeing) what it saw.

12. Will you then dispute with him concerning what he sees?

13. And verily he saw him yet another time.[258]

14. By the lote-tree of the utmost boundary,

15. Near to which is the Garden of Abode.

16. When that which shrouds did enshroud the lote-tree,

17. The eye turned not aside nor yet was in excess.

18. Verily he saw one of the greater revelations of his Lord.

19. Have you thought upon Al-Lat[259] and Al-'Uzza,[259]

20. And Manat,[259] the third, the other?

21. Are yours the males and His the females?[260]

22. That indeed would be an unfair division!

23. They are but names which you have named, you and your fathers, for which Allah has revealed no authority. They follow but a guess and that which (they) themselves desire. And now the guidance from their Lord has come to them.

24. Or shall man have what he desires?

25. But to Allah belongs the after (life), and the former.

26. And how many angels are in the heavens whose intercession benefits nothing except after Allah gives permission to whom He chooses and accepts.

27. It is those who disbelieve in the Hereafter who name the angels with the names of females.

---

257. This and the five following verses are generally accepted as referring to the Prophet's vision on Mt. Hira.

258. This is generally accepted as a reference to the Prophet's vision in which he ascended through the seven heavens.

259. An idol of pagan Arabs.

260. The pagan Arabs pretended that their idols were daughters of Allah.

28. And they have no knowledge of it. They only follow a guess, and a guess can never take the place of the truth.

29. Then withdraw (O Muhammad) from him who flees from Our remembrance and desires but the life of the world.

30. Such is their sum of knowledge. Your Lord is Best Aware of him who strays, and He is Best Aware of him who goes right.

31. And to Allah belongs whatever is in the heavens and whatever is in the earth, that He may reward those who do evil with that which they have done, and reward those who do good with goodness.

32. Those who avoid enormities of sin and abominations, except the unwilled offences - (for them) your Lord is of vast mercy. He is Best Aware of you (from the time) when He created you from the earth, and when you were hidden in the bellies of your mothers. Therefore ascribe not purity to yourselves. He is Best Aware of him who wards off (evil).

33. Did you (O Muhammad) observe him who turned away,

34. And gave a little, then was reluctant?

35. Has he knowledge of the Unseen so that he sees?

36. Or has he not had news of what is in the books of Moses

37. And Abraham who paid his debt:

38. That no laden one shall bear another's load,

39. And that man has only that for which he makes effort,

40. And that his effort will be seen.

41. And afterward he will be repaid for it with fullest payment;

42. And that your Lord, He is the goal;

43. And that He it is who makes laugh, and makes weep,

44. And that He it is Who gives death and gives life;

45. And that He creates the two spouses, the male and the female,

46. From a drop (of seed) when it is poured out;

47. And that He has ordained the second bringing out;

48. And that He it is Who enriches and contents;

49. And that He it is Who is the Lord of Sirius;

50. And that He destroyed the former (tribe of) 'Aad,[261]

51. And (the tribe of) Thamud He spared not;

52. And the people of Noah before, They were more unjust and more rebellious;

53. And Al-Mu'tafikah[262] He destroyed

54. So that there covered them that which did cover.

55. Concerning which then, of the bounties of your Lord, can you dispute?

56. This is a warner of the warners of old.

---

261. There was still in existence a tribe of that name.
262. Generally supposed to be a name for the villages of the people of Lot.

57. The threatened Hour is near.

58. None besides Allah can disclose it.

59. Are you then surprised at this statement,

60. And laugh and not weep,

61. While you amuse yourselves?

62. Rather prostrate yourselves before Allah and serve Him.

Surah 54: *Al-Qamar*
(The Moon)

Al-Qamar, "The Moon," takes its name from the first verse: "The hour drew near and the moon was split in two." A strange appearance of the moon in the sky, as if it had been split apart, is recorded in the traditions of several Companions of the Prophet as having astonished the people of Makkah about the time when the idolaters were beginning to persecute the Muslims.

An early Makkan Surah.

In the name of Allah,
the Beneficent, the Merciful.

1. The hour drew near and the moon was split in two.

2. And if they see a sign they turn away and say: Prolonged illusion.

3. They denied (the Truth) and followed their own lusts. Yet everything will come to a decision,

4. And surely there has come to them news of which the meaning should deter,

5. Effective wisdom; but warnings benefit not.

6. So withdraw from them (O Muhammad) on the day when the Summoner summons to a painful thing.

7. With downcast eyes, they come out from the graves as if they were locusts spread far and wide,

8. Hastening towards the summoner; the disbelievers say: This is a hard day.

9. The people of Noah denied before them, yes, they denied Our slave[263] and said: A madman; and he was repulsed.

10. So he called to his Lord, saying: I am vanquished, so give help.

11. Then We opened the gates of heaven with pouring water

12. And caused the earth to gush out springs, so that the waters met for a predestined purpose.

13. And We carried him upon a thing of planks and nails,

14. That ran (upon the waters) in Our sight, as a reward for him who was rejected.

15. And verily We left it as a sign; but is there anyone who remembers?

16. Then see how (dreadful) was My punishment after My warnings!

17. And in truth We have made the Qur'an easy to remember;[264] but is there anyone who remembers?

---

263. To be 'Abd Allah', is the proudest rank the Muslim can claim, bondage to Allah implying liberation from all other servitudes. All especially devoted men, all the chosen ones, are called slaves of Allah in the Qur'an.

264. It is a fact that the Qur'an is marvellously easy for the believers to commit to memory. Thousands of people in the East know the whole Book by heart. The translator, who finds great difficulty in remembering well-known English quotations accurately, can remember page after page of the Qur'an in Arabic with perfect accuracy.

18. (The tribe of) 'Aad rejected warnings. Then how (dreadful) was My punishment after My warnings.

19. We let loose on them a raging wind on a day of constant calamity,

20. Sweeping men away as though they were uprooted trunks of palm-trees.

21. Then see how (dreadful) was My punishment after My warnings!

22. And in truth We have made the Qur'an easy to remember; but is there anyone who remembers?

23. (The tribe of) Thamud rejected warnings

24. For they said; Is it a mortal man, alone among us, that we are to follow? Then indeed we should fall into error and madness.

25. Has the remembrance been given to him alone among us? No, but he is a rash liar.

26. (To their warner it was said): Tomorrow they will know who is the rash liar.

27. We are sending the she-camel as a test for them; so watch them and have patience;

28. And inform them that the water is to be shared between (her and) them. Every drinking will be witnessed.

29. But they called their comrade and he took and hamstrung (her).

30. Then see how (dreadful) was My punishment after My warnings!

31. We sent upon them one Shout, and they became as the dry twigs (rejected by) the builder of a cattle-fold.

32. And in truth We have made the Qur'an easy to remember; but is there anyone who remembers?

33. The people of Lot rejected warnings.

34. We sent a storm of stones upon them (all) except the family of Lot, whom We rescued in the last watch of the night,

35. As grace from Us. Thus We reward him who gives thanks.

36. And he indeed had warned them of Our blow, but they did doubt the warnings.

37. They even asked of him his guests for an ill purpose. Then We blinded their eyes (and said): Taste now My punishment after My warnings!

38. And in truth the punishment decreed befell them early in the morning.

39. Now taste My punishment after My warnings!

40. And in truth We have made the Qur'an easy to remember; but is there anyone who remembers?

41. And warnings came in truth to the house of Pharaoh

42. Who denied Our revelations, every one. Therefore We grasped them with the grasp of the Mighty, the Powerful.

43. Are your disbelievers better than those, or have you some immunity in the Scriptures?

44. Or do they say: We are a host victorious?

45. The hosts will all be routed and will turn and flee.

46. No, but the Hour (of doom) is their appointed time, and the Hour will be more wretched and more bitter (than their earthly failure).

47. The guilty are in error and madness.

48. On the day when they are dragged into the Fire upon their faces (it is said to them): Feel the touch of Hell.

49. We have created everything by measure.

50. And Our commandment is but one (commandment), as the twinkling of an eye.

51. And verily We have destroyed your fellows; but is there anyone who remembers?

52. And everything they did is in the Scriptures,

53. And every small and great thing is recorded.

54. The righteous will dwell among gardens and rivers,

55. Firmly established in the favour of a Mighty King.

Surah 55: *Ar-Rahman*
(The Beneficent)

Ar-Rahman, takes its name from the first verse. In the refrain: "Which is it, of the favours of your Lord, that you deny?" 'you' and the verb are in the dual form, and the question is generally believed to be addressed to mankind and the Jinn. Some have held that vv. 46-76 refer, not to the paradise hereafter, but to the later conquests of the Muslims, the four gardens being Egypt, Syria, Mesopotamia and Persia. There may well be a double meaning.

An early Makkan Surah.

In the name of Allah,
the Beneficent, the Merciful.

1. The Beneficent

2. Has made known the Qur'an.

3. He has created man.

4. He has taught him utterance.

5. The sun and the moon are made punctual.

6. The stars and the trees adore.

7. And the sky He has uplifted; and He has set the measure,

8. That you exceed not the measure,

9. But observe the measure strictly, and do not fall short of it.

10. And the earth has He appointed for (His) creatures,

11. In which are fruit and sheathed palm-trees,

12. Husked grain and scented herb.

13. Which is it, of the favours of your Lord, that you deny?

14. He created man of clay like the potter

15. And the jinn He created of smokeless fire.

16. Which is it, of the favours of your Lord, that you deny?

17. Lord of the two Easts,[265] and Lord of the two Wests![266]

18. Which is it, of the favours of your Lord, that you deny?

---

265. The two points where the sun rises in winter and in summer.
266. The two points where the sun sets in winter and in summer.

19. He has set free the two seas.[267] They meet.

20. There is a barrier between them. They encroach not (one upon the other).

21. Which is it, of the favours of your Lord, that you deny?

22. There comes out from both of them the pearl and coral-stone.

23. Which is it, of the favours of your Lord, that you deny?

24. His are the ships displayed upon the sea, like banners.[268]

25. Which is it, of the favours of your Lord, that you deny?

26. Everyone on it will pass away;

27. There remains but the Countenance of your Lord of Might and Glory.

28. Which is it, of the favours of your Lord, that you deny?

29. All in the heavens and the earth implore Him. Every day He exercises (universal) power.

30. Which is it, of the favours of your Lord, that you deny?

31. We shall dispose of you, O you two dependants (man and jinn).

32. Which is it, of the favours of your Lord, that you deny?

33. O company of jinn and men, if you have power to penetrate (all) regions of the heavens and the earth, then penetrate (them)! You will never penetrate them except with (Our) sanction.

34. Which is it, of the favours of your Lord, that you deny?

35. There will be sent, against you both, heat of fire and flash of brass, and you will not escape.

36. Which is it, of the favours of your Lord, that you deny?

37. And when the heaven splits apart and becomes rosy like red hide -

38. Which is it, of the favours of your Lord, that you deny? -

39. On that day neither man nor jinn will be questioned of his sin.

40. Which is it, of the favours of your Lord, that you deny?

41. The guilty will be known by their marks, and will be taken by the forelocks and the feet.

42. Which is it, of the favours of your Lord, that you deny?

43. This is Hell which the guilty deny.

44. They go circling round between it and fierce, boiling water.

45. Which is it, of the favours of your Lord, that you deny?

46. But for him who fears the standing before his Lord there are two gardens.

47. Which is it, of the favours of your Lord, that you deny?

48. Of spreading branches.

49. Which is it, of the favours of your Lord, that you deny?

50. In which are two fountains flowing.

51. Which is it, of the favours of your Lord, that you deny?

52. In which is every kind of fruit in pairs.

---

267. *i.e.* the salt water and the sweet.
268. The usual explanation of the commentators is "built into the sea like mountains."

53. Which is it, of the favours of your Lord, that you deny?

54. Reclining upon couches lined with silk brocade, the fruit of both the gardens near to hand.

55. Which is it, of the favours of your Lord, that you deny?

56. In it are those of modest gaze, whom neither man nor jinn will have touched before them.

57. Which is it, of the favours of your Lord, that you deny?

58. (In beauty) like the jacinth and the coral-stone.

59. Which is it, of the favours of your Lord, that you deny?

60. Is the reward for goodness anything except goodness?

61. Which is it, of the favours of your Lord, that you deny?

62. And beside them are two other gardens,

63. Which is it, of the favours of your Lord, that you deny?

64. Dark green with foliage.

65. Which is it, of the favours of your Lord, that you deny?

66. In which are two abundant springs.

67. Which is it, of the favours of your Lord, that you deny?

68. In which is fruit, the date-palm and pomegranate.

69. Which is it, of the favours of your Lord, that you deny?

70. In which (are found) the good and beautiful -

71. Which is it, of the favours of your Lord, that you deny?

72. Fair ones, close-guarded in pavilions -

73. Which is it, of the favours of your Lord, that you deny?

74. Whom neither man nor jinn will have touched before them -

75. Which is it, of the favours of your Lord, that you deny?

76. Reclining on green cushions and fair carpets.

77. Which is it, of the favours of your Lord, that you deny?

78. Blessed be the name of your Lord, Mighty and Glorious!

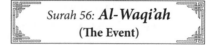

Surah 56: *Al-Waqi'ah*
(The Event)

Al-Waqi'ah, "The Event," takes its name from a word in v. 1.

An early Makkan Surah.

In the name of Allah,
the Beneficent, the Merciful.

1. When the event befalls -

2. There is no denying that it will befall -

3. Disgracing (some), exalting (others);

4. When the earth is shaken with a shock

5. And the hills are ground to powder

6. So that they become scattered dust,

7. And you will be three kinds:

8. (First) those on the right hand; what of those on the right hand?

9. And (then) those on the left hand; what of those on the left hand?

10. And the foremost in the race, the foremost in the race:

11. Those are they who will be brought near

12. In gardens of delight;

13. A multitude of those of old

14. And a few of those of later time.

15. On lined couches,

16. Reclining in it face-to-face.

17. There wait on them immortal youths

18. With bowls and ewers and a cup from a pure spring

19. From which they get no aching of the head nor any madness,

20. And fruit that they prefer

21. And flesh of fowls that they desire.

22. And (there are) fair ones with wide, lovely eyes,

23. Like hidden pearls,

24. Reward for what they used to do.

25. There they hear no vain speaking nor recrimination

26. (Nothing) but the saying: Peace, (and again) Peace.

27. And those on the right hand; what of those on the right hand?

28. Among thornless lote-trees

29. And clustered plantains,

30. And spreading shade,

31. And water gushing,

32. And fruit in plenty

33. Neither out of reach nor yet forbidden,

34. And raised couches;

35. We have created them a (new) creation

36. And made them virgins,

37. Lovers, friends,

38. For those on the right hand;

39. A multitude of those of old

40. And a multitude of those of later time.[269]

41. And those on the left hand: What of those on the left hand?

42. In scorching wind and scalding water

43. And shadow of black smoke,

44. Neither cool nor refreshing.

45. Prior to this they were indulgent with luxury

46. And used to persist in the awful sin.

47. And they used to say: When we are dead and have become dust and bones, shall we then, be raised again,

48. And also our forefathers?

49. Say (to them, O Muhammad): Those of old and those of later time

50. Will all be brought together at an appointed time on a day known (only to Allah).

51. Then you, the erring, the deniers,

52. You verily will eat of a tree called Zaqqum,

53. And will fill your bellies with it;

54. And after it you will drink of boiling water,

55. Drinking even as the camel drinks.

56. This will be their welcome on the Day of Judgement.

57. We created you. Will you then admit the truth?

---

269. This verse is said to have been revealed at Al-Madinah.

58. Have you seen that which you emit?

59. Do you create it or are We the Creator?

60. We mete out death among you, and We are not to be outrun,

61. That We may transfigure you and make you what you know not.

62. And verily you know the first creation. Why, then, do you not reflect?

63. Have you seen that which you cultivate?

64. Is it you who foster it, or are We the Fosterer?

65. If We willed, We verily could make it chaff, then you would cease not to exclaim:

66. We are laden with debt!

67. No, but we are deprived!

68. Have you observed the water which you drink?

69. Is it you who shed it from the rain cloud, or are We the Shedder?

70. If We willed, We verily could make it bitter. Why then, do you not give thanks?

71. Have you observed the fire which you strike out;

72. Was it you who made the tree of it to grow, or were We the Grower?

73. We, even We, appointed it a memorial and a comfort for the dwellers in the wilderness

74. Therefore (O Muhammad), praise the name of your Lord, the Tremendous.

75. No, I swear by the places of the stars -

76. And that verily is a tremendous oath, if you but knew -

77. That (this) is indeed a noble Qur'an

78. In a Book kept hidden,

79. Which no one touches except the purified,

80. A revelation from the Lord of the Worlds.

81. Is it this Statement that you despise,

82. And make denial of it your livelihood?

83. Why, then, when (the soul) comes up to the throat (of the dying),

84. And you are at that moment looking,

85. - And We are nearer to him than you are, but you see not -

86. Why then, if you are not in bondage (to Us),

87. Do you not force it back, if you are truthful?

88. Thus if he is of those brought near,

89. Then breath of life, and plenty, and a Garden of Delight.

90. And if he is of those on the right hand,

91. Then (the greeting) "Peace be to you" from those on the right hand.

92. But if he is of the rejecters, the erring,

93. Then the welcome will be boiling water

94. And roasting at Hell-fire.

95. This is certain truth.

96. Therefore (O Muhammad) praise the name of your Lord, the Tremendous.

Surah 57: **Al-Hadid**
(Iron)

Al-Hadid, "Iron," takes its name from a word in v. 25.

The reference in the word "victory" in v. 10, is undoubtedly to the conquest of Makkah, though Nöldeke[270] takes it to refer to the battle of Badr, and so would place the Surah in the fourth or fifth year of the Hijrah. The words of the verse are against such an assumption since no Muslims "spent and fought" before the battle at Badr, which was the beginning of their fighting.

The date of revelation must be the eighth or ninth year of the Hijrah.

In the name of Allah,
the Beneficent, the Merciful.

1. All that is in the heavens and the earth glorifies Allah; and He is the Mighty, the Wise.

2. His is the Sovereignty of the heavens and the earth; He gives life and He gives death; and He is Able to do all things.

3. He is the First and the Last, and the Outward and the Inward; and He is Knower of all things.

4. He it is Who created the heavens and the earth in six Days;[271] then He mounted the Throne. He knows all that enters the earth and all that emerges from it and all that comes down from the sky and all that ascends in it; and He is with you wherever you may be. And Allah is Seer of what you do.

5. His is the Sovereignty of the heavens and the earth, and to Allah (all) things are brought back.

6. He causes the night to pass into the day, and He causes the day to pass into the night, and He is knower of all that is in the hearts.

7. Believe in Allah and His messenger, and spend of that of which He has made you trustees; and such of you as believe and spend (aright), theirs will be a great reward.

8. What is the matter with you that you believe not in Allah, when the messenger calls you to believe in your Lord, and He has already made a covenant with you, if you are believers?

9. He it is Who sends down clear revelations to His slave, that He may bring you out from darkness to light; and for you, Allah is Full of Pity, Merciful.

10. And what is the matter with you that you spend not in the way of Allah when to Allah belongs the inheritance of the heavens and the earth? Those who spent and fought before the victory are not upon a level (with the rest of you). Such are greater in rank than those who spent and fought afterwards. To each has Allah promised good. And Allah is Informed of what you do.

11. Who is he that will lend to Allah a goodly loan,[272] that He may double it for him and his may be a rich reward?

---

270. Th. Nöldeke, Geschichte des Qorans, 2nd edn., Part I, Leipzig, 1909, p. 195.

271. See *Surah 22, Al-Hajj,* v. 47; *Surah 32, As-Sajdah,* v. 5 and *Surah 70, Al-Ma'arij,* v. 4.

272. A loan without interest or any thought of gain or loss.

12. On the day when you (Muhammad) will see the believers, men and women, their light shining out before them and on their right hands, (and will hear it said to them): Glad news for you this day: Gardens underneath which rivers flow, in which you are immortal. That is the supreme triumph.

13. On the day when the hypocritical men and the hypocritical women will say to those who believe: Look on us that we may borrow from your light! it will be said: Go back and seek for light! Then there will separate them a wall in which is a gate, the inner side of which contains mercy, while the outer side of it is towards the doom.

14. They will call to them (saying): Were we not with you? They will say: Yes, verily; but you tempted one another, and hesitated, and doubted, and vain desires deceived you till the ordinance of Allah came to pass; and the deceiver deceived you concerning Allah;

15. So this day no ransom can be taken from you nor from those who disbelieved. Your home is the Fire; that is your patron, and an unhappy journey's end.

16. Is not the time ripe for the hearts of those who believe to submit to Allah's reminder and to the truth which is revealed, that they become not as those who received the Scripture of old, but the term was prolonged for them and so their hearts were hardened, and many of them are evil-livers.

17. Know that Allah revives the earth after its death. We have made clear Our revelations for you, that perhaps you may understand.

18. Those who give alms, both men and women, and lend to Allah a goodly loan, it will be doubled for them, and theirs will be a rich reward.

19. And those who believe in Allah and His messengers, they are the loyal, and the martyrs are with their Lord; they have their reward and their light; while as for those who disbelieve and deny Our revelations, they are owners of Hell-fire.

20. Know that the life of the world is only play, and idle talk, and pageantry, and boasting among you, and rivalry in respect of wealth and children; as the likeness of vegetation after rain, of which the growth is pleasing to the farmer, but afterwards it dries up and you see it turning yellow, then it becomes straw. And in the Hereafter there is grievous punishment, and (also) forgiveness from Allah and His good pleasure, whereas the life of the world is only a matter of illusion.

21. Race one with another for forgiveness from your Lord and a Garden of which the breadth is as the breadth of the heavens and the earth, which is in store for those who believe in Allah and His messengers. Such is the bounty of Allah, which He bestows upon whom He wills, and Allah is of Infinite Bounty.

22. Nothing of disaster befalls in the earth or in yourselves but it is in a Book before We bring it into being - That is easy for Allah -

23. That you grieve not for the sake of that which has escaped you, nor yet rejoice because of that which has been given. Allah loves not all proud boasters,

24. Who hoard and who enjoin upon the people avarice. And whoever turns away, still Allah is the Absolute, the Owner of Praise.

25. We verily sent Our messengers with clear proofs, and revealed with them the Scripture and the Balance, that mankind may observe right measure; and He revealed iron, in which is mighty power and (many) uses for mankind, and that Allah may know him who helps Him and His messengers, though unseen. Allah is Strong, Almighty.

26. And We verily sent Noah and Abraham and placed the Prophethood and the Scripture among their seed, and among them there is he who goes right, but many of them are evil-livers.

27. Then We caused Our messengers to follow in their footsteps; and We caused Jesus, son of Mary, to follow, and gave him the Gospel, and placed compassion and mercy in the hearts of those who followed him. But monasticism they invented - We did not ordain it for them. (We commanded) only seeking Allah's pleasure, and they observed it not with right observance. So We give those of them who believe their reward, but many of them are evil-livers.

28. O you who believe! Be mindful of your duty to Allah and put faith in His messenger. He will give you twofold of His mercy and will appoint for you a

light in which you shall walk, and will forgive you. Allah is Forgiving, Merciful;

29. That the People of the Scripture[273] may know that they control nothing of the bounty of Allah, but that the bounty is in Allah's hand to give to whom He will. And Allah is of Infinite Bounty.

Surah 58: *Al-Mujadilah*
(She Who Disputes)

Al-Mujadilah, "She who Disputes," takes its name from a word in verse 1.

A woman complained to the Prophet that her husband had put her away for no good reason by employing an old formula of the pagan Arabs, saying that her back was for him as the back of his mother, and she "disputed" with the Prophet because he would take no action against the man before this revelation came to him. There is a brief reference to the same method of getting rid of wives in Surah 33, Al-Ahzab, v. 4. This Surah must therefore have been revealed before Surah 33.

The date of revelation is the fourth or fifth year of the Hijrah.

In the name of Allah,
the Beneficent, the Merciful.

1. Allah has heard the saying of her who disputes with you (Muhammad) concerning her husband, and complains to Allah. And Allah hears your conversation. Allah is Hearer, Seer.

2. Such of you as put away your wives (by saying they are as their mothers)

273. *i.e.* Jews and Christians.

- They are not their mothers;[274] none are their mothers except those who gave them birth - they indeed utter an ill word and a lie. And Allah is Forgiving, Merciful.

3. Those who put away their wives (by saying they are as their mothers) and afterwards would go back on that which they have said, (the penalty) in that case (is) the freeing of a slave before they touch one another. To this you are exhorted; and Allah is Informed of what you do.

4. And he who finds not (the means), let him fast for two successive months before they touch one another; and for him who is unable to do so (the penance is) the feeding of sixty needy ones. This, that you may put trust in Allah and His messenger. Such are the limits (imposed by Allah); and for disbelievers is a painful doom.

5. Those who oppose Allah and His messenger will be disgraced even as those before them were disgraced; and We have sent down clear signs, and for disbelievers is a shameful doom

6. On the Day when Allah will raise them all together and inform them of what they did. Allah has kept account of it while they forgot it. And Allah is Witness over all things.

7. Have you not seen that Allah knows all that is in the heavens and all that is in the earth? There is no secret conference of three but He is their fourth, nor of five but He is their sixth, nor of less than that or more but He is with them wherever they may be; and afterwards,

on the Day of Resurrection, He will inform them of what they did. Allah is Knower of all things.

8. Have you not observed those who were forbidden conspiracy and afterwards returned to that which they had been forbidden, and (now) conspire together for crime and wrongdoing and disobedience towards the messenger? And when they come to you they greet you with a greeting with which Allah greets you not, and say within themselves: Why should Allah punish us for what we say? Hell will suffice them; they will feel the heat of it - an unhappy journey's end!

9. O you who believe! When you conspire together, conspire not together for crime and wrongdoing and disobedience towards the messenger, but conspire together for righteousness and piety, and keep your duty towards Allah, to whom you will be gathered.

10. Conspiracy is only of the devil, that he may annoy those who believe; but he cannot harm them at all unless by Allah's permission. In Allah let believers put their trust.

11. O you who believe! when it is said to you, 'Make room!' in assemblies, then make room; Allah will make way for you (hereafter). And when it is said, 'Come up higher!' go up higher; Allah will exalt those who believe among you, and those who have knowledge, to high ranks. Allah is Informed of what you do.

12. O you who believe! When you hold conference with the messenger, offer alms before your conference.

274. See *Surah 33, Al-Ahzab,* v. 4.

That is better and purer for you. But if you cannot find (the means) then Allah is Forgiving, Merciful.

13. Fear you to offer alms before your conference? Then, when you do it not and Allah has forgiven you, establish worship and pay the poor-due and obey Allah and His messenger. And Allah is Aware of what you do.

14. Have you not seen those who take for friends a people with whom Allah is angry? They are neither of you nor of them, and they swear a false oath knowingly.

15. Allah has prepared for them a dreadful doom. Evil indeed is that which they used to do.

16. They make a shelter of their oaths and turn (men) from the way of Allah; so theirs will be a shameful doom.

17. Their wealth and their children will benefit them nothing against Allah. Such are rightful owners of the Fire; they will remain in it.

18. On the day when Allah will raise them all together, then they will swear to Him as they (now) swear to you, and they will think that they have some standing. Is it not they who are the liars?

19. The devil has engrossed them and so has caused them to forget remembrance of Allah. They are the devil's party. Is it not the devil's party who will be the losers?

20. Those who oppose Allah and His messenger, they will be among the lowest.

21. Allah has decreed: I verily shall conquer, I and My messengers. Allah is Strong, Almighty.

22. You will not find people who believe in Allah and the Last Day loving those who oppose Allah and His messenger, even though they be their fathers or their sons or their brothers or their clan. As for such, He has written faith upon their hearts and has strengthened them with a Spirit from Him, and He will bring them into Gardens underneath which rivers flow, in which they will remain. Allah is well pleased with them, and they are well pleased with Him. They are Allah's party. Is it not Allah's party who are the successful?

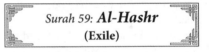

Surah 59: *Al-Hashr*
(Exile)

Al-Hashr, "Exile," takes its name from vv. 2-17, which refer to the exile of the Bani Nadir, a Jewish tribe of Al-Madinah (for treason and projected murder of the Prophet) and the confiscation of their property. The "Hypocrites," as the lukewarm Muslims were called, had secretly sympathised with these Jews, whose opposition had grown strong since the Muslims reverse at Mt. Uhud, and had promised to side with them if it came to a collision with the Muslims; and to emigrate with them if they were forced to emigrate. But when the Muslims marched against the Bani Nadir, and the latter took refuge in their strong towers, the Hypocrites did nothing. And when at length they were reduced and exiled, the Hypocrites did not go with them into exile.

The date of revelation is the fourth year of the Hijrah.

=====

In the name of Allah, the Beneficent, the Merciful.

1. All that is in the heavens and all that is in the earth glorifies Allah, and He is the Mighty, the Wise.

2. He it is Who has caused those of the People of the Scripture[275] who disbelieved to go out from their homes to the first exile. You did not think that they would go out, while they thought that their strongholds would protect them from Allah. But Allah reached them from a place of which they reckoned not, and cast terror in their hearts so that they ruined their houses with their own hands and the hands of the believers. So learn a lesson, O you who have eyes!

3. And if Allah had not decreed migration for them, He verily would have punished them in the world, and theirs in the Hereafter is the punishment of the Fire.

4. That is because they were opposed to Allah and His messenger; and whoever is opposed to Allah, (for him) verily Allah is stern in reprisal.

5. Whatever palm-trees you cut down or left standing on their roots, it was by Allah's permission, in order that He might confound the evil-livers.

---

275. The term for Jews and Christians. In this case it refers to Jews.

6. And that which Allah gave as spoil to His messenger from them, you urged not any horse or riding-camel for the sake of it, but Allah gives His messenger lordship over whom He will. Allah is Able to do all things.

7. That which Allah gives as spoil to His messenger from the people of the townships, it is for Allah and His messenger[276] and for the relatives and the orphans and the needy and the wayfarer, that it becomes not a commodity between the rich among you. And whatever the messenger gives you, take it. And whatever he forbids, abstain (from it). And keep your duty to Allah. Allah is stern in reprisal.

8. And (it is) for the poor emigrants who have been driven out from their homes and their belongings, who seek bounty from Allah and help Allah and His messenger. They are the loyal.

9. Those who entered the city and the faith before them love those who flee to them for refuge, and find in their hearts no need for that which has been given them, but prefer (the emigrants) above themselves though poverty become their lot. And whoever is saved from his own avarice - such are they who are successful.

10. And those who came (into the faith) after them say: Our Lord! Forgive us and our brothers who were before us in the faith, and place not in our hearts any rancour towards those who believe. Our Lord! You are Full of Pity, Merciful.

---

276. *i.e.* for the state.

11. Have you not observed those who are hypocrites, (how) they tell their brothers who disbelieve among the People of the Scripture: If you are driven out, we surely will go out with you, and we will never obey anyone against you, and if you are attacked we verily will help you. And Allah bears witness that they verily are liars.

12. (For) indeed if they are driven out they do not go out with them, and indeed if they are attacked they do not help them, and indeed if they had helped them they would have turned and fled, and then they would not have been victorious.

13. You are more awful as a fear in their hearts than Allah. That is because they are a people who understand not.

14. They will not fight against you in a body except in fortified villages or from behind walls. Their adversity among themselves is very great. You think of them as a whole whereas their hearts are diverse. That is because they are a people who have no sense.

15. On the likeness of those (who suffered) a short time before them, they taste the ill-effects of their own conduct, and theirs is painful punishment.

16. (And the hypocrites are) as the likeness of the devil when he tells man to disbelieve, then, when he disbelieves says: I am done with you. I fear Allah, the Lord of the Worlds.

17. And the consequence for both will be that they are in the Fire, remaining in it. Such is the reward of evildoers.

18. O you who believe! Observe your duty to Allah. And let every soul look to that which it sends on before for the next day. And observe your duty to Allah. Allah is Informed of what you do.

19. And be not as those who forgot Allah, therefore He caused them to forget their souls. Such are the evildoers.

20. Not equal are the owners of the Fire and the owners of the Garden. The owners of the Garden, they are the victorious.

21. If We had caused this Qur'an to descend upon a mountain, you (O Muhammad) verily would have seen it humbled, split apart by the fear of Allah. Such similitudes We coin for mankind that perhaps they may reflect.

22. He is Allah, other than Whom there is no God, the Knower of the Invisible and the Visible. He is the Beneficent, Merciful.

23. He is Allah, other than Whom there is no God, the Sovereign Lord, the Holy One, (the Source of) Peace, the Keeper of Faith, the Guardian, the Majestic, the Compeller, the Superb. Glorified is Allah from all that they ascribe as partner (to Him).

24. He is Allah, the Creator, the Shaper out of nothing, the Fashioner. His are the most beautiful names. All that is in the heavens and the earth glorifies Him, and He is the Mighty, the Wise.

Surah 60: *Al-Mumtahanah* (She Who Is To Be Examined)

Al-Mumtahanah, "She who is to be Examined," takes its name from v. 10, where the believers are told to examine women who come to them as emigrants from the idolaters, and if they find them sincere converts to *Al-Islam*, not to return them to the idolaters. This marked a modification in terms of the Truce of Hudeybiyah, by which the Prophet had engaged to return all emigrants, male and female, while the idolaters were not obliged to give up renegades of *Al-Islam*. The more terrible persecution which women had to undergo, if extradited, and their helpless social condition, were the causes of the change. Instead of giving up women refugees who were sincere, and not fugitives on account of crime or some family quarrel, the Muslims were to pay an indemnity for them; while as for Muslim husbands whose wives might flee to Quraysh, no indemnity was to be paid by the latter but, when some turn of fortune brought wealth to the Islamic State, they were to be repaid by the State what their wives had taken of their property. In v. 12 is the pledge which has to be taken from the women refugees after the examination.

The date of the revelation is the eighth year of the Hijrah.

In the name of Allah, the Beneficent, the Merciful.

1. O you who believe! Choose not My enemy and your enemy for allies. Do you give them friendship when they disbelieve in that truth which has come to you, driving out the messenger and you because you believe in Allah, your Lord? If you have come out to strive in My way and seeking My good pleasure, (show them not friendship). Do you show friendship to them in secret, when I am Best Aware of what you hide and what you proclaim? And whoever does it among you, he verily has strayed from the right way.

2. If they have the upper hand of you, they will be your enemies, and will stretch out their hands and their tongues towards you with evil (intent), and they long for you to disbelieve.

3. Your ties of relationship and your children will benefit you nothing upon the Day of Resurrection. He will part you. Allah is Seer of what you do.

4. There is a goodly example for you in Abraham and those with him, when they told their people: We are guiltless of you and all that you worship besides Allah. We are done with you. And there has arisen between us and you hostility and hate forever until you believe in Allah only - except for what Abraham promised his father (when he said): I will ask forgiveness for you, though I own nothing for you from Allah - Our Lord! In You we put our trust, and to You we turn repentant, and to You is the journeying.

5. Our Lord! Make us not a prey for those who disbelieve, and forgive us, our Lord! You, only You, are the Mighty, the Wise.

6. Verily you have in them a goodly example for everyone who looks to Allah and the Last Day. And whoever may turn away, still Allah, He is the Absolute, the Owner of Praise.

7. It may be that Allah will ordain love between you and those of them with whom you are at enmity. Allah is Mighty, and Allah is Forgiving, Merciful.

8. Allah forbids you not those who did not make war against you on account of religion and did not drive you out from your homes, that you should show them kindness and deal justly with them. Allah loves the just dealers.

9. Allah forbids you only those who made war against you on account of religion and have driven you out from your homes and helped to drive you out, that you make friends of them. Whoever makes friends of them - (All) such are wrongdoers.

10. O you who believe! When believing women come to you as emigrants, examine them. Allah is Best Aware of their faith. Then, if you know them to be true believers, send them not back to the disbelievers. They are not lawful for them (the disbelievers), nor are they (the disbelievers) lawful for them. And give them (the disbelievers) that which they have spent (upon them). And it is no sin for you to marry such women when you have given them their dues. And do not hold on to the ties of disbelieving women; and ask for (the return of) that which you have spent; and let them (the disbelievers) ask for that which they have spent. That is the judgement of Allah. He judges between you. Allah is Knower, Wise.

11. And if any of your wives have gone from you to the disbelievers and afterwards you have your turn (of triumph), then give to those whose wives have gone the like of that which they have spent, and keep your duty to Allah in Whom you are believers.

12. O Prophet! If believing women come to you, taking oath of allegiance to you that they will ascribe nothing as partner to Allah, and will neither steal, nor commit adultery, nor kill their children, nor produce any lie that they have devised between their hands and feet, nor disobey you in what is right,[277] then accept their allegiance and ask Allah to forgive them. Allah is Forgiving, Merciful.

13. O you who believe! Be not friendly with a people with whom Allah is angry, (a people) who have despaired of the Hereafter as the disbelievers despair of those who are in the graves.

Surah 61: **As-Saff**
(The Ranks)

As-Saff, " The Ranks," takes its name from a word in v. 4. In the copy of the Qur'an which I have followed, it is stated to have been revealed at Makkah, though its contents evidently refer to the Madinah period. It may have been revealed while the Prophet and his companions were encamped in the valley of Makkah during the negotiations of the Truce

277. This is called the women's oath of allegiance. It was the oath exacted from men also until the second pact of Al-Aqabah when the duty of defence was added to the men's oath.

of Hudeybiyah, with which some of its verses are associated by tradition.

In that case the date of revelation would be the sixth year of Hijrah.

In the name of Allah, the Beneficent, the Merciful.

1. All that is in the heavens and all that is in the earth glorifies Allah, and He is the Mighty, the Wise.

2. O you who believe! Why say you that which you do not?

3. It is most hateful in the sight of Allah that you say that which you do not.

4. Allah loves those who battle for His cause in ranks, as if they were a solid structure.

5. And (remember) when Moses said to his people: O my people! Why do you persecute me, when you well know that I am Allah's messenger to you? So when they went astray Allah sent their hearts astray. And Allah guides not the evil-living people.

6. And when Jesus son of Mary said: O Children of Israel! I am the messenger of Allah to you, confirming that which was (revealed) before me in the Torah[278] and bringing good tidings of a messenger who comes after me, whose name is the Praised One.[279] Yet when he has come to them with clear proofs, they say: This is mere magic.

7. And who does greater wrong than he who invents a lie against Allah when

he is summoned to *Al-Islam?*[280] And Allah guides not wrongdoing people.

8. They would like to put out the light of Allah with their mouths, but Allah will perfect His light however much the disbelievers are averse.

9. He it is Who has sent His messenger with the Guidance and the religion of truth, that He may make it conqueror of all religion however much idolaters may be averse.

10. O you who believe! Shall I show you a commerce that will save you from a painful doom?

11. You should believe in Allah and His messenger, and should strive for the cause of Allah with your wealth and your lives. That is better for you, if you only knew.

12. He will forgive you your sins and bring you into Gardens underneath which rivers flow, and pleasant dwellings in Gardens of Eden. That is the supreme triumph.

13. And (He will give you) another blessing which you love: help from Allah and present victory. Give good tidings (O Muhammad) to believers.

14. O you who believe! Be Allah's helpers, even as Jesus son of Mary said to the disciples: Who are my helpers for Allah? They said: We are Allah's helpers. And a party of the Children of Israel believed, while a party disbelieved. Then We strengthened those who believed against their enemy, and they became the uppermost.

---

278. Books of Moses.

279. Arabic: *Ahmad.* A name of the Prophet of Arabia. The promised "Comforter" was believed by many Christian communities of the East to be a prophet yet to come, and most of them accepted Muhammad as that prophet.

280. *Lit.* "The Surrender".

Surah 62: *Al-Jummu'ah*
(The Congregation)

Al-Jummu'ah, "The Congregation" takes its name from a word in v. 9, where obedience to the call to congregational prayer is enjoined. Tradition says that vv. 9-11 refer to an occasion when a caravan entered Al-Madinah with the beating of drums at the time when the Prophet was preaching in the mosque, and the congregation broke away to look at it except twelve men. If, as one version of the tradition says, the caravan was that of Dahya al-Kalbi, the incident must have occurred before the fifth year A.H. The date of revelation is between the years 2 and 4 A.H.

In the name of Allah,
the Beneficent, the Merciful.

1. All that is in the heavens and all that is in the earth glorifies Allah, the Sovereign Lord, the Holy One, the Mighty, the Wise.

2. He it is Who has sent among the unlettered ones a messenger of their own, to recite to them His revelations and to make them grow, and to teach them the Scripture and wisdom, though before that they were indeed in manifest error,

3. Along with others of them who have not yet joined them. He is the Mighty, the Wise.

4. That is the bounty of Allah; which He gives to whom He will. Allah is of Infinite Bounty.

5. The likeness of those who are entrusted with the Law of Moses, yet apply it not, is as the likeness of the donkey carrying books. Wretched is the likeness of people who deny the revelations of Allah. And Allah guides not wrongdoing people.

6. Say (O Muhammad): O you who are Jews! If you claim that you are favoured by Allah apart from (all) mankind, then long for death if you are truthful.

7. But they will never long for it because of all that their own hands have sent before, and Allah is Aware of evildoers.

8. Say (to them, O Muhammad): The death from which you shrink will surely meet you, and afterwards you will be returned to the Knower of the Invisible and the Visible, and He will tell you what you used to do.

9. O you who believe! When the call is heard for the prayer on the day of congregation, hasten to remembrance of Allah and leave your trading. That is better for you if you only knew.

10. And when the prayer is ended, then disperse in the land and seek of Allah's bounty, and remember Allah much, so that you may be successful.

11. But when they spy some merchandise or pastime they break away to it and leave you standing. Say: That which Allah has is better than pastime and than merchandise, and Allah is the best of providers.

Surah 63: *Al-Munafiqun*
(The Hypocrites)

Al-Munafiqun, " The Hypocrites" takes its name from a word occurring in the first verse. V. 8 refers to a remark by Abdullah Ibn Ubeyy, the "Hypocrite" leader, expressing the desire that the old aristocracy of Yathrib, of which he had been the acknowledged chief, might regain the ascendancy and turn out the refugees from Makkah, whom he regarded as intruders.

The date of the revelation is the fourth year of Hijrah.

In the name of Allah,
the Beneficent, the Merciful.

1. When the hypocrites come to you (O Muhammad), they say: We bear witness that you are indeed Allah's messenger. And Allah knows that you are indeed His messenger, and Allah bears witness that the hypocrites indeed are speaking falsely.

2. They make their faith a pretext so that they may turn (men) from the way of Allah. Verily evil is that which they used to do,

3. That is because they believed, then disbelieved, therefore their hearts are sealed so that they do not understand.

4. And when you see them, their appearance pleases, you; and if they speak you give ear to their speech. (They are) as though they were blocks of wood in striped cloaks.[281] They consider every shout to be against

281. Or propped up blocks of wood.

them. They are the enemy, so beware of them. Allah damn them! How they are perverted!

5. And when it is said to them: Come! The messenger of Allah will ask forgiveness for you! they avert their faces and you see them turning away, disdainful.

6. Whether you ask forgiveness for them or ask not forgiveness for them is all one for them; Allah will not forgive them. Allah guides not the evil-living people.

7. They it is who say: Spend not on behalf of those (who dwell) with Allah's messenger that they may disperse (and go away from you); when Allah's are the treasures of the heavens and the earth; but the hypocrites comprehend not.

8. They say: Surely, if we return to Al-Madinah the mightier will soon drive out the weaker; when might belongs to Allah and to His messenger and to the believers; but the hypocrites know not.

9. O you who believe! Let not your wealth nor your children distract you from remembrance of Allah. Those who do so, they are the losers.

10. And spend of that with which We have provided you before death comes to one of you and he says: My Lord! If only you would reprieve me for a little while, then I would give alms and be among the righteous.

11. But Allah reprieves no soul when its term comes, and Allah is Informed of what you do.

Surah 64: ***At-Taghabun***
(Mutual Disillusion)

At-Taghabun, "Mutual Disillusion" takes its name from a word in v. 9.

The date of revelation is possibly year 1 A.H., though it is generally regarded as a late Makkan Surah, vv. 14 ff. being taken as referring to the pressure being brought to bear by wives and families to prevent Muslims leaving Makkah at the time of Hijrah.

In the name of Allah,
the Beneficent, the Merciful.

1. All that is in the heavens and all that is in the earth glorifies Allah; to Him belongs Sovereignty and to Him belongs praise, and He is Able to do all things.

2. He it is Who created you, but one of you is a disbeliever and one of you is a believer, and Allah is Seer of what you do.

3. He created the heavens and the earth with truth, and He shaped you and made good your shapes, and to Him is the journeying.

4. He knows all that is in the heavens and the earth, and He knows what you conceal and what you publish. And Allah is Aware of what is in the hearts (of men).

5. Has not the story reached you of those who disbelieved before and so did taste the ill-effects of their conduct, and theirs will be a painful doom.

6. That was because their messengers (from Allah) kept coming to them with clear proofs (of Allah's Sovereignty), but

they said: Shall mere mortals guide us? So they disbelieved and turned away, and Allah was independent (of them). Allah is Absolute, Owner of Praise.

7. Those who disbelieve assert that they will not be raised again. Say (to them, O Muhammad): Yes, verily, by my Lord! you will be raised again and then you will be informed of what you did; and that is easy for Allah.

8. So believe in Allah and His messenger and the Light which We have revealed. And Allah is Informed of what you do.

9. The day when He shall gather you to the Day of Assembling, that will be a day of mutual disillusion. And whoever believes in Allah and does right, He will remit from him his evil deeds and will bring him to Gardens underneath which rivers flow, in it to remain forever. That is the supreme triumph.

10. But those who disbelieve and deny Our revelations, such are owners of the Fire; they will remain in it - an unhappy journey's end!

11. No calamity befalls except by Allah's permission. And whoever believes in Allah, He guides his heart. And Allah is Knower of all things.

12. Obey Allah and obey His messenger; but if you turn away, then the duty of Our messenger is only to convey (the message) plainly.

13. Allah! There is no God except Him. In Allah, therefore, let believers put their trust.

14. O you who believe! Among your wives and your children there are enemies for you, therefore beware of them. And if you let be and overlook and forgive, then Allah is Forgiving, Merciful.

15. Your wealth and your children are only a temptation, whereas Allah! with Him is an immense reward.

16. So keep your duty to Allah as best you can, and listen, and obey, and spend; that is better for your souls. And whoso is saved from his own greed, such are the successful.

17. If you lend to Allah a goodly loan,[282] He will double it for you and will forgive you, for Allah is Responsive, Clement,

18. Knower of the Invisible and the Visible, the Mighty, the Wise.

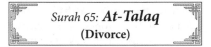

Surah 65: *At-Talaq*
(Divorce)

At-Talaq, "Divorce," is so called from vv. 1-7, which contains an amendment to the laws of divorce which are set forth in Surah 2, Al-Baqarah. This is generally referred traditionally to a mistake made by Ibn Umar in divorcing his wife, which is said to have happened in the sixth year of the Hijrah. But others relate that the Prophet on that occasion only quoted this verse which had already been revealed.

The date of revelation is the sixth year of the Hijrah or a little earlier.

===

In the name of Allah,
the Beneficent, the Merciful.

1. O Prophet! When you (men) divorce women, divorce them for

---

282. *i.e.* a loan without interest or any thought of gain or loss.

their (legal) period and reckon the period, and keep your duty to Allah, your Lord. Expel them not from their houses nor let them go out unless they commit open immorality. Such are the limits (imposed by) Allah; and whoever transgresses Allah's limits, he verily wrongs his soul. You know not: it may be that Allah will afterwards bring some new thing to pass.

2. Then when they have reached their term, take them back in kindness or part from them in kindness, and call to witness two just men among you, and keep your testimony upright for Allah. Whoever believes in Allah and the Last Day is exhorted to act thus. And whoever keeps his duty to Allah, Allah will appoint a way out for him,

3. And will provide for him from (a quarter) from where he has no expectation. And whoever puts his trust in Allah, He will suffice him. Allah brings His command to pass. Allah has set a measure for all things.

4. And for such of your women as despair of menstruation, if you are in doubt, their period (of waiting) shall be three months, along with those who have it not. And for those with child, their period shall be till they bring out their burden. And whoever keeps his duty to Allah, He makes his course easy for him.

5. That is the commandment of Allah which He reveals to you. And whoever keeps his duty to Allah, He will remit from him his evil deeds and magnify his reward for him.

6. Lodge them where you dwell, according to your wealth, and harass them not so as to narrow life for them. And if they are with child, then spend for them till they bring out their burden. Then, if they suckle for you, give them their due payment and consult together in kindness; but if you make difficulties for one another, then let some other woman suckle for him (the father of the child).

7. Let him who has abundance spend of his abundance, and he whose provision is measured, let him spend of that which Allah has given him. Allah asks nothing of any soul except that which He has given it. Allah will grant, after hardship, ease.

8. And how many a community revolted against the ordinance of its Lord and His messengers, and We called it to a stern account and punished it with dire punishment,

9. So that it tasted the ill-effects of its conduct, and the consequence of its conduct was loss.

10. Allah has prepared for them stern punishment; so keep your duty to Allah, O men of understanding! O you who believe! Now Allah has sent down to you a Reminder,

11. A messenger reciting to you the revelations of Allah made plain, that He may bring out those who believe and do good works from darkness to light. And whoever believes in Allah and does right, He will bring him into Gardens underneath which rivers flow, in it to remain forever. Allah has made good provision for him.

12. Allah it is Who has created seven heavens, and of the earth the like of it. The commandment comes down among them slowly, that you may know that Allah is Able to do all things, and that Allah surrounds all things in knowledge.

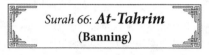

Surah 66: *At-Tahrim*
(Banning)

At-Tahrim, "Banning," takes its name from a word in v. 1.

There are three traditions as to the occasion of vv. 1-4:

(1) The Prophet was very fond of honey. One of his wives received a present of honey from a relative and by its means persuaded the Prophet into staying with her longer than was customary. The others felt aggrieved, and 'Ayeshah devised a little plot. Knowing the Prophet's horror of unpleasant smells, she arranged with two other wives that they should hold their noses when he came to them after eating the honey, and accuse him of having eaten the produce of a very rank-smelling tree. When they accused him of having eaten *Maghafir* the Prophet said that he had only eaten honey. They said : "The bees had fed on *Maghafir*." The Prophet was dismayed and vowed to eat no more honey.

(2) Hafsah found the Prophet in her room with Marya - the Coptic girl, presented to him by the ruler of Egypt, who became the mother of his only male child, Ibrahim - on a day which custom had assigned to 'Ayeshah. Moved by Hafsah's distress,

the Prophet vowed that he would have no more to do with Marya, and asked her not to tell 'Ayeshah. But Hafsah's distress had been largely feigned. No sooner had the Prophet gone than she told Ayeshah with glee how easily she had got rid of Marya.

(3) Before *Al-Islam* women had had no standing in Arabia. The Qur'an gave them legal rights and an assured position, which some of them were inclined to exaggerate. The Prophet was extremely kind to his wives. One day Omar had to rebuke his wife for replying to him in a tone which he considered disrespectful. She assured him it was the tone in which his own daughter Hafsah, 'Ayeshah and others of the Prophet's wives answered the Prophet. Omar went at once and remonstrated with Hafsah and with another of the Prophet's wives to whom he was related.

He was told to mind his own business which increased his horror and dismay. Soon afterwards the Prophet separated from his wives for a time, and it was thought that he was going to divorce them. Then Omar ventured to tell the story of his own vain effort to reform them, at which the Prophet laughed heartily.

Traditions (1) and (3) are better authenticated and are alone adduced by the great traditionalists. But the commentators generally prefer (2) as more explanatory of the text. All allude to a tendency on the part of some of the wives of the Prophet to presume on their new status and the

Prophet's well-known kindness - a tendency so marked that, if allowed to continue, it would have been a bad example to the whole community. The Qur'an first rebukes the Prophet for yielding to their desires to the extent of undertaking to forego a thing which Allah had made lawful for him - in the case of (2), fulfilment of his vow involved a wrong to Marya - and then reproves the women for their double-dealing and intrigue.

The above traditions have been made by some non-Muslim writers the text for strictures which appear irrelevant because their ideology is altogether un-Islamic. The Prophet has never been regarded by Muslims as other than a human messenger of God; sanctity has never been identified with celibacy. For Christendom the strictest religious idea has been celibacy, monogamy is already a concession to human nature. For Muslims, monogamy is the ideal, polygamy the concession to human nature. Polygamy is the nature of some men in all countries, and of all men in some countries. Having set a great example of monogamous marriage, the Prophet was to set a great example of polygamous marriage, by following which men of that temperament could live righteous lives. He encountered all the difficulties inherent in the situation, and when he made mistakes the Qur'an helped him to retrieve them. *Al-Islam* did not institute polygamy. It restricted an existing institution by limiting the number of a man's legal wives, by giving every woman a legal personality and legal rights which had to be respected, and making every man responsible for his conduct towards every woman. Whether monogamy or polygamy should prevail in a particular country or period is a matter of social and economic convenience. The Prophet himself was permitted to have more wives than were allowed to others because, as head of the State, he was responsible for the support of women who had no other protector. With the one exception of 'Ayeshah, all his wives had been widows.

───────────────

In the name of Allah,
the Beneficent, the Merciful.

1. O Prophet! Why prohibit you that which Allah has made lawful for you, seeking to please your wives? And Allah is Forgiving, Merciful.

2. Allah has made lawful for you (Muslims) absolution from your oaths (of such a kind), and Allah is your Protector. He is the Knower, the Wise.

3. When the Prophet confided a fact to one of his wives and when she afterwards divulged it and Allah informed him of it, he made known (to her) part of it and passed over part. And when he told it her she said: Who has told you? He said: The Knower, the Aware has told me.

4. If you both turn to Allah repentant, (you have cause to do so) for your hearts desired (the ban); and if you aid one another against him (Muhammad) then Allah, even He, is his Protecting Friend, and Gabriel and the righteous among the believers; and furthermore the angels are his helpers.

5. It may happen that his Lord, if he divorce you, will give him in your stead wives better than you, submissive (to Allah), believing, pious, penitent, devout, inclined to fasting, widows and maids.

6. O you who believe! Ward off from yourselves and your families a Fire of which the fuel is men and stones, over which are set angels strong, severe, who resist not Allah in that which He commands them, but do that which they are commanded.

7. (Then it will be said): O you who disbelieve! Make no excuses for yourselves this day. You are only being paid for what you used to do.

8. O You who believe! Turn to Allah in sincere repentance! It may be that your Lord will remit from you your evil deeds and bring you into Gardens underneath which rivers flow, on the day when Allah will not humiliate the Prophet and those who believe with him. Their light will run before them and on their right hands; they will say: Our Lord! Perfect our light for us, and forgive us! You are Able to do all things.

9. O Prophet! Strive against the disbelievers and the hypocrites, and be stern with them. Hell will be their home, an unhappy journey's end.

10. Allah cites an example for those who disbelieve: the wife of Noah and the wife of Lot, who were under two of Our righteous slaves yet betrayed them so that they (the husbands) benefitted them nothing against Allah and it was said (to them): Enter the Fire along with those who enter.

11. And Allah cites an example for those who believe: the wife of Pharaoh when she said: My Lord! Build for me a home with you in the Garden, and deliver me from Pharaoh and his work, and deliver me from evil-doing people;

12. And Mary, daughter of 'Imran, whose body was chaste, therefore We breathed in it something of Our Spirit. And she put faith in the words of her Lord and His Scriptures, and was of the obedient.

Surah 67: *Al-Mulk*
(The Sovereignty)

Al-Mulk takes its name from a word in the first verse. It belongs to the middle group of Makkan Surahs.

In the name of Allah, the Beneficent, the Merciful.

1. Blessed is He in Whose hand is the Sovereignty, and He is Able to do all things.

2. Who has created life and death that He may try you which of you is best in conduct; and He is the Mighty, the Forgiving,

3. Who has created seven heavens in harmony. You (Muhammad) can see no fault in the Beneficent One's creation; then look again: Can you see any rifts?

4. Then look again and yet again, your sight will return to you weakened and made dim.

5. And verily We have beautified the world's heaven with lamps, and We have made them missiles for

the devils,[283] and for them We have prepared the doom of flame.

6. And for those who disbelieve in their Lord there is the doom of Hell, an unhappy journey's end!

7. When they are flung in it they hear its roaring as it boils up,

8. As if it would burst with rage. Whenever a (fresh) group is flung in it the guardians of it ask them: Came there to you no warner?

9. They say: Yes, verily, a warner came to us; but we denied and said: Allah has revealed nothing; you are in nothing but a great error.

10. And they say: Had we listened or had sense, we would not have been among the dwellers in the flames.

11. So they acknowledge their sins; but far removed (from mercy) are the dwellers in the flames.

12. Those who fear their Lord in secret, theirs will be forgiveness and a great reward.

13. And keep your opinion secret or proclaim it, He is Knower of all that is in the hearts (of men).

14. Should He not know what He created? And He is the Subtle, the Aware.

15. He it is Who has made the earth subservient to you, so walk in the paths of it and eat of His provision And to Him will be the resurrection (of the dead).

---

283. On the authority of a tradition going back to Ibn' Abbas, the allusion is to the soothsayers and astrologers who saw the source of good and evil in the stars. See *Surah 72, Al-Jinn*, v. 9, footnote.

16. Have you taken security from Him Who is in the heaven that He will not cause the earth to swallow you when it is convulsed?

17. Or have you taken security from Him Who is in the heaven that He will not let loose on you a hurricane? But you shall know the manner of My warning.

18. And verily those before them denied, then (see) the manner of My wrath (with them)!

19. Have they not seen the birds above them spreading out their wings and closing them? Nothing upholds them except the Beneficent. He is Seer of all things.

20. Or who is he that will be an army to you to help you instead of the Beneficent? The disbelievers are in nothing but illusion.

21. Or who is he who will provide for you if He should withhold His provision? No, but they are set in pride and rebellion.

22. Is he who goes groping on his face more rightly guided, or he who walks upright on a straight road?

23. Say (to them, O Muhammad): He it is Who gave you being, and has assigned to you ears and eyes and hearts. Small thanks you give!

24. Say: He it is Who multiplies you in the earth, and to Whom you will be gathered.

25. And they say: When (will) this promise (be fulfilled), if you are truthful?

26. Say: The knowledge is with Allah only, and I am but a plain warner;

27. But when they see it near, the faces of those who disbelieve will be awry, and it will be said (to them): This is that for which you used to call.

28. Say (O Muhammad): Have you thought: Whether Allah causes me (Muhammad) and those with me to perish or has mercy on us, still, who will protect the disbelievers from a painful doom?

29. Say: He is the Beneficent. In Him we believe and in Him we put our trust. And you will soon know who it is who is in manifest error.

30. Say: Have you thought: If (all) your water were to disappear into the earth, who then could bring you gushing water?

Surah 68: **Al-Qalam**
(The Pen)

Al-Qalam, "The Pen," takes its name from a word in the first verse. A very early Makkan Surah.

In the name of Allah, the Beneficent, the Merciful.

1. *Nun.*[284] By the pen and that which they write (with it),

2. You are not, for your Lord's favour to you, a madman.

3. And yours verily will be a reward unfailing.

4. And you are of a tremendous nature.

5. And you will see and they will see

---

284. See *Surah 2, Al-Baqarah*, v. 1, footnote.

6. Which of you is the demented.

7. Your Lord is Best Aware of him who strays from His Way, and He is Best Aware of those who walk aright.

8. Therefore obey not you the rejecters

9. Who would have had you compromise, that they may compromise.

10. And do not obey each feeble oath-monger,

11. Detractor, spreader abroad of slanders,

12. Hinderer of the good, transgressor, malefactor

13. Greedy with it all, intrusive.

14. It is because he is possessed of wealth and children

15. That, when Our revelations are recited to him, he says: Mere fables of the men of old.

16. We shall brand him on the nose.

17. We have tried them as We tried the owners of the garden when they vowed that they would pluck its fruit next morning,

18. And made no exception (for the Will of Allah);[285]

19. Then a visitation from your Lord came upon it while they slept

20. And in the morning it was as if plucked.

21. And they called out one to another in the morning,

22. Saying: Run to your field if you would pluck (the fruit).

23. So they went off, saying one to another in low tones:

24. No needy man shall enter it to-day against you.[286]

25. They went early, strong in (this) purpose.

26. But when they saw it, they said: We are in error!

27. No, but we are desolate!

28. The best among them said: Did I not say to you: Why do you not glorify (Allah)?

29. They said: Glorified be our Lord! We have been wrongdoers.

30. Then some of them drew near to others, self-reproaching.

31. They said: Alas for us! In truth we were outrageous.

32. It may be that our Lord will give us better than this in place of it. We beseech our Lord.

33. Such was the punishment. And verily the punishment of the Hereafter is greater if they only knew.

34. For those who keep from evil are gardens of bliss with their Lord.

35. Shall We then treat those who have surrendered[287] as We treat the guilty?

36. What is the matter with you? How foolishly you judge!

37. Or have you a Scripture in which you learn

38. That you will indeed have all that you choose?

39. Or have you a covenant on oath from Us that reaches to the Day of Judgement, that yours will be all that you ordain?

---

285. *i.e.* they forgot to say: "If God wills."

286. It was a custom throughout the East to allow the poor a gleaning of all harvests.
287. Arabic: *Muslimin.*

40. Ask them (O Muhammad) which of them will vouch for that!

41. Or have they other gods? Then let them bring their other gods if they are truthful

42. On the day when it befalls in earnest, and they are ordered to prostrate themselves but are not able,

43. With eyes downcast, abasement stupefying them. And they had been summoned to prostrate themselves while they were yet unhurt.

44. Leave Me (to deal) with those who give the lie to this pronouncement. We shall lead them on by steps from where they know not.

45. Yet I bear with them, for My scheme is firm.

46. Or do you (Muhammad) ask a fee from them so that they are heavily taxed?

47. Or is the Unseen theirs that they can write (of it)?

48. But wait for your Lord's decree, and be not like him of the fish,[288] who cried out in despair.

49. Had it not been that favour from his Lord had reached him he surely had been cast into the wilderness while he was reprobate.

50. But his Lord chose him and placed him among the righteous.

51. And those who disbelieve would like to disconcert you with their eyes when they hear the Reminder, and they say: He is indeed mad;

52. When it is nothing else than a Reminder to creation.

288. *i.e.* Jonah

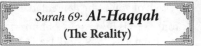

Surah 69: **Al-Haqqah**
(The Reality)

Al-Haqqah takes its name from a word recurring in the first three verses.

It belongs to the middle group of Makkan Surahs.

In the name of Allah,
the Beneficent, the Merciful.

1. The Reality!

2. What is the Reality?

3. Ah, what will convey to you what the reality is!

4. (The tribes of) Thamud and 'Aad disbelieved in the judgement to come.

5. As for Thamud, they were destroyed by the lightning.

6. And as for 'Aad, they were destroyed by a fierce roaring wind,

7. Which He imposed on them for seven long nights and eight long days so that you might have seen men lying overthrown, as if they were hollow trunks of palm trees

8. Can you (O Muhammad) see any remnant of them?

9. And Pharaoh and those before him, and the communities that were destroyed, brought error,

10. And they disobeyed the messenger of their Lord, therefore He gripped them with a tightening grip.

11. When the waters rose, We carried you upon the ship,

12. That We might make it a memorial for you, and that remembering ears (that heard the story) might remember.

13. And when the trumpet shall sound one blast,

14. And the earth with the mountains will be lifted up and crushed with one crash,

15. Then, on that day will the Event befall.

16. And the heaven will split apart, for that day it will be frail.

17. And the angels will be on the sides of it, and eight will uphold the Throne of your Lord that day, above them.

18. On that day you will be exposed; not a secret of yours will be hidden.

19. Then, as for him who is given his record in his right hand, he will say: Take, read my book!

20. Surely I knew that I should have to meet my reckoning.

21. Then he will be in a blissful state,

22. In a high garden,

23. Of which the clusters are in easy reach.

24. (And it will be said to those in it): Eat and drink at ease for that which you sent on before you in past days.

25. But as for him who is given his record in his left hand, he will say: Oh, would that I had not been given my book

26. And knew not what my reckoning was!

27. Oh, would that it had been death!

28. My wealth has not benefitted me,

29. My power has gone from me.

30. (It will be said): Take him and fetter him,

31. And then expose him to Hell-fire,

32. And then insert him in a chain of which the length is seventy cubits.

33. He did not believe in Allah the Tremendous,

34. And did not urge on the feeding of the wretched,

35. Therefore he has no lover here this day,

36. Nor any food except filth

37. Which none but sinners eat.

38. But no! I swear by all that you see,

39. And all that you see not,

40. That it is indeed the speech of an illustrious messenger.

41. It is not poet's speech - little is it that you believe!

42. Nor diviner's speech - little is it that you remember!

43. It is a revelation from the Lord of the Worlds.

44. And if he had invented false sayings concerning Us,

45. We assuredly would have taken him by the right hand,

46. And then severed his life-artery,

47. And not one of you could have held Us off from him.

48. And it is an authority to those who ward off (evil).

49. And We know that some among you will deny (it).

50. And it is indeed an anguish for the disbelievers.

51. And it is absolute truth.

52. So glorify the name of your Tremendous Lord.

Surah 70: *Al-Ma'arij*
(The Ascending Stairways)

Al-Ma'arij takes its name from a word in v. 3. An early Makkan Surah.

In the name of Allah,
the Beneficent, the Merciful.

1. A questioner questioned concerning the doom about to fall,

2. Upon the disbelievers, which no one can repel,

3. From Allah, Lord of the Ascending Stairways,

4. (By which) the angels and the Spirit ascend to Him in a Day of which the span is fifty thousand years.

5. But be patient (O Muhammad) with a patience fair to see.

6. They see it afar off

7. While we see it near:

8. The day when the sky will become as molten copper,

9. And the hills become as flakes of wool,

10. And no familiar friend will ask a question of his friend,

11. Though they will be given sight of them. The guilty man will long to be able to ransom himself from the punishment of that day at the price of his children,

12. And his spouse and his brother,

13. And his relative who protected him,

14. And all that is in the earth, if then it might deliver him.

15. But no! For it is the fire of Hell

16. Eager to roast;

17. It calls him who turned and fled (from truth),

18. And hoarded (wealth) and withheld it.

19. Man was created anxious,

20. Anxious when evil befalls him

21. And, when good befalls him, withholding;

22. Except worshippers.

23. Who are constant at their worship

24. And in whose wealth there is a right acknowledged

25. For the beggar and the destitute;

26. And those who believe in the Day of Judgement,

27. And those who are fearful of their Lord's doom -

28. The doom of their Lord is that before which no one can feel secure -

29. And those who preserve their chastity,

30. Except with their wives and those whom their right hands possess, for thus they are not blameworthy;

31. But whoever seeks more than that, those are they who are transgressors;

32. And those who keep their pledges and their covenant,

33. And those who stand by their testimony,

34. And those who are attentive at their worship.

35. These will dwell in Gardens, honoured.

36. What is the matter with those who disbelieve, that they keep staring towards you (O Muhammad), open-eyed,

37. On the right and on the left, in groups?

38. Does every man among them hope to enter the Garden of Delight?

39. No, verily. We created them from what they know.

40. But no! I swear by the Lord of the rising-places and the setting-places of the planets that We verily are Able

41. To replace them by (others) better than them. And We are not to be outrun.

42. So let them chat and play until they meet their Day which they are promised,

43. The day when they come out from the graves in haste, as if racing to a goal,

44. With eyes aghast, disgrace stunning them: Such is the Day which they are promised.

Surah 71: **Nuh**
(Noah)

Nuh takes its name from its subject, which is the preaching of the Prophet Noah. An early Makkan Surah.

====

In the name of Allah,
the Beneficent, the Merciful.

1. We sent Noah to his people (saying): Warn your people before the painful doom comes to them.

2. He said: O my people! I am a plain warner to you,

3. (Asking you): Serve Allah and keep your duty to Him and obey me,

4. That He may forgive you somewhat of your sins, and give you respite to

an appointed term. The term of Allah, when it comes, cannot be delayed, if you only knew.

5. He said: My Lord! I have called to my people night and day,

6. But all my calling only adds to their aversion;

7. And whenever I call to them that You may pardon them, they thrust their fingers in their ears and cover themselves with their garments and persist (in their refusal) and magnify themselves in pride.

8. And I have called to them aloud,

9. And I have made public proclamation to them, and I have appealed to them in private.

10. And I have said: Seek pardon of your Lord. He is always Forgiving.

11. He will let loose the sky for you in plenteous rain,

12. And will help you with wealth and sons, and will assign to you Gardens and will assign to you rivers.

13. What is the matter with you that you hope not towards Allah for dignity

14. When He created you by (diverse) stages?

15. Do you not see how Allah has created seven heavens in harmony,

16. And has made the moon a light in it, and made the sun a lamp?

17. And Allah has caused you to grow as a growth from the earth,

18. And afterwards He makes you return to it, and He will bring you out again, a (new) creation.

19. And Allah has made the earth a wide expanse for you

20. That you may thread the valley-ways of it.

21. Noah said: My Lord! They have disobeyed me and followed one whose wealth and children increase him in nothing except ruin;

22. And they have plotted a mighty plot,

23. And they have said: Forsake not your gods. Forsake not Wadd, nor Suwa', nor Yaghuth and Ya'uq and Nasr.[289]

24. And they have led many astray, and You increase the wrongdoers in nothing except error.

25. Because of their sins they were drowned, then made to enter a Fire. And they found they had no helpers in place of Allah.

26. And Noah said: My Lord! Leave not one of the disbelievers in the land.

27. If You should leave them, they will mislead Your slaves and will beget none except lewd ingrates.

28. My Lord! Forgive me and my parents and him who enters my house believing, and believing men and believing women, and increase not the wrongdoers in anything save ruin.

Surah 72: *Al-Jinn*

Al-Jinn takes its name from a word in the first verse, and also from the subject of verses 1-18. The meaning of the word jinn in the Qur'an has exercised the minds of Muslim commentators,

289. Idols of the pagan Arabs.

ancient and modern. Mr. Ya'qub Hasan of Madras, in the first volume of a remarkable work in Urdu, Kitabu'l-Huda, shows that it has at least three meanings in the Qur'an and that one of those meanings is something akin to "clever foreigners" as in the case of the jinn who worked for Solomon. But undoubtedly the first and obvious meaning is "elemental spirits," to whom, as to mankind, the Qur'an came as a guidance. The incident is said to have occurred during the Prophet's return from his unsuccessful missionary journey to Ta'if.

A late Makkan Surah.

======

In the name of Allah, the Beneficent, the Merciful.

1. Say (O Muhammad): It is revealed to me that a company of the Jinn gave ear, and they said: We have heard a marvellous Qur'an,

2. Which guides to righteousness, so we believe in it and we ascribe no partner to our Lord.

3. And (we believe) that He - exalted be the glory of our Lord! - has taken neither wife nor son,

4. And that the foolish ones among us used to speak concerning Allah an atrocious lie.

5. And we had supposed that humankind and jinn would not speak a lie concerning Allah -

6. And indeed (O Muhammad) individuals of humankind used to invoke the protection of individuals of the jinn, so that they increased them in revolt (against Allah);

7. And indeed they supposed, even as you suppose, that Allah would not raise anyone (from the dead) -

8. And (the Jinn who had listened to the Qur'an said): We had sought the heaven but had found it filled with strong guardians and meteors.

9. And we used to sit on places (high) in it to listen. But he who listens now finds a flame in wait for him;[290]

10. And we know not whether harm is promised to all who are on earth, or whether their Lord intends guidance for them.

11. And among us there are righteous people and among us there are those far from that. We are sects having different rules.

12. And we know that we cannot escape from Allah in the earth, nor can we escape by flight.

13. And when we heard the Guidance, we believed in it, and whoever believes in his Lord, he fears neither loss nor oppression.

14. And there are among us some who have surrendered (to Allah) and there are among us some who are unjust. And whoever has surrendered to Allah, such have taken the right path purposefully.

15. And as for those who are unjust, they are firewood for Hell.

16. If they (the idolaters) tread the Right Path, We shall give them to drink of water in abundance

17. That We may test them by it, and who turns away from the remembrance of his Lord; He will thrust him into ever-growing torment.

18. And the places of worship are only for Allah, so pray not to anyone along with Allah.

19. And when the slave of Allah[291] stood up in prayer to Him, they crowded on him, almost stifling.[292]

20. Say (to them, O Muhammad): I pray to Allah only, and ascribe to Him no partner.

21. Say: I control not hurt nor benefit for you.

22. Say: No-one can protect me from Allah, nor can I find any refuge besides Him

23. (Mine is) only conveyance (of the Truth) from Allah, and His messages; and whoever disobeys Allah and His messenger, his is fire of Hell, in which such dwell forever.

24. Till (the day) when they will see that which they are promised (they may doubt); but then they will know (for certain) who is weaker in allies and less in multitude.

25. Say (O Muhammad, to the disbelievers): I know not whether that

---

290. About the time of the Prophet's mission there were many meteors and other strange appearances in the heavens, which tradition says, frightened the astrologers from the high observatories where they used to watch at night, and threw out all their calculations.

291. *i.e.* the Prophet.

292. Generally taken to be an allusion to the rough treatment which the Prophet received at the hands of the people of Ta'if.

which you are promised is near, or if my Lord has set a distant term for it.

26. (He is) the Knower of the Unseen, and He reveals to no-one His secret,

27. Except to every messenger whom He has chosen, and then He makes a guard to go before him and a guard behind him,

28. That He may know that they have indeed conveyed the messages of their Lord. He surrounds all their doings, and He keeps count of all things.

Surah 73: *Al-Muzzammil*
(The Enshrouded)

Al-Muzzamil takes its title from a word in v. 1. After his first trance and vision, the Prophet went to his wife Khadijah and told her to wrap him up in cloaks, and that was afterwards his habit on such occasions, at any rate, in the early days at Makkah.

A very early Makkan revelation with the exception of the last verse, which all authorities assign to Al-Madinah.

In the name of Allah,
the Beneficent, the Merciful.

1. O you wrapped up in your garment!

2. Keep vigil the night long, except a little -

3. A half of it, or reduce a little of it

4. Or add (a little) to it - and chant the Qur'an in measure,

5. For we shall charge you with a word of weight.

6. The vigil of the night is (a time) when impression is more keen and speech more certain.

7. You have by day a chain of business.

8. So remember the name of your Lord and devote yourself with a complete devotion -

9. Lord of the East and the West; there is no God except Him; so choose Him alone for your defender -

10. And bear with patience what they utter, and part from them with a fair leave-taking.

11. Leave Me to deal with the deniers, lords of ease and comfort (in this life); and respite them a while.

12. With Us are heavy fetters and a raging fire,

13. And food which chokes (the eater), and a painful doom.

14. On the day when the earth and the hills rock, and the hills become a heap of running sand.

15. We have sent to you a messenger as witness against you, even as We sent to Pharaoh a messenger.

16. But Pharaoh rebelled against the messenger, upon which We seized him with no gentle grip.

17. Then how, if you disbelieve, will you protect yourselves upon the day which will turn children grey?

18. The very heaven being then split apart. His promise is to be fulfilled.

19. This is a Reminder. Let him who will, then, choose a way to his Lord.

20. Your Lord knows how you keep vigil sometimes nearly two-thirds of the night, or (sometimes) half or a third of it, as do a party of those with you. Allah measures the night and the day. He knows that you do not count it, and turns to you in mercy. Recite, then, of the Qur'an that which is easy for you. He knows that there are sick folk among you, while others travel in the land in search of Allah's bounty, and others (still) are fighting for the cause of Allah. So recite of it that which is easy (for you), and establish worship and pay the poor-due, and (so) lend to Allah a goodly loan.[293] Whatever good you send before you for your souls, you will find it with Allah, better and greater in recompense. And seek forgiveness of Allah. Allah is Forgiving, Merciful.

Surah 74: *Al-Muddaththir*
(The Cloaked One)

Al-Muddaththir takes its name from a word in v. 1. The Prophet was accustomed to wrap himself in his cloak at the time of his trances. A tradition says that some time - about six months - elapsed between the first revelation (Surah 96, vv.1-5) and the second revelation in this Surah. Then the Prophet suddenly again saw the Angel who had appeared to him on Mt. Hira, and wrapped himself in his cloak, upon which this Surah was revealed to him. Another opinion is that by this Surah the Prophet was ordered to begin the public preaching of *Al-Islam*, his preaching until then having been done privately among

293. *i.e.* a loan without interest or any thought of gain or loss.

his family and intimates. He is said to have begun his public preaching three years after his call.

In either case this is a very early Makkan Surah.

In the name of Allah,
the Beneficent, the Merciful.

1. O you enveloped in your cloak,

2. Arise and warn!

3. Your Lord magnify,

4. Your garment purify,

5. Pollution shun!

6. And show not favour, seeking worldly gain!

7. For the sake of your Lord, be patient!

8. For when the trumpet shall sound,

9. Surely that day will be a day of anguish,

10. Not of ease, for disbelievers.

11. Leave Me (to deal) with him whom I created lonely,

12. And then bestowed upon him ample means,

13. And sons remaining in his presence,

14. And made (life) smooth for him.

15. Yet he desires that I should give more.

16. No! For he has been stubborn to Our revelations.

17. On him I shall impose a fearful doom.

18. For he considered; then he planned -

19. (Self-) destroyed is he, how he planned!

20. Again (self-) destroyed is he, how he planned! -

21. Then he looked,

22. Then he frowned and showed displeasure.

23. Then he turned away in pride

24. And said: This is nothing else than magic from of old;

25. This is nothing else than speech of mortal man.

26. Him shall I fling to the burning.

27. - Ah, what will convey to you what that burning is! -

28. It leaves nothing; it spares nothing

29. It shrivels the man.

30. Above it are nineteen.

31. We have appointed only angels to be guardians of the Fire, and their number We have made to be a stumbling-block for those who disbelieve; that those to whom the Scripture has been given may have certainty, and that believers may increase in faith; and that those to whom the Scripture has been given and believers may not doubt; and that those in whose hearts there is disease, and disbelievers, may say: What does Allah mean by this similitude? Thus Allah sends astray whom He will, and whom He will He guides. None knows the forces of your Lord except Him. This is nothing else than a Reminder to mortals.

32. No, by the Moon,

33. And the night when it withdraws,

34. And the dawn when it shines forth,

35. This is one of the greatest (signs),

36. As a warning to men,

37. To any of you who will advance or hang back.

38. Every soul is a pledge for its own deeds;

39. Except those who will stand on the right hand.

40. In Gardens they will ask one another

41. Concerning the guilty:

42. What has brought you to this burning?

43. They will answer: We were not of those who prayed,

44. Nor did we feed the poor.

45. We used to enter (in vain dispute) with (all) who enter,

46. And we used to deny the Day of Judgement,

47. Till the Inevitable came to us.

48. The mediation of no mediators will benefit them then.

49. Why now do they turn away from the Admonishment,

50. As if they were frightened donkeys

51. Fleeing from a lion?

52. No, but every one of them desires that he should be given open pages (from Allah).

53. No, verily. They fear not the Hereafter.

54. No, surely this is an Admonishment.

55. So whosoever will may heed.

56. And they will not heed unless Allah wills (it). He is the source of fear. He is the source of Mercy.

Surah 75: *Al-Qiyamah*
(The Resurrection)

Al-Qiyamah takes its name from a word in the first verse.

An early Makkan Surah.

In the name of Allah,
the Beneficent, the Merciful.

1. No, I swear by the Day of Resurrection;

2. No, I swear by the accusing soul (that this Scripture is true).

3. Does man think that We shall not assemble his bones?

4. Yes, verily. Yes, We are Able to restore his very fingers!

5. But man would like to deny what is before him.

6. He asks: When will be this Day of Resurrection?

7. But when sight is confused,

8. And the moon is eclipsed,

9. And sun and moon are united,

10. On that day man will call: Where to flee!

11. Alas! No refuge!

12. To your Lord is the recourse that day.

13. On that day man is told the tale of that which he has sent before and left behind.

14. Oh, but man is a telling witness against himself,

15. Although he makes his excuses.

16. Stir not your tongue with it to hasten it.[294]

17. Upon Us (rests) the putting together of it and the reading of it.

18. And when We read it, follow the reading;

19. Then upon Us (rests) the explanation of it.

20. No, but you do love the fleeting now,

21. And neglect the Hereafter.

22. That day will faces be resplendent,

23. Looking towards their Lord;

24. And that day will other faces be despondent,

25. You will know that some great disaster is about to fall on them.

26. No, but when the life comes up to the throat,

27. And men say: Where is the wizard (who can save him now)?

28. And he knows that it is the parting;

29. And agony is heaped on agony;

30. To your Lord that day will be the driving.

31. For he neither trusted, nor prayed.

32. But he denied and showed contempt.

33. Then he went to his folk with glee.

34. Nearer to you and nearer,

35. Again nearer to you and nearer (is the doom).

36. Does man think that he is to be left aimless?

---

294. *i.e.* the Qur'an, which was revealed gradually, piece by piece.

37. Was he not a drop of fluid which gushed forward?

38. Then he became a clot; then (Allah) shaped and fashioned

39. And made of him a pair, the male and female.

40. Is not He (Who does so) Able to bring the dead to life?

Surah 76: *Al-Insan*
(Man)

Al-Insan or *Ad-Dahr* is in either case, so called from a word in the first verse. An early Makkan Surah.

In the name of Allah,
the Beneficent, the Merciful.

1. Has there come upon man (ever) any period of time in which he was a thing unremembered?

2. We create man from a drop of thickened fluid to test him; so We make him hearing, knowing.

3. We have shown him the way, whether he be grateful or disbelieving.

4. We have prepared for disbelievers manacles and iron collars and a raging fire.

5. The righteous will drink of a cup of which the mixture is of water of Kafur,

6. A spring from which the slaves of Allah drink, making it gush forward abundantly,

7. (Because) they perform the vow and fear a day of which the evil is widespread,

8. And feed with food the needy wretch, the orphan and the prisoner, for love of Him,

9. (Saying): We feed you, for the sake of Allah only. We wish for no reward or thanks from you;

10. We fear from our Lord a day of frowning and of fate.

11. Therefore Allah has warded off from them the evil of that day, and has made them find brightness and joy;

12. And has awarded them for all that they endured, a Garden and silk attire;

13. Reclining in it upon couches, they will find there neither (heat of) a sun nor bitter cold.

14. The shade of it is close upon them, and the clustered fruits of it bow down.

15. Goblets of silver are brought round for them, and beakers (as) of glass,

16. (Bright as) glass but (made) of silver, which they (themselves) have measured to the measure (of their deeds).

17. There they are watered with a cup of which the mixture is of *Zanjabil,*

18. The water of a spring in it, named *Salsabil.*

19. There wait on them immortal youths, whom, when you see, you would take them for scattered pearls.

20. When you see, you will see there bliss and high estate.

21. Their garments will be fine green silk and gold embroidery. Bracelets of silver they will wear. Their Lord will quench their thirst with a pure drink.

22. (And it will be said to them): This is a reward for you. Your endeavour (upon earth) has found acceptance.

23. We, even We, have revealed to you the Qur'an, a revelation;

24. So submit patiently to your Lord's command, and obey not of them any guilty one or disbeliever.

25. Remember the name of your Lord in the morning and evening.

26. And worship Him (a portion) of the night. And glorify Him through the long night.

27. These love fleeting life, and put behind them (the remembrance of) a grievous day.

28. We, even We, created them, and strengthened their frame. And when We will, We can replace them, bringing others like them in their stead.

29. This is an Admonishment, that whoever will may choose a way to his Lord.

30. Yet you will not, unless Allah wills. Allah is Knower, Wise.

31. He makes whom He will to enter His mercy, and for evildoers He has prepared a painful doom.

Surah 77: *Al-Mursalat*
(The Emissaries)

Al-Mursalat takes its name from a word in the first verse. Verses 1, 2 and 3 are taken to refer to winds, verses 4 and 5 to angels. An early Makkan Surah.

In the name of Allah,
the Beneficent, the Merciful.

1. By the emissary winds, (sent) one after another,

2. By the raging hurricanes,

3. By those which cause earth's vegetation to revive;

4. By those who winnow with a winnowing,

5. By those who bring down the Reminder,

6. To excuse or to warn,

7. Surely that which you are promised will befall.

8. So when the stars are put out,

9. And when the sky is split apart,

10. And when the mountains are blown away,

11. And when the messengers are brought to their time appointed -

12. For what day is the time appointed?

13. For the Day of Decision.

14. And what will convey to you what the Day of Decision is! -

15. Woe to the repudiators on that day!

16. Did We not destroy the former people,

17. Then caused the latter people to follow after?

18. Thus We deal with the guilty.

19. Woe to the repudiators on that day!

20. Did We not create you from a base fluid,

21. Which We laid up in a safe abode,

22. For a known term?

23. Thus We arranged. How excellent is Our arranging!

24. Woe to the repudiators on that day!

25. Have We not made the earth a receptacle

26. Both for the living and the dead,

27. And placed in it high mountains and given you to drink sweet water in it?

28. Woe to the repudiators on that day!

29. (It will be said to them:) Depart to that (doom) which you used to deny;

30. Depart to the shadow falling threefold.

31. (Which yet is) no relief nor shelter from the flame.

32. It throws up sparks like the castles,

33. (Or) as if camels of bright yellow hue.

34. Woe to the repudiators on that day!

35. This is a day in which they speak not,

36. Nor are they suffered to put forward excuses.

37. Woe to the repudiators on that day!

38. This is the Day of Decision, We have brought you and the men of old together.

39. If now you have any wit, outwit Me.

40. Woe to the repudiators on that day!

41. Those who kept their duty are amid shade and fountains,

42. And fruits such as they desire.

43. (To them it is said:) Eat, drink and welcome, O you blessed, in return for what you did.

44. Thus do We reward the good.

45. Woe to the repudiators on that day!

46. Eat and take your ease (on earth) a little. You are guilty.

47. Woe to the repudiators on that day!

48. When it is said to them: Bow down, they do not bow down!

49. Woe to the repudiators on that day!

50. In what statement, after this, will they believe?

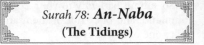

Surah 78: **An-Naba**
(The Tidings)

An-Naba takes its name from a word in the second verse. An early Makkan Surah.

In the name of Allah, the Beneficent, the Merciful.

1. Of what do they question one another?

2. (It is) of the awful tidings,

3. Concerning which they are in disagreement.

4. No, but they will come to know!

5. No, again, but they will come to know!

6. Have We not made the earth an expanse,

7. And the high hills bulwarks?

8. And We have created you in pairs,

9. And have appointed your sleep for rest,

10. And have appointed the night as a cloak,

11. And have appointed the day for livelihood.

12. And We have built above you seven strong (heavens),

13. And have appointed a dazzling lamp,

14. And have sent down from the rainy clouds abundant water,

15. By it to produce grain and plant,

16. And gardens of thick foliage.

17. The Day of Decision is a fixed time,

18. A day when the trumpet is blown and you come in multitudes,

19. And the heaven is opened and becomes as gates,

20. And the hills are set in motion and become as a mirage.

21. Hell lurks in ambush,

22. A home for the rebellious.

23. They will remain in it for ages.

24. In it they taste neither coolness nor (any) drink,

25. Except boiling water and a paralysing cold:

26. Reward proportioned (to their evil deeds).

27. For they looked not for a reckoning;

28. They called Our revelations false with strong denial.

29. Everything We have recorded in a Book.

30. So taste (of that which you have earned). No increase do We give you except of torment.

31. For the dutiful is an achievement -

32. Gardens enclosed and vineyards,

33. And maidens for companions,

34. And a full cup.

35. There they never hear vain discourse, nor lying -

36. Repayment from your Lord - a gift in payment -

37. Lord of the heavens and the earth, and (all) that is between them, the Beneficent; with Whom none can converse.

38. On the day when the angels and the Spirit stand arrayed, they speak not, except he whom the Beneficent allows and who speaks right.

39. That is the True Day. So whoever wills should seek recourse to his Lord.

40. We warn you of a doom at hand, a day on which a man will look on that which his own hands have sent before, and the disbeliever will cry: "Would that I were dust!"

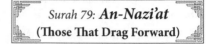

Surah 79: *An-Naziʿat*
(Those That Drag Forward)

An-Naziʿat takes its name from a word in the first verse.

An early Makkan Surah.

In the name of Allah, the Beneficent, the Merciful.

1. By those who drag forward to destruction,

2. By the meteors rushing,

3. By the lone stars floating,[295]

4. By the angels hastening,

5. And those who govern the event,

6. On the day when the first trumpet resounds,

7. And the second follows it,

8. On that day hearts beat painfully,

9. While eyes are downcast,

10. (Now) they are saying: Shall we really be restored to our first state,

11. Even after we are crumbled bones?

12. They say: Then that would be a vain proceeding.

295. Some commentators take vv. 2 and 3 as also referring to angels and explain them thus: " By those who console (the spirits of the righteous) tenderly." "By those who come floating (down from heaven with their Lord's command)." The rendering given in the text above is the more obvious.

13. Surely it will need only one shout,

14. And they will be awakened.

15. Has there come to you the history of Moses?

16. How his Lord called him in the holy vale of Tuwa,

17. (Saying:) Go to Pharaoh - He has rebelled -

18. And say (to him): Have you (will) to grow (in grace)?

19. Then I will guide you to your Lord and you shall fear (Him).

20. And he showed him the tremendous sign.

21. But he denied and disobeyed,

22. Then he turned away in haste,

23. Then he gathered and summoned

24. And proclaimed: "I (Pharaoh) am your Lord the Highest."

25. So Allah seized him (and made him) an example for the after (life) and for the former.

26. In this is indeed a lesson for him who fears.

27. Are you the harder to create, or is the Heaven that He built?

28. He raised the height of it and ordered it;

29. And He made dark the night of it, and He brought out the morning of it.

30. And after that He spread the earth,

31. And produced from it the water of it and the pasture of it,

32. And He made firm the hills,

33. A provision for you and for your cattle.

34. But when the great disaster comes,

35. The day when man will call to mind his (whole) endeavour,

36. And Hell will stand out visible to him who sees,

37. Then, as for him who rebelled

38. And chose the life of the world,

39. Hell will be his home.

40. But as for him who feared to stand before his Lord and restrained his soul from lust,

41. The Garden will be his home.

42. They ask you of the Hour: when will it come to pass?

43. Why (ask they)? What have you to tell of it?

44. To your Lord belongs (knowledge of) the term of it.

45. You are only a warner to him who fears it.

46. On the day when they see it, it will be as if they had only stayed for an evening or the morning of it.

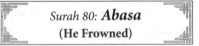

Surah 80: *Abasa*
(He Frowned)

Abasa, "He Frowned," takes its name from the first 2 words. One day when the Prophet was in conversation with one of the great men of Quraysh (his own tribe), seeking to persuade him of the truth of *Al-Islam,* a blind man came and asked him a question concerning the faith. The Prophet was annoyed at the interruption, frowned and turned away from the blind man. In this Surah he is told that a man's importance is not to be judged from his appearance or worldly station.

An early Makkan Surah.

**In the name of Allah,
the Beneficent, the Merciful.**

1. He frowned and turned away

2. Because the blind man came to him.

3. What could inform you but that he might grow (in grace),

4. Or take heed and so the reminder might benefit him?

5. As for him who thinks himself independent,

6. To him you pay regard.

7. Yet it is not your concern if he grows not (in grace).

8. But as for him who comes to you with earnest purpose,

9. And has fear,

10. From him you are distracted.

11. No, but verily it is an Admonishment,

12. So let whoever will pay heed to it,

13. On honoured leaves

14. Exalted, purified,

15. (Set down) by scribes,

16. Noble and righteous.

17. Man is (self-) destroyed: how ungrateful!

18. From what thing does He create him?

19. From a drop of seed. He creates him and proportions him.

20. Then makes the way easy for him.

21. Then causes him to die, and buries him;

22. Then, when He will, He brings him again to life.

23. No, but (man) has not done what He commanded him.

24. Let man consider his food:

25. How We pour water in showers,

26. Then split the earth in clefts

27. And cause the grain to grow in it,

28. And grapes and green fodder,

29. And olive trees and palm-trees,

30. And enclosed gardens of thick foliage,

31. And fruits and grasses:

32. Provision for you and your cattle.

33. But when the Shout comes,

34. On the day when a man flees from his brother,

35. And his mother and his father,

36. And his wife and his children,

37. Every man that day will have concern enough to make him heedless (of others).

38. On that day faces will be bright as dawn,

39. Laughing, rejoicing at good news;

40. And other faces, on that day, with dust upon them,

41. Veiled in darkness,

42. Those are the disbelievers, the wicked.

Surah 81: *At-Takwir*
(The Overthrowing)

At-Takwir takes its name from a word in verse 1. Verses 8 and 9 contain an allusion to the practice of the pagan Arabs of burying alive girl-children whom they deemed superfluous.

An early Makkan Surah.

In the name of Allah,
the Beneficent, the Merciful.

1. When the sun is overthrown,

2. And when the stars fall,

3. And when the hills are moved,

4. And when the camels big with young are abandoned,

5. And when the wild beasts are herded together,

6. And when the seas rise,

7. And when souls are reunited,

8. And when the girl-child who was buried alive is asked

9. For what sin she was slain,

10. And when the pages are laid open,

11. And when the sky is torn away,

12. And when Hell is lighted,

13. And when the Garden is brought near,

14. (Then) every soul will know what it has made ready.

15. Oh, but I call to witness the planets,

16. The stars which rise and set,

17. And the close of night,[296]

18. And the breath of morning[297]

19. That this is in truth the word of an honoured messenger,

20. Mighty, established in the presence of the Lord of the Throne,

21. (One) to be obeyed, and trustworthy;

22. And your comrade is not mad.

23. Surely he saw him on the clear horizon.[298]

---

296. *Lit.* "And the night when it closes."
297. *Lit.* "And the morning when it breathes."
298. The reference is to the Prophet's vision at Mt. Hira.

24. And he is not avid of the Unseen.

25. Nor is this the utterance of a devil worthy to be stoned.

26. Where then do you go?

27. This is nothing else than a reminder to creation,

28. To whomsoever of you wills to walk straight.

29. And you will not, unless (it be) that Allah wills, the Lord of Creation.

Surah 82: *Al-Infitar*
(The Cleaving)

Al-Infitar takes its name from a word in v. 1. An early Makkan Surah.

In the name of Allah,
the Beneficent, the Merciful.

1. When the heaven is cleft asunder,

2. When the planets are dispersed,

3. When the seas are poured out,

4. And the graves are overturned,

5. A soul will know what it has sent before (it) and what it left behind.

6. O man! What has made you careless concerning your Lord, the Bountiful,

7. Who created you, then fashioned, then proportioned you?

8. Into whatsoever form He will, He casts you.

9. No, but you deny the Judgement.

10. There are above you guardians,

11. Generous and recording,

12. Who know (all) that you do.

13. The righteous verily will be in delight.

14. And the wicked verily will be in Hell;

15. They will burn in it on the Day of Judgement,

16. And will not be absent from there.

17. Ah, what will convey to you what the Day of Judgement is!

18. Again, what will convey to you what the Day of Judgement is!

19. A day on which no soul has power at all for any (other) soul. The (absolute) command on that day is Allah's.

Surah 83: *Al-Mutaffiffin* (Defrauding)

Al-Mutaffifin, "Defrauding" takes its name from a word in verse 1.

An early Makkan Surah.

In the name of Allah, the Beneficent, the Merciful.

1. Woe to the defrauders:

2. Those who when they take the measure from mankind demand it in full,

3. But if they measure to them or weigh for them, they cause them loss.

4. Do such (men) not consider that they will be raised again,

5. To an Awful Day,

6. The day when (all) mankind stand before the Lord of the Worlds?

7. No, but the record of the vile is in *Sijjin* -

8. Ah! what will convey to you what *Sijjin* is! -

9. A written record.

10. Woe to the repudiators on that day!

11. Those who deny the Day of Judgement

12. Which none denies except each criminal transgressor,

13. Who, when you read to him Our revelations, says: (Mere) fables of the men of old.

14. No, but that which they have earned is rust upon their hearts.

15. No, but surely on that day they will be covered from (the mercy of) their Lord.

16. Then they verily will burn in Hell,

17. And it will be said (to them): This is that which you used to deny.

18. No, but the record of the righteous is in *'Illiyin* -

19. Ah, what will convey to you what *'Illiyin* is! -

20. A written record,

21. Attested by those who are brought near (to their Lord).

22. The righteous verily are in delight,

23. On couches, gazing,

24. You will know in their faces the radiance of delight.

25. They are given to drink of a pure wine, sealed,

26. Whose seal is musk - for this let (all) those strive who strive for bliss -

27. And mixed with water of Tasnim,

28. A spring from which those brought near (to Allah) drink.

29. The guilty used to laugh at those who believed,

30. And wink one to another when they passed them;

31. And when they returned to their own folk, they returned jesting;

32. And when they saw them they said: These have gone astray.

33. Yet they were not sent as guardians over them.

34. This day it is those who believe who can laugh at the disbelievers,

35. On high couches, gazing.

36. Are not the disbelievers paid for what they used to do?

Surah 84: *Al-Inshiqaq*
(The Splitting)

Al-Inshiqaq, "The Splitting", takes its name from a word in verse 1.

An early Makkan Surah.

═══════════════════

In the name of Allah, the Beneficent, the Merciful.

1. When the heavens is split apart

2. And attentive to her Lord in fear,

3. And when the earth is spread out

4. And has cast out all that was in her, and is empty

5. And attentive to her Lord in fear!

6. You verily, O man, are working towards your Lord a work which you will meet (in His presence).

7. Then who is given his account in his right hand

8. He truly will receive an easy reckoning

9. And will return to his people in joy.

10. But whoever is given his account behind his back,

11. He surely will invoke destruction

12. And be thrown to scorching fire.

13. He verily lived joyously with his people,

14. He verily thought that he would never return (to Allah).

15. No, but his Lord is always watching him!

16. Oh, I swear by the afterglow of sunset,

17. And by the night and all that it enshrouds,

18. And by the moon when she is at the full,

19. That you will journey on from plane to plane.

20. What is the matter with them, then, that they believe not,

21. And, when the Qur'an is recited to them, worship not (Allah)?

22. No, but those who disbelieve will deny;

23. And Allah knows best what they are hiding.

24. So give them tidings of a painful doom,

25. Except those who believe and do good works, for theirs is a reward unfailing.

Surah 85: *Al-Buruj*
(The Mansions of the Stars)

Al-Buruj takes its name from a word in verse 1 which I have translated "mansions of the stars". The word has the meaning of towers or mansions and is applied to the signs of the Zodiac. Verses 4 to 7 are generally taken to refer to the massacre of the

Christians of Najran in Al-Yaman by a Jewish King Dhu Nawas, an event of great historical importance since it caused the intervention of the Negus and led to the Abyssinian supremacy in the Yaman which lasted until the War of the Elephant (Surah 105) in the Prophet's year of birth. Professor Horowitz thinks that the words "owners of the ditch, of the fuel-fed fire" refer not to any historical event but to the condition of all persecutors in the Hereafter.[299]

An early Makkan Surah.

In the name of Allah, the Beneficent, the Merciful.

1. By the heaven, holding mansions of the stars,

2. And by the Promised Day.

3. And by the witness and that to which he bears testimony,

4. (Self-) destroyed were the owners of the ditch,

5. Of the fuel-fed fire,

6. When they sat by it,

7. And were themselves the witnesses of what they did to the believers.[300]

8. They had nothing against them except that they believed in Allah, the Mighty, the Owner of Praise,

9. Him to Whom belongs the Sovereignty of the heavens and the earth; and Allah is of all things the Witness.

299. See "Islamic Culture" (Hyderabad, Deccan), April 1929.
300. Or it might be: "(Self-) destroyed were the owners of the trench of fuel-fed fire (i.e. Hell) when they took their ease on earth and were themselves the witnesses," etc.

10. They who persecute believing men and believing women and repent not, theirs verily will be the doom of Hell, and theirs the doom of burning.

11. Those who believe and do good works, theirs will be Gardens underneath which rivers flow. That is the Great Success.

12. The punishment of your Lord is stern.

13. It is He Who produces, then reproduces,

14. And He is the Forgiving, the Loving,

15. Lord of the Throne of Glory,

16. Doer of what He will.

17. Has there come to you the story of the forces

18. Of Pharaoh and (the tribe of) Thamud?

19. No, but those who disbelieve live in denial,

20. And Allah, all unseen, surrounds them.

21. No, but it is a glorious Qur'an.

22. On a guarded tablet.

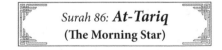

Surah 86: *At-Tariq*
(The Morning Star)

At-Tariq takes the name from a word in verse 1. There are other meanings to the word Tariq, but I have chosen that which must have occurred to every hearer of this Surah, especially in verse 3 it is stated that a star is meant. The Morning Star has here a mystic sense, and is taken to refer to the Prophet himself. Some have thought that it refers to the comet which alarmed the East about the time of the Prophet's call. Others believe that this and other introductory verses, hard to explain, hide scientific facts unimaginable at the period of revelation, and are related to the verses following them. Ghamrawi Bey, my collaborator in the revision of this work, informed me that the late Dr. Sidqi among others considered that the reference there is to the fertilising germ penetrating the ovary, the subject being the same as vv. 5-7.

An early Makkan Surah.

━━━━━━━━━━━━━━━

In the name of Allah, the Beneficent, the Merciful.

1. By the heavens and the Morning Star[301] -

2. Ah, what will tell you what the Morning Star is!

3. The piercing Star!

4. No human soul is without a guardian over it.

5. So let man consider from what he is created.

6. He is created from a gushing fluid

7. That issued from between the loins and the ribs.

8. He verily is Able to return him (to life)

9. On the day when hidden thoughts will be searched out.

10. Then he will have no might nor any helper.

---

301. The Arabic word means originally "that which comes at night" or "one who knocks at the door."

11. By the heavens which produce repeating rainfall,

12. And the earth which splits (with the growth of trees and plants)

13. This (Qur'an) is a conclusive word,

14. It is no pleasantry.

15. They plot a plot (against you, O Muhammad),

16. And I plot a plot (against them).

17. So give respite to the disbelievers. Deal gently with them for a while.

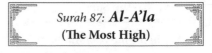

Surah 87: *Al-A'la*
(The Most High)

Al-A'la takes its name from a word in verse 1. An early Makkan Surah.

━━━━━━━━━━━━━━━

In the name of Allah, the Beneficent, the Merciful.

1. Praise the name of your Lord the Most High,

2. Who creates, then disposes;

3. Who measures, then guides;

4. Who brings out the pasturage,

5. Then turns it to brown stubble.

6. We shall make you read (O Muhammad) so that you will not forget,

7. Except that which Allah wills. He knows the disclosed and that which still is hidden;

8. And We shall ease your way to the state of ease.

9. Therefore remind (men), for the reminder is of use.

10. He will heed who fears,

11. But the most unhappy will violate it,

12. He who will be flung to the great Fire

13. In which he will neither die nor live.

14. He is successful who grows,

15. And remembers the name of his Lord, so prays,

16. But you prefer the life of the world

17. Although the Hereafter is better and more lasting.

18. This is in the former scrolls.

19. The Books of Abraham and Moses.

Surah 88: *Al-Ghashiyah*
(The Overwhelming)

Al-Ghashiyah takes its name from a word in verse 1. An early Makkan surah.

In the name of Allah,
the Beneficent, the Merciful.

1. Has there come to you tidings of the Overwhelming?

2. On that day (many) faces will be downcast,

3. Toiling, weary,

4. Scorched by burning Fire,

5. Drinking from a boiling spring,

6. No food for them except bitter thorn-fruit,

7. Which does not nourish or release from hunger.

8. In that day other faces will be calm,

9. Glad for their past effort,

10. In a high Garden,

11. Where they hear no idle speech,

12. In which is a gushing spring,

13. In which are couches raised,

14. And goblets set at hand,

15. And cushions ranged,

16. And silken carpets spread.

17. Will they not regard the camels, how they are created?

18. And the heaven, how it is raised?

19. And the hills, how they are set up?

20. And the earth, how it is spread?

21. Remind them, for you are but an admonisher,

22. You are not at all a guardian over them.

23. But who is averse and disbelieves,

24. Allah will punish him with dire punishment.

25. To Us is their return

26. And Ours their reckoning.

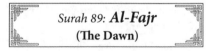

Surah 89: *Al-Fajr*
(The Dawn)

Al-Fajr takes its name from verse 1. A very early Makkan Surah.

In the name of Allah,
the Beneficent, the Merciful.

1. By the Dawn

2. And ten nights,[302]

3. And the Even and the Odd,

4. And the night when it departs,

5. There surely is an oath for thinking man.

---

302. Of the month of Pilgrimage.

6. Do you not consider how your Lord dealt with (the tribe of) 'Aad,

7. With many-columned[303] Iram,

8. The like of which was not created in the lands;

9. And with (the tribe of) Thamud, who clove the rocks in the valley;

10. And with Pharaoh, firm of might,

11. Who (all) were rebellious (to Allah) in these lands,

12. And multiplied iniquity in it?

13. Therefore your Lord poured on them the disaster of His punishment.

14. Your Lord is ever watchful.

15. As for man, whenever his Lord tries him by honouring him, and is gracious to him, he says: My Lord honours me.

16. But whenever He tries him by tightening his means of life, he says: My Lord despises me.

17. No, but you (for your part) honour not the orphan,

18. And do not urge the feeding of the poor,

19. And you devour heritages with devouring greed,

20. And love wealth with abounding love.

---

303. I had written "many-columned," following the run of commentators, who take the word *'imad* to mean columns, pillars, when I happened upon Ibn Khaldun's criticism against that rendering and all the legends to which it has given rise, in the preface to the Prolegomena. The word meant "tent-poles" to the Arabs of the Prophet's day, as Ibn Khaldun points out. In view of recent discoveries in the Yaman, however, I prefer the usual rendering.

21. No, but when the earth is ground to atoms, grinding, grinding,

22. And your Lord shall come with angels, rank on rank,

23. And Hell is brought near that day; on that day man will remember, but how will the remembrance (then benefit him)?

24. He will say: Ah, would that I had sent before me (some provision) for my life!

25. None punishes as He will punish on that day!

26. None binds as He then will bind.

27. But ah! you soul at peace!

28. Return to your Lord, content in His good pleasure!

29. Enter among My bondsmen!

30. Enter My Garden!

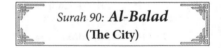

Surah 90: **Al-Balad**
(The City)

Al-Balad takes its name from a word in verse 1. A very early Makkan Surah.

In the name of Allah,
the Beneficent, the Merciful.

1. No, I swear by this city -

2. And you are a dweller of this city[304]

3. And the begetter and that which he begat,

4. We verily have created man in an atmosphere:[305]

5. Thinks he that none has power over him?

---

304. Or "when you have control over this city" (prophetically).
305. Or "in affliction."

6. And he says: I have destroyed vast wealth:

7. Does he think that no-one sees him?

8. Did We not assign to him two eyes

9. And a tongue and two lips,

10. And guide him to the parting of the mountain ways?

11. But he has not attempted the Ascent -

12. Ah, what will convey to you what the Ascent is! -

13. (It is) to free a slave,

14. And to feed in the day of hunger

15. An orphan relative,

16. Or some poor wretch in misery,

17. And to be of those who believe and exhort one another to perseverance, and exhort one another to pity.

18. Their place will be on the right hand.

19. But those who disbelieve Our revelations, their place will be on the left hand.

20. Fire will be an awning over them.

Surah 91: *Ash-Shams*
(The Sun)

Ash-Shams takes its name from a word in the first verse. A very early Makkan Surah.

**In the name of Allah,
the Beneficent, the Merciful.**

1. By the sun and his brightness,

2. And the moon when she follows him,

3. And the day when it reveals him,

4. And the night when it enshrouds him,

5. And the heavens and Him Who built it,

6. And the earth and Him Who spread it,

7. And a soul and Him Who perfected it

8. And inspired it (with conscience of) what is wrong for it and (what is) right for it.

9. He is indeed successful who causes it to grow,

10. And he is indeed a failure who stunts it.

11. (The tribe of) Thamud denied (the truth) in their rebellious pride,

12. When the lowest of them broke out,

13. And the messenger of Allah said: It is the she-camel of Allah, so let her drink!

14. But they denied him, and they hamstrung her, so Allah doomed them for their sin and levelled (their dwellings).

15. He dreads not the sequel (of events).

Surah 92: *Al-Lail*
(The Night)

Al-Lail takes its name from a word in verse 1. A very early Makkan Surah.

**In the name of Allah,
the Beneficent, the Merciful.**

1. By the night enshrouding,

2. And the day resplendent,

3. And Him Who has created male and female,

4. Your effort is dispersed (towards diverse ends).

5. As for him who gives and is dutiful (towards Allah),

6. And believes in goodness;

7. Surely We will ease his way to the state of ease.

8. But as for him who hoards and thinks himself independent,

9. And disbelieves in goodness;

10. Surely We will ease his way to adversity.

11. His riches will not save him when he perishes.

12. Ours it is (to give) the guidance

13. And to Us belong the latter portion and the former.

14. Therefore I have warned you of the flaming Fire,

15. Which only the most wretched must endure,

16. He who denies and turns away.

17. Far removed from it will be the righteous

18. Who gives his wealth that he may grow (in goodness),

19. And no-one has with him any favour for reward,

20. Except as seeking (to fulfil) the purpose of his Lord Most High.

21. He verily will be content.

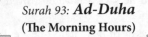

Surah 93: **Ad-Duha**
(The Morning Hours)

Ad-Duha, "The Morning Hours" takes its name from the first verse. There was an interval during which the Prophet received no revelation and the idolaters mocked him, saying: "Allah, of whom we used to hear so much, has forsaken poor Muhammad and now hates him." Then came this revelation. The Prophet had been a leading citizen of Makkah until he received his call. Now he was regarded as a madman. He was a man near fifty, and the prophecy in this Surah that "the later portion would be better for him then the former" must have seemed absurd for those who heard it. Yet the latter portion of the Prophet's life, the last ten years, is the most wonderful record of success in human history ever recorded.

***In the name of Allah,
the Beneficent, the Merciful.***

1. By the morning hours

2. And by the night when it is stillest,

3. Your Lord has not forsaken you nor does He hate you,

4. And verily the latter portion will be better for you than the former,

5. And verily your Lord will give to you so that you will be content.

6. Did He not find you an orphan and protect (you)?

7. Did He not find you wandering and direct (you)?

8. Did He not find you destitute and enrich (you)?

9. Therefore oppress not the orphan,

10. Therefore drive not away the beggar,

11. Therefore of the bounty of your Lord be your discourse.

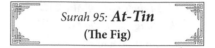

Surah 94: **Ash-Sharh**
(Solace)

Ash-Sharh "Solace," takes its name from a word in v. 1., and also from its subject, which is a relief from anxiety. It was probably revealed upon the same occasion as Surah 93, Ad-Duha; and, at a time when the Prophet was derided and shunned after having been respected and courted, must have struck the disbelievers as ridiculous. It refers to the inward assurance which the Prophet had received by revelation, and speaks of the future events as accomplished, as is usual in the Qur'an, the revelation coming from a plane where time is not. v. 4, speaking of his fame as exalted, must have seemed particularly absurd at that time of humiliation and persecution. But today, from every mosque in the world, the Prophet's name is called, as that of the messenger of God, five times a day, and every Muslim prays for blessing on him when his name is mentioned.

A very early Makkan Surah.

In the name of Allah,
the Beneficent, the Merciful.

1. Have We not caused your chest to dilate,

2. And eased you of the burden

3. Which weighed down your back;

4. And exalted your fame?

5. But with hardship goes ease,

6. With hardship goes ease;

7. So when you are relieved, still toil

8. And strive to please your Lord.

Surah 95: **At-Tin**
(The Fig)

At-Tin, "The Fig," takes its name from a word in verse 1. The sense is mystical, referring to man in relation to the revealed Law of God and His Judgement.

A very early Makkan Surah.

In the name of Allah,
the Beneficent, the Merciful.

1. By the fig and the olive,

2. By Mount Sinai,

3. And by this land made safe;

4. Surely, We created man of the best stature

5. Then We reduced him to the lowest of the low,

6. Except those who believe and do good works, and theirs is a reward unfailing.

7. So who after that will give the lie to you about the Judgement?

8. Is Allah not the most conclusive of all judges?

Surah 96: *Al-'Alaq*
(The Clot)

Al-Alaq takes its name from a word in verse 2. Verses 1-5 are the words which the Prophet received in the vision at Hira, therefore the first of the Qur'an to be revealed.

In the name of Allah, the Beneficent, the Merciful.

1. Read: In the name of your Lord Who creates,

2. Creates man from a clot.

3. Read: And your Lord is the Most Bounteous,

4. Who teaches by the pen,

5. Teaches man that which he knew not.

6. No, but verily man is rebellious,

7. That he thinks himself independent!

8. To your Lord is the return.

9. Have you seen him who dissuades

10. A slave when he prays?

11. Have you seen if he (relies) on the guidance (of Allah)

12. Or enjoins piety?

13. Have you seen if he denies (Allah's guidance) and is rebellious?

14. Is he then unaware that Allah sees?

15. No, but if he does not cease We will seize him by the forelock -

16. The lying, sinful forelock -

17. Then let him call upon his henchmen!

18. We will call the guards of Hell.

19. No! Do not obey him. But prostrate yourself, and draw near (to Allah).

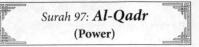

Surah 97: *Al-Qadr*
(Power)

Al-Qadr takes its name from the word in verse 1. It refers to the night (one of the last nights in Ramadan) on which the Prophet received his Call and the first verses of the Qur'an were revealed in the vision of Mt. Hira. It is said to be the night on which God's decrees for the year are brought down to the earthly plane.

A very early Makkan Surah.

In the name of Allah, the Beneficent, the Merciful.

1. We revealed it on the Night of Power.

2. Ah, what will convey to you what the Night of Power is!

3. The Night of Power is better than a thousand months,

4. The angels and the Spirit[306] descend in it, by the permission of their Lord, with all decrees.

5. (The night is) Peace until the rising of the dawn.

Surah 98: *Al-Bayyinah*
(The Clear Proof)

Al-Bayyinnah takes its name from a word in the first verse. There is no certainty as to the period of revelation. Many regard it as a late Makkan Surah. I follow the attribution in the Mushaf which I have followed throughout.

A probable date of revelation is the year 1 A.H.

---

306. *i.e.* Gabriel or, as some commentators think, a general term for angels of the highest rank.

**In the name of Allah,
the Beneficent, the Merciful.**

1. Those who disbelieve among the People of the Scripture and the idolaters could not have left off (erring) till the clear proof came to them,

2. A messenger from Allah, reading purified pages

3. Containing correct scriptures.

4. Nor were the People of the Scripture divided until after the clear proof came to them.

5. And they are ordered nothing else than to serve Allah, keeping religion pure for Him, as men by nature upright, and to establish worship and to pay the poor-due. That is the true religion.

6. Those who disbelieve, among the People of the Scripture and the idolaters, will remain in the fire of Hell. They are the worst of created beings.

7. (And) those who believe and do good works are the best of created beings.

8. Their reward is with their Lord: Gardens of Eden underneath which rivers flow, in which they dwell forever. Allah has pleasure in them and they have pleasure in Him. This is (in store) for him who fears his Lord.

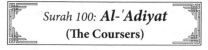

Surah 99: *Al-Zalzalah*
(The Earthquake)

Az-Zalzalah takes its name from a word in verse 1. A very early Makkan Surah.

**In the name of Allah,
the Beneficent, the Merciful.**

1. When the earth is shaken with her (final) earthquake,

2. And the earth yields up her burdens,

3. And man says, what is the matter with her?

4. That day she will relate her news,

5. Because your Lord inspires her.

6. That day mankind will come out in scattered groups to be shown their deeds.

7. And whoever does good an atom's weight will see it then,

8. And whoever does ill an atom's weight will see it then.

Surah 100: *Al-'Adiyat*
(The Coursers)

Al-Adiyat takes its name from a word in the first verse. A very early Makkan Surah.

**In the name of Allah,
the Beneficent, the Merciful.**

1. By the snorting coursers,

2. Striking sparks of fire

3. And scouring to the raid at dawn,

4. Then, with it, with their trail of dust,

5. Cleaving, as one, the centre (of the enemy),[307]

6. Man is ungrateful to his Lord,

7. And he is a witness to that;

307. The first five verses are eye-openers to one of the blessings of Allah, namely, horses that He made useful for use in wars; and yet man is ungrateful.

8. And in the love of wealth he is violent.

9. Does he not know that, when the contents of the graves are poured out

10. And the secrets of the breasts are made known,

11. On that day will their Lord be perfectly informed concerning them.

Surah 101: *Al-Qari'ah*
(The Calamity)

Al-Qari'ah takes its name from a word in verse 1 recurring in the next two verses. A very early Makkan Surah.

In the name of Allah, the Beneficent, the Merciful.

1. The Calamity!

2. What is the Calamity?

3. Ah, what will convey to you what the Calamity is!

4. A day in which mankind will be as thickly-scattered moths

5. And the mountains will become as carded wool.

6. Then, as for him whose scales are heavy (with good works),

7. He will live a pleasant life.

8. But as for him whose scales are light,

9. The Bereft and Hungry One will be his mother.

10. Ah, what will convey to you what she is!

11. Raging Fire.

Surah 102: *At-Takathur*
(Rivalry In Worldly Increase)

At-Takathur takes its name from a word in the first verse. A very early Makkan Surah.

In the name of Allah, the Beneficent, the Merciful.

1. Rivalry in worldly increase distracts you,

2. Until you come to the graves.

3. No, but you will come to know!

4. No, but you will come to know!

5. No, if only you knew (now) with a sure knowledge!

6. For you will see Hell-fire.

7. Aye, you will see it with sure vision.

8. Then, on that day, you will be asked concerning pleasure.

Surah 103: *Al-'Asr*
(The Declining Day)

Al-'Asr takes its name from a word in the first verse. A very early Makkan Surah.

In the name of Allah, the Beneficent, the Merciful.

1. By the declining day,

2. Man is in a state of loss,

3. Except those who believe and do good works, and exhort one another to truth and exhort one another to endurance.

Surah 104: **Al-Humazah**
(The Traducer)

Al-Humazah takes its name from a word in verse 1. The idolaters stopped all newcomers to Makkah and warned them against the Prophet, in order to prevent their listening to his preaching.

A very early Makkan Surah.

In the name of Allah,
the Beneficent, the Merciful.

1. Woe to every slandering traducer,

2. Who has gathered wealth (of this world) and arranged it.

3. He thinks that his wealth will render him immortal.

4. No, but verily he will be flung to the Consuming One.

5. Ah, what will convey to you what the Consuming One is!

6. (It is) the fire of Allah, kindled.

7. Which leaps up over the hearts (of men).

8. It is closed in on them

9. In outstretched columns.

Surah 105: **Al-Fil**
(The Elephant)

Al-Fil, "The Elephant," takes its name from a word in the first verse. The allusion is to the campaign of Abraha, the Abyssinian ruler of Al-Yaman, against Makkah, with the purpose of destroying the Ka'bah in the year of the Prophet's birth. He had with him an elephant which much impressed the Arabs. Tradition says that the elephant refused to advance on the last stage of the march, and that swarms of flying creatures pelted the Abyssinians with stones. Another tradition says that they retired in disorder owing to an outbreak of smallpox in the camp. At the time when this Surah was revealed, many men in Makkah must have known what happened. Dr. Krenkow, a sound Arabic scholar, is of the opinion that the flying creatures may well have been swarms of insects carrying infection. In any case the Ka'bah was saved from destruction after its defenders had despaired.

A very early Makkan Surah.

In the name of Allah,
the Beneficent, the Merciful.

1. Have you not seen how your Lord dealt with the owners of the Elephant?

2. Did He not bring their stratagem to nothing,

3. And send against them swarms of flying creatures,

4. Which pelted them with stones of baked clay,

5. And made them like green crops devoured (by cattle)?

Surah 106: **Quraysh**
(Quraysh)

Quraysh takes its name from a word occurring in the first verse. It is also called *Ash-Shita* (winter). A very early Makkan Surah.

***In the name of Allah,
the Beneficent, the Merciful.***

1. For the taming[308] of Quraysh.

2. For their taming (We cause) the caravans to set out in winter and summer.

3. So let them worship the Lord of this House,

4. Who has fed them against hunger and has made them safe from fear.

Surah 107: *Al-Ma'un*
(Small Kindness)

Al-Ma'un takes its name from a word in the last verse. An early Makkan revelation.

***In the name of Allah,
the Beneficent, the Merciful.***

1. Have you observed him who belies religion?

2. That is he who repels the orphan,

3. And urges not the feeding of the needy.

4. Ah, woe to worshippers

5. Who are heedless of their prayer;

6. Who would be seen (at worship),

7. Yet refuse small kindnesses!

Surah 108: *Al-Kauthar*
(The Abundance)

Al-Kauthar takes its name from a word in the first verse. The disbelievers used to taunt the Prophet with the fact that he had no son, and therefore no one to uphold his religion after him.

---

308. *i.e.* civilising

***In the name of Allah,
the Beneficent, the Merciful.***

1. We have given you Abundance;

2. So pray to your Lord, and sacrifice.

3. It is your insulter (and not you) who is without posterity.

Surah 109: *Al-Kafirun*
(The Disbelievers)

Al-Kafirun takes its name from a word in verse 1. It was revealed at a time when the idolaters had asked the Prophet to compromise in matters of religion.

***In the name of Allah,
the Beneficent, the Merciful.***

1. Say: O disbelievers!

2. I worship not that which you worship;

3. Nor do you worship that which I worship.

4. And I shall not worship that which you worship.

5. Nor will you worship that which I worship.

6. To you your religion, and to me my religion.

Surah 110: *An-Nasr*
(Triumph)

An-Nasr takes its name from a word in the first verse. It is one of the very last revelations, having come to the Prophet only a few weeks before his death. Though ascribed always to Al-Madinah, tradition says that it was actually revealed at Makkah during the days the Prophet spent there when he made his farewell pilgrimage. It is described in Ibn Hisham and elsewhere as the first announcement that the Prophet received of his approaching death.

The date of revelation is the tenth year of the Hijrah.

In the name of Allah,
the Beneficent, the Merciful.

1. When Allah's help and the triumph comes,

2. And you see mankind entering the religion of Allah in troops,

3. Then hymn the praises of your Lord, and seek forgiveness of Him. He is always ready to show mercy.

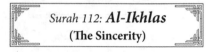

Surah 111: **Al-Masad**
(Palm-Fibre)

Al-Masad takes its name from a word (to the Arabs a very homely word) in the last verse. It is the only passage in the whole Qur'an where an opponent of the Prophet is denounced by name. Abu Lahab (The Father of Flame), whose real name was Abdul 'Uzza, was an uncle of the Prophet and was the only member of his own clan who bitterly opposed the Prophet. He made it his business to torment the Prophet, and his wife took pleasure in carrying thorn bushes and strewing them in the sand where she knew that the Prophet was sure to walk barefooted.

An early Makkan revelation.

In the name of Allah,
the Beneficent, the Merciful.

1. The power of Abu Lahab will perish, and he will perish.

2. His wealth and gains will not exempt him.

3. He will be plunged in flaming Fire,

4. And his wife, the wood-carrier,

5. Will have upon her neck a halter of palm-fibre.

Surah 112: **Al-Ikhlas**
(The Sincerity)

Al-Ikhlas, "The Sincerity," takes its name from its subject. It has been called the essence of the Qur'an, of which it is really the last Surah. Some authorities ascribe this Surah to the Madinah period, and think it was revealed in answer to a question from some Jewish doctors concerning the nature of God.

It is generally held to be an early Makkan Surah.

In the name of Allah,
the Beneficent, the Merciful.

1. Say: He is Allah, the One!

2. Allah, the Eternally Implored by all!

3. He does not give birth nor was He born,

4. And there is none like Him.

Surah 113: *Al-Falaq*
(The Daybreak)

Al-Falaq, "The Daybreak," takes its name from a word in the first verse. This and the following Surah are prayers for protection, this one being for protection against fears proceeding from the unknown. The two Surahs are known as Al-Mu'awwadhateyn, the two prayers for refuge and protection.

An early Makkan Surah.

***In the name of Allah,
the Beneficent, the Merciful.***

1. Say: I seek refuge in the Lord of the Daybreak

2. From the evil of that which He created;

3. From the evil of the darkness when it is intense,

4. And from the evil of malignant witchcraft,[309]

5. And from the evil of the envier when he envies.

Surah 114: *An-Nas*
(Mankind)

An-Nas, the second of the two prayers for refuge and protection, takes its name from a recurring word which marks the rhythm in Arabic. In this case protection is sought especially from the evil in a man's own heart and in the hearts of other men.

An early Makkan revelation.

***In the name of Allah,
the Beneficent, the Merciful.***

1. Say: I seek refuge in the Lord of mankind,

2. The King of mankind,

3. The God of mankind,

4. From the evil of the sneaking whisperer,

5. Who whispers in the hearts of mankind,

6. Of the jinn and of mankind.

---

309. *Lit.* "from the evil of blowers (feminine) upon knots," it having been a common form of witchcraft in Arabia for women to tie knots in a cord and blow upon them with an invocation.

Brief Index of Subjects

A

'Aad, people of 7:65-74; 9:70; 11:50; 11:59-60; 14:9; 22:42; 25:38; 26:123; 29:38; 38:12; 40:31; 41:13; 41:15; 46:21; 50:13; 51:41; 53:50; 54:18; 69:4-6; 89:6

Aaron [Harun], 2:248; 4:163; 6:84; 7:122; 7:142; 10:75; 19:53; 20:30; 20:70; 20:90; 20:92; 21:48; 23:45; 25:35; 26:13; 26:48; 28:34; 37:114; 37:120

Ablution, 4:43; 5:6

Abraham [Ibrahim], S. 14; 2:124-127; 2:130; 2:132-133; 2:135-136; 2:140; 2:258; 2:260; 3:33; 3:65; 3:67; 3:68; 3:84; 3:95; 3:97; 4:54; 4:125; 4:163; 6:74-75; 6:83; 6:161; 9:70; 9:114; 11:69; 11:74-76; 12:6; 12:38; 14:35; 15:51; 16:120; 16:123; 19:41; 19:58; 21:51; 21:60; 21:62; 21:69; 22:26; 22:43; 22:78; 26:69; 29:16; 33:7; 37:83; 37:104; 37:109; 38:45; 42:13; 43:26; 51:24; 53:37; 57:26; 60:4; 87:19

Abu Lahab (Father of Flame), 111:1-5

Adam, 2:31; 2:33-35, 2:37, 3:33, 3:59, 5:27, 7:11, 7:19, 7:26-27, 7:31, 7:35, 7:172, 17:61, 17:70, 18:50, 19:58, 20:115-117, 20:120-121, 36:60

Ahmad (Praised One), 61:6

Adultery, see Zina

Allah*,

    accepts repentance, 40:3; 42:25

    all beings in the Heavens and Earth declare His glory, 17:44; 21:19-20; 24:41; 57:1; 59:1; 59:24; 61:1; 62:1; 64:1

    all faces humble themselves before Him, 20:111

    all good is from Him, 4:79; 16:30; 16:53

    all power belongs to Him, 4:139; 10:65; 63:8

    all things are from Him, 4:78; 15:21

    answers the wronged one, 27:62

    ascribe no partners to Him, 3:64; 4:36; 4:48; 4:116; 5:72; 6:14; 6:81; 6:88; 6:136-137; 6:148; 6:151; 9:31; 10:28-29; 13:16; 13:33; 13:36; 16:51-57; 16:73; 16:86; 17:22; 17:39-40; 17:56-57; 18:110; 22:31; 23:59; 23:117; 24:55; 25:68; 28:87-88; 29:8; 30:31; 31:13; 35:13-14; 39:64-65; 40:41-43; 40:66; 41:6; 43:45; 46:4-6; 50:26; 51:51; 60:12; 72:2; 72:18

    belief in, 2:62; 2:177; 2:256; 3:179; 3:193; 4:38-39; 4:59; 4:136; 4:152; 4:162; 4:171; 4:175; 7:158; 9:18-19; 9:44-45; 24:2; 24:62; 36:25; 40:84; 49:15; 57:7-8; 57:19; 58:22; 60:4; 60:11; 61:11; 64:8; 64:11; 65:2; 67:29; 72:13; 85:8

    Blessed be He, 7:54; 23:14; 25:1; 25:10; 25:61; 40:64; 43:85; 55:78;

    bounty is in His hand, 3:73

    call upon, 6:52; 6:63; 7:29; 7:55-56; 7:180; 13:36; 18:28; 40:14; 40:60; 40:65

    creates what He will, 3:47; 5:17; 24:45; 28:68; 30:54; 35:1; 42:49; 82:8

    does what He will, 2:253; 3:40; 11:107; 14:27; 22:14-18; 85:16

    created you in the wombs, 3:6; 39:6

    does not give birth nor was he born, 112:3

    enlarges provision and tightens it, 2:245; 13:26; 17:30; 28:82; 29:62; 30:37; 34:36; 34:39; 39:52; 42:12; 42:27; 89:15-16

    feeds but is not fed, 6:14; 51:57-58

    forgives sins, 2:284; 3:31; 3:195; 4:116; 5:18; 5:39-40; 7:161; 8:29; 8:70; 12:92; 13:6; 14:10; 26:82; 28:16; 33:71; 36:27; 39:53; 40:3; 42:25; 42:30; 42:34; 46:31; 48:14; 57:28; 61:12; 64:17; 71:4

    gives life to the dead, 2:28; 2:243; 2:259-260; 3:27; 6:36; 7:57; 10:31; 22:6; 30:19; 30:40; 30:50; 36:12; 36:79; 41:39; 42:9; 46:33; 50:11; 75:40; 80:22; 86:8

    gives sustenance, 2:57; 2:126; 2:172; 3:27; 3:37; 3:169; 5:114; 6:151; 7:50; 7:160; 8:26; 10:31; 10:93; 11:88; 14:37; 16:72; 16:75; 17:31; 17:70; 20:81; 20:132; 27:64; 29:60; 30:40; 34:24; 35:3; 40:13; 40:40; 40:64; 42:19; 45:5; 45:16; 50:11; 65:3; 67:15; 67:21; 106:4

* Due to the recurrence of the mention of the name of Allah throughout the Qur'an, only verses containing specific information on the given subjects have been included for reference

Allah, *(cont'd.)*

guides whom He will, 2:213; 2:272; 10:25; 13:27; 13:31; 14:4; 16:93; 22:16; 24:35; 24:46; 28:56; 35:8; 39:23; 42:52; 74:31

has no partner, 6:163; 7:191-198; 9:31; 10:66; 17:111; 23:91; 25:2; 35:40; 42:21; 68:41; 72:3

has no son, 2:116; 4:171; 6:101; 9:30; 10:68; 17:111; 18:4; 19:35; 19:88-92; 21:26; 23:91; 25:2; 37:152; 39:4; 43:81-82; 72:3

hears the arguments from both husband and wife, 58:1

is not unaware of what you do, 2:74; 2:85; 2:140; 2:144; 2:149; 3:99; 6:132; 11:123; 14:42; 22:68; 23:17; 27:93

is sufficient, 2:137; 3:173; 4:6; 4:45; 4:70; 4:79; 4:81; 4:132; 4:166; 4:171; 8:62; 8:64; 9:59; 9:129; 10:29; 13:43; 17:17; 17:65; 17:96; 25:31; 25:58; 29:52; 33:3; 33:48; 39:38; 46:8; 48:28; 65:3

is the best of plotters, 3:54; 8:30; 13:42

knows all you disclose and hide, 2:33; 2:77; 2:284; 3:29; 5:99; 6:3; 11:5; 14:38; 16:19; 16:23; 21:110; 27:25; 27:74; 28:69; 33:54; 36:76; 60:1; 64:4; 87:7

knows best who is guided, 6:117; 16:125; 17:84; 28:56; 53:30; 68:7

knows what is hidden (the Unseen), 2:33; 5:109; 5:116; 6:59; 6:73; 9:78; 9:94; 9:105; 10:20; 11:123; 13:9; 16:77; 18:26; 20:7; 23:92; 25:6; 27:65; 32:6; 34:3; 34:48; 49:18; 72:26; 84:23

love for Him, 2:165; 2:177; 3:31; 5:54; 76:8

made all things good which He created, 32:7

meeting with Him, 2:46; 2:223; 2:249; 6:154; 10:11; 10:15; 10:45; 13:2; 18:110; 25:21; 29:5; 29:23; 30:8; 32:10; 33:44; 41:54; 84:6

nearness to Him, 2:186; 7:206; 11:61; 34:37; 34:50; 39:3; 50:16; 83:21; 83:28; 96:19

never breaks His promise, 3:9; 3:194; 13:31; 14:47; 30:6

no God but He (One God), 2:133; 2:163; 2:255; 3:2; 3:6; 3:18; 3:62; 4:87; 5:73; 6:102; 6:106; 7:59; 7:65; 7:85; 7:158; 9:31; 9:129; 11:14; 11:50; 11:61; 11:84; 16:2; 20:8; 20:14; 20:98; 21:22; 21:25; 21:87; 23:23; 23:32; 23:116-117; 27:26; 27:60-64; 28:70; 28:88; 35:3; 38:65; 39:6; 40:3; 40:62; 40:65; 44:8; 47:19; 52:43; 59:22-23; 64:13

no calamity befalls except by His permission, 64:11

no strength except in Him, 18:39

no refuge from Him except towards Him, 9:118; 72:22

obey Him, 3:132; 4:59; 4:69; 8:1; 8:20-21; 8:46; 9:71; 24:51-54; 33:33; 33:71; 47:33; 48:16-17; 49:14; 58:13; 64:12; 64:16

Praise be to Him, 1:2; 6:1; 6:45; 10:10; 14:39; 15:98; 16:75; 17:111; 18:1; 23:28; 25:58; 27:15; 27:59; 27:93; 28:70; 29:63; 30:18; 31:25; 34:1; 35:1; 35:34; 37:182; 39:29; 39:74-75; 40:55; 40:65; 50:39-40; 52:48-49; 64:1; 110:3

prostration to Him, 15:98; 16:49; 19:58; 20:70; 22:77; 25:64; 32:15; 39:9; 48:29; 50:40; 53:62; 76:26; 96:19

regulates affairs, 10:3; 10:31; 13:2; 32:5

the return to Him, 2:46; 2:156; 6:36; 6:60; 6:108; 10:23; 10:46; 10:70; 11:4; 11:34; 13:36; 19:40; 19:80; 21:93; 23:60; 26:50; 29:8; 29:17; 31:23; 39:7; 40:43; 40:77; 89:28; 96:8

says "Be" and it is, 2:117; 3:47; 3:59; 6:73; 16:40; 19:35; 36:82

seek His forgiveness, 2:285-286; 3:16; 3:135; 3:147; 3:193; 4:64; 5:74; 7:155; 11:3; 11:52; 11:61; 11:90; 12:29; 12:98; 14:41; 19:47; 23:109; 23:118; 24:62; 28:16; 40:55; 41:6; 47:19; 51:18; 60:5; 71:10; 71:28; 73:20: 110:3

seek His help, 1:5; 2:45; 2:153;

seek refuge in Him, 7:200-201; 16:98; 19:18; 23:97-98; 40:56; 41:36; 113:1; 114:1

there is none like Him, 42:11; 112:4

to Him belong the forces of the Heavens and the earth, 48:4; 48:7

to Him belong the keys of the Heavens and the Earth, 39:63; 42:12

to Him belong the Most Beautiful Names, 7:180; 17:110; 20:8; 59:24

to Him you shall be brought (returned) back, 2:28; 2:46; 2:156; 2:281; 3:158; 5:48; 5:96; 6:12; 6:36; 6:38; 6:60; 6:164; 8:24; 10:4; 10:23; 10:45; 10:56; 11:4; 15:25; 19:40; 21:35; 23:79; 23:115; 24:64; 28:70; 28:88; 29:8; 29:57; 30:11; 31:15; 32:11; 36:22; 36:32; 36:83; 39:44; 43:85; 45:15; 67:24; 96:8

Allah *(cont'd.)*

trust in, 3:159-160; 3:173; 4:81; 5:11; 5:23; 7:89; 8:2; 9:51; 9:129; 10:71; 10:84-85; 11:56; 11:88; 11:123; 12:67; 13:30; 14:11-12; 16:42; 16:99; 17:65; 25:58; 26:217; 27:79; 29:59; 33:3; 33:48; 39:38; 42:10; 42:36; 58:10; 60:4; 64:13; 65:3

will not change the condition of a people until they change, 13:11

will not suffer the reward to be lost, 3:195; 9:120; 12:56; 12:90; 18:30; 21:94; 52:21

worship Him (alone), 1:5; 3:64; 6:56; 6:102; 7:59; 7:65; 7:85; 7:206; 11:2; 11:26; 11:50; 11:61: 11:84; 11:123; 12:40; 13:36; 17:23; 19:65; 21:25; 22:77; 23:23; 24:55; 25:60; 39:66; 41:37; 46:21; 53:62; 71:3; 98:5; 106:3

Allah's attributes, 7:180; 17:110; 20:8, 59:24

Able to do all things *[Al-Muqtadir]* (Powerful), 18:45; 43:42; 54:42

Able to repay (the wrong) *[Dhu Intiqam]*, 3:4; 14:47; 39:37

Absolute (Has no needs) (Independent) (Rich) *[Al-Ghani]*, 2:263; 2:267; 4:131; 6:133; 10:68; 14:8; 22:64; 27:40; 29:6; 31:12; 31:26; 35;15; 39:7; 47:38; 57:24; 60:6; 64:6

Almighty (Absolute) *[Al-Qahhar]*, 12:39; 14:48; 38:65; 39:4; 40:16

All-Embracing (cares for all) *[Al-Wasi']*, 2:115; 2:247; 2:261; 2:268; 3:73; 4:130; 5:54; 24:32; 53:32;

Aware (Well-Informed) *[Al-Khabir]*, 2:234; 2:271; 3:153; 3:180; 4:35; 4:94; 4:128; 4:135; 5:8; 6:18; 6:73; 6:103; 9:16; 11:1; 11:111; 17:17; 17:30; 17:96; 22:63; 24:30; 24:53; 25:58: 25:59; 27:88; 31:16; 31:29; 31:34; 33:2; 33:34; 34:1; 35:14; 35:31; 42:27; 48:11; 49:13; 57:10; 58:3; 58:11; 58:13; 59:18; 63:11; 64:8; 66:3; 67:14; 100:11

Beneficent *[Al-Rahman]*, 1:1; 1:3; 2:163; 13:30; 17:110; 19:18; 19:26; 19:44-45; 19:58; 19:61; 19:69; 19:75; 19:78; 19:85; 19:88; 19:91-93; 19:96; 20:5; 20:90; 20:108-109; 21:26; 21:36; 21:42; 21:112; 25:26; 25:59-60; 25:63; 26:5; 27:30; 36:15; 36:23; 36:52; 41:2; 43:17; 43:20; 43:33; 43:36; 43:45; 43:81; 50:33; 55:1; 59:22; 67:3; 67:19-20; 67:29; 78:37-38;

Benign *[Al-Barr]*, 52:28

Benign (ever Clement) (Forgiving) (ever Forgiving) (Mild) *[Al-'Afu]*, 4:43; 4:99; 4:149; 22:60; 58:2

Best of all who show mercy, *[Khayr al-Rahimin]*, 23:109; 23:118

Best of deciders *[Khayr al-Fasilin]*, 6:57

Best of Providers (Best of all who make provision) *[Khayr al-Raziqin]*, 22:58; 23:72; 34:39; 62:11

Best to decide *[Ahkam al-Hakimin]*, 11:45; 95:8

Best to decide *[Khayr al-Hakimin]*, 7:87; 10:109; 11:45; 12:80

Bountiful (Grace) *[Al-Karim]*, 23:116; 27:40; 82:6

Calls to account *[Al-Hasib]*, 4:6; 4:86; 6:62; 17:14; 21:47; 33:39

Clement (Indulgent) *[Al-Halim]*, 2:225; 2:263; 3:155; 4:12; 5:101; 17:44; 22:59; 33:51; 35:41; 64:17

Compeller *[Al-Jabbar]*, 59:23

Creator *[Al-Khaliq; Al-Khallaq]*, 6:102; 13:16; 15:28; 15:86; 35:3; 36:81; 37:125; 38:71; 39:62; 40:62; 59:24

Creator (Originator) of the heavens and the earth *[Al-Fatir; Al-Badi']*, 2:117; 6:14; 6:101; 12:101; 14:10; 35:1; 39:46; 42:11

enlarges livelihood *[Yabsutu al-Rizq]*, 13:26;

Eternal *[Al-Qayyum]*, 2:255; 3:2; 20:111

Eternally implored by all *[Al-Samad]*, 112:2

Fashioner *[Al-Musawwir]*, 59:24

First *[Al-Awwal]*, 57:3

Forgiver *[Al-Ghaffar]*, 39:5; 40:42

Forgiving (Forgiver) *[Al-Ghafoor]*, 2:173; 2:182; 2:192; 2:199; 2:218; 2:225-226; 2:235; 3:31; 3:89; 3:129; 3:155; 4:23; 4:25; 4:43; 4:64; 4:96; 4:99-100; 4:106; 4:110; 4:129; 4:152; 5:3; 5:34; 5:39; 5:74; 5:98; 5:101; 6:145; 6:165; 7:153; 7:167; 8:69; 8:70; 9:5; 9:27; 9:91; 9:99; 9:102; 10:107; 11:41; 12:53; 12:98; 14:36; 15:49; 16:18; 16:110; 16:115; 16:119; 17:25; 17:44; 18:58; 22:60; 24:22; 24:33; 24:62; 25:6; 25:70; 27:11; 28:16; 33:5; 33:24; 33:50; 33:59; 33:73; 34:2; 35:28; 35:30; 35:34; 35:41; 39:53; 41:32; 42:5; 42:23; 46:8; 48:14; 49:5; 49:14; 57:28; 58:2; 58:12; 60:7; 60:12; 64:14; 66:1; 67:2; 71:10; 73:20; 85:14

Allah's attributes, *(cont'd.)*

full of Compassion *[Al-Ra'uf]*, 2:143; 2:207; 3:30; 9:117; 9:128; 16:7; 16:47; 22:65; 24:20; 57:9; 59:10

gives livelihood *[Al-Razzaq]*, 51:58

Great *[Al-Kabir]*, 4:34; 13:9; 22:62; 31:30; 34:23; 40:12

Guardian *[Al-Muhaymin]*, 59:23

Hearer *[Al-Sami']*, 2:127; 2:224; 2:256; 3:34; 4:58; 4:134; 4:148; 5:76; 6:13; 6:115; 8:17; 8:42; 8:53; 8:61; 9:103; 10:65; 14:39; 17:1; 21:4; 22:61; 22:75; 24:21; 24:60; 26:220; 29:5; 29:60; 31:28; 34:50; 40:20; 40:56; 41:36; 42:11; 44:6; 49:1; 58:1

Hearer of prayer (Responsive) *[Al-Mujib]*, 11:61; 37:75

Helper (Supporter) *[Al-Nasir]*, 3:150; 4:45; 8:40; 22:78; 25:31; 40:51

High Exalted *[Al-Muta'ali]*, 4:34; 13:9

Holy One *[Al-Quddus]*, 59:23; 62:1

Infinite Bounty *[Dhu al-Fadl al-'Azim]*, 2:105; 3:174; 57:21; 57:29; 62:4

Inheritor *[Al-Warith]*, 15:23

Inward *[Al-Batin]*, 57:3

Judge *[Al-Fattah]*, 34:26

King (Sovereign) *[Al-Malik; Al-Maalik]*, 1:4; 3:26; 20:114; 23:116; 54:55; 59:23; 62:1; 114:2

Knower of the invisible and visible *['Alim al-Ghayb wa al-Shahadah]*, 2:33; 6:59; 9:94; 9:105; 10:20; 11:123; 13:9; 16:77; 18:26; 23:92; 27:65; 32:6; 34:3; 35:38; 39:46; 49:18; 59:22; 62:8; 64:18; 72:26

Knows all things *[Al-'Alim]*, 2:224; 2:227; 2:256; 3:34; 3:73; 4:12; 4:17; 4:24; 4:26; 4:32; 4:39; 4:70; 4:147-148; 4:170; 4:176; 5:76; 5:97; 6:13; 6:83; 6:101; 6:115; 6:128; 8:17; 8:42; 8:53; 8:61; 8:71; 8:75; 9:15; 9:28; 9:98; 9:103; 9:106; 9:115; 10:36; 10:65; 12:76; 12:83; 12:100; 15:25; 15:86; 21:4; 22:52; 22:59; 24:18; 24:21; 24:28; 24:35; 24:41; 24:58-60; 24:64; 26:220; 27:6; 27:78; 29:5; 29:60; 29:62; 30:54; 31:23; 31:34; 33:34; 33:40; 33:51; 34:26; 35:8; 35:38; 35:44; 36:79; 36:81; 40:2; 41:12; 41:36; 42:12; 42:50; 43:9; 43:84; 44:6; 48:4; 48:26; 49:1; 49:16; 51:30; 57:3; 58:7; 60:10; 62:7; 64:11; 66:2-3; 67:13; 76:30

Last *[Al-Akhir]*, 57:3

Light of the heavens and the earth *[Al-Nur]*, 24:35

Living (Alive) *[Al-Hayy]*, 2:255; 3:2; 20:111; 25:58; 40:65

Lord of the Ascending Stairways, *[Dhu al-Ma'arij]*, 70:3

Lord of Majesty *[Rabb al-'Izzah]*, 37:180

Lord of Mercy *[Dhu al-Rahmah]*, 6:133; 6:147; 18:58

Lord of Might and Glory *[Dhu al-Jalal wa al-Ikram]*, 55:27; 55:78

Lord of the Daybreak *[Rabb al-Falaq]*, 113:1

Lord of unbreakable might *[Dhu al-Quwwah]*, 51:58

Lord of the East and the West *[Rabb al-Mashriq wa al-Maghirb; Rabb al-Mashriqayn wa al-Maghirbayn; Rabb al-Mashariq wa al-Magharib]*, 26:28; 37:5; 55:17; 70:40; 73:9

Lord of the heavens and the earth *[Rab al-Samawat wa al-Ard]*, 17:102; 18:14; 19:65; 21:56; 26:24; 37:5; 38:66; 43:82; 44:7; 45:36; 51:23; 78:37

Lord of the Tremendous Throne *[Rabb al-'Arsh]*, 9:129; 17:42; 21:22; 23:86-87; 23:116; 27:26; 40:15; 43:82; 85:15

Lord of the Worlds *[Rabb al-'Alamin]*, 1:2 2:131; 5:28; 6:45; 6:71; 6:162; 7:54; 7:61; 7:67; 7:104; 7:121; 10:10; 10:37; 26:16; 26:23; 26:47; 26:77; 26:98; 26:109; 26:127; 26:145; 26:164; 26:180; 26:192; 27:8; 27:44; 28:30; 32:2; 37:87; 37:182; 39:75; 40:64-66; 41:9; 43:46; 45:36; 56:80; 59:16; 69:43; 81:29; 83:6

Loving *[Al-Wadud]*, 11:90; 85:14

Master of the Day of Judgment *[Malik Yawm al-Din]*, 1:4

Mighty *[Al-'Aziz]*, 2:209; 2:220; 2:228; 2:240; 3:6; 3:18; 3:62; 3:126; 4:56; 4:158; 4:165; 5:38; 5:118; 6:96; 8:10; 8:63; 9:40; 9:71; 11:66; 14:4; 14:47; 16:60; 22:40; 22:74; 26:9; 26:104; 26:122; 26:140; 26:159; 26:175; 26:191; 26:217; 27:9; 27:78; 29:26; 29:42; 30:27; 31:9; 31:27; 32:6; 33:25; 34:6; 34:27; 35:2; 35:28; 36:5; 38:9; 38:66; 39:1; 39:5; 39:37; 40:2; 40:42; 41:12; 42:3; 42:19; 43:9; 44:42; 45:2; 45:37; 46:2; 48:7; 48:19; 54:42; 57:1; 57:25; 58:21; 59:1; 59:23-24; 60:5; 61:1; 62:1; 62:3; 64:18; 67:2; 85:8

Allah's attributes, *(cont'd.)*

Most Bounteous *[Al-Akram]*, 96:3

Most High *[Al-'Ali; Al-A'la]*, 22:62; 87:1

Merciful *[Al-Rahim]*, 1:1; 1:3; 2:160; 2:163; 2:192; 2:218; 2:226; 3:31; 3:89; 4:16; 4:23; 4:25; 4:29; 4:96; 4:100; 4:106; 4:110; 4:129; 4:152; 5:3; 5:34; 5:39; 5:74; 5:98; 6:145; 6:165; 7:153; 7:167; 9:91; 9:99; 9:102; 9:104; 9:117-118; 10:107; 11:90; 12:98; 15:49; 16:7; 16:18; 16:47; 16:110; 16:115; 16:119; 17:66; 22:65; 24:5; 24:20; 24:22; 24:33; 24:62; 25:6; 25:70; 26:9; 26:104; 26:122; 26:140; 26:159; 26:175; 26:191; 26:217; 27:11; 27:30; 28:16; 32:6; 33:5; 33:24; 33:43; 33:50; 33:73; 34:2; 36:5; 36:58; 39:53; 41:2; 41:32; 42:5; 44:42; 46:8; 48:14; 49:5; 49:12; 52:28; 57:9; 57:28; 58:12; 59:10; 59:22; 60:7; 60:12; 66:1; 73:20

Most Merciful of all (those) who show mercy *[Arham al-Rahimin]*, 7:151; 12:64; 12:92; 21:83

Near *[Al-Qarib]*, 2:186; 11:61; 34:50

Omnipotent *[Al-Qahir]*, 6:18; 6:61;

One God *[Al-Wahid; Al-Ahad]*, 2:133; 2:163; 4:171; 5:73; 6:19; 9:31; 12:39; 13:16; 14:48; 14:52; 16:22; 16:51; 18:110; 21:108; 29:46; 37:4; 38:65; 39:4; 40:16; 41:6; 112:1

Outward *[Al-Zahir]*, 57:3

Owner of Praise (Praiseworthy) *[Al-Hamid]*, 4:131, 11:73; 14:1; 14:8; 22:24; 22:64; 31:12; 31:26; 34:6; 35:15; 41:42; 42:28; 57:24; 60:6; 64:6; 85:8

Owner of Sovereignty *[Malik al-Mulk]*, 3:26

Peace *[Al-Salam]*, 59:23

Protecting Guardian (Guardian) (Protecting Friend) (Friend) *[Al-Wali]*, 2:107; 2:120; 2:257; 3:68; 4:45; 6:14; 7:155; 7:196; 9:116; 12:101; 34:41; 42:9; 42:28; 45:19;

Protector (Protecting Friend) (Befriender) (Patron) *[Mawlaa]*, 2:286; 3:150; 8:40; 9:51; 22:78; 47:11; 66:2; 66:4

Reckoner *[Al-Hasib]*, 4:6; 4:86; 6:62; 17:14; 21:47; 33:39

Relenting (Clement) *[Al-Tawwab]*, 2:37; 2:54; 2:160; 4:16; 4:64; 9:104; 9:118; 24:10; 49:12

Responsive (Bountiful) *[Al-Shakur]*, 35:30; 35:34; 42:23; 64:17

Seer *[Al-Basir]*, 4:58; 4:134; 8:72; 17:1; 17:30; 17:96; 22:61; 22:75; 25:20; 31:28; 33:9; 34:11; 35:31; 35:45; 40:20; 40:44; 40:56; 41:40; 42:11; 42:27; 48:28; 49:18; 57:4; 58:1; 60:3; 64:2; 67:19; 84:15

severe (stern; strong) in punishment (reprisal) *[Shadid al-'Iqab]*, 2:165; 2:196; 2:211; 3:11; 5:2; 5:98; 8:13; 8:25; 8:48; 8:52; 13:6; 40:3; 40:22; 59:4; 59:7

Shaper out of nothing *[Al Bari']*, 59:24

Strong *[Al-Qawi]*, 8:52; 11:66; 22:40; 22:74; 33:25; 42:19; 57:25; 58:21

Sublime (Exalted) *[Al-'Ali]*, 2:255; 31:30; 34:23; 40:12; 42:4

Subtle (gracious to His slaves) (tender to whom He will) *[Al-Latif]*, 6:103; 12:100; 22:63; 33:34; 42:19; 67:14

Superb *[Al-Mutakabbir]*, 59:23

Swift in prosecution *[Sari 'al-'Iqab]*, 6:165; 7:167

Swift at reckoning (Swift to take account) *[Sari 'al-Hisab]*, 2:202; 3:19; 3:199; 5:4; 6:62; 13:41; 14:51; 24:39; 40:17

Tremendous *[Al-'Azim]*, 2:255; 42:4; 56:74; 56:96; 69:52

Truth (True) *[Al-Haqq]*, 18:44; 22:6; 22:62; 23:116; 24:25; 31:30

Watcher *[Al-Raqib]*, 5:117

Wise *[Al-Hakim]*, 2:32; 2:129; 2:209; 2:220; 2:228; 2:240; 2:260; 3:6; 3:18; 3:62; 3:126; 4:11; 4:17; 4:24; 4:26; 4:56; 4:92; 4:104; 4:111; 4:158; 4:165; 4:170; 5:38; 5:118; 6:18; 6:73; 6:83; 6:96; 6:128; 6:139; 8:10; 8:49; 8:63; 8:67; 8:71; 9:15; 9:28; 9:40; 9:60; 9:71; 9:97; 9:106; 9:110; 11:1; 12:6; 12:83; 12:100; 15:4; 15:25; 16:60; 22:52; 24:10; 24:18: 24:58-59; 27:6; 27:9; 27:78; 29:26; 29:42; 30:27; 31:9; 31:27; 33:1; 34:1; 34:27; 35:2; 35:44; 36:38; 39:1; 40:8; 41:42; 42:3; 42:51; 43:84; 45:2; 45:37; 46:2; 48:4; 48:7; 48:19; 49:8; 51:30; 57:1; 59:1; 59:24; 60:5; 60:10; 61:1; 62:1; 62:3; 64:18; 66:2; 76:30

Witness over all things *[Al-Shahid]*, 4:33; 4:79; 4:166; 5:117; 6:19; 10:46; 13:43; 17:96; 29:52; 33:55; 34:47; 46:8; 48:28; 58:6; 85:9

Allah's blessings on the Prophet, 33:56

Allah's Bounty, 2:105; 2:251; 3:174; 4:130; 4:173; 8:29; 9:28; 9:59; 9:74-76; 10:58; 17:20-21; 30:45; 31:20; 35:30; 35:35; 38:54; 42:22-23; 42:26; 44:57; 57:21; 57:29; 62:4; 93:11;

seek of it, 4:32; 16:14; 17:12; 17:66; 28:73; 30:23; 30:46; 35:12; 45:12; 62:10; 73:20

Allah's Commands, 7:54; 11:76; 16:1-2; 16:33; 21:73; 22:65; 28:70; 28:88; 30:25; 30:46; 33:38-39: 40:15; 40:78; 51:44; 52:48; 57:14; 65:8; 68:48

His Command comes down, 65:12

His Command is like the twinkling of an eye, 54:50

Allah's Countenance, 2:115; 6:52; 13:22; 18:28; 28:88; 30:38; 30:39; 55:27

Allah's Covenant, 2:27; 3:77; 6:152; 9:75-77; 9:111; 13:20; 13:25; 16:91; 16:95; 33:23; 57:8;

with the Children of Israel, 2:40; 2:83-84; 2:93

Allah's curse, 2:89; 2:161; 3:61; 3:87; 7:44; 9:68; 11:18; 24:7; 28:42; 38:78; 47:23; 48:6; 63:4

Allah's help, 8:62; 8:64; 12:110; 22:40; 40:51; 61:13, 110:1

Allah's promise, 3:152; 4:122; 6:134; 10:4; 10:55; 14:22; 17:108; 18:21; 18:98; 20:86; 21:9; 21:104; 22:47; 25:15-16; 28:13; 28:61; 30:6; 30:60; 31:9; 31:33; 35:5; 36:52; 39:20; 39:74; 40:8; 40:55; 40:77; 45:32; 46:16-17; 48:20; 48:29; 51:5; 73:18

Allah's signs (revelations), 2:73; 2:242; 2:252; 3:103; 3:108; 4:155; 5:75; 5:89; 6:33; 6:35; 6:37; 6:157-158; 7:26; 7:40; 7:175-177; 8:2; 10:71; 16:104-105; 17:1; 18:9; 18:17; 18:57; 18:105; 19:58; 19:73; 19:77; 20:22-23; 20:42; 20:126-128; 21:37; 22:52; 23:30; 23:58; 24:1; 25:73; 27:13-14; 27:93; 28:87; 29:47; 29:49-50; 32:22; 32:24; 33:34; 36:46; 39:52; 40:4; 40:13; 40:34-35; 40:63; 40:81; 41:15; 42:35; 43:69; 45:6-9; 45:31; 46:27; 57:9; 62:2; 68:15; 74:16

explained, 2:187; 2:221; 6:46; 6:55; 6:65; 6:97-98; 6:105; 7:32; 7:58; 7:174; 9:11; 10:5; 10:24; 11:1; 13:2; 24:58-59; 24:61; 30:28; 41:3; 57:17

not for a little gain, 3:199; 5:44; 9:9

not to be treated as a jest or falsehood, 2:231; 4:140; 6:150; 7:37; 17:59; 18:56; 18:106; 23:105; 37:14; 45:9; 45:35; 46:26;
62:5; 64:10; 78:28

shown in the horizons and within themselves, 41:53

see also Signs in creation

Allah's Throne, 2:255; 7:54; 10:3; 11:7; 13:2; 20:5; 25:59; 39:75; 40:7; 57:4; 69:17

Alcohol, *see Intoxicants*

Alms, *[Sadaqah]*, 2:271; 2:276; 9:58; 9:60; 9:79; 9:103-104; 58:12-13

Angels, 2:161; 2:210; 2:248; 3:18; 3:39; 3:42; 3:45; 3:80; 3:87; 4:166; 6:8-9; 6:111; 6:158; 11:12; 13:23; 15:7-8; 16:32-33; 17:40; 17:92; 17:95; 21:103; 22:75; 23:24; 25:7; 25:21-22; 41:14; 43:60; 53:26-27; 66:4; 79:1-5

and Adam, 2:31; 2:34; 7:11; 15:28-30; 17:61; 18:50; 38:71-73

appointed over the fire, 39:71; 66:6-7; 67:8; 74:30-31; 96:18

ascent of, 70:4;

ask forgiveness for those on Earth, 42:5

ask forgiveness for those who believe, 40:7-9

belief in, 2:177; 2:285; 4:136

creation, of 35:1; 37:150; 43:19

descent, of 16:2; 19:64-65; 25:25; 41:30-32; 97:4

fighting, 3:124-125; 8:9; 8:12; 9:26

given female names by those who disbelieve in the Hereafter, 53:27-28

guardians, 6:61; 13:11; 82:10

on the Day of Judgment, 34:40-41; 39:75; 50:21; 69:17; 78:38; 89:22

recording, 50:17-18

send blessings, 33:43

send blessings on the Prophet, 33:56

serve and worship Allah, 2:30; 4:172; 13:13; 16:49-50; 21:19-20; 37:164-166; 39:75; 40:7; 42:5

take the souls of the dying, 4:97; 6:61; 6:93; 7:37; 8:50; 16:28; 16:32; 32:11; 47:27; 79:1-2

see also Gabriel and Michael

Apes, swine, transgressors became as, 2:65; 5:60; 7:166

Apostates, 47:25,

Arafat, 2:198

Argue, *see Plead*

B

Babel (Babylon), 2:102

Backbiting, 49:12; 104:1

Badr (battle of), 3:13
lessons from, 8:5-19, 8:42-48

Balance,
in Creation, 15:19; 55:7-9; 57:25
in weighing, 17:35; 26:182
on the Day of Judgement, 7:8-9; 21:47; 23:102-103; 42:17; 101:6-8

Barrier [*Barzakh*], 23:100
a barrier between (the two seas), 25:53 55:20
also see, 18:94-97; 34:54; 36:9

Beast (of the last days), 27:82

Bedouins (wandering Arabs), 9:90; 9:97-99; 9:101; 9:120; 33:20; 48:11; 48:16; 49:14

Bee, 16:68-69

Believers,
Allah accepts them, 42:26
Allah has attuned their hearts, 8:63
Allah has bought their lives, 9:111
Allah is with them, 8:19; 47:35
Allah pardons them, 33:73
Allah will remove their ills and improve their condition, 3:195; 47:2; 48:5; 64:9
among Egyptians, 7:120-126; 10:83; 20:70-73; 26:46-51; 40:28-45; 66:11
are nothing else than brothers, 49:10
best of created beings, 98:7
covenant with Allah, 33:23
delivered, 41:18
descriptions of, 2:285; 8:2-4; 8:74; 9:112; 13:19-22; 23:1-11; 24:51; 24:62; 27:2-3; 32:15-19; 47:3; 48:29; 49:15; 58:22; 66:5; 66:11-12; 70:22-35; 90:17; 103:3
do not disrespect one another, 49:11-12
do not malign them, 33:58;
loved by Allah, 19:96
make peace between your brothers, 49:9-10
men and women, 9:71-72; 33:35
might belongs to them, 63:8

on them is no fear, nor shall they grieve, 2:38; 2:62; 2:112; 2:262; 2:274; 2:277; 3:170; 5:69; 6:48; 7:35; 10:62; 39:61; 46:13

protectors of one another, 8:72; 9:71; 42:39

rewarded, 2:62; 2:277; 17:9; 18:2-3; 23:10-11; 32:17; 33:35; 33:44; 33:47; 34:4; 34:37; 41:8; 45:30; 48:29; 57:7; 57:19; 84:25; 95:6

rewarded with Gardens, 2:25; 9:72; 13:22-24; 14:23; 19:60-63; 20:75-76; 22:23; 32:19; 42:22; 43:68-73; 47:12; 48:5; 57:12; 58:22; 61:12; 64:9; 65:11; 66:8; 70:35; 76:22; 85:11; 98:8

saved, 10:103; 26:118-119; 27:53

stauncher in their love for Allah, 2:165

warded off from them evil, 51:35-36; 52:18; 52:27; 76:11

why say you that which you do not do?, 61:2

Bequest, 2:181; 2:240; 4:7; 4:12
see also Inheritance

Betray (deceive, fraud), 4:107; 8:27; 8:58; 8:71; 12:52; 66:10

Birds, 2:260; 3:49; 5:110; 6:38; 12:36-41; 16:79; 21:79; 22:31; 24:41; 27:16-20; 34:10; 38:19; 56:21; 67:19; 105:3

Blood-Money, 2:178-179; 4:92; 17:33

Bribery, 2:188

Burden,
Allah tasks not a person beyond his scope, 2:286; 6:152; 7:42; 23:62; 65:7
borne on the Day of Resurrection, 16:25; 20:100; 29:13
no burdened soul can bear another's burden, 6:164; 17:15; 35:18; 39:7; 53:38
removed by Muhammad, 7:157
removed from Muhammad, 94:1-6

C

Camel, 6:144; 7:40; 77:33; 88:17

Captives, 8:67; 8:70-71; 33:26; 76:8
see also Prisoners of War

Cattle, 3:14; 4:119; 5:1; 6:136; 6:138-139; 6:142; 7:179; 16:5-8; 16:66; 20:54; 22:28; 22:30; 23:21; 25:44; 26:133; 32:27; 35:28; 36:71-73; 39:6; 40:79; 42:11; 43:12; 43:13; 47:12; 79:33; 80:32

Cave, people of the, 18:9-22; 18:25-26

Cave of Thawr, 9:40

Charity *[Zakah]*, 2:43; 2:83; 2:110; 2:177; 2:270-274; 2:277; 4:77; 4:162; 5:12; 5:55; 7:156; 9:71; 19:31; 19:55; 21:73; 22:41; 22:78; 23:4; 23:60; 24:37; 24:56; 27:3; 28:54; 30:39; 31:4; 32:16; 33:33; 33:35; 35:29; 36:47; 41:7; 57:7; 57:10; 58:13; 63:10; 64:16; 70:24-25; 98:5

Children, 7:189-190; 8:28; 13:38; 16:72; 17:64; 24:31; 42:49-50; 46:15; 60:3; 63:9; 64:14-15; 71:12; 90:3

  after divorce, 2:233; 65:6

  and inheritance, 4:11

  do not kill, 6:137; 6:140; 6:151; 17:31; 60:12

Children of Israel, 2:211; 2:246-252; 3:49; 3:93; 5:12; 5:32; 7:159-171; 10:93; 17:2; 17:101; 20:80; 26:17; 26:22; 32:23-24; 40:53

  and Jesus, 3:49-51; 5:46; 5:72; 5:110; 61:14

  and the calf, 2:51-54; 2:93; 4:153; 7:148; 7:152; 20:87-97

  and the Qur'an, 26:197; 27:76; 46:10

  deliverance from Pharaoh, 2:48-49; 7:136-141; 10:90; 14:6; 20:77-80; 26:60-67; 44:30-33

  distort the book, 3:78; 7:162

  dwellings in Egypt, 10:87; 26:57-59

  forty years in the wilderness, 5:26

  granted Prophethood, 45:16

  hearts went astray, 61:5

  like a donkey carrying books, 62:5

  told to remember Allah's favours, 2:40; 2:47; 2:122; 5:20

  warning given to them, 17:4-8; 17:104

  see also Jews, People of the Scripture

Christ, *see Jesus*

Christians, 2:111; 2:113; 2:120; 2:135; 5:14; 5:18; 22:17

  believers rewarded, 2:62; 5:69; 5:82-85; 57:27-29

  Compassion and Mercy in their hearts, 57:27

  love for the believers, 5:82

  recognise the Truth, 5:83-84

  see also People of the Scripture

City (land) of security, 95:3

Communities that were destroyed, 69:9

Confederates, 33:22

Creation, 2:164; 3:190-191; 6:1-2; 6:73; 9:36; 10:6; 13:16; 14:19; 14:32-33; 15:85; 16:3; 17:70; 18:51; 20:50; 21:30-33; 21:56; 25:2; 27:64; 29:61; 30:8; 30:22; 31:10-11; 35:1; 36:81; 39:5-6; 39:38; 40:57; 42:29; 43:9-13; 45:4; 45:22; 46:3; 46:33; 51:47-49; 52:36; 56:59; 64:3; 65:12; 77:20; 78:6-16; 79:27-33; 88:17-20

  a new, 13:5; 14:19; 17:49; 17:98; 34:7; 35:16; 53:47

  in pairs 13:3; 35:11; 36:36; 42:11: 43:12; 51:49; 53:45; 78:8

  in six days, 7:54; 10:3; 11:7; 25:59; 32:4; 41:9-12; 50:38; 57:4

  not in play, 21:16; 38:27; 44:38-39

  purpose of, 51:56

  of which you have no knowledge, 16:8; 36:36

  see also Man, creation of; Signs in creation

Crow (raven), 5:31

Criterion, 2:53; 3:4; 21:48; 25:1

D

David *[Dawud]*, 4:163; 5:78; 6:84; 17:55; 21:78-80; 27:15; 27:16; 34:10; 34:13; 38:17-30

  fights Goliath, 2:251

Day of Resurrection (Judgment), 1:4; 2:281; 3:9; 3:25; 3:106; 3:161; 3:185; 3:194; 4:87; 4:109; 5:14; 6:12; 6:16; 6:22-23; 7:53; 7:59; 7:167; 10:45; 10:93; 11:3; 11:84; 11:103-108; 14:31; 14:41-42; 14:48-51; 16:25; 16:27-34; 16:92; 16:124; 17:13-14; 17:97; 18:98-101; 18:105; 19:37-40; 20:100-109; 22:7; 22:56; 23:16; 23:100; 25:17-30; 26:82; 26:87-102; 30:12-16; 30:43-44; 30:55-57; 39:15; 39:31; 39:47-48; 39:67-75; 40:15-20; 42:45-47; 43:65-77; 45:26-35; 50:42; 55:39-41; 56:1-56; 58:6-7; 58:18; 60:3; 60:6; 66:7-8; 67:27; 68:42-43; 69:13-37; 70:1-4; 75:1; 75:6; 75:7-15; 77:29-49; 78:17-40; 79:34-46; 80:33-42; 81:1-14; 84:1-15; 85:2; 86:9-10; 89:21-30; 99:1-8; 100:9-11; 102:8

  the Caller will call out from a near place, 50:41

Day of Resurrection (Judgment), *(cont'd.)*

a Day of Anguish, 19:39; 74:9

a Day of mutual disillusion, 64:9

a Day known (only to Allah), 56:50

all mankind will stand before the Lord of the Worlds, 83:4-6

appointed time of the Hour, 7:187; 10:48-51; 11:104; 16:61; 16:77; 18:21; 18:36; 20:15; 21:38-40; 27:71-72; 31:34; 32:28-30; 33:63; 34:3; 34:29-30; 36:48-50; 40:59; 41:47; 42:17-18; 43:61: 43:66; 43:85; 45:32; 47:18; 51:12-14; 54:1; 56:1; 67:25-26; 70:6-7; 72:25; 78:17; 79:42-46

awe, dread, fear, horror, and terror, 21:97; 22:1-2; 27:87; 34:23; 34:51; 73:17; 75:7; 79:6-9; 101:4

belief in, 2:177; 3:114; 4:38-39; 4:59; 4:136; 4:162; 5:69; 9:18-19; 9:44-45; 24:2; 40:27; 42:18; 58:22; 65:2; 70:26

covering is removed from your sight, 50:22

draws near, 21:1; 40:18; 53:57-58; 54:1; 70:7

Day of Reckoning, 38:16; 38:26; 38:53; 40:27

Day of Assembly, 42:7; 64:9

Day of Immortality, 50:34

Day of Gathering, 50:44

Day of Calamity, 101: 1-11

Day of Decision, 37:19-74; 44:40-42; 77:13-15; 77:38; 78:17

no excuses, 66:7; 75:13-15

no one can avail another, 31:33; 44:41; 80:34-37; 82:19

no speaking, 11:105; 77:35-36: 78:37-38

people will not be unjustly dealt with, 17:71; 18:49; 19:60; 21:47; 36:54; 39:69-70; 40:17; 43:76; 45:22

single Shout (Blast) (Cry), 36:49; 36:53; 38:15; 50:42; 69:13; 79:13-14; 80:33

Sovereignty shall be for Allah, 25:26; 82:19

the great, Overwhelming event, 88:1-16

the reality, 69:1-3

the True Day, 78:39

will surely come to pass, 51:5-6; 52:7-8; 74:47; 77:7

see also Hereafter; Hour; Resurrection; Balance; Trumpet

Death, 2:180; 2:243; 3:143-145; 3:154; 3:156-158; 4:78; 4:97; 4:100; 5:106; 6:61; 6:162; 7:25; 7:37; 8:50; 16:28; 16:32; 16:70; 23:15; 23:99; 31:34; 39:30; 45:21; 50:19; 56:60; 56:83-87; 62:6-8; 63:10; 67:2; 75:22-30; 80:21; 102:2

every soul shall taste, 3:185; 21:35; 29:57

only happens once, 37:58-60; 44:56

Debts, 2:280-282; 4:12; 56:66

Decree,

as a command from Our presence, We are always sending, 44:5

for everything there is, 13:38

We destroyed no township but there was a known, 15:4

when He (Allah) decrees a thing, He says only, "Be!" - and it is, 2:117

Deeds,

evil, beautified for them, 47:14

fastened man's, to his own neck, 17:13

right and wrong, are for and against his ownself, 41:46; 45:15

to us our, to you your works, 28:55; 42:15

Degrees (ranks),

from what they did, 6:132

Desire (Lusts),

those follow their, 47:14; 47:16

who chooses for his God his own, 25:43

Despair,

not of the mercy of Allah, 39:53

not of the Spirit of Allah, 12:87

Dhu'l-Kifl, 21:85

Dhu'l-Qarneyn, 18:83-98

Disbelievers, 3:156; 3:176-178; 3:196; 4:42; 4:76; 4.84; 4:151; 6:1; 8:30-40; 8:55; 9:73; 16:107; 22:72; 29:68; 32:22; 40:4; 61:8; 66:9-10; 74:43-53; 75:31-35; 78:40; 80:42; 88:23-24; 109:1-6

astray, 1:7; 4:136-137; 6:110; 14:2-3; 14:18; 17:48; 17:72; 23:106; 25:9; 25:34; 25:44; 27:4-5; 42:18; 42:44; 43:40; 45:23; 46:32

cannot outstrip (Allah's Purpose), 8:59;

covered with disgrace, 3:112; 3:192; 16:27; 68:42-43; 70:44

Disbelievers, *(cont'd.)*

cursed, 2:89; 2:161: 4:52

deaf, dumb, and blind, 2:18; 2:171; 6:39; 17:72; 17:97; 20:124-126; 21:45; 22:46; 27:66; 27:80-81; 28:66; 30:52-53; 31:7; 41:44; 47:23

deny the Day of Judgement, 34:3; 41:50; 42:18; 45:32; 52:11; 64:7; 82:9: 83:10-13; 84:13-15

despair of Mercy, 15:56; 41:49

despair of the Hereafter, 60:13

do not obey them, 3:149; 33:48; 96:19

do not take for friends or helpers, 3:28; 4:139; 4:144; 5:57; 9:23; 60:1-2; 60:9; 60:13

doubt Revelation, 6:7-8; 6:25; 16:101; 25:4-8; 30:58; 34:31; 37:12-17; 37:35-36; 37:170; 38:5-8: 40:70; 43:31; 45:11; 50:2; 52:30-44; 67:9; 68:15; 74:24-25; 84:20-22

forbidden Paradise, 7:50; 70:38-39

fuel for the Fire (Companions of the Fire), 3:10-12; 3:151; 5:10; 5:86; 21:98; 22:19; 40:6; 57:19; 67:10-11; 72:15

hearts are sealed, 2:7; 7:101; 10:74; 16:108; 30:59; 40:35: 45:23; 47:24; 63:3

in illusion, 67:20-21

makes as his god his own desire, 45:23

ordered to prostrate, but do not, 68:42-43; 77:48

persecuting the Believers, 85:4-8; 85:10

plotting and planning, 8:30; 13:42; 14:46; 52:42; 71:22; 74:18-20; 86:15-17; 105:2

protectors of one another, 8:73; 45:19

ransom not accepted, 3:91; 5:36; 13:18

render their actions vain, 47:1; 47:8-9

their deeds are as a mirage, 24:39

their own deeds made fair-seeming, 6:122: 8:48; 9:37; 27:4; 35:8

will blame each other on the Day of Resurrection, 34:31-33; 37:24-32; 38:59-64

will not be successful, 23:117

wish to be Muslims, 15:2

Distress (grief), 3:154

be not in distress, 16:127

distress and anguish, 12:86

tribulation and distress, 7:95

Ditch (pit), people of the, 85:4-10

Divorce, 2:227-232; 2:236-237; 2:241; 33:49; 58:2-3; 65:1-7

see also, 4:35

Donkeys (ass), 2:259; 16:8; 31:19; 62:5; 74:50

Drink,

alcoholic, 2:219; 5:90

cup from a gushing spring, pure, 37:45; 76:21

pure wine, 83:25

white, delicious, 37:46

E

Earth,

becomes green, 22:63

created seven, 65:12

creation in four days, 41:9-10

for a dwelling place, 40:64

for the living and dead, 77:25-26

is Allah's, 7:128

mischief (corruption; evil) in, 2:251; 7:56; 7:74; 8:73; 11:116; 12:73; 13:25; 26:152; 26:183; 27:48; 30:41; 47:22

noble things of, 26:7; 31:10; 50:7

on the Day of Judgment. 14:48; 18:47; 20:105-107; 39:67; 39:69; 50:44; 52:10; 56:4-6; 69:14; 70:9; 73:14; 77:10; 78:20; 81:3-6; 82:3-4; 84:3-5; 89:21: 99:1-5

revive it after its death, 2:164; 7:57; 16:65; 22:5; 25:49; 29:63; 30:19; 30:24; 30:50; 35:9; 36:33-36; 41:39; 43:11; 45:5; 50:11; 57:17

split, 80:26; 86:12

spread out, 13:3; 15:19; 51:48; 71:19-20; 79:30; 88:20; 91:6

subservient to humans, 67:15

sustenance, 41:10

wide and spacious, 4:97; 4:100; 29:56; 39:10; 78:6

Elephant army, 105:1-5

Elias *[Elijah; Ilyasin; Ilyas]*, 6:85; 37:123-132

Elisha, 6:86

Emigration, 2:218; 3:195; 4:97; 4:100; 8:72; 8:74; 9:20; 16:41; 16:110; 22:58; 24:22; 59:3

Event, 56:1; 69:15

Evil, 4:123; 10:27-30; 19:83; 59:15

    appears on land and sea, 30:41

    changed, for the good, 7:95

    consequence for those who dealt, 30:10

    ever forgiving, 4:149

    good from Allah, evil from yourselves, 4:79; 42:48

    plan ill deeds, 16:45-47

    recompensed, 6:160; 42:40

    repel; overcome, with better, 13:22; 23:96; 41:34

    those who follow their, lusts, 47:14; 47:16

    utterance of harsh speech, 4:148

Evil One, *see Satan*

Excess forbidden,

    in food, 5:87; 20:81

    in religion, 4:171; 5:77-81

Eyes, ears and skins will testify against sinners, 41:20-23

Ezekiel, see Dhu'l Kifl

Ezra *[Uzayr]*, 9:30

F

Faith (belief), 2:108; 3:167; 3:177; 3:193; 5:5; 9:23; 16:106; 30:56; 40:10; 42:52; 49:11; 49:14; 52:21; 58:22; 59:9; 59:10

    disbelieve, 3:116

    He has led you to the, 49:17

    increased, 3:173

    is sure, 44:7; 45:4; 45:20; 51:20

False Gods,

    besides Allah, idols and so-called partners, vanity, 7:194-198; 16:20-21; 16:73; 16:86; 21:22; 21:24; 34:22; 34:27; 41:47; 41:48; 46:5-6; 53:19-24; 71:23-24

    revile not those whom they worship besides Allah, 6:108

Falsehood *[Batil]*, 2:42; 3:71; 8:8; 13:17; 17:81; 22:62; 29:52; 29:67; 31:30; 34:49; 40:5; 41:42; 42:24; 47:3

    perishes, 21:18

Fasting,

    in expiation, 2:196; 4:92; 5:89; 5:95; 58:4

    in Ramadan, 2:183-185; 2:187

    men and women, 33:35

Fear of Allah, 2:223; 3:175; 4:77; 7:56; 9:13; 9:18; 22:1; 23:57; 32:16; 33:37; 35:28; 39:23; 59:21; 64:16; 70:27; 79:26; 79:40; 87:10; 98:8

    in secret, 35:18; 36:11; 50:33; 67:12

Fear no evil, 3:175

Fear, none for the Righteous, 2:38;

    or for Believers, 2:62

    or those who submit to Allah, 2:112

    or whoever spends for Allah, 2:262, 274

    or those who believe and do good, 2:277; 5:69

    or whoever believes and does right, 6:48; 7:35

    or for friends of Allah, 10:62

    or for Allah's devotees (slaves), 43:68

    or for those who remain firm in Allah, 46:13

Fear of mankind, 4:77

Female infanticide, 16:58; 81:8-9

Fig, 95:1

Fighting (striving),

    against those who believe not in Allah, 9:29

    by Children of Israel, 2:246-251

    in the Cause of Allah, and oppressed men and women, 4:74-77

    in the way of Allah against disbelievers (who fight against you), 2:190-193; 2:244; 4:84; 4:95; 8:72; 8:74-75; 9:12-16; 9:20; 9:36; 9:123; 47:4; 61:11

    in sacred months, 2:217; 9:5

    no blame for the blind, lame and sick, 48:16-17

    ordained, 2:216

    sanction given to those who are wronged, 22:39-41

    until persecution is no more, 8:39

    twenty overcoming two hundred, 8:65

    whose heart is a disease (hypocrites), 47:20

Food,

    in paradise, 2:25; 19:62; 37:41-42; 38:51; 43:73; 44:55; 47:15; 52:22; 55:52-54; 55:68; 56:20-21; 56:32-33; 69:23-24; 76:14; 77:42-43

Food, *(cont'd.)*

   lawful and unlawful (Halal and Haram), 2:168; 2:172-173; 5:1; 5:3-5; 5:88; 6:118-119; 6:121; 6:136-146; 10:59; 16:114-115; 22:30; 66:1

   make not unlawful which Allah has made lawful, 7:32

   no sin for what ate in the past, 5:93

   transgress not, 5:87-88

Forbidden conduct, 6:151-152; 7:33

Forgiveness, 7:199; 39:53; 45:14; 53:32; 57:20-21

   a duty of Believers, 45:14

   Allah forgives all sins, 39:53

   Allah forgives to whom He will, 4:48

   Allah pardons not that partners should be ascribed to him, 4:116

   Angels ask for, for those on the Earth, 42:5

   forgive, when they are angry, 42:37

   forgive and make reconciliation, 42:40-43

   not to pray for forgiveness of idolaters, 9:113

   people of the Scripture long to make you disbelieve, 2:109

   race one with another in, 57:21

   seeks pardon of Allah, 4:110

Fornication, *see Zina*

Fraud, 83:1-6

Free will,

   choose a way to his lord, 76:29

   limited by Allah's will (plan), 6:107; 10:99; 74:56; 76:31; 81:28-29

   to walk straight, 81:28

   whosoever wills, let him: believe and disbelieve, 18:29

Friday prayers, 62:9-11

Fruit, 16:11

   as they desire, 77:42

   every kind, of 47:15

   in Paradise, plenty, 43:73

G

Gabriel, 2:97-98; 66:4

   true spirit, 26:193

   see also Jesus, and the Holy Spirit;

Gambling, 2:219; 5:90; 5:91

Gardens, 6:141; 13:4; 23:19; 26:57; 26:134; 26:147; 34:15-16; 44:25; 50:9; 71:12; 78:16; 80:30

Gardens of Paradise, 3:15; 3:133; 3:136; 3:195; 3:198; 4:57; 4:122; 5:85; 5:119; 7:19; 7:42-43; 7:49; 9:21-22; 13:35; 15:45-48; 18:31; 18:107-108; 20:76; 22:14; 22:23; 25:10; 25:15-16; 25:24; 29:58; 30:15; 31:8-9; 35:33-35; 36:26; 36:55-58; 38:49-54; 39:73-74; 40:40; 43:70-73; 44:51-57; 51:15; 52:17-28; 54:54; 56:11-40; 59:20; 76:5-22; 77:41-44; 78:31-36; 79:41; 89:30

   abode of Peace, 6:127; 10:25

   bliss and high estate, 76:20

   breadth of the heaven and earth, 57:21

   brought near. 50:31-75; 81:13

   carpets (couches), 55:54; 55:76

   drink in, 37:45-47; 38:51; 52:23; 56:18-19; 76:5-6; 76:15-18; 76:21; 77:43; 78:34: 83:25-28; 88:14

   see also Food, in Paradise;

   firmly established, 54:55

   Garden of Abode, 53:15

   Garden of Immortality, 25:15

   Gardens of Bliss, 68:34: 76:20

   Gardens of Delight, 5:65; 10:9; 22:56; 26:85; 31:8; 37:43-49; 56:12; 56:89

   Gardens of Eden, 9:72; 13:23; 16:31; 18:31; 19:61; 20:76; 35:33; 38:50; 40:8; 61:12; 98:8

   Grief removed, 35:34

   in a high garden, 69:22-24; 88:10-16

   lofty halls, 39:20

   Mansions of eternity, 35:35

   no toil nor weariness, 35:35

   reclining on thrones and couches, 18:31; 36:56; 52:20; 56:15-16; 56:34; 76:13: 83:23; 83:35; 88:13

   secure (safe) place, 44:51; 44:55

   similitude of, 47:15

   two Gardens, 55:46-47

   with Allah, 50:35; 68:34; 73:20

   youths (menservants), 52:24; 56:17; 76:19

Game, in a state of Ihram, 5:94; 5:96

Gog and Magog, *[Ya'juj and Ma'juj]*, 18:94-99; 21:96

Goliath, 2:249-251

Good,

Allah rewards those who do, with goodness, 53:31

be, as Allah has been kind to you, 28:77

for those who do, there is a, (reward) and the home of Hereafter, 16:30

increased, 42:23

is there any reward for, other than goodness, 55:60

repel evil with, 23:96; 28:54; 41:34

rewarded double, 4:40; 28:54

rewarded ten times, 6:160

those who do, in this world there is, 39:10

you hate a thing which is, and that you love a thing which is bad, 2:216

Good and Evil,

every soul will be confronted with all that he has done, 3:30

Good is from Allah, and evil is from yourself, 4:79

if you do good, for your own souls, and if you do evil, 17:7; 41:46

Good deed,

openly or keep it secret, 4:149

vie one with another in, 5:48

Gospel, 3:3; 3:48; 3:65; 5:46; 5:47; 5:66; 5:68; 5:110; 7:157; 9:111; 48:29; 57:27

Greeting (Salutation), 4:86; 10:10; 14:23; 24:61; 25:75; 33:44

H

Hail, 24:43

Haman, 28:6; 28:8; 28:38; 29:39; 40:24; 40:36-37

Hands and Feet will speak out, 36:65

Hardship, with it goes ease, 94:5-6

Hearts,

diverse, 59:14

hardened, 2:74; 22:53; 39:22; 57:16

in whose, there is a disease, 2:10; 5:52; 8:49; 9:125; 22:53; 24:50; 33:12; 33:32; 33:60; 47:20; 47:29; 74:31

locks, 47:24

print upon, 7:100; 7:101; 40:35

sealed, 47:16; 63:3

veil, 17:46; 41:5

whose, fear when Allah is mentioned, 22:35

Heavens,

as a canopy (roof), 2:22; 21:32; 40:64; 52:5; 79:28

built with might, 51:47

full of Paths, 51:7

(hypothetical) ladder (stairway) to, 6:35; 52:38

no rifts in it, 50:6; 67:3-4

on the Day of Judgment, 14:48; 21:104; 25:25; 39:67; 52:9; 55:37; 69:16; 70:8; 73:18; 77:8-9; 78:19; 81:1-2; 81:11; 82:1-2; 84:1-2

ordained in two days, 41:12

raised by Allah, 13:2; 55:7; 79:27-28

returning rain, 86:11

seven in number, 2:29; 17:44; 23:17; 23:86; 41:12; 65:12; 67:3; 71:15; 78:12

split apart, 42:5

starry, 85:1; 86:1

when it was smoke (primeval matter), 41:11

Hell, 2:206; 3:12; 3:103; 3:131; 3:151: 3:191-192; 3:197; 4:56; 4:121; 7:18; 7:38; 9:35; 9:81: 14:16; 14:28-30; 15:43-44; 16:29; 17:97; 18:29; 21:98-100; 22:19-22; 23:103-108; 25:65-66; 29:54-55; 32:20; 36:63-64; 38:55-64; 39:16; 39:60; 40:71-76; 43:74-77; 44:43-50; 45:10; 50:24-26; 52:13-16; 54:48; 55:43-44; 56:41-56; 56:94; 57:14-15; 58:8; 59:3; 69:30-37; 70:15-18; 72:23; 73:12-13; 74:26-31; 74:42-48; 76:4; 77:29-33; 81:12; 82:14-16; 83:16-17; 88:4-7; 90:20; 102:6-7

lurks in ambush, 78:21-30

blazing in fury, 25:11-12; 67:7-8; 77:31-33; 92:14-16; 101:11; 111:3

filled with Jinn and men, 7:18; 7:179; 11:119; 32:13; 38:85

fuel is men and stones, 2:24; 66:6

inhabitants of Paradise talk about comrade in, 37:51-59

insatiable, 50:30

neither dying nor living there, 14:16-17; 20:74; 35:36; 43:77; 87:13

Hell, *(cont'd.)*

penalty of Eternity, 10:52; 32:14; 41:28

placed in full view, 79:36-39; 89:23

Hereafter, 2:94; 2:200-201; 2:220; 3:22; 3:85; 3:145; 3:148; 4:77; 4:134; 9:69; 10:64; 12:57; 12:101; 13:34; 16:107; 16:122; 17:72; 20:127; 22:11; 22:15; 24:14; 24:19; 24:23; 27:66; 29:27; 38:46; 39:9; 39:26; 40:43; 41:16; 41:31; 59:3; 60:13; 68:33; 75:21

belief in, 6:92; 6:113; 6:150; 11:19; 16:22; 17:19; 27:3; 31:4; 34:21; 39:45; 41:7

better than worldly life, 2:86; 2:201; 3:77; 3:152; 4:74; 6:32; 7:169; 9:38; 13:26; 14:27; 16:30; 20:131; 28:80; 29:64; 40:39; 42:20; 43:35; 57:20; 87:14-17

see also Day of Resurrection; Gardens of Paradise; Hell; Resurrection

Horses, 3:14; 16:8

Hour (of Doom) (the Final),

but as a twinkling of the eye, or it is nearer still, 16:77

comes upon you, 6:40; 20:15; 34:3

drew near, 54:1-5

earthquake of the, 22:1

no doubt of the, coming, 40:59; 45:32

the knowledge of it is with Allah only, 7:187; 33:63; 41:47

they will be divided, 30:14

unrighteous will despair, 30:12

will come suddenly, 6:31; 12:107; 43:66

Houses, manners about entering, 24:27-29

Huneyn (battle), 9:25

Hur (females in Paradise), 44:54; 52:20; 56:22

Hypocrites,

afraid of being found out, 9:64-65

Allah punishes, 33:73

are the enemy, so beware of them, 63:4

comprehend not (know not), 63:7; 63:8

deceive themselves, 2:9

deaf, dumb and blind, 2:17-18

disbelievers success, 4:141

disease in their hearts, 2:10; 8:49; 22:53; 33:12; 47:29

go for judgment to false deities, 4:60-62

in fear of death and darkness, 2:19-20

in the lowest depths of Fire, 4:145

losers; Allah curses them, 9:67-69

make faith a pretext to misguide men, 63:2

mischief makers, 2:11-12

mockers, 2:13-15

most rigid of opponents, 2:204-206

not to be taken as friends, 4:89

not to pray for, 9:84

seek to deceive Allah, 4:142-143

strive against them, 66:9

their hearts are sealed, 63:3

they utter a thing which is not in their hearts, 3:167

they verily are liars, 59:11-14

when they believe not, 2:8

I

Imran,

daughter of, 66:12

wife of, 3:35

Inheritance, 2:180; 2:240; 4:7-9; 4:11; 4:12; 4:19; 4:33; 4:176; 5:106-108

Injustice, 4:30

one who has been wronged, 4:148

Intercession, 6:51; 6:70; 6:94; 10:3; 19:87; 20:109; 30:13; 34:23; 39:44; 40:18; 43:86; 53:26; 74:48

Interest, *see Usury*

Intoxicants

strong drink, 2:219; 5:90; 5:91

Isaac *[Ishaq]*, 2:133; 4:163; 6:84; 19:49; 21:72; 29:27; 37:112; 37:113

Ishmael *[Isma'il]*, 2:125-129; 2:133; 4:163; 6:86; 19:54-55; 21:85; 38:48

Islam, 3:19; 3:85; 5:3; 6:125; 39:22; 61:7

as a favour, 49:17

first of those who submit as Muslims, 6:14; 6:163; 39:12

whose heart Allah has expanded for, 39:22

J

Jacob *[Yaqub]*, 2:132; 2:133; 2:136; 2:140; 3:84; 4:163; 6:84; 11:71; 12:6; 12:38; 12:68; 19:6; 19:49; 21:72; 29:27; 38:45

Jesus, son of Mary

    and the Holy Spirit, 2:87; 2:253; 5:110; 19:17

    annunciation of, 3:45-51; 19:16-21

    a sign, 21:91; 23:50; 43:57-61

    belief in, 4:159

    covenant with Allah, 33:7

    cursed the Children of Israel, 5:78

    disciples of, 3:52-54; 5:111-113; 57:27; 61:14

    given the revelation, 2:87; 2:136; 2:253; 3:48; 3:84; 4:163; 5:46; 19:30; 57:27

    gives good tidings of the Praised One (Ahmad), 61:6

    is not Allah, 5:17; 5:72; 9:30-31

    like Adam, 3:59

    messenger to Children of Israel, 3:49-51; 5:46; 5:72; 43:59; 61:6; 61:14

    miracles of, 5:110; 5:113-115

    no more than a Messenger, 4:171; 5:75; 43:59

    raised to Allah, 3:55; 4:158

    religion of, 42:13

    serves Allah, 4:172; 19:30; 43:64

    spoke in the cradle, 3:46; 5:110; 19:30-33

    testifies before Allah, 5:116-118

    was of the righteous, 6:85

    was not killed, 4:157

    wisdom of, 43:63

Jews, 2:111; 2:113; 2:120; 2:135; 4:160; 5:18; 16:118; 22:17

    among them some believe, 2:62; 4:162; 5:69

    became apes and swine, 2:65; 5:60; 7:166

    claim that they are favoured by Allah, 62:6-8

    cursed, 4:46-47; 5:78; 9:30

    enmity, of 5:64; 5:82

    greediest of mankind for life, 2:96

    judged by the Torah, 5:44

    slew prophets, 2:87; 2:91; 3:21; 3:181; 4:155; 5:70

    took usury, 4:161

    unbelief and blasphemy of, 5:41; 5:64; 59:2; 59:11

    work iniquity, 5:41-42; 5:78-81; 59:2-4; 59:11-17

    write the Book with their own hands, 2:79

    see also Children of Israel; People of the Scripture

Jinn, 6:100; 6:112; 15:27; 34:41; 46:18; 46:29; 55:15; 55:33; 55:39; 72:1-15

Job *[Ayyub]*, 4:163; 6:84; 21:83;

    he suffered, 21:84; 38:41-44

John, the Baptist *[Yahya]*, 19:7

    glad tidings of, 3:39; 21:90

    righteous, 6:85

    wise; compassionate; pure; dutiful, 19:12-15

Jonah *[Jonas or Yunus]*, 4:163; 6:86; 10:98; 37:139-148

Joseph *[Yusuf]*, 6:84; 12:4-101; 40:34

Judgment Day, *see Day of Resurrection*

Judi, Mount, 11:44

Justice, 2:282; 4:58; 4:135; 7:29; 16:90

    see also, 4:65; 4:105

K

Ka'bah (Inviolable Place of Worship), 2:144; 2:149-150; 2:158; 3:96-97; 5:2; 5:95-97; 9:19; 17:1; 22:29; 22:33; 48:27; 52:4; 106:3

    and the disbelievers, 8:34-35; 9:7; 9:17; 9:28; 22:25; 48:25

    built by Abraham and Ishmael, 2:125-127; 22:26

    fighting at, 2:191; 2:217;

Keys,

    of the Heavens and the Earth, 39:63; 42:12

    of the invisible, 6:59

Killing,

    do not slay anyone, 17:33

    if anyone killed a human being, 5:32

Kind words 2:263

Kindred, rights of, 4:7-9; 4:36; 8:41; 16:90; 17:26; 24:22; 30:38; 42:23

Knowledge,

    know with a sure, 102:5-7

Knowledge, *(cont'd.)*
    not a leaf falls, but He knows it, 6:59
    of five things, with Allah alone, 31:34
    slain their children without, 6:140

Korah *[Qarun]*, 28:76-82; 29:39; 40:24

L

Lamp, 25:61; 67:5; 71:16

Languages,
    difference in, 30:22

Last Day, *see Day of Resurrection*

Law,
    prescribed, 5:48

Liars, 26:221-223

Life,
    if anyone saves the, 5:32

Life of the world,
    bought the, at the price of the Hereafter, 2:86
    desire for, 11:15-16; 17:18; 42:20
    good tidings in the, 10:64
    is but comfort of illusion, 3:185
    little is the enjoyment of the, 9:38; 13:26; 28:60
    love for the, and neglecting the Hereafter 75:20-21; 76:27
    pageantry and boasting, 57:20
    pastime and a sport, 6:32; 29:64: 47:36
    sell the, for the other, 4:74
    similitude of the, 10:24
    tricked Jinns and humans, 6:130
    you prefer the, over the Hereafter, 87:16

Light,
    of Allah, 5:15-16; 9:32; 24:35-36; 39:22; 61:8; 64:8
    of the Believers, 57:12-13; 57:19; 57:28; 66:8; 76:11

Lightning, 24:43; 69:5
    fear and hope, 13:12-13; 30:24
    parable of, 2:19-20

Lion, 74:51

Loan,
    lend to Allah a goodly, 2:245; 73:20

    doubled for them, 57:11; 57:18; 64:17

Loss, manifest, 39:15

Lot *[Lut]*, 6:86; 7:80; 11:70; 11:74; 11:77; 11:81; 11:89; 21:71; 21:74; 22:43; 26:160; 26:161; 26:167; 27:54-56; 29:26; 29:28; 29:32; 29:33; 37:133; 38:13; 50:13; 54:33; 54:34
    his disobedient wife, 11:81; 15:60; 66:10

Lote tree, 34:16; 53:14-16; 56:28

Luqman, 31:12-14

M

Madinah *[Yathrib]*, 9:120; 33:13; 63:8

Midian, 7:85-93; 11:84-95; 20:40; 22:44; 28:22; 28:23; 29:36-37

Mahr (bridal-money), 2:229; 2:236; 2:237; 4:4; 4:19-21; 4:24; 4:25; 5:5; 33:50; 60:10; 60:11

Makkah (Becca), 3:96; 48:24

City, 90:1; 90:2
    land made safe, 95:3

Man,
    Allah is nearer to him than his jugular vein, 50:16
    argumentative, 18:54; 22:3; 22:8; 36:49
    assumed the Trust, 33:72
    created according to the will of Allah, 30:30; 82:8
    created anxious, 70:19-21
    created in affliction, 90:4
    created of the best stature, 95:4
    created to worship Allah, 51:56
    created weak, 4:28; 30:54
    creation of, 2:30; 4:1; 6:2; 6:98; 7:11; 7:189; 15:26; 15:28-29; 15:33; 16:4; 18:37; 19:67; 22:5; 23:12-14; 25:54; 30:20; 30:54; 32:7-9; 35:11; 36:36; 36:77-78; 37:11; 38:71-72; 39:6; 40:57; 40:64; 40:67; 45:4; 49:13; 50:16; 53:45-46; 55:3-4; 55:14; 56:57-59; 67:23; 71:14; 74:11; 75:36-39; 76:2; 76:28; 77:20-23; 78:8; 79:27; 80:18-19: 82:7-8; 86:5-7; 90:4-9; 96:2
    is an open opponent, 16:4; 36:77
    is hasty, 17:11; 21:37
    journey from plane to plane, 84:19
    not assigned with two hearts, 33:4

Man, *(cont'd.)*

   stages of growth, 46:15

   was a thing unremembered, 76:1

   work towards Allah, 84:6

Mankind,

   be careful of your duty to your Lord, 4:1

   created you in the wombs of your mothers, 39:6

   made you nations and tribes, 49:13

   one community, 2:213; 10:19

   rebellion is only against yourselves, 10:23

   witnesses over, 2:143

Manna and Quails, 2:57; 7:160; 20:80-81

Manners,

   about entering houses, 24:27-29

   in assemblies, 58:11

   in the home, 24:58-61

   in the Prophet's house, 33:53

   in the Prophet's presence, 2:104; 4:46; 24:62; 49:1-5

   not to scoff another, 49:11

   to greet and send blessings on the Prophet, 33:56

Marriage, 2:221; 4:3-4; 4:20-21; 4:24-25; 4:34:35; 4:128-130; 7:189; 23:6; 24:3; 24:26; 24:32-33; 25:54; 30:21; 60:10

   of Muhammad, 33:50-52; 66:5

   prohibited degrees in, 4:22-24; 24:31; 33:37

   with women of the People of the Book, 5:5

   see also Wives

Martyrs,

   not dead, 2:154; 3:169

   rejoice in grace and bounty from Allah, 3:170; 3:171

   receive forgiveness and mercy, 3:157-158

   will receive good provision, 22:58; 22:59

Mary (mother of Jesus),

   a sign for all people, 21:91; 23:50

   birth, 3:35-77

   brought Jesus to her own people, 19:27-33

   false charge, 4:156

   glad tidings of Jesus, 3:42-51; 19:16-21

   guarded her chastity, 21:91; 66:12

   in childbirth, 19:23-26

Measure and weight, 11:85; 17:35; 83:1-5

Meeting,

   with Allah, 6:31

   of an Awful Day, 19:37

   of the Hereafter, 30:16

Messengers, 2:253; 4:164; 4:165; 14:44; 57:27

   an angel as a, 17:95; 25:7

   and their wives and offspring, 13:38

   as a witness from every nation, 16:89

   belief in, 2:177; 2:285; 3:179; 4:171; 5:12; 57:19; 57:21

   believing in some and rejecting others, 4:150-152

   for every nation, there is a, 10:47; 16:36

   gathering of the, 5:109

   mocked, 6:10; 13:32; 15:11; 21:41

   narrate Allah's verses, 7:35-36

   no more than human beings, 14:10-12; 17:94; 21:8; 25:7-8; 25:20

   rejected by their people, 3:184; 4:150; 5:70; 6:34; 7:101; 10:13; 10:74; 14:9-13; 16:113; 22:42-44; 23:44; 23:69; 26:105-191; 30:9; 34:34-35; 34:45; 35:4; 35:25; 36:13-19; 38:12-14; 40:22; 40:83; 41:14; 43:24; 50:12-15; 51:52; 54:9; 54:18; 54:23; 54:33; 54:42; 64:6; 67:9; 69:9-10

   slay, 3:183

   sent as bearers of good news and warners, 6:48; 14:4-8

   succession of, 2:87; 23:44

   threatened, 14:13

   testify before Allah, 5:109; 7:6; 39:69; 40:51; 43:45; 77:11

   see also Prophets

Messiah, *see* Jesus

Michael, 2:98

Misfortune, because of your hands, 42:30

Monasticism,

   not prescribed, 57:27

Months, number of, 9:36; 9:37

Moon, 7:54; 10:5; 16:12; 22:18; 25:61; 36:39; 36:40; 71:16; 91:2;

   split in two, 54:1

Moses *[Musa]*,

and calf-worship of his people, 7:148-156; 20:86-98

and his people, 2:51-61; 5:20-29; 7:138-141; 7:159-162; 14:5-8; 61:5

called and given messengership, 19:51-53; 20:9-56; 28:29-35

came to them with clear proofs, 29:39

given the Criterion, 21:48

given the Scripture, 17:2

guided by Allah, 6:84

guided to the Right path, 37:114-122

Pharaoh, and his people (chiefs), 2:49; 2:50; 7:103-137; 10:75-92; 11:96-99; 17:101-103; 20:17-53; 20:56-79; 23:45-49; 25:35-36; 26:10-69; 28:4-21; 28:31-42; 40:23-46; 43:46-56; 51:38-40; 73:16; 79:15-26

his book, differences arose in it, 11:110

his childhood, mother and sister, 20:38-40; 28:7-13

his mishap in the city, 28:15-21

in Midian, 20:40; 28: 22-28

magicians converted, 20:70-73; 26:46-52

mountain and Lord's appearance, 7:142-145

mystic fire, 27:7-12; 28:29-35

nine Clear signs, 7:133; 17:101

Scripture (books), 53:36; 87:19

to the junction of the two seas, 18:60-82

Mosque (of Jerusalem),

temple, 17:7

Mosque (of Quba), 9:107; 9:108

Mosques, 2:187; 22:40

sanctuaries, 9:17-19

to tend, of Allah, 9:18

Mountains (hills), 15:19; 16:15; 20:105-107; 21:31; 22:18; 31:10; 59:21; 77:10; 77:27; 81:3; 101:5

Muhammmad,

a mercy to the believers, 9:61

a plain warner, 7:184; 7:188; 11:2; 15:89; 53:56

a warner and bearer of good tidings, 7:188; 11:2; 15:89; 33:45; 34:28; 48:8

a witness over believers, 2:143

Allah is Witness between me and you, 13:43; 29:52; 46:8

and the blind man, 80:1-12

as a mercy from Allah, 28:46-47

ask no reward (fee), 25:57; 38:86; 42:23

close to the believers, 33:6

covenant to believe in, 3:81

devoted to prayer, 73:1-8; 73:20

foretold by Jesus, 61:6

from darkness to light, 65:11

good example to follow, 33:21

has been commanded to, 27:91-93; 30:30; 66:9

his sayings, 11:2-4; 12:108; 34:46-50

his work, 3:164; 7:157; 36:6; 52:29

is but a Messenger, 3:144

lenient with them, 3:159

men who annoy the, 9:61

mercy for the peoples, 21:107

mocked, 25:41-42; 34:7; 34:8

not a madman, 68:2; 81:22

not a poet or a soothsayer, 69:41-42

not made as a keeper, 6:107

not to be distressed, 16:127; 18:6

nothing new among the Messengers, 46:9

only a mortal, 41:6

only follows that which is inspired, 10:15-16; 46:9

oppose him not, 58:20-22

reading purified pages, 98:2

respect the Messenger, 2:104; 49:1-5

reward is from Allah only, 34:47

saw Gabriel, 53:4-18; 81:22-25

seal of the Prophets, 33:40

send salutations on, 33:56

sent as a great favour to the believers, 3:164

sent to all mankind, 34:28

sent to be a witness, 16:89; 22:78; 33:45; 48:8; 73:15

sent to mankind as the Messenger of Allah, 7:158; 48:9; 48:29

sent with the truth, 4:170

Muhammmad, *(cont'd.)*

swore allegiance beneath the tree, 48:18

those who swear allegiance to him, 48:10

to make Religion of truth victorious over all religions, 61:9

to prostrate and draw near to Allah, 96:19

to strive hard against disbelievers and hypocrites, 66:9

unlettered, 7:157; 62:2

verses regarding family, of 33:28-34; 33:50-53; 33:55; 33:59; 66:1; 66:3-6

who defames you, 9:58

witness of the Children of Israel, 46:10

you are of a tremendous nature, 68:4

see also Messengers; Prophets

Mules, Horses, 16:8

Murder, 2:178-179

Muslims,

first of the, 6:14; 6:163; 9:100; 39:12

forgiveness and a vast reward for them who are, 33:35

He has named you, 22:78

N

Names, see Allah's Attributes

Necessity, if one is forced by, 2:173; 6:145

Neighbour, 4:36

New moons, 2:189

News, to be tested, 4:83

Niggards condemned, 17:29; 47:38

Night (as a symbol), 92:1; 93:2

for rest, 10:67

as a covering, 13:3;

as a cloak, 78:10

Night of Decree (Al-Qadr), 44:3-4; 97:1-5

Noah *[Nuh]*, 3:33; 4:163; 6:84; 7:59-69; 9:70; 10:71; 11:25; 11:32; 11:36; 11:42; 11:43; 11:46; 11:48; 17:3; 21:76; 23:23; 25:37; 26:105; 29:14; 37:75; 51:46; 54:9; 71:1- 28

with them for a thousand years, except fifty years, 29:14

unrighteous son not saved, 11:45-47

unrighteous wife, 66:10

O

Oaths, 2:224-227; 3:77; 5:89; 6:109; 16;38; 16;91; 16:92; 16:94; 24:22; 24:53; 66:2; 68:10; 68:39

Obedience, 3:132; 4:34; 4:59; 4:64; 4:66; 4:80; 4:81; 24:51-52; 24:53; 24:54; 47:33; 64:12

Offspring,

He bestows male and female, upon whom he will, 42:49-50

Olive, 6:99; 6:141; 16:11; 23:20; 24:35; 80:29; 95:1

Orphans, 2:83; 2:177; 2:215; 2:220; 4:2; 4:3; 4:8; 4:10; 4:36; 4:127; 6:152; 8:41; 17:34; 18:82; 59:7; 76:8; 89:17; 90:15; 93:6; 107:2

guardians of, 4:6

P

Pairs,

in all creatures, 13:3; 36:36; 42:11; 43:12; 51:49; 53:45

Palm tree, 13:4; 19:23; 19:25; 20:71; 59:5

Parables (likeness, example, similitudes),

a fly, 22:73

a man belonging to several partners, 39:29

ashes which the wind blows hard upon, 14:18

bad tree, 14:26

blind and deaf, 11:24

darkness on a vast, abysmal sea, 24:40

dog who pants with his tongue, 7:176

donkey, 62:5

dumb man who is a burden to his owner, 16:76

fallen from the sky and snatched by birds, 22:31

garden, 2:265-266

goodly tree, 14:24-25

grain of corn, 2:261

icy wind, 3:117

life of the world like water from the sky, 18:45

light is a niche, 24:35-36

mirage, 24:39

mountain humbled, 59:21

Parables *(cont'd.)*

partners, 30:28

people of the city, 36:13-32

people of the garden, 68:17-33

rain, 10:24

rainstorm from the sky, 2:19-20

rope, 3:103

seed growing, 48:29

slave and a man, 16:75

smooth rock, 2:264

spider, 29:41

township, secure and well content, 16:112-113

two men with gardens of grapes, 18:32-44

vegetation after rain, 57:20

water were to disappear, 67:30

who kindles fire, 2:17-18

who shout, 2:171

Paradise, *see Gardens of Paradise*

Parents,

kindness to 2:83; 2:215; 4:36; 6:151; 17:23; 29:8; 31:14; 46:15-17

Pasturage, 87:4-5

Path,

right 42:52-53; 43:43

plain road 5:77

see also Way

Patience 11:115; 40:55; 40:77; 42:43; 46:35; 70:5; 73:10

seek help in, and prayer 2:45; 2:153

endure 3:200; 16:126; 16:127

forbear (bear)10:109; 20:130

steadfast 3:186; 8:46; 39:10

Peace,

after war, 8:61; 9:11

greeting in Paradise, 10:10; 13:24; 14:23; 15:46; 16:32; 19:62; 25:75; 33:44; 36:58; 39:73 56:26; 56:91

sent down by Allah, 9:26; 9:40: 48:4; 48:26

upon Allah's servants and Messengers, 27:59; 37:79-81; 37:108-111; 37:119-122; 37:129-132; 37:181

Pen 68:1; 96:4

People of the Scripture (Book), 2:146; 3:20; 3:98; 3:110-115; 3:187; 4:51; 4:123; 4:131; 4:153; 4:159; 4:171; 5:65-66; 5:68; 6:20; 74:31

among them are those who believe, 2:62; 3:113-115; 3:199; 4:162; 5:66; 5:83; 28:53; 29:47; 57:27-29

among them are unbelievers, 59:2; 59:11; 98:1; 98:6

differed among themselves, 2:213; 3:19; 3:66; 27:76; 32:25; 41:45; 42:14; 43:65; 45:17; 59:14; 98:4

do not exceed the bounds, 5:77

relationship to Muslims, 3:64-80; 3:99-101; 4:44; 5:5; 5:57-59; 5:82; 29:46

treachery of, 33:26-27; 59:2-4

warner has come to them, 5:15-16; 5:19

see also Christians; Jews

Pharaoh,

a believing man of Pharaoh's family 40:28-44

building of a tower, 40:36; 40:37

claims to be god 28:38; 79:24

dead body out from sea 10:90-92

dealings with Moses 7:103-137; 10:75-92

destroyed 29:39

drowned 2:50

people of 2:49; 3:11; 7:141; 44:17-33

righteous wife of 28:9

transgressed beyond bounds; committed sins and disobeyed 20:24; 20:43; 69:9; 73:16; 89:10-14

Plead,

not on behalf of those who deceive themselves, 4:107

who will, on the Day of Resurrection, 4:109

Pledge (Allegiance),

covenant of Allah, 16:91

every man, what he has earned, own deeds, 52:21; 74:38

of the Believers, 48:18; 60:12

swear allegiance to you (Muhammad), 48:10

Poetry, 36:69

Poets, 26:224-227; 69:41

Pomegranates, 6:99; 6:141; 55:68

Poor, 2:177; 2:215; 2:273; 2:277; 4:8; 4:36; 8:41; 9:60; 17:26; 24:22; 24:32; 30:38; 47:38; 51:19; 59:7; 69:34; 74:44; 76:8; 89:18; 90:16; 93:8-9; 107:2-3

Prayer, 1:1-7; 3:8; 3:26; 3:27; 3:147; 3:191-194; 4:103; 17:80; 23:118

   do not be loud voiced nor yet silent, 17:110

   draw not near to, when you are drunken, 4:43

   facing towards Qiblah, 2:144; 2:149; 2:150

   guard your prayers, 2:238

   in travel and attack, 2:239; 4:101; 4:102

   not to pray for idolaters, 9:113; 9:114

   of disbelievers, 13:14

   prescribed at fixed times, 4:103

   purifying for, 5:6

   times of, 11:114; 17:78; 17:79; 20:130; 30:17; 30:18; 50:39; 50:40; 52:48-49; 73:1-6; 73:20

Precautions in danger, 4:71

Prisoners of war, 8:67-71

   see also Captives

Promise of Truth, 46:16

Property, wealth, 2:188; 3:186; 4:5; 4:7; 4:29; 51:19; 59:7-9

Prophets, 3:33; 3:146; 4:163; 6:84-90; 23:23-50; 57:26

   covenant of, 3:81; 33:7-8

   not for any Prophet to deceive, 3:161

   an adversary (enemy) to every Prophet, 6:112

   see also Messengers

Provision, 10:59; 14:32; 16:73; 34:36; 34:39; 42:12; 67:21; 79:33

   livelihood, 13:26; 51:57

Psalms, 4:163

Punishment, 3:178

   cutting of hands or feet, 5:33

   in the World and the Hereafter, 24:19; 68:33

Purification,

   bodily, 4:43; 5:6

Q

Qur'an, 4:82; 9:111; 10:15-16; 11:1; 12:1-3; 13:1; 13:31; 14:1 ;15:1; 15:91; 17:41; 17:89; 18:54; 21:106; 25:30; 26:2; 27:1; 28:2; 30:58; 36:69-70; 39:27; 43:44; 47:20; 47:24; 50:45; 55:2; 69:43-51; 86:13-14;

   a Light, 42:52

   a message to all the creation, 38:87; 68:52; 81:26-28

   a reminder for the heart, 50:37

   Arabic, 12:2; 13:37; 16:103; 20:113; 26:195; 39:28; 41:3; 41:44; 42:7; 43:3; 46:12

   belief in, 2:177; 17:107; 42:15; 72:2; 77:50

   Book of Wisdom, 10:1; 31:2; 36:2;

   confirms earlier Scripture, 5:48; 6:92; 10:37; 46:12

   full of blessings, 38:29

   Glorious, 50:1; 85:21

   guarded by Allah, 15:9; 85:22

   guidance, 2:2; 2:159; 12:111; 16:64; 16:89; 16:102; 17:9; 27:2; 27:76-77; 31:3; 41:44; 42:52; 45:20; 72:2

   heard by Jinn, 46:29-32; 72:1-2

   honourable, 56:75-82; 80:11-16

   inimitability of, 17:88

   made easy, 44:58; 54:17; 54:22; 54:32; 54:40

   makes (things) plain, 43:2; 44;2

   no falsehood can come at it, 41:41-42

   ponder its revelations, 38:29

   power of, 13:31; 59:21

   purified, 98:2-3

   recitation of, 10:61; 16:98; 17:45-46; 17:106; 18:27; 27:92; 29:45; 35:29; 73:4; 73:20; 75:18; 84:21; 96:1; 96:3

   renowned, 38:1

   revelation of, 2:176; 2:185; 2:213; 2:231; 3:3; 3:7; 4:105; 4:113; 5:48; 5:101; 6:19; 6:114; 6:155-157; 7:2-3; 14:1; 15:87; 16:64; 17:82; 17:105-106; 18:1; 20:2-4; 20:114; 21:10; 24:1; 25:6; 26:192-199; 29:51; 32:2 36:5; 38:29; 39:1-2; 39:23; 40:2; 41:2-4; 42:17; 44:3-6; 45:2; 46:2; 69:43; 75:16-19; 87:6-7

   when recited pay head, 7:204; 41:26; 46:29

   with truth, 17:105; 32:3; 34:6; 35:31; 39:2; 39:41; 46:30; 47:2-3; 51:23; 56:95; 57:16; 69:51

Quraysh, 106:1-4

R

Rabbis and Monks, 9:31; 9:34

Rain, sent down by Allah, 2:22; 2:164; 6:6; 6:99; 7:57; 8:11; 11:52; 13:17; 14:32; 15:22; 16:10; 16:65; 18:45; 20:53; 22:5; 22:63; 23:18; 24:43; 25:48-49; 27:60; 29:63; 30:24; 30:48-49; 31:10; 31:34; 32:27; 39:21; 41:39; 42:28; 43:11; 45:5; 50:9; 56:68-69; 57:20; 71:11; 78:14

Ramadan, 2:185

Ransom,
    none can be taken, 57:15
    offered as, by disbelievers, 10:54; 13:18
    of fasting or almsgiving, 2:196

Reconciliation,
    whoever pardons and amends, 42:40
    between man and wife 4:35
    between believers, 49:9; 49:10

Record,
    a written, 83:7-9; 83:18-21
    each nation summoned to its, 45:28-29
    written pages of deeds of every person, 81:10
    which speaks the truth, 23:62

Recording angels, 50:17; 50:18; 50:23

Religion
    do not exaggerate, 4:171;
    fathers following a, 43:22-24
    no compulsion in, 2:256
    not laid upon you in, any hardships, 22:78
    of Allah, 3:83-84
    other than the surrender (Islam), 3:85
    perfected, 5:3
    same, for other Prophets, 42:13-15
    set your purpose (O Muhammad) for, 30:30
    stress not in your, 5:77
    the surrender (Islam), 3:19
    who divide their, into sects, 6:159; 23:53; 30:32
    who take, for a pastime and a jest, 6:70
    see also 42:13; 42:14; 43:65; 45:17

Remembrance of Allah, 63:9
    in the hearts find rest, 13:28

Repentance, 2:54; 2:160; 3:89-90; 4:17-18; 5:34; 5:74; 6:54; 7:153; 9:3; 9:112; 9:118; 9:126; 11:3; 11:52; 11:61; 11:90; 16:119; 17:25; 19:60; 24:5; 25:70-71; 28:67; 30:33; 39:8; 39:17; 39:54; 40:7; 46:15; 60:4
    accepted by Allah, 40:3; 42:25
    of Adam and Eve, 2:37; 7:23
    of Moses, 7:143

Respite for evil, 3:178; 10:11; 12:110; 14:42; 14:44; 29:53-55; 86:15-17

Restraint from evil, 7:26

Resurrection, 16:38-40; 17:49-52; 19:66-72; 22:5; 23:15-16; 46:33-34; 50:3; 50:20-29; 50:41-44; 75:1-15; 79:10-12; 86:5-8

Revelation, 6:93; 10:2; 10:109; 12:102; 17:86; 40:15; 42:3; 42:7; 42:51; 42:52; 53:4; 53:10
    a guidance and a mercy, 7:203; 16:64; 31:3
    Allah's guidance, 3:73
    detailed; explained, 6:98; 41:2-4
    for people who have understanding, 6:98
    if you are in doubt, 2:23-24
    is not abrogated or forgotten except that one better than it is brought, 2:106
    revealed from your Lord, in truth, 6:114
    the Holy Spirit, 16:102; 26:192-193
    the, of the scripture is from Allah, 46:2
    see also Qur'an

Righteous,
    amid gardens and watersprings, 51:15-19; 76:5-12
    the best of company, 4:69
    will inherit the Earth, 21:105
    see also Good

Righteousness, 2:112; 2:177; 2:207; 2:208; 3:16; 3:17; 3:92; 3:133-135; 3:191-195; 4:36; 4:125; 5:93; 7:42; 7:43

Rivalry in worldly increase, 102:1-4

Roads, way, 43:10

Rocky Tract [Al-Hijr], dwellers in 15:80-85

Romans, 30:2-5

S

Sabbath,

transgress not the, 2:65; 4:154; 7:163-166

appointed only for, 16:124

Sabaeans, 5:69; 22:17

Sacrifice, 2:67-71; 6:162; 22:28; 22:32-34; 22:36-37; 48:25; 108:2

of Abraham, 37:102-107

Safa and Marwah, 2:158

Salih, 7:73-79; 11:61-68; 26:141-159; 27:45-53

Samiri, 20:85

Satan, 2:36; 2:168; 2:208; 2:268; 2:275; 3:36; 3:155; 3:175; 4:38; 4:60; 4:76; 4:83; 4:119; 4:120; 5:91; 6:43; 6:68; 6:142; 7:20; 7:22; 7:27; 7:175; 7:200; 7:201; 8:48; 16:63; 16:98; 20:120; 24:21; 25:29; 27:24; 41:36; 58:10; 58:19

cast among you enmity and hatred, 5:91

has no power over those who believe, 16:99; 16:100

is open enemy 12:5; 35:6; 36:60

made their deeds seem fair to them, 8:48

promised you, then failed you, 14:22

proposes a temptation, 22:52-53

slander, 7:200

spell from the, 7:201

Saul, *see Talut*

Scripture,

belief in 2:285; 4:136; 6:92

Seas,

the ships, 42:32-33; 45:12

the two, 25:53; 35:12; 55:19-20

when the, are poured out, 82:3

Secret,

conferences, 4:114

conference of three, 58:7

conference with the Messenger, 58:12; 58:13

Sects and division in religion, 23:53; 30:32; 42:13-14; 45:17

Security,

after grief, He sent down, 3:154

Senses (ears, eyes), 23:78

Shadow,

falls prostrate to Allah, 13:15

incline to the right and to the left 16:48

spread the 25:45

She-camel as a clear sign to the people of Thamud, 7:73; 17:59; 26:155-158

Ships,

and of His signs are the, 42:32-33

and you see the, cleaving them, 35:12

appointed for you, 43:12

displayed upon the sea, 55:24

glide on the sea, 31:31

is of use to men, 2:164

makes the, to be of service to you, 14:32

runs upon the seas by His command, 22:65; 45:12

the, ploughing, 16:14

who drives for you the, upon the sea, 17:66

Siege of Al-Madinah, 33:9-27

Signs of Allah, *see Allah's signs*

Signs in creation, 2:164; 3:190; 6:99; 10:6; 10:67; 16:69; 17:12; 20:53-54; 24:44-46; 26:8; 27:86; 29:44; 30:20-25; 30:46; 31:31; 32:26-27; 34:15; 36:33-34; 41:37; 41:39; 42:29; 42:32; 45:3-6; 45:12-13; 50:7-11; 51:20; 71:14-20; 78:6-16; 79:27-33; 88:17-20

Sin, 7:100; 74:43-56

Allah pardons not that partners should be ascribed to him, 4:116

Allah, who forgives all, 39:53

if you avoid the great things (sin), 4:31

illegal sexual intercourse, 4:15; 4:16; 24:2

the guilty never are successful, 10:17

they seek to hide from men, and seek not to hide from Allah, 4:108

those who amass, will be awarded that which they have earned, 6:120

those who shun the worst of sins, 42:37

who commits a crime, then throws (the blame) of it upon the innocent, 4:112

who commits, commits it only against himself, 4:111

Sinai, Mount, 19:52; 23:20; 95:2

Sinners, their ears, eyes and skins testify against them, 41:20-23

Slanderer, 68:11-12 104:1

Slaves, 2:177; 2:178; 4:25; 4:36; 4:92; 5:89; 24:33; 58:3; 90:13

Sleep, for rest, 78:9

Sodomy, 7:80-82; 11:77-83; 29:28-29

Solomon [Sulaiman], 2:102; 4:163; 6:84; 21:78-82; 27:15-44; 34:12-14; 38:30-40

  and the ants, 27:18-19

  and the Queen of Saba, 27:22-44; 34:15

Soul,

  Allah tasks not a, beyond its scope, 2:286; 7:42; 23:62

  by the accusing, 75:2

  every, is a pledge for its own deeds, 74:38

  every, will be confronted with all the good and evil he has done, 3:30

  every, will come pleading for himself, 16:111

  no, knows what it will earn tomorrow, 31:34

Spending in the cause of Allah, 2:177; 2:195; 2:215; 2:261-274; 3:134; 4:39; 8:60; 9:34; 9:60; 25:67; 47:38; 92:18-20

Spirit, the 15:29; 16:102; 17:85; 21:91; 26:193; 38:72; 40:15; 58:22; 70:4; 78:38; 97:4

Spoils of war, 3:152-153; 8:1; 8:41; 8:69; 48:15

Spying, 49:12

Star, 16:16; 53:1; 86:1-4

Stars, 7:54; 16:12; 22:18; 37:6-10: 56:75; 77:8; 81:2

Straight Path, 1:6; 6:153

Striving, 4:95; 8:72; 8:74; 8:75; 9:20; 9:24; 9:81; 22:78; 25:52; 29:69; 60:1; 61:11

Suckling, the term of, 2:233

Suffering (tribulation; adversity), 7:94-99

Sun, 7:54; 10:5; 14:33; 16:12; 22:18; 36:38; 36:40; 71:16; 81:1; 91:1

Supreme triumph, 9:72; 44:57

Suspicion, 49:12

Sustenance (food), 19:62

  see also Provision

T

Tabuk, battle of, 9:40-59; 9:81-89

Talut (Saul), 2:247-249

Term, every nation has its, 7:34; 10:49; 15:4-5; 16:61; 20:129

Test, by Allah, 3:154

Thamud, 7:73-79; 11:61-68; 17:59; 25:38; 26:141-159; 27:45-53; 29:38; 41:17; 51:43-45; 54:23-31; 69:4-8; 85:17-20; 89:9-14; 91:11-15

Thief, punishment of, 5:38-39

Throne, 7:54; 9:129; 10:3; 13:2; 20:5; 23:86; 23:116; 32:4; 40:15; 57:4; 85:15

  angels gathered around the, 39:75

  eight will uphold the, 69:17

  those who bear the, 40:7

  upon the water, 11:7

Thunder, 13:13; 69:5

Time, 9:36; 10:5; 17:12; 22:47; 32:5; 76:1; 103:1-2

  destroys disbelievers, 45:24

Torah, [Tawrah], 3:3; 3:48; 3:50; 3:65; 3:93; 5:43-44; 5:66; 5:68; 5:110; 6:91; 7:157; 9:111; 11:17; 48:29; 61:6; 62:5

  confirmed by the Gospel, 5:46

  confirmed by Jesus, 61:6

  confirmed by the Qur'an, 46:12

  mention of Muhammad in, 7:157

  revelation of, 7:144-145

  see also Moses

Torment, 3:188; 6:15-16; 10:50-53; 13:34; 16:88; 46:20; 70:1-2

Township, 15:4

Trade and wealth, 4:29

Travel, in the land, 6:11; 10:22; 12:109; 22:46; 27:69; 29:20; 30:9; 30:42; 34:18; 35:44; 40:21; 40:82; 47:10

Treachery, 8:58; 22:38

Treasures of Allah, 6:50

Tree of Immortality, 20:120

Trees, 22:18

Trials and tests, 2:49; 2:124; 2:155; 2:214; 2:249; 3:142; 3:154; 3:186; 5:48; 5:94; 6:53; 6:165; 7:141; 7:155; 7:163; 7:168; 8:17; 8:28; 9:49; 9:126; 11:9-10; 14:6; 16:92; 16:110; 17:60; 18:7; 21:111; 22:11; 23:30; 25:20; 27:47; 33:11; 34:21; 37:106; 39:49; 44:17; 47:4; 47:31; 49:3; 64:15; 67:2; 68:17; 72:17; 89:15-16

Trumpet, on the Day of Resurrection, 6:73; 18:99; 20:102; 23:101; 27:87; 36:51; 39:68; 50:20; 69:13; 74:8; 78:18; 79:6-7

Trusts (pledges), 2:283; 8:27; 33:72; 70:32

Truth, 5:48; 23:70-71; 23:90; 25:33; 69:51
    has come and falsehood has vanished, 17:81
    mix not, with falsehood, 2:42
    the promise of Allah, 46:16-17

Tubba', people of, 44:37; 50:14

Tuwa, valley of, 20:12; 79:16

U

Uhud, battle of, 3:121-128; 3:140-180

Unseen, the
    belief in, 2:3; 52:41
    keys of, 6:59

Usury [Riba], 2:275; 2:276; 2:278-280; 3:130; 4:161; 30:39

V

Veiling, 24:31; 33:59

Verses, seven often repeated, 15:87

Victory,
    given you a signal, 48:1
    help from Allah, 61:13

W

Wait, 7:71; 9:52; 10:102; 11:122; 20:135; 44:59; 52:31

Waste not, 6:141; 7:31; 17:26

Water, 13:4; 13:14; 16:91; 18:41; 24:39; 25:48-50; 25:53; 35:12; 38:42; 47:15; 54:11-12; 54:28; 55:19-20; 56:31; 56:68-70; 67:30; 77:27; 79:31; 80:25
    Allah's Throne upon the, 11:7
    every living thing made of, 21:30; 24:45; 25:54

Way, right (straight) path, 1-6; 42:52-53

Wayfarer, 2:177; 2:215; 8:41; 17:26; 30:38; 59:7

Wealth, 104:2-4
    and children are an ornament of the life of the world, 18:46

Widows, 2:234; 2:240

Will of Allah, 10:99-100; 30:5; 81:29; 82:8

Winds, 7:57; 30:46; 77:1-3
    fertilising, 15:22
    who sends the, so that they raise clouds, 30:48

Wine, 2:219; 5:90-91; 12:36; 12:41; 47:15; 76:21; 83:25-27

Wish (Desire),
    not a thing which Allah has made some of you excel others, 4:32

Witnesses, 3:81
    against mankind, 2:143; 22:78
    when you contract, 2:282
    illegal sexual intercourse, 4:15; 24:4
    hands and legs will bear, 36:65
    man is a telling, against himself, 75:14

Wives,
    are a tilth for you, 2:223
    garment for you, 2:187
    of your own kind, 16:72

Women, 2:222; 2:223; 3:14; 4:15; 4:19-25; 4:34; 4:127; 9:71; 24:26; 24:31; 24:60; 33:32; 33:35; 33:73; 47:19; 48:5; 48:25; 65:1-2; 65:6; 66:5; 71:28
    in pregnancy, 7:189; 31:14; 39:6; 41:47; 46;15; 65:4; 65:6
    modesty of, 24:30-31; 33:53
    see also Wives

Wood, dwellers of the, 15:78; 26:176-191 38:13; 50:14;

Wrongdoers, 11:18-22; 11:101-104; 11:116; 11:117; 39:47

X

No references

Y

Yathrib [Al-Madina], people of, 33:13

Z

Zechariah [Zakariya], 3:37-41; 6:85; 19:2-11; 21:89-90

Zakat, *see Charity* (Almsgiving)

Zeyd bin Haritha, 33:37

Zina (Adultery), 4:15-56; 17:32; 24:2-4; 25:68; 60:12
    accusations of, 24:4-9; 24:11-19; 24:23